Early Chinese Texts

EARLY CHINA SPECIAL MONOGRAPH SERIES NO. 2

Early Chinese Texts:
A Bibliographical Guide

Edited by

Michael Loewe

THE SOCIETY FOR THE STUDY OF EARLY CHINA

AND

THE INSTITUTE OF EAST ASIAN STUDIES, UNIVERSITY OF CALIFORNIA, BERKELEY

1993

Set in Zapf Calligraphic (Bitstream), titles in Centaur (Monotype),
by Birdtrack Press, New Haven

Library of Congress Cataloging-in-Publication Data

Early Chinese texts : a bibliographical guide / edited by Michael
Loewe
    p.   cm. — (Early China special monographs series ; no. 2)
    Includes bibliographical references and index.
    ISBN 1-55729-043-1
    1. Bibliography — China — Best books. 2. China — Imprints.
    3. Chinese classics — History and criticism.   I. Loewe, Michael.
    II. Series.
Z1035.8.C5E2   1993   93-40281
015.51'073 — dc20   CIP

Contents

Preface

This corporative project started as a result of a conversation held with David Keightley while awaiting the delivery of a lecture in the Mill Lane Lecture Rooms, Cambridge, England. We were lamenting the absence of a work of reference which we could recommend to students as a means of providing the basic information and aids with which to embark on the study of an early Chinese text, to solve some of the obvious and unavoidable problems that present themselves at the outset of such a study and to gain familiarity with the outstanding questions that yet await solution. We had in mind a book that would state established conclusions, describe the contents of each work, discuss its date of composition and indicate questions of authorship and authenticity.

We thought that it would be possible and valuable to state clearly which parts of a given work, if any, are suspect or known to be later interpolations; to list its most important traditional and modern commentators; to trace the history of the text through its more important editions and prints; to name the most useful translations into Western languages together with some of the Japanese editions; and to identify the principal aids to research, including indexes and concordances. The book was never conceived as being a forum for arguing out new theories but it was hoped that contributors would take note of newly found evidence, such as that of manuscripts, which demands recognition and the consequent modification of existing views.

In the hope that the necessary work could be completed reasonably quickly we determined to invite scholars who had already made a specialised study of a particular text to contribute to a corporate volume. A number of those who were invited to do so responded magnificently to the call; and it is to the great credit of those who did so immediately that they have refrained from displays of impatience in the intervening years, when for various reasons long delays have been unavoidable. These have been due chiefly to the impossibility of identifying a scholar with specialist experience in and knowledge of a particular text. The task of filling the deficiency fell on the shoulders of one of the editors, who included William Boltz at the outset of the project; but owing to their regular commitments, principally as university teachers, neither editor was free to devote sufficient time to the concentrated effort needed for such research for more than a limited period in each year. A debt of gratitude is owed to Professor Shaughnessy for nobly stepping into the breach and undertaking some of this work. It is a matter of profound regret that two of the contributors, Timoteus Pokora and Angus Graham, did not live to see their work published.

From the outset it was necessary to determine the scope of the literature that would be handled in the volume, and it was decided to include only those items of which the greater parts could reasonably be accepted as having reached their present form before the end of the Han dynasty. This decision rested on the need to define a limit at some convenient, if arbitrarily chosen, point; it did not derive from literary, philosophical or historical considerations. No decisions of this type can be wholly satisfactory, and readers will note for themselves the absence of certain items, such as the *Hou Han shu* 後漢書, which certainly bear a strong claim for inclusion but which were completed after the accepted dateline. At the same time it has not been possible to include an account of all extant works that had been completed by then. Some, but not all, of those works which exist now in no more than fragmentary form have been treated; each case has been decided on its own merits. It is a matter of satisfaction to the editor that it has been possible to accommodate to a remark of Professor Shaughnessy, made perhaps more in jest than in earnest, that the most appropriate number of texts to be handled would be sixty-four.

Apart from general guidance, the treatment of each item has been left to the judgement of the contributor. Each text has its own problems and technicalities, and the type of coverage that has been possible varies widely in proportion to its inherent difficulties, the extent of the scholarly effort that it has attracted and the degree of certainty that may be suggested by way of conclusion. In this respect certain anomalies will be immediately obvious. Readers will observe cases of a work which has taken a prominent place in Chinese literature but which receives comparatively small attention here; in other cases, texts which are known far less widely and whose influence on China's literary and scholarly heritage has been less marked, are treated at comparatively greater length.

Such differences are understandable; for the *Shih ching* 詩經, to take an obvious example, has been subject to repeated and lengthy comment over the centuries. It would hardly be possible to summarise the results of such work justly within the scope of the present volume, and the

principal conclusions may be found without undue difficulty in a number of western writings. For such cases the entries here may be limited
to pointing out the chief references to a few of the leading writings on
the subject. By contrast, more lengthy and detailed treatment has been
deemed justifiable for items which cannot be studied without access to
recondite scholarly writings or where a new situation has arisen thanks
to the discovery of a manuscript, or the completion of recent research.
Dating of the texts is not always possible within the limits that readers
might wish to find; in this respect contributors have often preferred to
err on the side of caution.

In no case is it claimed that an entry provides a complete list of all
publications that concern the item that is under consideration. Nor is it
possible at this stage of scholarship to embark on text critical studies of
all the items that are treated. While it is hoped that the basic information has been supplied, readers are also referred to the bibliographies or
lists that are to be found in some of the secondary works that are listed,
and which will direct them to some of the more modern writings which
may not be named here. Some contributors may take it for granted that
readers will of their own initiative consult certain well-known works
with which they are assumed to be familiar, such as the *Ssu k'u ch'üan
shu tsung mu t'i yao* 四庫全書總目提要, the *Wei shu t'ung k'ao* 偽書通考,
Juan Yüan's 阮元 annotation to the *Thirteen Classics* or the mammoth
collations of Yen Ling-feng 嚴靈峯. Nor has it been thought necessary
to remind readers where citations of a work appear in anthologies or
encyclopaedias, unless such citations are germane to a problem under
discussion. In some cases it has been possible to supplement a contribution with notes of a few important publications that have appeared
since the time when it was originally drafted. Regrettably it has been
possible to include mention of no more than a few of the contributions
written in recent years in Russian.

Each text that is treated is necessarily *sui generis*; contributors have
been free to adopt divisions and to choose those headings that they
believe to be appropriate; and while the intention has been to cover the
same basic questions for each text, there has been no call to impose a
uniformity of treatment or to require consistency for its own sake, at the
expense of compromising with clarity or with an individual contributor's preference. In particular the ways chosen to list secondary writings
may vary from one item to another; some authors prefer to give full
bibliographical details within their text, others have chosen to append
separate lists. Such lists may be given either in chronological or in alphabetical order, as may be appropriate; in a few instances it has been

necessary to refer to secondary writings by the author and year of publication.

This book is not designed for those who are new to Chinese Studies; it is addressed principally to those who are embarking on research after completing some three or four years of a course of basic training and are therefore familiar with the fundamental developments of China's literary and historical traditions. It has therefore not been felt necessary to include certain well known facts, such as the dates of the principal dynasties. In most cases it has not been thought desirable or necessary to duplicate information which is readily available; for example, the titles of the constituent parts of a work, which may be found immediately in a table of contents; they call for comment here only in cases of problems.

The book is best used in conjunction with three copies of a text that is under study; one of these should best derive from a traditional edition, and one should be a reputable modern print, with punctuation, but without the use of simplified characters; a third copy should be from one of the Japanese series of editions. Readers should also refer to the textual notes of Professor D.C. Lau that are available in the concordances published by the Institute of Chinese Studies of the Chinese University of Hong Kong.

My thanks are due to a number of colleagues whose encouragement and advice has been invaluable over the years, and especially to William Boltz who shouldered the burdens of co-editor during the early years of the work. I am grateful to Dr. Bertil Lundahl for his valuable corrections for one entry and to Dr. P. Kornicki for guidance over the intricacies of Japanese names and bibliography. I am glad to acknowledge with deep thanks the help provided by the staff of the East Asian collections of the Joseph Regenstein Library, Chicago, and of the University Library, Cambridge, England. Above all, the speedy preparation of the text for publication, as became possible in the final stages, has been due to Professor Shaughnessy's initiative and the skilled assistance of Fangpei Cai, Magnus Fiskesjö, Amy J. Mayer and Laura A. Skosey, of the University of Chicago. Without David Goodrich's professional advice and skillful help, this book would never have reached its present form.

The following conventions have been adopted:

1. The names of Chinese and Japanese scholars are given without the style (*tzu* 字 or *hao* 號), unless this is of material significance.
2. For Chinese and Japanese scholars who wrote before the twentieth century, dates (at times no more than a general indication such as

'Ming period') are given on the first occurrence in each entry. These
are repeated in the index, where such details as can be ascertained
for more recent scholars are also included. These dates, sometimes
included in recent Japanese publications, are otherwise taken from
the following sources:

(a) Arthur W. Hummel, *Eminent Chinese of the Ch'ing Period*, 2 vols.;
Washington D.C.: Library of Congress, 1943.

(b) Yves Hervouet (ed.), *A Sung Bibliography (Bibliographie des Sung)*,
initiated by Etienne Balazs; Hong Kong: the Chinese University
Press, 1978.

(c) T'an Cheng-pi 譚正璧 *Chung kuo wen hsüeh chia ta tzu tien* 中國文
學家大辭典; reprinted Hong Kong: Wen shih ch'u pan she, 1961.

(d) Ch'ang Pi-te 昌彼得, Wang Te-i 王德毅, Ch'eng Yüan-min 程元
敏 and Hou Chün-te 侯俊德 *Sung jen chuan chi tzu liao so yin* 宋人
傳記資料索引, 6 vols.; Taipei: Ting wen, 1974–76.

(e) Wang Te-i 王德毅, Li Jung-ts'un 李榮村 and Pan Po-teng 潘柏
澄 *Yüan jen chuan chi tzu liao so yin* 元人傳記資料索引 5 vols.;
Taipei: Hsin wen feng 新文豐, 1979–82.

(f) Chu Pao-chiung 朱保烱 and Hsieh P'ei-lin 謝沛霖, *Ming Ch'ing
chin shih t'i ming pei lu so yin* 明清進士題名碑錄索引, 3 vols.;
Shanghai: Ku chi, 1980.

(g) *Kokuritsu kokkai toshokan chosha mei ten kyoroku* 國立國會圖書館
著者名典據錄, 4 vols.; Tokyo: National Diet Library, 1991 (distributed by Kinokuniya).

(h) *Jimbutsu refuarensu jiten IV: Nihon jimmei ten kyoroku* 人物レフアレ
ンス事典VI日本人名典據錄 2 vols.; Tokyo: Nichigai Associates,
1983.

3. Chinese characters, which are given regularly in full rather than in
simplified forms, are not usually included on a second or subsequent
occurrence of a Chinese or Japanese proper name in the same entry.
They do not appear for references to titles of the sixty-four items that
are treated in this book; or necessarily for the following: kings of
Chou and emperors of the Han and T'ang Dynasties; kingdoms of
the *Chan kuo* period; *nien hao* 年號; titles of the Standard Histories;
the titles of the select number of *ts'ung shu* 叢書 and other works
listed in the Appendix; the frequently recurring name Fujiwara
Sukeyo 藤原佐世 and the frequently recurring terms *chüan* 卷, *p'ien*
篇, and *k'ao cheng* 考證; Chinese and Japanese publishing houses of
the twentieth century; and titles of the series of *Kambun* 漢文 editions, which will be found in the Appendix. In order to save excessive

duplication the names of *Kambun* editors, which repeat very frequently, are not printed in each entry; they will be found in the index.
4. Chinese names and terms are rendered in the Wade-Giles system,
   with hyphenation being restricted to elements of proper names and
   to place names; *Pinyin* 拚音 is used only when that form is used in a
   title that is quoted. To avoid undue pedantry incorrect forms such as
   Peking, Tientsin, now hallowed by traditional usage, have been retained.
5. Unless stated otherwise, references to the Standard Histories are to
   the punctuated edition published by the *Chung hua shu chü* from 1959
   onwards.
6. Page references are given to the bibliographical lists that are included in the Standard Histories, but not to other regular catalogues
   that are cited unless location is likely to present difficulty. No pagination is provided for the references to Fujiwara Sukeyo's catalogue;
   none is marked on the original copy which is available in facsimile.
7. Where appropriate, references to sections of texts are given in the
   form of *Chan kuo ts'e* 戰國策 11 ('Ch'i 2').
8. In most cases the terms *chüan* and *p'ien* have been retained as such;
   'chapter' is used as a neutral word, where it may not necessarily be
   possible or desirable to distinguish between the two Chinese expressions.
9. Individual contributors have in general been left to choose between
   terms such as *Ch'un ch'iu* or *Spring and Autumn*. Where dates may be
   in question (e.g., in respect of the discovery of the documents at the
   Wei 魏 tomb of Chi hsien 汲縣) contributors have in general been
   left to specify the particular year that they believe to be correct.
10. A number of references are made to the comments of Yü Yüeh 俞樾
    (1821–1907). These will be found in separately published items for the
    work that is concerned, in which the title is preceded by the word *tu*
    讀, or in his *Chu tzu p'ing i* 諸子平議) of 1870.

Grantchester
February 1992   M.L.

Chan kuo ts'e 戰國策

1. Content

Among the few surviving pre-Ch'in documents, the *Chan kuo ts'e* is probably the only work which deals with all the states of the Chan kuo period. It includes stories of warfare and political manipulation and concerns the personalities of that period, which marked a major transition from ancient times to a new era in Chinese history. As with the term *Ch'un ch'iu*, so with the term *Chan kuo*, the title of a text came to be used to denote an historical period (variously taken to refer to 481 or 403 to 221 B.C.). The unique style and content of the book set a precedent in explaining the strategies of power politics by means of diplomatic argument. The clever methods of persuasion with their vivid characterizations, their wit and humour impart to the work a literary merit that is higher than its historical value.

The *Chan kuo ts'e* is concerned with the use of intrigue to secure advantage in a manner that is contrary to the principles of Confucian morality. Since compilation in its present form at the beginning of the present era the book has not received the same degree of respect that other old books in China have merited. Almost all Confucian scholars, including Liu Hsiang 劉向 (79–8 B.C.), the original compiler, have attacked its historical implications. In his preface to the work, Liu Hsiang condemned the Chan kuo rulers for 'renouncing courteousness but honouring warfare, and for rejecting benevolence and justice, using improper means for the sole end of achieving power'. Other scholars, while disapproving of the moral implications of the book, were nevertheless attracted by its refined rhetoric and vigorous literary style. The opinion of Lu Lung-ch'i 陸隴其 (1630–93) that the book 'is almost like poison in delicious food' represents the traditional attitude towards the *Chan kuo ts'e*, i.e. that of appreciating it as literature while condemning it as history.

2. Sources of the work

Opinions vary as to the meaning of the title and the origin and nature of the book. Some scholars interpret the word *ts'e* to mean 'schemes',

1

'intrigues' or 'plots'; others believe that it should be taken to refer to the bamboo or wooden tablets used in writing, and thus to mean 'documents'. Liu Hsiang, who gave the work this title, expressed his view clearly. He wrote that 'the book contains materials used by the diplomats of the Warring States to advise those states that employed them by contriving plans and plots for their use; it is therefore proper to call the book *Chan kuo ts'e*. There is thus good reason to follow Liu Hsiang's original intention and to interpret the title as meaning 'Plots of warring states'. Some renderings of the title use the term 'intrigues' or 'stratagems'.

Controversy has also arisen as to the nature and style of this writing, and as to whether it should be regarded as history or fiction. Although most of the standard histories and bibliographies list the work in the class of *tsa shih* 雜史, the *Sung shih* (205, p. 5203) and some other bibliographies place it within the category of *tsung heng chia* 縱橫家.

Liu Hsiang wrote of the confused fragments of records that he had found in the imperial library, in addition to eight incomplete *p'ien* that concerned various states. He had arranged such material in rough chronological order for those states, and supplemented it with other writings that had not been set out in any sequence; and after eliminating material that was found to be duplicated, he had made a total of 33 *p'ien*. From Liu Hsiang's reference to named documents that were present in the archive (i.e., *Kuo ts'e* 國策, *Kuo shih* 國事, *Tuan ch'ang* 短長, *Shih yü* 事語, *Ch'ang shu* 長書 and *Hsiu shu* 脩書), it is apparent that at least six different sources of the same nature and scope were used in the compilation of the *Chan kuo ts'e*. Although none of these documents exist today, they may be classified in three distinct categories, on the basis of their titles.

(a) Regional records of various states, including the *Kuo ts'e* (state documents) and *Kuo shih* (state affairs). Since these two titles begin with the word *kuo*, the documents must have been arranged in order according to the states that were concerned, as is the case with the *Kuo yü* 國語. This is evidently the material to which Liu Hsiang referred as the eight *p'ien* arranged for the various states. The received text of the *Chan kuo ts'e* includes sections on the royal house of Chou 周; the seven major states of Ch'in 秦, Ch'i 齊, Ch'u 楚, Chao 趙, Wei 魏, Han 韓 and Yen 燕; and the three minor states of Sung 宋, Wei 衛 and Chung shan 中山. Thus, the eight *p'ien* that Liu Hsiang mentions specifically seem to have concerned Chou and the seven major states, with the latter three occupying only a very small portion of the material. These documents were probably not official histories of the states, which are known to have been written in the form of annals and to have been destroyed under Ch'in; the *Kuo ts'e* and the *Kuo shih* more probably were other records arranged by state and concerning state affairs.

Throughout the whole text, each paragraph, whether short or long, usually represents an independent incident that is unconnected with those that precede and follow it. Some of these stories relate to authenticated historical facts and were probably drawn from state documents. For example, the initial passage that concerns Ch'in records that Wei Yang 衛鞅 (better known as Shang Yang 商) left Wei for Ch'in, there to put his reforms into practice for eight years before dying in a violent circumstances, after the death of Duke Hsiao 孝. This paragraph includes information which is similar to that included in *Shih chi* ch. 68. Other stories, such as those about the physician Pien Ch'üeh 扁鵲, Wang-sun Ku 王孫賈 and Chih Po 知伯, or about political relations among the six states, can be confirmed in the *Shih chi* or other historical documents.

(b) Anecdotes, such as those in the item which Liu Hsiang identified as *Shih yü* (topical discourses). This was probably a collection of historical romances of various states, written in the form of discourses and arranged by topic. The term *yü* is seen in the title *Kuo yü*, which is a collection of anecdotes from the Ch'un ch'iu period arranged by state. The *Shih yü* must have consisted of the same kind of material for the Chan kuo period, as may be exemplified in the story of Su Ch'in 蘇秦 and his change of loyalties from an alliance that was pro-Ch'in to one that was anti-Ch'in. The Confucian tradition strongly disapproved of the moral implications of the story, but for literary merit it has been considered the best of the historical romances. The vivid if greatly exaggerated presentation may have been derived from anecdotes transmitted by story-tellers which gradually became popular legends among various states. Because these stories were written mostly in the form of highly imaginative discourses, there is reason to believe that this kind of narration was probably based on the anecdotes or *Shih yü* described above.

(c) Material concerning the theories and practices of the diplomats, including the *Tuan ch'ang, Ch'ang shu* and *Hsiu shu*, which were probably arranged by types of argument. The term *tuan ch'ang* (short and long, wrong and right, loss and gain or defects and merits) seems to refer to the presentation of contradictory arguments from each of two sides. It was apparently the practice of some diplomats to present their case by exaggerating one point and belittling another; or to please a person by praising (*ch'ang*) him to his face while decrying (*tuan*) others behind their backs.

Some scholars have thought that the term *tuan ch'ang* refers to the use of pieces of wooden stationery of differing lengths for the composition of one and the same document. In fact no examples of such a usage have come to hand. Even if documents had been made up on long and short tablets, there is no reason to suppose that the term should refer particularly to diplomatic writings.

The items named *Ch'ang shu* and *Hsiu shu* may have set forth only one aspect of a plot, or they may have included a longer version of an argument. The *Chan kuo ts'e* is especially rich in such augmentation of the plans and plots of various diplomats; less common are stories, anecdotes or fables; and probably those passages that can be considered as historical records are rather few. It is clear that the *Chan kuo ts'e* is a work of a composite nature, which draws on materials of different sources; it cannot therefore be classified arbitrarily within a single category of either history or fiction.

3. Dating and authorship

The dating of the events narrated in the *Chan kuo ts'e* is generally in agreement with the statement in Liu Hsiang's preface that the book covers a period of 245 years, from the end of the Ch'un ch'iu until the rise of Ch'u 楚 and Han 漢. The rise of Ch'u as a contender for imperial power is dated in 209 B.C.; 245 years earlier brings the date to 454 B.C. All the incidents included in the book fall within this period, except for one which concerns Duke Ling 靈 of Wei 衛, who reigned from 534 to 493. According to some scholars, this passage was inserted as a quotation, in connection with the preceding and following paragraphs, rather than as a separate incident from the Ch'un ch'iu period. Most of the book deals with the middle part of the Chan kuo period; only a few incidents are of earlier date, such as the stories about Chih Po, whose fief was divided by Chao, Wei and Han in 453 B.C.

The latest events that are described in the book date from around 221 B.C. (e.g., the unsuccessful attempt to assassinate the king of Ch'in in 227 B.C.; the second attempt to do so, after he had become emperor, in 221 B.C.). Since there is a gap of about 200 years between the latest of the events mentioned and the compilation of the *Chan kuo ts'e* at the end of the first century B.C., it is possible that some material written during Former Han may have been included.

The question of authorship of the book has long come into question, with some scholars ascribing this to Liu Hsiang ever since the T'ang dynasty. The bibliography of the *Chiu T'ang shu* (46, pp. 1993–94) includes the note that the book was written (*chuan* 撰) by Liu Hsiang; the bibliography of the *Hsin T'ang shu* (58, p. 1463) names the item as 'Liu Hsiang's *Chan kuo ts'e*'. Ku Kuang-ch'i 顧廣圻 (1776–1835) even wrote that 'the *Chan kuo ts'e* derives from Liu Hsiang's own school and it is therefore not hard to understand why it is different from the writings of Han Fei, Ssu-ma Ch'ien and other schools'. Since it is clearly stated in the preface that the book was collated and compiled by Liu Hsiang from various early sources then extant, it is evident that Liu Hsiang was the compiler and not the author of the work.

Some scholars (e.g. Lo Ken-tse 羅根澤) have suggested that the *Chan kuo ts'e* is the same as the lost work entitled *Chün yung* 雋永, which was written by K'uai T'ung 蒯通 (*c.* 236–196 B.C.). Their argument is based on the statement in the *Shih chi* that K'uai T'ung was an expert in diplomatic theory and discussed the intrigues of the warring states in 81 headings (*shou* 首). This theory rests on the arbitrary association of the term *chün yung* (delicious and lasting) with the terms *ch'ang shu* and *hsiu shu*, and it is assumed that Liu Hsiang must have taken 33 *p'ien* from the 81 *shou* of the *Chün yung* with which to make the *Chan kuo ts'e*. Liu Hsiang, however, does not mention *Chün yung* in his sources, and there is no positive evidence with which to support this view.

All attributions of the *Chan kuo ts'e* to one individual author have been based on the mistaken assumption that the book originally existed as a complete work; and they have ignored Liu Hsiang's statement in his preface that the book was a collection based on various sources that existed during the Chan kuo period. With his reorganisation of the original materials that were then in the imperial archives, the new title *Chan kuo ts'e* that was assigned by Liu Hsiang naturally replaced old titles such as *Kuo ts'e*, or *Kuo shih*; for this reason the original titles were no longer used and they were not recorded in the bibliography that is now in the *Han shu*. Other works, however, which were listed in that bibliography, do not feature as items on which the compiler of the *Chan kuo ts'e* drew. There is little doubt that this work is an anthology of existing materials written by unknown authors of the Chan kuo period.

4. Transmission of the text, and the early commentaries

The *Chan kuo ts'e* was compiled by Liu Hsiang between 26 and 8 B.C., at a time when a whole variety of documents in the imperial archives were being examined by the commission which he led. The text was first annotated by Kao Yu 高誘 (*c.* 168–212), also known as a commentator of the *Huai nan tzu*. Kao Yu's annotation is entered in the bibliography of the *Sui shu* (33, p. 959) as an item of 21 *chüan*, and the same list includes an entry for the *Chan kuo ts'e* compiled by Liu Hsiang, in 32 *chüan*. The lists in both the *Chiu t'ang shu* and the *Hsin t'ang shu* include entries both for Kao Yu's annotation and for Liu Hsiang's text, each of 32 *chüan*. By Sung times it had become customary to include both text and commentary together, as one item. The bibliography of the *Sung shih* (205, p. 5203) carries an entry for Kao Yu's *Chan kuo ts'e*, in 33 *chüan*; a copy of 33 *chüan*, with Kao Yu's notes, was entered in Fujiwara Sukeyo's catalogue.

During the Sung period, parts of the text, together with Kao Yu's annotation, gradually disappeared. According to the *Ch'ung wen tsung mu* (compiled 1034–42), 12 *p'ien* of the text (nos. 2–10 and 31–33) and 12 *p'ien* of the annotation (nos. 1, 5 and 11–20) were missing from the copy kept in the imperial library. Some time later, when a number of scholars began to work on the recovery of the book, the most important contribution was made by Tseng Kung 曾鞏 (1019–83), who had been working on the collation of ancient documents as editor in the Historical Commission, between 1060 and 1067. By searching for all copies that were then available in private collections, he was able to examine 21 *p'ien* (nos. 1 and 11–30) of the original text and 10 *p'ien* (nos. 2–4, 6–10 and 32–33) of the annotation; and by reconstructing two *p'ien* (nos. 5 and 31) he was able to recover a text with a total of 33 *p'ien*. It is clear that Tseng Kung's version is not identical with Liu Hsiang's original text, particularly in respect of *p'ien* nos. 5 and 31; nevertheless Tseng's text, which was collated and revised three times, has been considered the authoritative version; all later editions have been based upon it.

Almost contemporary with Tseng Kung, a private scholar named Wang Chüeh 王覺 was also working on the collation of the book; this was in about 1064–67, but his edition does not survive. When, in 1086, Sun P'u 孫朴 (*c.* 1050–93) was appointed editor in the Imperial Library, he made further collations of the text, with corrections of some 550 words. This text was termed the *Huang pen* 黃本, and was copied for the Imperial Library in 1093.

During Southern Sung, two scholars were working on the book almost simultaneously, but independently, and their collations have become the direct progenitors of the various editions that are available today. Yao Hung 姚宏 (*c.* 1100–1146) made some 480 corrections to the book on the basis of Tseng Kung's work and other editions; his preface, dated 1146, was copied by his brother Yao K'uan 姚寬 (1104–1161) in 1160.

A second, popular, commentary was made by Pao Piao 鮑彪 (1106–49). In this edition, which carries a preface dated 1147 and a revision of

1149, the complete text is rearranged into 10 *chüan* according to the states, and then in chronological order. Although Pao did not follow the traditional practice of preserving the original text and order, some of his corrections and judgments show outstanding ability and scholarship and have served to settle a great many problems that were previously unsettled.

During the Yüan dynasty Wu Shih-tao 吳師道 (1283–1344) wrote what was the most highly critical study of the *Chan kuo ts'e*, which was based on Pao Piao's edition but also used the commentaries of Yao Hung. This work was completed in 1325, with a postscript dated in 1333. First printed in 1355, the work was praised by the editors of the *Ssu k'u* project as being 'the best commentary ever made on the study of this work since ancient times'.

No important studies were contributed by Ming scholars, except for the many reprints with some additional notes that were based on the Pao-Wu edition. These included those by Wang T'ing-hsiang 王廷相 (1522), Ko Tzu 葛鼎 (1523), Kung Lei 龔雷 (1528), Tu Shih 杜詩 (1552), Chang Wen-huan 張文爟 (1587) and Li K'o-chia 李克家; there was also a three colour edition, made by the well-known printer Min Ch'i-chi 閔齊伋 in 1619. During the Ch'ing period, the last edition was reprinted by K'ung Kuang-sen 孔廣森 (*c.* 1780) and Li Hsi-ling 李錫齡 (*c.* 1850). Later it was included in several *ts'ung shu* of the 19th and early 20th centuries. The edition has been very popular in Japan, forming the basis of most of the Japanese reprints and translations.

Probably for political reasons, Yao Hung's version did not become popular until the middle of the 18th century, when Lu Chien-tseng 盧見曾 (1690–1768) found and reproduced a Sung printing (1756). Another Sung print with Yao Hung's commentary was re-engraved in facsimile in 1803 by Huang P'ei-lieh 黃丕烈 (1763–1825), who followed the copy in his own library exactly, adding his own critical notes as a supplement in 3 *chüan*. This edition is prized for its rarity, its faithful reproduction and the careful notes that are appended, and it has subsequently been collated or emended by several scholars. This edition was used for the *Ssu pu pei yao* series in 1927.

Pao Piao's edition, as transmitted with Wu Shih-tao's commentary, was popular throughout the Ming and early Ch'ing periods, when Yao Hung's edition was unknown. It was first included in the *Ssu pu ts'ung k'an* series in 1922.

These two rival editions, one by Yao Hung in 33 *p'ien* arranged by states, and the other by Pao Piao with Wu Shih-tao's revisions rearranged in chronological sequence, in 10 *chüan*, have thus become the most influential and popular texts and commentaries on the *Chan kuo ts'e*, on which all other modern editions are based.

5.   Newly discovered manuscripts of Chan kuo documents

The manuscript documents discovered at Ma wang tui in 1973 included some texts which are related to the *Chan kuo ts'e* and which have been variously termed *pieh pen* 別本, *po shu* 帛書 and *Chan kuo tsung heng chia shu* 戰國縱橫家書. These manuscripts carry 27 items of text in which 11,000 out of a total of some 17,000 characters survive; about 60% of the material does not appear in the received text of the *Chan kuo t'se*. The new texts include correspondence, dialogues and argumentation of the diplomatic school, and the content is similar in nature and style to that of the *Chan kuo ts'e*; but the material is not arranged according to the states that are concerned or in chronological sequence. As certain misplaced passages of length equal to that of individual wooden strips can clearly be identified, the text is believed to have been copied, on silk, from one that that had been written on wooden or bamboo strips.

Nine items of this material (nos. 15–16 and 18–24) have counterparts in the received text of the *Chan kuo ts'e* and the *Shih chi*, and two items (nos. 4 and 5) are partly identical with parts of the *Chan kuo ts'e*. The other 16 items are not found in any other extant literature. The material may be divided into three groups, according to content and layout:

(a) Items 1 to 14 are all stories which relate to three members of the Su 蘇 family and two other persons. The coherence of the contents and the uniform style in which certain characters are written indicate that all these items derive from one single source.

(b) The contents of items 15 to 19 are unrelated to one another. However, there is a note at the end of each item giving the number of characters therein, and at the end of the group the total number is given as 2870. This figure agrees exactly with the sum of the figures given at the end of each of the five items, thus testifying that they were taken from a single source.

(c) Items 20 to 27 are unrelated in content; no numbering of characters is given, and they appear to have been taken from other sources.

The events recorded in these documents all relate to the middle and late parts of the Chan kuo period. The stories in items 1 to 14 concern events which can be dated to about 300–286 b.c.; those in items 15 to 27 concern events of 353 to 235 b.c.. Twenty four of these items concern the period 307 to 221 b.c., and 16 of these concentrate on 289 to 283 b.c.

The value of the newly discovered texts is clear. They represent a different source of information, which is perhaps older than those sources on which Liu Hsiang based his work, and there is nothing to show that their text had been seen by Ssu-ma T'an 司馬談 (d. *c.* 110 B.C.) or Ssu-ma Ch'ien 司馬遷 (?145-?86 B.C.). In addition the new material is of considerable importance for the textual criticism of the received text of the *Chan kuo ts'e* and for the study of China's history during the Chan kuo period. The chronology of the later part of that period has been based primarily on the historical events related in the *Chu shu chi nien*, which end at 299 B.C., and in the *Shih chi*, and there is thus a gap of 78 years between 299 B.C. and the unification of 221 B.C. The newly found documents, which mostly concern events dating to the later part of the Chan kuo period, are especially useful for the reconstruction of the chronology of that time.

For transcriptions and critical studies, see the following and below under 6 (d):

(i) Ma wang tui Han mu po shu cheng li hsiao tsu (ed.), *Ma wang tui Han mu po shu chan kuo tsung heng chia shu* 馬王堆漢墓帛書戰國縱橫家書; Peking: Wen wu, 1976; text of the 27 items transcribed in abbreviated characters (previously published in *Wen wu* 1975.4, 14–26), followed by articles by T'ang Lan 唐蘭, Yang K'uan 楊寬 and Ma Yung 馬雍 (for earlier versions of the latter two items, see WW 1975.2, 26–34, and WW 1975. 4, 27–40).

(ii) Ma wang tui Han mu po shu cheng li hsiao tsu (ed.), *Ch'ang sha Ma wang tui Han mu po shu* 長沙馬王堆漢墓帛書 (3); Peking: Wen wu, 1978; facsimiles and annotated transcriptions.

(iii) Tseng Ming 曾鳴, 'Kuan yü po shu "Chan kuo ts'e" chung Su Ch'in shu hsin jo kan nien tai wen t'i ti shang ch'üeh 關於帛書《戰國策》中蘇秦書信若干年代問題的商榷'; WW 1975.8, 23–30.

(iv) Kudō Motoo 工藤元男, 'Maōtai shutsudo "Sengoku jūōka sho" to "Shiki" 馬王堆出土 "戰國縱橫家書" と "史記"'; Chūgoku seishi no kisoteki kenkyū 中國正史の基礎的研究; Tokyo: Waseda daigaku, 1984, pp. 1–26.

6. Principal editions

(a) *Chan kuo ts'e chu* 戰國策注, 33 *p'ien*, annotated by Kao Yu and with commentary of Yao Hung; collated by Lu Chien-tseng; in *Ya yü t'ang ts'ung shu* and *Chi fu ts'ung shu*.

(b) *Chan kuo ts'e chu*, 33 *p'ien*; text of a Sung edition, collated by Huang P'ei-lieh, with critical notes in 3 *chüan*; facsimile blockprint in *Shih li*

chü Huang shih ts'ung shu (1803); recut by Hu-pei Ch'ung wen shu
chü (1869); type-set reprint in *Ssu pu pei yao* (1927) and *Ts'ung shu chi
ch'eng* (punctuated, 1936).

(c) *Chan kuo ts'e chiao chu* 戰國策校注; 10 *chüan*, with commentary by
Pao Piao and Wu Shih-tao; in *Hsi yin hsüan ts'ung shu* (1846); facsimile reprint of 1355–65 ed. in *Ssu pu ts'ung k'an* (1922).

(d) *Chan kuo ts'e*, 3 vols., Shanghai: Ku chi, 1978; punctuated text (unabbreviated characters), based on Yao Hung's text, with variant
readings and collected annotation from other editions; followed by
(i) a chronology of the *Chan kuo ts'e*, by Yü Ch'ang 于鬯 (from a
manuscript in the Shanghai library); (ii) index of names mentioned
in the text; and (iii) transcription of texts from Ma wang tui.

7.   Selected studies

(a) Chang Ch'i 張琦 (1764–1833), *Chan kuo ts'e shih ti* 戰國策釋地, 2
chüan; in *Kuang ya shu chü ts'ung shu* (1900); reprinted *Ts'ung shu chi
ch'eng* (1936).

(b) Chung Feng-nien 鍾鳳年, *Kuo ts'e k'an yen* 國策勘研; Peiping:
Harvard-Yenching Institute, 1936.

(c) Ch'i Ssu-ho 齊思和, 'Chan kuo ts'e chu tso shih tai k'ao 戰國策著作
時代考'; *Yen-ching hsüeh pao* 34 (1948), 257–78.

(d) Crump, J.I. Jr, 'The *Chan-kuo ts'e* and its fiction'; *TP* XLVIII (1960),
305–75.

(e) Cheng Liang-shu 鄭良樹, *Chan kuo ts'e yen chiu* 戰國策研究; Singapore: Yu lien, 1972; also Taipei: Taiwan hsüeh sheng, 1972.

(f) Chu Tsu-keng 諸祖耿, *Chan kuo ts'e chi chu hui k'ao* 戰國策集注彙
考; 3 vols. ; Yang-chou: Chiang-su ku chi, 1985.

(g) Ho Chien-chang 何建章, *Chan kuo ts'e chu shih* 戰國策注釋; 4 vols.;
Chung hua, 1990.

(h) Feng Tso-min 馮作民, *Pai hua Chan kuo ts'e* 白話戰國策; 3 vols.,
Taipei: Hsing kuang, 1979.

(i) Meng Ch'ing-hsiang 孟慶祥, *Chan kuo ts'e i chu* 戰國策譯注; Hei-
lung-jiang: Jen min, 1986.

8.   Translations

(a) Crump, J.I., Jr., *Intrigues: studies of the Chan-kuo ts'e*; Ann Arbor, Michigan: University of Michigan Press, 1964.; contains 50 selected items
with a critical analysis of the content, treated as fiction; reviewed by
T. H. Tsien, *JAS* 24 (1965), 328–29.

(b) Crump, J.I., Jr., *Chan-kuo ts'e*; Oxford: Clarendon Press, 1970; a complete translation of the text.

9.　Japanese editions

A. *Kambun taikei*; no. 19, 1915, edited by Yokota Ikō and Yasui Sokken (Mamoru); new edition with commentaries by Nagasawa Kikuya 長澤規矩也 and index, 1958.
B. *Kanseki kokujikai zensho*; nos. 38–40, 1917, edited by Makino Kenjirō (Sōshū).
D. *Kokuyaku kambun taisei*; no. 12, 1920, edited by Uno Tetsuto.
E. *Kambun sōsho*, 1927, edited by Nakamura Kyūshirō.
H. *Shinshaku kambun taikei*; nos. 47–49, 1977, 1981, edited by Hayashi Hideichi.
I. *Tōyō bunko*; nos. 64, 74, 86, 1966–67, edited by Tsuneishi Shigeru.
J. *Chūgoku no shisō*; no. 2, 1964, edited by Moriya Hiroshi.
K. *Chūgoku koten bungaku taikei*; no. 7, 1972, edited by Tsuneishi Shigeru.
L. *Chūgoku koten shinsho*, 1968–69, edited by Sawada Masahiro.

10.　Indexes

(a) *Chan kuo ts'e t'ung chien* 戰國策通檢; Peiping; Centre franco-chinois, 1948.
(b) *Sengokusaku koyū meishi sakuin* 戰國策固有名詞索引; compiled under the direction of Shigezawa Toshio 重澤俊郎; Kyoto: Kyōto daigaku bungakubu tetsugaku shi kenkyūshitsu, 1960; based on Yao Hung's edition.
(c) Fidler, Sharon J., with J.I. Crump, *Index to the* Chan-kuo ts'e; Ann Arbor, Michigan: University of Michigan,1973.
(d) *A Concordance to the Zhanguoce* 戰國策逐字索引, ed. D.C. Lau and Chen Fong Ching; *ICS* series, Hong Kong: Commercial Press, 1992.

— Tsuen-hsuin Tsien

Ch'ien fu lun 潛夫論

1. Content

The *Ch'ien fu lun* 潛夫論, in 10 *chüan*, contains 36 essays (*p'ien*) by Wang Fu 王符 (*c.* 90–165). The last essay is in the form of an epilogue, in which the author enumerates the headings of the preceding 35 essays and states his reason and purpose in writing them. Nos. 25 to 28 and no. 35 concern miscellaneous topics of divination, shamanistic practice, physiognomy, the interpretation of dreams, the Five Elements and Virtues and the origin of surnames. The other *p'ien* discuss a variety of important issues, tracing their historical background and expounding the author's viewpoints or solutions.

The subjects of discussion range from problems of scholarship and morality (nos. 1, 4, 32) to those of enlightened rulership and government (nos. 6, 9, 10, 17). Some refer to the selection of meritorious officials (nos. 7, 14, 15), the administration of justice (nos. 16, 18, 19, 20), social and economic conditions and policies (nos. 2, 3, 4, 12, 13) and matters of military strategy and frontier defence (nos. 21, 22, 23, 24). Many of these issues, which are inter-dependent, are discussed together from different perspectives. Altogether the 35 *p'ien* cover almost all the important aspects of state, society, thought and religion of Later Han times.

2. Authorship and date of composition

According to Fan Yeh 范曄 (398–446; *Hou Han shu* 後漢書 49, p. 1630), Wang Fu, style Chieh-hsin 節信, was a native of Lin-ching 臨涇, in An-ting 安定 commandery. Born in a humble status, he took no part in the social activities that were popular among the political factions and élite circles of his time, and he was not successful in seeking to enter government service. Frustrated and embittered, he lived as a recluse and wrote his work in some thirty *p'ien*, in order to criticize current affairs. Not wishing to publicize his own name, he entitled the book *Ch'ien fu lun* (A hermit's discourses). His essays enable a reader to get a good view of the social and political situation of the time.

Fan Yeh does not mention the dates of Wang Fu's birth or death, nor does he specify his age at death. Although Wang Fu was unsuccessful in political affairs, he is stated to have been friendly with prominent scholar officials such as Ma Jung 馬融 (79–166), Chang Heng 張衡 (78–139), Ts'ui Yüan 崔瑗 (78–173) and Tou Chang 竇章 (d. 144). In addition, on returning to An-ting after his dismissal (c. 163), the general Huang-fu Kuei 皇甫規 (104–174) is said to have treated Wang Fu with special courtesy. On the basis of such information, Hou Wai-lu 侯外廬 and others have suggested that Wang Fu was born during the period 88 to 125, and that he died sometime between 146 and 189. In what is so far the most detailed study, Chin Fa-ken 金發根 suggested c. 90 to 165 as Wang Fu's dates, and these are also given in Balazs' work. Liu Chi-hua 劉紀華 has suggested revised dates of c. 80 to 164.

According to Chin Fa-ken, and as re-iterated by Liu Chi-hua, Wang Fu wrote the four *p'ien* on military and frontier defence (nos. 21–24) in reaction to the first major uprising of the Ch'iang 羌 in 107–18, and they were composed probably between 112 and 118 (revised to 111–116 by Liu). The editors of the *Ssu k'u ch'üan shu* suggested that the *Ch'ien fu lun* was written during the reign of Huan ti (146–68), but this view has been criticized by Liu Chi-hua. Liu supported the conclusion of Chin Fa-ken that, as the work does not mention the *tang ku* 黨錮 incidents of 166–84, it was completed between 111 and 152.

3.   Traditional assessments and textual history

Fan Yeh, who valued Wang Fu's critical appraisal of current affairs, included an abridged version of five *p'ien* of the *Ch'ien fu lun* (nos. 11, 12, 14, 18 and 16) in *Hou Han shu* 49, pp. 1630f.; the text is substantially identical with that of the received version, with some differences of wording. Han Yü 韓愈 (768–824) praised Wang Fu as being one of the three worthy men of later Han (see the citation in *Ssu k'u ch'üan shu tsung mu t'i yao*). In *Cheng t'ang tu shu chi* 鄭堂讀書記 (Basic Sinological Series, 1940, 36, p. 665), Chou Chung-fu 周中孚 (1768–1831) stated that the *Ch'ien fu lun* had been continuously recorded and listed in all important bibliographical works and library catalogues, beginning with that of the *Sui shu* (34, p. 998; under *ju chia*). The work appears in Fujiwara Sukeyo's catalogue, with 10 *chüan*. Authenticity and authorship pose no serious problems.

4.   Editions

The earliest text available is that of a Sung manuscript (format 10 by 18), reproduced in the *Ssu pu ts'ung k'an* series; another Sung version was used in the *Liang ching i pien*. In 1305 the text was printed along with the

Pai hu t'ung and *Feng su t'ung i*, on the basis of earlier editions which are unspecified. Little is known of this print, which was however available to Wang Chi-p'ei 汪繼培 (b. 1775), who noted that its text was defective, as compared with that of the *Han Wei ts'ung shu* of 1592. Other Ming editions include that of Kuei Yu-kuang 歸有光 (1506–71; in *Chu tzu hui han*).

The best collated edition, and the only one with extensive annotations, is that of Wang Chi-p'ei (preface 1814); this was included, with a further preface by Wang Shao-lan 王紹蘭, in the *Hu hai lou ts'ung shu*. This is based on the edition of 1305, taking full account of the text of the *Han Wei ts'ung shu* (1592), an edition by Ho T'ang 何鏜 (*cs* 1547), citations of the *Ch'ien fu lun* that appear in other works such as the *Ch'ün shu chih yao*, and notes by Lu Wen-ch'ao 盧文弨 (1717–96) and other scholars. Wang Chi-p'ei's edition is available in the *Ssu pu pei yao* series, the *Pai pu ts'ung shu* and a modern, punctuated, edition, of 1978 (Shanghai: Ku chi). A few revisions have been made to Wang Chi-p'ei's text in that print, notably by re-arranging part of *p'ien* no.32; Wang's notes have been recast in Western style; and notes, as well as text, are punctuated.

Other recent editions include:

(a) Hu Ch'u-sheng 胡楚生, *Ch'ien fu lun chi shih* 潛夫論集釋 (Taipei: Ting wen,1979). Hu compares the text of Wang Chi-p'ei's edition with that of the Sung copy, which had not been available to Wang.

(b) P'eng To 彭鐸, *Ch'ien fu lun chien* 潛夫論箋(Peking: Chung hua, 1979); punctuated text with notes by Wang Chi-p'ei and P'eng; appendixes include biographical notes on Wang Fu, assessments of his work and prefaces.

(c) P'eng To, *Ch'ien fu lun chiao cheng* 潛夫論校正; Peking: Chung hua, 1979.

5. Traditional comments printed without text

(a) By Yü Yüeh 俞樾 (1821–1907); see 'Tu *Ch'ien fu lun*' 讀潛夫論, in *Ch'un tsai t'ang ch'üan shu* 春在堂全書, and notes in *Chu tzu p'ing i pu lu*.

(b) By Sun I-jang 孫詒讓 (1848–1908); see *Cha i 8*.

(c) By Wang Jen-chün 王仁俊 (1866–1913); see 'Ch'ien fu lun i wen' 潛夫論佚文, in *Ching chi i wen* 經籍佚文.

6. Secondary studies

(a) Balazs, Etienne, *Chinese Civilization and Bureaucracy*; New Haven and London: Yale University Press, 1964; see pp. 198–205.

(b) Chin Fa-ken 金發根, 'Wang Fu sheng tsu nien sui ti k'ao cheng chi Ch'ien fu lun hsieh ting shih chien ti t'ui lun' 王符生卒年歲的考證及潛夫論寫定時間的推論; *BIHP* 40:2 (1969), 781–99.

(c) Liu Chi-hua, *Wang Fu yü Ch'ien fu lun* 王符與潛夫論; Taipei: 1977.

(Of the foregoing items (c), though based on the original research of (b), is the most comprehensive).

(d) Huang Chen-ch'iu 黃振球, 'Wang Fu che hsüeh ssu hsiang' 王符哲學思想; *Tai-wan Shih ta Chiao yü yen chiu suo chi k'an* 2 (1948), 109–111.

(e) Ch'en Ch'i-yün; see *The Cambridge History of China*, vol. I (Cambridge: Cambridge University Press, 1986), pp. 789–96.

7. Translations

(a) Pearson, Margaret J., *Wang Fu and the comments of a recluse* (Tempe, Arizona: Center for Asian Studies, Arizona State University, 1989); introductory chapters, which concern the life and times of Wang Fu and his political thought are followed by translations of 14 *p'ien*.

(b) Kamenarović, Ivan P., *Wang Fu: propos d'un ermite (Qianfu lun); introduction et traduction du chinois*; Paris, Éditions du Cerf, 1992; the translation of the 36 *p'ien* is accompanied by notes which (i) indicate where this is based on an emended text and (ii) provide the basic information needed by non-specialist readers.

8. Indexes

(a) *Ch'ien fu lun t'ung chien* 潛夫論通檢 (Index du Ts'ien Fou Louen); centre franco-chinois d'études sinologiques no.6, Peking, 1945. This is based on the *Ssu pu pei yao* version, and includes a summary of the contents of the work.

(b) *A Concordance to the Qianfu lun* 潛夫論逐字索引, ed. D.C. Lau and Chen Fong Ching; *ICS* series, Hong Kong: Commercial Press, forthcoming 1995.

— Ch'i-yün Ch'en
— Margaret Pearson

Chiu chang suan shu 九章算術

1. Content

This work is a classified collection of 246 problems with accompanying solutions, evidently designed to give a comprehensive account of the mathematical knowledge of its day. The contents of the book follows a set form: immediately after a statement of a problem there is a numerical answer, after which details of the method of solution are given. All problems are formulated as particular numerical examples. In the absence of an algebraic notation methods of solution are given rhetorically, i.e., in the form of instructions to perform a series of arithmetical operations on the data. No explicit attempt is made to prove the validity of the methods used.

The *Chiu chang suan shu* classifies its problems under the following headings:

(a) *Fang t'ien* 方田 ('square fields'); rules are given for finding the areas of fields of various shapes, including rectangles, triangles, trapezoids, circles, segments, sectors and annuli. The rules given for rectilinear figures are exact; in calculating the area of a circle it is assumed that $\pi=3$, and approximate rules are given for segments and sectors. Rules for the manipulation of fractions are also stated.

(b) *Su mi* 粟米 ('cereals'); the section opens with a tabulation of equivalent amounts of different grains, and deals with the exchange of a given quantity of one type of grain for that of another variety. Related problems of pricing are also treated.

(c) *Ts'ui fen* 衰分 ('differential allocation'); problems deal with the distribution of quantities amongst groups at different rates, according to rank rating, tax liability etc., and with further questions of proportion.

(d) *Shao kuang* 少廣 ('diminishing breadth'); given the area and one side of a figure, the unknown side is found. Rules are also given for finding the side of a square of given area (extracting the square root), and of a cube of given volume (extracting the cube root). These are stated in terms of the manipulation of counting rods on a calculating board.

16

(e) *Shang kung* 商功 ('consultations on works'); the volumes of earth-works and excavations of a variety of shapes are calculated.

(f) *Chün shu* 均輸 ('equal supply'); problems of alligation arising from the assessment of tax burdens are treated. In the latter part of the section questions involving pursuit are solved.

(g) *Ying pu tsu* 盈不足 ('excess and deficiency'); problems of joint purchase are considered, equivalent to equations of the form y = ax. These are solved on the basis of the excess or deficiency arising from given trial solutions (equivalent to the mediaeval European 'rule of false position').

(h) *Fang ch'eng* 方程 ('the square array'); the problems solved in this section are equivalent to systems of simultaneous linear equations. The data are arranged on the counting board in a rectangular matrix, and manipulations are performed corresponding to the successive elimination of unknowns in a modern algebraic treatment. The handling of both positive *cheng* 正 and negative *fu* 負 numbers is described.

(i) *Kou ku* 句股 ('base and altitude'); this section deals with applications of Pythagoras' theorem. Some of the later problems involve what is in effect the solution of quadratic equations. At least two of these examples re-appear in identical form in the repertoire of Indian mathematics of the ninth century A.D. (Mahavira of Mysore).

The *Chiu chang suan shu* is the world's earliest extant comprehensive arithmetical textbook. Although its problems are all stated in the context of supposedly practical situations, it is far more than an official's hand-book for reckoning and gauging, and its unknown author was clearly interested in mathematical theory for its own sake. The authority and influence of the book in the later development of Chinese mathematics were very great. One unfortunate result of this was that Chinese mathematicians felt constrained to conform to the model that it had set. What-ever the theoretical interest of a problem, it had to be motivated (often with evident artificiality) by some practical requirement.

2. Composition

The *Chiu chang suan shu* is consistent and orderly enough to make it likely that it was written, or perhaps edited, by a single author. It has never been doubted that it is a Han work, but much of the mathematical knowledge that it contains must go back at least as far as the Warring States. Quite apart from the improbability of such a rich body of theory developing suddenly, even the smallest of the pre-Ch'in states could not have run its affairs without the services of reckoning clerks able to solve many of the problems of gauging and the allocation of finance and manpower that are dealt with in the *Chiu chang suan shu*.

The tradition that there were nine divisions of mathematics may have antedated the *Chiu chang suan shu* considerably, and thus influenced the form that the work took. The ninefold scheme first appears in the *Chou li*, which is at least as old as the early Han. According to the idealised scheme of ancient government that it purports to record, noble youths were instructed in the six arts (*liu i* 六藝) by an official known as the Guardian (*pao shih* 保氏). Each art was subdivided: thus there were the five kinds of ritual (*wu li* 五禮), the six kinds of music (*liu yüeh* 六樂), etc. The last art taught was the *chiu shu* 九數, the nine ways of reckoning. As with the other arts, the *Chou li* gives no indication what these might be.

The earliest extant attempt at an explanation of the *chiu shu* is that given by Cheng Chung 鄭衆 (d. 83) and quoted by Cheng Hsüan 鄭玄 (127–200) in his comment on the relevant passage of the *Chou li* (*SPTK* ed. 4.8b). The first eight headings are identical with those of the *Chiu chang suan shu* as received today, except that the seventh and eighth are interchanged, and trivially different characters are used in two of the titles (i.e., *ch'a fen* 差分 for *ts'ui fen* 衰分 and *ying pu tsu* 贏不足 for *ying pu tsu* 盈不足; the latter change may have been introduced so as to avoid the use of Hui ti's name). The ninth heading is entitled not *kou ku* but *p'ang yao* 旁要, which is a term of unknown significance. Cheng is clearly giving a list that was out of date in his time, for he adds 'nowadays there are also the *ch'ung ch'a* 重差 ('repeated differences'; the usual term for the use of similar right triangles), the *hsi chieh* 夕桀 (significance unknown) and the *kou ku'*. The old list almost certainly goes back to Former Han, and it is highly suggestive that the three modern innovations mentioned include *kou ku*, which has replaced *p'ang yao* in the received text. The *Chiu chang suan shu* was current in the time of Cheng Hsüan, who is said to have understood it thoroughly (see *Hou Han shu* 35, p. 1207). More significantly, the same claim is made for Ma Hsü 馬續, who, as the elder brother of Ma Jung 馬融, must have studied the work shortly after Cheng Chung's death (*Hou Han shu* 24, p. 862).

It seems clear that the *Chiu chang suan shu* was already current in the early years of Later Han, but its earlier history is obscure. In his preface, the third century A.D. commentator Liu Hui 劉徽 (see below) observed correctly that the *Chiu chang suan shu* shows signs of being a Han book; e.g., those of its problems which concern travel often involve trips to Ch'ang-an. Since he accepted the *Chou li* as a canonical scripture giving a true account of early Chou government, he felt sure that there must have been a pre-Ch'in forerunner of the *Chiu chang suan shu*. Further, he evidently accepted Cheng Hsüan's list as a description of the contents of such an older work, for he notes that the present work 'differs somewhat from the ancient one'. There seems no other basis for his claim that the *Chiu chang suan shu* was compiled from ancient fragments by the early Han statesman Chang Ts'ang 張蒼 (d. 152 B.C.), apart from the fact that Chang was the first Han personage to be well known for mathematical skill (*Shih chi* 96, p. 2676).

Until recently it seemed clear that the *Chiu chang suan shu* could not possibly date from as early as the time of Chang Ts'ang. The earliest known use of the sixth heading, *chün shu*, was as a term taken from the economic measures introduced by Wu ti in 110 B.C. (*Shih chi* 30, p. 1441), and the Shang lin 上林 pleasure palace and park mentioned in the ninth problem of this section were famous constructions of the same emperor. Further, the *Chiu chang suan shu* does not appear with the other mathematical books listed in *Han shu* chapter 30, which reproduces the titles in a listing that was submitted to the throne *c.* 6 B.C., after exhaustive researches by Liu Hsin 劉歆 (46 B.C.–A.D. 23) and his father Liu Hsiang 劉向 (79–8 B.C.). It was hard to believe that a work which was so influential in the Later Han would have escaped notice if it had been current in the first century B.C.; it therefore seemed quite possible that it was not compiled until as late as the time of Wang Mang (reigned 9–23). Ostensible adherence to the forms of the *Chou li* was a major element in Wang Mang's statecraft, and his reign would have been a favourable time for an attempt at reconstituting the ancient curriculum of the *chiu shu*.

The authorship of the *Chiu chang suan shu* remains a mystery. Some light has however been shed on its possible background by the discovery in 1983–84 of several books on bamboo strips in the Han dynasty tomb M 247 near Chang chia shan 張家山, Hupei province. One of these bore the title *Suan shu shu* 算數書 'The Book of Reckoning', and it appears that its form and content bear a close relation to those of the *Chiu chang suan shu*. The work is in poor condition and so far only a brief preliminary description of its contents has been published: see Tu Shih-jan 杜石然, 'Chiang-ling Chang-chia-shan chu chien "Suan shu shu" ch'u t'an' 江陵張家山竹簡《算數書》初探, *Tzu jan k'o hsüeh shih yen chiu* 自然科學史研究 vol. 7 no. 3, 1988, 210–204. The tomb dates from the first half of the second century B.C., intriguingly close to the time of Chang Ts'ang. Since another text from the same tomb also contains an instance of the term *chün shu* previously thought to have been introduced *c.* 110 B.C. (see above), an early dating of the *Chiu chang suan shu* seems less unlikely than before.

3. Commentaries

The earliest commentator on the *Chiu chang suan shu* seems to have been Hsü Yüeh 徐岳 (*fl.* A.D. 220), supposed author of the still exant mathematical work *Shu shu chi i* 數術記遺. His commentary was still known in the Sui and T'ang but it had been lost by the Sung period. The first extant commentary is that by Liu Hui, who, according to *Sui shu* 16, p. 404, did his work under the Wei 魏 kingdom, at a date corresponding with A.D. 263. However, in his comments on the area of a circular field, Liu mentions a bronze measure kept in the arsenal of the Chin dynasty (established 265); it appears that he must have continued to write while in the service of the new government.

Liu's commentary is one of the great achievements of ancient mathematics. He is especially famous for his work on the ratio between the circumference and diameter of a circle. Like the *Chou pi suan ching*, the *Chiu chang suan shu* uses the approximation $\pi=3$. Liu attacks the problem of obtaining a better value by the use of inscribed polygons with increasing numbers of sides, thus reaching an increasingly closer approximation. His final value is equivalent to $\pi=3.14$. As already mentioned, the *Chiu chang suan shu* itself does not attempt to prove the validity of the methods of solution it prescribes. Perhaps it was enough that they were seen to produce the right answers. Liu Hui however was clearly interested in giving general justifications of the methods laid down in the text. He did this by reinterpreting the algorithmic procedures of the text in geometrical terms. The diagrams he supplied did not survive the T'ang period, but an attempted restoration was given by Tai Chen (see below).

In addition to his comments throughout the *Chiu chang suan shu*, Liu added a new chapter on the *ch'ung ch'a*, discussing the use of gnomons for surveying purposes. Under the Sui this text was still attached to the *Chiu chang suan shu* as a tenth chapter (*Sui shu* 34, p. 1025), but by the T'ang it had begun to circulate as a separate work and was given the title *Hai tao suan ching* 海島算經 ('Sea island mathematical classic'), after the subject of its first problem (*Chiu T'ang shu* 47, p. 2039; *Hsin T'ang shu* 59, p. 1546). This work is still extant.

A commentary by Chen Luan 甄鸞 (*fl.* A.D. 560), who also wrote on the *Chou pi suan ching*, was likewise lost after the T'ang period. Although it is not listed in the Sui or T'ang bibliographies, a commentary by Tsu Chung 祖中 (elsewhere Tsu Chung 祖仲) is mentioned in Fujiwara Sukeyo's list. This commentator is probably to be identified with the great fifth century mathematician Tsu Ch'ung-chih 祖沖之, whose work may have been among those which perished when most of the Sui imperial library sank in the Yellow River in the disaster of 622.

In 656 Li Ch'un-feng 李淳風 (602–670) was instructed to prepare editions of mathematical texts for use in the state College (*Chiu T'ang shu* 79, p. 2719), and for this purpose he wrote a subcommentary on the *Chiu chang suan shu*, taking as a basis the text bearing Liu Hui's commentary. Li's notes preserve some interesting early material, and it was his work which fixed the version of the received text. Further explanatory material was supplied under the Northern Sung by Li Chi 李籍, a member of the staff of the imperial library, who added an appendix entitled *Chiu chang suan shu yin i* 九章算術音義 before the book was printed in 1084.

4. Text history

There are no grounds for suspecting the authenticity of the received text of the *Chiu chang suan shu*. All extant editions of the work can be traced back to a printed collection of nine mathematical books (also including the *Chou pi suan ching*) issued in 1084 by the imperial library of Northern Sung. The *Chiu chang suan shu* was printed with the commentaries of Liu Hui and Li Ch'un-feng and the appendix of Li Chi. No examples of this printing are extant, and we owe the preservation of the text to a reprint made by Pao Huan-chih 鮑澣之 in 1213. According to his postface the study of the *Chiu chang suan shu* had ceased almost completely after the collapse of the Northern Sung dynasty in 1126. Not only were there very few scholars interested in such subjects, but the only available texts lacked the essential commentaries of Liu and Li, and bore attributions to the Yellow Emperor. Such an edition appears to have been reprinted by Jung Ch'i 榮棨 in 1148; his preface is printed in the *I chia t'ang ts'ung shu* edition of Yang Hui's 楊輝 *Hsiang chieh chiu chang suan fa* 詳解九章算法 (1261).

Fortunately in the summer of 1200 a copy of the old imperial library print of 1084 came to light in the house of one of Pao's friends in Hangchou, and he had it copied and reprinted. Under the Ming dynasty, Pao's text was copied into the *Yung lo ta tien*. A surviving incomplete copy (sections 1 to 5) of his printing is now preserved in the Shanghai library. A late seventeenth century tracing of this defective version has been reproduced in the *T'ien lu lin lang ts'ung shu*. A photographic reproduction of the Shanghai text is included in *Sung k'o suan ching liu chung* 宋刻算經六種 (Peking: Wen wu 1980).

When Tai Chen 戴震 (1724–77) edited the *Chiu chang suan shu* for the *Ssu k'u* project he evidently did not know of the surviving Southern Sung print and worked solely from the *Yung lo ta tien*. He made many

emendations to the text and its commentaries, and added reconstructions of the lost illustrations by Liu Hui. Apart from the instance mentioned above, Tai's edition is the one reproduced in all *ts'ung shu*.
Caution is necessary in one respect; some collections, such as the *Ts'ung
shu chi ch'eng*, reproduce the fine Wu ying tien print in which the unaltered, but punctuated, text from the *Yung lo ta tien* is accompanied by
notes in the text giving Tai Chen's comments and emendations. Others,
such as the *Ssu pu ts'ung k'an*, collect Tai's notes together at the end of
each section, but print a text which has already been emended in accordance with Tai's ideas. A critical text with introduction was published
by Ch'ien Pao-ts'ung 錢寶琮, in his *Suan ching shih shu* 算經十書
(Peking: Chung-hua, 1963). In addition to the principal sources described above, Ch'ien makes use of quotations from the *Chiu chang suan
shu* in Yang Hui's work. The best edition of the text so far is however
that established by Kuo Shu-ch'un 郭書春 in his *Chiu chang suan shu*
(Shen-yang: Liao-ning chiao yü ch'u pan she, 1990). Kuo includes important introductory essays and copious explanatory notes.

5.   Studies and translations

A full collection of bibliographical material on the *Chiu chang suan shu* is
given in Ting Fu-pao 丁福保 and Chou Yün-ch'ing 周雲青, *Ssu pu
tsung lu suan fa pien* 四部總錄算法編 (Shanghai: Shang-wu, 1957). A
detailed study by Li Huang 李潢 *Chiu chang suan shu hsi ts'ao t'u shuo* 九
章算術細草圖說 (*c.* 1790) is still useful. For an important modern study,
see Pai Shang-shu 白尚恕, *Chiu chang suan shu chu shih* 九章算術注釋
(Peking: K'o hsüeh, 1983), as well as the work of Kuo mentioned above
which takes issue with Pai on several points. A convenient introductory
discussion is given in Joseph Needham *et al.*, *Science and Civilisation in
China* vol. 3 (Cambridge: Cambridge University Press, 1959), pp. 24–29,
and also (with sample problems) in Yoshio Mikami, *The development of
mathematics in China and Japan* (Leipzig: Abhandlungen zur Geschichte
der Mathematische Wissenshaften 30, 1913), pp. 8–25. Two more recent
general histories of Chinese mathematics in Western languages discuss
the *Chiu chang suan shu*. See Li Yan and Du Shiran, *Chinese Mathematics:
A Concise History* (Oxford: Clarendon Press, 1987), pp. 33–59, and J. C.
Martzloff, *Histoire des Mathematiques Chinoises* (Paris: Masson, 1988), pp.
115–26.

The following translations have appeared in western languages:

(a) E.I. Berezkina, 'Drevnekitajskij Traktat *Matematika v devjati Knigach'*,
    in *Istoriko-matematiceskie issledovaniya* (Moscow) 1957:10, 423–584.

(b) Vogel, Kurt, *Neun Bucher arithmetischer Technik*; Ostwalds Klassiker der exacten Wissenshaften, n.s., vol.IV; Braunschweig, 1968.

(c) At the time of writing (1992), a full French translation of the text and Liu Hui's commentary is in preparation by Karine Chemla (Centre Nationale de la recherche scientifique, Paris).

6. Index

A Concordance to the Zhou bi suanjng and Jiu zhang suanshu 周髀算經, 九章算術逐字索引, ed. D.C. Lau and Chen Fong Ching; *ICS* series, Hong Kong: Commercial Press, forthcoming 1996.

— Christopher Cullen

Chou li 周禮

1. Content and structure

The *Chou li*, originally known as the *Chou kuan* 周官, and sometimes also called the *Chou kuan li* 周官禮, gives an elaborately laid out and detailed description of what purports to be the governmental and administrative structure and organisation of the royal state of Chou. The text is divided into six major sections, each one corresponding with one of the six primary titles and offices of the Chou royal hierarchy, each of which was responsible for one general area or domain of governmental administration, as follows:

(a) *T'ien kuan chung tsai* 天官冢宰; celestial offices, [domain of the] Prime Minister (matters of general administration).
(b) *Ti kuan ssu t'u* 地官司徒; terrestrial offices, [domain of the] Overseer of Public Affairs (education).
(c) *Ch'un kuan tsung po* 春官宗伯; spring offices, [domain of the] patriarch of ancestral affairs (sacrifices and rites).
(d) *Hsia kuan ssu ma* 夏官司馬; summer offices, [domain of the] overseer of military affairs.
(e) *Ch'iu kuan ssu k'ou* 秋官司寇; autumn offices, [domain of the] overseer of penal affairs.
(f) *Tung kuan k'ao kung chi* 冬官攷工記; winter offices, records of the scrutiny of crafts.

With the exception of (f), each of these sections starts with an enumeration of the various governmental officials and staff titles at every level from the highest to the lowest, arranged and listed hierarchically. Section (a), for example, begins with the *chung tsai* 'Prime Minister', or 'Chancellor of State', the highest non-proprietary office of a state, and ends with such quotidian staff of the court as palace gate-keepers, tailors, dyers and cobblers. A systematic, detailed description of the responsibilities and duties of every title and office mentioned then follows. The descriptions are normally phrased at the outset with a kind of formula that states the name of the office, followed by the word *chang* 掌 'is in charge of', or 'has charge of'; that is then followed by the appropriate specification of the duties incumbent on the office in question. Each of the six sections was, apparently, designed to comprise sixty offices, giving a total of 360 for the *Chou li* in its entirety. Kuo Mo-jo (see 4 (a) below) has suggested that this structure of six times sixty offices has an astronomical or cosmological significance of the kind that was characteristic of the late Spring and Autumn or Warring States periods, and thus argues against an early date for the origin of the work. In any case, according to the tabulation and enumeration by Sven Broman (see 4 (c) below), the actual number of offices in each section varies from the ideal of sixty, in all cases being more rather than fewer than that number.

The original sixth section (*Tung kuan*) was the domain of the *ssu k'ung* 司空 'Overseer of public works'. That section had already been lost at the time when the *Chou li* first became known in Former Han, and the *K'ao kung chi* was substituted in its place. This text varies somewhat from the model of the preceding five sections in that it does not list administrative offices, titles and duties, but rather gives an enumeration and description of the various craftsmen attached to the royal court and the technical details of their crafts, including, for example, the making of carriages, weapons and boats. In each case the text describes in considerable detail the component parts of the item in question. It gives the names and sizes of different types, and specifies the artisan or craftsman responsible for each part or stage of the construction. The *K'ao kung chi* is thought by Chiang Yung 江永 (1681–1762) to be a work of the late Warring States period, compiled by a person from the state of Ch'i. He bases this conclusion on the place names of the Warring States period and the Ch'i dialect expressions that he finds occurring in the text; see his *Chou li i i chü yao* 周禮疑義舉要, ch.6.

2. Origin and authenticity

The *Chou li* is not known before Former Han. It is first mentioned, by its original name of *Chou kuan*, in the 'Feng shan' 封禪 chapter of the *Shih chi* (28, p. 1357), and then, by the name *Chou kuan ching* 周官經, in *Han shu* 30, p. 1709, where it is entered as a work with 6 *p'ien*; in *Han shu* 99C, p. 4187, it is referred to as the *Chou li*. The change of name from *Chou kuan* to *Chou li* is attributed by Hsün Yüeh 荀悅 (148–209) to Liu Hsin 劉歆 46B.C–A.D. 23 (*Ch'ien Han chi*, SPTK ed., 25.2b), and this statement is reiterated by Lu Te-ming 陸德明 (556–627) in his preface to the *Ching tien shih wen*. Hsün Yüeh states that Liu Hsin also proposed calling the text *Li ching* 禮經, a title that is occasionally used in reference to the *Chou li*. Liu Hsin sought to have the post of an official scholar estab-

lished for the *Chou li;* since the name whereby the work is entered in
Han shu ch.30 is *Chou kuan ching,* it may be said that from the time of Liu
Hsin the *Chou li* has been regarded as a classical text.

According to the traditional account of the emergence of the *Chou li*
in the mid-second century B.C., as reflected in varying degrees of detail
in *Han shu* 30, p. 1710, *Han shu* 53, p. 2410, *Sui shu* 32, p. 925 and the
summary of Ma Jung 馬融 (79–166) partially preserved in the essay
'Chou li fei hsing' 周禮廢興 of Chia Kung-yen 賈公彥 (*fl.* 650; usually
seen as the preface to his *Chou li shu* 周禮疏), the text came to light
when a certain Mr. Li 李 presented it to the Hsien 獻 king of Ho-chien
河間 (reigned 155–129 B.C). This was in fact Liu Te 劉德, son of Han
Ching ti and younger brother of Wu ti. He was well known as an avid
collector and afficionado of old texts. When he received the *Chou li,* the
sixth section (*Tung kuan*) was already missing; so he is said to have
offered a reward of 1000 cash to anyone who could provide him with it.
When this was still not forthcoming, he substituted the *K'ao kung chi* in
its place. The king is then reported to have presented the *Chou li* to the
imperial archives in the court of his brother, Wu ti.

At that time, not only did the text fail to receive any serious consideration from official scholars; it was actually criticised and scorned,
presumably for not being in accord with the prevailing tradition as
expressed in other texts. No details of this criticism survive, but it may
be assumed that it arose at least from the fact that official scholarship of
this period was dominated by what would soon come to be known as
the 'New Text school'. Being an Old Text work, the *Chou li* was not likely to be looked upon with much favour or objectivity by the established
scholars of the court.

Ma Jung says that the *Chou li* was a particular target for elimination
by the First Ch'in Emperor at the time of the burning of the books in 213
B.C. because it represented the traditional, orthodox governmental system of the Chou kings so fully, and therefore flew directly in the face of
the centralised legalist authoritarian administration of his own regime.
This suggests that anyone who was pre-disposed to hide away copies of
proscribed texts would have been taking an especially grave risk in the
case of the *Chou li.* It might also explain the absence of any reference to
the text prior to the time of the king of Ho-chien.

After its presentation by that king the *Chou li* seems to have lingered
in the Han imperial archives largely untouched, save for the aforementioned scorn, until the time of Wang Mang. At that time, because
Wang Mang strove to invest his rule with legitimacy by deliberately establishing a government modelled after that of Chou kung; and because

the *Chou li* had already come to be regarded as the work of the latter, it was natural for this text to be adopted as the principal authority on state organization. In the course of his service to Wang Mang, Liu Hsin not only promoted the *Chou li*, rescuing it from the obscurity of the Han archives; as mentioned above, he was also instrumental in getting a post established for an official scholar of the work.

With the end of the regime of Wang Mang, not surprisingly the *Chou li* fell out of imperial favour. Nevertheless, orthodox Juist scholars of later Han, especially Cheng Hsüan 鄭玄 (127–200), continued to hold the work in high regard, not primarily for political reasons, but as an important ancient text, which was thought, at least by some, to have been written by Chou kung and therefore to lie at the heart of the orthodox tradition. The immediate disciple of Liu Hsin who prepared a commentary to the *Chou li* was a certain Tu Tzu-ch'un 杜子春. Cheng Hsing 鄭興 (*fl.* A.D. 30), his son Cheng Chung 鄭眾 (d. 83) and Chia K'uei 賈逵 (30–101) are all also known to have compiled notes to the work, now all lost save for fragments cited elsewhere.

While the belief that the work had been written by Chou kung must already have been held before the Wang Mang period, the first time that it is expressly stated is in the opening line of Cheng Hsüan's commentary to the text. Although that belief seems to have prevailed until as late as the Sung period, already in Cheng Hsüan's own time there were sceptics such as Ho Hsiu 何休 (129–82) who had doubts. It is now no longer seriously maintained that the *Chou li* was written by Chou kung. There are many specific textual references reasons for this; the two most important general considerations being: (i) the language of the text is clearly the classical Chinese of the late Spring and Autumn and Warring States periods, not the pre-classical language of Western Chou; and (ii) in many places the content of the text involves concepts and concerns that are identifiably characteristic of the late Spring and Autumn and Warring States periods, and are incompatible with an early Western Chou provenance. Among such features are references to the *wu hsing* 五行, *wu ti* 五帝 and *wu yüeh* 五嶽, none of which is appropriate to a text prior to the fourth century B.C., at the earliest. Moreover, the *Chou li*'s descriptions of sacrifices, laws, burial customs, agricultural techniques, enfeoffment procedures and tenets, etc., all largely conform to what is known from other sources about the society of the Warring States period and not to that of Western Chou.

At the other chronological extreme, it has been suggested since Sung times that the *Chou li* was 'forged' by Liu Hsin as one of his ostensible textual efforts to lend legitimacy to Wang Mang's rule. Among the early

proponents of this charge were the noted scholars Ssu-ma Kuang 司馬
光 (1019–86), Hung Mai 洪邁 (1123–1202) and Su Ch'e 蘇轍 (1039–1112);
more recent advocates included the reformist K'ang Yu-wei 康有爲
(1858–1927). The general basis for this suspicion is the fact that prior to
its appearance in the imperial archives, under the superintendency of
Liu Hsin, the *Chou li* appears scarcely to have been known. Before Liu
Hsin's generation there is in fact no reference to it at all. The fact that
the *Chou li* was highly favoured by Wang Mang, whose interests Liu
Hsin served, also encouraged the suspicion of forgery.

Many reputable scholars have rejected the notion that the work is a
concoction of Liu Hsin. Ch'en Chen-sun 陳振孫 (*c.* 1190–after 1249)
points out that the *Chou li*'s use of many ancient forms of characters and
names of things unknown in the Han period clearly suggests a pre-Han
origin (*Chih chai shu lu chieh t'i* 直齋書錄解題, *Ssu k'u ch'üan shu chen pen*
ed., 2, 21b–22b;). Mao Ch'i-ling 毛奇齡 (1623–1716) also argues against
its having been forged by Liu Hsin. He points out that *Han shu* 30 says
that as early as the time of Wei Wen hou 魏文侯 (445–396 B.C.) a musi-
cian named Tou Kung 竇公 from the state of Wei had a book known as
the *Yüeh shu* 樂書; this was presented at the time of Han Wen ti (reigned
180–157), and turned out to be nothing other than the music section (*ta
ssu yüeh* 大司樂) of the 'Ta tsung po' 大宗伯 part of the *Chou li* (*Ching
wen* 經文; *Huang Ch'ing ching chieh* ed., 163,1a–2a).

In response to K'ang Yu-wei's strident attacks on the authenticity of
many pre-Han texts, including the *Chou li*, several modern scholars
have undertaken to demonstrate that Liu Hsin was not the great forger
that he has been accused of being. In regard to the *Chou li*, the most important western study of this kind is Karlgren's article 'The Early History
of the *Chou li* and *Tso chuan* Texts' (see 4 (c) below). By showing that
numerous passages of the *Chou li* appear in other texts well before the
time of Liu Hsin (e.g., the *Shih chi*, the *Mao shih* commentary and the *Erh
ya*), Karlgren concludes that the *Chou li* must have existed in something
close to its known form and scope in the mid-second century B.C., if not
earlier, and could not have been forged by Liu Hsin. This date is consistent with the traditional record of when the text first became known.

Ku Chieh-kang 顧頡剛 (1893–1980) and Kuo Mo-jo 郭沫若 (1892–
1978) likewise determined that the *Chou li* is a genuine work of the late
Warring States period, and even went so far as to speculate on the particular identity and provenance of the author. In a long study that took
into account Eastern Chou bronze inscriptions, omitted in Karlgren's
article, Kuo Mo-jo concluded that the *Chou li* was probably compiled by
a disciple of Hsün Ch'ing 荀卿 in the state of Chao in the late Chou

period. Ku Chieh-kang by contrast suggests that it was compiled by someone from the state of Ch'i, but stops short of linking it with any particular individual (see 4 (a) below). While such hypotheses must perforce remain speculative, the conclusion that the *Chou li* is a genuine pre-Han text remains convincing.

3. Commentaries and editions

The earliest wholly extant commentary to the *Chou li* is that by Cheng Hsüan, which includes *inter alia* some of the notes of the several earlier Han commentaries. All of the extant fragments of those Han scholars' notes have been collected by Ma Kuo-han 馬國翰 (1794–1857) in his *Yü han shan fang chi i shu*. Ma Jung's notes have also been assembled by Wang Mo 王謨 (*cs* 1778) in his *Han Wei i shu ch'ao* 漢魏遺書鈔. The next major extant commentary is the *shu* 疏 compiled by Chia Kung-yen. These two, along with Lu Te-ming's *yin i* 音義, constitute the principal pre-Ch'ing commentaries to the work.

Of the extensive Ch'ing scholarship on the *Chou li*, three names should be mentioned in particular; Juan Yüan 阮元 (1764–1849), because of his collation notes; Chiang Yung 江永 (1681–1762), who, in addition to his general philological and phonological studies, took a special interest in the three *li* texts, and as a consequence wrote the *Chou li i i chü yao* 周禮疑義舉要; and Sun I-jang 孫詒讓 (1848–1908) who compiled the *Chou li cheng i* 周禮正義 in 86 chapters.

The history of the text between the end of the Han and the beginning of the T'ang periods is obscure. The *Sui shu* (32, p. 919) records a total of 15 *Chou li* works, two of which are marked as lost already. The fifteen titles include the commentaries by Ma Jung and Cheng Hsüan, as well as those of Wang Su 王肅 (195–256) and Kan Pao 干寶 (*fl.* 320), and a *shu* 疏 or sub-commentary in 40 chapters by Shen Chung 沈重 (*fl. c.* 570). Sun I-jang, following a suggestion of Ch'en Chen-sun, suspects that this last is the basis for Chia Kung-yen's *shu* of a century or so later, because, among other things, the number of chapters in both cases is the same. Fujiwara Sukeyo's list includes nine entries for the main work, entitled variously *Chou kuan li*, *Chou li i* or *Chou li*; there is also an entry for *Chou li yin* 周禮音 in 1 *chüan*, and two entries for a work entitled *Chou kuan t'u* 周官圖, in 15 and 10 *chüan* respectively.

Apart from this bibliographic record we know that the *Chou li* was important during the Western Wei dynasty, when Yü-wen T'ai 宇文泰 (507–556) made a deliberate attempt to institute a government that reflected the administrative structure of the book. Ku Chieh-kang says that this was the first time that the administrative system laid out in the *Chou li* was actually put into practice.

The *Chou li* was not one of the classical texts engraved on stone in A.D. 175. It was only in the K'ai ch'eng period (836–840) that it was thus engraved as part of the canon, along with the other eleven classical texts, as may be seen in the Pei lin 碑林 (Hsi-an).

The *Chou li* first appeared in print as one of the Nine Classics for which Feng Tao 馮道 ordered wood blocks to be cut in 932. The text used for this task, which was completed in 953, was based on that of the T'ang Stone Classics, and this first printed text is known as the *Wu tai chien pen* 五代監本 *Chou li*. The transmission of the text thereafter can generally be traced from the printing history of the Classics as a set. The second officially sponsored carving of blocks and printing of the Classics came between 988 and 994. A new set of blocks was cut, based on the text of the *Wu tai* print, and this printing was called the *Kuo tzu chien ch'ung hsing chiao k'o chiu ching* 國子監重行校刻九經.

According to the *Yü hai*, Li Hang 李沆 (947–1004) and Tu Hao 杜鎬 were ordered in 996 to collate and edit the texts of Chia Kung-yen's *shu* for the *Chou li* and the *I li*, along with a number of other texts. Their work was finished and presented to the court in 1001, and at that time the emperor ordered blocks to be cut for the printing of these texts in Hang-chou. This was the first printing of Chia Kung-yen's *shu* for both the *Chou li* and the *I li*. As was then customary, the commentaries were printed separately from the texts of the Classics themselves. The habit, with which we are familiar from Ming and Ch'ing times, of printing the *Chou li* together with Cheng Hsüan's *chu* and Chia Kung-yen's *shu* in a single work, was first seen in the Shao hsing period (1131–1162). This printing is known as the *Ch'a yen ssu* 茶鹽司 edition, or alternatively the *Huang T'ang* 黃唐 edition, after the name of the man who was in charge of cutting the blocks.

A later Southern Sung printing, which was destined to have a greater influence on the subsequent history of the text than the *Ch'a yen ssu* edition, was the *Shih hang pen* 十行本, so called because its format consisted of ten columns to the half folio. It is properly known as the *(Fu) shih yin Chou li chu shu* (附) 釋音周禮注疏, and was printed in Fu-chou. All subsequent printings of the *chu shu* editions of the *Chou li* stem from this 'ten column' edition, the most important being the following:

(a) Ming (Chia ching: 1532–1567): edition of Li Yüan-yang 李元陽 printed from blocks with 9 columns of text to the half folio; also called the *chiu hang pen* 九行本, and known as the *Min pen* 閩本, because Li had served as *Yü shih* 御史 in the Min area.

(b) Ming (Wan li: 1573–1620): the *Chien pen* 監本 or 'Palace edition', known as *Pei chien pen* 北監本, 'Northern Palace Edition'; based on Li Yüan-yang's print.

(c) Ming (Ch'ung chen: 1628–44): the *Chi ku ko* 汲古閣 edition of Mao Chin 毛晉 (1599–1659), based on the Northern Palace edition.

(d) The *Wu ying tien pen* 武英殿本, 1736. Based on the Northern Palace edition, the text was also collated with that of a number of other editions, thus allowing for a number of corrections and emendations of corrupt readings that had accrued to the text since Sung times. This print is considered to be superior to both the Mao Chin and the Northern Palace editions.

(e) Ch'ing (Chia ch'ing: 1796–1820): Juan Yüan's edition (see above). This is based directly on the *Shih hang pen*, but was also collated comprehensively with (a) (b) and (c) as well as with some other editions. It is known under the title (*Fu*) *chiao k'an chi* (附) 校勘記 and is a much superior edition in comparison with other descendants of the *Shih hang pen*, with the possible exception of the *Wu ying tien* print. See also Katō Toranosuke 加藤虎之亭, *Shūrai kyō chūso ongi kōkanki* 周禮經注疏音義校勘記 (Tokyo: Kiyota Kiyoshi, 1958).

Apart from the printings already mentioned, one of the best known private editions of the *Chou li* is the one that Yüeh K'o 岳珂 (1183–1240) included as part of the Nine Classics, in what is known as the *Hsiang t'ai* 相臺 print. If we may believe Yüeh K'o's *Chiu ching san chuan yen ko li* 九經三傳沿革例, he had access to more than fifteen editions of the Classics in his own household, to which he could freely refer in establishing his own text for printing. His work is considered one of the best of the Southern Sung privately printed editions. Both the *Ssu pu ts'ung k'an* and the *Ssu pu pei yao* texts of the *Chou li chu* are based on the *Hsiang t'ai* edition.

4. Major studies, translations and reference works

Major twentieth century studies of the *Chou li* include the following items:

(a) Chinese: Kuo Mo-jo, *Chou kuan chih i* 周官質疑, in *Chin wen ts'ung k'ao* 金文叢考 (revised ed., Peking: Jen min, 1954), 49a–81b; and Ku Chieh-kang, 'Chou kung chih li ti chuan shuo ho Chou kuan i shu ti ch'u hsien' 周公制禮的傳說和周官一書的出現, *Wen shih* 6 (1979), 1–4.

(b) Japanese: Hayashi Taisuke 林泰輔 (1854–1922), *Shūkō to Shūkan Girai Shūeki to no kankei* 周公と周官儀禮周易との關係. This appeared as

Part III of the author's *Shūkō to sono jidai* 周公と其時代 (Tokyo: Okura shoten, 1915), with an appended essay 'Shūkan seisaku jidai kō' 周官制作時代考. Two additional studies by Hayashi, 'Shūkan ni mietaru jinrin no kankei' 周官に見えたる人倫の關係, and 'Shūkan ni mietaru eisei seido' 周官に見えたる衛生制度 appear in *Shina jōdai no kenkyū* 支那上代の研究 (Tokyo: Kōfūkan, 1927; republished Okazaki: Shinkōsha, 1944), pp. 335–345 and 347–354 respectively. Also worthy of note is Tanaka Toshiaki 田中利明, 'Shūrai no seiritsu ni tsuite no ichi kōsatsu' 周禮の成立についての一考察 (*Tōhōgaku* 42, August 1971, 16–31). Honda Jirō 本田二郎, *Shūrai tsūshaku* 周禮通釋 (Tokyo: Shūei, 1977–79) sets out the text with *Kambun* notation and Japanese translation and notes. The work is not included in the major series of *Kambun* editions.

(c) Western: see Charles De Harlez, 'Le Tcheou-li et le Shan-hai-king, leur origine et leur valeur historique' (*TP* 5, 1894, 11–42, 107–22); Bruno Schindler, *Das Priestertum im alten China*; Leipzig: Spaniersche Buchdruckerei, 1919, pp. 55–77; Bernhard Karlgren, 'The Early History of the *Chou li* and *Tso chuan* Texts'(*BMFEA* 3, 1931, 1–59); and Sven Broman, 'Studies on the *Chou li*' (*BMFEA* 33, 1961, 1–89; republished Stockholm, 1961).

There is one translation of the *Chou li* into a Western language: Édouard Biot, *Le Tcheou-li ou Rites des Tcheou*, 3 volumes; Paris: Imprimerie Nationale, 1851; reprinted Taipei; Ch'eng-wen, 1975.

5.　Indexes

(a) *Chou li yin te fu chu shu yin shu yin te* 周禮引得附注疏引書引得 (Index to Chou li and to the titles quoted in the commentaries); Harvard-Yenching Institute Sinological Index Series no.37, Peking 1940; reprinted Taipei; Ch'eng-wen, 1966.

(b) Noma Fumichika 野間文史, *Shūrei sakuin* 周禮索引; Fukuoka: Chūgoku shoten, 1989; based on the text of Juan Yüan's edition of the Thirteen Classics.

(c) *A Concordance to the Zhouli* 周禮逐字索引, ed. D.C. Lau and Chen Fong Ching; *ICS* series, Hong Kong: Commercial Press, forthcoming 1993.

— William G. Boltz

Chou pi suan ching 周髀算經

1. Title

Various renderings have been proposed for the title of this book, but the text itself explains that *Chou pi* means 'the gnomon of Chou'; it also claims that the observations which it contains were made with a gnomon at the Chou capital. The words *suan ching* 'mathematical classic' were not added to the title until the T'ang period. Western scholars have frequently romanised the title as *Chou pei*, but the reading *pi* is attested by an early authoritative source (*Chou pi yin i*; see below).

2. Content

The *Chou pi* is a varied collection of material in two chapters, mainly on the subjects of calendrical astronomy and the *kai t'ien* 蓋天 ('umbrella-[like] heaven') cosmology. It opens with a short dialogue between Chou kung and the otherwise unknown Shang Kao 商高, who explains the mathematical significance of the trysquare *chü* 矩 and refers briefly to a round heaven lying above a square earth. In connection with the trysquare, Shang Kao states Pythagoras' theorem for the case of a 3-4-5 right-angled triangle. There is no connection between this dialogue and the next section, considerably longer and written in a different style, in which Jung Fang 榮方 is described as seeking instruction in astronomy from Ch'en Tzu 陳子; neither of these figures is known to history.

Ch'en Tzu discusses the use of the gnomon (a vertical pole) for observing the shadow cast by the noon sun. Here and throughout the *Chou pi* the height of the gnomon used is given as eight *ch'ih* 尺 (about six feet), which remained the standard used by Chinese astronomers until the Yüan dynasty. A simple rule is propounded: the length of the noon shadow increases or decreases by one *ts'un* 寸 (ten *ts'un* = one *ch'ih*) for every thousand *li* 里 (about 400 miles) whereby an observer moves north or south. On the basis of this rule and with the benefit of certain other assumptions the form and dimensions of the universe are laid out in detail. The shadow-rule used is quite false, but it was not seriously challenged until Li Ch'un-feng 李淳風 (602-70) wrote his commentary to the text in the seventh century.

The second chapter begins with a brief cosmographical passage, and then describes the use of the gnomon for making stellar observations. The rest of the chapter deals with such matters as the annual change in noon shadow-length, the motion of the moon and the cyclical periods on which calendars of the *ssu fen* 四分 ('quarter [day]') type were based. Such calendars used a tropical year of length 365¼ days; in correspondence with this figure the *Chou pi* divides the circumference of the heavens into 365¼ degrees (*tu* 度).

The general mathematical level of the work is equivalent to that of the relevant sections of the *Chiu chang suan shu*, with which the *Chou pi* is roughly contemporary. Fractions are handled readily, simple proportion is applied and square roots are extracted. The properties of similar right-angled triangles are understood, and Pythagoras' theorem is used in a quite general way, although no proof is given. The approximation $\pi = 3$ is used throughout. Although it is based on the assumption of a flat earth, the *kai t'ien* cosmography is fairly successful in giving a qualitatively correct account of diurnal and seasonal phenomena and their variation from place to place over the earth's surface. Polar and tropical conditions are clearly described and accounted for, including the six-month alternation of day and night at the pole itself. When the *kai t'ien* was discarded in favour of the *hun t'ien* 渾天 theory (see below), these features were lost, although the new theory gave an accurate prediction of the phenomena seen by an observer at the centre of the celestial sphere, which was also the centre of the (still flat) earth, the privileged position where Chinese astronomers assumed themselves to be. According to the *Chou pi*, the Chou capital was 103,000 *li* away from the centre of the earth.

3. Composition

The text is clearly an assembly of material by different hands, and in places there are signs of corruption and disorder. The traditional view, based on the opening dialogue involving Chou kung (*fl. c.* 1050 B.C.), was that the *Chou pi* dated from the early Western Chou, but this is certainly much too early. While the work may contain some material and ideas from the time of the Warring States, its final assembly seems likely to have occurred within the approximate limits 50 B.C.–A.D. 100. The latter date is fixed by two factors:

(a) The first commentary (see below), which dates from the third century A.D.;
(b) A reference to the title of the book in a memorial by Ts'ai Yung 蔡邕 (133–92) *c.* A.D. 180 (*Hou Han shu* (tr.) 10, p. 3217; see commentary).

The earlier limit is rather less definite. The *Chou pi* is not mentioned in *Han shu* ch. 30 (completed *c.* A.D. 90), which reproduces the listing of Liu Hsin's 劉歆 (46 B.C.–A.D. 23) *Ch'i lüeh* 七略 (submitted *c.* 6 B.C.). While this omission does not prove that the *Chou pi* did not exist in Western Han, it does suggest that the book was not a work of wide currency or repute. There are a number of indications that it may have been compiled in the later part of Western Han:

(a) It shows signs of being connected with the apocryphal *wei shu* 緯書 then current. A fragment of one of these, the *Hsiao ching yüan shen ch'i* 孝經援神契, is very similar to part of the *Chou pi* (see *TPYL* 1.10b). Like the *Chou pi*, the *wei shu* favour calendars of the *ssu fen* type, which had been officially abandoned in 104 B.C., but were to be re-adopted in A.D. 85, partly on the basis of the support of the *wei shu*.

(b) Its detailed justification of the *kai t'ien* cosmography suggests the need for defence of the theory in the face of criticism from protagonists of the rival *hun t'ien* ('continuous, i.e., spherical, heaven') cosmography. The *hun t'ien* theory may have been current by the middle of the first century B.C.; the first indications of controversy with the *kai t'ien* theory occur in the writings of Yang Hsiung 揚雄 (53 B.C.–A.D. 18; see *Fa yen* 法言, *SPPY* ed., 10.1b).

(c) Similarly, parts of the *Chou pi* describe quite impracticable methods for using a gnomon to make measurements of right ascension. Such methods are possible only with the use of an armillary sphere (*hun t'ien i* 渾天儀), an instrument closely associated with the *hun t'ien* theory.

Parts of the *Chou pi* may well have circulated independently for a considerable time before it was assembled as a unity. Similar ideas can be traced in the *Huai nan tzu*, compiled by 139 B.C., and the *Lü shih ch'un ch'iu* (compiled *c.* 239 B.C.); at one point the *Chou pi* quotes directly from the latter work. The identity of the person or group who put together the *Chou pi* remains a mystery. As in the case of the anonymous *wei shu* apocrypha, it may have been hoped that the book would pass for a work of high antiquity, and consequently wield a greater influence than if it had been seen to be recent.

4. Commentaries

We owe the preservation of the *Chou pi* to its first commentator, Chao Shuang 趙爽. At one point Chao refers to the Ch'ien hsiang 乾象 calendrical system, which was in official use in the kingdom of Wu 吳 from 223 to 280. Some of the material in his commentary is closely related to the commentary of Liu Hui 劉徽 on the *Chiu chang suan shu*, which we know was begun in 263 and was not yet complete in 265. There are fairly good grounds for believing that Chao drew on Liu rather than *vice versa*, so it seems likely that Chao did his work some time between c. 270 and 280. In his preface, Chao states that he added the diagrams which now accompany the text. Further, as he notes in his commentary, he discarded the original list of the seasonal noon shadow lengths and substituted his own (ch. 2, pp. 63–5 in Ch'ien Pao-ts'ung's edition; see below). Parts of Chao's work are of considerable interest in their own right.

Chao's *ming* 名 was certainly Shuang, as is evident from the occasions in the preface and elsewhere, when he uses this in reference to himself. His *tzu* 字, Chün-ch'ing 君卿, is authenticated by the sub-commentators of the sixth and seventh centuries (see below). It is therefore puzzling that the Sui (*Sui shu* 34, p. 1018) and both T'ang catalogues (*Chiu T'ang shu* 47, p. 2036; *Hsin T'ang shu* 59, p. 1543) list commentaries by Chao Ying 趙嬰, and do not mention Shuang, although their listing of the sub-commentaries proves that his work was known. It seems highly unlikely that there is any question of a second commentator with the same surname, and it is possible that, as Pao Huan-chih 鮑澣之 first conjectured (see below), this is a case of the confusion of two characters.

Chen Luan 甄鸞 (*fl.* 560) added detailed workings for all calculations in the text and Chao's commentary. The main interest of these today is that they suggest that, at the time when Chen was writing, students of the *Chou pi* were expected to have no more than a very basic mathematical ability. Under the T'ang, Li Ch'un-feng added a sub-commentary which discusses the *Chou pi* and its previous commentaries in detail and with much critical insight. When the book was printed in 1084, a member of the staff of the imperial library named Li Chi 李籍 added an appendix with the title *Chou pi yin i* 周髀音義, in which he gave explanations of the meaning and pronunciation of terms used in the text and its commentaries. This work is customarily printed with the *Chou pi* (as in *SPTK* and *SPPY*), although it is not given by Ch'ien Pao-ts'ung.

5. Text history

Current versions of the text are substantially identical in form and content. Comparison of text and commentary suggests that no significant textual revisions have been made since Chao wrote his commentary in the third century. Further, apart from one case which he mentions explicitly (see above), it is clear that Chao was content to leave the text as he evidently found it, that is as a loosely connected compilation that had already suffered a certain amount of corruption and disorder; at some points he expresses doubt whether the material presented is really 'the original text of the *Chou pi*'.

The nature of the disorders in the text suggests that it had passed through a stage of being written on wooden strips, as was usual in Han times for most works. Such strips could all too easily be broken or slip out of proper sequence. Since Chao added diagrams, it is possible, but not certain, that he copied the text on to a silk roll. If this had already been done it might explain Chao's reluctance to edit the text, as would have been the obvious procedure if he had been given a bundle of disordered strips. After Chao's time textual changes were confined to the corruption of individual characters and the garbling of the diagrams through repeated copying.

The continuity of the text is well attested up to the time of the first extant printed versions. A copy of the *Chou pi* in one chapter was presented to Wen ti of the Liu Sung dynasty in 437, along with other books from the calendrical expert Chao Fei 趙歐 (fl. 412; see *Sung shu* 98, p. 2416). Chao Fei had been in the service of the Northern Liang dynasty, and was the creator of the Hsüan shih 玄始 calendrical system. He may well have been a descendant of Chao Shuang, whose text could have been handed down in the family. In the next century the *Chou pi* was worked on by Chen Luan. Under the Sui, three examples of the text are recorded, each in one *chüan*, one with the commentary of Chao Ying [sic], one with Chen Luan's comments and one with illustrations (*t'u* 圖).

In 656, Li Ch'un-feng was instructed to prepare annotated editions of ten mathematical texts for use in the T'ang state College. These included the *Chou pi* and the *Chiu chang suan shu*. In addition to his own comments, he included those of Chao and Chen; and he added the term *suan ching* to the title of the work. Both T'ang histories continue to list the one chapter versions under the names of Chao Ying and Chen Luan. Presumably because of its increased bulk, the text with Li's comments is listed as divided into two *chüan*, as are all modern editions.

All received texts of the *Chou pi* can be traced to three sources:

(a) The first printed edition, together with eight other mathematical works including the *Chiu chang suan shu*, issued by the Imperial Library of Northern Sung in 1084. This was reprinted under Southern Sung by Pao Huan-chih (postface 1213). A copy of Pao's print survives in the Shanghai library, and an early Ch'ing tracing of the same copy has been reproduced photographically in the *T'ien lu lin lang ts'ung shu* (1932). The original Southern Sung text is reproduced photographically in *Sung k'o suan ching liu chung* 宋刻算經六種 (Peking: Wen wu, 1980).

(b) A text of unknown antecedents printed by Hu Chen-heng 胡震亨 in the *Pi ts'e hui han* 祕冊彙函 (Wan li period, 1573–1619). This is the text that is followed by a number of *ts'ung shu*, including *Ssu pu ts'ung k'an* and *Ssu pu pei yao*; there are many errors.

(c) A text copied into the *Yung lo ta tien*, now lost. It was collated with Hu's text by the editors of the *Ssu k'u* project, and appears not to have differed significantly from the Sung print. The resultant text is available in the *Wan yu wen k'u* and *Ts'ung shu chi ch'eng* series.

All other editions have now been superseded by the excellent critical text of Ch'ien Pao-tsung 錢寶琮 (Peking: Chung hua, 1963), which includes a useful introduction.

6. Studies and translations

A collection of bibliographical material on the *Chou pi* is given in Ting Fu-pao 丁福寶 (1874–1952) and Chou Yün-ch'ing 周雲青, *Ssu pu tsung lu suan fa pien* 四部總錄算法編 (Shanghai: Shang-wu yin shu kuan, 1957).

The *Chou pi* is discussed in Joseph Needham *et al.*, *Science and Civilisation in China*, Vol. 3 (Cambridge: Cambridge University Press, 1959), pp. 19–24 and 210–15; for cosmography, Needham follows the somewhat misleading account of Chatley (*Observatory* 61, 1938, 10). A better description is given by S. Nakayama, in *A History of Japanese Astronomy* (Cambridge, Mass.: Harvard University Press, 1969). A detailed study in Japanese, with English summary, by Nōda Chūryō 能田忠亮, in *Shūhi sankei no kenkyū* 周髀算經の研究 (Kyoto: Academy of Oriental Culture, 1933), covers all important previous scholarship.

The translation of E. Biot in *Journal Asiatique*, 3rd series, 11 (1841), 593–638 is useful for general orientation but unreliable in detail. A full translation and study of the *Chou pi* has now been completed by the present writer, and is forthcoming as *Astronomy and Mathematics in Ancient China: The Zhou Bi Suan Jing* (Cambridge: Cambridge University Press: Needham Research Institute Research Monograph Series).

7. Index

A Concordance to the Zhou bi suanjing and Jiu zhang suanshu 周髀算經, 九章算術逐字索引, ed. D.C. Lau and Chen Fong Ching; *ICS* series, Hong Kong: Commercial Press, forthcoming 1996.

— Christopher Cullen

Chu shu chi nien 竹書紀年

The *Chu shu chi nien*, 'Annals written on bamboo strips' or 'Bamboo Annals', sometimes called *Chi chung chi nien* 汲冢紀年 'Annals from the tomb in Chi hsien, Ho-nan', is a chronicle which was discovered, probably, in A.D. 281. It begins with Huang ti 黃帝 and extends to the year 299 B.C., with exact dates from the first year of Yao 堯, set in the text at 2145 B.C. One must distinguish between an original text or texts, now perhaps partly lost; the 'Current Text' (*Chin pen* 今本) in 2 *chüan*, which may be in large part original; and collections of quoted fragments called the 'Old Text' (*Ku pen* 古本), on the assumption that they are remnants of the supposedly otherwise wholly lost original text. The prevailing opinion in the past two centuries has been that the 'Current Text', of 2 *chüan*, is a fake, often said, e.g. by Ch'ien Ta-hsin 錢大昕 (1728–1804) and Shinjō Shinzō 新城新藏 (1873–1938) to be of Ming date. Wang Kuo-wei 王國維 (1877–1927) is especially well-known for research which supports this view. A lucid presentation of the view is found in David N. Keightley, 'The *Bamboo Annals* and Shang-Chou chronology'; *HJAS* 38, 1978, 423–38. More recent research argues that the 'Current Text' in 2 *chüan* is not a fabrication, though it contains deviations from a still older original; see Edward L. Shaughnessy, 'On the authenticity of the *Bamboo Annals*', *HJAS* 46 (1986), 149–80; and 'The "Current" *Bamboo Annals* and the date of the Zhou conquest of Shang', *EC* 11–12 (1985–87), 33–6; and David S. Nivison, 'The dates of Western Chou', *HJAS* 43 (1983), 481–580; and 'Response'; *EC* 15 (1990) 'The Early China Forum', 151–172.

1. Content

(a) The 'Current Text' (*Chin pen*)

The 'Current Text' is a very spare chronicle, beginning with Huang ti (in all probability a mythical figure) in the third millennium B.C. Exact dates are not given until the time of Yao (at least partly mythical), dated according to the the *kan chih* system at 2145–2046 B.C. The chronicle continues to 299 B.C., i.e. the 20th, and last, year of King Ai Hsiang 哀襄

(or Ai, or Hsiang) of the state of Wei 魏, and the 16th year of King Nan 赧 of Chou (for the hypothesis that 'Ai Hsiang' was the actual name of the Wei king who is sometimes also called 'Ai wang', and sometimes 'Hsiang wang', see D.C.Lau, *Mencius*; Harmondsworth: Penguin Books, 1970, p. 206). All events of the Chou era are dated in the royal calendar of Chou, even though for the period of Eastern Chou (770–299) events are presented from the perspective of the states of Chin 晉 and Wei.

The first *chüan*, which is approximately the first half of the text, concludes with the last ruler of the Shang dynasty, who is dated here from 1558 to 1051 B.C. The second *chüan* is divided almost equally between Western and Eastern Chou; but concrete historical detail is richer for the latter part; long fanciful passages on auspicious portents (usually identical with text in *Sung shu* 27, 'Fu jui chih 符瑞志', pp. 759f.) occur in the earlier parts of the chronicle at intervals. These are apparently a kind of commentary; none appear in the Eastern Chou part of the chronicle. There is an occasional textual commentary through the whole book, identified as being written by Shen Yüeh 沈約 (441–513), who compiled the *Sung shu* in 488–89. Perhaps the earlier part of this commentary is Shen's work, as some entries (again dated through to the time of Ch'eng Wang 成王) begin with the words '[I, Shen] Yüeh note . . . '. A significant feature of the text that concerns the period from 784 B.C. onwards is the listing of certain years in the royal calendar with no event being recorded, but with a commentary; this commentary explains that the year in question was the first year of a named ruler of Chin, or (later) of Wei. During the last two reigns of Wei, i.e. from 370 B.C., every year is listed, whether or not there is an event to record.

(b) The Original Text

The term 'Original Text' is used here to refer to the actual text that was interred with the burial of the king of Wei, after his death in 299 B.C., along with many other texts. This was discovered during the Western Chin dynasty, when the tomb was plundered by thieves, probably in A.D. 281. According to one theory, the cache was found not in a tomb but in a royal store house; see, e.g., Wei T'ing-sheng 衛挺生, 'Lun chi chung yü ch'i chu shu 論汲冢與其竹書', *Ssu hsiang yü shih tai yüeh k'an* 思想與時代月刊 (1964) 121, 9–13; 122, 7–10; and 123, 26–28.

This text was reconstituted, perhaps in more than one version, by court scholars who worked on the finds. Tu Yü 杜預 (222–84), who saw the texts soon after their discovery, reports on them in his *Tso chuan hou hsü* 左傳後序, to the effect that although much had been destroyed by the thieves, the *Chu shu chi nien* text was relatively complete. Tu makes three important points about the document: (i) It began with Hsia, Yin and Chou, i.e. not with Huang ti, as does the 'Current Text'; but it may be remarked that since it is hardly possible to give an account of Yü 禹, first ruler of Hsia, without first recounting Yao and Shun, Tu may have meant that the text began with Yao; (ii) It used the Hsia calendar scheme, beginning each year with the lunar month preceding that of the spring equinox; (iii) For the Chou period it used the royal calendar only to the last part of the reign of Hsüan Wang 宣王. Beginning with Shang Shu 殤叔 of Chin (784 B.C.), it used the ducal calendar of Chin; after the end of Chin it used the state calendar of Wei. As Tu notes, this implies that the book served as a state chronicle of the state of Wei.

The *Chin shu*'s biography of Shu Hsi 束晳, who, with Hsün Hsü 荀勗 and Ho Ch'iao 和嶠, had worked on the discovery of the texts (see *Chin shu* 51, p. 1432; for Hsün and Ho, see below) refers, without quoting Shu, to the '*Chi nien* in 13 *p'ien*', and repeats that the chronicle began with Hsia; the *Sui shu* (33, p. 957) lists a '*Chi nien* in 12 *chüan*, with variants in 1 *chüan*', identified as 'one of the books from the Chi tomb'. Both of these works are compilations of the T'ang period; there is no entry for the work in Fujiwara Sukeyo's catalogue. The original was thus probably much longer than the 'Current Text', which may be either a reduction of the original or just the chronicle portion out of a collection of various materials. The original also lacked the *kan chih* identifications of the first years of the reigns. The use of *kan chih* to specify years came into use only during the Han dynasty; Nivison believes that there must have been some form of absolute dating therein; Shaughnessy thinks not (see Nivison and Shaughnessy as already cited).

It is probable that, as in the 'Current Text', the totals of the number of years were given at the end of each dynasty. P'ei Yin 裴駰 (5th century) quotes the *Chi nien* as saying that 'From Wu Wang's 武王 destruction of Yin 殷 until Yu wang 幽王 [i.e. through 771 B.C.] was 257 years (see the *Chi chieh* 集解 comment to *Shih chi* 4, p. 149, note 4, at the death of Yu Wang). This statement is the basis for the widely accepted date of 1027 for the Chou conquest. However P'ei Yin also says (*Shih chi* 44, p. 1849, note 1) that 'Hsün Hsü says that Ho Ch'iao said that the *Annals* begin with Huang ti and continue to the present ruler of Wei'. This not only authoritatively refutes Tu Yü as to the scope of the book, it also reveals that P'ei Yin himself never saw it. It can be argued that internal consistency in some stage of the text's history during the Chou period would have required it to read '275 years', thus dating the conquest to 1045. Shaughnessy (1986) has shown that the date 1050, now in the text, requires that editors at some stage moved a bamboo strip from the chronicle of Ch'eng Wang to that of Wu Wang. Sometimes a quotation from a lost part of the original contains important accurate information that is not found elsewhere; e.g., correct dates for the rulers of Ch'i 齊 (see Henri Maspero, 'La chronologie des rois de Ts'i au IVe siècle avant notre ère'; *TP* 25, 367–86). Shaughnessy's work however has demonstrated that substantial portions of the 'Current Text', dealing with early Chou, must be exactly the same text as that which came from the Chi hsien tomb.

(c) The 'Old Text' (*Ku pen*)

This is the supposed 'original' as represented by collections (such as that of Wang Kuo-wei) of quotations from the *Chu shu chi nien* found in early commentaries, encyclopaedias or other sources. The concept presupposes that the 'Current Text' (*Chin pen*) is a forgery perpetrated after the original had been lost. Actually, such quotations can come from the original, or from some reconstitution of it, or from the 'Current Text' itself, or from some other derivative text; or they may sometimes be merely loose paraphrases. It follows that strictly speaking, there is no *Ku pen* text, although for convenience one may use the term for such collections of quotations. These quotations are important repositories of material for research.

2.   Date of composition and authenticity

The original text taken from the Wei tomb reached its final form by the date of the last entry, i.e. 299 B.C., and before the interment of the king of Wei who died in that year. In one passage the *Chin shu* (3, p. 70), gives the date of the discovery as A.D. 279, but this is perhaps a manufactured date. A.D. 279 was the thousandth anniversary of the first year recorded in the *Ch'un ch'iu* 春秋 of Lu 魯, i.e. in 722 B.C. The *Chi nien* apparently came to be regarded as a '*ch'un ch'iu*' of Chin and Wei, from which the post-Han state of Wei and the Chin dynasty took their names. Hsün Hsü, one of the court scholars who worked on the discoveries, gives the date of 281 (see his preface to the *Mu t'ien tzu chuan*, itself one of the texts from the Chi tomb), and this date is also seen elsewhere in the *Chin shu* (51, p. 1432). Yet a further reference in the *Chin shu* (39, p. 1154) reports the discovery after events dated early in the Hsien-ning period (275–80).

The 'Current Text', with its *Kan chih* dates and its use of the Eastern Chou royal calendar, must have been produced in the Chin period, and altered slightly over the next several centuries. Part of it, perhaps most, as Nivison argues, is copied exactly from the original. On the important matter of the Chou conquest, the date of 1050 B.C. was apparently accepted by some scholars in Former Han, and serves to glorify the pre-imperial state of Chin, and so, indirectly, the Chin dynasty. Astrological arguments require that, if the beginning of the state of Chin were to be at 1035 B.C., as stated in the 'Current Text', then the conquest must have been in 1050 B.C. 1035 was just 400 years before 635, i.e. the first year, according to the *Ch'un ch'iu*, of the great Duke Wen 文 of Chin. Recent work by Nivison suggests that the date of 1050 results from a reworking of the text in the fourth century B.C., and that an earlier version (probably not the earliest) had the date of 1045.

Discrepancies between the 'Current Text' and passages from the *Annals* as quoted in other books were great enough to move 18th century historians such as Wang Ming-sheng 王鳴盛 (1722–98) to denounce the 'Current Text' as a fake (see Legge, as cited under (5) below, *Prolegomena*, p. 176). Wang thought that the forger must have been Shu Hsi. The more usual charge of forgery takes the form of the one that is usual in the twentieth century, i.e. that the 'Current Text' was fabricated many centuries later, from quoted fragments and sheer imagination, after the original had disappeared. This belief has to be rejected, because, as Nivison shows (see Nivison 1983), it turns out to be possible to reconstruct an independently verifiable late Shang and Western Chou chronology through inferences based on the dates of reigns in the 'Current Text'. A putative forger could not have invented such a 'Current Text' by using the 'Old Text'(*Ku shu*) fragments; they give us almost no dated entries. Indeed Nivison and Pang claim to show, on the basis of astronomical arguments, that it is possible to reconstruct a chronology for early Hsia (19th and 20th centuries B.C.), from the 'Current' *Annals* (see David S. Nivison and Kevin Pang, 'Astronomical Evidence for the *Bamboo Annals*' chronicle of early Hsia'; *EC* 15, 1990, 'The Early China Forum', pp. 87–95).

3. Textual history

It is generally assumed that the book remained unknown between 299 B.C. and A.D. 281; but as Édouard Chavannes pointed out a century ago there is a relationship between the chronology of Lu in the *Shih chi* and the dating of Chou in the *Annals* that can hardly be accidental (see *Mémoires Historiques*, vol. I, pp. cxcii–iii). In any case, in the Chin period the texts from Chi hsien were a discovery; rescued from thieves, they reached the Chin court, and were put in order and transcribed by court scholars, including Shu Hsi, Ho Ch'iao and Hsün Hsü in a space of two years. There may have been disputes about transcription, as the commentary in the present text sometimes refers to other versions. The long portent passages, also found in Shen Yüeh's *Sung shu*, are puzzling. It has usually been supposed that Shen Yüeh inserted them as more 'commentary'; but Ch'ien Ta-hsin pointed out (*Shih chia chai yang hsin lu* 十駕齋養新錄) that P'ei Yin's commentary to the *Shih chi*, written half a century before the *Sung shu*, sometimes quotes these texts. Ch'ien Ta-hsin took this as evidence of late forgery; but when this idea is discarded, one is forced to the likelihood that these passages about portents too were part of the text from Chi hsien.

Early bibliographies do not mention the 'Current Text' of 2 *chüan*, and this omission has made the charge of forgery seem plausible. The *Hsin T'ang shu* 58, p. 1459, lists a long version in 14 *chüan*; the *Sung shih*, compiled under the Yüan period, (203, p. 5088) lists only a *Chu shu*, in 3 *chüan*, compiled by Hsün Hsü and Ho Ch'iao. This may be another short version, long since lost; but Lei Hsüeh-ch'i 雷學淇 suspected that it was ancestral to the 'Current Text' (see *Chu shu chi nien i cheng* 竹書紀年義證 preface, dated 1810); and it could well just be the 'current' text, divided into three parts instead of two. It is more likely, however, that it consisted of three chapters taken out of a lost longer text. The *Yü hai* (ch. 47) describes three chapters said already to be lost; all are said to have been 'copied by Mr Hsün', but only one was actually a 'chronicle'. So the long versions contained a variety of material; one of the chapters, identified as the 6th, was 'Commands and Responses'. The earliest extant editions of the 'Current Text' of 2 *chüan* are of the Ming dynasty; Lin Ch'un-p'u 林春溥 lists six (*Chu shu pen mo* 竹書本末: see under Yang Chia-lo 楊家駱 in (4) below).

4. Editions

(a) Of the widely available *Ts'ung shu*, the *Kuang Han Wei ts'ung shu* carries the T'ien i ko edition of Ho Yün-chung 何允中; the *Ssu pu ts'ung k'an* has the T'ien i ko edition of Fan Ch'in 范欽 (1508–85), who has been accused of being the forger of the text; see Wu Yü, under (6) below.

(b) Two 20th century editions by Wang Kuo-wei are indispensable for research: (i) *Ku pen Chu shu chi nien chi chiao* 古本竹書紀年輯校, by Chu Yu-tseng 朱右曾, supplemented by Wang. This work collects fragments supposed to be the remnants of the original text. (ii) *Chin pen Chu shu chi nien shu cheng* 今本竹書紀年疏證. In this work Wang attempts to prove the 'Current' (*Chin pen*) text to be a fake, by producing a possible forger's source (or source of inspiration) for nearly every line. Both books are to be found in *Wang Kuan-t'ang hsien sheng ch'üan chi* 王觀堂先生全集 (Taipei: Wen hua ed., vol. 13).

(c) Wang's two books are also included in a valuable small collection of eight *Chu shu chi nien* texts and studies edited by Yang Chia-lo, under the title of *Chu shu chi nien pa chung* 竹書紀年八種 (Taipei: Shih chieh, 1963).

(d) This collection also includes an annotated edition, in 4 *chüan*, by Lin Ch'un-p'u, entitled *Chu shu chi nien pu cheng* 竹書紀年補證, together with two of Lin's other studies that repay attention. Of these, the *Chu shu pen mo* copies out early references to the text, including those of Tu Yü that are used above.

(e) Yang Chia-lo also includes two supplements to the attempts of Chu and Wang to recover a *Ku pen*: (i) Ch'ien Mu 錢穆, *Ku pen Chu shu chi nien chi chiao pu cheng* 古本竹書紀年輯校補正, in 1 *chüan*; (ii) Fan Hsiang-yung 范祥雍, *Ku pen Chu shu chi nien chi chiao ting pu* 古本竹書紀年輯校訂補 (107 pp.; uncredited; previously published Shanghai: Jen min, 1962). Another recent work of this type is seen in Fang Shih-ming 方詩銘 and Wang Hsiu-ling 王修齡, *Ku pen Chu shu chi nien chi cheng* 古本竹書紀年輯證 (Shanghai: Ku chi, 1981).

(f) Lists of Ch'ing or later annotated editions will be found in Legge (as cited under (5) below, *Prolegomena*, p. 206); in Fan Hsiang-yung (as cited above, p. 105); and in Lin Ch'un-p'u's *Chu shu pen mo*. Descriptions and evaluations of thirteen studies of the text by scholars of the Ch'ing period and early Republic, by Yang Chung-hsi 楊鍾羲, are provided in *Hsü hsiu Ssu k'u ch'üan shu t'i yao* 續修四庫全書提要 (Taipei: Wan yu wen k'u, n.d.), vol. 4, pp. 77–88.

(g) Ch'en Feng-heng 陳逢衡 (1778–1855), *Chu shu chi nien chi cheng* 竹書紀年集證 in 50 *chüan*, used by Legge and Biot (see under (5) below).

(h) Lei Hsüeh-ch'i, *Chu shu chi nien i cheng*, in 14 *chüan* (preface 1810), which does not give a faithful reproduction of a received text. Instead Lei has used the 'Current Text', which he does not dismiss as a fake, to rediscover the original, restoring the Chin-Wei calendar arrangement as described by Tu Yü, but still starting with Huang ti. He strips out the portent passages, makes additions and corrections based on his own scholarship, and provides a very full and valuable commentary. A fine edition of this work was published in Peking in 1939 (photographic reprint, in two volumes; Taipei: I wen).

5. Translations ('Current Text')

(a) For a translation into French, by Édouard Biot, see *Journal Asiatique*, Third Series, vol. XII (December 1841), 537–78, and vol. XIII (May 1842), 381–431, with a supplementary note on the translation of the first book in vol. III, 203–07. Biot dates the discovery of the strips to 284; he omits the portent texts.

(b) For an English translation that is good and very convenient, but not flawless, see James Legge, *The Chinese Classics, vol.III, The Shoo King or Book of Historical Documents* (original preface 1865), *Prolegomena*, Ch. iv, 'The Annals of the Bamboo Books', pp. 105–07 (introduction), pp. 108–76, Chinese text and commentary by Shen Yüeh, Legge's translation and notes; and pp. 176–83 for Legge's evaluation. Legge's rendering of dates must be used with caution, as they are usually one year late.

6. Other recent studies (select items only)

(a) Chinese

    (i) Chao Jung-lang 趙榮琅, 'Chu shu chi nien chih chin ku pen wen t'i chi ch'i p'ing chia 竹書紀年之今古本問題及其評價'; *Ta lu tsa chih* 1954.8,10, 9–16.

    (ii) Ch'en Meng-chia 陳夢家, *Liu kuo chi nien* 六國紀年; Shanghai: Jen min, 1957.

    (iii) Chu Hsi-tsu 朱希祖, *Chi chung shu k'ao* 汲冢書考 original print 1939; reprinted Peking: Chung hua, 1960.

    (iv) Wu Yü 吳璵, 'Liu shih nien lai Chu shu chi nien chih k'ao ting 六十年來竹書紀年之考訂'; in Ch'eng Fa-jen 程發軔, ed., *Liu shih nien lai chih kuo hsüeh* 六十年來之國學, Taipei: Cheng Chung, 1972–74, vol. 3, pp. 555–73.

(b) Japanese

    (i) Hara Tomio 原富男, 'Chikusho kinen ni tsuite 竹書紀年につい て'; *Kambun gakkai kaihō* 漢文學會會報, 1933, 52–83.

    (ii) Kanda Ki'ichiro 神田喜一郎, 'Kyū chō sho shutsudo shimatsu kō 汲冢書出土始末考'; in *Shinagaku setsurin* 支那學說林 1934, 10–32.

(c) Western languages

    (i) Creel, Herrlee G., *The origins of statecraft in China, vol. 1, the Western Chou Empire*: Chicago: The University of Chicago Press, 1970; see Appendix A 'The sources', pp. 483–85.

    (ii) Debnicki, Aleksy, *The 'Chu-shu-chi-nien' as a source to the social history of ancient China*; Warsaw: Panstwowe Wydawnictwo Naukowe, 1956.

    (iii) Eberhard, Wolfram and Rolf Müller, 'Contributions to the astronomy of the Han period III: astronomy of the later Han period', *HJAS* 1 (1936), 194–241, especially 220–25.

(iv) Pankenier, David W., 'Mozi and the Dates of Xia, Shang and Zhou; a Research Note', *EC* 9–10 (1983–85), 175–81.

(v) Pankenier, David W., 'The *Bamboo Annals* revisited: problems of method in using the chronicle as a source for the chronology of Early Zhou, Part I'; *BSOAS* LV.2 (1992), 272–97.

7. Index

A Concordance to the Zhu shu jinian 竹書紀年傳世本及輯本逐字索引, ed. D.C. Lau and Chen Fong Ching; *ICS* series, Hong Kong: Commercial Press, forthcoming 1995.

— David S. Nivison

Ch'u tz'u 楚辭

1. Composition of the text

The term *Ch'u tz'u* was first used to designate a poetic corpus or 'tradition' rather than a specific text; thus when we are told that Chu Mai-ch'en 朱買臣 (*fl.* 120–110 B.C.) was first recommended to the attention of Han Wu ti 漢武 as a *Ch'u tz'u* expert, it is in this sense that the term is to be understood (see *Han shu* 64A, p. 2791). The corpus so designated seems to have comprised the poetical works of Ch'ü Yüan 屈原, a Ch'u nobleman contemporary with king Huai 懷 of Ch'u (reigned in the last quarter of the fourth century B.C.), together with a smaller number of works ascribed to his followers and imitators.

The earliest known book to be given this title, the *Ch'u tz'u chang chü* 楚辭章句 was compiled and annotated by Wang I 王逸, a collator (*chiao shu lang* 校書郎) at the court of Shun ti (r. 125–144) in the early part of the second century A.D.; this purports to be based on an earlier *Ch'u tz'u* compiled by Liu Hsiang 劉向 (79–8 B.C.). The *Han shu i wen chih*, which was compiled by Liu Hsiang's son, makes no mention of this work, though it begins the section on *fu* 賦 with the entry 'The *fu* of Ch'ü Yüan in 25 *p'ien*', followed by separate entries for the *fu* of T'ang Lo 唐勒 and Sung Yü 宋玉 (two later Ch'u poets); see *Han shu* 30, p. 1747.

Attempts to relate the entry of the *Han shu* to the contents of Wang's collection are doomed to failure because the titles of the 25 *p'ien* are not given. The 17 *chüan* of Wang I's collection consist half of works which he ascribes to Ch'ü Yüan, and half of works by later poets. Seven of these were Han poets, including Wang I himself, whose effusions make up the final *chüan* of the book. The titles of the 17 *chüan*, together with the authors to whom Wang I attributes them, are as follows:

1. *Li sao* 離騷 'On encountering trouble'; by Ch'ü Yüan.
2. *Chiu ko* 九歌 'Nine songs'; by Ch'ü Yüan.
3. *T'ien wen* 天問 'Heavenly questions'; by Ch'ü Yüan.
4. *Chiu chang* 九章 'Nine pieces'; by Ch'ü Yüan.
5. *Yüan yu* 遠遊 'Far-off journey'; by Ch'ü Yüan.

6. *Pu chü* 卜居 'Divination'; by Ch'ü Yüan.
7. *Yü fu* 漁父 'The fisherman'; by Ch'ü Yüan.
8. *Chiu pien* 九辯 'Nine changes'; by Sung Yü 宋玉.
9. *Chao hun* 招魂 'Summons of the soul'; by Sung Yü.
10. *Ta chao* 大招 'The great summons'; by Ch'ü Yüan ('some say by Ching Ts'o 景瑳').
11. *Hsi shih* 惜誓 'Sorrow for troth betrayed'; by Chia I 賈誼.
12. *Chao yin shih* 招隱士 'Summons for a recluse'; by Liu An 劉安.
13. *Ch'i chien* 七諫 'Seven remonstrances'; by Tung-fang Shuo 東方朔.
14. *Ai shih ming* 哀時命 'Alas that my lot was not cast'; by Yen Chi 嚴忌 (originally named Chuang 莊 Chi, and called such in *Han shu* 30, p. 1747).
15. *Chiu huai* 九懷 'Nine regrets'; by Wang Pao 王褒.
16. *Chiu t'an* 九歎 'Nine laments'; by Liu Hsiang.
17. *Chiu ssu* 九思 'Nine longings'; by Wang I.

Two of the above works (*Chiu ko* and *Chiu chang*), attributed by Wang I to Ch'ü Yüan, themselves consist of a series of separate poems, each with its own title.

The order of the 17 *chüan* listed above, which is the order found in all extant editions, is evidently intended to be a chronological one. An earlier and more haphazard order, said by Sung editors to have been found in a no longer extant edition entitled *Ch'u tz'u shih wen* 楚辭釋文, would appear to have been the original one, since it had *Chiu pien* in the second place after *Li sao*, and Wang I's commentary on *Chiu chang* assumes that *Chiu pien* occurs earlier in the collection by referring back to it. If the order given in the *Ch'u tz'u shih wen* was the original order, that is an additional reason for discounting the assertion that Liu Hsiang compiled the anthology, since the *Ch'u tz'u shih wen* had included Liu Hsiang's own *Chiu t'an* in the thirteenth place.

All subsequent works which incorporate the words 'Ch'u tz'u' in their titles derive ultimately from Wang I's anthology, although they do not all contain exactly the same collection of poems. For example, Chu Hsi's 朱熹 (1130–1200) *Ch'u tz'u chi chu* 楚辭集註 omits *Ch'i chien, Chiu t'an* and *Chiu ssu*, but incorporates two *fu* by Chia I which are not included in Wang I's collection; Wang Fu-chih's 王夫之 (1619–92) *Ch'u tz'u t'ung shih* 楚辭通釋 retains all the first twelve titles of Wang I's collection but replaces the last five with four other works, including one of his own composition. What such books have in common is that all include all the poems which their editors believe to be attributable to Ch'ü Yüan, whatever else they may decide to add or to omit.

Exclusive editions confined to what their editors believe to be the works of Ch'ü Yüan appear under such titles as *Ch'ü Yüan fu chu* 屈原賦 注, *Ch'ü fu t'ung chien* 屈賦通箋. There are also numerous separate editions or independent studies of individual works from the collection, particularly of *Li sao*, *Chiu ko* and *T'ien wen*. A selection of the *Ch'u tz'u* poems is to be found in *Wen hsüan* (*chüan* 32–33), where it appears as an independent genre, distinct from *shih* 詩 and *fu* 賦, entitled *sao* 騷. The *Wen hsüan* selection comprises all of *Li sao*, six songs from *Chiu ko*, one poem from *Chiu chang*, *Pu chü* and *Yü fu*, four poems from *Chiu pien*, *Chao hun* and *Chao yin shih*. The poems selected are accompanied, in the *Liu ch'en* 六臣 edition of the *Wen hsüan*, by a slightly abridged version of Wang I's commentary.

The earliest occurrence of the title *Chiu chang* is in a poem by Liu Hsiang. In his biography of Ch'ü Yüan, Ssu-ma Ch'ien 司馬遷 (?145– ?86 B.C.) mentions one of the *Chiu chang* poems (*Ai ying* 哀郢) by name (*Shih chi* 84, p. 2503) and cites another of them (*Huai sha* 懷沙) in full (*Shih chi* 84, pp. 2486f.); but he appears to know nothing of the collective title, which may in fact have been Liu Hsiang's own creation (see Lu K'an-ju 陸侃如 and Feng Yüan-chün 馮沅君, *Chung kuo shih shih* 中國 詩史; Peking: Tso chia, 1957, p. 125). The suggestion that *Chiu chang* is a collection of individual works put together not by the poet — or poets — but by a later compiler goes back at least as far as Chu Hsi (see *Ch'u tz'u chi chu*, ch. 4).

2.   Nature of contents

Two of the individual works to be found in nearly all editions of the *Ch'u tz'u*, i.e., *Pu chü* and *Yü fu*, are not, strictly speaking, poems at all, but anecdotes in poetical prose of the kind frequently encountered in the *Chuang tzu*. Quite apart from these, the other *Ch'u tz'u* works differ greatly, both from each other and from earlier Chinese poetry as exemplified in the poems and songs of the *Shih ching*. To begin with, most of the poems are very much longer; e.g., the *Li sao* is more than eight times as long as the longest poem in the *Shih ching*. A modified form of the quadruple metre characteristic of *Shih ching* verse is found in *T'ien wen*, *Chao hun*, *Ta chao* and parts of *Chiu chang*, but the form most characteristic of the *Ch'u tz'u* is a long line, often of thirteen or more characters, divided midway by the meaningless refrain word *hsi* 兮; this is a form that is most suitable for recitation and which was subsequently employed and developed in the *fu* of the Han dynasty. It is used throughout the long poem *Li sao*, a strange mixture of allegorized autobiography and moralizing reflections on court politics with excursions into the super-natural world of shamanism and mythology. A shorter verse-form more suitable for singing is found in the lyrical parts of the collection, such as *Chiu ko.*

All the earlier *Ch'u tz'u* poems (i.e., those traditionally attributed to Ch'ü Yüan or his disciple Sung Yü) are often influenced by or con-nected with the beliefs and practices of shamanism. Some (*Chiu ko*, *Chao hun*, *Ta chao*) are explicitly concerned with these practices; but even in those which are not, the supernatural world of the shamans makes intermittent appearances.

3. Authorship and authenticity

There is no mention of Ch'ü Yüan in any pre-Han text. The earliest ref-erence to him occurs in a work of Chia I, who died in 169 B.C.; the earliest reference to his authorship of *Li sao* occurs in a fragment from a lost work of Liu An 劉安, who died in 122 B.C. The biography of Ch'ü Yüan in Ssu-ma Ch'ien's *Shih chi* (84, p. 2484) does not purport to give an exhaustive list of his works, but even those pieces which it names (*Li sao*, *T'ien wen*, *Chao hun* and two of the *Chiu chang* poems) include one (*Chao hun*) which Wang I attributes to Sung Yü.The very existence of Ch'ü Yüan has at times been doubted (see, e.g., Hu Shih's 胡適 (1891-1962) essay 'Tu Ch'u tz'u' 讀楚辭 in *Hu shih wen ts'un* 胡適文存, vol.2); and his authorship of every work ever ascribed to him has at one time or another been called into question; for an extreme example of such scepticism, see Ho T'ien-hsing 何天行, *Ch'u tz'u tso yü Han tai k'ao* 楚辭作於漢代考 (Shanghai: Chung-hua, 1948).

In the course of this century extreme scepticism has at times given way to extreme credulity, to which political and patriotic considerations have often contributed. But even the most enthusiastic upholders of Ch'ü Yüan's authorship have reservations about some of Wang I's attri-butions. For example, Kuo Mo-jo 郭沫若 (1892-1978) considered *Yüan yu* to be a work of early Han provenance, being an early draft of the *Ta jen fu* 大人賦 of Ssu-ma Hsiang-ju 司馬相如 (c. 179-117), which in many ways it resembles. In the case of *Chiu ko*, even Wang I himself says that the songs represent a re-working by the poet of pre-existing mate-rial. During the past twenty years or so the earlier tide of scepticism seems to have receded. Probably a majority of *Ch'u tz'u* scholars would nowadays ascribe the authorship of *Li sao*, *Chiu ko*, *T'ien wen* and two or three of the *Chiu chang* poems to a great poet who can conveniently be identified with the subject of Ssu-ma Ch'ien's biography.

4. Commentaries and texts

Apart from a small fragment of a *Ch'u tz'u yin* 楚辭音, listed in the *Sui shu ching chi chih* (*Sui shu* 35, p. 1055), which was found among the Tun-huang manuscripts deposited in the Bibliothèque Nationale, Wang I's *Ch'u tz'u chang chü* is the only pre-Sung commentary to have survived. The commentary on his own *Chiu ssu* in the final *chüan* is thought to be by someone else unknown, since in one place it grotesquely misinter-prets the text. For no discernible reason, his commentaries on *Yüan yu*, *Chiu pien*, *Chao yin shih*, *Chiu huai* and on the poems *Ai ying*, *Ch'ou ssu* 抽思, *Ssu mei jen* 思美人, *Hsi wang jih* 惜往日 and *Pei hui feng* 悲回風 (in *Chiu chang*) are entirely written in rhyming verse.

Because of its antiquity and the fact that Wang I was himself a native of Ch'u and familiar with that dialect, his *chang chü* must be regarded as an indispensable aid. However, Wang I is unfortunately not one of the great Han annotators, and the lameness of his commentary has often been remarked on. Usually it is read in combination with an excellent 'amplification' (*pu chu* 補注) by the Sung scholar Hung Hsing-tsu 洪興祖 (1090–1155). Hung Hsing-tsu incorporated the work of Su Tung-p'o 蘇東坡 (1037–1101) and other Sung scholars in his *Apparatus* (*k'ao i* 考異), which in all extant editions is printed not as a separate appendix but dispersed throughout the book. (The textual variants given after Wang's commentary and before the words *pu yüeh* 補曰 which precede Hung's amplifications are in fact from the *k'ao i*). Hung's amplification of Wang I's *chang chü*, the *Ch'u tz'u pu chu* 楚辭補注, has become the standard form in which the *Ch'u tz'u* is read. This is the only *Ch'u tz'u*, for ex-ample, to be found in both the *Ssu pu ts'ung k'an* and the *Ssu pu pei yao* series.

Chu Hsi's *Ch'u tz'u chi chu* 楚辭集註 (late twelfth century) breaks entirely with Wang's commentary and contains a somewhat different selection of texts (see above). Chu's imaginative and interesting, but rather subjective, interpretations represent a deliberate departure from the more narrowly philological approach of Wang and Hung. These two works, i.e., of Wang/Hung and Chu are the most important tradi-tional commentaries. Of the numerous Ming and Ch'ing commentaries available, Chiang Chi's 蔣驥 *San lü Ch'u tz'u* 三閭楚辭, sometimes re-ferred to as the *Shan tai ko chu Ch'u tz'u* 山帶閣註楚辭 (prefaces dated 1712 and 1727) deserves special mention for its fertility of ideas and rich-ness of content. It contains several maps. In modern times, Wen I-to's 聞一多 (1899–1946) *Ch'u tz'u chiao pu* 楚辭校補 is indispensable for text-critical studies (see *Wen I-to ch'üan chi* 聞一多全集; Shanghai: K'ai ming, 1948, vol.II, pp. 339–495). Chiang Liang-fu's 姜亮夫 *Ch'ü Yüan fu chiao chu* 屈原賦校註 (Peking: Jen min, 1957) is the best all-round modern commentary in both textual and exegetic areas. For a recent set of interpretative essays, see T'ang Ping-cheng 湯炳正, *Ch'u tz'u lei kao* 楚 辭類稿 (Ch'eng-tu: Pa Shu shu she, 1988).

5. Editions etc.

The earliest text of the *Ch'u tz'u* is contained in two sections of a fragmentary T'ang manuscript edition of the *Wen hsüan*, entitled *Wen hsüan chi chu* 文選集注. It consists of the first half of *Li sao* and the whole of *Chao hun* and *Chao yin shih* (see *Kyōtō teikoku daigaku bungakubu eiin kyū shōhon san shū* 京都帝國大學文學部景印舊鈔本三集). The text differs slightly from that found in standard editions of the *Wen hsüan*.

All *Wen hsüan* texts of the *Ch'u tz'u*, printed and manuscript alike, differ from all other texts of that work in substituting synonyms for the T'ang tabooed words *shih* 世 and *min* 民. The only Sung and Yüan prints of the *Ch'u tz'u* to have survived are editions of Chu Hsi's *Ch'u tz'u chi chu*. One of these, published by Chu Hsi's grandson in 1235, was reproduced by photolithography in 1953 by the *Jen min wen hsüeh* publishing house. Only Ming reprints of Sung editions have survived of Wang I's *Ch'u tz'u chang chü*, without Hung's amplification, and of Hung Hsing-tsu's *Ch'u tz'u pu chu*. There are two such editions of *Ch'u tz'u chang chü* generally thought to be based on the same Sung edition, one of 1518 and one of 1571.

The latter, the so-called *Fu jung kuan* 夫容館 edition, is the ancestor of most modern reprints. For example, the *Ch'u tz'u chang chü* printed in the *Ts'ung shu chi ch'eng* is there described as having been 'based on the *Hu pei ts'ung shu* edition' (of 1891); but the *Hu pei ts'ung shu* edition has itself been described as a 'faithful copy' of the *Fu jung kuan* reprint. Chu Hsi is thought to have used Hung Hsing-tsu's text and *k'ao i* without acknowledgement. As Hung Hsing-tsu's text is eclectic and the variants that he supplies are mostly unidentified, this means that the *Ch'u tz'u chang chü* is the critic's most important edition. For further information about editions and commentaries, the reader is recommended to consult one of the bibliographies of the *Ch'u tz'u*, i.e., Jao Tsung-i's 饒宗頤 *Ch'u tz'u shu lu* 楚辭書錄 (Hong Kong: Tong nam, 1956); or Chiang Liang-fu's *Ch'u tz'u shu mu wu chung* 楚辭書目五種 (Peking: Chung hua, 1961).

6. Aids to study

A concordance to the *Ch'u tz'u*, entitled *Soji sakuin* 楚辭索引, by Takeji Sadao 竹治貞夫, based on the *Ssu pu ts'ung k'an* edition of *Ch'u tz'u pu chu*, was published by Tokushima University 德島大學 in 1964. Takeji's *Soji kenkyū* 楚辭研究 (Tokyo, 1978) contains an excellent survey of the whole range of *Ch'u tz'u* studies and an index with more than 1200 entries.The section on editions may be specially recommended as being a more concise and more easily assimilable exposition than the larger, somewhat confusing catalogues mentioned above.

Among translations into modern colloquial Chinese, those of Kuo Mo-jo are probably the most widely known. His *Ch'ü Yüan fu chin i* 屈原賦今譯 (Peking: Jen-min Press, 1953) contains translations into modern Chinese of *Chiu ko, Chao hun, T'ien wen, Li sao, Chiu chang, Pu chü* and *Yü fu* (in that order). The translation of *Li sao* is, with very few alterations, the same as the one appearing in his earlier *Chü Yüan* 屈原 (Shanghai: K'ai ming, 1935). Wen Huai-sha's 文懷沙 more scholarly translations might be found more useful by the foreign student; see *Ch'ü Yüan chiu ko chin shih* 屈原九歌今釋 (Shanghai: T'ang ti, August 1952), *Ch'ü Yüan chiu chang chin shih* 屈原九章今釋 (Shanghai: T'ang ti, December 1952) and *Ch'ü Yüan Li sao chin shih* 屈原離騷今釋 (Shanghai: Wen i lien ko, 1954).

7. Translations

The English translation *Li sao and other poems of Ch'ü Yüan* by Yang Hsien-yi and Gladys Yang (Peking:Foreign Languages Press, 1957) is based on Kuo Mo-jo's modern Chinese versions. Arthur Waley's *The Nine Songs: a study of shamanism in ancient China* (London: George Allen and Unwin, 1956) contains, along with translations of all but the last of the *Chiu ko* poems, a useful summary of the information on shamanism to be culled from traditional Chinese sources. Translations of the remaining *Chiu ko* poem *Kuo shang* and of *Ta chao* are to be found in his *Chinese poetry* (London: George Allen and Unwin, 1956). David Hawkes, *Ch'u tz'u: The songs of the south, an ancient Chinese anthology* (Oxford: Clarendon Press, 1959; second revised edition: *The songs of the south: an anthology of ancient Chinese poems by Qu Yuan and other poets*; Harmondsworth: Penguin Books Limited, 1985) contains translations of all the poems in Wang I's anthology. The first edition included a short section of textual notes mostly derived from Wen I-to's *Ch'u tz'u chiao pu*.

8. Japanese editions

A. *Kambun taikei;* no. 22, 1916, edited by Inoue Tetsujirō, Okada Masayuki.

B. *Kanseki kokujikai zensho;* no.17, 1911, edited by Asami Keisai.

D. *Kokuyaku kambun taisei*; no.1 (literary series), 1922, edited by Shaku Seitan.

E. *Kambun sōsho*, 1928, edited by Okada Masuyuki.

G. *Chūgoku koten bungaku zenshū*; no.1, 1960, edited by Mekata Makoto.

H. *Shinshaku kambun taikei*; no.34, 1970, edited by Hoshikawa Kiyotaka.

K. *Chūgoku koten bungaku taikei*; no.15, 1969, edited by Mekata Makoto.

L. *Chūgoku koten shinsho*, 1970, edited by Hoshikawa Kiyotaka.

9. Indexes

(a) See under (6) above.

(b) *A Concordance to the Chu ci* 楚辭逐字索引, ed. D.C. Lau and Chen Fong Ching; *ICS* series, Hong Kong: Commercial Press, forthcoming 1996.

— David Hawkes

Chuang tzu 莊子

1. Content, date and authenticity

Authorship of the *Chuang tzu*, one of the two basic texts of the Taoist tradition, has traditionally been ascribed to Chuang Chou 莊周, who is described in *Shih chi* 63, p. 2143, as a contemporary of the Hui 惠 king of Liang 梁 (370–319 B.C.) and the Hsüan 宣 king of Ch'i 齊 (319–301 B.C.). It has long been recognised that the received text is not an homogeneous collection made by a single author, but that it contains a considerable amount of miscellaneous material, some of which appears to be related only marginally to the main themes of the book.

Possibly from the time of its initial compilation the text has been divided into the three sections of *nei p'ien, wai p'ien* and *tsa p'ien*; the extant recension of 33 *p'ien*, which dates from Kuo Hsiang 郭象 (d. 312), includes 7 'inner chapters', 15 'outer chapters' and 11 'mixed chapters'. From earliest times the *nei p'ien* have been considered to be the actual work of Chuang Chou (or Chuang Tzu), and modern scholars generally concur with this view, on the basis of the style, vocabulary, grammar and philosophical content of the text. This section of the work contains all the major themes for which the *Chuang tzu* has been renowned, i.e. the 'free and easy wandering' of the sage who is grounded in the *Tao*, the relativity of all conceptual categorization and equanimity towards life and death.

Although commentators have usually treated the text as a whole, since at least the Northern Sung period it has been recognised that the work includes much material that could not have been written by Chuang Chou. Recent scholars, such as Kuan Feng 關鋒 and A.C. Graham, discern several distinct groupings of some of the *p'ien* in the outer and mixed sections of the book:

(a) Nos. 8–11 (the 'Primitivist' material); essays by an individual who was strongly influenced by the *Lao tzu*, variously dated to later Ch'in (Kuan) and *c.* 205 B.C. (Graham); possibly including only the first part of no. 11 and two passages of nos. 12 and 14.

(b) Nos. 12–16 and 33 (the 'Syncretist' material); attributed to the eclectic Taoists who probably compiled the text *c.* 180 B.C. (Graham), or to

the lost school of Sung Hsing 宋鈃 (?360–?290 B.C.) and Yin Wen 尹
文 (4th century, from Ch'i); for details see works by Kuan and
Graham under (7) below.

(c) Nos. 17–22; material from later followers of Chuang Chou, often
imitating the style and themes of the *nei p'ien*; Kuan adds no. 23 to
this group.

(d) Nos. 23–27 and 32; heterogeneous collections of fragments, including some material from Chuang Chou which belongs in the *nei p'ien*.

(e) Nos. 28–31; a collection of material from the school of Yang Chu 楊
朱 (5th century B.C.), dated by Graham to *c.* 200. Kuan questions the
inclusion of no. 30.

The text of the *Chuang tzu* thus seems to have taken its form in a
period of over a century as an heterogeneous collection of material from
Chuang Chou or his followers and from other sources believed to be
related to him in some way. This raw textual material may have initially
been compiled during the first few decades of the Han dynasty by the
eclectic Taoists who contributed several essays to the book. A new study
by H.D. Roth argues that these eclectic Taoists could not have also compiled the book, and that instead the *Chuang tzu* was initially compiled
by retainers at the court of Liu An 劉安 (king of Huai-nan 淮南, died
122 B.C.) in *c.* 130 B.C. (see Roth, 'Who Compiled the *Chuang tzu*', in
Chinese Texts and Philosophical Contexts, ed. Henry Rosemont, Jr., La
Salle, Illinois: Open Court Press, 1992, 79–128). Roth argues further that
the Syncretist *Chuang tzu* and the *Huai nan tzu* are both products of the
Huang-Lao philosophical lineage that was the principal representative
of Taoism in the early Han. If these conclusions are correct, they suggest
the possibility that the philosophical positions represented in the text
are not all miscellaneous, but, instead, indicate different strata in the
development of early Taoist thought.

However, the recension of the book in 33 *p'ien*, upon which these conclusions are based, dates from Kuo Hsiang, and it cannot be known how
far that recension relates to an original compilation, especially in so far
as the arrangement of material among the three sections is concerned.

2. Transmission of the text

Shih chi 63, pp. 2143f., refers to a text of some 100,000 words, and cites
the titles of several *p'ien* that are still in the text (nos. 31, 29, 10 and possibly 23). The *Shih chi* also provides a complete version of a story about
Chuang Chou that is fragmentary in the received text of *p'ien* no. 32;
nothing is stated about the organization of the work. As the *Huai nan*

tzu clearly includes material that had been adopted from the *Chuang tzu*, it is evident that an early version of that text was present at the court of Liu An. In addition, two essays on the *Chuang tzu* which survive only in small fragments in Li Shan's (d. 689) 李善 commentary to the *Wen hsüan* are attributed to Liu An.

Han shu 30, p. 1730, lists the *Chuang tzu* in 52 *p'ien*, and it is believed, but not certain, that such a redaction, which existed in Former Han, represented an original form of the text. During the late third and fourth centuries a number of commentaries were written on the *Chuang tzu*, of which two were based on the redaction in 52 *p'ien*. Of these, that of Ssu-ma Piao 司馬彪 (240–306) contained 7 inner, 28 outer and 14 mixed chapters, together with 3 chapters of interpretative material, which may have included Liu An's essays. Three other commentaries, which were based on redactions with a different number of *p'ien*, apparently all contained 7 inner but no mixed *p'ien* (those of Ts'ui Chuan 崔譔 (3rd–4th century) and Hsiang Hsiu 向秀 (?221–?300), of 27 *p'ien*, and that of Li I 李頤 (3rd–4th century), of 30 or 35 *p'ien*); these are more likely to represent revisions of the redaction of 52 *p'ien* than alternative original versions of the work. All of these redactions survived into the T'ang period, but they were gradually replaced by a shorter and more popular version, arranged by Kuo Hsiang.

All extant editions derive from Kuo Hsiang's recension, and as is clear from Lu Te-ming's 陸德明 (556–627) remarks (preface to *Ching tien shih wen; c.* 625) and from Kuo's own colophon (see 5 (b) below), Kuo Hsiang himself completed a major revision of the text of the *Chuang tzu*. Probably beginning from the redaction in 52 *p'ien*, he reduced the text by about 30%, removing passages that he could not comprehend and those which resembled other works such as the *Shan hai ching* and the *Huai nan tzu*. In addition he probably reorganized some of the *p'ien* that he preserved, since early sources refer to some passages of the *Chuang tzu* as being in one section of the text, while they are now to be found in another (see preface to Wang Shu-min 王叔岷, 1947, as in 7 below). There are a large number of passages attributed to the *Chuang tzu* in various encyclopaedias and in the commentaries to other works that are not present in the received text, and these probably constitute indirect testimony to the material which Kuo Hsiang excised. While the work of collecting these passages really began with the redactions of Sun P'ing-i 孫馮翼 (1799), the most reliable collections are to be found in the appendixes of the works of Wang Shu-min and Ma Hsü-lun 馬敘倫 (1884–1970); for an analysis of this material, see Fukunaga Mitsuji and Livia Kohn (see 7 below).

The recension in 33 *p'ien* that Kuo Hsiang created has been transmitted continuously until the present time, being in fact the sole recension available since the T'ang period.

The practice of calling the *Chuang tzu* by the alternative title of *Nan hua chen ching* 南華眞經 that is followed in many extant editions originated in an imperial edict of 742. This was made to honour Chuang Chou and three other Taoist authors, by giving their works honorific titles that were based on the alternative names they were reputed to have possessed.

3.   Commentaries

The great popularity of the *Chuang tzu* has given rise to extensive commentaries on the text and to this day that of Kuo Hsiang remains one of the most important. However, this is due more to the exposition of his own philosophy of the inherent spontaneity of all phenomena (*tzu jan* 自然) than to the light that it throws on the text itself. Kuo Hsiang's philosophy struck a note to which Chinese men of letters were responding, and this undoubtedly helped to assure the success of his recension in 33 *p'ien*.

Five other commentaries of the Chin period, by Ssu-ma Piao, Meng Shih 孟氏, Hsiang Hsiu, Li I and Ts'ui Chuan focussed more closely on the text but they survive only in indirect testimony. The single most important source for these is Lu Te-ming's *Ching tien shih wen*, whose section on the *Chuang tzu* is sometimes published separately as the *Chuang tzu wen chü i* 莊子文句義. Taken together these commentaries with several others of a later date and Lu's own additional notes (based on Kuo Hsiang's recension in 33 *p'ien*) constitute an important source of glosses on the text. Lu Te-ming's commentary has also proved to be extremely popular and is now extant in several forms; it is usually published together with that of Kuo Hsiang.

Except for that of Mr. Meng, all the above Chin commentaries seem to have survived until the end of the T'ang period. The most popular of these must have been that of Ssu-ma Piao, since sufficient indirect testimony has survived to form a number of reconstituted redactions by Ch'ing scholars; the earliest and most important of these is that of Sun P'ing-i (*Ssu-ma Piao Chuang tzu chu* 司馬彪莊子注, 1799).

Owing to certain comments in the *Shih shuo hsin yü* 世說新語, it has long been assumed that Hsiang Hsiu's commentary was largely incorporated into that of Kuo Hsiang. However, careful comparison of the fragments of Hsiang Hsiu's notes with the commentary of Kuo Hsiang (undertaken by a number of Chinese and Japanese scholars) has cast doubt on this traditional belief; for details, see Fukunaga.

By the Sui dynasty, at least 11 other expository studies of varying lengths and types had been written. None of these has survived, but some of the 30 or more new commentaries that date from the T'ang or Sung periods are extant. The most important of these is the sub-commentary (*shu* 疏) of the Taoist master Ch'eng Hsüan-ying 成玄英 (*fl.* 630–60), which is valuable for its concise explanations and its new phonetic glosses. Ch'eng wrote these notes in order to expand on Kuo Hsiang's commentary, with which it has always been transmitted.

Four Sung interpretative studies have been influential both in China and Japan:

(a) Wang P'ang 王雱 (1042–76), *Nan hua chen ching hsin chuan* 南華眞經 新傳, of 1096; see *Tao tsang* 503–06.

(b) Lin Hsi-i 林希逸 (*c.* 1200–*c.* 1273), *Chuang tzu k'ou i* 莊子口義, of 1261; see *Tao tsang* 488–94.

(c) Lo Mien-tao 羅勉道, *Nan hua chen ching hsün pen* 南華眞經循本, of *c.* 1270; see *Tao tsang* 498–502.

(d) Ch'u Po-hsiu 褚伯秀 (*c.* 1230–after 1287), *Nan hua chen ching i hai tsuan wei* 南華眞經義海纂微, of 1270; see *Tao tsang* 467–87. This is a collection of 13 Sung philosophical commentaries, including those of Wang P'ang and Lin Hsi-i.

The most important Ming interpretative study of the *Chuang tzu* is the *Chuang tzu i* 莊子翼 of Chiao Hung 焦竑 (1541–1620), of 1588; this carries the comments of 22 Sung and Ming scholars, including the four named above.

4.   Editions

There are over 100 extant complete editions, which can be classified into a number of major redactions as follows:

(a) Text only: the oldest of the 28 editions of this category is that of the *Tao tsang* (1445), in 5 *chüan* (344–51). In all probability this version did not derive directly from a text that as yet had no commentary; it was probably created by removing the commentaries from one of the editions in the following three categories.

(b) With Kuo Hsiang's commentary only: there are two extant editions only, both originating from Northern Sung.

   (i) That of Chao Chien-i 趙諫議, printed between 1163 and 1190, but based on a Northern Sung edition.

(ii) The second part (*chüan* 7–10) of the reprint (Northern Sung) published in the *Hsü ku i ts'ung shu*. (The first part of this reprint (*chüan* 1–6) is from a Southern Sung edition as described in (c)).

An early copy features among the 21 items listed for the *Chuang tzu* in Fujiwara Sukeyo's catalogue.

(c) With Kuo Hsiang's commentary followed by Lu Te-ming's notes: this is the single most popular redaction, which has appeared in over 65 editions.

(i) The oldest edition is that included in the *Hsü ku i ts'ung shu* (see (b) (ii) immediately above).

(ii) The Kung Shih-hsieh 龔士卨 (Ma sha 麻沙 print) of 1260, included in his collection *Liu tzu* 六子 (issued in a revised printing of 1533 by the Shih te t'ang 世德堂 as the *Liu tzu shu* 六子書; reprinted 1573 as *Liu tzu ch'üan shu* 六子全書). The Shih te t'ang *Chuang tzu* was the basis for 37 subsequent editions, including the *Ssu pu ts'ung k'an* and the *Ssu pu pei yao*.

(d) With Kuo Hsiang's commentary and Ch'eng Hsüan-ying's subcommentary; there are 18 editions, mostly published during the nineteenth century. The two oldest are:

(i) The Southern Sung edition reproduced in the *Ku i ts'ung shu* and entitled *Nan hua chen ching chu shu* 南華眞經注疏; this formed the basis for Kuo Ch'ing-fan's 郭慶藩 (1844–96) annotated edition (see 6 (a) below), that was used for the Harvard-Yenching Sinological Index series.

(ii) *Tao tsang* 507–19.

In general, textual criticism requires consultation of the oldest extant edition of each of the foregoing redactions (a) to (d), and, of these, that of the *Hsü ku i ts'ung shu* is the most reliable. But as that version is not free of textual errors, it should be used at the very least in conjunction with one of the modern text-critical studies that are listed below.

5. Major fragments

The following are the principal sources of the considerable body of fragmentary material:

(a) Manuscripts from Tun-huang. Fragments constituting most of twelve *p'ien* of an edition in the Kuo Hsiang redaction, dating from early T'ang, were discovered at Tun-huang. Most of these are kept at the British Library or the Bibliothèque Nationale; some are held in Japan and China. The most complete of a number of publications of collections of these fragments is Teraoka Ryūgan 寺岡龍含, *Ton-kō bon Kaku Zō chū Sōshi Nanka shinkei kōkan ki* 敦煌本郭象注莊子南華眞經校勘記 (Fukui: Kambun gakkai, 1961); the author collates fragments with six of the oldest editions of the *Chuang tzu*.

For a smaller group of fragments from three other sources at Tun-huang, see Teraoka, *Tonkō bon Kaku Zō chū Sōshi Nanka shinkei kenkyū sōron* 敦煌本郭象注莊子南華眞經研究總論 (Fukui: Kambun gak-kai, 1966). This work also includes a number of valuable essays on different aspects of the material from Tun-huang.

(b) The Kōzanji 高山寺 manuscript. The Kōzanji monastery, Kyoto, possesses a manuscript of the Muromachi period (1392–1568) which carries seven *p'ien* of an edition with the notes of Kuo Hsiang and Ch'eng Hsüan-ying. All seven *p'ien* are complete, being from the outer and the mixed sections of the text. Variants indicate that this manuscript was based on a very old edition, in all probability from early T'ang, and hence very close to Ch'eng Hsüan-ying's original work. It also contains the only extant copy of Kuo Hsiang's draft colophon that has been mentioned above. The manuscript has been published by Kano Naoki 狩野直喜 in *Kyū shō kansuhon Sōshi zankan kō kan ki* 舊鈔卷子本莊子殘卷校勘記 (Tokyo: Tōhō bunka gakuin, 1932), where the text is collated with several major Sung and Ming editions.

(c) The *Ching tien shih wen*. Lu Te-ming's work includes frequent cita-tions of textual variants which he sporadically identifies and which are most frequently drawn from two sources: (i) Ts'ui Chuan's edi-tion (*c.* 290); and (ii) an edition dated between 424 and 454. All Lu's textual variants are conveniently listed at the foot of each page of the Harvard-Yenching print of the the text, but Lu's identification of the sources of his variants is unfortunately omitted.

(d) The *Nan hua chen ching chang chü yin i* 南華眞經章句音義, by Ch'en Ching-yüan 陳景元 (dated 1084; *Tao tsang* 495–97). This work con-tains annotations of words and phrases from a critical text that Ch'en had established, primarily on the basis of the edition of the *Kuo tzu chien* 國子監 of 1007. In an appendix (*ch'üeh wu* 闕誤) he lists 349 variants between his basic text and seven other T'ang and Sung edi-tions, including three by Chang Chün-fang 張君房, who was one of the editors of the Northern Sung Taoist Canon (1019). In fact these three editions are identified by Ch'en as deriving from the Canon.

6. Studies of the Ch'ing period

The Ch'ing scholars continued the traditional work of interpreting the *Chuang tzu* that had been started by Kuo Hsiang and developed during the Sung and Ming periods. While many scholars, including Wang Fu-chih 王夫之 (1619–92; *Chuang tzu chieh* 莊子解 of 1669) wrote interpretations of the meaning of the text, only a few stand out. Lin Yün-ming 林雲銘, *Piao chu Chuang tzu yin* 標註莊子因 (1663) and Lu Shu-chih 陸樹芝, *Chuang tzu hsüeh* 莊子雪 (1796) are generally regarded as the best examples of this genre.

The textual criticism that began in the middle of the 18th century, under the impact of the *Han hsüeh* movement, was of greater importance. Of a number of the major Ch'ing textual critics who included sections on the *Chuang tzu* in their large works, the most valuable are Wang Nien-sun 王念孫 (1744–1832), Yü Yüeh 俞樾 (1821–1907) and Sun I-jang 孫詒讓 (1848–1908).

Two late Ch'ing annotated editions of the *Chuang tzu* are worthy of mention:

(a) Kuo Ch'ing-fan, *Chuang tzu chi shih* 莊子集釋 (1894), based on the *Ku i ts'ung shu* reproduction of an edition (Southern Sung) of Ch'eng Hsüan-ying, with Lu Te-ming's *shih wen* distributed throughout the text. Owing to copyist's errors, only the *Chiao cheng Chuang tzu chi shih* 校正莊子集釋 (Taipei: Shih chieh, 1974) can be recommended.

(b) *Chuang tzu chi chieh* 莊子集解 (1909), by Wang Hsien-ch'ien 王先謙 (1842–1918; a pupil of Kuo Ch'ing-fan), and of somewhat less value. This distributes a collection of interpretative and philological comments by Wang himself and other Ch'ing scholars in an unidentified edition (probably a descendant of the Shih te t'ang edition of 1533).

7. Recent studies

(a) Annotations without complete text:

(i) Ma Hsü-lun, *Chuang tzu i cheng* 莊子義正 (Shanghai: Shang wu, 1930).

(ii) Wang Shu-min, *Chuang tzu chiao shih* 莊子校釋 (Shanghai: Shang wu, 1947); revised and expanded as *Chuang tzu chiao ch'üan* 莊子校詮 (Taipei: Institute of History and Philology, 1988), thus superseding the earlier work.

Based on reliable editions, these collate text where desirable, add critical comments by Ch'ing scholars and include reconstituted redactions of lost fragments of the *Chuang tzu*. Wang Shu-min's book has the added advantage of incorporating most of the fragmentary and indirect testimony to the text, and is the most valuable work of textual criticism ever written on the *Chuang tzu*. Wang's later textual research was included in his volume of 1988.

(b) Edition with text:

Liu Wen-tien 劉文典, *Chuang tzu pu cheng* 莊子補正 (Shanghai; Shang wu, 1947); annotated edition based on Kuo Ch'ing-fan's text, with valuable text-critical commentary of earlier scholars, but subject to methodological errors, as is his edition of the *Huai nan tzu* (see appendix, in Wang Shu-min, *Chuang tzu chiao shih*).

(c) Other works:

> (i) Ch'ien Mu 錢穆, *Chuang tzu tsuan chien* 莊子纂箋 (Hong Kong: Tung nan yin wu, 1925; reprinted 1951); succinct summaries of selections from a long list of commentators.
>
> (ii) Yen Ling-feng 嚴靈峯, *Lao Lieh Chuang san tzu chih chien shu mu* 老列莊三子知見書目 (3 vols., Taipei: Chung hua, 1965); includes a thorough bibliography.
>
> (iii) Yen Ling-feng, *Chou Ch'in Han Wei chu tzu chih chien shu mu* 周秦漢魏諸子知見書目 (Taipei: Cheng chung, 1975); an updated bibliography, including western publications.
>
> (iv) Yen Ling-feng, *Wu ch'iu pei chai Chuang tzu chi ch'eng* 無求備齋莊子集成 (Taipei: I wen, 1972-74); facsimile reproductions of most of the important editions and of extant scholarship, back to the Sung period.
>
> (v) Kuan Feng 關鋒, 'Chuang tzu "wai tsa p'ien" ch'u t'an' 莊子 "外雜篇" 初探; in Che hsüeh yen chiu pien chi pu 哲學研究編輯部 (ed.), *Chuang tzu che hsüeh t'ao lun chi* 莊子哲學討論集 (Peking: Chung hua, 1962), pp. 61-98.
>
> (vi) Graham, A.C., 'How much of *Chuang tzu* did Chuang Tzu write?' (*Studies in Chinese Philosophy and Philosophical Literature*, Singapore, 1986, and New York: State University of New York Press, 1990, pp. 283-321).
>
> (vii) Kohn, Livia, 'Lost *Chuang Tzu* Passages'; *Journal of Chinese religion* 10 (1982), 53-79.
>
> (viii) Roth, H.D., 'Who compiled the *Chuang Tzu*?'; in *Chinese Texts and Philosophical contexts*, ed. Henry Rosemont, Jr., LaSalle, Illinois: Open Court Press, 1992, 79-128.

(d) Japanese writings; the following items stand out in an extensive body of writing:

(i) Takeuchi Yoshio 武内義雄, Sōshi kō 莊子考 and Rōshi to Sōshi 老子と莊子; available most conveniently in *Takeuchi Yoshio zenshū* 武内義雄全集 (Tokyo: Kadokawa, 1979).

(ii) Fukunaga Mitsuji 福永光司, 'Sōshi no yū ni tsuite 莊子の遊について,' *Shinagaku*, 12, 1946, 33–73; *Sōshi* (Tokyo: Chūō kōronsha, 1964); and 'Kaku Shō no Sōshi chū to Kō Shu no Sōshi chū 郭象の莊子注と向秀の莊子注'; *THG* 36 (1964), 187–215.

8. Translations (selected items only)

(a) Legge, *Sacred books of the East*, vol. XXXIX, XL.

(b) Giles, Herbert, *Chuang Tzu, Mystic, Moralist and Social Reformer*; London: Bernard Quaritch, 1889; second edition, revised, Shanghai: Kelly and Walsh, 1926 (reprinted London: George Allen and Unwin, 1961).

(c) Fung Yu-lan, *Chuang Tzu, a new selected translation with an exposition of the philosophy of Kuo Hsiang*; Shanghai: Shang wu, 1933 (includes translation of *p'ien* nos. 1–7).

(d) Ware, James, *The sayings of Chuang Chou*; New York: Mentor Classics, 1963.

(e) Watson, Burton, (i) *Chuang tzu: Basic writings*; New York and London: Columbia University Press, 1964; (ii) *The complete works of Chuang Tzu*; New York and London: Columbia University Press, 1968.

(f) Graham, A.C., *Chuang-tzu, The Seven Inner Chapters and other writings from the book Chuang-tzu*; London: George Allen and Unwin, 1981; also published paperback, 1986. (Notes to this translation were published separately as *Chuang-tzu: textual notes to a partial translation*; London: School of Oriental and African Studies, 1982).

9. Japanese editions

A. *Kambun taikei*; no. 9, 1911, edited by Hattori Unokichi.

B. *Kanseki kokujikai zensho*; (a) no. 9, 1910, edited by Mōri Teisai; (b) nos. 28, 29, 1914, edited by Makino Kenjirō (Sōshū).

D. *Kokuyaku kambun taisei*; no. 7, 1920, edited by Kimida Rentarō.

E. *Kambun sōsho*, 1928, 1928, edited by Hattori Unokichi.

F. *Keisho taikō*; nos. 10–12, 1938–39.

H. *Shinshaku kambun taikei*; nos. 7–8, 1966–67, edited by Ichikawa Yasuji and Endō Tatsuo.

J.   *Chūgoku no shisō*; no. 12, 1965, edited by Kishi Yōko.

K. *Chūgoku koten bungaku taikei*; no. 4, 1973, edited by Kuraishi Takeshirō and Seki Masao.

L. *Chūgoku koten shinsho*, 1968, edited by Abe Yoshio.

M. *Shintei Chūgoku koten sen*; nos. 7–9, 1966–67, edited by Fukunaga Mitsuji.

10. Indexes

(a) *Chuang tzu yin te* 莊子引得 (A concordance to Chuang Tzu); Harvard-Yenching Institute Sinological Index series no. 20. Peking, 1947, compiled by Ch'i Ssu-ho 齊思和 (b. 1907); based on an early reprint of Kuo Ch'ing-fan's edition, without correction of copyist's errors.

(b) *A Concordance to the Zhuangzi* 莊子逐字索引, ed. D.C. Lau and Chen Fong Ching; *ICS* series, Hong Kong: Commercial Press, forthcoming 1996.

— H. D. Roth

Ch'un ch'iu 春秋, Kung yang 公羊, Ku liang 穀梁 and Tso chuan 左傳

1. Content

The *Ch'un ch'iu* is one of the traditional classical texts, whose content is best described by Burton Watson: 'The *Ch'un-ch'iu* or *Spring and Autumn* is a chronicle of the reigns of twelve dukes of the state of Lu 魯 covering the period from 722 to 481 B.C. It contains, in barest outline, notations of the internal affairs of Lu, of diplomatic conferences, feudal wars, and Lu's other relations with neighboring states, and occasional records of eclipses, floods, earthquakes and prodigies of nature. The account is entirely impersonal, with no trace, at least to the untutored eye, of the personality or attitude of the recorder or recorders.' (Burton Watson, *Ssu-ma Ch'ien, Grand Historian of China*; New York: Columbia University Press, 1958, pp. 75–6). The *Ch'un ch'iu* appears to be a bare record of facts, composed in an extremely terse style and arranged in chronological order. The title is usually taken to stand as a synecdoche for the four seasons of the year, and therefore to be a generic term for annals; it gives its name to the period that it covers, i.e., 722–481 B.C.

2. Authorship and authenticity

Mencius was the first to claim that Confucius himself was the actual author of the *Ch'un ch'iu*. He was followed on this point by the whole of traditional scholarship, and the revered character of the *Ch'un ch'iu* as a classical text was not brought into question until early in the 20th century. But, whoever the author may have been, the *Ch'un ch'iu* was most probably known to Confucius, and in any case constitutes a valuable source of historical information.

The work is now currently known under the headings of its three main commentaries, the *Kung yang* 公羊, the *Ku liang* 穀梁 and the *Tso* 左 or *Tso shih* 左氏. In *Han shu* 30, p. 1713, two other commentaries, now lost, are listed, the *Tsou shih* 鄒氏 and the *Chia shih* 夾氏; they are both entered as being in 11 *chüan*. The three extant commentaries must have stemmed originally from different schools of interpretation, and were the objects of passionate discussion during the Han dynasty, with each school of thought claiming to be the bearer of Confucius' authentic teaching. Furthermore, the three commentaries were based on different versions of the *Ch'un ch'iu*, and the textual variants have been studied, chiefly by Ch'ing scholars (e.g., Mao Ch'i-ling 毛奇齡 (1623–1716), Chao T'an 趙坦 (*fl.* 1820) and Chu Chün-sheng 朱駿聲 (1788–1858)). The *Kung yang* and *Ku liang* were taken to represent the New Text school, in that they were based on a version of the *Ch'un ch'iu* in modern script (*chin wen* 今文), i.e., the script current in Han times; these were already officially acknowledged as the orthodox interpretations in the Former Han period. The *Tso chuan*, on the other hand, is associated with the Old Text school, because, when it was brought to imperial attention at the end of Former Han, it was claimed to be based on an older version of the *Ch'un ch'iu* in the pre-Ch'in 'ancient' script (*ku wen* 古文).

Of a number of similarities between the *Kung yang* and the *Ku liang* commentaries, the most important is that they are both in the form of a catechism: they comment on the text of the *Ch'un ch'iu* by means of questions and answers, thus illustrating the 'praise and blame' theory of historical writing that was formulated by Mencius, and according to which Confucius composed the *Ch'un ch'iu* in order to pass judgement on the violence, lawlessness and corruption of his age. Both the *Kung yang* and the *Ku liang* read into the *Ch'un ch'iu* a political and moral lesson, and make much of the omission or inclusion of particular information, and of the choice of particular words, as bearing and conveying a profound significance.

According to the traditional theory, as summed up by Ho Hsiu 何休 (129–182; see *Kung yang chuan chieh ku* 公羊傳解詁, Duke Yin, 2nd year), the *Kung yang* was the result of a continuous oral tradition which originated with Tzu Hsia 子夏, one of Confucius' disciples, and was transmitted to a Kung yang shih 公羊氏, who wrote down the *Kung yang* on bamboo and silk during the reign of Han Ching ti (reigned 157 to 141 B.C.). According to modern scholarship, however, the *Kung yang* already existed in written form by the end of the Warring States period; the text was dispersed and damaged under the Ch'in empire and put together again early in the Han period. It is usually believed that, given its numerous borrowings from and elaborations upon the *Kung yang*, the *Ku liang* was written later (see P'i Hsi-jui 皮錫瑞 (1850–1908), as cited below, 5.16b–18a). It was granted official recognition as a result of the Shih ch'ü ko 石渠閣 discussions of 51 B.C.

The *Tso shih* is somewhat different from the other two commentaries in that it covers a longer period than the *Ch'un ch'iu* (722 to 463 B.C.) and lays greater emphasis on the historical background of the events mentioned, thus providing valuable additional information about the period. It is also by far the longest of the three commentaries.

The traditional theory about its authorship, as seen in *Shih chi* 14, pp. 509-10, is a straightforward statement grounded on two main assumptions: (a) that the author of the *Tso shih* is the Tso Ch'iu-ming 左丘明 mentioned in the *Lun yü* and taken to be a contemporary of Confucius; and (b) that the *Tso shih* was composed as a commentary on the *Ch'un ch'iu*. The former assumption was already challenged by T'ang scholars such as Tan Chu 啖助 (fl. 750) and Chao K'uang 趙匡 (early 8th century), who were followed by a number of scholars of the T'ang, Sung, Ming and Ch'ing periods (see Lu Ch'un 陸淳 (late 8th century) and Chu I-tsun 朱彝尊 (1629–1709), as cited below).

The second assumption raises a particularly intricate issue since there were originally two versions of the *Tso shih*: one, which was circulating during the Former Han period; and one which, being kept in the Han imperial archives, was another version of the *Tso shih* and the *Ch'un ch'iu* in ancient script. This copy of the *Ch'un ch'iu*, which was not attached to any commentary and carried the chronicle two years further than the *Kung yang* and *Ku liang* versions, was brought to light by Liu Hsin 劉歆 (46 B.C.–A.D. 23) during the reign of Ai ti (reigned 7–1 B.C.). The story of the find is told in *Han shu* 36, p. 1967: 'When Liu Hsin examined the books of the secret archives, he found a *Ch'un ch'iu* and *Tso shih* in ancient characters and was delighted with them. . . . Originally the *Tso shih* had many ancient characters and ancient expressions, and scholars had done no more than transmit explanations of their meaning. When Liu Hsin put the *Tso shih* in order, he quoted the words of the commentary in order to explain the text of the *Ch'un ch'iu*, thus getting them to clarify each other. From this time onwards, the chapters and clauses and their meanings were complete.' (The two works to which this passage refers were respectively the *Ch'un ch'iu ku ching* 春秋古經, in 12 *p'ien*, and the *Tso shih chuan* 左氏傳 in 30 *chüan*, as listed in *Han shu* 30, pp. 1712–13).

Liu Feng-lu 劉逢祿 (1776–1829) initiated a long drawn-out controversy by emphasizing the discrepancies between the texts of the *Tso shih* commentary and that of the *Ch'un ch'iu*, on which it was supposed to be commenting, as these have been handed down. This was not, in fact, Liu's original idea, but one which was typical of the New Text school as a whole; as early as the Han period, we find the idea that the *Tso shih* was not written as a commentary to the *Ch'un ch'iu*. Indeed, a large number of discrepancies are to be found, to the extent that sometimes there are passages of the *Ch'un ch'iu* without 'commentary', or 'commentary' where there is no text to which it applies. These discrepancies have been accounted for in many ways. Liu Feng-lu's thesis, as revised and nearly caricatured by K'ang Yu-wei 康有為 (1858–1927) , was that Liu Hsin, who, with his father Liu Hsiang 劉向 (79–8 B.C.) was the first to have access to rare and hitherto unknown documents in the imperial archives, used the opportunity to serve the interests of Wang Mang 王莽; to do so, he forged the *Tso shih* as a commentary to the *Ch'un ch'iu*, thereby justifying Wang Mang's policy; his work was largely based on the *Kuo yü* 國語, also ascribed to Tso Ch'iu-ming of Lu.

This thesis was taken up by a number of Ch'ing scholars, and it was later followed by some non-Chinese scholars such as Otto Franke (see his *Studien zur Geschichte des konfuzianischen Dogmas und der chinesischen Staatsreligion*; Hamburg: L. Friedrichsen, 1920, pp. 60f.). More recently attempts have been made to counter the accusation of forgery from every possible angle. Henri Maspero cited textual evidence against it. From a philological approach, Bernhard Karlgren concluded that the *Tso shih* is neither the work of Tso Ch'iu-ming nor a forgery by Liu Hsin, but that it is 'probably to be dated between 468 and 300 B.C.' In a debate which is grounded on astronomical evidence, two Japanese scholars have come to opposite conclusions. Iijima Tadao 飯島忠夫, followed by Tsuda Sōkichi 津田左友吉, verifies the theory of forgery by placing the compilation of the *Tso shih* in the first century B.C.; Shinjō Shinzō 新城新藏, in agreement with Kamata Tadashi 鎌田正, places it in the third century B.C. at the latest, thus establishing Liu Hsin's innocence.

Another hypothesis is presented by William Hung, who starts from the assumption that the *Tso shih* was indeed composed as a commentary to the *Ch'un ch'iu*, and at a relatively late date. Hung assigns it to the reign of Hui ti (reigned 195–88 B.C.), and even goes so far as to attribute it to the scholar and astronomer Chang Ts'ang 張蒼 (d. 152 B.C.). This hypothesis is still open to controversy, the actual revival of interest in the *Tso shih* in the early Han period not being sufficient proof of Chang Ts'ang's authorship. Hung then proceeds to account for the discrepancies between the *Tso shih* and its version of the *Ch'un ch'iu* by drawing a distinction between what it terms *Tso shih ching* 左氏經 (i.e., the text of the *Ch'un ch'iu* as we find it attached to the received *Tso shih*) and the *Tso chuan ching* 左傳經 (i.e., the text of the *Ch'un ch'iu* originally used by the author of the *Tso shih* in the second century B.C.). Hung believes the former to have been derived directly from the *Ch'un ch'iu ku ching* in 12 *p'ien*, which was associated with the *Tso shih* by Liu Hsin. As to the latter, it differed from the *ku ching* in that it had already been in circulation before Liu Hsin's discovery, and was a text lacking in homogeneity, made up of additions, modifications and loans from the other commentaries of the *Ch'un ch'iu* and various other texts such as the *Kuo yü*. According to Hung, this latter version disappeared at a very early stage, but is still to be perceived intermittently in the received *Tso shih*. In this connection, see also the works of Hou K'ang 侯康 (1798–1837), Li Fu-sun 李富孫 (1764–1843), Liu Shih-p'ei 劉師培 (1884–1919) and Tuan Yü-ts'ai 段玉裁 (1735–1815).

Maspero propounded a third theory, which differed from that of Hung in respect of the explanation of the discrepancies between the *Tso shih* and the *Ch'un ch'iu*. According to Maspero, the *Tso shih* that we know was originally made up of two distinct works: (a) a small literal commentary on the *Ch'un ch'iu*, mainly concerned with rites and ethics and analogous to the *Kung yang* and *Ku liang*, but stemming from a different school; and (b) a long, purely historical chronicle that originally had nothing to do with the *Ch'un ch'iu* or even with the state of Lu. Maspero thought that this component had been mainly concerned with the state of Chin 晉, being thus very closely affiliated to the *Kuo yü*. These two works, which Maspero dates back to the early 5th or late 4th century B.C. must have been amalgamated shortly afterwards to form the received *Tso shih*, the historical chronicle being cut up so as to fit the entries of the *Ch'un ch'iu*.

Maspero's theory of a purely historical component in the *Tso shih* seems to be somewhat supported by the discovery at Ma-wang-tui in 1973 of a badly damaged and fragmentary text written on silk (see *Ma-wang-tui Han mu po shu* 馬王堆漢墓帛書, 3; Peking: Wen wu, 1983). This records historical events of the *Ch'un ch'iu* period, some of which correspond with those described in the *Tso shih*, but with a different type of interpretation, and without chronological details. Some of the events that are recorded are not seen in the *Tso shih*.

3. Textual history and reliability of extant editions

Both the *Kung yang* and the *Ku liang* are entered in *Han shu* 30, p. 1713 as consisting of 11 *chüan* (one for each of the twelve dukes of Lu, except for the very short reign of Duke Min 閔, which was attached to that of Duke Chuang 莊 in the original edition). Beginning with Lu Te-ming's 陸德明 (556–627) *Ching tien shih wen hsü lu* 經典釋文敘錄, the *Kung yang* is reported as having 12 *chüan*; entries for the *Ku liang* in 12 and 13 *chüan* appear in *Sui shu* 32, p. 931.

The question arises of when the *Kung yang* and the *Ku liang* were first cut up and intercalated with the entries of the *Ch'un ch'iu*, as they are today, and it is very likely that they were not presented in that way originally. The fragments of the *Kung yang* seen in the classical texts carved on stone by Ts'ai Yung 蔡邕 (133–192) in A.D. 175 do not include the text of the *Ch'un ch'iu*. Yen K'o-chün 嚴可均 (1762–1843) argues that the intercalation must have been made by Ho Hsiu 何休 (129–82) in the Later Han period, but in his glosses on the *Kung yang* that writer does not comment on the *Ch'un ch'iu* itself.

The sub-commentary (*shu* 疏) is recorded for the first time as having 30 *chüan*, without the name of the author, in the *Ch'ung wen tsung mu* (completed 1041), and is subsequently attributed to Hsü Yen 徐彥 (T'ang or earlier). In the *Ssu k'u ch'üan shu tsung mu t'i yao* the *shu* is entered as having 28 *chüan*, and it is supposed there that the two missing chapters must have corresponded with the text of the *Ch'un ch'iu*, which would therefore have been distinct from that of the *Kung yang*. However, Sugiura Toyoji 山浦豐治 writes on the basis of an ancient manuscript of the *shu* alone in 30 *chüan*, which was based originally on a Sung edition, and which is now kept in the Nagoya shi Hōsa bunko 名古屋市蓬左文庫; he shows that the hypothesis of the *Ssu k'u ch'üan shu* on the reduction of the *shu* from 30 to 28 *chüan* proves to be wrong, and that it is in any case to be dated later than the T'ang period.

It is usually agreed that it was Fan Ning 范甯 (339–401) who intercalated the *Ku liang* with the *Ch'un ch'iu*, in his *Ch'un ch'iu Ku liang chuan chi chieh* 春秋穀梁傳集解. Two fragments, both dated in the Lung shuo period (661–64) were discovered by Pelliot at Tun-huang; they may be parts of the same manuscript, and they present interesting variants from the received versions (see Lo Chen-yü 羅振玉, *Ming sha shih shih ku chi ts'ung ts'an* 鳴沙石室古籍叢殘; Kanda Kiichirō 神田喜一郎, *Tun-huang mi chi liu chen hsin pien* 敦煌秘籍留真新編; Taipei: National Taiwan University, 1947); and the explanatory notes in Wang Chung-min 王重民, *Tun-huang ku chi hsü lu* 敦煌古籍敘錄; Peking: Shang wu, 1956).

The intercalation of the *Tso shih* with its version of the *Ch'un ch'iu* was effected by Tu Yü 杜預 (222–84), in his *Ch'un ch'iu ching chuan chi chieh* 春秋經傳集解, in 30 *chüan*. Four fragments in manuscript, dating back to the Six Dynasties, and two, dated in early T'ang, have been found at Tun-huang (see Lo Chen-yü, as cited immediately above). These constitute the oldest extant pieces available, together with the more complete 'ancient manuscript scroll' which is kept in the Kanazawa bunko 金澤文庫, and represents a textual tradition that goes back to the Six Dynasties (see Takezoe Shinichirō, in the *Kambun taikei* edition; and Shimada Kan 鳥田翰, *Kobun kyūsho kō* 古文舊書考; Tokyo: Minyūsha, 1905). This scroll was taken as the basis for many of the later editions of the *Tso shih* in Japan.

4. Current editions

These generally include the standard glosses and critical notes on the three commentaries, all accompanied by Lu Te-ming's *yin i* 音義, i.e.:

(i) *Kung yang*: Ho Hsiu's *chieh ku*, and a *shu* whose author is unknown;

(ii) *Ku liang*: Fan Ning's *chi chieh*, and the *shu* by Yang Shih-hsün 楊士勛 (T'ang);

(iii) *Tso shih*: Tu Yü's *chi chieh* and the *cheng i* 正義 of K'ung Ying-ta 孔穎達 (574-648).

(a) The *Ssu pu pei yao* series follows an edition of 1604, by Chin P'an 金蟠 and Ko Tzu 葛鼐 (c. 1523).

(b) Other reprints are chiefly based on the *Ch'ung k'an Sung pen shih san ching chu shu* 重刊宋本十三經注疏, edited with textual criticism (*chiao k'an chi* 校勘記) by Juan Yüan 阮元 (1764-1849) in 1815. This follows a late Sung edition of Yüeh K'o 岳珂, and it has been reprinted on a number of occasions from 1926 onwards in Shanghai, Taipei and Kyoto; it is also in the *SPPY* (*chu shu*) series.

    A recent punctuated edition based on Juan Yüan's text and including supplementary notes that take account of new material, e.g., from Tun-huang, has been published by Yang Po-chün 楊伯峻, as *Ch'un ch'iu Tso chuan chu* 春秋左傳注, 4 vols. (Peking: Chung hua, 1981).

(c) The texts of the *Ssu pu ts'ung k'an* and *Ts'ung shu chi ch'eng* series are based on a slightly earlier edition, dated in the Shao hsi period (1190-95); block-printed by Yü Jen-chung 余仁仲 during the Chia ch'ing period (1796-1820).

5. Principal secondary studies

(a) Chao T'an 趙坦, *Ch'un ch'iu i wen chien* 春秋異文箋; in *Huang Ch'ing ching chieh*, ch. 1303-15.

(b) Chu Chün-sheng 朱駿聲, *Ch'un ch'iu san chia i wen ho* 春秋三家異文疀; in *Chü hsüeh hsüan ts'ung shu* 聚學軒叢書, series 2.

(c) Chu I-tsun 朱彝尊, *Ching i k'ao* 經義考 (*SPPY*).

(d) Fu Li-p'u 傅隸樸, *Ch'un ch'iu san chuan pi i* 春秋三傳比義, Peking: Chung hua yu i, 1984.

(e) Hou K'ang 侯康 (1798–1837) ,*Ch'un ch'iu ku ching shuo* 春秋古經說 (*TSCC*).

(f) *Huang Ch'ing ching chieh* 皇清經解, and *hsü pien* 續編; originally published 1829.

(g) Hung, William; see introduction to item 8 (d) below.

(h) Iijima Tadao 飯島忠夫; (i) in *Tōyō gakuhō* 2:1 (1912), 28–57; and 9:2 (1919), 155–94; (ii) *Shina kodai shiron* 支那古代史論, revised ed., Tokyo: Kōseisha, 1941.

(i) K'ang Yu-wei 康有爲, *Hsin hsüeh wei ching k'ao* 新學僞經考, 1891.

(j) Karlgren, Bernhard: (i) 'On the authenticity and nature of the Tso-chuan' (*Götesborgs högskolas arsskrift* 32 (1926), 365; reprinted Taipei, 1965); (ii) 'The early history of the Chou li and Tso chuan texts', *BMFEA* 3 (1931), 1–59.

(k) Li Fu-sun 李富孫 (1764–1843), *Ch'un ch'iu san chuan i wen shih* 春秋三傳異文釋 (*TSCC*).

(l) Liu Shih-p'ei 劉師培, *Ch'un ch'iu ku ching chien* 春秋古經箋, in *Liu Shen-shu hsien sheng i shu* 劉申叔先生遺書.

(m)Lu Ch'un 陸淳, *Ch'un ch'iu Tan Chao chi chuan tsuan li* 春秋啖趙集傳纂例; in *Ku ching chieh hui han* 古經解彙函.

(n) Ma Heng 馬衡, *Han shih ching chi ts'un* 漢石經集存, Peking: K'o hsüeh, 1957.

(o) Mao Ch'i-ling 毛奇齡, *Ch'un ch'iu chien shu k'an wu* 春秋簡書刊誤; in *Huang Ch'ing ching chieh*, ch. 156–57.

(p) Maspero, Henri, 'La composition et la date du Tso-chuan', *Mélanges chinois et bouddhiques* I (1931–32), 137–215.

(q) P'i Hsi-jui 皮錫瑞, *Ching hsüeh t'ung lun* 經學通論 1923 ed. vol.5, 16b–18a.

(r) Shinjō Shinzō 新城新藏, *Tōyō temmongaku shi kenkyū* 東洋天文學史研究; Kyoto: Kōbundō, 1928.

(s) Sugiura Toyoji 杉浦豐治, *Kōyōso ronkō* 公羊疏論考 (*kobun hen* 古文編); Anjō: Gakuyūkai, 1961.

(t) Tsuda Sōkichi 津田左友吉, *Saden no shisōshiteki kenkyū* 左傳の思想史的研究, Tokyo: Tōyō bunko, 1935.

(u) Tuan Yü-ts'ai 段玉裁, *Ch'un ch'iu Tso shih ku ching* 春秋左氏古經 in *Tuan Yü-ts'ai i shu* 段玉裁遺書, rpt. Taipei: Ta hua, 1977.

(v) *T'ung chih t'ang ching chieh* 通志堂經解; dated 1677.

(w)Yen K'o-chün 嚴可均, *T'ang k'ai ch'eng shih ching chiao wen* 唐開成石經校文, 1926.

6. Translations

(a) Legge, *The Chinese Classics*, Vol. V, Parts I, II.

(b) Couvreur, Séraphin, *Tch'ouen ts'ieou et Tso tschouan*, vols. 1–3; Ho Kien Fou, 1914; reprinted Paris: Cathasia, 1951.

(c) For translations of passages of the *Kung yang* and *Ku liang*, see Göran Malmqvist, 'Studies on the Gongyang and Guliang commentaries,' *BMFEA* 43 (1971), 67–222; 47 (1975) 19–69; and 49 (1977) 33–215.

7. Japanese editions

A. *Kambun taikei*; nos. 10, 11, 1911, edited by Takezoe Shin'ichirō (no.10) and Hattori Unokichi (no.11).

B. *Kanseki kokujikai zensho*; nos. 13–15, 1910–11, edited by Katō Seian.

D. *Kokuyaku kambun taisei*; nos. 5–6, 1920–22, edited by Kojima Kenkichirō.

E. *Kambun sōsho*, 11927, edited by Nakamura Kyūshirō.

G. *Chūgoku koten bungaku zenshū*; no.3, 1958, edited by Takeuchi Teruo.

H. *Shinshaku kambun taikei*; nos. 30–33, 1971–81, edited by Kamata Tadashi.

J. *Chūgoku no shisō*; no. 11, 1965, edited by Matsueda Shigeo.

K. *Chūgoku koten bungaku taikei*; no.2, 1968, edited by Takeuchi Teruo.

L. *Chūgoku koten shinsho*, 1937, edited by Kamata Tadashi.

8. Indexes

(a) Fraser, Everard D.H., and James Haldane Stewart Lockhart, *Index to the Tso chuan*; London: Oxford University Press, 1930; reprinted Taipei, 1966.

(b) Shigezawa Toshio 重澤俊郎 and Satō Kyōgen 佐藤匡玄, *Saden jimmei chimei sakuin* 左傳人名地名索引; Tokyo: Daitō bunka kyōkai, 1935.

(c) Yasui Kotarō 安井小太郎 and Morohashi Tetsuji 諸橋轍次, *Sōgō Shunjū Sashiden sakuin* 綜合春秋左氏傳索引, Tokyo: Daitō bunka kyōkai, 1935.

(d) *Combined concordances to Ch'un-ch'iu, Kung-yang, Ku-liang and Tso-chuan*, 4 vols., Harvard-Yenching Index no. 11 (1st ed. Peiping, 1937; reprinted Taipei, 1966). (Text in vol. 1; indexes in vols. 2–4).

(e) Nakamura Junya 中村俊也 and Mashima Jun'ichi 間島潤一, *Shunjū Kōyōden jimmei chimei sakuin* 春秋公羊傳人名地名索引, Tokyo: Ryūkei shosha, 1979.

(f) Yang Po-chün 楊伯峻 and Hsü T'i 徐提, *Ch'un ch'iu Tso chuan tz'u tien* 春秋左傳詞典; Peking: Chung hua, 1985.

(g) *A Concordance to the Chunqiu and Zuo zhuan* 春秋經, 左傳逐字索引, ed. D.C. Lau and Chen Fong Ching; *ICS* series, Hong Kong: Commercial Press, forthcoming 1994.

(h) *A Concordance to the Chunqiu Gongyang zhuan* 春秋公羊傳逐字索引, ed. D.C. Lau and Chen Fong Ching; *ICS* series, Hong Kong: Commercial Press, forthcoming 1994.

(i) *A Concordance to the Chunqiu Guliang zhuan* 春秋穀梁傳逐字索引, ed. D.C. Lau and Chen Fong Ching; *ICS* series, Hong Kong: Commercial Press, forthcoming 1994.

— Anne Cheng

Ch'un ch'iu fan lu 春秋繁露

1. Content and title

The *Ch'un ch'iu fan lu*, in 17 *chüan*, is a philosophical text ascribed to Tung Chung-shu 董仲舒 (?179–?104 B.C.), who served as an academician at the courts of Han Ching ti (reigned 157–141) and Han Wu ti (reigned 141–87). It is a work in the New Text tradition describing the ethical and political principles found in the *Ch'un ch'iu*, as interpreted through the medium of the *Kung yang chuan*, and corroborated in terms of the Yin-Yang and *wu hsing* beliefs that were prevalent at the time. The *Ch'un ch'iu fan lu* has been regarded by some as the fullest expression of what was adopted as the orthodox doctrine of state, in 134 B.C.

In the items that it lists under *ju chia*, the *Han shu* includes an entry with 123 *p'ien* under Tung Chung-shu's name (*Han shu* 30, p. 1727); that chapter does not include the title *Ch'un ch'iu fan lu*. Under *Ch'un ch'iu* it includes the item *Kung yang Tung Chung-shu chih yü* 公羊董仲舒治獄 in 16 *p'ien* (*Han shu* 30, p. 1714). In its biography of Tung Chung-shu, which refers to a total of 123 *p'ien* of his writings, the term *fan lu* occurs as the name of one of his expository essays on the *Ch'un ch'iu* (*Han shu* 56, pp. 2525–26). The title *Ch'un ch'iu fan lu tz'u* 春秋繁露詞 appears in the *Hsi ching tsa chi* 西京雜記 (2.4a; *SPTK* ed.) of the fifth or early sixth century; in the *Ch'i lu* 七錄 of Juan Hsiao-hsü 阮孝緒 (479–536), the title *Ch'un ch'iu fan lu* is associated with the entry given for Tung Chung-shu in *Han shu* 30.

The meaning of the term is by no means certain. In interpreting *fan lu* as an expression for the gems which hang down from a ceremonial hat, being strung together like the drops of dew, the *Nan Sung (Chung hsing) kuan ko shu mu* (as cited in the *Ssu k'u ch'üan shu tsung mu t'i yao*) sought by means of metaphor to show how Tung's writings were closely related to the lessons of the *Ch'un ch'iu*; very often the title is simply and literally translated as 'Luxuriant dew of the Spring and Autumn Annals'.

The received version comprises 82 *p'ien*, of which the text of three (nos. 39, 40 and 54) is no longer extant; the individual *p'ien* vary in form and content, and in the time of their composition. Most give definitions of terms, explanations of events and interpretations of passages of the

Ch'un ch'iu; they may also relate its ethical and political ideas to recognised cosmic principles. *P'ien* nos. 1–6, 23, 25, 28, 30 and 46 are written as reports of responses of Tung, either in respect of specific doctrinal questions or in answer to critics. *P'ien* no. 71 is a report of Tung's response to a question posed by a court official about a matter of ritual; *p'ien* nos. 32 and 38 are reports of Tung's responses to requests made by kings of the empire whom Tung had served as chancellor. *P'ien* nos. 32, 38 and 71 were undoubtedly written by Tung's disciples, rather than by Tung Chung-shu personally. *P'ien* no. 73 is quite unlike the others, being in the form of an eulogy (*sung* 頌).

References in different *p'ien* to various stages in Tung's official career, and to his retirement, necessarily imply different occasions and dates of composition. According to the biography in the *Han shu* (56, p. 2525), Tung Chung-shu submitted all 123 *p'ien* to the emperor; they were completed by 104 B.C. at the latest.

2.   Subject matter

The work may be divided into two main sections. In the first, which comprises *p'ien* nos. 1 to 17, no. 17 serves as a postface. These *p'ien* form a relatively straightforward set of analyses of the ethical and political lessons to be derived from incidents in the *Ch'un ch'iu*, the wording of which was assumed to have been intentionally obscured by Confucius. Confucius is regarded as an 'uncrowned king' who lacked political power but nevertheless had received the Mandate of Heaven. Concealed beneath the surface of the *Ch'un ch'iu* is a record of his wisdom, which he had intended to be passed on in preparation for a future appearance of a sage-king who would put the world in order. In this section reference is made not only to the events mentioned in the *Ch'un ch'iu*, but also to that work as a whole, the purpose for which it was written and its general meaning.

The specific events to which the *Ch'un ch'iu* refers are used to derive ethical and political models and precedents by a comparative analysis of the wording of the text. In most cases the events which Tung calls to mind are described in the *Kung yang* commentary; at times the events under reference are found today only in the *Tso chuan*. Topics discussed in this section include the rectification of names; the reason for the extinction of some states; the meaning of portents; the role of the sages; differences between righteousness and lawfulness; the relation between changeable regulations of state and the constancy of the *tao*; the importance of emphasising root (*pen* 本) rather than branch (*mo* 末), and intention rather than result; and other standard concerns. The wisdom that is passed on is to be used in making personal decisions as well as in ordering the state.

The second section (*p'ien* nos. 18 to 82) is more theoretical. While referring to ideas expressed in the first section, it seeks to show how Confucius' ethical and political notions are consistent with *Yin-Yang* and *wu hsing* metaphysics. The difference in emphasis in this section from that of the preceding one has led critics either to doubt its authenticity or to regard it as being unrelated to the first 17 *p'ien*. To some, however, (e.g. Davidson) the two sections seem to form one consistent whole.

In general, the second section confronts the microcosmic relations of man that are discussed in the first 17 *p'ien* with the macrocosmic relations of Heaven and Earth, *Yin-Yang*, the *wu hsing* and the Four Seasons. It is explained here that Heaven uses things to show its intention. The *k'o* 科 (categories or classes) that inform the natural world represent Heaven's way. Moreover, the nature and relation of all things also express Heaven's intentions. Heaven and Earth and Yin and Yang are used for the most part as models for hierarchic and complementary relations and forces; the *wu hsing* describe functional specialization; and the Four Seasons set the pattern for spatial, temporal and sequential relations, i.e., through the image of the seasons following each other in proper sequence as the sun changes its positions in the sky.

The relation of yin and yang and of Heaven and Earth thus reveal the proper relations of ruler and minister; the relation of the *wu hsing* reveal the proper relations among the various officials and are even presented as expressing the meaning of filial piety (*p'ien* no. 42). Human language too is shown to be among the Heavenly manifestations expressing Heaven's intentions.

Heaven's intentions are explained to be such things as the virtues of *jen* 仁, *i* 義, *chih* 智 and *chung* 忠. Heaven's Way is also presented as working through the cosmic principles including, for example, those that mutual opposites cannot both emerge at the same time, and that things of similar categories activate each other. These principles lend structure to the world so as to manifest Heaven's intentions. Knowledge of these principles helps man to establish guidelines for his behaviour.

In all, the levels of man, state and universe are shown to reflect each other in such a way that what is known of one category reveals what is known of the others. In this way, the author offers an epistemological foundation for his explanation of the purpose of the *Ch'un ch'iu* and the truth of its lessons. He explains that the *Ch'un ch'iu* establishes regulations and patterns for government, including sumptuary laws, rewards and punishments, and prescribed official activities, in accordance with this revealed Way of Heaven.

This section of the book further develops the idea that man should practise the rites and sacrifices, especially the *chiao* 郊 sacrifice, which expresses the supreme importance of Heaven. This is in order to accord properly with Heaven's will and way. The ruler's ritual and sacrificial actions, as all actions, have short and long range historical and cosmic repercussions, being part of the complex and ever present causal processes of the world. The essays on sacrifices further attempt to reduce any expectation of their efficacy as acts of magic. They are to be understood in terms of Heaven's will and way.

In addition, there are essays on the ceremonies designed to start or to stop rain, devoid of shamanistic content and reliant almost totally on explanations based on an understanding of Yin-Yang. A closing section concerns the function of man, in particular that of the sage, as the pivot in cosmic activity that relates Heaven to the ten thousand things of creation. Heterogeneous though they are, the *p'ien* of the two sections are interconnected.

In all the *Ch'un ch'iu fan lu* is a rich source of what some may regard as early Han thought. Furthermore it is a storehouse of quotations from pre-Ch'in and Han texts. Quotations are found from works such as the *Shang shu, Shih ching, Lun yü* and the *Kuan tzu*. Parallel statements are found to texts such as the *Li chi*, the *Hsiao ching*, the *Kuan tzu*, the *Yüeh ling*, the *Huai nan tzu* and the *Han shih wai chuan*. Terms such as *t'ai p'ing* 太平, *san t'ung* 三統, *san kang* 三綱, *kai chih* 改制 and *su wang* 素王, all of which became standard concepts in New Text vocabulary, appear in the *Ch'un ch'iu fan lu*. That they do not appear as well developed theories, as they do in Ho Hsiu's 何休 (129–82) commentary to the *Kung yang chuan*, perhaps lends credence to an earlier date for the composition of the work; in the *Ch'un ch'iu fan lu* these terms do not reflect sophisticated metaphysical notions.

Tung Chung-shu is known to have written legal decisions based on precedent from the *Ch'un ch'iu* (see *Hou Han shu* 48, p. 1612, which refers to 232 items; the notes in *Han shu pu chu* 30.16b,17a; and *T'ung tien* 69 (*li* 29), Shang wu ed. 381c; punctuated ed., Peking: Chung hua, 1988, p. 1911); this type of reasoning is also found in the *Ch'un ch'iu fan lu*. For collected fragments, see *Yü han shan fang chi i shu* 31, 45a–47a.

3. Authenticity of the work

Doubts have been raised in regard to the authenticity of the work since the Sung period, and it has been asked how far the surviving 79 *p'ien* relate to the original 123 *p'ien* that are mentioned twice in the *Han shu*.

Chu Hsi 朱熹 (1130–1200) and Ch'en Chen-sun 陳振孫 (c. 1190–after 1249) to name but two well-known critics, doubted whether the work is authentic. Huang Chen 黃震 (1213–80) expressed the view that the *Ch'un ch'iu fan lu* that had been available in the Sui and T'ang periods was not entirely the work of Tung Chung-shu; and that the text that became available subsequently was not the one that had been seen in Sui and T'ang times. He also pointed to a number of passages whose inconsistencies could not be reconciled with Confucian doctrine or thought.

The questions discussed by Hu Ying-lin 胡應麟 (1551–1602), Yao Chi-heng 姚際恆 (b. 1647) and Chin Te-chien 金德建 (20th century) included the validity of attaching the terms *Ch'un ch'iu* and *fan lu* to the received work; how far the contents of the received text, of which something less than half concerns the *Ch'un ch'iu*, can be regarded as parts of a text which bears that term in its title; how far the received 82 (or rather 79) *p'ien* can be identified with the 123 *p'ien* that the *Han shu* lists under *ju chia*; and whether the 16 *p'ien* of the *Kung yang Tung Chung-shu chih yü* had been incorporated, along with parts of other writings of Tung, to form the received version of the work.

The *Ssu k'u* editors concluded that while the text cannot entirely derive from Tung Chung-shu, there are many expressions therein on which later writers would not have been able to call. The following points have been brought into question:

(a) There are internal inconsistencies, along with *lacunae* and anachronistic use of taboo terms.

(b) There are variations as between citations that appear in the T'ang and Sung encyclopaedias and the received text. In particular Ch'eng Ta-ch'ang 程大昌 (1123–95) pointed out that the copy that was available to him did not include quotations to be found in the *T'ung tien*, *T'ai p'ing yü lan* and *T'ai p'ing huan yü chi* 太平寰宇記; he therefore concluded that the text before him was not the original version. Lou Yüeh 樓鑰 (1137–1213) commented that Ch'eng's copy was clearly incomplete as compared with the one mentioned in the *Ch'ung wen tsung mu* and the one of 82 *p'ien* that was seen by Ou-yang Hsiu 歐 陽脩 (1007–72). One recent scholar (Tzey-yueh Tain, pp. 12–3) has replied by observing that only 4 of the 50 quotations in the *T'ai p'ing yü lan* are missing from the received text.

(c) Tai Chün-jen 戴君仁 (pp. 32–31) has pointed to the treatment of the *wu hsing* concept in *p'ien* nos. 18 to 82 of the *Ch'un ch'iu fan lu*, as compared with the absence of mention in the three memorials of Tung that are retained in the *Han shu* (56, pp. 2498f.) Hsü Fu-kuan has replied (pp. 314–16) that the points at issue in those three memo-

rials did not warrant a discussion of *wu hsing*, whose absence from
mention therefore bears no significance.

(d) Hsü Fu-kuan 徐復觀 has also attempted to answer the charge
brought by Ch'eng Ta-ch'ang of the shallow nature of the contents,
by maintaining that the text upon which such an opinion was based
was incomplete, and that the Neo-Confucian philosophers of Sung
were unable to transcend their own world view so as to appreciate
Tung's ideas (see Hsü, pp. 312–13).

In conclusion it may thus be observed that Hsü Fu-kuan, Tzey-yueh
Tain and S. Davidson remain convinced of the authenticity of the received text, incomplete as it is. Davidson adduces further reason on
conceptual grounds. He believes that there is a good match between the
ideas in the *Ch'un ch'iu fan lu* and those of Tung that are expressed in
the *Shih chi* and *Han shu*, and that those ideas fit historically between
those of Lu Chia 陸賈 and Chia I 賈誼 on the one hand and those of the
Pai hu t'ung on the other. It may also be urged that the existence of inconsistencies and other imperfections of the text is itself an argument in
favour of its originality and against that of the more polished effort that
would be expected of a fabricator.

As against this there are grounds for believing (Loewe) that by no
means all portions of the received text are entirely authentic. As will be
seen, the textual transmission is somewhat tenuous; and there is an absence of full annotation or comment until the 18th century; this is somewhat odd for a work that was supposedly one of the mainstays of the
Confucian tradition. In addition, in at least one instance (*p'ien* 25, where
the text is defective and perhaps subject to transposition), Su Yü 蘇輿
(for his edition see below) has argued on conceptual grounds that the
text could not have derived from Tung Chung-shu; these views have,
however, been subject to question by a number of scholars.

4. Traditional assessments

Traditional assessments have in general been laudatory. In its appreciation of Tung Chung-shu the *Han shu* (56, p. 2526) cites the views of Liu
Hsiang 劉向 (79–8 B.C.) and Liu Hsin 劉歆 (46 B.C.–A.D. 23), but does not
mention the *Ch'un ch'iu fan lu* by name. The passage explains that Tung
was highly respected by scholars of his time, and that he was in fact the
leader of the scholastics of the day.

The *Lun heng* refers to Tung Chung-shu on at least 30 occasions, but
the title *Ch'un ch'iu fan lu* does not appear to be mentioned, and it has
yet to be investigated how far these passages necessarily or specifically

relate to parts of that work. In a number of other passages, where Tung is not named, the *Lun heng* carries a strong attack on one of the principal concepts that is expressed in the three memorials of Tung that are included in the *Han shu*, i.e. the idea that Heaven conveys warnings to the ruler of mankind by way of strange phenomena.

5.　Textual history and editions[1]

Considerable differences are to be observed in the early references to the work. Following the various entries in the *Han shu*, the *Lun heng* (Huang Hui ed., 30, p. 1194) refers to Tung's composition of 100 or more *p'ien*. In the *Sui shu* (32, p. 930), *Chiu T'ang shu* (46, p. 1979) and *Hsin T'ang shu* (57, p. 1437) the work is entered under *Ch'un ch'iu*, with 17 *chüan*; it does not appear in Fujiwara Sukeyo's catalogue.

In a notice dated 1037, Ou-yang Hsiu wrote that the extant work had no more than 40 *p'ien*; he had however seen a copy of 80 or more *p'ien*, but this had been in a state of considerable disarray, with some duplication of text. He added that, in response to a general appeal for books, a copy with some 30 *p'ien* had been produced, and that some of those 30 were external to the 80. In a preface to the book which was dated in 1047, Lou Yu 樓郁 (*chin shih* 1053) wrote that the extant version consisted of 10 *chüan*; that figure, with 37 *p'ien*, is mentioned in the *Nan Sung kuan ko shu mu* (late 12th century).

The *Ch'ung wen tsung mu* (completed possibly in 1041) enters the work with 17 *chüan*, and the author noted that this corresponded with the entries in the Sui and T'ang histories. He added that while the content of the 82 *p'ien* did not derive from recent times, the order had at times become disarrayed, and he suspected that the work included later interpolations.

In a postface dated 1211 Hu Chü 胡榘 (Chung fang 仲方), states that he acquired a copy of the work from Lo Chün 羅濬 (died after 1228), and had the text, together with some annotation, printed in P'ing hsiang 萍鄉, where he was posted. This text included no more than 37 *p'ien* in 10 *chüan*; subsequently he acquired a collated copy of the work from Lou Yüeh 樓鑰 (1137-1213; also known as Kung k'uei 攻媿; grandson of Lou Yu) in 17 *chüan* that had contained 82 *p'ien*, and of which three were missing; this was printed in the first instance by Hu Chü's brother. From Huang Chen we learn that it was reprinted by Yüeh K'o 岳珂

---

1. The prefaces and other notices that are under reference in this section will in general be found in the *SPPY* edition and Su Yü's edition, as well as in the entry for *Ch'un ch'iu fan lu* in the *Wei shu t'ung k'ao*.

(1183–1240), being subsequently regarded as the definitive text. In his postface, which is included in most editions, Lou Yüeh records how he had acquired the copy.

In their preface to the text that is printed in the *Ssu k'u chüan shu chü chen* series, which is dated variously at 1773 or 1777, the editors noted that there had been four Sung copies of the work. They accepted Lou Yüeh's text as the definitive version, despite the missing three *p'ien*, a number of other *lacunae* which they identified (in *p'ien* nos. 48, 55, 56 and 75), and the transposition of at least one page (in *p'ien* no. 25); and they added that no complete text had been available for three or four centuries. For their edition they adopted Lou Yüeh's text as preserved in the *Yung lo ta tien*; and they noted that they had restored 1100, eliminated 110 and emended 1820 characters (these figures are sometimes given as 1121, 121 and 1829). The *Ssu pu ts'ung k'an* reproduces a print of this version, together with Lou Yu's preface.

Other editions include:

(a) Lu Wen-ch'ao's 盧 文 弨 (1717–96) annotated text, which was included in the *Pao ching t'ang ts'ung shu*, preface dated 1785. Lu adopted the *Ssu k'u* editors' text as his basis, while taking note of:

  (i) An edition with a preface by Chao Wei-yüan 趙維垣 (*chin shih* 1532), dated 1554. A copy of this print which was held in the former Peiping Metropolitan Library includes 79 of the 82 *p'ien*, in 17 *chüan*, in a format of 9 by 17; it also carries prefaces and notices about the work, and there is some annotation at the heads of the pages, some of which are defective. At one point (3.6b) a passage of 241 characters had been inserted in small type, in double column, having evidently been omitted at an earlier stage. In a colophon which is dated in 1804 (with a further note of 1814), Huang P'ei-lieh 黃 丕 烈 (1763–1825) expressed the view that the text derived from a Sung print, which was based on the same source as that of the *Yung lo ta tien*'s copy. He had himself inserted corrections to the text, thereby bringing it into conformity with the *Ssu k'u*'s version.

    The *Liang ching i pien*, of 1582, includes 8 *chüan* (30 *p'ien*) of this text, without Lou Yu's preface and the table of contents that are present in the complete copy; Huang P'ei-lieh's notes and corrections are not present.

  (ii) The prints of Ch'eng Jung 程 榮 (1447–1520) and Ho Yün-chung 何 允 中 in the *Han Wei ts'ung shu* and *Kuang Han wei ts'ung shu*. The text of the *Han Wei ts'ung shu* varies in minor respects from (i), and its readings are sometimes adopted in the *Ssu k'u* edition, which sometimes carries breaks between sections of text within a single *p'ien* that are not carried either in (i) or (ii).

Lu Wen-ch'ao's edition was reprinted in the *Ssu pu pei yao* series, with a supplement that includes most of the prefaces and notices regarding the work.

(b) Mo Yu-chih 莫友芝 (1811–71) and Yeh Te-hui 葉德輝 (1864–1927) refer to a movable type edition of 1516, with format of 9 by 18, and lacunae as in other Ming prints. In this connection the length of the passages whose omission was noted by the *Ssu k'u* editors, i.e. 396 and 180 characters (sometimes given as 398 and 179) is of interest.

(c) Annotated text, edited by Ling Shu 凌曙 (1775–1829), with his own extensive commentary and preface (dated 1815). The text is based on that of the *Ssu k'u* editors, and includes notes by Wang Tao-hun 王道焜 (Ming period) and Lu Wen-ch'ao. This edition is included in the *Lung hsi ching she ts'ung shu* and in the *Huang Ch'ing ching chieh hsü pien*.

(d) The *Tseng ting Han Wei ts'ung shu* includes a punctuated text, without notes. It follows Lou Yüeh's text and includes Lou Yu's preface and a postface by Wang Mo 王謨 (*chin shih* 1778).

(e) What is probably the most valuable edition of the work is that of Su Yü, entitled *Ch'un ch'iu fan lu i cheng* 春秋繁露義證 (first published 1914; reprinted Taipei: Ho lo t'u shu, 1973). The work includes a preface by Wang Hsien-ch'ien 王先謙 (1842–1918), dated 1914, which is not seen in other editions; Su Yü's own preface (1909), and an introductory statement in which he mentions a number of editions that he consulted. There is also a biographical table of Tung Chung-shu's life, together with most of the prefaces and notices of earlier scholars. Su Yü's own extensive notes supplement those of Lu Wen-ch'ao and Ling Shu. He also had access to a critical edition by Sun K'uang 孫鑛 of the T'ien ch'i period (1621–27), and cites variants from this version in his notes.

(f) Lai Yen-yüan 賴炎元, *Ch'un ch'iu fan lu chin chu chin i* 春秋繁露今註今譯; Taipei: Taiwan Shang wu, 1984, with annotation and modern Chinese version.

6. Translations

There is no full translation of the *Ch'un ch'iu fan lu* into a Western language. For a list of partial translations of some 55 *p'ien*, see Pokora, pp.

267–68, to which one subsequent item may be added: Gassmann, Robert H., *Tung Chung-shu ch'un ch'iu fan lu: Übersetzung und Annotation der Kapitel eins bis sechs*; Bern: Peter Lang, 1988 (reviewed by Gary Arbuckle, 'Some remarks on a new translation of the *Chunqiu fanlu*'; *EC* 17 (1992), 215–38).

7. Japanese edition

L.   *Chūgoku koten shinsho*, 1977, edited by Hihara Toshikuni.

8. Indexes

(a) *Ch'un ch'iu fan lu t'ung chien* 春秋繁露通檢 (Index du Tch'ouen Ts'ieu Fan Lou); centre franco-chinois d'études sinologiques no. 4, Peking, 1944; reprinted Taipei: Ch'eng wen, 1968; based on Lu Wen-ch'ao's edition.

(b) *A Concordance to the Chunqiu fanlu* 春秋繁露逐字索引, ed. D.C. Lau and Chen Fong Ching; *ICS* series, Hong Kong: Commercial Press, forthcoming 1993.

9. Secondary writings, including those under reference above

(a) Ch'eng Ta-ch'ang, *Yen fan lu* 演繁露 1.1b–2a; in *Ju hsüeh ching wu* 儒學警悟 11.

(b) Chin Te-chien 金德建, *Ku chi ts'ung k'ao* 古籍叢考; Shanghai: Chung hua, 1941, pp. 108–13.

(c) Chou Fu-ch'eng 周輔成, *Lun Tung Chung-shu ssu hsiang* 論董仲舒思想; Shanghai: Jen min, 1961.

(d) Chu Hsi, *Chu tzu yü lei* 朱子語類; 1473 edition, 83.27a; reprinted Taipei: Cheng chung, 1962, p. 3509.

(e) Franke,Otto, *Studien zur Geschichte des konfuzianischen Dogmas und der chinesischen Staatsreligion; das Problem des Tsch'un-t'siu und Tung Tschung-schu's Tsch'un-tsiu fan lu*; Hamburg: L. Friedrichsen & Co., 1920.

(f) Hsü Fu-kuan 徐復觀, *Liang Han ssu hsiang shih* 兩漢思想史; Taipei: Taiwan hsüeh sheng, 1964.

(g) Hu Ying-lin, *Chiu liu hsü lun* 九流緒論 *chung* 中; in *Shao shih shan fang pi ts'ung* 少室山房筆叢; *Kuang ya ts'ung shu* 28.1b; and Peking: Chung hua, 1958, p. 360.

(h) Huang Chen; see *Huang shih jih ch'ao* 黃氏日抄, as cited in most editions and *Wei shu t'ung k'ao*.

(i) K'ang Yu-wei 康有爲, *Ch'un ch'iu Tung shih hsüeh* 春秋董氏學; Shanghai, 1894.

(j) Pokora, Timoteus, 'Notes on New Studies on Tung Chung-shu'; *Archiv Orientální* 33 (1965), 256–71.

(k) Sun I-jang; see notes in *Cha i.*

(l) Tai Chün-jen 戴君仁, "Tung Chung-shu pu shuo wu hsing k'ao" 董仲舒不說五行考; in *Mei yüan lun hsüeh chi* 梅園論學集; Taipei: K'ai ming, 1970, pp. 319–34.

(m) Tain Tzey-yueh, *Tung Chung-shu's System of Thought: Its Sources and its Influences on Han Scholarship*; PhD thesis, University of California, Los Angeles, 1974.

(n) Woo, Kang, *Les trois théories politiques du Tch'ouen Ts'ieu interpretées par Tong Tchong-chou*; Paris: Ernest Leroux, 1932.

(o) Yao Chi-heng 姚際恆 (b. 1647), *Ku chin wei shu k'ao* 古今僞書考; Ch'ang-sha: 1889, 44b–45b.

(p) Yü Yüeh; see notes in *Chu tzu p'ing i.*

— Steve Davidson
— Michael Loewe

Chung lun 中論

1. Authorship of the work

The *Chung lun* is a collection of essays that are principally concerned with philosophical questions, written by Hsü Kan 徐幹 (*tzu* Wei-ch'ang 偉長), whose dates are given variously as 171–218 (see the unsigned preface to the work) and as d. 217 (see *San kuo chih* 21 (Wei 21), pp. 602, 608; and Ts'ao P'i's 曹丕 (186–226) letter to Wu Chih 吳質, *Wen hsüan*, SPPY ed., 42.5b). Brief notes in *San kuo chih* 21, p. 599 and its comments state that he was appointed, but never served, as magistrate (chief) of Shang-ai 上艾 county, probably after taking part in Ts'ao Ts'ao's 曹操 (155–220) campaigns. He also held positions on the staff of the Minister of Works (*Ssu k'ung* 司空), probably between 197 and 208, and as literary adviser to the *Wu kuan chiang* 五官將, after Ts'ao P'i's appointment to that position in 211. As one of the 'Seven masters of the Chien an period' (196–220) he was most renowned for his composition of poetry, *fu* 賦 and discourses (*lun* 論). The author of the *Chung lun* is to be distinguished from a man of the same name who served with Pan Ch'ao 班超 (d. 102) in campaigns in the north-west *c.* 80 (see *Hou Han shu* 47, p. 1576).

2. Content

The twenty-two surviving *p'ien* of the *Chung lun* range over a wide variety of topics, including disputation (*p'ien* no. 8), calendrical calculations (no. 13), population figures (no. 20) and re-institution of the three year mourning period (no. 21). As a whole the text can best be described as a philosophical enquiry into the causes of political and social breakdown and the presentation of various ethical and political remedies. While much of Hsü's argumentation appeals to the authority of traditional Confucian ethics, a range of influences may be discerned that derives eclectically from other sources. The work is classified under *ju chia* in all bibliographical lists of the Standard Histories except for that of the *Sung shih*, where it is placed among miscellaneous writers.

The single most important concept that is employed in the *Chung lun* is the recurring distinction between *ming* 名 and *shih* 實 which Hsü inherited from pre-Han philosophical traditions and developed in a number of discourses. Other topics such as the relationship between wisdom (*chih* 智) and moral action (*hsing* 行), as discussed in *p'ien* no. 9, were later to become central issues of debate in the Wei and Chin periods (e.g., see the discusssions regarding *ts'ai hsing* 才性).

3. Traditional Chinese evaluation of the work

Apart from remarks in the unsigned preface to the work, the earliest critical evaluation is that of Ts'ao P'i: 'Hsü Kan . . . wrote the *Chung lun* in some twenty *p'ien*, establishing a school in his own right. His phrases are classical and refined, worthy of transmission to posterity; this man will be immortal' (*Wen hsüan* 42.6b). In the *Chen kuan cheng yao* 貞觀政要 (compiled by Wu Ching 吳競, 670–749; see entry for 643; *SPPY* ed. 6.20a), T'ang T'ai tsung 太宗 (reigned 626–49) is reported to have seen the *Fu san nien sang* 復三年喪 chapter and to have remarked on its profundity of thought. The work is acclaimed by Tseng Kung 曾鞏 (1019–83; preface to the *Chung lun*) and Ch'ao Kung-wu 晁公武 (d. 1171) for its literary and philosophical value. In his posface of 1502, Tu Mu 都穆 (1458–1525) commends the work as being on a par with the *Yen t'ieh lun*.

4. Structure and arrangement of the text

(a) The number of *p'ien*. According to the preface and Li Shan's 李善 (d. 689) comment to Ts'ao P'i's letter to Wu Chih, the *Chung lun* comprised 20 *p'ien*, but there is reason to believe that these accounts may have been mistaken. There are at least two references to the work as consisting of more than 20 *p'ien* (see *Wei lüeh* 魏略, as cited in the commentary to *San kuo chih* 21, p. 608; and the versions of Ts'ao P'i's letter in *San kuo chih* 21, p. 602 and in *Wen hsüan* 42.5b). In addition, the *Ch'ün shu chih yao* 群書治要 includes substantial parts of two *p'ien* that have been transmitted nowhere else. There are also statements in the *Chen kuan cheng yao*, as cited, and in the *Chün chai tu shu chih* 郡齋讀書志 to the effect that the book included two *p'ien*, entitled respectively *Fu san nien* 復三年 [sic] and *Chih i* 制役. The material which is included in the *Ch'ün shu chih yao* is of a nature that matches those two titles and may be regarded as being abridged versions of the two *p'ien*. It is not possible to determine whether the book had originally contained more than twenty-two *p'ien*.

(b) The number of *chüan*. The entries in different books vary as follows:

(i) 1 *chüan*: the note to the entry in the Sui catalogue (*Sui shu* 34,

p. 998) refers to an item listed in the Liang catalogue, i.e., the *Ch'i lu* 七錄 of Juan Hsiao-hsü 阮孝緒 (479–536), of 1 *chüan*.

(ii) 2 *chüan*: this figure is given in *Chün chai tu shu chih, Chih chai shu lu chieh t'i* 直齋書錄解題 and *Wen hsien t'ung k'ao* 文獻通考. The notes to the *Chung lun* (usually printed as a postface) by Shih Pang-che 石邦哲 (dated 1158; first appended in the edition of Huang Wen 黃紋, 1502) and Lu Yu-jen 陸友仁 (dated 1323) refer to the work in 2 *chüan* as a 'personally collated copy of Chu Ch'eng's 朱丞 book'. (For these notes, see 5 (a) below).

(iii) 5 *chüan*: Ch'ien Tseng 錢曾 (1629–1701) lists a hand copied text in 5 *chüan*; see *Yü shan Ch'ien Tsun-wang ts'ang shu mu lu hui pien* 虞山錢遵王藏書目錄彙編 (Shanghai: Ku tien, 1958, p. 124).

(iv) 6 *chüan*: this figure is given in the *I lin, Sui shu* 34, p. 998, *Ch'ung wen tsung mu, Chiu T'ang shu* 47, p. 2024, *Hsin T'ang shu* 59, p. 1510, and *Chien an ch'i tzu chi* 建安七子集 (revised ed. 1768; Taiwan: Taiwan Chung hua, 1971, 26a–28a).

(v) 7 *chüan*: the *Wen hsien t'ung k'ao* cites the *Ch'ung wen tsung mu* as listing an edition of 7 *chüan*.

(vi) 8 *chüan*: according to Kao Ssu-sun 高似孫 (c. 1160–c. 1230), this figure apears in a list used by Yü Chung-jung 庾仲容 (476–549) for compilation of his *Tzu ch'ao*; see *Tzu lüeh* (*mu* 目), *SPPY* revised ed. 11b, where the entry reads 徐幹四論八卷.

(vii) 10 *chüan*: *Sung shih* 205, p. 5208 (under miscellaneous schools) and *Yü hai* 玉海 (citing the *Chung hsing [kuan ko] shu mu* 中興 [館閣] 書目) give this figure.

5.   Editions of the text

(a) Arranged in 2 *chüan*

(i) Yen Ling-feng's 嚴靈峯 copy (format 8 by 16). The earliest extant copy of the *Chung lun* is allegedly the one belonging to Yen Ling-feng, and which is now (1989) held in the Central Library, Taipei. Yen Ling-feng claims that this may be a copy of the redaction made in 1323 by Lu Yu-jen of the collated edition of Shih Pang-che (of 1158); he dates the calligraphic style at anywhere between the Southern Sung and the Ming periods. Yen Ling-feng further claims that this redaction served as an exemplar for Huang Wen's edition of 1502, which had hitherto been considered the earliest available print of the *Chung lun*. It is equally possible that both Yen Ling-feng's copy and the Huang Wen 黃紋 edition derived from a common source, which was reproduced more faithfully in the latter; there is no evidence to prove which of the two prints was the earlier. Yen Ling-feng's copy appends both the original preface and that of Tseng Kung; see Yen Ling-feng, 'Wu ch'iu pei chai hsien ts'ang Hsü Kan Chung lun t'i chi' 無求備齋見藏徐幹 中論題記 (see Lo Chien-jen, *Hsü Kan Chung lun yen chiu* 徐幹中論 研究, as cited below).

(ii) Huang Wen's edition (1502); text with original preface and that of Tseng Kung, notes by Shih Pang-che and Lu Yu-jen, and postface by Tu Mu 都穆 (dated 1502), from which Huang Wen is identified as being responsible for printing the edition; there are some *lacunae*; format 8 by 16.

(iii) Hsüeh Ch'en's 薛晨 edition (1565); text with prefaces, etc. as in (ii) and lacunae as in (ii); format 8 by 16. A note on the first folio of each *chüan* ascribes collation to Hsüeh Ch'en; printed by Tu Ssu 杜思, as stated in his preface (1565). This edition has been reproduced in the *SPTK* series.

(iv) *Liang ching i pien* edition (1582); punctuated text in 9 by 17 format, with material as in (iii).

(v) *Han Wei ts'ung shu* (1592); format 9 by 20, with material as in (iii); also in *Kuang Han Wei ts'ung shu*, with Tseng Kung's preface and an appended note by Sun Yin-chi 孫胤奇 (*fl.* 1622), and in *Tseng ting Han Wei ts'ung shu*, format 9 by 20, with postface by Wang Mo 王謨.

(vi) Ch'ien P'ei-ming's 錢培名 edition (1854); a revised edition of (iii) including Ch'ien P'ei-ming's notes and the text of the two lost *p'ien* (*Fu san nien sang* and *Chih i*); format 10 by 20; first published in the *Hsiao wan chüan lou ts'ung shu*. A punctuated edition of the text, based on the re-cut edition of this *ts'ung shu* of 1878 and edition (iv) above, was included in the *Ts'ung shu chi ch'eng* series (reproduced Taipei: Taiwan Shang wu, 1968, in the *Kuo hsüeh chi pen ts'ung shu* series).

(vii) Cheng Kuo-hsün's 鄭國勳 edition (1917); included in the *Lung hsi ching she ts'ung shu*; text with prefaces as in (iii); format 9 by 17. A note preceding the prefaces states that this edition took Lu Yu-jen's edition as its exemplar, thus putatively claiming it to be a redaction of the oldest edition then extant. Some commentators, seemingly with good reason, have implicitly denied that Lu cut a new edition, as his note states only that he had acquired the version which had been personally edited by Shih Pang-che; there is no specific reference to a new edition. Indirect support for the view that Lu did indeed produce his own edition and that this served as the exemplar for Cheng Kuo-hsün is forthcoming from a note by Chang Wen-hu 張文虎 (1808–85) (*Shu i shih hsü pi* 舒藝室續筆, 1879, 1.30a). He writes that in 1876 he saw a Yüan redaction of a Sung edition of the *Chung lun* in 20 *p'ien*. Almost all the variants which he cites (30a–31a) are identical with those in Cheng Kuo-hsün's edition, the differences being obviously due to Cheng's preference for another, more coherent reading. It would thus appear that Lu Yu-jen's redaction existed until the early years of the Republic.

No modern Chinese study of the *Chung lun* cites Cheng Kuo-hsün's edition. The only scholar who appears to have done so is Ikeda Shūzō (see under Japanese editions).

While all the foregoing editions are almost certainly derivatives from Chu Ch'eng's copy, as used by Lu Yu-jen, no single one is sufficient to serve as a standard text. As they all include textual variants, they should be consulted along with the edition in 6 *chüan*. Of the editions in 2 *chüan*, the most important are either (i) or (ii), and (vii).

(b) Arranged in 6 *chüan*

The only extant edition in 6 *chüan*, entitled *Hsü Wei-ch'ang chi* 徐偉長集, is included in the *Chien an ch'i tzu chi* (revised edition, edited by Ch'en Ch'ao-fu 陳朝輔, 1768). A work entitled *Hsü Kan chung chi* 徐幹中集, which is listed in Chao Yung-hsien 趙用賢 (1535–96), *Chao Ting-yü shu mu* 趙定宇書目 (Shanghai: Ku tien, 1957), p. 72, may be related to this edition. The text includes some poetry as well as the twenty *p'ien*, whose order varies from that of the editions in two *chüan*. Some of the variants are similar to the text given in the *Ch'ün shu chih yao* and Hao Ching 郝經 (1223–75), *Hsü Hou Han shu* 續後漢書 (1841 ed.), 69B.1a–6b.

6. Textual and secondary studies

(a) Selections of text are printed with emendations and recorded variants in the *Cha chi* 札記 of Ch'ien P'ei-ming.

(b) Chang Wen-hu, *Shu i shih hsü pi*; Chang compares the Yüan edition with that of Ch'ien P'ei-ming, recording variants that are not noted there.

(c) Lo Chien-jen 駱建人, *Hsü Kan Chung lun yen chiu* 徐幹中論研究 (Taipei: Taiwan shang wu, 1973). This study includes a bibliographical section, detailed commentary on selections from the text (based essentially on Ch'ien P'ei-ming's work) and traditional literary evaluations of Hsü's *fu*, poetry and the *Chung lun*.

(d) Liang Jung-mao 梁榮茂, *Hsü Kan Chung lun chiao shih* 徐幹中論校釋 (Taipei: Mu t'ung, 1979); revised edition, entitled *Hsü Kan Chung lun chiao cheng* 徐幹中論校證 (Taipei: Mu t'ung, 1980). Selections from the text are printed with annotations, the most complete to appear in Chinese studies. There are also a few pages of general interpretation.

(e) Notes to the text will be found in Sun I-jang 孫詒讓 (1848–1908), *Cha i* 10, and Yü Yüeh 俞樾 (1821–1907), *Chu tzu p'ing i pu lu* 諸子平議補錄, 10.

7. A recent edition

Ting Lü-chuan 丁履譔, 'Chung lun chiao chu' 中論校注, *Kao hsiung shih fan hsüeh yüan hsüeh pao* 高雄師範學院學報 2 (December 1973), 255–337; punctuated text, with notes derived mainly from those of Ch'ien P'ei-ming and Lo Chien-jen.

8. Japanese editions

(a) A work entitled *Chū ron kō* 中論考, which is attributed to Okamoto Hōkō 岡本保考 (1797–1878; see Ozawa Masatane 小澤政胤, ed., *Keichō irai kokugakka ryakuden* 慶長以來國學家略傳, Tokyo: Kokkōsha, 1900, p. 692) appears to be no longer extant. The Seikadō library holds a copy of a Ch'ing print of the *Chung lun*, annotated in manuscript by Okamoto Hōkō.

(b) Tada Kensuke 多田狷介, 'Chūron yakukō' 中論譯稿; *Nihon joshi daigaku kiyō* 日本女子大學紀要 31 (1981), 91–134, and 32 (1982), 39–65; an annotated translation into modern Japanese.

(c) Ikeda Shūzō 池田秀三, 'Jo Kan Chū ron kōchū' 徐幹中論校注, *Kyōto daigaku bungakubu kenkyū kiyō* 京都大學文學部研究紀要 23 (1984), 1–62; 24 (1985), 73–112; and 25 (1986), 117–200; punctuated Chinese text followed by the most complete annotation of any study; *Kambun* transcription.

9. Index

A Concordance to the Shen jian, Zhong lun and Xin yu 申鑑, 中論, 新語逐字索引, ed. D.C. Lau and Chen Fong Ching; *ICS* series, Hong Kong: Commercial Press, forthcoming 1995.

— John Makeham

Erh ya 爾雅

1. Nature and content

The earliest source to discuss the title of this text is the *Shih ming*, where the word *erh* is glossed paronomastically as *ni* 昵 'close, intimate' and *ya* is taken in its common sense of 'correct, refined'. The interpretation of the title as something like 'approaching what is correct, proper, refined' is now widely accepted.

The *Erh ya* is often called the earliest Chinese dictionary, but in fact it is actually a kind of thesaurus or compendium of what are often rather cryptic glosses that were probably in origin annotations to passages in early texts. The received version consists of nineteen sections, the first of which is divided into two parts in most editions. The title of each section begins with the word *shih* 釋 to explain, which is followed by a word denoting the nature of the material treated in the chapter. The titles and general content of the sections are as follows:

1. *Shih ku* 釋詁. Verbs, words that are commonly used as adjectives or adverbs, and a few grammatical particles.
2. *Shih yen* 釋言. Verbs.
3. *Shih hsün* 釋訓. Primarily stative or descriptive verbs, many of which are reduplicative binomes.
4. *Shih ch'in* 釋親. Kinship terms.
5. *Shih kung* 釋宮. Architectural terms.
6. *Shih ch'i* 釋器. Names of a wide range of utensils and tools, together with verbs having to do with the use of these items.
7. *Shih yüeh* 釋樂. Names of musical instruments and certain other items of musical terminology.
8. *Shih t'ien* 釋天. Astronomical, calendrical, and meteorological terms.
9. *Shih ti* 釋地. Geographical and geological terms.
10. *Shih ch'iu* 釋丘. Terms having to do with hills.
11. *Shih shan* 釋山. Terms pertaining to mountains, and names of famous mountains.

12. *Shih shui* 釋水. Terms having to do with rivers and streams and also a variety of related items such as islands and boats.
13. *Shih ts'ao* 釋草. Names of grasses, herbs, and vegetables.
14. *Shih mu* 釋木. Names of trees and shrubs.
15. *Shih ch'ung* 釋蟲. Names of insects, spiders, reptiles, etc.
16. *Shih yü* 釋魚. Names of various aquatic creatures such as fish, amphibians, and crustaceans.
17. *Shih niao* 釋鳥. Names of wildfowl.
18. *Shih shou* 釋獸. Names of wild and legendary animals.
19. *Shih ch'u* 釋畜. Names of domestic animals and poultry.

A significant division is discernible in the text between the first three and the last sixteen sections. The first part deals with a rather heterogeneous corpus of 'abstract' words, while the second is made up of topically arranged glosses on specific items. It may be that the first portion of the text was compiled by excerpting and combining material from early commentaries on works such as the *Shih ching* and *Shang shu*. Some recent research suggests that this may not be true of sections in the second part, for these contain many glosses that cannot be associated with any known early texts (see Carr, under (5) below). In any case the work is clearly a result of a conscious effort to collect and arrange systematically a large body of lexical material, and as such it occupies an important place in the development of early Chinese lexicography. In the late Han and Six Dynasties periods the *Erh ya* was venerated as an authoritative guide to the language of the ancient texts, and its coverage in the *Ching tien shih wen* indicates that by T'ang times it had itself been elevated to the status of a classic.

2. Date of origin and early history

The earliest known reference to the *Erh ya* text is in *Han shu* 30, p. 1718, where it is listed as a work of three *chüan* and twenty *p'ien*. The discrepancy between this listing and the division of the received version into nineteen sections has never been satisfactorily explained. The text is quoted in a number of Later Han sources, and it is clear that its form in this period was essentially that of the received version. The authenticity of this received version has never been seriously questioned.

Chang I 張揖 (*fl.* 227–233) in his *Shang Kuang ya piao* 上廣雅表 (*Huang Ch'ing ching chieh* 667a, pp. 1a–2a) attributed the *Erh ya* to Chou kung, and this view was followed by Lu Te-ming 陸德明 (556–627), in his preface to the *Ching tien shih wen*. Later scholars rejected this ascription because the *Erh ya* contains glosses on texts that were written in middle or late Chou times. Later and current opinion is perhaps best summarized by Karlgren, who concluded that the *Erh ya* is a work of different hands and probably dates from the third century B.C. ('The Early History of the *Chou Li* and *Tso Chuan* Texts', *BMFEA* 3 (1931), 1–59 especially pp. 44–54). Internal analysis confirms this conclusion for the first major portion of the text (see Coblin, under (5) below). Internal dating of the second part remains to be suggested.

3.   Text history and current editions

Current editions of the *Erh ya*, of which there are a great many, derive for the most part directly or indirectly from printed editions of Sung and Yüan times. The most important of these early versions were used by Juan Yüan in the compilation of his great 1815 critical edition, published together with his *Erh ya chiao k'an chi* 爾雅校勘記 by the Nan-ch'ang prefectural academy as part of the *Shih san ching chu shu fu chiao k'an chi* edition of the Thirteen Classics. Juan took the text of the *Ming Wu yüan kung fang Sung k'o Erh ya ching chu* 明吳元恭仿宋刻爾雅經注 of 1538, based on a Sung original, and which he considered the finest edition available in Ch'ing times, as the basis for his critical edition of the primary text and of the commentary by Kuo P'u 郭璞 (276–324; see under (4) below). This work may be considered the standard, as well as the best, version of the *Erh ya* text, but there are several interesting editions not included in this collation, e.g.:

(a) A Sung edition of the *Erh ya chu* discovered in Japan by Li Shuch'ang 黎庶昌 (1837–97) and published by him in the *Ku i ts'ung shu*; described as a traced copy of a large character print from Shu, commonly known as the *Ying Sung Shu ta tzu pen Erh ya* 影宋蜀大字本爾雅.

(b) The version of Lu Tien 陸佃 (1042–1102), which served as the basis of his *Erh ya hsin i* 爾雅新義 reproduced in the *Ts'ung shu chi ch'eng* series and in the *Yüeh ya t'ang ts'ung shu*, ch. 187–190.

(c) The version of Cheng Ch'iao 鄭樵 (1104–1160), used in his *Erh ya chu* and reprinted in the *Hsüeh chin t'ao yüan* 學津討源. Cheng does not mention the origin of the text that he used, but the striking resemblance of this to the later standard versions of the *Erh ya* make it almost certain that he based himself on Kuo P'u's *Erh ya chu* text. Chang Hai-p'eng 張海鵬 (1755–1816), the compiler of the *Hsüeh chin t'ao yüan*, says in his postface to that edition of Cheng Ch'iao's *Erh ya* (dated 1805) that he has reprinted the Mao Chin 毛晉 version of the text. This refers to the version reprinted in Mao Chin's *Chin tai pi shu* between 1630 and 1642, which was based on a very fine Southern Sung printed edition that Mao had acquired. Mao had changed a few characters to accord with the Kuo P'u text, as noted in his Preface, and Chang restored those characters to their original Sung form.

(d) Tun-huang fragments, preserved in the Bibliothèque Nationale, where they are catalogued as *Fonds Pelliot Chinois* nos. 2661, 3719, 3735, and 5522.

4. Commentaries and research aids

The earliest extant commentary on the *Erh ya* is the *Erh ya chu* 爾雅注 of Kuo P'u. By T'ang times it was already considered to be the best *Erh ya* commentary available, and this probably accounts for the fact that it is the only pre-Sung commentary on the text to have survived intact to modern times. Kuo P'u's version of the text and his commentary on it became the basis for almost all *Erh ya* studies of Sung and later. The *Ssu pu ts'ung k'an* reproduces one of the earliest Southern Sung versions, the edition listed in the *T'ieh ch'in t'ung chien lou ts'ang shu mu lu* 鐵琴銅劍樓藏書目錄 of 1898 by Ch'ü Yung 瞿鏞 (1860–98). The *Ssu pu pei yao* version of the *Erh ya Kuo chu* text is based on the Wan li (1573–1619) wood-block edition of Ko Tzu 葛鼐 (c. 1523).

The principal subcommentary is the *Erh ya shu* 爾雅疏 of Hsing Ping 邢昺 (931–1010), which was undertaken on imperial orders in 994. Juan Yüan used a Sung wood-block edition as the basis of his *Erh ya chiao k'an chi* 爾雅校勘記. From his description of it (in his preface, *hsü* 序, to that work) this appears to be identical with a print registered in Lu Hsin-yüan's 陸心源 (1834–1894) *Pi sung lou ts'ang shu chih* 皕宋樓藏書志. Lu thinks that this edition is from the early part of the Hsien p'ing (993–1004) era, and it may thus be an original first printing of Hsing Ping's *shu*.

From Southern Sung times on Kuo P'u's *chu* and Hsing Ping's *shu* are often combined and issued together. The earliest known *chu shu* versions of the *Erh ya* are from the Yüan period, and the origins of the various *chu* and *shu* versions used to form these and the later combined *chu shu* editions are not known. The most important *Erh ya chu shu* edition is, as mentioned above, that prepared by Juan Yüan and published in 1815.

The two major Ch'ing commentaries on the *Erh ya* are:

(a) Shao Chin-han 邵晉涵 (1743–1796), *Erh ya cheng i* 爾雅正義, *Huang Ch'ing ching chieh*, ch. 504–513; and

(b) Hao I-hsing 郝懿行 (1757–1825), *Erh ya i shu* 爾雅義疏, *Huang Ch'ing ching chieh*, ch. 1247–76.

5.   Twentieth century studies

(a) Carr, Michael E., *A Linguistic Study of the Flora and Fauna Sections of the Erh ya*. Doctoral Dissertation, University of Arizona 1972. This work provides a detailed study of the flora and fauna sections of the text, with a gloss by gloss analysis of sections 13 and 14. Particular attention is devoted to the nature of early Chinese botanical terminology.

(b) Chou Tsu-mo 周祖謨, *Wen hsüeh chi* 問學集, Peking: Chung hua, 1966 'Erh ya chih tso che chi ch'i ch'eng shu chih nien tai' 爾雅之作者及其成書之年代, pp. 670–675; 'Erh ya Kuo P'u chu ku pen pa' 爾雅郭璞注古本跋 pp. 676–682; and 'Kuo P'u Erh ya chu yü Erh ya yin i' 郭璞爾雅注與爾雅音義 pp. 683–686.

(c) Coblin, W. South, *An Introductory Study of Textual and Linguistic Problems in Erh ya*. Doctoral Dissertation, University of Washington 1972. This work provides a detailed study of the nature, origin, and text history of the *Erh ya* and a gloss by gloss analysis of the first three sections.

(d) Hsieh Yün-fei 謝雲飛, *Erh ya i hsün shih li* 爾雅義訓釋例 Yang ming shan, Hua Kang, 1969.

(e) Huang K'an 黃侃 (1886–1935), (i) 'Erh ya lüeh shuo' 爾雅略說, *Huang K'an lun hsüeh tsa chu* 黃侃論學雜著, pp. 361–401. Shanghai: Chung hua; 1964; reprinted Taipei: Chung hua, 1969. (ii) *Erh ya cheng ming p'ing* 爾雅正名評, Hong Kong: Hsin Ya Shu Yüan; actually written by Wang Ying (16th century) with comments by Huang K'an.

(f) Kaga Eiji 加賀榮治, 'Jiga moji ko' 爾雅文字考 *Morohashi hakushi koki shukuga kinen rombunshū*. 諸橋博士古稀祝賀紀念論文集 Tokyo: Morohashi tetsuji sensei koki shukuga kinenkai, 1953, pp. 372–393.

(g) Ku Chieh-kang 顧頡剛, 'Tu Erh ya shih ti i hsia ssu p'ien' 讀爾雅釋地以下四篇 *Shih hsüeh nien pao* 史學年報 2.1 (1934), pp. 247–266.

(h) Naitō Torajirō 內滕虎次郎, 'Jiga no shin kenkyū' 爾雅の新研究 *Shinagaku* 支那學 2.1. (1921), pp. 1–11; 106–110.

(i) Wen I-to 聞一多, *Erh ya hsin i* 爾雅新義, in *Ku tien hsin i* 古典新義, Peking: Ku chi, 1956, pp. 209–231.

6. Translations

Given the nature of the text, it is not surprising that there are no translations of the *Erh ya*.

7. Indexes

(a) *Erh ya yin te* 爾雅引得 (*Index to Erh ya*), Harvard-Yenching Institute Sinological Index Series, supplement no.18; Peking, 1941.

(b) *Erh ya chu shu yin shu yin te* 爾雅注疏引書引得 (*Index to the Titles Quoted in the Commentaries on Erh Ya*); Harvard-Yenching Institute Sinological Index Series, no. 38; Peking, 1941.

(b) *A Concordance to the Erya and Xiaojing* 爾雅孝經逐字索引, ed. D.C. Lau and Chen Fong Ching; *ICS* series, Hong Kong: Commercial Press, forthcoming 1994.

— W. South Coblin

Fa yen 法言

1. Content

The *Fa yen* is a collection of aphorisms composed by the poet-philosopher Yang Hsiung 揚雄 (53 B.C.–A.D. 18). The text, in thirteen *p'ien*, is structured around a dialogue between an anonymous interlocutor and Yang Hsiung, who responds to a variety of questions on philosophical, political, literary and scholarly matters. According to Yang Hsiung, the questions that he answers were actually posed by his contemporaries. Because his answers were in the form of *exempla* (*fa*), drawn usually from orthodox history and the classics, he entitled the book 'Exemplary Sayings'. The model for the *Fa yen* was the *Lun yü*, and its style is thus deliberately archaic and elliptical. Most of the responses are in the form of terse pronouncements and rely on wit and puns rather than on logical exposition to make their point.

Yang Hsiung's avowed purpose in compiling the work was to counter what he considered to be the deleterious influence of the 'heterodox' (*tsa* 雜) thinkers, who had corrupted Confucian doctrine and 'confused the affairs of the world' with their 'strange convolutions, hairsplitting arguments and paradoxical language' (see Yang Hsiung's autobiographical postface, in *Han shu* 87B, p. 3580). Yang was particularly critical of the eclectic thinkers of the pre-Ch'in and Han periods, whom he derisively called the *chu tzu* 諸子 or 'Masters', for incorporating in their texts theories and sayings that were contrary to the teachings of the sages and the classics. Thus, except for Confucius and his immediate disciples, and Meng tzu 孟子, almost every important philosopher of the pre-Ch'in and Former Han eras receives some measure of censure and ridicule in Yang's barbed comments.

Although the *Fa yen* is divided into chapters, like the *Lun yü* their titles are not indicative of the content, but are formed of the first two characters of the text. Most of the chapters do not focus on a single subject, but contain random discussions of a variety of topics. The initial chapters are mainly concerned with ethical questions; i.e., the role of learning in cultivating the good man (no. 1); the classics and the sage as arbiters of moral wisdom (nos. 2–4); the concept of *shen* 神 (spirit, godliness), which, through prescience (*hsien chih* 先知) enables the mind to perceive the Way (nos. 5, 6 and 9); and the notion of sagehood as the highest embodiment of this prescience (nos. 7–8). The later chapters (nos. 10–13) consist mostly of praise-and-blame type comments on historical figures as well as acerbic remarks on contemporary practices and theories (e.g., alchemy, numerology and other occult sciences), that Yang considered absurd and contrary to classical teachings.

2. Date of composition

The *Fa yen* was not composed all at one time, but represents Yang Hsiung's random jottings written over a decade or more. In the last chapter, Yang gives what can be construed as the *terminus ad quem* for the book, for he refers to Wang Mang 王莽 as the Duke of Han 漢, and claims that the Han dynasty had at that point ruled for 210 years. The Duke of Han is an abbreviated form of Wang Mang's title An Han kung 安漢公, which he held from A.D. 1 until A.D. 9. The figure of 210 years for the duration of the Han dynasty is subject to various interpretations, but it most likely represents the period beginning in 202 B.C., when Liu Pang 劉邦 formally assumed the title of emperor. If this assumption is correct, the final sections of the *Fa yen* must have been written in A.D. 9 or shortly thereafter. As corroboration, it may be noted that Wang Mang mentions the same span of 210 years for the Han dynasty, in his mandate or charter issued to the deposed prince, Liu Ying 劉嬰, in A.D. 9 (see *Han shu* 99B, p. 4099).

The earliest mention of the *Fa yen* is in Yang Hsiung's autobiographical postface, which he must have written *c.* A.D. 10 (*Han shu* 87B, p. 3580). Here he describes the *Fa yen* as a work in 13 *chüan*, and he provides brief outlines of each one. According to the *Han shu* (87B, p. 3585), some forty years after Yang Hsiung's death, the *Fa yen* was widely circulated among scholars. Pan Ku 班固 (32–92) also includes it as one of his additions in the notes to the *Ch'i lüeh* 七略 of Liu Hsin 劉歆 (46 B.C.–A.D. 23; *Han shu* 30, p. 1727), where he lists it as a work of thirteen *p'ien*. This text is undoubtedly the same as the version in 13 *chüan* and is probably the text that survives today. One of the reasons for the extremely good condition of the *Fa yen* may be that the first editor was Yang Hsiung's disciple Hou Pa 侯芭 (1st century A.D.), who also wrote a commentary to the work; this was lost in the sixth century (*Sui shu* 34, p. 998, where Hou Pa's name is incorrectly given as Hou Pao 侯苞). Another early commentary by the later Han or Wei scholar Sung Chung 宋衷, who was also responsible for editing the *T'ai hsüan ching*, was still extant in the eleventh century (see *Hsin T'ang shu* 59, p. 1510).

3. Textual history

Extant editions fall into two groups: (a) in 13 *chüan* and (b) in 10 *chüan*.

(a) Editions in 13 *chüan* are based on a text prepared by Li Kuei 李軌 (*fl.* 317) whose paraphrases and word glosses form the earliest commentary. The work is first listed in the *Sui shu* (34, p. 998) with 15 *chüan* and one further *chüan* of 'exegesis' (*chieh* 解), and the note to that entry refers to the existence of a text in six *chüan* during the sixth century that had subsequently been lost. But there is also an entry for the work in the *Sui shu* in 13 *chüan*; by the middle of the T'ang period, Li Kuei's *Fa yen* appears as an item of 13 *chüan* (*Chiu T'ang shu* 47, p. 2024; see also the entry in Fujiwara Sukeyo's catalogue), with each *chüan* presumably corresponding to one *p'ien*.

The earliest extant version of the text with the Li Kuei commentary is the so called *Chih p'ing chien pen* 治平監本 which was prepared by the *Kuo tzu chien* 國子監 and *Chih mi ko* 直祕閣 between 1037 and 1065. The editors also added a supplement of pronunciation and glosses on meaning by an unknown early Sung scholar in one *chüan*. In 1820 Ch'in En-fu 秦恩復 (1760–1843) issued a facsimile reproduction of this edition, which was adopted for both the *Ssu pu ts'ung k'an* and the *Ssu pu pei yao* series. Although this edition is valuable for preserving the most complete version of Li Kuei's commentary, in many places the text includes incorrect and corrupt readings; see Ch'in En-fu's table of emendations that is prefaced to his reprint of the *Chih p'ing chien pen* copy.

(b) Although a version in 10 *chüan* was already known in the middle of the T'ang period (see *Chiu T'ang shu* 47, p. 2024), the extant text is based on an edition prepared during Northern Sung by Sung Hsien 宋咸 (*chin shih* 1150). In the same period a printer in the Chien-ning 建寧 area (modern Fukien) issued an edition with four commentaries, which included that of Li Kuei, and those of Liu Tsung-yüan 柳宗元 (773–819), Wu Mi 吳祕 (*chin shih* 1034) and Sung Hsien. With Sung Hsien's edition as his basis, in 1081 Ssu-ma Kuang 司馬光 (1019–86) issued a text in 13 *chüan* that included portions of the four-commentary edition, supplemented by his own explanatory notes. This work is no longer extant; it is listed in *Sung shih* 205, p. 5173, and it exists only as a work of 10 *chüan*. The earliest known version is the *Tsuan t'u hu chu Yang tzu Fa yen* 纂圖互注揚子法言, issued by a Northern Fukien printer in the early 1260's. In 1533 Ku Ch'un 顧春 printed a modified version of that edition under the title of *Hsin tsuan men mu wu ch'en yin chu Yang tzu Fa yen* 新纂門目五臣音注揚

子法言. This edition, which is commonly called the *Shih te t'ang pen* 世德堂本 was reprinted in 1914 by the Yu wen she 友文社.

The only major difference between the editions grouped as (a) and (b) lies in the distribution of the *p'ien*; in (b) *chüan* nos. 2, 5 and 6 each contain 2 *p'ien*; in (a) each of the 13 *chüan* corresponds to one *p'ien*.

4.　Recent editions

(a) Text with annotation: Wang Jung-pao 汪榮寶, *Fa yen i shu* 法言義疏, 20 *chüan*, 1933; reprinted, with punctuation, by Ch'en Chung-fu 陳仲夫 (Peking: Chung hua, 1987). This is a revision of the same author's *Fa yen shu cheng* 法言疏證 of 1911. It is an extremely detailed commentary that offers many original interpretations, particularly on the meaning of rare words; it explains much of the text as a tract against Wang Mang.
(b) Annotations without text: apart from Wang Nien-sun's 王念孫 (1744–1832) valuable philological commentary (in *Tu shu tsa chih yü pien* 讀書雜誌餘編) and Yü Yüeh's 俞樾 (1821–1907) anti-Wang Mang interpretation (in *Chu tzu p'ing i* 34), see three works of Liu Shih-p'ei 劉師培 in *Liu Shen-shu hsien sheng i shu* 3.

5.　Recent studies

(a) Kano Naoki 狩野直喜, 'Yō Yū to Hōgen' 揚雄と法言, *Shinagaku* 3:6 (1923), 399–420.
(b) Jäger, Fritz, 'Yang Hiung und Wang Mang', *Sinica-Sonderausgabe* (1937), 14–34. This concerns the passages of the *Fa yen* that purport to criticize Wang Mang.
(c) Hsü Fu-kuan 徐復觀, 'Yang Hsiung lun chiu' 揚雄論究; *Ta lu tsa chih* 大陸雜誌 50:3 (1975), 1–43; reprinted *Liang Han ssu hsiang shih* 兩漢思想史 (Hong Kong: Chinese University Press, 1975). This concerns Yang Hsiung's thought, with a long section on the *Fa yen*.
(d) Lan Hsiu-lung 藍秀隆, *Yang Hsiung Fa yen yen chiu* 揚雄法言研究; Taipei: Wen shih che, 1989.

6.　Translations

(a) von Zach, Erwin, *Yang Hsiungs Fa-yên (Worte strenger Ermahnung)*, *Sinologische Beiträge* IV:1, Batavia, 1939. A complete, reasonably accurate, unannotated rendering of the whole text; reprinted San Francisco: Chinese Materials Center, 1976.

(b) Belpaire, Bruno, *Le Catechisme philosophique de Yang Hiong-tse*, Brussels, 1960. This work is replete with errors.

7. Japanese editions

L. *Chūgoku koten shinsho*, 1972, edited by Suzuki Yoshikazu.

Momoi Hakuroku 桃井白鹿, *Zōchū Yōshi Hōgen* 增註揚雄法言, 1796; Ssu-ma Kuang's version (10 *chüan*, with five commentaries), together with Momoi's annotation.

8. Index

A Concordance to the Fa yan and Tai xuan jing 法言, 太玄經逐字索引, ed. D.C. Lau and Chen Fong Ching; *ICS* series, Hong Kong: Commercial Press, forthcoming 1995.

— David R. Knechtges

Feng su t'ung i 風俗通義

1. The author and his aims

Ying Shao 應劭 (*c*. 140 to before 204) was a social critic who lived at the end of the Later Han period, when regional strong men were threatening the continuation of the Han dynasty and political theorists were questioning some of the basic premises of Han society and government. Thanks to a family tradition of scholarship and the patronage of one of the clans of Ju-nan 汝南, Ying Shao advanced along the path of an official career, until his appointment as governor (*T'ai shou* 太守) of T'ai-shan 泰山 commandery in 189. In T'ai-shan he bravely routed one rebel band which was associated with the Yellow Turban movement, only to flee from his post several years later, lest he should become involved in a feud which was developing between local overlords. In 197 he demonstrated his loyalty to the Han house by reconstructing the law codes and case-books that had been lost in the move of the capital from Lo-yang 洛陽 to Hsü 許 (later called Hsü-ch'ang 許昌) in the previous year. A number of other compilations, including the *Feng su t'ung i*, were written during the following years before his death some time before 204. For his biography and date of death, see *Hou Han shu* 48, pp. 1609–15, and *San kuo chih* 1 ('Wei' 魏 1) p. 11, note 1.

In the *Feng su t'ung i*, also called *Feng su t'ung*, and now extant only in an incomplete form, Ying Shao was hoping to support the imperial house at a time when, as he himself wrote in his preface 'the ruling house had collapsed and the provinces were rent asunder like a length of cloth' (*SPTK* ed., 5b). He saw a paramount need of greater perception, integrity and courage, if the Han Dynasty was to return to the Golden Age of the past. The work is now best known for its vivid descriptions of contemporary cults and beliefs, which the *Ssu k'u* editors compare favourably with those of the *Lun heng*. In his preface, Ying Shao confesses his fear that in describing such ordinary topics he hazards the condemnation of his readers. Thanks to his breadth of interest and keen observation, however, the work not only provides a unique record of Han beliefs, but also reveals the complex philosophy of one of the best informed intellectuals of the day.

2.   Textual history

One of the first references to the *Feng su t'ung i* was made by Hua Ch'iao 華嶠 (d. 293), who mentions it as one of Ying Shao's writings (see Hua Ch'iao's *Hou Han shu* 1, p. 22a, in Wang Wen-t'ai 汪文臺, *Ch'i chia Hou Han shu* 七家後漢書; preface dated 1882; reprinted Taipei: Chin sheng ko ta shu chu, 1972; see pp. 534–35). A similar reference in the *Hou Han shu* of Fan Yeh 范曄 (398–446; see ch. 48, p. 1614) adds that, apart from his commentaries to the *Han shu*, his works amounted to 136 *p'ien*. No extant citation predating the *Sui shu* (completed 656) gives more precise bibliographical information about the *Feng su t'ung i*; the received text of the *Sui shu* (34, p. 1006, where the work is listed under *tsa chia* 雜家) reads *Feng su t'ung i* 31 *chüan; lu* 錄 1 *chüan*. The *Chiu T'ang shu* (47, p. 2033) and *Hsin T'ang shu* (59, p. 1534) list the book with 30 *chüan*.

It has been suggested that in the *Sui shu* the entry for the *lu* in 1 *chüan* was included in the total count of 31, but that it was not included in the counts given in the two T'ang histories. From this it has been concluded that the original *Feng su t'ung i* amounted to 30 chapters. However, such a view ignores information given by Su Sung 蘇頌 (1020–1101) in the preface that he wrote for an edition which he collated between 1078 and 1085. According to Su Sung, the entry in the *Sui shu* for the *Feng su t'ung i* read '32 *chüan, lu* 1 *chüan*'. This difference should not be explained as being due to error; Su Sung's statement is corroborated by the entry for *Feng su t'ung* in Fujiwara Sukeyo's catalogue, which reads 32 *chüan*.

By comparing material given in his copies of Yü Chung-jung's 庾仲容 (476–549) *Tzu ch'ao* (Liang period, 502–556) and Ma Tsung's 馬總 (d. 823) *I lin*, Su Sung arrived at what he believed to be a rough outline of the original text of the *Feng su t'ung i* (see Su Sung, *Chiao Feng su t'ung i t'i hsü* 校風俗通義題序, in *Su Wei kung wen chi* 蘇魏公文集; *Feng su t'ung i* 66, p. 5b–7a, in *Ssu k'u ch'üan shu chen pen* 四庫全書珍本, collection 4; reprinted Peking: Chung hua, 1988, pp. 1006–07). He renumbered ten extant chapters and gave the titles of 20 other chapters that had already been lost; finally he stated that both the title and the text of the original chapter no. 8 were missing. In this way he brought the total number of *chüan* up to 31, i.e. the number mentioned by Yü Chung-jung; with the addition of the *lu*, in 1 *chüan*, the total tallies with Su Sung's reading of the entry in the *Sui shu*.

If due credit is given to Su Sung's argument and its compelling consistency, the figures reflect a real rather than an apparent loss of one *chüan* that must have taken place between the compilation of the lists in the Sui and the T'ang histories. By the eleventh century, twenty more chapters had been lost, and thereafter a *Feng su t'ung i* in no more than

10 *chüan* is listed in the catalogues (e.g., *Ch'ung wen tsung mu, Chün chai tu shu chih, Chih chai shu lu chieh t'i* and *Sung shih* 206, p. 5208). The loss of the 20 chapters presumably occurred after the compilation of the *I lin* and the imperially sponsored *T'ai p'ing yü lan* of 983, as these works preserve considerable portions of the original text that are not found in the editions available either to Su Sung or to Ting Fu 丁黼, a later editor whose postface was dated in 1220; there is no apparent reason to identify him with the Ting Fu whose short biography is included in *Sung shih* 454, p. 13, 345.

It was with Su Sung that the task of reconstructing the original format and text of the *Feng su t'ung i* began. In his preface he renumbered the ten chapters that were available to him, in accordance with the information given in the *Tzu ch'ao* and the *I lin*. However, this numbering was challenged by the editors of the *Ssu k'u*, as may be seen:

Extant editions	Su Sung	*Ssu k'u*
1 'Huang pa' 皇霸	1	5
2 'Cheng shih' 正失	6	11
3 'Yen li' 愆禮	8	9
4 'Kuo yü' 過譽	7	8
5 'Shih fan' 十反	9	10
6 'Sheng yin' 聲音	13	28
7 'Ch'iung t'ung' 窮通	15	12
8 'Ssu tien' 祀典	20	17
9 'Kuai shen' 怪神	31	15
10 'Shan tse' 山澤	24	19

The received texts of the *Tzu ch'ao* and the *I lin* do not include information seen by Su Sung, and the authority of the *Ssu k'u* editors is uncertain. As a result, the original arrangement of the chapters cannot be determined for certain.

Su Sung's preface also gives the titles of the missing 20 chapters, as follows: 'Hsin cheng' 心政; 'Ku chih' 古制; 'Yin chiao' 陰教; 'Pien huo' 辨惑; 'Hsi tang' 析當; 'Shu tu' 恕度; 'Chia hao' 嘉號; 'Hui ch'eng' 徽稱; 'Ch'ing yü' 情遇; 'Hsing shih' 姓氏; 'Hui p'ien' 諱篇; 'Shih chi' 釋忌; 'Chi shih' 輯事; 'Fu yao' 服妖; 'Sang chi' 喪祭; 'Kung shih' 宮室; 'Shih ching' 市井; 'Shu chi' 數紀; 'Hsin Ch'in' 新秦; 'Yü fa' 獄法. In citing Su Sung's preface, Lu Hsin-yüan 陸心源 (1834–94; see *I ku t'ang chi* 儀顧堂集; preface by Yü Yüeh 俞樾, 1821–1907, dated 1898; facsimile reprint Taipei: T'ai lien, 1970, 2.4b–5b) gave the alternative titles of 'Shih wang' 釋忘, 'Shih yü' 恃遇 and 'Hui ch'eng' 穢稱 for three of these; Wu Shu-p'ing 吳樹平 ('Feng su t'ung i tsa k'ao' 風俗通義雜考, *Wen shih* 文史 7, December 1979, pp. 59–72) argues persuasively that only the last of these three alternatives is correct.

There is no question of forgery in the case of the *Feng su t'ung i*. The few textual variants may be attributed either to printing errors or to editorial correction. For the incorrect attribution of a few fragments to the work, see Wu Shu-p'ing, *op. cit.*, p. 71. It is also clear that the received text of 10 *chüan* is not complete (see Wu Shu-p'ing, pp. 63f.)

3. Principal early editions

All extant editions may be traced to Ting Fu's collation of three copies, one of which he described as being 'all but unreadable'. His work resulted in a text corresponding to the first ten chapters of the work; his postface is dated in 1220. No Sung edition of this collation survives; a Yüan edition of 1307, to be described immediately below, is based on Ting Fu's work. For further details of rare copies, see Wu Shu-p'ing's edition, as noted under 6 (a) below.

(a) The *Ta te hsin k'an chiao cheng Feng su t'ung i* 大德新刊校證風俗通義, format 9 by 17, prefaces by Hsieh Chü-jen 謝居仁, dated 1305, and Li Kuo 李果 dated 1307; postfaces by Ting Fu and Huang T'ing-chien 黃廷鑑 (b. 1762), dated 1841. Two copies are held in the National Library of China, one complete and one incomplete, including chapters 8–10 only; reproduced in the *Ssu pu ts'ung k'an*, and the *Sui-an Hsü shih ts'ung shu hsü pien* (1916), and used as the basis for the print of the *Liang ching i pien* of 1582 (facsimile in *Ts'ung shu chi ch'eng*).

There are also references to a second 'small character' print, with a format of 10 by 16. Wu Shou-yang 吳壽暘, *Pai ching lou ts'ung shu ti pa chi* 拜經樓叢書題跋記 (preface 1847, 4, p. 6a–7a; *Ts'ung shu chi ch'eng* reprint, p. 80), believed that it was such a print which Lu Wen-ch'ao 盧文弨 (1717–96) had consulted prior to preparing his annotation; see also the revised edition of the work of Shao I-ch'en 邵懿辰 (1810–61), i.e. *Tseng ting Ssu k'u chien mu lu piao chu* 曾訂四庫簡目錄標注 (Peking: Chung hua, 1959), p. 527; Shao identifies this as a Yüan edition and mentions two other editions of Yüan date. Wu Shu-p'ing correctly doubts the attribution of a small character print to this period.

(b) Four chapters only are included in the *Ku chin i shih* of Wu Kuan 吳琯, *cs* 1571, of *c.* 1580.

(c) The text which is included in the *Ko chih ts'ung shu* 格致叢書 of Hu Wen-huan 胡文煥 (1603); stated by Lu Wen-ch'ao to be full of errors.

(d) *Han Wei ts'ung shu*; used as the basis in the *Ssu pu pei yao* series.

(e) Chung Hsing 鍾惺 (?1574–?1624): edition with scant annotation; available in a *Kambun* reprint (see under (7) below).

(f) The National Library of China holds a copy of an edition printed in Kuang-chou in 1826; stated by Huang T'ing-chien to be based on the edition of 1307.

4. Traditional commentaries

The only annotation prior to the Ch'ing period consists of the few comments included in Chung Hsing's edition. Many of the Ch'ing scholars were concerned with collecting fragments of the work.

(a) Ch'ien Ta-hsin 錢大昕 (1728–1804), *Feng su t'ung i i wen* 風俗通義佚文; a collection of some 600 fragments, of which 350 are concerned with surnames from 20 sources ranging from the *So yin* 索引 commentary to the *Shih chi* by Ssu-ma Chen 司馬貞 (8th century) to the *T'ai p'ing yü lan*. Lu Wen-ch'ao included this text in his *Ch'ün shu shih pu* 群書拾補 of 1787 (*Pao ching t'ang ts'ung shu*, 75); Sun Chih-tsu 孫志祖 (1737–1801) copied 17 more fragments found by Tsang Yung 臧庸 (1767–1811), and added one further one of his own discovery in his *Tu shu tso lu* 讀書脞錄 4, pp. 13b–15a, of 1799 (reprinted Taipei: Kuang wen, 1963). Further fragments were assembled by Chu Yün 朱筠 (1729–81), Chang Chu 張澍 (1781–1847) and Ku Huai-san 顧槐三 (19th century), as may be seen below. Ch'ien Ta-hsin is criticised by Wu Shu-p'ing for failing to comb through the works which he claimed to have consulted.

(b) Lu Wen-ch'ao's work on the *Feng su t'ung i*, i.e. *Feng su t'ung i shih pu* 風俗通義拾補, in *Pao ching t'ang ts'ung shu* 75, consists of four parts: (i) annotation of the text, with comparison of different editions; (ii) prefaces to the Sung and Yüan editions; (iii) fragments collected by Tsang Yung; and (iv) fragments collected by Ch'ien Ta-hsin. In his notes to the text, Lu Wen-ch'ao considers the opinions of scholars such as Ho Ch'o 何焯 (1661–1722), Chai Hao 翟灝 (d.1788), Ch'ien Ta-hsin and Sun Chih-tsu. Hsieh Kuo-chen 謝國楨 (20th century) included a few examples of Lu Wen-ch'ao's hasty judgement or excessive eagerness to emend characters, but most of his errors were corrected by Sun I-jang 孫詒讓 (1848–1908) or Liu Shih-p'ei 劉師培 (1884–1919), for whose contributions see below.

(c) Chu Yün began work in 1767 on two studies: (i) *Feng su t'ung pu i* 風俗通補逸, which collects 170 fragments; and (ii) *Feng su t'ung chiao cheng* 風俗通校證, which collates the text of the *Kuang Han Wei ts'ung shu* with that of the Yüan print, and offers its own solution to some of the difficult problems of the text. Chu Yün's manuscript copies are held in the National Library of China.

(d) In his *Feng su t'ung hsing shih p'ien* 風俗通姓氏篇, of 1821, Chang Chu 張澍 (1781–1847) provides full entries for 488 fragments that concern matters of genealogy; in *Lung hsi ching she ts'ung shu* (also in *Ts'ung shu chi ch'eng*).

(e) Ku Huai-san, *Pu chi Feng su t'ung i i wen* 補輯風俗通義佚文 published 1854; included in the *Chin ling ts'ung shu* 金陵叢書; criticised for unscholarly citation of sources and a less than rigorous search for fragments. The work is valuable for the inclusion of six surnames that appear for the first time, nineteen entries that are longer than the versions of these fragments seen elsewhere, and there are some variant readings. Ku Huai-san was one of the first scholars to point out that some of the fragments that had been traditionally ascribed to the *Feng su t'ung i* may instead have been drawn from works such as the *T'ung su wen* 通俗文 of Fu Ch'ien 服虔 (c. 125–95); see *Yü han shan fang chi i shu* 61, 1a–28b.

(f) Sun I-jang; see *Cha i* 10 for the correction in 26 items of Lu Wen-ch'ao's commentary, on the basis of parallel anecdotes of Han date in other texts.

(g) Liu Shih-p'ei; see *Tso an chi* 左盦集 (preface 1928) 7.37b, 38a (*Liu Shen-shu hsien sheng i shu* 7.29a–b) for the correction of a few items of Lu's commentary, on the basis of better readings in different editions of the works consulted by Lu.

(h) Hsieh Kuo-chen, *Hsü hsiu Ssu k'u ch'üan shu t'i yao* 續修四庫全書提要 (Taipei: Shang wu, 1971–72); criticised Ch'ien Ta-hsin for failing to consult a sufficient number of reference works; praised Lu Wen-ch'ao as a 'meritorious official who had served Ying Shao'; and evaluated Lu Wen-ch'ao's work as 80% correct.

5. Recent studies

(a) Liu P'ei-yü 劉培譽, 'Kuan yü Feng su t'ung' 關於風俗通; *Li hsüeh* 1/2 (1935) 67–72. This article includes a brief biography of Ying Shao, an assessment on various editions and notes on their variant readings. A final section discusses the attempts to reconstruct the text and concludes with the author's own additions to the chapter on surnames.

(b) Shih Shu-ch'ing 史樹青, *Feng su t'ung chiao pu* 風俗通校補; manuscript dated 1943–44; facsimile copy available in the Gest Oriental

Library, Princeton. A brief discussion of the available editions is followed by (i) notes on the text, concerning glosses, the use of loan characters and variant readings; (ii) comments on earlier compilations of fragments; (iii) an examination of variant readings for 28 fragments; (iv) additional fragments; and (v) Sun Chih-tsu's collection of fragments. If Shih Shu-ch'ing is somewhat precipitate in his revisions, his suggestions are consistently thought provoking and his comparison of early texts is apposite.

(c) Wu Shu-p'ing, 'Feng su t'ung i tsa k'ao 風俗通義考雜, *Wen shih* 7 (December 1979) 53–72. This article explores five topics: (i) Ying Shao's biography; (ii) the number of chapters and their titles; (iii) the fragmentary nature of the ten chapters of the received text; (iv) the reconstruction of the other chapters; and (v) the editions.

6.　Modern editions and commentaries

(a) Wu Shu-p'ing, *Feng su t'ung i chiao shih* 風俗通義校釋; Tientsin: Jen min, 1980; text in unabbreviated characters, with the editor's own notes. The introduction discusses Ying Shao's life and times and provides basic information on textual history, editions and commentaries. The main text is followed by the fragments, with identification of their provenance, arranged in 27 sections, according to subject matter (surnames in no. 27) and a list of sources from which they are drawn. The prefaces, postfaces and notice by the *Ssu k'u* editors are followed by indexes of (i) proper names and (b) books cited in both the text and the fragments.

(b) Wang Li-ch'i 王利器, *Feng su t'ung i chiao chu* 風俗通義校注, 2 vols.; Peking: Chung hua, 1981; text in unabbreviated characters, with a shorter introduction but more extensive notes than in (a). The main text is followed by the fragments, with a note of their provenance, arranged according to the *p'ien* from which they are said to have been drawn. Appended are the biography of the *Hou Han shu*, references in other histories or works, and a wider collection of prefaces and bibliographical notes than those included in (a).

7.　Japanese edition

Chung Hsing's edition, with *Kambun* notation of 1660 by Iida Chūbei 飯田忠兵衞, is reprinted in Nagasawa Kikuya 長澤規矩也 (1902–80), ed., *Wa kokubon Kanseki zuihitsu shū* 和刻本漢籍隨筆集; Tokyo: Koten ken-kyūkai, 1974.

8. Indexes

(a) *Feng su t'ung i t'ung chien* 風俗通義通檢 (*Index du Feng su t'ung i*); Centre franco-chinois d'études sinologiques, Peking, 1943; reprinted Taipei: Ch'eng wen, 1968. This volume reprints the text from the *Ssu pu ts'ung k'an* (with punctuation), together with most of Lu Wen-ch'ao's annotations, Sun I-jang's notes, six *chüan* of fragments drawn from Yen K'o-chün's 嚴可均 (1762–1843) *Ch'üan Hou Han wen* 全後漢文, and compilations by Lu Wen-ch'ao and Chang Chu.

(b) *A Concordance to the Fengsu tongyi* 風俗通義逐字索引, ed. D.C. Lau and Chen Fong Ching; *ICS* series, Hong Kong: Commercial Press, forthcoming 1995.

— Michael Nylan

Han chi 漢紀

1. Content

The *Han chi*, sometimes known as the *Ch'ien Han chi* 前漢紀, was written by Hsün Yüeh 荀悅 (A.D. 148–209). It is an abstract of Pan Ku's 班固 (32–92) *Han shu* in which the author in 30 *chüan* epitomizes the contents of the hundred *chüan* of the *Han shu*. The period covered by the *Han chi* is therefore identical with that of the *Han shu*, viz. from *c.* 210 B.C. to A.D. 23. Inspired by the venerable example of the *Ch'un ch'iu*, Hsün Yüeh rearranged the *Han shu* material in a strictly chronological order, inserting relevant passages from the *Han shu* treatises and biographies in the framework of his abbreviated imperial annals. About one third of the *Han chi* text consists of material taken from the annals, the other two thirds deriving from the other parts of the *Han shu*. On thirty-nine occasions Hsün Yüeh inserts remarks of his own into the narrative. These remarks, called *lun* 論, 'discourses', are of varying length. It is possible that Hsün Yüeh included passages from the now lost *Han yü* 漢語 compiled by his uncle Hsün Shuang 荀爽, a work reputedly also based on the *Han shu*.

Hsün Yüeh's biography in the *Hou Han shu* includes a passage said to be his preface to the *Han chi* that is completely different from the preface that usually accompanies the text (*Hou Han shu* 62, p. 2062). For the relation between these two prefaces see Ch'en Ch'i-yün, *Hsün Yüeh and the Mind of Late Han China* (Princeton: Princeton University Press, 1980), pp. 75 f.

2. Date of composition and authenticity

The *Han chi* may have been started as a private venture, but Hsün Yüeh was formally ordered to compile an epitome of the *Han shu* in A.D. 198, because the emperor considered the latter work too long. The *Han chi* was completed and presented to the throne in A.D. 200.

The *Han chi* is well attested through the centuries and, although it has suffered in the long course of its transmission, there exist no reasons to doubt its authenticity. It should be noted that, according to Hsün Yüeh's preface, he wrote his work on paper, with the result that it cannot have suffered from any disarrangement of wooden or bamboo strips.

3.   Editions

Several Sung editions of the *Han chi* are known, but they are said to be very corrupt. Three Ming editions are recorded:

(a) Of Lü Nan 呂柟 (1479–1542).

(b) Of Huang Chi-shui 黃姬水, 1548; reproduced in the *Ssu pu ts'ung k'an*. It was further reproduced as a separate publication by the Shang wu yin shu kuan in Taiwan, in 1973. Some pages used for the reproduction were defective. The text has been emended and punctuated by a scholar whose name is not given.

(c) The *Nan chien* 南監 edition of 1598, prepared by the Nanking academy.

(d) An edition of 1696 by Chiang Kuo-hsiang 蔣國祥 based on editions (b) and (c) above. This edition, together with Chiang's *Liang Han chi tzu chü i t'ung k'ao* 兩漢紀字句異同考, was re-set and punctuated in the series *Jen jen wen k'u* 人人文庫; Taipei: Shang wu, 1971.

(e) An edition of 1876 produced by the Hsüeh-hai t'ang 學海堂.

(f) The version included in the *Lung hsi ching she ts'ung shu* based on edition (d) above.

4.   Translations

Western or Japanese translations of the *Han chi* do not seem to exist.

5.   Recent studies and research aids

(a) Niu Yung-chien 鈕永建 (Ch'ing period), *Ch'ien Han chi chiao shih* 前漢紀校釋, included in the *Nan ching cha chi* 南菁札記. Niu compares *Han chi* passages with corresponding passages in the *Han shu* and *Shih chi*, and evaluates the validity of the *Han chi* version.

(b) Ch'en Ch'i-yün, 'Textual problems of Hsün Yüeh's (A.D. 148–209) writings: the *Han-chi* and the *Shen-chien* 申鑑', in *Monumenta Serica* 24 (1968), pp. 208–232.

(c) Chi-yun Chen, *Hsün Yüeh (A.D. 148–209); the Life and Reflections of an Early Medieval Confucian* (Cambridge: Cambridge University Press, 1975); see pp. 84–126.

6.   Index

A Concordance to the Qian Han ji 前漢紀逐字索引, ed. D.C. Lau and Chen Fong Ching; *ICS* series, Hong Kong: Commercial Press, forthcoming 1995.

— A.F.P. Hulsewé

Han fei tzu 韓非子

1. Content

The work is concerned with a theory of state power which combines the ideas of Shang Yang 商鞅, Shen Tao 慎到 and Shen Pu-hai 申不害: absolute order can be maintained only by means of *fa* 法 (law), *shu* 術 (political expedients) and *shih* 勢 (the authority of an acknowledged position). In so far as the *Han fei tzu* brings into question the way in which a ruler conducts an investigation, the work also concerns epistemology. For Han Fei's political ideas and his concept of knowledge, see Léon Vandermeersch, *La Formation du Légisme* (Paris: École Française d'extrême orient, 1965), Part 3 and bibliography, pp. 296–99.

2. Form of the work

The 55 *p'ien* of the text, which are arranged in 20 *chüan*, include a collection of essays each one of which, while being of very different form, yet constitutes a coherent whole. The importance of the book lies as much in the light that it throws on the history of literary genres as it does on the history of ideas; for it gives a general view of all types of argued writing that were current in the fourth and third centuries B.C., of which some were destined to flourish during the Han period and the Six Dynasties. In addition to memorials or addresses to a ruler, such as *Ch'u chien Ch'in* 初見秦 (*p'ien* no. 1), *Ts'un Han* 存韓 (no. 2), and *Yu tu* 有度 (no. 6), there are examples of specialised types of writing such as the form that was named 'connected pearls' (*lien chu* 連珠) during the Six Dynasties (e.g., *Nei, Wai chu shuo* 內外儲說 *p'ien* nos. 30–15); or arguments followed by their rebuttal such as *Nan i, Nan erh, Nan san, Nan ssu* 難一, 難二, 難三, 難四, nos. 36–39, whose influence was very great with philosophers such as Wang Ch'ung 王充; and collections of stories such as *Shuo lin* 說林 (nos. 22–3) that formed a model for the *Chan kuo ts'e*.

3. The author

Han Fei (*c.* 280–*c.* 233 B.C.), whose name appears in the title of the book, was descended from the royal family of Han 韓. Together with Li Ssu

115

李斯 (?280–208 B.C.) he had been a pupil of Hsün Ch'ing 荀卿 (*c*. 335–*c*. 238 B.C.); he met his death in a dramatic manner at the hands of Ch'in, thanks to the accusations framed by his former comrade, who had by then become a minister of the First Ch'in Emperor. Han Fei's tragic end stirred the imagination of his contemporaries, with the result that there are a number of references to his life in works written at the close of Ch'in and during the Han period; e.g., see *Shih chi* 6, p. 230, 63, p. 2157 and 45, p. 1878 and *Chan kuo ts'e* 'Ch'in ts'e'. Modern studies of his life will be found in Vandermeersch *La Formation du Légisme*, Part 1; Ch'en Ch'i-yu 陳奇猷, *Han fei tzu chi shih* 韓非子集釋 (revised edition, Peking: Chung hua, 1962), pp. 1171–84; and Lundahl (see 12 (c) below).

4.   Date of compilation, and authenticity

Han shu 30, p. 1735 lists a work entitled *Han tzu* 韓子 by Han Fei, in 55 *p'ien*, under the section *fa chia*. *Shih chi* 63, p. 2147 mentions five titles of works by Han Fei, amounting to 11 *p'ien* of the received text. While a number of scholars of the 1930s regarded a large number of chapters of the work as suspect (e.g., Jung Chao-tsu 容肇祖 (1899–). *Han fei tzu k'ao cheng* 韓非子考證), most specialists today incline to the view that most of the book derives from Han Fei's own hand, even though certain parts had been restyled. The following *p'ien* raise a number of questions which cannot be solved for certain:

(a) No. 1 *Ch'u chien Ch'in*; a similar version is known in the *Chan kuo ts'e*.
(b) No. 53 *Ch'ih ling* 飭令; there is a parallel version in the *Shang Chün shu*, and it is possible that Han Fei was presenting a résumé of Shang Yang's thought. In any event there is little doubt that the text had been included in the *Han fei tzu* from Han times.
(c) No. 52 *Jen chu* 人主 and no. 55 *Chih fen* 制分 have been regarded as suspect by Ch'en Ch'i-yu and some Japanese scholars, either on the grounds that they summarize other parts of the *Han fei tzu*, or because of stylistic differences with other parts of the work.
(d) The rebuttals of nos. 37 (*Nan erh*) and 39 (*Nan ssu* 難四) are the work of other writers that has been incorporated in the text.
(e) It has been suggested that all passages starting with the formula *I yüeh* 一曰 in *p'ien* nos. 30–35 likewise derived from a later period, being added to the original text by commentators. There is no proof of this suggestion.
(f) The final part of *p'ien* no. 2, *Ts'un Han* 存韓 includes the two speeches of Li Ssu. Here there is no question of Han Fei's own writings; the passages were included as being relevant when Han Fei's

written works were brought together into a book during the Han period.

It may be concluded that most of the *p'ien* of the received text derived from Han Fei's own hand. The book was compiled from his scattered writings since the Han period and it has been subject to very little interpolation. From citations which are included in other works and in the encyclopaedias it appears that the text has suffered very few losses. The book may therefore be accepted as authentic.

5. Textual history

The book was first entitled the *Han tzu*, as may be seen in *Han shu* 30, p. 1735. In view of the possible confusion with the works of Han Yü 韓愈, from the T'ang period onwards it usually appears as *Han fei tzu*, in the catalogues of both private and public collections, the bibliographical lists of the Standard Histories and in critical editions of the work itself.

The *Han shu* enters the book with 55 *p'ien*, and it is only from the Liang period (i.e. in Juan Hsiao-hsü's 阮孝緒 (479–536) *Ch'i lu* 七錄, and notices in the Standard Histories such as the *Sui shu* 34, p. 1003, and the *Sung shih* 205, p. 5202, that are thereon based) that the number of *chüan* is mentioned. There appears to have been no variation in the number given for the *p'ien*, apart from references to 56 *p'ien*, in the *Han i wen chih kao cheng* 漢藝文志考證, and the *Yü hai* 玉海, of Wang Ying-lin 王應麟 (1223–96); these are without doubt due to copyists' errors. Fujiwara Sukeyo's catalogue includes the entry *Han tzu shih cheng lun wu chüan* 韓子十政論五卷, under *fa chia*.

Owing to their political ideas, the writings of Han Fei were circulated widely during Ch'in and even Han. References may be found both in the *Huai nan tzu*, *Shih chi* and *Yen t'ieh lun* and in a large number of other writers, such as Wang Ch'ung who devotes a complete part of his work to refuting Han Fei's ideas (see 'Fei Han p'ien' 非韓篇). Interest in the work showed no sign of abatement during the Six Dynasties and the T'ang periods, owing to the attention then being paid to literary forms and styles. In the Sung period a number of men of letters such as Ou-yang Hsiu 歐陽修 (1007–72), Su Shih 蘇軾 (1036–1101) and Su Ch'e 蘇轍 (1039–1112) engaged in refuting its ideas.

6. Early commentators

(a) The notes of Liu Ping 劉昞 (452–533), the first known commentator, have been lost, but it is possible that some of the interpolations in the *Han fei tzu* are due to the incorporation of his comments in the text.

(b) Yin Chih-chang's 尹知章 (d. 718) commentary, of the T'ang period, in 3 *chüan*, had already been lost, when the *Hsin Tang shu*, was compiled.

(c) In his preface to the critical edition of the Yüan period, Ho Fan 何犿 writes that he had suppressed the old notes of Li Tsan 李瓚. Li Tsan may perhaps be identified with the man of that name stated in the *Chiu T'ang shu* to have achieved the degree of *chin shih* 進士 between 847 and 859. The intercolumnar notes printed in small characters and printed in the extant *Tao tsang* 道藏 and Ch'ien tao 乾道 editions (see below) make no mention of the name of the commentator; thus the notes may nonetheless be supposed to have been written by Li Tsan. They are in any case to be dated before the Sung period, appearing as they do in some of the encyclopaedias of the tenth century.

7. Early editions

Three groups of editions may be distinguished, all deriving from a single source.

(a) Editions with the last 76 characters of *p'ien* no. 50 missing.

To this group there belongs the oldest printed edition, carefully made by Huang San pa lang 黃三八郎 of Chien-ning 建寧 in 1165, and known as the Ch'ien tao 乾道 (1165–73) edition. This edition had become extremely rare by the Ch'ing period, when it was re-edited by Wu Tzu 吳鼐 in 1818, on the basis of (i) a copy belonging to Li Shu-nien 李書年 and (ii) a tracing which had been made from a different copy of the same edition which was in the possession of Huang P'ei-lieh 黃丕烈 (1763–1825). The latter scholar, who had borrowed Li Shu-nien's copy, had himself completed the text of the two copies, each of which was defective. Wu Tzu added three chapters of critical notes by Ku Kuang-ch'i 顧廣圻 (1776–1835). Wu Tzu's edition was republished in the *Ku shu ts'ung k'an* series, and by the *Che chiang shu chü* and in the *Ssu pu pei yao* series; the *Ssu pu ts'ung k'an* reproduces Huang Pei-lieh's version.

(b) Editions in 53 *p'ien*

Certain editions no longer include *p'ien* no. 14, nor do they divide the *p'ien* 'Shuo lin' 說林 (nos.22 and 23 of other editions) into two, the latter part being missing. In fact the loss is not very great; in the first case *p'ien* no. 13 and the first two thirds of *p'ien* no. 14 of other editions; in the second case the first 16 passages of *p'ien* no. 23. As the titles disappeared together with the text, it would seem that the loss of these parts had been complete. This group of is represented by three editions:

(i) Ho Fan's 何犿 edition, published in 1267, on the basis of two printed copies, one belonging to the imperial library (*Chung mi shu* 中秘書) and one to Hsü Ch'ien 許謙 (659–729). Although this edition is no longer available in China, it formed the basis for Men Wu-tzu's 門無子 edition (see below). Japanese catalogues mention a second version of Ho Fan's edition, of 1744.

(ii) The *Tao tsang* edition, without table of contents; this may derive from the same source as that of Ho Fan's edition, but it is not directly based on Ho's print. For whereas Ho Fan had substituted his own notes in place of the early glosses, the *Tao tsang* copy reproduces the earlier notes in small characters. There is however one problem, in that the text of the *Cheng t'ung tao tsang* 正統道藏 is not identical with the citations ascribed to the *Tao tsang* by Ku Kuang-ch'i in his *Han fei tzu chih wu* 韓非子識誤. Only two copies of the *Cheng t'ung tao tsang* existed, together with the supplement of the Wan li period, when that work was re-issued in 1924 (photographic edition published in reduced size in 1962 by Taiwan, I-wen yin shu kuan).

(iii) The edition of Men Wu-tzu 門無子, entitled *Han fei tzu yü p'ing* 韓非子迂評; also called Ch'en Shen's 陳深 edition, in view of the inclusion of a preface by the latter of 1578; although the table of contents lists no more than 53 *p'ien*, the text is complete. This is because Chao Yung-hsien's 趙用賢 (1535–96) edition (see below) appeared just at the time when Men Wu-tzu was editing Ho Fan's text, thereby both obliging and enabling Men Wu-tzu to include the newly found lost portions of the book.

Men Wu-tzu's edition, which was printed with very great care, includes prefaces by Ch'en Shen, Men Wu-tzu (pseudonym of a man called Yü 俞) and Ho Fan; there is also a preface to the new version together with introductory notes for the guidance of the reader (*fan li* 凡例). An appendix comprises references to and judgements upon the author, which date fom the Ch'in to the Sung periods; the text is accompanied by a large number of critical notes, and notes also appear both before and after every *p'ien*. It is thanks to this edition that it is possible to know the form that Ho Han's edition had taken.

It would seem that both groups (a) and (b) derived from a common source; group (a) was made on the basis of a print that was already incomplete in the Sung period; group (b) came from a copy of the same print in which the *lacunae* had been filled from another version, whether manuscript or printed.

(c) Editions of the complete text

> (i) Chang Ting-wen's 張鼎文 edition appeared in 1561. It was based on a contemporary print that had derived from Ho Fan's version, and the text had been completed on the basis of a Sung edition that may without doubt be identified as the Ch'ien tao print. This somewhat poor version was corrected and reprinted by Feng Shu 馮舒 in about 1640.
>
> (ii) Chao Yung-hsien's 趙用賢 edition of 1582 has won a considerable reputation. Being a re-issue of the Sung edition it has served as one of the best versions that are available. It would appear that this edition as based on a version in 53 *p'ien* that derived from Ho Fan's print and was current at the beginning of the Ming period, on the text of the *Tao tsang* and on a Sung print which can without doubt be identified as that of 1165. As is frequently the case with prints that were made at this time, the text includes a number of emendations that are often of an arbitrary nature, thus rendering it difficult if not impossible to re-establish the original text.

This edition was included in the *Ssu k'u ch'üan shu* and by the Chung wen shu chü. It also served as a model for a number of other editions, often of good quality, where it was used as a basis for correcting Men Wu-tzu's print. Such editions include those of the following:

(a) Wang Shih-chen 王世貞 (1526–90); printed *c*.1583, together with the *Kuan tzu*.

(b) Wu Mien-hsüeh 吳勉學 (*fl*. 1600); included in the *Erh shih tzu* 二十子 between 1583 and 1620.

(c) Chou K'ung-chiao 周孔教; published between 1583 and 1620.

(d) Ling Ying-ch'u 凌瀛初; a carefully edited version (*c.* 1600) which repeats the notes of the *Han fei tzu yü p'ing*, and of Chao Yung-hsien.

(e) Chang Pang 張榜; at the end of the Ming period (incomplete).

(f) Chao Ju-yüan 趙如源 and Wang Tao-kun 王道焜, 1625; often neglected, this edition has the advantage of including the critical notes of a number of writers.

(g) Ch'en Jen-hsi 陳仁錫 (*c*.1580–*c*.1635) and Sun K'uang 孫鑛; published in *Chu chia p'ing tien* 諸家評點 between 1620 and 1627.

8.   Modern critical editions

(a) Wang Hsien-shen 王先慎, *Han fei tzu chi chieh* 韓非子集解; based on the Sung edition, with emendations and notes of the Ch'ing scholars. The work includes Wang's preface; an essay on the authenticity of the text, and a collection of fragments of Han Fei's writings; first published 1896, reprinted 1925, 1930 and Taipei: Shih chieh, 1955; Taiwan: Shangwu, 1956; Taiwan: I wen, 1959.

(b) Wu Ju-lun 吳汝綸 (1840–1903), *Han fei tzu tien k'an* 韓非子點勘, based on the Sung edition. A new annotation summarises the work of earlier scholars; published in late Ch'ing.

(c) Yin T'ung-yang 尹桐陽, *Han fei tzu hsin shih* 韓非子新釋, 1919; a somewhat poorly printed and poorly researched edition.

(d) Ch'en Ch'i-t'ien 陳啓天, *Han fei tzu chiao shih* 韓非子校釋, Shang-hai: Chi cheng t'u shu kung ssu, 1940; second edition Taiwan: Chung hua, 1958; revised edition (*Tseng ting* 增訂), 1969. This is one of the better editions, calling on more than 30 sets of annotations and the results of Japanese scholarship. The text is introduced by ex-planatory notes on the titles of the *p'ien* and a résumé of their ideas; critical notes follow each paragraph. Unfortunately the order of the *p'ien* has been changed. The author's *Han fei tzu ts'an kao shu chi yao* 韓非子參考書輯要, published independently by the Chung hua shu chü in 1945, and including a critical bibliography and a study of Han Fei's life and political ideas, is attached as an appendix in the revised edition. The volume includes a list of citations from works which concern the *Han fei tzu*, and the prefaces of the principal editions.

(e) Ch'en Ch'i-yu 陳奇猷, *Han fei tzu chi shih* 韓非子集釋, first edition Shanghai: Chung-hua, 1958, with a number of errors and misprints. Corrections and some new textual references were published in *Han fei tzu chi shih pu* 韓非子集釋補, in 1961 (Peking: Chung hua). A cor-rected edition of the book was published by Peking: Chung hua in 1962, with the addition of some new notes. A further edition, with-out the appendix, was published by Shanghai: Jen min, in 1974.

This is perhaps the best of all editions, giving all the variant read-ings and references to the text that have been noted elsewhere. The author consulted some 90 different commentaries, which he cites be-fore expressing his own opinion. The appendix includes most of the prefaces of the editions that had been consulted; fragments of lost text; studies of textual authenticity; an account of the relationship of the various editions; notes on the early commentaries, on the life of the author and on early sources. There is a bibliography of the works under reference.

(f) Liang Ch'i-hsiung 梁啓雄, *Han tzu ch'ien chieh* 韓子淺解, Peking: Chung hua, 1960. In his notes Liang Ch'i-hsiung selects the princi-pal points raised by Wang Hsien-shen and both earlier and later commentators, giving a summary of the conclusions without the supporting reasons; Liang's own suggestions are also included.

(g) T'ang Ching-chao 湯敬昭, Li Shih-an 李安仕 and others, *Han fei tzu chiao chu* 韓非子校注; Nanking: Chiang su jen min, 1982. This edition, in simplified characters, is the work of members of the Institute of Chemistry and other scholars at Nanking University. An explanatory passage is appended at the head of each chapter, and the text is accompanied by a paraphrase in modern Chinese. An appendix includes an index of proper names, a map and short notes on some of the editions.

9. Notes printed without the text

The following is a selection of the many publications of this type that have appeared, in addition to the notes of the well-known scholars Wang Nien-sun 王念孫 (1744–1832), Hung I-hsüan 洪頤煊 (1765–1837), Yü Yüeh 俞樾 (1821–1907) and Sun I-jang 孫詒讓 (1848–1908).

(a) Lu Wen-ch'ao 盧文弨 (1717–96), *Han fei tzu shih pu* 韓非子拾補; first published independently some time after 1736; included in the *Ch'ün shu shih pu* 群書拾補 in 1787.

(b) Ku Kuang-ch'i 顧廣圻 (1776–1835), *Han fei tzu chih wu* 韓非子識誤; completed in 1816, and included as an appendix in Wu Tzu's edition.

(c) T'ao Hung-ch'ing 陶鴻慶, in *Tu chu tzu cha chi* 讀諸子札記 (preface 1920); published in complete form Peking: Chung hua, 1959.

(d) Sun K'ai-ti 孫楷第, 'Tu Han fei tzu cha chi 讀韓非子札記', in *Pei p'ing t'u shu kuan yüeh k'an* III:6 (1926).

(e) Liu Shih-p'ei 劉師培 (1884–1919), *Han fei tzu chiao pu* 韓非子斠補, in *Liu Shen-shu hsien sheng i shu*, 1937.

10.   Translations

(a) Liao, W.K., *The complete works of Han fei-tzu*; London: Arthur Probsthain, vol.I, 1939 (reprinted 1959); vol.II, 1959.

(b) Watson, Burton, *Han Fei Tzu; basic writings*; New York and London: Columbia University Press, 1964.

11.   Japanese editions

A. *Kambun taikei*; no. 8, 1911, edited by Hattori Unokichi; annotation by Ōta Zensai.

B. *Kanseki kokujikai zensho*; nos. 24, 25, 1911; edited by Matsudaira Yasukuni.

D. *Kokuyaku kambun taisei*; no. 9, 1921, edited by Uno Tetsuto.
E. *Kambun sōsho*, 1928, edited by Koyanagi Shikita.
F. *Keisho taikō*; nos.19–22, 1938–39.
H. *Shinshaku kambun taikei*; nos.11,12, 1960,1964, edited by Takeuchi Teruo.
J. *Chūgoku no shisō*; no. 1, 1964, edited by Nishino Hiroyoshi and Ichikawa Hiroshi.
K. *Chūgoku koten bungaku taikei*; no. 5, 1968, edited by Kakimura Takashi.
L. *Chūgoku koten shinsho*, 1968, edited by Onozawa Sei'ichi.

In addition the work has been handled independently as follows:

(a) *Kampishi kaiko* 韓非子解詁, edited by Tsuda Gokō (Hōkei) 津田梧岡 (鳳卿) and written from dictation by Yasue Nobukimi 安江信君; preface, by Tsuda, dated 1816; printed *c.*1855. Chinese text with *Kambun* notation; notes also with *Kambun* notation.
(b) *Kampishi kōgi* 韓非子講義, editor unnamed; Tokyo: Kōbunsha, 1933; text with *Kambun* notation followed by Japanese version.
(c) Tsuneishi Shigeru 常石茂, *Kampishi*; Tokyo: Kadokawa bunko, nos. 2519–20, 1968; Japanese version without Chinese text.
(d) Honda Wataru 本田濟, *Kampishi*; Tokyo: Chikuma shobō, 1969; Japanese version without Chinese text.

12. Recent studies

The following items are selected from among a large number of publications; references to general works on Chinese philosophy are not included.

(a) Chou Chung-ling 周鍾靈, *Han fei tzu ti luo chi* 韓非子的邏輯, Peking: Jen min, 1958.
(b) Hsieh Yün-Fei 謝雲飛, *Han fei tzu hsi lun* 韓非子折論; Taipei: Ta lin shu tien, 1973.
(c) Wang Pang-hsiung 王邦雄, *Han fei tzu ti che hsüeh* 韓非子的哲學; Taipei: Ts'ang hai ts'ung k'an, 1977.
(d) Wang Hsiao-po 王曉波 and Chang Ch'un 張純, *Han fei tzu ssu hsiang ti li shih yen chiu* 韓非子思想的歷史研究; Taipei: Lien ching, 1983; second edition, Chung hua, 1986.
(e) Lundahl, Bertil, *Han Fei Zi: the Man and the Work* (Stockholm East Asian Monographs No. 4); Stockholm: Institute of Oriental Languages, Stockholm University, 1992. This full length study covers the historical and philosophical background; Han Fei's life and

works; and the authenticity of the various parts of the *Han fei tzu*.

(f) For a study of the content of the *Han fei tzu*, see also Liang Ch'i-ch'ao 梁啓超 (1873–1929), *Chung kuo liu ta cheng chih chia* 中國六大政治家 Shanghai: Kuang chih (1911), section 2.

13. Indexes

(a) Wallace Johnson, *A concordance to Han-Fei tzu (Han fei tzu yin te)*; San Francisco: Chinese materials Center Inc., Research Aids Series No. 13, 1975; references are to *Han fei tzu chi chieh* of Wang Hsien-shen (Taiwan: Shih chieh, 1955).

(b) Chou Chung-ling 周鍾靈, Shih Hsiao-shih 施孝適 and Hsü Wei-hsien 許惟賢, eds., *Han fei tzu so yin*; Peking: Chung hua, 1982. References are to the punctuated text printed in unabbreviated characters at the end of the volume. That text is based on Wu Tzu's version of the Ch'ien tao edition. Variant readings are given in the notes after each *p'ien*.

(c) *A Concordance to the Hanfeizi* 韓非子逐字索引, ed. D.C. Lau and Chen Fong Ching; *ICS* series, Hong Kong: Commercial Press, forthcoming 1996.

                                                                — Jean Levi

Han shih wai chuan 韓詩外傳

1. Content

The *Han shih wai chuan* is an heterogeneous collection of 306 anecdotes, moral disquisitions, prescriptive ethics and practical advice, each entry normally concluding with an appropriate quotation from the *Shih ching* which serves to reinforce the point of the story or argument. This is the extent of the relationship of the book to the *Shih ching*, to which it contributes neither commentary nor exegesis. *Han shu* 30, p. 1708 lists other works of the Han 韓 school of the *Shih ching* which are now lost, but which presumably performed that function; the *Han shih wai chuan* served to provide illustrations of one practical use of the poems, i.e. that of the illustrative quotation, as frequently used in works such as the *Hsün tzu*.

Although nominally attached to one of the classical texts, the materials used in the *Han shih wai chuan* are eclectic, deriving from writings of several philosophical schools. The *Hsün tzu* is a favoured source, but the *Chuang tzu*, *Han fei tzu* and *Lü shih ch'un ch'iu* are also used, as well as the *Yen tzu ch'un ch'iu*, the *Lao tzu* and the *Meng tzu*. The dominant tone is moralizing, but some amusing anecdotes lack any apparent ethical point. The absence of a concluding quotation from the *Shih ching* for twenty-four paragraphs suggests a defective text. The *Han shih wai chuan* is more a compilation than an original composition, judging from the fact that extant pre-Han texts supply more than a third of its material, some of them already complete with a *Shih ching* quotation. Parallel passages in other Han dynasty works, in particular the *Shuo yüan*, *Hsin hsü* and *Lieh nü chuan* 列女傳, show that the *Han shih wai chuan* was itself a source and possibly the inspiration for other anthologies of excerpts which were compiled for different purposes.

2. Date of composition and authenticity

The book is attributed to Han Ying 韓嬰 , an academician (*po shih* 博士) of the time of Wen ti 文帝 (reigned 180–157 B.C.), who lived to dispute

with Tung Chung-shu 董仲舒 (*c.*179–*c.*104) in the presence of Wu ti 武
帝 (reigned 141–87). His biography (*Shih chi* 121, p. 3124 and *Han shu* 88,
p. 3613) provides no more clues than these to his dates, which must lie
between 200 and 120 B.C.. The *Han shih wai chuan* should therefore date
from *c.*150 B.C..

The attribution to Han Ying has never been challenged, and it is hard
to conceive of a motive for a forger to put together such a work. However, the integrity of the text is in some doubt, since *Han shu* 30, p. 1708
lists a work entitled *Han wai chuan* 韓外傳 in six *chüan* and one named
Han nei chuan 韓內傳 in four *chüan*, and the biography of Han Ying in
the *Han shu* also mentions the two texts. By the time of the bibliography
of the *Sui shu* (32, pp. 915–16) the *Nei chuan* had disappeared, although
commentators of the T'ang period quote a few lines which they attribute to a *Han shih nei chuan*. The *wai chuan* is listed with 10 *chüan* in the
catalogues of the *Sui shu*, both T'ang histories (*Chiu T'ang shu* 46, p.
1970; *Hsin T'ang shu* 57, p. 1429), the *Sung shih* (202, p. 5045) and that of
Fujiwara Sukeyo. All modern editions contain 10 *chüan*.

It has been suggested by Yang Shu-ta 楊樹達 (*Han shu pu chu pu cheng*
漢書補注補正; Shanghai: Shang wu, 1925, p. 28) that the two texts, *wai
chuan* and *nei chuan*, were combined under the single title of *Han shih
wai chuan*, as there was never any difference in the kind of material that
they contained, neither being a work of exegesis. Further evidence for
such an amalgamation has been found in the sequence of quotations
from the *Shih ching*, though this indicates that more was involved than
the simple juxtaposition that was suggested by Yang; see Hightower, as
under 5 (a) below. A number of quotations attributed to the *Han shih wai
chuan* in the T'ang encyclopaedias and by T'ang commentators on the
classics and histories are not to be found in the received text. There are
157 quotations from the work in the *T'ai p'ing yü lan*, 23 of which are
now missing.

3.   Editions

(a) The earliest known published text was a Sung edition described by
    Hung Mai 洪 邁 (1746–1809) as dating from the Ch'ing li period
    (1041–48). Mao Chin 毛晉 (1599–1659) believed that he had a copy of
    this edition, which he reprinted in the *Chin tai pi shu*. Of the several
    Ming editions, one by Shen Pien-chih 沈辨之, which is reproduced
    in the *Ssu pu ts'ung k'an* series, is derived from a Yüan print (preface
    by Ch'ien Wei-shan 錢惟善, 1355).

(b) Critical editions, with commentary, were published independently
    by Chao Huai-yü 趙懷玉 (1747–1823) in his *I yu sheng chai* 亦有生

齋, with prefaces dated in 1790 (reprinted in the *Lung hsi ching she ts'ung shu*), and by Chou T'ing-ts'ai 周廷寀, as *Han shih wai chuan chiao chu* 韓詩外傳校注 (reprinted in *An hui ts'ung shu*), with preface dated 1791. The second of these, by Chou, is the more conservative text, and it was taken as the basis for the combined edition of the two commentaries, which was brought out in 1875 by Wu T'ang 吳棠 (*Wang san i chai* 望三益齋; reprinted in *Chi fu ts'ung shu* and, with punctuation, in the *Ts'ung shu chi ch'eng*; also typeset by Shanghai: Shang wu, 1917). An edition of unknown provenance that includes most of the parallel passages was published in 1818 by Ch'en Shih-k'o 陳士珂, under the title *Han shih wai chuan shu cheng* 韓詩外傳疏證 (in the *Wen yüan lou ts'ung shu*).

(c) Other *ts'ung shu* which carry the *Han shih wai chuan* include the *Han Wei ts'ung shu, Kuang Han Wei ts'ung shu, San shih san chung ts'ung shu*.

(d) Hsü Wei-yü 許維遹 (1905–51), *Han shih wai chuan chi shih* 韓詩外傳集釋; Peking: Chung hua, 1980; published posthumously, with punctuated text in unabbreviated characters, and annotation that includes some uniquely available material and Hsü's own views.

(e) Lai Yen-yüan 賴炎元, *Han shih wai chuan chin chu chin i* 韓詩外傳今注今譯; annotated and punctuated text, with a version in modern Chinese; Taipei: Taiwan Shang wu, 1972.

4. Annotations available without text

(a) Sun I-jang 孫詒讓, in *Cha i* 2, deals with ten passages.
(b) Yü Yüeh 俞樾, in *Tu Han shih wai chuan* 讀韓詩外傳, proposes emendations for 22 difficult passages; see *Ch'ü yüan tsa tsuan* 曲園雜纂 17, (*Ch'un tsai t'ang ch'üan shu*).
(c) Chao Shan-i 趙善詒, in *Han shih wai chuan pu cheng* 韓詩外傳補正 (Ch'angsha: Shang wu,1938), treats difficult or uncertain passages from almost every paragraph of the text supporting his comments and emendations with citations from parallel passages, and always referring to previous annotations of the same passage (in *Kuo hsueh hsiao ts'ung shu*). His work is incorporated in Lai Yen-yüan's *Han shih wai chuan k'ao cheng* (see item 5 (b) below).

5. Recent studies and research aids

(a) Hightower, James R., 'The *Han-shih wai-chuan* and the *san chia shih*'; *HJAS* 11 (1948), 241–310. This article develops the suggestion of Yang Shu-ta that the present text of the *Han shih wai chuan* combines the six original *chüan* of that work and the four *chüan* of the no longer extant *nei chuan*. It traces the history of the Three Schools of the *Shih ching* in Han times.

(b) Lai Yen-yüan, *Han shih wai chuan k'ao cheng* 韓詩外傳考徵, 2 vols.; Taipei: Shih fan ta hsüeh, 1963. Volume 1 is a detailed study of the Han school of the *Shih ching*, editions of the *Han shih wai chuan*, collation notes and differences between *Han shih* readings and those of the other schools, including the *Mao shih*. Volume 2 examines parallels to *Han shih wai chuan* passages from earlier and later texts and concludes with an exhaustive list of attributions to the *Han shih wai chuan* that are not found in modern editions.

(c) Nishimura Fumiko 西村富美子, 'Kanshi gaiden no ichi kōsatsu' 韓詩外傳の一考察; *Chūgoku bungaku hō* 中國文學報 19 (1963), 1–16. This article argues that Han Ying wrote the *Han shih wai chuan* for the edification of Liu Shun 劉舜 (king of Ch'ang shan 常山 from 145 to 114 B.C., whom he served as tutor).

6. Translation

Hightower, James R., *Han-shih wai-chuan, Han Ying's illustrations of the didactic application of the Book of Songs*; Cambridge, Mass.: Harvard University Press, 1952; a complete, annotated translation.

7. Japanese edition

By Toriyama Shūgaku 鳥山崧岳 punctuated with *kaeriten*, 1759.

8. Indexes

(a) Toyoshima Mutsu 豐島睦, *Kanshi gaiden sakuin* 韓詩外傳索引. Hiroshima: Hijiyama joshi tanki daigaku, 1972; reproduces the entire text, based on Toriyama's edition (see (7) above), with numbered paragraphs; essentially a concordance, but without entries for final particles.

(b) *A Concordance to the Hanshi waizhuan* 韓詩外傳逐字索引, ed. D.C. Lau and Chen Fong Ching; *ICS* series, Hong Kong: Commercial Press, 1992.

— James R. Hightower

Han shu 漢書

1. Content

The *Han shu*, often called *Ch'ien Han shu* 前漢書, describes the history of
the Former or Western Han Dynasty, beginning with the early life of its
founder, Liu Pang 劉邦 in about 210 B.C., and ending with the fall of
Wang Mang 王莽 in A.D. 23. The *Han shu* is the work of Pan Ku 班固,
tzu 字 Meng-chien 孟堅 (32–92), inspired by the work of his father, Pan
Piao 班彪 (A.D. 3–54). The latter, dissatisfied with those parts of the *Shih
chi* that dealt with the history of the Han dynasty, wrote 'several tens of
p'ien' (perhaps 65) called *Hou chuan* 後傳 'Later traditions'. This work is
lost, if it ever existed as an independent text, and a few passages in the
present *Han shu* are its sole testimony.

The *Han shu* consists of one hundred *chüan*, i.e. twelve imperial annals,
(*pen chi* 本紀), eight tables (*piao* 表), ten treatises (*chih* 志), and seventy
biographies and accounts of foreign peoples, *lieh chuan* 列傳. The
treatises contain several innovations when compared with those of the
Shih chi: new ones have been added on the organisation of the administration (19, *Pai kuan kung ch'ing piao* 百官公卿表), on the development
in penal law (23, *Hsing fa chih* 刑法志), on administrative geography (28,
Ti li chi 地理志), and on the extant literature (30, *I wen chih* 藝文志).

In his division of the material Pan Ku followed the example of Ssu-ma
Ch'ien's (?145–?86 B.C.) 司馬遷 *Shih chi*, only omitting the latter's category of 'hereditary families' *shih chia* 世家.

2. Date of composition and authenticity

Pan Piao compiled his *Hou chuan* sometime after A.D. 36. Pan Ku started
work on the *Han shu* shortly after his father's death in A.D. 54, but this
was interrupted about A.D. 60. During the years 62 to 74 he was ordered
by the emperor to take part in the writing of the history of the founding
of the Later Han. Upon the completion of his task he continued to work
on the *Han shu*. When he died in A.D. 92, the eight tables and the chapter
on astronomy (26, *T'ien wen chih* 天文志) were still unfinished. These

parts were completed by his sister Pan Chao 班昭 (?48–?116), eventually assisted by Ma Hsü 馬續, who was known as a mathematician in his youth, and was still active as a general in 141.

There have never been any doubts about the authenticity of the *Han shu*. Like any other ancient work, the text has suffered in the course of its transmission in manuscript and in print, but not extensively.

The early commentaries to the *Han shu*, written between the 2nd and the 6th century, were no longer transmitted independently once they had been collected by Yen Shih-ku 顏師古 (581–645) who carefully lists them in his Foreword (*Hsü li* 敘例) to the *Han shu*. He completed his commentary in 641, and it is now included in all editions. Two copies of the book appear in Fuijwara Sukeyo's catalogue; one, in 115 *chüan*, included notes by Ying Shao 應劭 (*c.* 140 to before 204), one, in 120 *chüan*, included Yen Shih-ku's notes.

3. Sources

It is generally assumed that Pan Ku copied the chapters concerning the early history of the Han from the *Shih chi*, only altering the wording occasionally and adding incidental new material. This is nowhere stated in the ancient texts, and some possibility remains that it was the *Han shu* which instead served as the basis for the reconstruction of a badly damaged *Shih chi*. Pan Ku's sources are to a large extent official documents, for he was given access to the court archives. He is therefore able to quote at length from imperial edicts as well as from memorials to the throne. In many cases he reproduces or extracts the details of law suits or the service records of military men. The Tables of the kings and the nobles (13–18) are either copies or extracts of their official genealogies, whereas his chronological list of the holders of high offices with its detailed dates (19) must have been taken from official files.

Pan Ku also made considerable use of the works of other authors. The Treatise on Harmonics and the Calendar (*Lü li chih* 律曆志) is based on a work by Liu Hsin 劉歆 (46 B.C.–A.D. 23), whereas the latter's descriptive catalogue of the imperial library constitutes the basis of the Treatise on Literature (30, *I wen chih*). The aforementioned Ma Hsü was the author of the Treatise on Astronomy (26, *T'ien wen chih*). The Memoir on the Western Regions (96, *Hsi yü chuan* 西域傳) is undoubtedly based on reports from the Chinese officials stationed in Central Asia. In the biographies of literary figures, especially poets, Pan Ku inserts extensive quotations from their works.

4. Editions

For surviving manuscript fragments, on wood, of edicts whose text is included in the *Han shu*, see Loewe, *Records of Han Administration* (Cambridge: Cambridge University Press, 1967), vol. II, p. 230. For a fragment of manuscript text, on paper, which carries an abbreviated version of passages to be found in *Han shu* 96A, p. 3981, see *Wen wu* 1985.8, 54–55 and Plate 1.

An account of the manuscripts of isolated chapters that have been preserved and of the earliest prints (Sung, Yüan and Ming) is provided by Kurata Junnosuke (see (5) below).

The principal editions are:

(a) of 1035, the earliest extant complete print, sometimes called the Ching yu 景祐 edition (after the Ching yu reign period); reproduced in the Po-na series of the *Ssu pu ts'ung k'an*, and used as the basis for both the *Ssu pu pei yao* and the *K'ai ming* editions of the histories;

(b) of the Ch'ing-yüan period (1195–1200), called the Liu Chih-wen 劉之問 edition after one of the editors, or the Chien-an 建安 edition after his prefecture;

(c) the Nan chien 南監 or Nanking Academy edition of 1529–1533;

(d) the Wu ying tien 武英殿, or 'Palace' edition of 1739, reproduced in the T'ung wen 同文 edition of the twenty-four histories (1884), and in the Han fen lou 涵芬樓 edition of the Commercial Press in 1916.

Another line of transmission is seen in:

(e) Mao Chin's 毛晉 *Chi ku ko* 汲古閣 edition of 1641, based on an unknown Ming edition;

(f) the Chin ling shu chü 金陵書局 edition of 1869, made using the printing blocks of (e) preceding.

The *Chi ku ko* edition of 1641 was used as the basis for the *Han shu pu chu* 漢書補注 compiled by Wang Hsien-ch'ien 王先謙 (1842–1918), published in Ch'ang-sha in 1900; this was reproduced, four pages on one, by the I-wen publishers in Taiwan (1955). This work includes the commentary by Yen Shih-ku, and in addition Wang's own remarks and those of a host of other scholars, whose notes on the *Han shu* had appeared since 641. It is an indispensable tool, though caution is sometimes necessary, because Wang occasionally abbreviates the statements that he quotes.

The *Han shu pu chu* was reprinted in several newly composed editions: in the nineteen twenties by the Wen-jui lou 文瑞樓 Press in

Shanghai with punctuation *more sinico;* in 1941 in the Basic Sinological Series, *Kuo hsüeh chi pen ts'ung shu:* and most recently in Peking in 1983 by the Chung hua shu chü reproducing the Hsü shou t'ang 虛受堂 woodblock edition of 1900, four pages on one.

The text of the *Han shu* and that of Yen Shih-ku's commentary as found in the *Han shu pu chu* were used for the punctuated edition of the *Han shu* in the Chung hua shu chü (Peking) series in 1962. Although Wang Hsien-ch'ien's own additional notes have been omitted, the editors of this new edition have added text critical notes at the end of each chapter, often, but not exclusively, based on Wang Hsien-ch'ien's suggestions.

Annotations printed without the text include:

(a) An anonymous *Han shu shu cheng* 漢書疏證 in manuscript was published in facsimile by the Naigai 內外 Press in Tokyo in or shortly after 1939. This is perhaps a work by Hang Shih-chün 杭世駿 (1696–1773). See the remarks by M. A. N. Loewe, as cited under (5) below.

(b) Yang Shu-ta 楊樹達, *Han shu k'uei kuan* 漢書窺管 (Peking: K'o hsüeh, 1955); 662 pages of text critical and explanatory notes, with direct reference to the pagination of the first edition of *Han shu pu chü*.

(c) Ch'en Chih 陳直 (died 1980), *Han shu hsin cheng* 漢書新證 (Tientsin: Jenmin; 1st ed. 1959, 208 pp.; 2nd ed. 1979, 496 pp.). The author's remarks, often based on archaeological evidence, follow the pagination of the *Ssu pu ts'ung k'an* edition.

(d) Shih Chih-mien 施之勉, *Han shu pu chu pien cheng* 漢書補注辨證 (Kowloon: Hsin Ya Yen chiu so 新亞研究所, 1961); 368 pages with about 1100 notes of varying length, both text critical and explanatory; intended to correct Wang Hsien-ch'ien's *Han shu pu chu*, but without reference to the studies of Yang Shu-ta or Ch'en Chih.

(e) Kano Naoki 狩野直喜. *Han shu pu chu pu* 漢書補注補, notes in Chinese to the first twenty-two *chüan* of the *Han shu*, *Tōhō Gakuhō* (Kyoto): 9:1 (1938), 1–9; 10:1 (1939), 35–48; 10:3 (1939), 1–12; 10:4 (1940), 1–9; 11:2 (1940), 1–12; 11:4 (1941), 1–4; 12:1 (1941), 34–48; 12:2 (1941), 1–10.

5.   Recent studies and research aids

(a) Kurata Junnosuke 倉田淳之助, *Kanjo hanpon-kō* 漢書板本考, in *Tōhō gakuhō* 27 (Kyoto, 1957), pp. 255–284.

(b) Loewe, M.A.N., 'Some recent editions of the Ch'ien *Han shu*', *Asia Major* X (1963), pp. 162–172.

6. Bibliographies to *Han shu* studies

(a) Ma Hsien-hsing 馬先醒, *Han shih lun chu lei mu* 漢史論著類目, in *Chinese Culture* (Taipei), vol. X.3 (1969), pp. 103–170, and X.4, pp. 105–159; vol. XI.1 (1970), pp. 124–178, and XI.2, pp. 69–187.

(b) Sanae Yoshio 早苗良雄, *Kan-dai kenkyū bunken mokuroku hōbun-hen* 漢代研究文獻目錄邦文編 (Kyoto: Hōyū shoten, 1979). This is an index to modern Japanese books and articles.

7. Other studies

(a) Lo Tchen-ying, *Une famille d'historiens et son oeuvre; les formes et les méthodes historiques en Chine* (Paris: Paul Guethner, 1938); Université de Lyon: Bibliotheca Franco-sinica lugdunensis. Études et documents publiés par l'Institut franco-chinois de Lyon, IX.

(b) Swann, Nancy Lee, *Pan Chao, foremost woman scholar of China, 1st century A.D.* (New York: Century, 1932)

(c) Hulsewé, A.F.P., 'Notes on the historiography of the Han period', in W.G. Beasley and E.G. Pulleyblank, eds., *Historians of China and Japan* (London: Oxford University Press, 1961), pp. 31–43.

(d) van der Sprenkel, O.B., *Pan Piao, Pan Ku and the Han History*. Occasional Paper 3, The Australian University Centre of Oriental Studies (Canberra, 1964).

(e) Hervouet, Yves, 'La valeur relative des textes du *Che-ki* et du *Han chou*; in *Mélanges de Sinologie offerts à Monsieur Paul Demiéville* (Études chinoises XX, Paris: Bibliothèque de l'Institut des Hautes Études Chinoises, 1974, Vol. II, 55–76).

(f) Hulsewé, A.F.P., 'The problem of the authenticity of *Shih Chi* ch. 123, the memoir on Ta Yüan'; *TP* 61:1–3 (1975), 83–147.

(g) Sinicyn, E.P., *Ban' Gu — istorik drevnego Kitaya*, Moscow: Nauka, 1975.

(h) Studies on particular *Han shu* chapters, assembled in *Erh shih wu shih pu pien* 二十五史補編 (Shanghai: K'ai ming, 1936; reprinted by the Chung hua shu chü in Peking, 1956), vol. I, pp. 0135–1385; vol. II, pp. 1387–1774.

8. Translations

A. *Western languages*

There does not exist a complete translation of the *Han shu*. The following list includes only translations that have appeared in book form.

chüan

1–5   Dubs, Homer H., with the collaboration of Jen T'ai and P'an

Lo-chi, *History of the Former Han Dynasty*, vol. I (Baltimore: Waverly Press, 1938).

6–10   as above, vol. II (1944).

11–12   Dubs and P'an, vol. III (1955), pp. 15–87.

22 (partial)   Hulsewé, A.F.P., *Remnants of Han Law* (Leiden: E.J.Brill, 1955), pp. 429–455.

23   as above, pp. 309–422.

24   Swann, Nancy Lee, *Food and money in ancient China: the earliest economic history of China to A.D. 25. Han shu 24, with related texts Han shu 91 and Shih Chi 129.* (Princeton, N.J.: Princeton University Press, 1950), pp. 109–359.

26 (partial)   Eberhard, Wolfram, *Beiträge zur kosmologischen Spekulation der Chinesen der Han-Zeit.* Inaug.-diss. Berlin, 1933; Bässler Archiv, XVI. 1–2.

54, 63, 65,   Watson, Burton, *Courtier and Commoner in Ancient China:*
67, 68, 71,   *Selections from the History of the Former Han by Pan Ku* (New
74, 78, 92,   York and London: Columbia University Press, 1974).
97A–B

52, 54, 70,   Taskin, V.S., *Materialy po istorii Syunnu po kitaiskim*
94A–B,   *istočnikam* (Moscow: Nauka, 1968–1973), vol. I and II.
96A

(57)   Hervouet, Yves, *Le Chapitre 117 du Che-ki; biographie de Sseu-ma Siang-jou* (Paris: Presses universitaires de France, 1972). This work is a translation of the *Shih chi* text that is parallel to *Han shu* 57.

61   Hulsewé, A.F.P. and M.A.N. Loewe, *China in Central Asia; the early stage: 125 B.C.–A.D. 23. An annotated translation of chapters 61 and 96 of the History of the Former Han dynasty* (Leiden: E.J. Brill, 1979).

68   Jongchell, Arvid, *Huo Kuang och hans tid* (Göteborg: Elander, 1930).

88 (partial)   Tjan Tjoe Som, *Po Hu T'ung, The Comprehensive Discussions in the White Tiger Hall*, vol. I (Leiden: E.J. Brill. 1949), p. 85 ff.

91   Swann, *Food and money* (see above), pp. 414–462.

94   de Groot, J.J.M., *Chinesische Urkunden zur Geschichte Asiens*, vol. I: *Die Hunnen der vorchristlichen Zeit* (Berlin and Leipzig: de Gruyter, 1926).

94   Taskin, *Materialy* (see above).

96   de Groot, J.J.M., *Chinesische Urkunden zur Geschichte Asiens*, Vol. II: *Die Westlande Chinas in der vorchristlichen Zeit* (Berlin and Leipzig: de Gruyter, 1926). Hulsewé and Loewe, *China in Central Asia* (see above), pp. 71–203.

99   Stange, Hans O.H., *Die Monographie über Wang Mang*. Abhandlungen für die Kunde des Morgenlandes XXIII, (Leipzig: Brockhaus, 1938).

          Sargent, Clyde Bailey, *Wang Mang, a translation of the official account of his rise to power as given in the History of the Former Han dynasty* (Shanghai: printed by the Graphic Art Book Co., 1950); 99A only.

          Dubs, *The History of the Former Han Dynasty*, vol. III (see above), pp. 125–474.

B.   *Japanese.*

chüan

23   Uchida Tomoo 內田智雄, *Kanjo keihōshi* 漢書刑法志 Kyoto: Dōshisha University, 1958.
          Uchida Tomoo, ed. *Yakuchū Chūkoku rekidai keihōshi* 譯注中國歷代刑法志 Tokyo: Sobunsha, 1964), pp. 1–57.

24   Katō Shigeru 加藤繁, *Shiki Heijun-sho Kanjo Shokka-shi yakuchū* 史記平準書漢書食貨志譯注 (Tokyo: Iwanami, 1942), pp. 115–221.

30   Suzuki Yoshijirō 鈴木由次郎, *Kanjo geimonshi* 漢書藝文志 (Tokyo: Meitoku shuppansha, 1968).

For a translation of the whole work, with brief notes, see Otake Takeo 小竹武夫 *Kanjo* 漢書, 3 volumes; Tokyo: Chikuma, 1977–79.

9.   Indexes

(a) *Combined indices to Han shu and the notes of Yen Shih-ku and Wang Hsien-ch'ien.* Harvard-Yenching Index no. 36 (Peking 1940; reprinted Taipei 1966). This index is based on the T'ung wen edition.

(b) Wong Fook-luen 黃福巒, ed., *Index to Han shu* (The Chinese University of Hong Kong, 1966). This is an index to both the *Ssu pu ts'ung k'an* and the *Ssu pu pei yao* editions of the *Han shu*. The indexed items are divided into twenty-five groups such as personal names, geographical names, natural phenomena, wearing apparel, official titles etc., the items being arranged according to number of strokes.

(c) Wei Lien-k'o 魏連科, ed. *Han shu jen ming so yin* 漢書人名索引. (Peking: Chung hua, 1979). This includes references to names that appear in the text but not the commentaries. References are to the punctuated edition (Peking: Chung hua, 1962). Entries are listed according to the four corner system.

(d) *Twenty-five Dynastic Histories Full Text Data Base* 廿五史全文資料庫; Taipei: Institute of History and Philology, 1988.

— A.F.P. Hulsewé

Ho kuan tzu 鶡冠子

1. Content

The *Ho kuan tzu* purports to be a Taoist philosophical treatise of the Chou period, attributed to a hermit of Ch'u who wrote under the pseudonym of 'Pheasant Cap Master'. Although the identity of Ho kuan tzu is not known, it is thought that he was a military officer; for, beginning at least in the Warring States period, snow pheasant plumes, symbolic of ferocity, were worn in a warrior's cap. The present version of the text is a miscellany of essays on Huang-Lao philosophy, legalist doctrine and military strategy, tempered by Confucian moralism. Some of the chapters (nos. 7–9 and 14–15) consist of dialogues between Ho kuan tzu and a general of Chao named P'ang Hsüan 龐煖 (*c.* 295–*c.* 240 B.C.). A major theme that is expressed throughout the text is the Taoist idea of the cyclical movement of nature, and the necessity for the ruler to bring histhought and action into harmony with the cosmic process, particularly the workings of heaven, which by its constant movement establishes the norms (*fa* 法) for human society. The military chapters stress the importance of the ruler's attracting the most able advisers (preferably those who were 'one hundred times better than oneself') and following the precepts of propriety, duty, loyalty and fidelity.

2. Date of composition and authenticity

The book was listed twice in the *Ch'i lüeh* 七略, once under *Tao chia* and once under *ping ch'üan* 兵權. When Pan Ku 班固 (32–92) incorporated the *Ch'i lüeh* into the *Han shu*, he listed the *Ho kuan tzu*, in 1 *p'ien*, under *Tao chia*, and eliminated the entry from the category of *ping ch'üan* (see *Han shu* 30, pp. 1730, 1757).

The entry in the *Han shu* is thus for a book of 1 *p'ien*; later catalogues (e.g., *Sui shu* 34, p. 1001, *Chiu T'ang shu* 47, p. 2029, *Hsin T'ang shu* 59, p. 1516) list it as a work of 3 *chüan*; and the received text is likewise of 3 *chüan*. For this reason, some scholars have concluded that portions of the *Ho kuan tzu* must have been forged after the Han dynasty. Thus Liu Tsung-yüan 柳宗元 (773–819) noted that many lines of the 'Shih ping' 世兵 chapter are virtually identical with lines in Chia I's 賈誼 (201–169

B.C.) Owl Rhapsody ('Fu niao fu' 鵩鳥賦), and concluded that 'some overzealous person must have forged the book' (see *Liu Ho-tung chi* 柳河東集, *SPPY* ed., 4. 10b–11a). The 'Owl Rhapsody' passage of the *Ho kuan tzu*, which is a poetic discourse on the vagaries of fate, is actually an intrusion into a treatise on military tactics and is very likely a later addition to the text.

The discrepancy between the entries in the *Han shu* and the later catalogues is less significant than might be supposed. It is possible that the text of 1 *p'ien* contained only the Taoist sections of the work, and that the *Ho kuan tzu* which Pan Ku eliminated from the category of *ping ch'üan* contained that portion of the work which is concerned with military strategy. It is even conceivable that the portions of the text that contain the discourses of P'ang Hsüan may have been drawn from a text of that name, which is listed by Pan Ku twice; first as a work of 2 *p'ien* under *Tsung heng chia* 縱橫家 (*Han shu* 30, p. 1737); and secondly as a work of 3 *p'ien* under *Ping ch'üan* 兵權 (*Han shu* 30, p. 1757).

Use of substitute characters for *cheng* 正 and *cheng* 政 in chapters 1 and 2 (see Wu Kuang, as cited under (6) below, pp. 157f.) shows that those parts of the work must be earlier than Former Han, to which the rest of the material may be dated. The work was apparently unknown to Ssu-ma Ch'ien 司馬遷 (?145–?86 B.C.), who cites Chia Tzu 賈子 (i.e., Chia I) but not *Ho kuan tzu* as the source of four lines that are in the 'Owl Rhapsody' interpolation (see *Shih chi* 61, p. 2127). In addition to the intrusion from the 'Owl Rhapsody', part of the 'Shih ping' chapter is virtually identical with Lu Chung-lien's 魯仲連 letter to the king of Yen (*Chan kuo ts'e* 13. 2a–4b (*SPPY* ed.) and *Shih chi* 83, pp. 2465–66), and much of the chapter 'Po hsüan' 博選 is adapted from a Warring States' attempt at persuasion (*Chan kuo ts'e* 29. 8a). Several passages are also similar to lines in the *Ching fa* 經法, which was discovered at Ma-wang-tui 馬王堆 (see *Ma-wang-tui Han mu po shu* 馬王堆漢墓帛書, vol. 1, Peking: Wen wu, 1980, notes to transcription, p. 44; and Li Hsüeh-ch'in 李學勤, 'Ma-wang-tui po shu yü "Ho kuan tzu" 馬王堆帛書與 "鶡冠子"', in *Jianghan kaogu* 7 (1983: 2), 51–6). Although there is insufficient evidence with which to determine which text may be drawing from which, the textual parallels at least prove that some of the *Ho kuan tzu* material, if not the *Ho kuan tzu* text itself, existed in Former Han.

3. Textual history

All extant editions contain 19 *p'ien*. Han Yü 韓愈 (768–824) saw a text of 16 *p'ien* in which there were *lacunae* and errors (see Ma T'ung-po 馬通

伯, ed., *Han Ch'ang-li wen chi chiao chu* 韓昌黎文集校注; Shanghai: Ku tien, 1957, p. 21). Ch'ao Kung-wu 晁公武 (d. 1171) extracted a text of 3 *chüan* (19 *p'ien*) from a text of 8 *chüan* that had included 3 *chüan* (13 *p'ien*) of interpolations from the *Mo tzu* and 2 *chüan* (19 *p'ien*) of discursive essays from the post-Han period. More recently Fu Tseng-hsiang 傅澄 湘 (1872–1950) discovered a Tun-huang manuscript (unpublished) of the first *chüan* that consists of the first 8 *p'ien* and half of *p'ien* no. 9; the text also has a commentary by an unnamed scholar from the pre-Sui period (see Fu Tseng-hsiang, *Ts'ang yüan ch'ün shu t'i chi hsü chi* 藏園群 書題記續集; Peking: 1938, 2. 37a–38a).

4. Editions

(a) The extant printed editions are all based on a text in 3 *chüan* with commentary prepared by Lu Tien 陸佃 (1042–1102). Lu's commentary, with the complete text, exists in:

  (i) the *Tao tsang*;
  (ii) *Hsüeh chin t'ao yüan*; this text was reprinted in the *Ssu pu pei yao* series;
  (iii) *Wu ying tien chü chen pan ts'ung shu*;
  (iv) *Tzu hui*; reprinted, with punctuation, in the *Ts'ung shu chi ch'eng* series.

(b) The *Ssu pu ts'ung k'an* text; reprint of a Ming facsimile of a Sung edition of unknown provenance.

(c) Chang Chin-ch'eng 張金城, 'Ho kuan tzu chien shu 鶡冠子箋疏'; in *Kuo li T'ai wan shih fan ta hsüeh kuo wen yen chiu suo chi k'an* 國立臺 灣師範大學國文研究所集刊 19 (1975), 641–793; the most extensive commentary on the complete text.

5. Annotations without text

(a) Yü Yüeh 俞樾 (1821–1907), 'Tu Ho kuan tzu 讀鶡冠子'; in *Ch'ü yüan tsa tsuan* 曲園雜纂 20. 1a–9a.

(b) Sun I-jang 孫詒讓 (1848–1908); see *Cha i*.

6. Recent studies

(a) Sun Jen-ho 孫人和, 'Ho kuan tzu chü cheng 鶡冠子舉正'; *Kuo li Pei p'ing t'u shu kuan yüeh k'an* 國立北平圖書館月刊 3:2 (1929), 159–66.

(b) Hosokawa Kazutoshi 細川一敏, 'Katsu Kanshi to Kansho Kōrō shi-sō to no kankei to sono igi 鶡冠子と漢初黄老思想との關係とそ

の意義'; *Bunkei ronsō, Hirosaki daigaku bungakubu* 文經論叢弘前大
學文學部 14:2 (1979), 1–14.

(c) Ch'en K'o-ming 陳克明, 'Shih lun Ho kuan tzu yü Huang Lao ssu
hsiang ti kuan hsi 試論鶡冠子與黃老思想的關係'; in *Che hsüeh
shih lun ts'ung* 哲學史論叢, Ch'ang-ch'un: Chi lin jen min, 1980, pp.
224–44.

(d) Ōgata Toru 大形徹, 'Katsu kanshi—fukyū no kokka wo gensō shita
inja no sho 鶡冠子不朽の國家を幻想した隱者の書'; *Tōhō shūkyō*
東方宗教 59 (1982), 43–65.

(e) Wu Kuang 吳光, *Huang Lao chih hsüeh t'ung lun* 黃老之學通論;
Hang-chou: Che chiang jen min, 1985.

(f) Peerenboom, R.P., '*Heguanzi* and Huang-Lao Thought'; *EC* 16 (1991),
169–86.

7. Translations

(a) Rand, Christopher C., 'Chinese Military Thought and Philosophical
Taoism'; *Monumenta Serica* 34 (1979–80), 206–10; translation of short
excerpts.

(b) Neuberger, K.K., *Hoh-kuan tsï*; Frankfurt, 1986; annotated German
translation of chapters 7–9, 14–16 and 19.

8. Index

A Concordance to the Heguanzi, Wenshi zhenjing and Wei guzi 鶡冠子, 文始
眞經, 鬼谷子逐字索引, ed. D.C. Lau and Chen Fong Ching; *ICS* series,
Hong Kong: Commercial Press, forthcoming 1995.

— David R. Knechtges

(The editor is indebted to the late A.C. Graham for information commu-
nicated privately and incorporated above; see his article 'A neglected
pre-Han philosophical text: *Ho-kuan-tzu*'; *BSOAS* 52:3 (1989), 497–509).

Hsiao ching 孝經

1. Nature and structure

The *Hsiao ching* is a comparatively small work, of not more than two thousand characters, dealing with the virtue of *hsiao* 'filial piety' in its predictable contexts, i.e., with respect to one's behaviour towards parents and other seniors, and also in connection with the comparable attitude of fealty and duty one is traditionally called upon to show towards one's lord (*chün* 君). The work begins with Confucius giving a short lecture on the fundamental nature of *hsiao* to his disciple Tseng tzu 曾子 (Tseng Ts'an 曾參), who appears waiting in attendance on his master. It continues in a didactic, sometimes aphoristic, vein with comments on filial piety and allied virtues as they ostensibly characterized a 'golden age' of past kings, and as they ought, according to Confucius, to be practised in the socially and politically disrupted age of his own time. Tseng tzu injects comments or raises questions intermittently allowing Confucius to carry the discussion forward. No other one of Confucius' disciples figures in the text.

The text is in nine *chüan*, divided into eighteen sections (*chang* 章), but not in a regular two-to-one ratio. Each section is either a single dialogue between Confucius and Tseng tzu, or what appears to be a continuation of an immediately preceding dialogue. Typically each section ends with a short citation from the *Shih ching*; in one case from the *Shang shu* and in seven cases without such a citation at all. All cited lines from those classics conform exactly with the received versions of the texts from which they are taken, and offer no textual variants.

The *Hsiao ching* bears a general similarity in style and context to the 'Tseng tzu wen' 曾子問 sections of the *Li chi* but differs primarily in that Tseng tzu's questions and Confucius' answers here never stray far from the subject of filial piety, whereas in the *Li chi* the 'Tseng tzu wen' sections are concerned largely with matters of ceremony and ritual, especially funeral and burial rites. The two texts complement each other in content, and resemble each other in style. To that extent they might be regarded as reflecting a contemporary and homogeneous provenance.

2.   Origin of the text

Because the *Hsiao ching* appears in large part to be a record of questions
and answers between Confucius and Tseng tzu, it was early on assumed
that Confucius or perhaps Tseng tzu was the author. The *T'ai p'ing yü
lan* ch. 610, for example, cites two apocryphal texts, the *Hsiao ching kou
ming chüeh* 孝經鉤命訣 and the *Hsiao ching chung ch'i* 孝經中契 (neither
now extant) that attribute authorship to Confucius. *Shih chi* 67, p. 2205,
says that Confucius *tso hsiao ching* 作孝經, which is interpreted conventionally to mean that Confucius composed the *Hsiao ching* orally, and
recited it to Tseng tzu who in turn wrote it down.

Between the Han and the T'ang periods the prevalent opinion was
that Tseng tzu wrote the book, either as a consequence of Confucius'
direct recitation or as a later record of those earlier dialogues that he
had had with Confucius on the theme of filial piety. By Sung times it
was suggested instead that the substance of Confucius' *Hsiao ching* and
Tseng tzu's discussions about *hsiao* was recorded by their later followers
and that that record became the text of the *Hsiao ching*.

Ch'ao Kung-wu 晁公武 (d. 1171) wrote that the book was the work of
Tseng tzu's disciples alone, i.e., not of the disciples of Confucius, nor of
those of both masters jointly (*Chün chai tu shu chih*, Taipei: Shang wu,
1978, pp. 75–6). Chu Hsi 朱熹 (1130–1200) identified what he thought
were two distinct temporal strata in the text of the *Hsiao ching*. He suggested that the earlier stratum consisted of the specific questions posed
by Tseng tzu together with Confucius' direct answers; he thought that
this dated from the time of Confucius and Tseng tzu themselves. He
recognized that the rest of the text must date from a later time, because
it incorporates lines from both the *Tso chuan* and the *Kuo yü*, two texts
that did not yet exist at the time of Confucius and Tseng tzu.

Chu Hsi argued that it could not be that the *Tso chuan* and *Kuo Yü*
were instead citing lines from an already extant *Hsiao ching*, because it
was clear from both style and context that the cited lines were well integrated in their *Tso chuan* or *Kuo Yü* settings, whereas they were mani-
festly not of a piece contextually in their occurrences in the *Hsiao ching*
(see *Chu tzu yü lei* 朱子語類 82; Peking: Chung hua, 1986, pp. 2141–44).

Han shu 30, pp. 1718–19 and *Sui shu* 32, pp. 933–35 both record the
Hsiao ching as having been extant at the start of the Han period, and as
having been transmitted by Chang Yü 張禹, (d. 5 B.C.). Yao Chi-heng 姚
際恆 (b.1647) observes, as Chu Hsi had done before him, that the *Hsiao
ching* contains several lengthy passages taken from the *Tso chuan*. He
thus claims that because the *Tso chuan* did not gain any appreciable cir-

culation until the time of Liu Hsin 劉歆 (46 B.C.–23), who is credited by Pan Ku 班固 (32–92) with rescuing it from oblivion when he was keeper of the imperial archives, the *Hsiao ching* could not have cited these *Tso chuan* passages unless it was written after Liu Hsin's time. This would mean a date later than A.D. 23 (see Yao Chi-heng, *Ku chin wei shu k'ao* 古今偽書考, Taipei: K'ai ming, 1969, p. 13).

Yao's argument fails on two counts. First, there are at least two size-able citations from the *Hsiao ching* found in the *Lü shih ch'un ch'iu* (see SPPY ed., 14, 2a and *Hsiao ching*, SPPY ed., 1, 2a, with some textual dif-ferences; and 16, 14a and *Hsiao ching* 2,1a, without textual differences and introduced with the words *Hsiao ching yüeh* 孝經曰). The date of the compilation of the *Lü shih ch'un ch'iu*, about 239 B.C., gives us there-fore a date by when the *Hsiao ching* must have been composed and in circulation. Yao ignores the presence of these citations of the *Hsiao ching* in the *Lü shih ch'un ch'iu*.

Secondly, Karlgren has shown that even though Liu Hsin himself knew nothing of the *Tso chuan* before he discovered it in the archives, the text was not entirely unknown at that time, having in fact its own school, together with a following even prior to Liu Hsin's discovery of the text ('On the authenticity and nature of the *Tso chuan*'; Göteborgs Högskolas Arsskrift XXXII, 1926:3, 16–7). Yao's argument, therefore, is not well founded, and the date of the *Lü shih ch'un ch'iu* can safely be taken as a *terminus ante quem* for the composition of the *Hsiao ching*.

In his *Ming t'ang lun* 明堂論, Ts'ai Yung 蔡邕 (133–192) cites a text called the *Hsiao ching chuan* 孝經傳 by Wei Wen hou 魏文侯 presum-ably Wei Ssu 魏斯, founder of the state of Wei in the mid fifth century, who died in 396 B.C. This reference (*Ch'üan Hou Han wen* 80, 6b) is some-times taken to refer to a commentary on the extant *Hsiao ching*, which would mean that the *Hsiao ching* itself would have predated Wei Wen hou's death. But it is unlikely that Ts'ai Yung's note has anything to do with the *Hsiao ching* known to have been extant in the Han period, and transmitted until now as one of the Thirteen Classics. There are three reasons for this.

First, *Han shu* 30 makes no mention of a *Hsiao ching chuan* by Wei Wen hou or any other author. Secondly, the word *chuan* 傳 was not typically used in pre-Han times to refer to textual commentaries; whatever the *Hsiao ching chuan* might have been in the fifth century B.C., it is not likely that it was a commentary to a text called *Hsiao ching*. Finally, if Wei Wen hou as cited by Ts'ai Yung is really the historically attested founder of the state of Wei, he would have been older than the disciples of Tseng tzu who are presumed to have compiled the *Hsiao ching* in the first place; he would not therefore have been in a position to write a commentary to that work.

3. History of the text

There are historical records of both a *chin wen* 今文 and a *ku wen* 古文 *Hsiao ching*, both being found registered in *Han shu* chapter 30.

(a) *Early history, to the T'ang period*

The *chin wen* text of the *Hsiao ching* underlies all extant versions of the work, save for the ostensible *Ku wen Hsiao ching* found in Japan in the eighteenth century (see (d) below); it can be traced back to the version that is recorded in *Han shu* ch.30, in 18 *chang*. Pan Ku states that it was transmitted by five different individuals, implying that there were correspondingly five different schools of interpretation. The text itself is explicitly said to have been without variants in all five cases; thus we may safely presume that it was only the interpretations that varied. The five transmitters were: a certain Chang-sun shih 長孫氏 about whom nothing is known; Chiang Weng 江翁, who was an academician at the time of Hsüan ti 宣帝 (reigned 74–49 B.C.), from the area of Hsia ch'iu 瑕丘; Hou Ts'ang 后蒼, also of the time of Hsüan ti, with whom versions of some of the other classical texts, such as the *I li*, are associated; I Feng 翼奉, also of Hsüan ti's time; and Chang Yü 張禹 (d. 5 B.C.). None of these texts survives intact; fragments of those of Hou Ts'ang and Chang Yü may be found in the *Yü han shan fang chi i shu*, ch. 40.

The preface of Lu Te-ming's 陸德明 (556–627) *Ching tien shih wen* (*c.* A.D. 625) states that at the time of the burning of the books by Ch'in a certain Yen Chih 顏芝 of Ho chien 河間 hid a copy of the text, which was retrieved by his son Yen Chen 顏貞 in the Former Han period. This same account is repeated a few years later in *Sui shu* 32, p. 935. Nonetheless there is no independent corroboration of the role of either Yen Chih or Yen Chen in the preservation and transmission of the *Chin wen Hsiao ching*; in any event its veracity has no bearing on the subsequent history of the text.

According to the *Sui shu*, Liu Hsiang 劉向 (79–8 B.C.) compared the Yen text (i.e., the *chin wen* text circulating in Former Han) with the *ku wen* text, and established a definitive edition of eighteen sections, having excised those portions that he considered doubtful. This can be regarded as the first edited text of the *Hsiao ching*.

At the end of the Later Han dynasty, a version of the *chin wen* text appeared accompanied by a commentary (*chu* 注), identified as being written by a scholar named Cheng 鄭. Later this was taken to refer to

Cheng Hsüan 鄭玄 (127–200), but that attribution is highly doubtful (see (c) below). Nevertheless the *Hsiao ching Cheng chu*, whoever Cheng may have been, constituted the second edited text of the *Hsiao ching*.

Han shu 30, p. 1718 records an item entitled *Hsiao ching ku K'ung shih* 孝經古孔氏 in one *p'ien*; the note adds that it is in twenty-two sections (*chang*). Yen Shih-ku 顏師古 (581–645) cites Liu Hsiang as his authority to explain the difference from the number of 18 sections of the *Chin wen Hsiao ching*. This resulted from the fact that the 'Shu Jen' 庶人 portion consisted of a single section in the *chin wen* text, but of two sections in the *ku wen* text; and from the fact that the single section 'Tseng tzu kan wen' 曾子敢問 of the *chin wen* text corresponded to three sections of the *ku wen*, which also included an additional section not found in the *chin wen* text at all. Yen Shih-ku does not name this additional section, but we know from the preface to the *Ching tien shih wen* that it was called 'Kuei men' 閨門. *Sui shu* 32, p. 935 seems to suggest that the Chang-sun version of the (*chin wen*) text included the 'Kuei men' section. But we have it on the authority of *Han shu*, 30, p. 1719, that the texts of the five different schools of the *Chin wen Hsiao ching* did not vary from one another. It would thus appear that the *Sui shu*'s statement about the Chang-sun version including the 'Kuei men' section is in error.

In its account of the *Shang shu*, *Han shu* 30, p. 1706, includes mention of the *ku wen* texts found when Lu Kung wang 魯恭王 demolished Confucius' house, at a time specified as being towards the 'end of Wu ti's 武帝 (reigned 141–87) reign', but which actually could not have been later than 128 B.C., when Lu Kung wang died (for the chronological disparity, see William Hung, as cited below, p. 115). This account in the *Han shu* puts the *Ku wen Hsiao ching* squarely within the tradition of *ku wen* texts said to have been pulled from a hiding place in the walls of Confucius' house, and associated with transmission and commentaries at the hands of the Han *ku wen* scholar K'ung An-kuo 孔安國 (d. *c.* 100 B.C.).

A fragment of the *Hsin lun* of Huan T'an 桓譚 (*c.* 43 B.C.–A.D.28) notes that the *ku wen* version of the *Hsiao ching* amounted to twenty sections (*chang*) and 1872 characters, differing from the *chin wen* version in more than four hundred places (see *T'ai p'ing yü lan* 608; *Ch'üan Hou Han wen* 14, 8b–9a; Pokora's collected fragments of Huan T'an 90A). Yen Shih-ku's note to *Han shu* 30, p. 1719 cites the same passage from the *Hsin lun*.

Hsü Ch'ung's 許沖 memorial, composed to accompany the presentation to the throne of his father's *Shuo wen chieh tzu* (A.D. 121) gives a slightly different account of the appearance of the *ku wen* text. It claims that it was presented to the court at the time of Chao ti 昭帝 (reigned 86–74 B.C.) by an Elder (*san lao* 三老) of the state of Lu 魯; that it was collated, presumably with the *chin wen* text, by Wei Hung 衛宏 in the first years of Later Han; and that it was transmitted orally. Tuan Yü-ts'ai 段玉裁 (1735–1815) suggests (*Shuo wen chieh tzu chu*, SPPY ed., 15B, 8b) that this *ku wen* text of the *Hsiao ching* could have been the same one which was reported to have been found much earlier in the wall of Confucius' house. It may have been, he speculates, that it simply was not presented until the time of Chao ti. Only the *Shang shu* is explicitly said to have been presented by K'ung An-kuo some decades previously.

Both the *Chin wen Cheng chu Hsiao ching* and the *Ku wen K'ung An-kuo chuan Hsiao ching* were backed by officially established schools during the Liang dynasty, but with the political turmoil at the end of that time, the *ku wen* version is thought to have been lost. By the latter half of the sixth century, in the Ch'en, Chou and Ch'i dynasties, only the *Cheng chu chin wen* text appears to have been transmitted.

With the Sui unification, a text purporting to be the K'ung An-kuo commentary, presumably accompanied by the *Ku wen Hsiao ching*, is said to have been obtained by Wang Shao 王劭, Director of the Palace Library, who turned it over to Liu Hsüan 劉炫 of Ho chien 河間 (died *c.* 613; *Sui shu* 32, p. 935). This text is said to have been given official status on a par with that of the *Chin wen Cheng chu* text, but in the ensuing debate regarding its authenticity it was widely believed that it was actually a fabrication, made perhaps by Liu Hsüan himself. Nevertheless, both this and the *Cheng chu* text existed side by side and were transmitted to the T'ang period.

(b) *The debate at the court of T'ang Hsüan tsung*

Early in 719 T'ang Hsüan tsung 玄宗 (reigned 712–56), observing the numerous interpretative contradictions between the K'ung An-kuo and Cheng commentaries, ordered an enquiry into the question of which of the two was to be preferred. In response Liu Chih-chi 劉知幾 (661–721), then First Secretary to the Heir Apparent, presented a treatise entitled *Hsiao ching chu i* 孝經注議 in which he argued in detail that the Cheng commentary was not in fact recognized or sanctioned. Instead Liu praised the K'ung An-kuo commentary, and, *inter alia*, the *ku wen* version of the text which it accompanied. This was most probably the same *ku wen* text that had been turned over to Liu Hsüan by Wang Shao more than a century earlier. The opposite view, preferring the *chin wen* text and the Cheng commentary, was defended by Ssu-ma Chen 司馬貞 (early 8th century) and other unnamed scholars. They submitted a treatise to the Board of Rites attacking both the then current K'ung An-kuo commentary and the companion *ku wen* text itself as spurious. The substance of this treatise is known from lengthy citations in a memorial prepared by the President of the Board of Rites (unidentified) for presentation to the throne.

T'ang Hsüan tsung appears to have been something less than completely satisfied with the results that his command had elicited. His final edict on the subject said, in part, 'the discussions . . . have not expounded [the substantive differences between the Cheng and the K'ung commentaries], but have been given to picking petty faults not of the slightest importance . . . Let the Cheng commentary remain in use, . . . [and] let encouragement be given to the study of the K'ung commentary so that its transmission might not terminate' (translation adapted from Hung, p. 83).

(c) *The Cheng chu Hsiao ching* 鄭注孝經

The *Cheng chu Hsiao ching* apparently circulated widely in the Nan-pei ch'ao period, but even then its currency was accompanied by a question about the identity of the scholar, named Cheng, to whom the commentary was ascribed. The first to suggest that the name Cheng referred to Cheng Hsüan seems to have been a certain Hsün Ch'ang 荀昶 (*fl. c.* 424) who compiled a record of court expositions of the *Hsiao ching* under the Eastern Chin emperors Mu ti 穆帝 and Hsiao Wu ti 孝武帝 in 355 and 376 (see Hung, note 14). Hsün Ch'ang's work, entitled *Chi i hsiao ching* 集議孝經 in *Sui shu* 32, p. 933, is not extant.

The earliest record of any doubt about the attribution to Cheng Hsüan is to be found in *Nan Ch'i shu* 39, p. 684. In the last passage of a letter written to Wang Chien 王儉 (452–489) in 483, Lu Cheng 陸澄 (423–494) wrote that the *Hsiao ching* that was said 'to carry a commentary by Cheng Hsüan' 題為鄭玄注 ought not to be the version of the text accorded official status because it was not, to his mind, likely to be a work genuinely by Cheng Hsüan. Lu based his scepticism on two points: (i) the language of the commentary was not of a style characteristic of Cheng Hsüan's other works; and (ii) there was no reference to a *Hsiao ching chu*, either in Cheng Hsüan's otherwise quite thorough record of his own writings, or by his disciples and followers. Wang Chien responded by allowing the *Cheng chu Hsiao ching* to remain with the status that it had already achieved, deeming the question of authorship as being secondary to that of content, which he found acceptable.

Sui shu 32, p. 935 already registers some doubt about the attribution of the Cheng commentary to Cheng Hsüan. In his memorial of 719, Liu Chih-chi specified twelve points that gave rise to doubt, and these all derived from the absence of any clear reference to a commentary on the

Hsiao ching by Cheng Hsüan in any of the numerous bibliographical, literary and historical sources where such a mention might be expected (see Hung, pp. 75–77).

The *Cheng chu Hsiao ching* was supplanted by the imperial commentary (*yü chu* 御注) of Hsüan tsung himself, and is not extant in its original transmitted form. It had been included in the *Ch'ün shu chih yao* compiled a century earlier on the order of T'ai Tsung, and is known, apart from a few citations in extant Chinese works, only from that version recovered in Japan. It was edited by Okada Shinsen 岡田新川 (1737–1799) and sent by him to the Hangchow book collector and scholar Pao T'ing-po 鮑廷博 (1728–1814) specifically in the hope that it would be included in Pao's *Chih pu tsu chai ts'ung shu*, where in fact it is now found in the 21st *chi* (集).

The Ch'ing philologists P'i Hsi-jui 皮錫瑞 (1850–1908) and Yen K'o-chün 嚴可均 (1762–1843), have also edited and attempted to reconstruct the *Cheng chu Hsiao ching* on the basis of the *Ch'ün shu chih yao*, together with citations culled from Chinese works, and have defended its attribution to Cheng Hsüan. P'i Hsi-jui's work is in the *ching* 經 section of the *SPPY* collection, and that of Yen K'o-chün is in the *Chih chin chai ts'ung shu*, third chi (集).

Except for a few *lacunae* due to damage on the manuscript, the whole of the Cheng commentary is preserved on two Tun-huang rolls in the Bibliothèque National, Paris (P. 2674 and P. 3428); these are judged by William Hung (p. 130) to be in the same handwriting and to be dated in the period 860–73.

(d) The *K'ung An-kuo chuan* 孔安國傳

Han records identify K'ung An-kuo as the figure associated with finding the *Ku wen Hsiao ching* in the wall of Confucius' house when it was being demolished, in the same way that he is associated with the *ku wen* versions of other texts said to have been discovered in this way. But there is no record, of the Han period, of a commentary (*chuan* 傳) by K'ung An-kuo to the *Hsiao ching*. That tradition is first mentioned in a second postface of the *K'ung tzu chia yü*, compiled perhaps as late as *c.* 250 (see *Ying Sung Shu pen K'ung tzu chia yü* 影宋蜀本孔子家語; Taipei: Chung hua, 1968, 10, 16b). William Hung points out that while the K'ung An-kuo *chuan* to the *Hsiao ching* is mentioned here by name as early as 250, we do not have any evidence for such a commentary being actually in circulation until early in the fifth century, when it is said to have figured in Hsün Ch'ang's *Chi i hsiao ching* (Hung, p. 117, note 67). The authenticity of the K'ung An-kuo commentary is thus very much in doubt, owing to (i) the sketchy evidence for its early history; and (ii) its mention in the *K'ung tzu chia yü* postface along with the alleged K'ung An-kuo commentaries to the *Lun yü* and the *Shang shu*, both of which are generally and with good reason regarded as spurious.

Liu Hsüan is known to have written a commentary to the *Hsiao ching* in five *chüan*, around 600. The work is entered in *Sui shu* 32, p. 934, under the title *Ku wen Hsiao ching shu i* 古文孝經述議, where it is noticed that the first character *ku* is sometimes erroneously written as ch'ien 千. The work is also registered in Fujiwara Sukeyo's catalogue, and it is the first major work known on the *ku wen* text and on the *K'ung An-kuo chuan*. Only volumes 1 and 4 are now extant, having been discovered in Tokyo in the twentieth century, by Takeuchi Yoshio 武内義雄. In 1951 Hayashi Hideichi 林秀一 completed a major study of the work, including a reconstruction of the lost volumes 2, 3 and 5 (see under 4 below).

In his defence of the *chin wen* text and the Cheng commentary in 719, Ssu-ma Chen criticized the *ku wen* text as being unauthentic and the accompanying K'ung An-kuo commentary as being 'superficial and false' (Hung, p. 81). He charged that its language and sentiments are both vulgar and uncouth.

The bibliographical lists of the *Chiu T'ang shu* (46, pp. 1980–81) and the *Hsin T'ang shu* (57, pp. 1442–43) each include 27 items for the *Hsiao ching*. After the T'ang period, the K'ung An-kuo commentary was lost in China, but seemingly preserved and transmitted in Japan. The *ku wen* text of the *Hsiao ching* itself seems to have been preserved in the Sung imperial library, as may be suggested by two eleventh century works: (i) Ssu-ma Kuang 司馬光 (1019–86), *Ku wen Hsiao ching chih chieh* 古文孝經指解, presented to the court in 1055; and (ii) Fan Tsu-yü 范祖禹 (1041–98), *Ku wen Hsiao ching shuo* 古文孝經說 presented between 1086 and 1093. Both texts, along with T'ang Hsüan tsung's *yü chu*, are currently extant as parts of the *Hsiao ching chu chieh* 孝經注解 (see *T'ung chih t'ang ching chieh*; Hung, p. 127, note 119).

In 1945 a nearly complete and intact version of Fan Tsu-yü's *ku wen* text, inscribed on stone, was discovered in a grotto in Ssu-ch'uan. The inscription closes with the words *Fan Tsu-yü ching shu* 范祖禹敬書, which is understood to mean that it was inscribed by Fan himself. It need hardly be stressed that this discovery has been of extraordinary value for the study and analysis of the textual history of the *Ku wen Hsiao ching*; see Ma Heng 馬衡, in *BIHP* 20.1 (1948), pp. 19–24, which includes a transcription.

A facsimile of a copy of the *Ku wen Hsiao ching* made by Fujiwara Chikanaga 藤原親長 in 1493 was published in the Sonkeikaku sōkan

(Tokyo) in 1935. The version of this text edited by Dazai Jun 太宰純 (Shundai 春臺; 1680–1747), preface dated 1731, is better known than Fujiwara Chikanaga's copy, being published by Pao T'ing-po under the title *Ku wen Hsiao ching K'ung chuan* (see the *Chih pu tsu chai ts'ung shu* and *Ssu k'u ch'üan shu*). Pao added the Sung *ku wen* text from the *Hsiao ching chu chieh* for comparative purposes.

Dazai's text is commonly believed to be a late Japanese forgery of the already spurious mediaeval *K'ung An-kuo chuan*. William Hung (p. 128) points out that Ting Yen 丁晏 (1794–1875) argued, persuasively as he thinks, that Dazai's text was in fact likely to be an authentic version of Liu Hsüan's text of the Sui period; and that that text, for its part often thought to have been fabricated by Liu Hsüan himself, was in all probability forged before it came into Liu Hsüan's hands; see Ting Yen, *Lun yü K'ung chu cheng wei* 論語孔注證偽 (*Ho chung t'u shu kuan ts'ung shu* XII, 1, 48a–49b) and *Hsiao ching cheng wen* 孝經徵文 (*Huang Ch'ing ching chieh hsü pien* 847, 15a).

In concluding his remarks on the *Ku wen Hsiao ching* and the *K'ung An-kuo* commentary, William Hung recognizes that in origin there probably was no authentic *Ku wen Hsiao ching* text at all; in his opinion the classic was not old enough to have had a genuine *ku wen* version. He further recognizes that the *K'ung chuan* must have been forged repeatedly, beginning from the third century A.D. It is of little significance now who the various forgers were, since we know *a priori* that any purported *ku wen* text or *K'ung chuan* is not genuine (Hung, p. 129).

(e) *The T'ang Hsüan tsung commentary*

First in 722, and then again in a revised form in 743, T'ang Hsüan tsung issued and circulated his own preface (*hsü* 序) and commentary (*chu* 注) to the *Hsiao ching*. These are known as the 'imperial commentary' *yü chu* 御注. The former is called the *K'ai yüan shih chu* 開元始注, and the latter the *T'ien pao ch'ung chu* 天寶重注. Both commentaries enjoyed wide distribution throughout China as a result of Hsüan tsung's own imperial decree. In 745 he had his preface and the revised commentary, along with the text of the *Hsiao ching* proper, engraved on stone tablets, which were then set out at the Imperial University in Ch'ang-an. This text is known as the *Shih t'ai Hsiao ching* 石臺孝經, and is presumably still extant in Hsi-an. This text and commentary supplanted both the Cheng *chu* and the *K'ung chuan* versions, and it is the one that underlies all modern editions, save for the spurious *ku wen* version. The *K'ai yüan shih chu* was lost in China, and is now known only as recovered in Japan. It is included in Li Shu-ch'ang's 黎庶昌 (1837–1897) *Ku i ts'ung shu*.

On instructions from Hsüan tsung, Yüan Hsing-ch'ung 元 行 沖 (653–729) wrote a sub-commentary (*shu* 疏) to the Imperial commentary. (See *Chiu T'ang shu* 102, p. 3178, *Hsin T'ang shu* 125, p. 5691). This sub-commentary is not now extant, except in fragments collected by Ma Kuo-han 馬 國 翰 (1794–1857; see *Yü han shan fang chi i shu*). What is identified as the *shu* in current versions, in particular in the *Shih san ching chu shu* text, is actually the *cheng i* 正義 of Hsing Ping 邢昺 (931–1010), which dates from the Sung, and is based on the earlier *shu* of Yüan Hsing-ch'ung.

In 1987 the Ku chi shu tien 古籍書店 in Tientsin issued a photographic facsimile of the Sung wood-block text of the *Hsiao ching* with Hsüan tsung's preface and revised commentary that is preserved in the Ch'ien lung imperial archives, titled *Sung k'o Hsiao ching* 宋刻孝經.

(f) *Other commentaries and manuscript versions*

Apart from the principal 'schools' of commentaries discussed above, a list of the most important textual studies should include the *yin i* 音義 of Lu Te-ming (*Ching tien shih wen*, ch.23). The most important of the 'Sung' school works is Chu Hsi's *Hsiao ching k'an wu* 孝經刊誤 which is divided into one section (*chang*) of text (*ching*) followed by fourteen of *chuan*. The two main successors to this approach are (i) Tung Ting 董鼎 (Sung to Yüan periods), *Hsiao ching ta i* 孝經大義 (1305); and (ii) Wu Ch'eng 吳澄 (1247–1331), *Hsiao ching chang chü* 孝經章句.

Of the voluminous Ming and Ch'ing studies, two deserve particular mention: (i) Mao Ch'i-ling 毛奇齡 (1623–1716) *Hsiao ching wen* 孝經問 because it is a direct criticism of the 'Sung *hsüeh*' works; and (ii) Juan Yüan's 阮元 (1764–1849) textual collation, the *Hsiao ching chiao k'an chi* 孝經校勘記, appended to his edition of the *Hsiao ching chu shu*. A full list of Ming and Ch'ing works can be found in Ts'ai Ju-k'un's work (see immediately below). For a list of studies of its various manuscripts from Tun-huang, see Cheng (4 (g) below).

4. Recent studies

(a) Ts'ai Ju-k'un 蔡汝堃, *Hsiao ching t'ung k'ao* 孝經通考. Shanghai: Shang-wu, 1937; reprinted Taipei: Shang-wu, 1967. This is the most comprehensive modern Chinese study of the work. Pages 103–34 give, in the form of a chart, a very useful history of the text, commentaries and traditional studies.

(b) Hayashi Hideichi 林秀一, *Kōkyō jutsugi fukugen ni kansuru kenkyū* 孝經述議復原に關する研究; Tokyo: Bunkyōdo, 1953. Hayashi

Hideichi is one of the foremost Japanese scholars of the Chinese classics, especially with respect to the study of the *Hsiao ching*. Pages 341–42 give a detailed listing of his earlier research and publications on this text, amounting to a total of twenty-one items.

(c) Itano Chōhachi 板野長八, 'Kōkyō no seiritsu' 孝經の成立; *Shigaku zasshi* 64.3–4, 188–214, 282–296; see also *RBS* 1 (1955) no.408. The author holds the unlikely view that the *Hsiao ching* was written before the *Lü shih ch'un ch'iu*.

(d) Hung, William, 'A Bibliographical Controversy at the T'ang Court A.D. 719'; *HJAS* 20.1–2 (1957), 74–134.

(e) Yen, Isabella Y., *A Grammatical Analysis of* Syau Jing; Bloomington, Indiana: Indiana Research Center in Anthropology, Folklore, and Linguistics, 1960; see *RBS* 6 (1960), no.394.

(f) Hayashi Hideichi 林秀一 'Kōkyō no denrai to sono eikyō: shabon jidai wo chūshin to shite' 孝經の傳來とその影響: 寫本時代を中心として. *Tōhō gakkai sōritsu jūgo shūnen kinen tōhōgaku ronshū* 東方學會創立十五周年記念東方學論集, Tokyo: Tōhō Gakkai, 1962, pp. 235–244. See also *RBS* 8 [1962], no. 155 (for Hayashi's *summa* on this text, see under (6) L below).

(g) Cheng A-ts'ai 鄭阿財 and Chu Feng-yü 朱鳳玉 *Tun-huang hsüeh yen chiu lun chu mu lu* 敦煌學研究論著目錄 Taipei: Han hsüeh yen chiu tzu liao chi fu wu chung hsin 漢學研究資料及服務中心, 1987. For the *Hsiao ching* see p. 97.

(h) Ho Kuang-yen 何廣棪. 'Wan chin "*Hsiao ching*" yen chiu lun wen hui mu' 晚近《孝經》研究論文彙目. *Shu mu chi k'an* 書目季刊 (1989) 32.4, pp. 91–97.

5.   Translations

(a) Legge, *Sacred Books of the East*, vol. III.

(b) de Rosny, Leon, *Le Hiao-king*; Paris: Maisonneuve et Ch. Leclerc, 1889; and *Le morale de Confucius, le livre sacré de la piété filiale*; Paris: J. Maisonneuve, 1893.

(c) Chen, Ivan, *The Book of Filial Piety*; London: J. Murray, 1908, 1920; New York: E.P. Dutton & Co., 1908, 1909.

(d) Wilhelm, Richard, *Hiau Ging; das Buch der Ehrfurcht*; Peking: Verlag der Pekinger Pappelinsel, 1940.

(e) Makra, Mary Lelia, *The Hsiao ching*; ed. Paul K.T. Sih; New York: St. John's University Press, 1961.

(f) Tomassini, Fausto, *Testi confuciani*; Turin: Unione tipografica-editrice torinese, 1974; see pp. 69–83.

6. Japanese editions

A. *Kambun taikei*; no.5, 1910, edited by Shigeno Yasutsugu and Hoshino Tsune.

B. *Kanseki kokujikai zensho*; no.7, 1909, based on the work of Kumazawa Banzan.

C. *Kōchū kambun sōsho*; no.3, 1913, edited by Katsuta Sukeyoshi.

D. *Kokuyaku kambun taisei*; no.1, 1922, edited by Hattori Unokichi and Yamaguchi Satsujō.

E. *Kambun sōsho*, 1927, edited by Hayashi Taisuke.

F. *Keisho taikō*; no, 5, 1939.

H. *Shinshaku kambun taikei*; no. 35, edited by Kurihara Keisuke.

L. *Chūgoku koten shinsho*, 1979, edited by Hayashi Hideichi.

7. Indexes

(a) *Hsiao ching yin te; a concordance to Hsiao ching*; Harvard-Yenching Institute Sinological Index Series Supplement no. 23, 1950, reprinted 1966.

(b) *A Concordance to the Erya and Xiaojing* 爾雅 孝經逐字索引, ed. D.C. Lau and Chen Fong Ching; *ICS* series, Hong Kong: Commercial Press, forthcoming 1994.

(I am indebted to Laura E. Hess for much of the information on the *Hsiao ching* in Japan, though the formulation given here is my own responsibility)

— William G. Boltz

Hsin hsü 新序

1. Content

The *Hsin hsü* is a collection of moralistic anecdotes and historical tales reputedly assembled or written by Liu Hsiang 劉向 (79–8 B.C.). The received text contains 166 entries, in 10 *chüan*. Fragments of 59 entries have also been collected from various sources. Most of the entries are paraphrases or verbatim extracts from earlier philosophical and historical texts, notably the *Lü shih ch'un ch'iu, Han shih wai chuan, Shih chi, Chan kuo ts'e*, the three commentaries to the *Ch'un ch'iu* (with a notable bias towards the *Ku liang*), the *Chuang tzu* and the *Hsün tzu*.

Most of the historical tales concern the Spring and Autumn period; the final *chüan* (no.10) consists entirely of stories from the Han period; and the first five *chüan* are all entitled *tsa shih* 雜事. Hirotsune Jinsei (see under (9) below, pp. 17–19) has argued that in spite of the inclusion of the word *tsa* in their titles, these *chüan* are a unified whole that presents a series of *exempla* which illustrate the basic elements of good government. Other *chüan* contain stories about extravagant and sybaritic rulers (no. 6), officials of integrity and loyalty (no. 7), men of principle and courage (no. 8) and examples of clever stratagems devised by wise ministers (nos. 9 and 10). The basic philosophy of the text is Confucian, with an emphasis on the necessity for the ruler to govern his realm by cultivating rectitude, listening to public opinion and heeding the advice of worthies and virtuous men, who should not shrink from their duty of admonishing and reproving a cruel and foolish lord.

2. Date of composition and authorship

Although early sources credit Liu Hsiang as the 'author' of the *Hsin hsü*, he would be described more accurately as the 'editor', as there is virtually nothing in the text that was original with Liu Hsiang, the substance being derived from other sources. The attribution of authorship, as opposed to editorship, to Liu Hsiang stems from a misinterpretation of the entry for the *Hsin hsü* in the *Ch'i lüeh* 七略, which lists it along with three other works among 67 *p'ien* 'arranged' (i.e., *hsü* 序) by Liu Hsiang (see *Han shu* 30, p. 1727). According to another passage in the *Han shu* (36, p. 1958), Liu Hsiang 'selected deeds and events from biographical records' and wrote (*chu* 著) the *Hsin hsü* and the *Shuo yüan* in a total of 50 *p'ien* and presented them to the emperor. Yen Ling-feng 嚴靈峯 has argued (see under (7) below) that in this passage the expression *Hsin hsü* was not the title of a book, and that Pan Ku 班固 (32–92) simply used the term in the sense of 'newly arranged'. Thus, the work of 50 *p'ien* that Pan Ku attributes to Liu Hsiang could be a single book, the 'Newly arranged *Shuo yüan*'.

Later catalogues and works refer to the work as being 'composed' (*chuan* 撰) by Liu Hsiang (see *Sui shu* 34, p. 997; *Chiu T'ang shu* 47, p. 2024; and Ssu-ma Chen's 司馬貞 (early eighth century) note in *Shih chi* 68, p. 2238). However, they likewise describe the *Shuo yüan* and the *Lieh nü chuan* 列女傳 as being 'composed' by Liu Hsiang, whereas the entries in Liu Hsiang's own *Ch'i lüeh pieh lu* 七略別錄 for those two works clearly indicate that he edited (*chiao* 校) them from pre-existing materials; for this reason, some scholars have argued that Liu Hsiang did not compose the material that is in the *Hsin hsü* and that he merely collected and edited it. Hsü Fu-kuan 徐復觀 has argued that modern scholars have misconstrued the sense of *hsü* as used in the Han period, and claims that the term also meant to 'compose'.

Liu Hsiang presented the *Hsin hsü* to the throne in 24 or, as in one source, 25 B.C. According to a tradition that is first recorded in Lu Hsi's 陸喜 autobiography (third century; see *Chin shu* 54, p. 1486), Liu Hsiang modelled the *Hsin hsü* directly on the *Hsin yü* of Lu Chia 陸賈 (*c.* 228–*c.* 140 B.C.). A close comparison of the *Hsin yü* as received and the *Hsin hsü* does not reveal any close textual or structural similarities. The only features which the two works share is their overt Confucian moralism.

3. Textual history

Although the *Han shu* does not indicate the exact size of the *Hsin hsü*, scholars have assumed that the original work was in 30 *chüan*. Thus the *Sui shu* (34, p. 997), *Chiu T'ang shu* (47, p. 2024) and *Hsin T'ang shu* (59, p. 1510) both list it as a text in 30 *chüan*, under *ju chia*. By the Northern Sung period only 10 *chüan* were extant. Tseng Kung 曾鞏 (1019–1083) edited these fragments to form the received version, in 10 *chüan*.

4. Editions

(a) A Sung edition is held in the National Library of China, but the most widely available print is a facsimile of a Sung edition that was prepared in the period 1552–1566, and which was incorporated in the *Ssu k'u ch'üan shu* and the *Ssu pu ts'ung k'an*.

(b) An edition of unknown provenance is to be found in the *Han Wei ts'ung shu* (including the *Kuang* and *Tseng ting* editions).

(c) An edition based on Chiang Feng-tsao's 蔣鳳藻 (19th century) collation of several Sung editions is included in the *T'ieh hua kuan ts'ung shu*; this has been reproduced in the *Ts'ung shu chi ch'eng* series.

(d) Chang Kuo-ch'üan 張國銓, *Hsin hsü chiao chu* 新序校注; Ch'eng tu: Ju ku, 1944.

The *Hsin hsü* is also included in the *T'ien i ko ts'ung shu*, the *Tzu shu pai chia* and the *Lung hsi ching she ts'ung shu*.

5.   Annotation without text

(a) Lu Wen-ch'ao 盧文弨 (1717–96), *Hsin hsü chiao pu* 新序校補; in *Ch'ün shu shih pu (Pao ching t'ang ts'ung shu)*.

(b) Sun I-jang 孫詒讓 (1848–1908), in *Cha i*.

(c) Meng Chuan-ming 蒙傳銘, 'Hsin hsü chiao chi' 新序校記; *Hsin ya shu yüan hsüeh shu nien k'an* 12 (1970), 19–73.

(d) Liang Jung-mao 梁榮茂, *Hsin hsü chiao pu* 新序校補; Taipei: Shui niu, 1971.

6.   Fragments

(a) Yen K'o-chün 嚴可均 (1762–1843), *Ch'üan shang ku san tai Ch'in Han San kuo Liu ch'ao wen* 39.1a–10a.

(b) Lu Wen-ch'ao, *Hsin hsü i wen* 新序逸文; printed with 5 (a) above.

See also Chang Kuo-ch'üan under 4 (d) above.

7.   Recent studies

(a) Yü Chia-hsi 余嘉錫 (1883–1955), *Ssu k'u t'i yao pien cheng* 四庫提要辨證, 10, pp. 544–54.

(b) Lo Ken-tse 羅根澤, 'Hsin hsü Shuo yüan Lieh nü chuan pu tso shih yü Liu Hsiang k'ao' 新序說苑列女傳不作始於劉向考, *Ku shih pien* 古史辨 4; reprinted *Chu tzu k'ao so* 諸子考索, Peking: Jen min, 1958, pp. 540–42.

(c) Chao Chung-i 趙仲邑, 'Hsin hsü shih lun' 新序試論, *Chung shan ta hsüeh hsüeh pao* 中山大學學報 3 (1957), 170–83.

(d) Meng Chuan-ming, 'Liu Hsiang Hsin hsü chih ch'ung hsin k'ao ch'a' 劉向新序之重新考察, *T'u shu kuan hsüeh pao* 圖書館學報 7 (1965), 77–86.

(e) Hsü Fu-kuan, 'Liu Hsiang Hsin hsü Shuo yüan ti yen chiu' 劉向新序說苑的研究, *Ta lu tsa chih* 55:2 (1977), 51–74.

(f) Ikeda Shūzō 池田秀三, 'Ryū Kō no gakumon to shisō' 劉向の學問と思想, *Tōhōgaku hō* 東方學報 (Kyoto) 50 (1978), 109–90 (see especially pp. 110–16).

(g) Yen Ling-feng, 'Liu Hsiang Shuo yüan pieh lu yen chiu' 劉向說苑別錄研究, *Ta lu tsa chih* 56:6 (1978), 287–92.

(h) Hsü Su-fei 許素菲, *Liu Hsiang Hsin hsü yen chiu* 劉向新序研究; Taipei: 1980.

8. Modern Chinese version

Lu Yüan-chün 盧元駿, *Hsin hsü chin chu chin i* 新序今註今譯; Taipei: Shang wu, 1975.

9. Japanese edition

L. *Chūgoku koten shinsho*, 1973, edited by Hirotsune Jinsei.

10. Indexes

(a) *Hsin hsü t'ung chien* 新序通檢; Peking: Centre franco-chinois, 1946, reprinted Taipei: Ch'eng wen, 1968; based on the *SPTK* edition.

(b) *A Concordance to the Xinxu* 新序逐字索引, ed. D.C. Lau and Chen Fong Ching; *ICS* series, Hong Kong: Commercial Press, 1992.

— David R. Knechtges

Hsin lun 新論

1. Subject matter and assessment

The surviving fragments of a book written by Huan T'an 桓 譚 (*c.* 43
B.C.–A.D. 28) represent what had originally been a long text which was
concerned with a variety of opinions on philosophical, cultural and
economic matters. The book had also included highly interesting information on natural phenomena, the practices of masters of the occult arts
and contemporary figures such as Wang Mang 王莽 (*r.* 9–23), Liu Hsin
劉歆 (46 B.C.–A.D. 23) and Yang Hsiung 揚雄 (53 B.C.–A.D. 18). The text
was also concerned with matters of everyday life.

The importance of the *Hsin lun* lies both in its expression of the somewhat independent ideas of the Old Text school and in its criticism of the
contemporary Confucian attention to prognostication texts. The work
also throws light on contemporary political conditions at a time of social
unrest and military upheaval. Huan T'an's writings exercised a profound influence on Wang Ch'ung 王充 (27–*c.* 100) and others.

While not being concerned exclusively with philosophical ideas, the
Hsin lun was perhaps intended to provide Kuang-wu ti 光武帝 (*r.* 25–
57) with advice on how to maintain Confucian practice alongside some
Legalist methods. The admiration felt by Wang Ch'ung for Huan T'an's
ideas, the production of several books after the Han period which were
also entitled *Hsin lun*, the preservation of a large number of fragments
and the inclusion of some important examples of these in the *Ch'ün shu
chih yao* 群書治要 of Wei Cheng 魏徵 (580–643) together suggest that
Huan T'an attained considerable recognition and respect. Such admiration as he may have received may have been due as much to his
character as a courageous critic as to his writings. From the Sung period
onwards his reputation began to decline, until it was revived in the
1930's.

2. Compilation of the work and authenticity of its fragments

Huan T'an presented his work to Kuang-wu ti, probably in A.D. 26,
while the last chapter was still incomplete. According to Li Hsien's 李賢

(651–84) statement (see his note to *Hou Han shu* 28A, p. 961) the book had included 16 *p'ien*; thirteen of these had been divided into two parts, thus making a total of 29 *p'ien*. Probably lost from after the T'ang dynasty, the book was not available in the imperial library in 1091, when the Sung emperor sought to obtain a copy from Korea. Quotations of the work which are not attested in Sung encyclopaedias but which are sometimes found independently as late as the 17th century do not necessarily suggest that a complete text of the *Hsin lun* had survived in some places at that time; for such quotations may have been drawn from certain *lei shu* 類書 or, alternatively, ascribed to Huan T'an without any foundation for so doing. That the authenticity of such quotations can at times be of crucial significance may be illustrated in the case of a passage in the *Ch'i kuo k'ao* 七國考 of Tung Yüeh 董說 (1620–80). This purports to reproduce, as from Huan T'an, a consideraton of the *Fa ching* 法經 of Li K'uei 李悝 (5th or 4th century B.C.); in all probability such a work never existed (See Tung Yüeh, *Ch'i kuo k'ao*, Peking: Chung hua, 1956, pp. 366–67; and Timoteus Pokora, 'The Canon of Laws by Li K'uei – A Double Falsification'; *Archiv Orientální* 27, 1959, 96–121). The authenticity of fragments that appear in pre-Sung sources need not be questioned, whereas those that are found in later sources require individual examination. The longest fragment known is to be found in the *Hung ming chi* 弘明集 (*Ssu pu ts'ung k'an* edition, 5.4b–5b); for ascription of this to Huan T'an rather than to a later writer, see Chung Chao-p'eng 鍾肇鵬 'Hsin lun Hsing shen ti tso che ying tuan kuei Huan T'an' 新論形神的作者應斷歸桓譚 (*Jen wen tsa chih* 人文雜誌 1959.2, 34–6).

3. Collections of the fragments

The fragments of the *Hsin lun* have been collected as follows:

(a) By Sun P'ing-i 孫馮翼, in *Wen ching t'ang ts'ung shu* 問經堂叢書 (1797–1802); also included in *Ssu pu pei yao*. The fragments are arranged according to the sources where they originate.
(b) By Yen K'o-chün 嚴可均 (1762–1843), in *Ch'üan Hou Han wen* 全後漢文 (compiled 1808–36, printed 1887–93), where there is an attempt to reconstruct the text in the form of the *p'ien* mentioned by Li Hsien. On occasion several different versions of a passage are combined so as to complete the text; such procedure is not without its dangers.
(c) By Ch'ien Hsi-tso 錢熙祚 (1801–44), in *Chih hai* 指海 (1839–46) compiled with full knowledge of (a) and (b).
(d) There is an unpublished reconstruction by Huang I-chou 黃以周 (1828–99) who was also aware of (a) and (b).

(e) An edition published in 1977 (Shanghai: Jen min) has not been available for consideration.

For an account of editions or partial collections of these fragments, see Timoteus Pokora, *Hsin-lun (New Treatises) and Other Writings by Huan T'an (43 B.C.–28 A.D.)* (Ann Arbor: Center for Chinese Studies, the University of Michigan, 1975), pp. 271–72. This book includes translations of all fragments to be found in the works of Sun P'ing-i and Yen K'o-chün, of thirty other fragments which may be attributed to the *Hsin lun* and of eleven others that derived from different writings of Huan T'an; in all 214 fragments are treated. The translations are accompanied by notes which call attention to textual variants; the bibliographies list works in Chinese, Japanese and Western languages; and the whole is supported by an index of names, terms and subjects.

4. Further studies

For a list of the small number of studies of Huan T'an, see Pokora, *op. cit.*, pp. 273–275; see also Timoteus Pokora, 'The Life of Huan T'an', in *Archiv Orientální* 31 (1963), 1–79 and 521–576.

— Timoteus Pokora

Hsin shu 新書

1. Size and contents of the work

The received text of the *Hsin shu*, traditionally ascribed to Chia I 賈誼 (201–169 B.C.),is composed of either 55 or 56 *p'ien*, arranged in 10 *chüan*, with the variation in the number of *p'ien* depending on the division of the essay 'Kuo Ch'in' 過秦 into either two or three sections. The received text also includes the titles, without text, of two additional *p'ien*, 'Wen hsiao' 問孝 (in *chüan* no. 5) and 'Li jung yü, shang' 禮容語, 上 (in *chüan* no. 10). Numbers are not usually assigned to the *p'ien*; most editions of the work append a biography of Chia I to the text. When allowance is made for these differences, the total number of *p'ien* reaches 58.

In some editions the titles of the *p'ien* are followed by a descriptive term or short annotation: (a) in *chüan* nos. 1–4, the *p'ien* that are subtitled 'Shih shih' 事勢 consist of memorials submitted to Wen ti 文帝 concerning political issues, also recorded in slightly abbreviated form in *Han shu* 24 or 48; (b) in *chüan* nos. 5–8, the *p'ien* that are subtitled 'Lien yü' 連語 include discussions on ritual in what are apparently rough transcripts of Chia I's talks with his disciples; 'Lien yü' is itself the main title of one of the *p'ien* in *chüan* no. 5; and (c) in *chüan* no. 10, those *p'ien* that are subtitled 'Tsa shih' 雜事 include historical anecdotes illustrating political homilies, many of which also appear in contemporary works such as the *Han shih wai chuan*. These subtitles were known to Ch'ao Kung-wu 晁公武 (d. 1171), and they are included in the entry for the *Hsin shu* in the *Yü hai*.

2. Editions

Early editions of the work are known as follows:

(a) The T'an 潭 or Ch'ang-sha edition. A copy of the work was acquired by an official named Ch'eng 程, who is described as a transport officer and superintendent of training but is otherwise unknown; this was used as a basis of a print made by him and Hu Chieh 胡价,of T'an-chou 潭州, in 1181. A recut version of this edition, in which

'Kuo Ch'in' is divided into three *p'ien*, was issued in 1248. A copy of this print (1248) was available to Wang Ming-sheng 王鳴聲 (1722–98), but by the end of the Ming period it had already become rare.

(b) The Chien 建 edition. As the preface to this Sung edition was lost before late Ming, the year of publication is unknown. The table of contents was followed by the note 'Printed by Ch'en Pa-lang 陳八郎 of Chien-ning 建寧'. This edition has been identified by Hu Yü-chin 胡玉縉 (d. 1940) with a Southern Sung Ma-sha 麻沙 print. Between 1488 and 1505 Tu Mu 都穆 (1458–1525) acquired a copy of this text and had it printed. Tu's edition can probably be identified, in its turn, with an edition collated by Shen Hsieh 沈頡 in 1505, which is known to us through two Ming redactions. Of these, the first, that of Mao Fu-chi 毛斧季, omits the *p'ien* 'T'ui jang' 退讓 in *chüan* no. 7. The second, that of Wu Yüan-kung 吳元恭, supplies the missing text for this *p'ien* from elsewhere. A copy of Wu's redaction is available in the Seikadō library.

By the end of the Ming period the Chien edition, like the T'an edition, had become rare. Neither of these appear to be available today except by way of Lu Wen-ch'ao's 盧文弨 (1717–96) notes and editions (see (h) below). Wu Yüan-kung's redaction of the 1505 edition is also rare. The principal surviving witnesses to these and other early editions which were consulted by Lu Wen-ch'ao can be divided into two groups as follows:

(i) exemplified in Lu Liang-pi's 陸良弼 (16th century) edition (see (c) below), now available in the *Ssu pu ts'ung k'an* series; descriptive subtitles are appended to the titles of some of the *p'ien*. In eight *p'ien* (e.g.,'Ch'un ch'iu' 春秋 in *chüan* no.6) the text is separated into paragraphs; 'Kuo Ch'in' is divided into two sections; the two *p'ien* 'Fu i' 服疑 and 'I jang' 益壤 are included as the last two *p'ien* in *chüan* no.1; the last few columns only of the *p'ien* 'T'ui jang' 退讓 are included,being joined without break to the text of the preceding *p'ien*, 'Yü cheng' 諭誠; the biography of Chia I, appended at the end, is long.

(ii) exemplified in Li Meng-yang's 李夢陽 (16th century) edition (see (d) below, now available in the *Liang ching i pien* series); there are no subtitles after the titles of the *p'ien*; the entire text lacks indication of paragraphing; 'Kuo Ch'in' is divided into three sections; 'Fu i' and 'I jang' are included as the first two *p'ien* of *chüan* no.2; even fewer columns of 'T'ui jang' are included after a break in the text and the proper title; the biography of Chia I is short.

In group (i), 'Kuo Ch'in, shang' 上 includes the first section of the essay; 'Kuo Ch'in, hsia' 下 includes the second and the third sections. In both groups (i) and (ii),the order of the three sections varies from, but is more logical than, that given in *Shih chi* 6 where they appear jumbled, with: section 1 in *Shih chi* 6, pp. 278–82; also in *Shih chi* 48, pp. 1962–65 and *Han shu* 31, pp. 1821–25; section 2 in *Shih chi* 6, pp. 283–84; section 3 in *Shih chi* 6, pp. 276–78. There are textual variants between the versions of this essay in the Standard Histories and the *Hsin shu*.

The appended biography of Chia I varies, depending on whether it follows *Shih chi* 84, pp. 2491–2505 or *Han shu* 48, pp. 2221–66 more closely. Both of these histories include the text of two of Chia I's *fu* 賦. The *Han shu* also includes a number of his memorials on political subjects. The editions of the *Hsin shu* assigned to group (i) include both the *fu* and the memorials; they are omitted in group (ii).

The relationship between these two groups of editions, (i) and (ii), and the *T'an* and *Chien* editions (including that of Shen Hsieh) cannot be wholly determined. Both groups apparently derived from a copy or copies in which two complete folios were missing, carrying respectively the text of 'Wen hsiao' and 'Tui jang' in *chüan* nos. 5 and 7. Lu Wen-ch'ao supplies the missing 'T'ui jang' text from the *Chien* edition, and states that it was missing in the *T'an* edition. From other notes of Lu it may be inferred that group (i), as seen in the *Ssu pu ts'ung k'an* copy, nearly always follows the readings of the *Chien* edition, while group (ii), as seen in the *Liang ching i pien*, generally follows the readings of the *T'an* edition.

(c) Lu Liang-pi's edition was cut in 1513 for the governor of Ch'ang-sha 長沙 of that name. It includes a preface written by a local official named Huang Pao 黃寶 (1456–1523), possibly the most fulsome praise of Chia I ever composed, and a postface written by the Sung scholar Hu Chieh 胡价 (*cs* 1166?) for the edition of 1181. New woodblocks for a second printing, known as the *Chi fu* 吉府 or *Chi p'an* 吉潘 edition, were cut in the following year (1514). The second printing varies from the original Lu edition only by the addition of a postface by Yang Chieh 楊節, a local official, which explains the decision to cut a second set of blocks. In both cases the title of the *p'ien* 'Chieh hsüan' 解縣 is omitted in the table of contents, although the text is included in *chüan* no. 3 as usual. Copies of the *Chi fu* edition are held in the National Library, Peking.

While these are praised by the *Ssu k'u* editors as being the best of the Ming editions, they are marked by a large number of scribal errors (e.g., *hsüeh* 雪, *mai* 買, *she* 舍, and *fu* 夫 in place of *nüeh* 虐, *mao* 冒, *ho* 合 and *t'ien* 天 respectively). A few glosses concern pronunciation.

This edition has been reproduced in the *Ssu pu ts'ung k'an* series; it also forms the basis for the text included in the *Kuang Han Wei ts'ung shu* and Wang Mo's 王謨 (*cs* 1778) *Han Wei ts'ung shu*. Ch'eng Jung's 程榮 (1447–1520) *Han Wei ts'ung shu* carries a text that is closely related to the Lu Liang-pi edition, but Ch'eng draws indiscriminately on other versions and includes a number of characters, especially particles, not seen elsewhere.

(d) The *Chia tzu hsin shu* 賈子新書 of Li Meng-yang (also known by his *hao* of K'ung-t'ung 空同) was also printed in 1513. Li's preface states that he had consulted a variety of editions then circulating, including the *T'an* edition. His work is available in the *Liang ching i pien* series of 1582. At a later date this text was re-edited by a certain Ch'in Yüan-yu 欽遠猷, of unknown date, who followed the lead of Ho Meng-ch'un 何孟春 (*cs* 1493; see below). According to Lu Wen-ch'ao, Ho had appended a *p'ien* entitled 'Shen ch'ü she' 審取舍 after 'Kuo Ch'in'; in reality the text of that *p'ien* is identical with the 'Li ch'a' 禮察 section of the *Ta Tai li chi*.

Ch'ien Chen-lung's 錢震瀧 (*cs* 1631) edition, printed in Japan in 1749, is also based on Li Meng-yang's edition. It includes Huang Pao's preface, a general critique of the *Hsin shu* and various remarks by P'i Jih-hsiu 皮日休 (*cs* 860–73).

(e) The *T'ai fu Chia Hsin shu* 太傅賈新書 of 1519 with commentary by Ho Meng-ch'un (also called the *Tien* 滇 edition) is identified by the distinctive title of the book itself and the titles of some of the *p'ien* (e.g., the *p'ien* 'Hsiung nu' 匈奴 in *chüan* no. 4 is entitled 'San piao wu erh' 三表五餌). In its arrangement of the text, 'Kuo Ch'in' is divided into three sections while five *fu* attributed to Chia I and a short biography follow *chüan* no.10. Finally, as stated above, Ho Meng-ch'un was the first to add textual material from the *Ta Tai li chi* to *chüan* no. 1. This edition was severely criticised by Sun Chih-tsu 孫志祖 (1737–1801) and Cheng Chen 鄭珍 (1806–64).

(f) The *Chia tzu Hsin shu* of Ch'ien Yen-tzu 潛菴子 (1577) arranges the entire text in two *chüan* (*shang* and *hsia*), rather than the usual ten. Descriptive subtitles follow the titles of some of the *p'ien* as in Lu Liang-pi's edition. The text is divided into paragraphs in some, but not all, of those *p'ien* that are treated in that way in Lu's edition. 'Kuo Ch'in' is divided into two sections. The order of the *p'ien* varies considerably from that found in groups (i) and (ii). A fuller version of 'T'ui jang' than that found in groups (i) and (ii) is included, together

with a *p'ien* entitled 'Ting [sic] ch'ü she' 定取舍, whose text is equivalent to the 'Li ch'a' section of the *Ta Tai li chi*.

(g) The late Ming *Hsin shu* in the Hang-chou 杭州 collection of Chu
T'u-lung 朱圖隆 was edited by Huang Fu-lung 黃甫龍 and T'ang
Lin 唐琳. Copies of this text in ten *chüan*, with an appended biography of Chia I, are to be found in the rare book collections of the
National Central Library (Taiwan) and the Gest Oriental Library
(Princeton University). The copy which is held in Taiwan has been
annotated by Huang T'ing-chien 黃廷鑑 (b. 1762). The copy which
is held in Princeton includes a manuscript introduction by its owner,
Kan P'eng-yün 甘鵬雲, which discusses the merits of various
editions; there are marginal notes by a number of scholars, mainly
of the Ming period, such as Yang Shih-ch'i 楊士奇 (1365–1444), Kuei
Yu-kuang 歸有光 (1506–1571), Mao K'un 茅坤 (1512–1601), Wang
Tao-k'un 汪道昆 (1525–1593), Wang Shih-chen 王世貞 (1526–1590)
and Ch'en Jen-hsi 陳仁錫 (*c.* 1580–*c.* 1635).

(h) The late 18th century edition of Lu Wen-ch'ao is based upon eight
editions which he names; he divides 'Kuo Ch'in' into three sections,
following the *T'an* edition. Lu also took note of parallel passages in
texts such as the *Ta Tai li chi* and the *Han shu*. The edition has been
criticised by Yü Chia-hsi 余嘉錫 (1883–1955) and Yü Yüeh 俞樾
(1821–1907) for modifying the text in the light of the biography of
Chia I in the *Han shu*; the *Hsü hsiu Ssu k'u ch'üan shu tsung mu t'i yao*
續修四庫全書總目提要 (Taipei: Shang wu, 1971–72; *tzu* 子, p. 1016)
accuses Lu of ignorance of philological studies. Other scholars, however, have regarded this edition as the best that is available. It appeared first in the *Pao ching t'ang ts'ung shu* (reproduced in the *Lung
hsi ching she ts'ung shu*); the text was also followed in the *Ssu pu pei
yao*, *Ts'ung shu chi ch'eng* (where it is punctuated), *Nien erh tzu*, and
Tzu shu erh shih wu chung.

(i) The 1904 edition of Wang Keng-hsin 王耕心, entitled *Chia tzu tz'u ku
賈子次詁*, has been praised by some scholars such as Ch'en Chao-
ch'en 陳兆琛, but it may be criticized on the grounds of its anachronistic comparison of the *Hsin shu* with Buddhist philosophical
tenets. The National Central Library of Taiwan holds Wang's draft
manuscript, rendered nearly illegible by revisions in red or black
ink. A copy is also held by the University of Chicago.

The editions of both Lu Wen-ch'ao and Wang Keng-hsin should be
consulted by serious students of the *Hsin shu*. Other editions of secondary importance include those of Ho T'ang 何鐺 (printed some time
between 1522 and 1566), Ho Liang-chün 何良俊 (also known as Ho

Yüan-lang 何 元 朗) and Chao Hsi-ming 趙 曦 明, whose annotated edition was available to Lu Wen-ch'ao.

3.   Textual history and authenticity

Two passages in the *Han shu*'s biography of Chia I mention his writings. *Han shu* 48, p. 2230 states that the biography includes many of his memorials in abbreviated form; *Han shu* 48, p. 2265 (Pan Ku's appreciation) elaborates this statement, by remarking that 'Chia I's written works amount to 58 *p'ien*, from which those that have a direct bearing on the issues of his time have been selected for inclusion in the biography'. The same figure of 58 *p'ien* is given for Chia I's writings in *Han shu* 30, p. 1726 under the category of *ju chia* 儒 家, but apart from this entry we know little more about the early history of these works. The *Ch'ung wen tsung mu* of 1038 records the tradition that Liu Hsiang 劉 向 (79–8 B.C.) had reduced the 72 *p'ien* of Chia I's collected works to 58; a brief note by Ying Shao 應 劭 (c. 140 to before 204) mentions the existence of 'Kuo Ch'in', in two *p'ien*, as part of Master Chia's corpus. A suggestion by Wen Ying 文 穎 (fl. 196–200) that would identify a reference in *Han shu* 7, p. 223 with the extant *p'ien* 'Pao fu' 保 傅 cannot necessarily be sustained (see commentary in *Han shu pu chu* 7.4b).

Reconstruction of the early text is complicated by the absence of references, before the Liang dynasty, either to the title *Hsin shu* or to the number of *chüan*. The *I lin* and the *Tzu ch'ao* list the work under the title *Chia I Hsin shu*. In the *I lin* it is twice described as consisting of eight *chüan*; in the *Tzu ch'ao* and the bibliographical list of the *Chiu T'ang shu* 47, p. 2024 the figure of nine is given. According to the *Ch'ung wen tsung mu*, the same figure was given in the bibliographical treatise of the *Sui shu*, but in the received text (34, p. 997) this appears as ten, as it also does in the *Hsin t'ang shu* 59, p. 1510. There is no entry for the work in Fujiwara Sukeyo's 藤 原 佐 世 catalogue. Ch'en Chen-sun 陳 振 孫 (c. 1190–after 1249) refers to a copy with the *fu* 'Tiao hsiang' 弔 湘 appended, together with Chia I's biography, in an eleventh *chüan*. Yü Chia-hsi persuasively argues that it is possible to account for the discrepancy in the number of the *chüan* without postulating major differences between different editions.

Two questions arise regarding the authenticity of the received text; (i) whether those parts which also appear in the *Shih chi* or the *Han shu* were drawn from an existing collection of Chia I's writings, in 58 *p'ien*, or whether the *Hsin shu* drew on the histories for those sections; and (ii) whether those sections of the *Hsin shu* that do not have a counterpart in the histories should be regarded as a late fabrication. The possibility has been raised that different selections of Chia I's writings were circulating at one time under the three separate titles of *Chia I*, *Chia tzu* and *Hsin shu*. As the work occasionally refers to 'Master Chia' it is clear that parts cannot have originated from the hand of Chia I himself, but must be due to compilation by his immediate pupils or followers; herein may lie a simple explanation for the use of *Chia tzu* as a title for the book. Sun I-jang 孫詒讓 (1848–1908) offers a plausible explanation for the title *Hsin shu*; i.e., that, as was the case with certain other texts such as the *Hsün tzu, Lieh tzu* and *Kuan tzu*, the term *Hsin shu* was adopted so as to distinguish the new version, collated by Liu Hsiang, from earlier collections; and for some reason *Hsin shu* was erroneously retained as the principal title for Chia I's writings.

Doubts regarding the authenticity of the *Hsin shu* have been voiced since Sung times. Some scholars, including Ch'en Chen-sun and Yao Nai 姚鼐, (1732–1815) dismiss those parts of the book that are not reproduced in the *Han shu* as clumsy forgeries that are unworthy of attention. Their attempts to disprove the authenticity of the text focus on issues of literary style, grammar and supposed anachronisms. Despite this the *Hsin shu* has had its supporters. Lu Wen-ch'ao took the view that the work had been put together by near contemporaries of Chia I who were well acquainted with his opinions. The *Ssu k'u* editors believed that a basis for the work had been available in the *Han shu* in T'ang times, and that the received text, while not dating from the Sung period, was undoubtedly of sufficient authenticity to merit study.

The opinion of the *Ssu k'u* editors that the text before them was not identical with that of the Sung period has been refuted by Yü Chia-hsi, who concludes that the *Han shu* took its selections from the *Hsin shu* rather than vice versa. The validity of the received text also gains support from Liu Shih-p'ei's 劉師培 (1884–1919) comparison with quotations that are ascribed to Chia I in T'ang works; only three T'ang passages do not correspond with material that is in extant editions. In recent times the most spirited defence of the *Hsin shu* has been presented by Wang Chou-ming 王洲明 (see his 'Hsin shu fei wei shu k'ao' 新書非 偽書考, in *Wen hsüeh i ch'an* 1982:2, 17–28). Wang ably covers most points in the debate, but inexplicably fails to provide a linguistic analysis of the particles used in the memorials that are included in the *Han shu* and those in the *Hsin shu* that do not correspond with usage of the *Han shu*. Further research is needed in this respect. See also Reinhard Emmerich, 'Untersuchungen zu Jia Yi (200–168 v.Chr.) (Habilitationsschrift, Hamburg, August 1991), which follows on from the work of Yü

Chia-hsi and Yoshinami Takashi 好並隆司, 'Ka Gi to koso kōchū hō' 賈
誼 と 顧租公鑄法, *Shigaku kenkyū* 史學研究 (Hiroshima) 100 (1967),
77–86.

4. Critical scholarship

A number of essays and poems, including the Chia I lun 賈誼論 of Su
Tung-p'o 蘇東坡 (1036–1101), have been devoted to an appreciation of
Chia I, often as a talented man of letters who was ignored or rejected by
his emperor. The following notes are concerned with work which fo-
cusses on the text of the *Hsin shu* and its problems.

(a) Liu Shih-p'ei's notes appear under various titles in *Kuo ts'ui hsüeh pao*
    61:2833–42; 62:2951–65; 63:3175–84; 64:3343–48; 65:3475–80; 66:3611–
    19; 67:3749–56; 69:4031–36; 70:4187–95; and 71:4331–37 (1909–10). They
    are included with some change of title in *Liu Shen-shu hsien sheng i
    shu* 2:1167–89 (Taiwan: Ta-hsin Press, 1965). These notes mainly con-
    cern variant readings and the identification of loan characters.
(b) Yü Yüeh's 俞樾 (1821–1907) comments in *Chu tzu p'ing i* 諸子平議
    attempt to reconstruct the characteristic style of an original text of
    Chia I and act as a valuable corrective to Lu Wen-ch'ao's edition.
(c) In *Tu chu tzu cha chi* 讀諸子札記 (Peking: Chung hua ch'ien yin,
    1959) pp. 140–238, T'ao Hung-ch'ing 陶鴻慶 (1859–1918) assumes
    that the *Hsin shu* should be corrected in the light of passages in the
    Han shu, and suggests the removal of passages thought to be redun-
    dant or incomprehensible.
(d) In his *Cha i*, Sun I-jang discusses nineteen passages, suggesting
    emendations on the basis of other texts, and citing opinions of Hung
    I-hsüan 洪頤煊 (1765–1837) and Tai Wang 戴望 (1783–1863) that are
    otherwise difficult or impossible to find.
(e) Chang Chih-ch'un 張之純, in *Chu tzu ch'ing hua lu shih pa chung* 諸
    子精華錄十八種 (dated 1939: reprinted Taipei: Hung yeh, 1970);
    comments to Lu Wen-ch'ao's edition which often discuss the struc-
    ture and style of Chia I's writings.
(f) Chiang Jun-hsün 江潤勳, Ch'en Wei-liang 陳煒良 and Ch'en Ping-
    liang 陳炳良, *Chia I yen chiu* 賈誼研究; Hong Kong: Ch'iu ching,
    1958, reprinted 1969. This book derived from research projects writ-
    ten by undergraduates at the University of Hong Kong who were
    studying under the direction of Jao Tsung-i 饒宗頤. Jao's preface is
    followed by Ch'en Wei-liang's essay on the authenticity of the *Hsin
    shu*; this includes comparative tables that show the correspondence
    between the text of the *Hsin shu* and other works. Ch'en Wei-liang's

second chapter discusses the synthesis of ideas in Chia I's philosophy. The third essay, by Chiang Jun-hsün and Ch'en Ping-liang, is a commentary on 'Kuo Ch'in'. The book forms an excellent introduction to the literary, historical and philosophical problems of the *Hsin shu*.

(g) Ch'i Yü-chang 祁玉章, *Chia tzu t'an wei* 賈子探微 (Taipei: San min, 1969); a summarized account of textual transmission, Chia I's biography and problems of authenticity, with lists of available editions and studies of Chia I.

(h) Ch'i Yü-chang, *Chia tzu Hsin shu chiao shih* 賈子新書校釋 (Taipei: Tung ya, 1974); a commentary to the *Hsin shu* which compares parallel passages and identifies place names and historical personages. Also included is a chronology of Chia I's life.

(i) *Chia I chuan chu* 賈誼傳注, Shanghai: Jen min, 1975; this includes an essay by Hung Hsüan 紅宣 (reprinted from *Chieh fang jih pao* of 26–11-74) which comments on the tension in Chia I's philosophy between his advocacy of the consolidation of imperial power and his concern with the use of ethical values to maintain the political balance. There is a commentary to the *Han shu*'s biography of Chia I and to the two essays 'Kuo Ch'in' and 'Chih an' 治安.

(j) Ts'ai T'ing-chi 蔡延吉, *Chia I yen chiu* (Taipei: Wen shih che hsüeh, 1984) presents, often uncritically, materials on a variety of subjects related to Chia I, including early biographical accounts; the authenticity of the *Hsin shu*; the origins and expressions of Chia I's philosophical political and economic thought; and his literary achievements.

(k) Satō Akira 佐藤明, 'Shinsho yōkei hen ni tsuite' 新書容經篇につい て; *Chūgoku kankei ronsetsu shiryō* 中國關係論說資料 23 (1981), 309–16. By means of a comparison of intellectual trends during the reigns of Wen ti and Wu ti, Satō makes the case that the 'Jung ching' 容經 *p'ien* must be genuine, despite allegations that it is among the forged sections.

(l) Uno Shigehiko 宇野茂彥, 'Ka Gi Shinsho satsuki' 賈誼新書札記, *Nagoya daigaku bungakubu kenkyū ronshū (Tetsugaku)* 102 (1988), 177–87. Uno argues that the *Hsin shu* cannot be a forgery, on the grounds of its consistency with texts assigned to the same period, its unique manner of citation from early texts of Former Han, and its deft use of philosophical terms.

(m) For a list of studies on the *Hsin shu* by scholars of the Tokugawa and Meiji periods, see *Kokusho sōmokuroku* 國書總目錄 (Tokyo: Iwanami, 1989) II, pp. 71, 116.

5. Japanese edition

D. *Kokuyaku kambun taisei*; no.18, 1924, edited by Yamaguchi Satsujō.

6. Index

A Concordance to the Xin shu 新書逐字索引, ed. D.C. Lau and Chen Fong Ching; *ICS* series, Hong Kong: Commercial Press, forthcoming, 1994.

— Michael Nylan

Hsin yü 新語

1. Content

The received text is divided into two *chüan*, each of which comprises six *p'ien*. These are all entitled with a phrase of two characters which summarises or relates to the subject; they are not catch-phrases taken from the opening words of the text. The work discusses various aspects of the government of man and the duties of a ruler; it praises the value of government by a true king (*wang* 王) and decries that of an overlord (*pa* 霸). There are allusions to the *Ch'un ch'iu* and the *Lun yü* by way of support for the theme, and the book has been described by the *Ssu k'u* editors as being the most mature expression of Confucian opinion for the Han period, apart from the writings of Tung Chung-shu 董仲舒 (*c.* 179–*c.* 104 B.C.). The text cites from the *Lao tzu* once. One critic (Huang Chen 黃震 1213–80) remarks that the book is in many respects highly logical and that it rejects rash statements that concern superhuman or supernatural elements. One *p'ien* (no. 6; *SPTK* ed. *shang* 15b) includes what must be one of the earliest criticisms of the habits and austerities associated with the cult of mountains.

2. Date of composition and authenticity

The authorship of the book is ascribed to Lu Chia 陸賈, whose life may have extended from the time of the First Ch'in Emperor (died 210 B.C.) until the reign of Ching ti 景帝 (reigned 157–141 B.C.); he is known for undertaking two diplomatic missions to Nan Yüeh 南越. According to a well-known incident recorded in the *Shih chi* 97, p. 2699 and the *Han shu* 43, p. 2113, Lu Chia had been in the habit of admonishing Kao ti 高帝 (reigned as emperor 202–195), first of the Han emperors, on the nature of a sovereign's duties and the circumstances of the rise and fall of dynasties. Somewhat mortified, Kao ti asked Lu Chia to prepare a written version of his homilies; the resulting twelve *p'ien*, submitted in turn to the emperor, received his approbation and were entitled the *Hsin yü*.

The *Shih chi* (97, p. 2705) carries the specific statement that the author of that work had read the twelve *p'ien* of the *Hsin yü* of Mr. Lu, and there are two entries for Lu Chia's writings in the *Han shu*. One of these (30, p. 1726) credits him with 23 *p'ien* of writings, without title, under the category of *ju chia* 儒家; the other lists him as the author of three *p'ien* of *fu* 賦 (30, p. 1748). There appear to be no specific references to other works in prose that are attributed to Lu Chia other than the *Ch'u Han ch'un ch'iu* 楚漢春秋, in 9 *p'ien* (*Han shu* 30, p. 1714). The text of this work had been lost by the Southern Sung period, and it has been suggested by Wang Hsien-ch'ien 王先謙 (1842–1918) (*Han shu pu chu* 30.18a) that the work of this name that was available during the T'ang period was not Lu Chia's original text. The *Ch'u Han ch'un ch'iu* exists now solely as a collection of fragments; for a study of this question by J.L. Kroll, see *RBS* no. 7 (for 1961), item 77.

The statement that the *Hsin yü* consisted of two *chüan* is seen in a citation from the *Ch'i lu* 七錄 of Juan Hsiao-hsü 阮孝緒 (479–536) and in the *I lin* 意林 of Ma Tsung 馬總 (prefaces 787 and 804); it is repeated in bibliographical lists such as *Sui shu* 34, p. 997, *Chiu T'ang shu* 47, p. 2024 and *Hsin T'ang shu* 59, p. 1510. The same figure occurs in the entries of the *Ch'ung wen tsung mu* (1034–42) and the *Sung shih* 205, p. 5207, where the work is placed in the category of miscellaneous rather than Confucian philosophies. There is no entry for the work in the *Chün chai tu shu chih* (compiled 1151–1249) or the *Chih chai shu lu chieh t'i* (completed 1249). In the list of titles appended to the *Tzu lüeh* (*SPPY* ed., 10b), Kao Ssu-sun 高似孫 (c. 1160–1230) enters the figure of '2 *chüan*, 10 *p'ien*' for the *Hsin yü*. This can probably be ignored as an error, as he likewise (*SPPY* ed., 7a) cites the figure of 20 *chüan* for the work, as from the *T'ang shu*, and this is wholly unsupported.

Huang Chen quotes the titles of the 12 *p'ien* in a form that is identical with that of the received text. In the *Yü hai* his contemporary Wang Ying-lin 王應麟 (1223–96) writes that seven *p'ien* survived, and he lists the titles of nos. 1, 2, 3, 4, 7, 8 and 9 as they are known today. In commenting on the two different copies that were evidently seen by these two scholars in the 13th century, Yen K'o-chün 嚴可均 (1762–1843; in a preface dated 1815) suggests that the book had been lost by the Sung period, when it was again brought to light; but even then it was in an incomplete form. As against this suggestion, Yü Chia-hsi 余嘉錫 (1883–1955) prefers the view that there were two different copies in the Sung period, of which one, which was incomplete, was seen by Wang Ying-lin, and one, which was complete, was seen by Huang Chen. The same view is taken by Hsü Fu-kuan 徐復觀 (1976).

Huang Chen had expressed doubts about the authenticity of the text that he saw, on the somewhat questionable grounds that the content did not entirely correspond with the account of the book and its origins as given in the *Shih chi* and *Han shu*. He suggests that part of the text could hardly have been relevant to, or acceptable, in the times in which Lu Chia was supposedly tendering his advice. In a notice which is not free entirely from error, the *Ssu k'u* editors expressed their doubts about the *Hsin yü*'s authenticity on three grounds:

(a) Despite the statement in the *Han shu* that Ssu-ma Ch'ien 司馬遷 (?145–?86 B.C.) had drawn on the *Hsin yü* as source material, there are no traces to show that parts of the work were incorporated in the *Shih chi*. Both Hu Shih 胡適 (1891–1962) and Yü Chia-hsi have shown that the statement which the *Ssu k'u* editors ascribed to the *Han shu* is in fact not to be found there and that it originated only from Kao Ssu-sun.

(b) The *Lun heng* carries a citation from Lu Chia which is not to be found in the received text of the *Hsin yü*. To this objection, Yen K'o-chün and Yü Chia-hsi counter that the reference in the *Lun heng* is simply to the writings of Lu Chia and not specifically to the *Hsin yü*.

(c) The *Hsin yü* carries a citation from the *Ku Liang chuan*; however, as that text was first produced only in the time of Wu ti 武帝 (reigned 141–87), it could not have been available for Lu Chia to see. This objection has been refuted by Yen K'o-chün, T'ang Yen 唐晏 (1857– 1920), Yü Chia-hsi and Lo Ken-tse 羅根澤, on the grounds that Lu Chia could easily have had access to the *Ku Liang chuan* before its disappearance under Ch'in, and that he was referring to passages omitted in the later version of that work.

The *Ssu k'u* editors suggest that, in view of these reasons and the *Yü hai*'s limitation to 7 *p'ien*, at least part and possibly all of the text is not authentic. However, they take note of the citations that are seen in the *I lin* and in Li Shan's 李善 (d. 689) comments to the *Wen hsüan* 文選, which are identical or almost identical with the received text; they therefore infer that any interpolations that there are date from before the T'ang period. In view of the *Yü hai*'s limitation to 7 *p'ien*, they suggest that the other five were written by a scholar who wished to make the text conform with the statements of the *Shih chi* and *Han shu* that it consisted of 12 *p'ien*.

Sun Tz'u-chou 孫次舟 gives what is possibly a more significant reason for doubting the authenticity of the received text. He points out (1936–37) that one, and possibly two, *p'ien* (nos. 1 and 2) refer to the *wu ching* 五經, and that this expression had not come into use in Lu Chia's own time. However, Hsü Fu-kuan 徐復觀 apparently does not regard this as a serious objection. Sun mentions that other scholars who entertained suspicions about the *Hsin yü* included Liang Ch'i-ch'ao 梁啓超 (1873–1929) and Chang Hsi-t'ang 張西堂.

The authenticity of the *Hsin yü* is re-affirmed by a number of notable scholars such as Yü Yüeh 俞樾 (1821–1907), Sun I-jang 孫詒讓 (1848–1908), Yü Chia-hsi, Hu Shih, Lo Ken-tse, Hsü Fu-kuan and Miyazaki Ichisada 宮崎市定. In addition to their refutation of the suspicions of the *Ssu k'u* editors, Yen K'o-chün draws attention to the inclusion in the *Ch'ün shu chih yao* and elsewhere of citations from four of the five *p'ien* whose titles were omitted from mention by Wang Ying-lin. Those citations are identical with the received text, which must thus originate from copies of the Sui and T'ang periods. No evidence can be adduced to support the supposition that the book had been lost by the Sung period and discovered in an incomplete state. In insisting on the authenticity of the *Hsin yü*, Miyazaki points out that the received text is marred by a large number of errors and omissions, and by the disarrangement of a number of strips. In his reconstruction of the text of *p'ien* no. 1, he is at pains to produce a version that reads coherently and logically as a statement of 'Confucian' philosophy.

3.   Text history

Prints of the *Hsin yü* that date from the Sung or Yüan periods are unknown, and the first print to be found is that of 1502, with a preface by Ch'ien Fu 錢福 (1461–1504) and a postface by Tu Mu 都穆 (1458–1525), both dated in that year. This text is divided into two *chüan* (*shang* and *hsia*), each of which includes six *p'ien*. At least one recut edition of this print is known (1621).

According to Tu Mu, whose postface curiously enough describes the book, quite erroneously, as consisting of three *chüan*, copies of the *Hsin yü* were scarce in his time and the text was defective. Li T'ing-wu 李廷梧 (style Chung-yang 仲陽; graduated with a *chin shih* degree in 1499) acquired a copy, and had the text cut on blocks. This print (format 10 by 17) is reproduced in the *Ssu pu ts'ung k'an* and was used as a basis for the *Ssu pu pei yao*, and, possibly, for the *Liang ching i pien* (1582). The punctuated text of the *Chu tzu chi ch'eng* follows the *Ssu pu ts'ung k'an*.

Yen K'o-chün states that all copies derive from this print, but, as will be seen, this statement is not entirely acceptable. The text of the print of 1502 is almost identical with one of 1591, which carries a preface by Fan Ch'in 范欽 (Ta-ch'ung 大沖 1506–85) (reproduced in *Hu pei hsien cheng i shu*, from a *T'ien i ko* print). The same text is followed in the *Han Wei ts'ung shu* and the *Tseng ting Han Wei ts'ung shu*; the former one of these includes Ch'ien Fu's preface; the latter includes a page of independent and unsigned criticism immediately before the text, and a postface by Wang Mo 王謨 (*cs* 1778). There are a number of *lacunae* in the text, particularly in the later *p'ien* of the book.

Despite Yen K'o-chün's statement, it may be suggested that the print in the *Tzu hui* (1576–77), with a format of 10 by 21, is of an independent lineage, but deriving from the same source as the print of 1502. The reasons for this suggestion are:

(a) The text is entitled *Lu tzu* 陸子 and not *Hsin yü*.
(b) The text is presented in one *chüan* without break; the division into 12 *p'ien* is identical.
(c) There are textual variants, and the size of the *lacunae* as indicated varies from that noted in the print of 1502.
(d) In at least one instance, the order of two half-folios of text varies as between (i) the *Tzu hui* and (ii) the 1502 print and its derivatives, where it is incorrect. From this difference it may be inferred that both editions were copied from a text whose half-folio carried 13 columns, usually of 17 characters each. Whereas the *Tzu hui* copied the half-folios in the correct order, the print of 1502 retained the original column length, which was changed in the *Tzu hui*.

There is one further print which it has not been possible to trace. This is described as a small character edition, superior to others, but with text and notes defective; see Ch'ü Yung 瞿鏞, *T'ieh ch'in t'ung chien lou ts'ang shu mu lu* 鐵琴銅劍樓藏書目錄 (1898), 13.4a.

An annotated text which is included in the *Lung hsi ching she ts'ung shu* under the title *Lu tzu Hsin yü chiao chu* 陸子新語校注 includes an annotation by T'ang Yen. The text is divided into two *chüan* and is stated to be based on the *Tzu hui* edition, with full reference to the *T'ien i ko* print. This edition is dated in 1917; it includes the critical notes of the *Ssu k'u* editors together with T'ang Yen's own preface and postface. *Lacunae* in the text are marked by symbols for each missing character, i.e., not simply as a statement of the length of the deficiency. The text usually follows the *Tzu hui*, but occasionally emends that version so as to follow the *T'ien i ko* edition; references in the notes sometimes mention an unspecified print, which can almost certainly be identified as that of the *Han Wei ts'ung shu*. The notes also refer to textual variants (e.g., as seen in the citations in the *I lin*); they draw attention to textual peculiarities and difficulties, to rhymes and to parallels in other books. Of all editions, this is probably the most valuable, as is agreed by Hu Shih (in a postface) and Miyazaki.

4. Recent studies and research aids

No index or concordance to the work seems to have been published. Annotations by Lu Wen-ch'ao 盧文弨 (1717–96) to a copy of the *Han Wei ts'ung shu* are preserved in one collection of rare books (see Ting Ping 丁丙, *Shan pen shu shih ts'ang shu chih* (1901) 15.3a). A copy of an annotated edition by Sung Hsiang-feng 宋翔鳳 (1776–1860) which was available to Sun I-jang is held in the National Library of China, Peking. Works to which reference has been made above will be found as follows:

(a) Chang Hsi-t'ang, 'Lu Chia Hsin yü pien wei 陸賈新語辨僞'; *Ku shih pien* no.4, 1933:4, 214–15.

(b) Hsü Fu-kuan; 'Han ch'u ti ch'i meng ssu hsiang chia—Lu Chia 漢初的啓蒙思想家 —— 陸賈'; *Ta lu tsa chih* 52:2 (1976) 1–9; revised in *Liang Han ssu hsiang shih* 兩漢思想史, vol. II (Taipei: Taiwan hsüeh sheng, 1976), pp. 85–108.

(c) Hu Shih 胡適 (i) 'Lu Chia Hsin yü k'ao 陸賈新語考'; first written as a postface to T'ang Yen's edition of the *Hsin yü* (1930), and printed in the *Bulletin of the National Library Peiping* IV:1 (Shanghai: 1930) 1–4; included in *Ku shih pien* no.4, 1933:4, 195–98, and in Hu Shih's collected works, series III, pp. 873–77. (ii) 'Shu Lu Chia ti ssu hsiang 述陸賈的思想', *Hu Shih hsüan chi* 胡適選集 (Taipei: Wen hsing shu tien, 1966) *hsüeh* section, pp. 109f; first appeared 1937.

(d) Lo Ken-tse, 'Lu Chia Hsin yü k'ao cheng 陸賈新語考證'; *Hsüeh wen* 1 (November 1930) 2–7; reprinted in *Ku shih pien* no. 4, 1933:4, 198–202.

(e) Miyazaki Ichisada, 'Riku Ka Shingo dōki hen no kenkyū 陸賈新語道基篇の研究'; *Tōhō gaku* 25 (March 1963), 1–10. A vindication of the authenticity of the work is followed by the attempted reconstruction of the text of *p'ien* no. 1, whose content is regarded as fundamental to Lu Chia's thought. See also his article 'Riku Ka "Shingo" no kenkyū' 陸賈《新語》の研究 (*Kyoto daigaku bungakubu kenkyū kiyō* 9, 1965).

(f) Sun I-jang; see *Cha i* 7.8b (1894).

(g) Sun Tz'u-chou, 'Lun Lu Chia Hsin yü ti chen wei 論陸賈新語的眞僞'; *Ku shih pien* no.6, 1936–37, 112–22.

(h) Yen K'o-chün, 'T'ieh ch'iao man kao 鐵橋漫稿', 5.22b (1885).

(i) Yü Chia-hsi; see *Ku shih pien* no.4, 1933, 203–14; *Ssu k'u t'i yao pien cheng*, 10.518–32.

(j) Yü Yüeh; see *Chu tzu p'ing i pu lu* (1922) 14.1a.

Other studies include:

(k) Ho Ling-hsü 賀凌盧, 'Lu Chia ti cheng chih ssu hsiang 陸賈的政治思想'; *Ssu yü yen* 6:6 (1969), 30–5.

(l) Kanaya Osamu 金谷治, 'Riku Ka to Rō Kei 陸賈と婁敬'; *TSK* 15 (1957), 309–30; see *RBS* 3, item 816.

5. Translations

(a) von Gabain, Annemarie, 'Ein Fürstenspiegel: Das Sin-yü des Lu Kia'; *MSOS* 33:1 (1930) 1–82; reviewed by Paul Pelliot in *TP* 27 (1930) 429–34.

(b) An annotated translation, with introduction, was presented as a thesis for the degree of Master of Arts (Asian Studies) at the Australian National University (April 1974) by Ku Mei-kao, under the title 'A New Discourse On the Art of Government being a translation of *Hsin yü* of Lu Chia (? –178 B.C.) of the Western Han Dynasty'.

6. Japanese editions

There is no record of an early entry of the *Hsin yü* into Japan. A recut print of the 1591 edition held in the Naikaku Library (dated 1748, with corrections of 1796) includes *kambun* diacritical marks; a further copy of this print may be available in the Seikaku Library. Miyazaki has appended a Japanese version to his reconstructed text of *p'ien* no.1 (see under (4) above).

D. *Kokuyaku kambun taisei*; no.10, 1921, edited by Kojima Kenkichirō.

7. Index

A Concordance to the Shen jian, Zhong lun and Xin yu 申鑑, 中論, 新語逐字索引, ed. D.C. Lau and Chen Fong Ching; *ICS* series, Hong Kong: Commercial Press, forthcoming 1995.

— Michael Loewe

Hsün tzu 荀子

1. Origin of the work

According to a short biographical note in the *Shih chi* (74, p. 2348), Hsün Ch'ing 荀卿 of Chao 趙 served in the pre-imperial kingdoms of Ch'i 齊 and Ch'u 楚, and died after dismissal from the post of magistrate of Lan-ling 蘭陵; Li Ssu 李斯 (?280–208 B.C.) had been one of his pupils. Being dismayed at the contemporary lack of political stability and at the addiction to occult practices, Hsün Ch'ing responded by propounding the ethical ideals of the scholastics (*ju chia* 儒家) and Mo tzu, producing an ordered set of writings of 'several myriads of words'.

This bare statement may be supplemented from other sources. Hsün Ch'ing's given name is said to have been K'uang 況; and Sun 孫 sometimes replaces the Hsün of his surname, allegedly in deference to the taboo on Han Hsüan ti's 宣帝 (reigned 74–49 B.C.) personal name of Hsün 詢. Precise dates for Hsün Ch'ing's life are difficult to determine, but it seems that he lived to a great age. Some references suggest that he may have been born as early as *c.* 335 B.C. and to have died as late as *c.* 238. His pupils included Han Fei 韓非. Ten *p'ien* of *fu* are listed under the name of Sun Ch'ing (*Han shu* 30, p. 1750), but there is nothing to indicate that this entry refers to the work of Hsün Ch'ing of Chao.

2. The arrangement and divisions of the work

The list of *ju chia* writings in the *Han shu* includes an entry for the *Sun ch'ing tzu* 孫卿子 in 33 *p'ien* (*HS* 30, p. 1725); this figure is believed by Wang Ying-lin 王應麟 (1223–96) and Shen Ch'in-han 沈欽韓 (1743–96) to be an error for 32, which appears consistently elsewhere. Two notices to the work are ascribed to Liu Hsiang 劉向 (79–8 B.C.); in the longer of these, which probably first appeared in the print of 1068, we are told that, in the course of collating copies of the text, Liu Hsiang had at his disposal a total of 322 *p'ien*. He had rejected 290 of these as being duplicates, and had settled on a definitive text of 32 *p'ien*, to be written out on strips of seasoned bamboo. This statement is repeated by a number of bibliographers, including Ch'ao Kung-wu 晁公武 (d. 1171), Ch'en

Chen-sun 陳振孫 (*c.* 1190–after 1249), Wang Ying-lin and Ma Tuan-lin 馬端臨 (1254–1325); later, however, Lü Ssu-mien 呂思勉 (1884–1957) rejected the whole of this longer notice as being spurious and not the work of Liu Hsiang.

In the catalogue of Fujiwara Sukeyo (died 898), the *Sun ch'ing tzu* is listed as consisting of 10 *chüan*, but the figure of 12 is given in the bibliographical lists of the *Sui shu* (34, p. 997), *Chiu T'ang shu* (47, p. 2024) and *Hsin T'ang shu* (59, p. 1510) (all under *ju chia*). The *Hsin T'ang shu* also includes a second entry for the work with Yang Liang's 楊倞 annotation, in 20 *chüan*; entries for the work in 20 *chüan* appear also in the *Sung shih* (205, p. 5172), *Ch'ung wen ts'ung mu*, *Chih chai shu lu chieh t'i* and *Wen hsien t'ung k'ao*.

In the *Chün chai tu shu chih*, Ch'ao Kung-wu includes the statement that Liu Hsiang had set out his text of 32 *p'ien* in 12 *chüan*. In the preface to his annotated edition of the work, which is dated in 819, Yang Liang noted the different degree of attention that the work had received, in comparison with that given to the *Meng tzu*; and he explained the reasons why he was preparing his annotation. To accommodate the enlarged work with its comments, he had redistributed the 32 *p'ien* into 20 *chüan*. In addition he had changed the order of the *p'ien* so that they would be grouped together more logically; the order that he chose and which has been adopted subsequently may be compared with the different order that is printed along with Liu Hsiang's long notice about the work. Yang Liang also records that he changed the title of the work from *Sun Ch'ing hsin shu* 孫卿新書 to *Hsün ch'ing tzu* 荀卿子. These statements are accepted and repeated in the *Ch'ung wen ts'ung mu* and the *Yü hai*.

Yang Liang's preface was included in the *Ch'üan T'ang wen* 全唐文 ch. 729, together with an epitaph inscription that he wrote for one Ma Shu 馬紓 (died 844). Yang Liang is identified there as the son of Ju shih 汝士; during the Yüan ho 元和 period (806–20) he held the office of *Ta li p'ing shih* 大理平事. His identification as the son of Yang Ju-shih has however been brought into question.

3. Authenticity

The following summary of views on the authenticity of the received text of the *Hsün tzu* takes into account opinions expressed by a number of contemporary critics (for details, see *Wei shu t'ung k'ao*, pp. 734f.). There is in fact a considerable difference of views, e.g. from that of Tu Kuo-hsiang 杜國庠 (1889–1961), who believed that in general all 32 *p'ien* can be accepted as being reliable, to that of Lü Ssu-mien, who thought that the teachings of Hsün Ch'ing, if really represented in the *Hsün tzu*, are not compatible with *ju chia* doctrine; he suggested that comparison with other texts shows that the *Hsün tzu* is a result of some measure of fabrication.

Between these extremes, Hu Shih 胡適 (1891–1962) took the view that four *p'ien* (nos. 17, 21, 22 and 23) form the essence of Hsün Ch'ing's thought. In addition, doubts have been cast on the authenticity of all or parts of various *p'ien*, on grounds such as their mention of 'Sun Ch'ing tzu'; parallels with, or citations from, later works; differences in style; contradictions in the argument, especially in relation to *shu* 術; differences in emphasis on the main theme, in respect of *li* 禮; variation in the types of title of the *p'ien*; the incomplete nature of some *p'ien*; or obvious interpolations. For these reasons some *p'ien* are accepted as being authentic without doubt; some are regarded as being partly reliable, and some as compilations which were the work of Hsün Ch'ing's school. Other *p'ien* are described as being unrelated to Hsün Ch'ing; authorship by Li Ssu is suggested for *p'ien* no. 26; and some commentators date some of the *p'ien* to Former Han. The views that have been put forward may be summarised as follows:

(a) *p'ien* where no doubts have been raised: nos. 1, 2, 3, 6, 11
(b) *p'ien* generally accepted as authentic but doubted by some scholars: nos. 7, 14; not by Hsün Ch'ing, according to Chang Hsi-t'ang 張西堂; possibly Han, according to Kuo Mo-jo 郭沫若 (1892–1978); nos. 9, 20 (thought by Kuo Mo-jo to derive from his school); no. 10 (where Yang Yün-ju 楊筠如 questioned the authenticity of some parts)
(c) *p'ien* where the greater parts are accepted as authentic, with some interpolation: nos. 4, 5, 13, 17, 18, 19, 21, 22, 23; and no. 12 (except by Kuo Mo-jo)
(d) *p'ien* compiled by Hsün Ch'ing's school: nos. 8, 15, 16
(e) *p'ien* variously described as of mixed authorship, as being unrelated to Hsün Ch'ing in person, or as being compiled by his school: no. 12 (Kuo Mo-jo); nos. 24–32; Chang Hsi-t'ang dates nos. 27–32 in Han; Yang Liang is thought to have deliberately placed nos. 28–32 at the end of the work, in the belief that they were citations.

4.　Early prints

(a) By Lü Hsia-ch'ing 呂夏卿 in 1068. A tracing of this official publication was used as the basic text by Lu Wen-ch'ao (see under (5) below) who refers to it as the *Ta tzu Sung pen* 大字宋本. Derivative copies include the print made by T'ang Chung-yu 唐仲友, entitled *T'ai chou pen* 台州本 (preface 1181). This was made available thanks to Li Shu-ch'ang 黎庶昌 (1837–97), minister to Japan, who acquired the sole surviving copy of the print as a gift. This text is now available in the *Ku i ts'ung shu* (printed in Tokyo 1882–84) and reproduced in the *SPTK* series. The format is 8 by 16; the names of Lü Hsia-ch'ing and Wang Tzu-shao 王子韶 are given as the editors. An undated reprint, by the *Ju ku shu chü* 茹古書局 of Ch'eng-tu includes two sets of *k'ao-cheng* (i) unsigned and undated, citing remarks of Wang Hsien-ch'ien 王先謙 (1842–1918) and Liu Shih-p'ei 劉師培 (1884–1919); and (ii) that of Wang Hsien-ch'ien.

(b) A print made by Ch'ien Tien 錢佃 (Chung-keng 仲耕) dated 1181 has been lost, as was observed by Miao Ch'üan-sun 繆荃孫 (1844–1919) in 1905. However there survives Ch'ien Tien's *Hsün tzu k'ao-i* 荀子考異 in one *chüan* (available, e.g., in the *Chou Ch'in chu tzu chiao chu* 周秦諸子斠註). In his colophon to these notes, Ch'ien Tien deplored the absence of good copies of the text. Although he did see some provincial copies, he makes no reference to Lü Hsia-ch'ing's print. Eventually he acquired a copy of a print of 1078–85 which he used as the basis of his edition. In addition to making 154 textual emendations, he appended as his *k'ao i* a list of 126 variant readings, where questions were in his opinion still outstanding. This list survives, but it was apparently not seen by Lu Wen-ch'ao 盧文弨 (1717–96), Wang Nien-sun 王念孫 (1744–1832) or Ku Kuang-ch'i 顧廣圻 (1776–1835). In a postface to the *k'ao i*, Miao Ch'üan-sun states that Ch'ien Tien obtained his degree in the period 1111–17.

(c) A Yüan illustrated and annotated print, entitled *Tsuan t'u hu chu Hsün tzu* 纂圖互註荀子. The text, preceded by Yang Liang's preface and illustrations of a few terms to which the book refers (e.g., in *p'ien* nos. 13, 20), is set out with Yang Liang's notes in 11 by 21 format. The book was available to Lu Wen-ch'ao, and a partially defaced copy is held in the National Library, Peking. A tracing of the edition, made by Fujiwara Hisashi 藤原榮 in 1739, is available in Kyoto. A copy in 8 by 17 format was printed by Ku Ch'un 顧春 in the period 1522–66, without illustrations. This is known as the *Shih te t'ang* 世德堂 edition, being included in the *Liu tzu ch'üan shu* 六子全書.

Notes on the provenance and history of illustrated editions were included in the *T'ien lu lin lang shu mu* 天祿琳瑯書目 (1775; cited in Wang Hsien-ch'ien's 王先謙 (1842–1918) *k'ao cheng*). Yeh Te-hui 葉德輝 (1864–1927) identified the print as a Yüan re-issue of a Southern Sung edition, and lists a number of variants where he regards this text as being superior to that of the T'ai chou print. Comparison of a sample *p'ien* (no. 2) shows at least 21 variants, not counting any that occur in the text of the notes.

5. Annotated editions

For long the *Hsün tzu* received comparatively little attention as compared with that lavished on pre-imperial texts associated with Confucian teaching. The views expressed in the book about human nature stand in contrast with those of the *Meng tzu*, which conformed with the philosophical trends of the T'ang and Sung periods. Whereas the *Meng tzu* attracted scholarly comment from the second century onwards (e.g. by Chao Ch'i 趙岐, died A.D. 201), it is necessary to wait until the ninth century for the appearance of the earliest surviving commentary on the *Hsün tzu*, i.e. that of Yang Liang.

Apparently the work is not mentioned in the *T'ung tien*. Apart from the few Sung and Yüan prints and the entries in bibliographies, it seems that the book escaped attention until the 18th century. The two standard editions that have the merit of including the notes of contemporary scholars are those of Lu Wen-ch'ao (dated 1786) and Wang Hsien-ch'ien (dated 1891). More recently the editions of Liang Ch'i-hsiung 梁啓雄 (1936, 1956) take account of the work of Chinese scholarship, and of some Japanese commentators, that was not available to Wang Hsien-ch'ien. Notes on the principal editions that carry annotation follow.

(a) *Hsün tzu fu chiao k'an pu i i chüan* 荀子附校勘補遺一卷. Bearing the joint names of Hsieh Yung 謝墉 (1719–95) and Lu Wen-ch'ao (1717–96), this edition is ascribed sometimes to the one, and sometimes to the other scholar. The main work of the annotation was completed by Lu Wen-ch'ao. Hsieh Yung's preface, in which he discusses the relationship of the *Hsün tzu* to the *Li chi* and the *Ta Tai li chi*, and the place of Hsün Ch'ing's ideas in pre-imperial thought, is dated in 1786. The edition was first printed with the single *chüan* of supplementary notes following the text in the *Pao ching t'ang ts'ung shu*; that print is reproduced in the *Ts'ung shu chi ch'eng* series with at least one half folio missing (at the end of *chüan* 2). The edition has been reprinted on a number of occasions, e.g., in the *Shih tzu* 十子 (under the title *Hsün tzu chien shih* 荀子箋釋) in 1804; in the *Erh shih erh tzu* 二十二子 (4–5) in 1877; in the *Ssu pu pei yao* series; and, punctuated, in the *San shih liu tzu ch'üan shu* 三十六子全書 (10) in 1923. It was also used as the basis of a *kambun* edition by Asakawa Kanae 朝川鼎 in 1830 (see under (8) below).

This edition includes Yang Liang's notes, which are followed by, but clearly separated from, Lu Wen-ch'ao's own annotation. This took account of a tracing of Lü Hsia-ch'ing's edition, the *Tsuan t'u hu chu* print and Ku Ch'un's *Shih te t'ang* edition. Hsieh Yung also lists two Ming editions which were available: (i) by Yü Chiu-chang 虞九章 and Wang Chen-heng 王震亨; according to Wang Hsien-ch'ien's later observation, this is actually cited in a note to one passage only; and (ii) by Chung Jen-chieh 鍾人傑, style Jui-sheng 瑞生, editor of the *T'ang Sung ts'ung shu*; for his notes on the *Hsün tzu*, see *Hsing li ta ch'üan hui t'ung* 性理大全會通 57.27b. In addition Hsieh Yung names the following scholars as authorities on whose work the edition drew: Chao Hsi-ming 趙曦明 (Ching-fu 敬夫; early 17th century); Tuan Yü-ts'ai 段玉裁 (1735–1815); Wu Ch'ien 吳騫 (Ch'a-k'o 槎客; 1733–1813); Chu Huan 朱奐 (Wen-yu 文游; *fl. c.* 1760); and Wang Chung 汪中 (Jung-fu 容甫; 1745–94).

(b) *Hsün tzu chi chieh* 荀子集解, edited by Wang Hsien-ch'ien. Originally published in the series *Ssu hsien shu chü k'an shu* 思賢書局刊書, with a preface dated in 1891, this edition has been re-issued on a number of occasions, sometimes with punctuation (e.g., *Wan yu wen k'u*, Basic Sinological series, *Chu tzu chi ch'eng*, Peking/Shanghai 1954; and by the *Shih chieh shu chü*, Taipei, 1983). It has also formed the basis on which subsequent editors such as Liang Ch'i-hsiung and Li Ti-sheng 李滌生 relied; and it is available in the *Kambun taikei* series. As is usual with Wang Hsien-ch'ien's work, there is a copious annotation, including that of Yang Liang, Lu Wen-ch'ao, Ch'ing dynasty scholars whose work was not included by Lu, and that of Wang Hsien-ch'ien himself. The supplementary notes which Lu Wen-ch'ao published at the end of his edition have been included here in the appropriate part of the text to which they refer.

The text is preceded by extensive prolegomena, including a preface, introductory remarks and Wang Hsien-ch'ien's own *k'ao cheng*, in two *chüan*. This gives the basic information regarding Hsün Ch'ing's life and the history of the work, citing from most of the more important notes, prefaces and postfaces of bibliophiles and earlier editions. These include: notices in the *Ssu k'u ch'üan shu tsung mu*; the *T'ien lu lin lang shu mu*; the *Tu shu min ch'iu chi* 讀書敏求記 of Ch'ien Tseng 錢曾 (1726); the *Ai jih ching lu tsang shu chih* 愛日精廬藏書志 of Chang Chin-wu 張金吾 (1826); Ku Kuang-ch'i's postface to the *Shih te t'ang* edition 1796); a postface by Ch'ien Ta-hsin 錢大昕 (1728–1804) of 1786; various notes by Hao I-hsing 郝懿行 (1757–1825); Wang Nien-sun's note of 1830 (concerning differences between

the Lü Hsia-ch'ing edition and the tracing of it that was available to
Lu Wen-ch'ao); postfaces to the T'ai chou edition in the *Keiseki hōko-shi* 經籍訪古志 (1885) and by Yang Shou-ching 楊守敬 (1884); the
Hsün Ch'ing t'ung lun 荀卿通論 of Wang Chung (where he seeks to
establish Hsün Ch'ing's part in perpetuating the traditional teachings
of Confucius); a chronological table of Hsün Ch'ing's life; and Hu
Yüan-i's 胡元儀 long biographical note, including citations from the
work and tracing Hsün Ch'ing's descendants to the Liu ch'ao period.

(c) *Hsün tzu chien shih* 荀子簡釋, edited by Liang Ch'i-hsiung 梁啓雄.
This scholar's first edition of the *Hsün tzu* was published by Shang
wu in 1936, under the title *Hsün tzu chien shih* 荀子柬釋. It had followed the help and instruction given by his elder brother Liang
Ch'i-ch'ao 梁啓超 (1873–1929) and protracted discussions with Yang
Shu-ta 楊樹達 and Kao Heng 高亨 (b. 1900). The work was republished after revision in 1956, under the title of *Hsün tzu chien shih* 荀
子簡釋. The punctuated text is based on that of Wang Hsien-ch'ien;
but being aware of its imperfections, Liang Ch'i-hsiung attempted to
eliminate interpolations and to restore *lacunas* by reference to other
editions, i.e., the T'ai chou and *Shih te t'ang* edition, and the *Junshi
zōchū* of Kubo Chikusui 久保築水 (see under (8) below). The annotation is intended to select the most important opinions of the principal
Ch'ing scholars and to save readers the tedium of working through
all their extensive notes. In addition Liang Ch'i-hsiung draws on
some works which Wang Hsien-ch'ien omitted to mention or which
were published subsequently to his edition, and the comments of
several Japanese scholars. Occasionally he quotes the opinion of
Liang Ch'i-ch'ao.

The text, which is not divided into *chüan*, is preceded by the prefaces of Yang Shu-ta (1929), Kao Heng (1934) and Liang Ch'i-hsiung
himself (1934 and 1955). These discuss the earlier work of the commentators to the text, but they do not refer to questions of authenticity. Following the text there is a biographical account of Hsün
Ch'ing and a chronological table showing events of 321 to 213 B.C.
which were of relevance to his life and writings.

(d) Chang Shih-t'ung 章詩同, *Hsün tzu chien chu* 荀子簡注; Shanghai:
Jen min, 1974; punctuated text in simplified characters, with brief
annotation.

(e) Hsiung Kung-che 熊公哲, *Hsün tzu chin chu chin i* 荀子今註今譯;
Taipei: Shang wu, 1975; annotated text with a version in modern
Chinese.

(f) *Hsün tzu chi shih* 荀子集釋, edited by Li Ti-sheng 李滌生; Taipei:

T'ai-wan hsüeh sheng shu chü, 1979. This annotated text is based on that of Wang Hsien-ch'ien's edition. The author of the new commentary sets out to collect the notes of both early and recent Chinese scholars, and of some Japanese scholars, that lie dispersed in a number of sources and may be difficult to find. Writing deliberately for those embarking on a study of the text for the first time, and wishing to save them time and trouble, Li Ti-sheng presents the conclusions reached by his predecessors without repeating their supporting arguments. Each *p'ien* is preceded by an introductory note, and the comments to the text result from frequent exchanges of view with Mou Tsung-san 牟宗三, whose preface (1977) is included, without those of the earlier editors. The text is punctuated, with no lines that identify proper names; suggested emendations are marked clearly. Shih Chih-mien's 施之勉 chronological table of Hsün Ch'ing's life follows at the end of the volume.

(g) Yang Liu-ch'iao 楊柳橋, *Hsün tzu ku i* 荀子詁譯; Chi-nan: Ch'i-Lu, 1985; fully annotated edition, with text in unabbreviated characters, and a modern Chinese version.

6. Studies, comments and notes published without the text

The principal matters of controversy have concerned details of Hsün Ch'ing's life and his dates; the use of the character Sun 孫 in place of Hsün 荀; the authenticity of some of the *p'ien*; and the identification of Yang Liang. In addition the assessment and classification of the views expressed in the *Hsün tzu*, especially in regard to the nature of man and ethical questions, have engaged some of China's most famous writers. These have included Han Yü 韓愈 (768–824), (see his *Tu Hsün tzu* 讀荀子), who was concerned with Hsün Ch'ing's place in comparison with that of Mencius and Yang Hsiung 揚雄, and with evaluating the *Hsün tzu* within the context of the Confucian tradition. Su Tung-p'o 蘇東坡 (1036–1101) (see his *Hsün Ch'ing lun* 荀卿論) was concerned with the influence that Hsün Ch'ing exercised over Li Ssu and his effect on the political measures of the Ch'in empire. The following are included among the scholars of the Ch'ing period and later who wrote on these subjects and examined questions of the text (publications which concern a single *p'ien* are not listed here).

(a) Fang Pao 方苞 (1668–1749): *Shan ting Hsün tzu* 刪定荀子, 1 *chüan*; in *K'ang hsi t'ang shih liu chung* 抗希堂十六種.

(b) Wang Chung (Jung-fu; 1745–94): *Hsün Ch'ing t'ung lun* 荀卿通論.

(c) Liu T'ai-kung 劉台拱 (Tuan-lin 端臨; 1751–1805): *Hsün tzu pu chu* 荀

子補注, 1 *chüan*; in *Liu Tuan-lin hsien sheng i shu* 劉端臨先生遺書, 4; included in *Chou Ch'in chu tzu chiao chu shih chung*.

(d) Hao I-hsing (1757–1825): *Hsün tzu pu chu* 荀子補注, 2 *chüan*; in Hao I-hsing's posthumous works; also in *Chou Ch'in chu tzu chiao chu shih chung*.

(e) Wang Nien-sun (1744–1832): notes on *Hsün tzu* in 8 *chüan* and one supplement; in *Tu shu tsa chih* 8 (published 1812–31).

(f) Ku Kuang-ch'i (1776–1835): *Hsün tzu chiao* 荀子校, 1 *chüan*; in *Chiao pu yü lu* 斠補隅錄, which is included in *She wen tzu chiu* 涉聞梓舊 20, dated 1829.

(g) Yü Yüeh 俞樾 (1821–1907); notes on *Hsün tzu* in 4 *chüan*; in *Chu tzu p'ing i* 諸子平議 12 (1870); punctuated text in the Basic Sinological Series.

(h) Sun I-jang 孫詒讓 (1848–1908): *Hsün tzu Yang Liang chu* 荀子楊倞註; in *Cha i* 6. 9a–15b (1894).

(i) Liu Shih-p'ei 劉師培 (Shen shu 申叔; 1884–1919); *Hsün tzu chiao pu* 荀子斠補, 4 *chüan*; and *Hsün tzu pu shih* 荀子補釋, 1 *chüan*; in *Liu Shen-shu hsien sheng i shu* (1936).

(j) Liang Ch'i-ch'ao (1873–1929); there are several writings; see principally *Ku shih pien* 4 (1933), 104f., *Hsün Ch'ing chi Hsün tzu* 荀卿及荀子.

(k) Yü Hsing-wu 于省吾: *Shuang chien ch'ih Hsün tzu hsin cheng* 雙劍誃荀子新證, 4 *chüan*, 1937; reprinted, Peking: Chung hua shu chü, 1962.

(l) Yü Chia-hsi 余嘉錫, in *Ssu k'u t'i yao pien cheng* (1958), pp. 513f. He is concerned with the use of the character Sun and with the identification of Yang Liang.

(m) Yang Yün-ju 楊筠如: *Hsün tzu yen chiu* 荀子研究; Taiwan: Shang wu, 1966; see also *Ku shih pien* 6 (1938), 130–47.

(n) Mou Tsung-san: *Ming chia yü Hsün tzu* 名家與荀子; Taipei: T'ai-wan hsüeh sheng shu chü, 1979.

Also:

(o) Ogyū Sorai 荻生徂來 (1666–1728): *Toku Junshi* 讀荀子; original undated; available in a facsimile of the author's own manuscript, printed *c*. 1940.

(p) Duyvendak, J.J.L., 'Hsün-tzu on the rectification of names'; *TP* 23 (1924), 221–54.

(q) Duyvendak, J.J.L., 'The chronology of Hsün-tzu'; *TP* 26 (1929), 73–95.

(r) Malmqvist, N.G.D., 'A note on the *Cherng shiang* ballad in the *Shyun Tzyy*' *BSOAS* 36. 2 (1973), 352–8.

(s) Jao Pin 饒彬, *Hsün tzi i i chi shih* 荀子疑義輯釋; Taipei: Lan t'ai, 1977; with notes to select difficult terms and passages of the text.

(t) Lung Yü-ch'un 龍宇純, *Hsün tzu lun chi* 荀子論集; Taipei: Hsüeh sheng, 1987; collected essays on a variety of topics, including the authenticity of the work, and Hsün Ch'ing's thought, together with the author's notes to the text and to the traditional commentaries.

7. Translations

(a) Dubs, Homer H., *The works of Hsüntze*; London: Arthur Probsthain, 1928. The author presents translations of *p'ien* nos. 1–2, 4–11 and 15–23 being 'all the writings of Hsüntze that are both genuine and important'. The text used was that of Wang Hsien-ch'ien, and references to this edition are printed in the margins. The notes are minimal, concerning technical terms and names, and not questions of textual criticism. This volume follows the author's earlier *Hsüntze the Moulder of Ancient Confucianism* (London: Arthur Probsthain, 1927), which considers the life, writings and ideas of Hsün Ch'ing; see Duyvendak's review of this translation in *TP* 29 (1932) 1–42.

(b) Kanaya Osamu 金谷治, *Junshi*; Japanese version without Chinese text, with an index; Iwanami Bunko nos. 6344–51 (1961–62).

(c) Watson, Burton, *Hsün Tzu, Basic Writings*; New York and London: Columbia University Press, 1963. This volume contains translations of ten select *p'ien* (nos. 1, 2, 9, 15, 17, 19–23).

(d) Köster, Hermann, *Hsün-tzu ins Deutsche übertragen*; Kaldenkirchen: Steyler Verlag, 1967. The translation of all 32 *p'ien* is based on the text of Liang Ch'i-hsiung's edition of 1936.

(e) Malmqvist, Göran, 'The Cherng shianq ballad of the Shyun tzyy', in *BMFEA* 45 (1973), 63–89.

(f) Knoblock, John, *Xunzi: a Translation and Study of the Complete Works*; 3 volumes, Stanford: Stanford University Press, 1988, 1990, and forthcoming. A long and valuable introduction discusses Hsün Ch'ing's life and his contribution to Chinese thought, and the history and authenticity of the text. Translations are furnished with prefatory remarks and annotation; *p'ien* nos. 1–6 in vol. I, nos. 7–16 in vol. II, nos. 17–32 in vol. III.

(For translations of single *p'ien* or their parts by Legge, Evan Morgan, Duyvendak, Wieger and O. Franke, see Dubs, *Hsüntze the Moulder of Ancient Confucianism*, p. 47, note 3).

8. Japanese editions

A. *Kambun taikei*; no. 15, 1913, edited by Hattori Unokichi, with notes by Kubo Chikusui 久保築水 and Igai Hikohiro 豬飼彥博 included (see below under (b)).
B. *Kanseki kokujikai zensho*; nos. 22, 23, 1911, edited by Katsura Koson.
D. *Kokuyaku kambun taisei*; no. 8, 1920, edited by Sasakawa Rimpū.
E. *Kambun sōsho*, 1927.
F. *Keisho taikō*; nos. 13–15, 1938–39.
H. *Shinshaku kambun taikei*; nos. 5, 6, 1966–69, edited by Fujii Sen'ei.
J. *Chūgoku no shisō*; no. 4, 1964, edited by Sugimoto Tatsuo.
K. *Chūgoku koten bungaku taikei*; no. 3, 1970, edited by Takeoka Yatsuo and Hihara Toshikuni.
L. *Chūgoku koten shinsho*, 1973, edited by Kimata Tokuo.

The text has also been treated independently as follows:

(a) *Junshi ihei* 荀子遺秉, edited by Momoi Hakuroku 桃井白鹿; preface 1798, published 1800.
(b) *Junshi zōchū* 荀子增注, edited by Kubo Chikusui; preface dated 1820. The edition includes Yang Liang's preface and text with Yang Liang's notes, followed by Kubo's own notes; supplementary comments by Igai Hikohiro follow.
(c) *Junshi senshaku* 荀子箋釋, edited by Asakawa Kanae 朝川鼎, with notes by Katayama Keizan 片山兼山, 1830; this follows Lu Wen-ch'ao's edition.

9. Indexes

(a) *Hsün tzu yin te* 荀子引得; no. 22 in the *Harvard-Yenching Institute Sinological Index series*. This full concordance was prepared by Ch'i Ssu-ho 齊思和, whose preface is dated in 1949. The punctuated text which precedes the index is based on Wang Hsien-ch'ien's edition, with variant readings being shown in the footnotes.
(b) *A Concordance to the Xunzi* 荀子逐字索引, ed. D.C. Lau and Chen Fong Ching; *ICS* series, Hong Kong: Commercial Press, forthcoming, 1995.

— Michael Loewe

Huai nan tzu 淮南子

1. Content

The *Huai nan tzu* is a collection of essays, resulting from the scholarly debates that took place under the patronage and at the court of Liu An 劉安 (?179–122 B.C.), King of Huai-nan, sometime before 139 B.C. The work encompasses a wide variety of subjects, from ancient myths to contemporary government, from didactic historical anecdotes to topography, astronomy and philosophy. The diversity of contents is compounded by the many pre-Han schools of thought that find a voice in the text as indicated by the more than 800 citations from other texts found in the work. Finally, one finds many instances of stylistic discontinuity, not only from one chapter to the next, but also from one paragraph to the next within the same chapter. At the same time, one senses an indisputable stylistic and conceptual consistency running throughout the work. This character of simultaneous homogeneity in some respects and heterogeneity in others arises in all likelihood as a consequence of the way the text was compiled.

One overriding concern pervades the *Huai nan tzu*, namely, the attempt to define the essential conditions for a perfect socio-political order. The perfect order is seen to derive primarily from the perfect ruler, conceived as the True Man (*chen jen* 眞人). We may characterize the basic intent of the *Huai nan tzu* as political utopianism and the work as a handbook for the instruction of an enlightened ruler and his court. As a philosophical foundation for this programme, the *Huai nan tzu* argues that political rule is bound by the same patterns that govern the natural world. The universal patterns are conceived along the lines of what is sometimes called Huang-Lao 黃老 Taoism of the Former Han dynasty and of the school of Yin-Yang and the Five Phases. One of the main concepts elaborated in the *Huai nan tzu* is that of the *kan ying* 感應 'stimulus and response', or better, 'resonance'.

The twenty-one chapters of the *Huai nan tzu* may be divided into three parts according to contents:

1. Basic principles (chapters 1–8);
2. Applications and illustrations (chapters 9–20);
3. Postface: summary and outline (chapter 21).

2. Composition and Authenticity

On the basis of both internal and external evidence we may speculate on a provisional theory of the method of composition of the *Huai nan tzu* and of its authorship:

Liu An was a gifted and prolific writer who, from his youth, was interested in every aspect of learning and tried his hand successfully at many styles. He conceived the general design and format for a book, which came to be known as the *Huai nan tzu*. For the purpose of drafting his projected work, he convened a 'literary symposium' at his court, in which a large number of scholars participated. The literary and philosophical debates that took place at the symposium resulted in rough drafts penned by the close collaborators of Liu An (eight are named by Kao Yu 高誘 (*c.* 168–212) in his preface to the *Huai nan tzu*), each marked by its particular genius and style. Liu An revised these drafts doctrinally and stylistically, but did not obliterate all of the idiosyncrasies of the initial compositions. A scheme such as this would explain both the apparent unity and diversity of the work. Liu An presented the finished product to Wu Ti (r. 141–87) on his first state visit in 139 B.C.

3.   Text history and editions

(a) The Liu Hsiang 劉向 (79–8 B.C.) edition.

   Han shu 30, p. 1741, lists *Huai nan wai* 淮南外 in 33 *p'ien* (for which see *Han shu pu chu* 漢書補注 30, 47a note) and *Huai nan nei* 淮南內, i.e. Liu Hsiang's text, in 21 *p'ien*. These are placed under the *tsa chia* 雜家, and we find thereafter a continuous bibliographic tradition, both private and public, which lists the *Huai nan tzu* in 21 *p'ien*. There are variations in the title of the work, the one used most often being *Huai nan hung lieh chieh* 淮南鴻烈解. From the sixth century onwards, bibliographers speak of 21 *chüan* rather than 21 *p'ien* (*Chiu T'ang shu* 47, p. 2032; *Hsin T'ang shu* 59, p. 1533; Fujiwara Sukeyo enters copies in 21 and 31 chapters). These changes have no bearing on the integrity of the work.

(b) The Hsü Shen 許慎 (*c.* 55–*c.* 149) and Kao Yu commentaries and editions.

   Sui shu 34, p. 1006 enters two copies of the *Huai nan tzu*, each of 21 *chüan*, one with comments by Hsü Shen and one with those of Kao Yu. Whether Kao Yu commented on all 21 chapters is open to question. At any rate, the titles of the 21 chapters seem to have been part of the original edition, since they are mentioned in *Huai nan tzu* 21 and are glossed by Hsü and Kao, the earliest two commentaries on the *Huai nan tzu* still extant. These two commentaries may have been attached to two slightly different redactions of the *Huai nan tzu,* being blended together sometime before the eleventh century. This composite commentary was then attached to the Kao Yu edition and, in different printed editions, it was attributed arbitrarily either to Hsü Shen or to Kao Yu. This is the case for all block-printed editions, starting with the *Pei Sung hsiao tzu pen* 北宋小字本, printed between 1023–1063, and the *Tao tsang.* While quotations from the *Huai nan tzu* preserved in pre-Sung sources may shed some faint light on the possible differences between the Hsü Shen and Kao Yu commentaries, comparison between the early printed editions and such quotations of the text reveals little more than character variants, so that the body of the text and the order of the chapters seem to have remained remarkably stable over more than two thousand years of transmission.

(c) The Northern Sung edition.

In his 'Chiao Huai nan tzu t'i hsü' 校淮南子題序 Su Sung 蘇頌 (1020–1101) states that he establised a critlcal text of the *Huai nan tzu* on the basis of a comparison of seven different copies that were current in his time; he also defined a set of criteria to discriminate between the Hsü and Kao editions and commentaries. There is evidence to suggest that Su's text may well be the Northern Sung small character edition of 1023–1063. The first critical description of this text was given by Huang P'ei-lieh 黃丕烈 (1763–1825). After passing through various hands, a copy of the Northern Sung edition was acquired by the Library of the University of Dairen at the beginning of this century, at which point we lose sight of it. Fortunately, traced copies were made of the original on behalf of Ku Kuang-ch'i 顧廣圻 (1776–1835) and Wang Nien-sun 王念孫 (1744–1832), who both wrote extensive critical notes on the edition. Finally, a facsimile of Wang's copy by Liu Lü-fen 劉履芬 (1827–79) was printed in the first series of the *Ssu-pu ts'ung k'an.* While enjoying the prestige of having been printed in the early Sung, it is not the best edition.

(d) The *Tao tsang* edition.

According to the greatest of modern commentators on the *Huai nan tzu,* Wang Nien-sun, the most reliable text in his day was that of the *Tao tsang* (1445). It derives basically from the Northern Sung edition but the editors used other early editions (now lost) to correct mistakes in the Northern Sung text. One distinctive feature of the *Tao tsang* edition is its division into 28 *chüan* rather than the 21 *chüan* of the Northern Sung and earlier. This difference does not entail any interpolation or change in the content, for the 28 *chüan* are obtained simply by dividing into two each of the *chüan* nos. 1–5, 8, and 13. The reason for such a division remains obscure, but it may be related to Taoist speculations about the twenty-eight heavenly mansions.

(e) Ming and Ch'ing editions.

More than fifteen editions of the *Huai nan tzu* were prepared during the Ming dynasty, nine of them during the Wan li period (1573–1620). These editions derived from the *Tao tsang* copy, not from the Northern Sung edition. The first generations of editions were in 28 *chüan*, the most important being those of Wang P'u 王浦 (printed 1488–1505), Wang Ying 王瑩 (printed 1522–1566), and Chu Tung-kuang 朱東光 (printed 1573–1620). During the Wan li period, we find editions that derive from the *Tao tsang* text, but revert to the more traditional arrangement in 21 *chüan*. The first and most important of these is that of Mao I-kuei 毛一桂 (printed 1573–1620), which was the ancestor of four important editions, including that of Mao K'un 茅坤 (printed 1573–1620) and the *Han Wei ts'ung shu* version (*kuang* and *tseng ting* editions.) The Mao K'un text and critical annotations were reprinted in several Japanese collections of Chinese books.

Two valuable editions appeared during the Ch'ing dynasty, both based on the *Tao tsang* text: the Chuang K'uei-chi 莊逵吉 (1760–1813) edition of 1789 (21 *chüan*) and the *Tao tsang chi yao* edition of 28 *chüan* (printed 1796–1820). The latter, prepared by Chiang Yüan-t'ing 蔣元廷 (1755–1819), was based directly on the *Tao tsang* edition.

Textual variants seem to indicate that Chiang also used some other unidentified editions to establish his text. For a study of its filiation, see Harold D. Roth, as cited under (6) below, and 'Filiation Analysis and the Textual Criticism of the *Huai nan tzu*', in *Transactions of the International Conference of Orientalists in Japan*, No. XXVII, 1982, 60–81 (published by Tōhō Gakkai). The Chuang edition was based on an emended version of the *Tao tsang* text collated by Ch'ien Tien 錢坫 (1744–1806). Despite Chuang's critical glosses on the main text and the commentary, his edition contains many mistaken characters. It has been reprinted, with Chuang's preface and notes, in the *Ssu pu pei yao*. In 1875, T'ao Fang-ch'i 陶方琦 (1845–1884) and others revised Chuang's edition. This has become the standard Chuang edition, probably the best available text of the *Huai nan tzu*.

(f) The revised Chuang text has been made the *textus receptus* of most recent editions of the *Huai nan tzu*, among others:

(1) Liu Chia-li 劉家立, *Huai nan chi cheng* 淮南集證, Peking: Chung hua, 1924.

(2) Liu Wen-tien 劉文典, *Huai nan hung lieh chi chieh* 淮南鴻烈集解, Shanghai: Shang wu, 1923; Taipei reprint, 1968.

(3) *Chu tzu chi ch'eng*, Peking: Chung hua, 1935; reprint 1954. The text prepared by Liu Wen-tien is unpunctuated and beautifully printed. The critical annotations of the foremost Ch'ing commentators of the *Huai nan tzu*, especially Wang Nien-sun and Yü Yüeh 俞樾 (1821–1907), are added to the standard commentary. It is the most reliable and useful edition of the *Huai nan tzu*.

4. Translations

There are no complete translations of the *Huai nan tzu* in Western languages. Besides Morgan (see below) who translated eight chapters, most recent translations deal with only one chapter. There are a number of excellent unpublished translations of individual chapters. Partial translations include:

(a) Balfour, Frederic Henry, *Taoist Texts, ethical, political, and speculative*, London: Trubner, and Shanghai: Kelly and Walsh, 1884 (translation of ch. 1). This is a remarkable translation, given the state of research on the *Huai nan tzu* at the time.

(b) Morgan, Evan, *Tao, the Great Luminant: essays from the Huai nan tzu*, London: Kegan Paul, Trench, Trubner & Co., 1933 (translation of chs. 1, 2, 7, 8, 12, 13, 15, and 19); a pioneering effort marred by theological preconceptions and an excessive freedom with the Chinese text.

(c) Kraft, Eva, 'Zum *Huai-nan-tzu*. Einführung, Übersetzung (Kapitel I und II) und Interpretation', *Monumenta Serica* 16 (1957), 191–286; 17 (1958), 128–207.

(d) Wallacker, Benjamin, *The Huai-nan-tzu, Book Eleven: Behavior Culture and the Cosmos*. New Haven: American Oriental Society, 1962.

(e) Larre, Claude, *Le Traité Vlle du Houai nan tseu. Les esprits légers et subtils animateurs de l'essence*. Variétés sinologiques, 67 (Nouvelle serie), Taipei, Paris, Hong Kong, 1982.

(f) Ames, Roger T., *The Art of Rulership: A Study in Ancient Chinese Political Thought*. Honolulu: University of Hawaii Press, 1983.

(g) Le Blanc, Charles, *Huai nan tzu; Philosophical Synthesis in Early Han Thought: The Idea of Resonance* (Kan-Ying) *With a Translation and Analysis of Chapter Six*. Hong Kong: Hong Kong University Press, 1985.

(h) Major, John S., *Heaven and Earth in Early Han Thought: Chapters Three, Four and Five of the Huainanzi*. Albany: State University of New York Press, 1993.

(i) Larre, Claude, Isabelle Robinet and Elisabeth Rochet de la Vallée, *Les grands traités du Huainan zi*; Paris: Éditions du Cerf, 1993; translation of chs. 1, 7, 11, 13 and 18.

5. Japanese Editions.

A. *Kambun taikei*; no. 20, 1915, edited by Hattori Unokichi.
B. *Kanseki kokujikai zensho*, nos. 43-4, 1917, edited by Kikuchi Sankurō (Bankō).
D. *Kokuyaku kambun taisei*; no. 11, 1921, edited by Gotō Asatarō.
E. *Kambun sōsho*, 1928.
H. *Shinshaku kambun taikei*; nos. 54, 55, 62, 1979, 1982, 1988 edited by Kusuyama Haruki.
K. *Chūgoku koten bungaku taikei*; no. 6, 1974, edited by Togawa Yoshio, Kiyama Hideo and Sawaya Harutsugu.
L. *Chūgoku koten shinsho*, 1972, edited by Kusuyama Haruki.

Editions D and E above contain the Mao K'un text of the *Huai nan tzu* along with a full Japanese translation and extensive critical notes.

6. Recent Studies and Research Aids

(a) Shimada Kan 島田翰 (1879-1915), *Kobun kyūsho kō* 古文舊書考, Tokyo: Minyūsha, 1905, Ch. 4, 21a-436 (in Chinese).
(b) Wu Tse-yü 吳則虞, 'Huai nan tzu shu lu' 淮南子書錄, *Wen shih* 2 (1963), 291-315.
(c) Yü Ta-ch'eng 于大成, *Huai nan tzu chiao shih* 淮南子校釋, 2 vols., Taipei: National Normal University, Chinese Literature Department, 1969.

The three foregoing works present the essential data relating to the composition, transmission, editions, and textual criticism of the *Huai nan tzu*.

(d) Kanaya Osamu 金谷治, *Rōsō teki sekai, Enanji no shiso* 老莊的世界, 淮南子の思想, Kyoto: Heirakuji, 1959. This is one of the most elaborate attempts to interpret the underlying ideas of the *Huai nan tzu* as a whole.
(e) Feng Yu-lan 馮友蘭; *Chung kuo che hsüeh shih hsin pien* 中國哲學史新編, vol. 2, Peking: Jen min, 1964. The long section devoted to the *Huai nan tzu*, focusing mainly on *ch'i* 氣, is a most perceptive effort to bring out the basic philosophy of the work.

(f) Roth, Harold D., *The textual history of the Huai-nan tzu*; Ann Arbor, Michigan: The Association for Asian Studies, 1992.

7. Indexes

(a) *Huai nan Tzu t'ung chien* 淮南子通檢, Peking: Centre franco-chinois, 1944; Taipei reprint, 1968.

(b) *Enanji Sakuin* 淮南子索引, Kyoto: Kyōto daigaku jimbun kagaku kenkyūjo, 1976.

(c) *A Concordance to the Huainanzi* 淮南子逐字索引, ed. D.C. Lau and Chen Fong Ching; *ICS* series, Hong Kong: Commercial Press, 1992.

— Charles Le Blanc

Huang ti nei ching 黃帝內經

1. Title of the work

The name 'Huang ti nei ching' is usually prefixed to the titles of four books, *Su wen* 素問, *Ling shu* 靈樞, *T'ai su* 太素, and *Ming t'ang* 明堂.*
Since the Northern Sung it has been used as a collective title for the first two, and in this usage it is often abbreviated to *'Nei ching.'* Critical scholarship over many centuries has established that none of the four is a pristine Han text, and that none is a fabrication. The issue is rather the violence done in each case by editors aiming to 'restore' the text. All except *Su wen* are T'ang or Sung reconstructions from recensions and fragments of Han origin. Although the *Su wen* was not lost, it shows signs of more substantial revision by its T'ang and Sung editors than the other books. It thus is best studied in conjunction with parallel passages in *T'ai su* (which greatly overlaps it and shows fewer signs of revision), *Ling shu*, and the early syntheses based on it such as *Huang ti pa shih i nan ching* 黃帝八十一難經 (or *Nan ching*, probably second century A.D.), *Huang ti chia i ching* 黃帝甲乙經 (or *Chia i ching*, 甲乙經 between 256 and 282), and *Mo ching* 脈經 (c. 280).

The 'Huang ti' in the titles of the books just mentioned (including the earliest known titles for *Nan ching* and *Chia i ching*) affiliates them with the Yellow Lord, who takes his place in mythology among the first rulers of mankind. Wang Mang claimed descent from him. As for *'nei ching,'* *Han shu* 30, p. 1776, lists canons of medicine belonging to lineages of masters associated with the Yellow Lord, with the legendary physician Pien Ch'üeh 扁鵲 (his exploits are dated *c*. 501 B.C.), and with a Master Po (Po shih 白氏). In each instance inner and outer canons are paired. Of these six, only the *Huang ti nei ching* survived past Former Han.

No evidence has come to light that enables a choice between the various senses of 'inner' and 'outer' in Han book titles. The title has at-

---

* In view of the large number of works cited in this account, these have been listed separately under (10) (a) Primary sources and (b) Secondary sources, below. References in the text identify items by the author and date of publication; characters for such names will be found in (10) below.

196

tracted both uninformed translations ('The Yellow Emperor's classic of
internal medicine') and speculative ones freely extrapolated from ambiguous evidence ('The Yellow Emperor's manual of corporeal [medi-
cine]', contrasted with 'incorporeal [or extra-corporeal medicine]' for the
Wai ching, about the contents of which nothing is known). Most specialists translate '*nei ching*' unexceptionably as 'inner canon', and register a
frank confession of ignorance with respect to what was originally
intended by 'inner'. The title *Su wen* is first mentioned in the preface to
Shang han tsa ping lun 傷寒雜病論 (Treatise on Cold Damage and miscellaneous disorders, before A.D. 220). The earliest surviving commentaries on *Su wen* gloss the title as 'basic questions' (Ch'üan Yüan-ch'i 全
元起, c. 503, lost) and 'plain or pristine questions' (Wang Ping 王冰, 672;
see under (5) below for both). Because Wang's commentary is ubiqui-
tous, his interpretation is seldom challenged. The dialogues and the
questions they contain can hardly be considered either plain or pristine,
however, but are incontestably basic.

The title *Ling shu* does not appear until the T'ang. Huang-fu Mi 皇甫
謐 (215–282), in the preface to *Chia i ching*, identifies a *Su wen* and a
'Needling canon' (*Chen ching* 鍼經) in 9 *chüan* each, available in his time,
with the lost *Huang ti nei ching* of 18 *chüan* listed in '*Ch'i lüeh i wen chih*
七略藝文志' (a term that presumably refers to the bibliography preserved in *Han shu* 30). He evidently uses *Chiu chüan* 九卷, 'Nine
chapters,' as a variant title for the *Chen ching*. In the text of *Chia i ching*,
passages parallel to the extant *Ling shu* are simply labelled 'Huang ti.'
Because the *Ling shu* transmitted since the Sung is based on a *Huang ti
chen ching* retrieved from Korea, historians of medicine generally believe
that the original *Huang ti nei ching* is represented in the surviving *Su wen*
and *Ling shu*. As the examination of textual history below will show, this
belief is neither unfounded nor unchallengeable.

The meaning of the title *T'ai su* is also vexed. Lu and Needham translate as 'The great clarity' (1970, p. 270), but 'clarity' is not a documented
meaning of *su*. The only monographic Western study based on this text
prefers 'The grand basis,' also used by other recent publications (Chiu
1986; see Morohashi, 27300 (5)). The *Ming t'ang* remains practically un-
explored, but its title clearly refers to the cosmic theory of monarchy embodied in what Soothill called 'the Hall of Light' (1951). Except for the
preface and one *chüan*, the book is known only from quotations. Yang
Shang-shan's 楊上善 preface to the extant recension acknowledges that
it is his re-arrangement of fragmentary materials.

The remainder of this account will concentrate on what is reliably
and generally known about the first three titles as reflections of the Han

Huang ti nei ching, considering the *T'ai su* as a variant recension that overlaps the content of both *Su wen* and *Ling shu.*

2. Content

The *Huang ti nei ching* is composed of dialogues between the Yellow Lord and one of six no less legendary ministers. In the best-known parts the Yellow Lord poses questions and Ch'i Po 岐伯 replies, but in others the subordinate is the interlocutor. The dialogues add up to a broad basis for medical reasoning. They provide a view of the relation between the cosmos, the immediate environment, and the human body and emotions, of the relation between living habits and health, of the body contents, of vital and pathological processes, of signs and symptoms, and of how diagnoses and therapeutic decisions are formed by evaluating the patient in all these contexts. *Su wen* does not dwell on details of therapy, but *Ling shu* is much concerned with applying acupuncture to the circulation tracts.

These dialogues bring the evolution of cosmological doctrine based on Yin-Yang and Five Phases thought to its culmination, and in this sense they are essential sources for the formation of Chinese philosophy (Graham so uses *Su wen* in 1986, pp. 60–63, 87). As in predecessors from *Lü shih ch'un ch'iu* on, this cosmology remains tightly linked to rationales for the Han model of centralized monarchy.

Archaeological finds of the 1970's have vindicated the opinion voiced from time to time over four hundred years that *Huang ti nei ching* is not by one author and was not written at one time (e.g., *Ku chin i t'ung* 古今 醫統 of 1556, 3, 47a–47b). It is now seen not as a single book but as a collection of inter-related short writings from distinct medical lineages at different times. Some of these present alternative explanations of the same phenomenon; some annotate or expand on others; in some a copyist has merged a text and a commentary; some parts of *Ling shu* repeat parts of *Su wen.* Ma Chi-hsing 馬繼興 (1990, pp. 68–69) has listed many such relationships, and Keegan (1988) has traced the descent of particular subtexts. Thus the extant texts are now understood to record the process of discussion and dispute by which classical medical doctrine was first formed. Several scholars have compared them with fragments of earlier texts cited in *Huang ti nei ching* or recently excavated at Ma-wang-tui 馬王堆, and with the three later syntheses that attempted to impose a coherent overview on the diversity and frequent internal contradictions of the Inner Canon (see above). Such comparisons are locating that process in the longer evolution of classical medicine (see the various publications of Akahori and Yamada, Keegan 1988, and, for an overview, Sakurai 1985).

3. Authorship and authenticity

Nothing is known about the authors of the writings gathered in *Huang ti nei ching*, nor about those who compiled the Han precursors of the extant texts. The only controversy attaches to part of *p'ien* 9 and all of 66–71 and 74 on 'phase energetics' (Porkert 1974, ch. 2), missing from Ch'üan Yüan-ch'i's recension and generally considered late fabrications. The notes in the 1067 edition (*Su wen*, 3:78, 21:409, 447) suggest that these portions were interpolated by Wang Ping. This view has been accepted by later scholars, with the notable exception of Fan Shih 范適 (Hsing-chun 行準, 1951), whose convoluted argument that they were inserted by an unknown hand in the Five Dynasties or early Sung has been summarized by Lu and Needham (1980, pp. 139–40). Wang himself was unable to reconstruct *p'ien* 72 and 73, so that only their titles appear in the current *Su wen*.

4. Dates of composition

Most critical philologists from Shao Yung 邵庸 (1011–77) on have refused to associate the writing of *Huang ti nei ching* with the Yellow Lord (see the many citations in *Wei shu t'ung k'ao*, pp. 969–78). Until recently the majority, assuming that it was by a single author, tended to place its composition in the Warring States period. Among the pioneers who began sorting out strata and dating them to different times in the last three centuries B.C., Lung Po-chien 龍伯堅 (1957) stands out.

Medical texts excavated at Ma-wang-tui have prompted a decisive shift of opinion toward dating in the first century B.C. That is, the most incisive scholars now judge that the book was compiled at that time from parts written over perhaps a century. The pertinent texts found at Ma-wang-tui, named by modern scholars *Tsu pi shih i mo chiu ching* 足臂十一脈灸經 and *Yin yang shih i mo chiu ching* 陰陽十一脈灸經 (two copies), were buried in 168 B.C. In the absence of detailed studies of their dates by the few scholars who have access to the MSS, one has only the judgment of two authorities that the MS was written in a script intermediate between seal and clerical in the Ch'in period (Ma Chi-hsing and Li Hsüeh-ch'in 1975, 49–50). No proof has appeared to support a much earlier date of composition.

The content of these documents is closely related to parts of *T'ai su*, *chüan* 8–10, which correspond to *Ling shu*, *p'ien* 13 and 10, in that order.

But the Ma-wang-tui writings reflect a considerably earlier understanding. There are eleven tracts instead of twelve; all lead toward the seat of cardiac functions; they are not associated with a circulation of *ch'i* and other vital fluids; and therapy does not include acupuncture with metal needles. Japanese and Chinese scholars have remarked that three other fragmentary Ma-wang-tui MSS show a similar ancestral relation to parts of *T'ai su*. Even between *Tsu pi shih i mo chiu ching* and *Yin Yang shih i mo chiu ching*, terminological and other differences consistently reflect in a complex way different stages of conceptual elaboration (Yamada 1979b, 75–78, 86, Yao Ch'un-fa 1982). The burden of proof is now taken to fall upon those who insist that the great gaps between the two MSS and *Huang ti nei ching* were bridged in much less than two centuries, i.e., that any significant part of the latter text was set down before the mid-first century B.C.

This shift in views about the dates of the *Nei ching* texts has been ignored by many scholars in China and some elsewhere, but the few attempts to halt it repeat old arguments rather than provide new counter-evidence.

The new archaeological evidence has prompted historians to re-examine familiar external and internal evidence. The compilation of case studies from the practice of Ch'un-yü I 淳于意 (*c.* 154 B.C.; *Shih chi* 105, pp. 2796f.), for instance, does not mention *Huang ti nei ching* among the ten books he received, but eight of the latter are cited in *Huang ti nei ching* (Jen Ying-ch'iu 1984, pp. 346–49). Ch'un-yü I relies on stone-needle therapy more than acupuncture and, like the Ma-wang-tui MSS, does not stimulate at named loci (or 'points'). His use of Yin-Yang and the Five Phases is less consistent and more superficial than in *Nei ching*. Wei Yao-hsi (1983) has drawn attention to Ch'in and Han degree subdivisions, land taxation terminology, and so on within the *Ling shu*. Sun Man-chih 孫曼之 notes that the correspondences of the yin visceral systems of functions (*wu tsang* 五藏) to the Five Phases in the *Huang ti nei ching* texts do not tally with those in pre-Han classics, but first appear in the New Text *Book of Documents* (*Chin wen Shang shu* 今文尚書). He argues that this clear-cut division did not develop until the late part of Former Han, and should be understood in connection with the political agenda of this polemic (1988; see also Wang Yü-ch'uan 1988).

This new dating, like the older ones, assumes that the content of extant recensions (the T'ang *T'ai su*, the Northern Sung *Su wen*, and the Southern Sung *Ling shu*, to be discussed below) corresponds in a general way to the 'original' *Huang ti nei ching*, a problematic entity. This assumption has been borne out by comparison between versions, and with frequent quotations and epitomes in other early writings. Significant discrepancies in content can be accounted for in several ways. For instance, of 37 citations from 'the canons' (*ching*) in *Nan ching*, 18 are not found in *Su wen* or *Ling shu* (Wu K'ao-p'an 1983, 85; see also *Nan ching ching shih* of 1727); but there is no reason to understand 'the canons' so narrowly.

On the whole, citations in pre-T'ang sources, particularly in *Nan ching, Chia i ching* and *Mo ching*, indicate that the three *Nei ching* texts are not so much re-written as re-arranged versions of the books available to Later Han authors. An exemplary formal analysis by Keegan (1988) shows that the three versions draw on and relate very differently a common pool of short texts, some mentioned by name in the biography of Ch'un-yü I, also incorporating various explanations, often discrepant, of such texts. No consistent pattern allows one to conclude that one version consistently represents an earlier stage than the others. Keegan concludes that it is impossible to establish a simple relationship between the Han and T'ang recensions.

T'ai su was compiled by Yang Shang-shan from fragments of a post-Han recension of *Huang ti nei ching*. Comparing it with *Su wen* and *Ling shu* reveals many shifts. The latter two on the whole contain less archaic and obscure language; they rearrange *p'ien* in the interest of systematic, functional discourse; and they separate (even between *Su wen* and *Ling shu*) what in *T'ai su* are patently text and comment (Yamada 1979b, 71–72). But as Keegan shows, this pattern is not consistent; *Su wen* and *Ling shu* contain precursors of texts in *T'ai su* (p. 208). Consulting all three versions is essential.

5. Textual history and major recensions

Many scholars have noted that there was a *Huang ti t'ai su* 黃帝太素 of 20 *p'ien* in the imperial library at the end of the Former Han. Since nothing is known about it except that the *Ch'i lüeh* 七略 put it in the Yin-Yang rather than the medical class (*Han shu* 30:1732), this listing is hardly evidence for a Han exemplar. The *Huang ti nei ching t'ai su* is still dated *c.* 600 by some medical historians, but Yang Shou-ching 楊守敬 (1839–1915) refuted this opinion in 1901 (9, la–3b), and more recent inquiries suggest 666/683 (Sivin forthcoming). It is listed in *Chiu T'ang shu* 47, p. 2047, and *Hsin T'ang shu* 59, p. 1566, as 30 *chüan*. It does not figure in Fujiwara Sukeyo's catalogue, and it is given in *Sung shih* 207, p. 5303, with 3 *chüan* only. The book is very rarely cited after the Sung period. After the *T'ai su* was lost in China, only a copy made in 1167–1168 of a recension that entered Japan in the first half of the eighth century survived at Ninnaji in Kyoto to serve as the basis of all twentieth-century editions. This copy preserves only 25 out of the original 30 *chüan*, and 180 out of an unknown number of *p'ien*.

Su wen and *Ling shu*, despite variations in the number of *chüan* recorded at various times, have consistently included 81 *p'ien* each, with much duplication. In *Su wen*, as already noted, two *p'ien* are missing, and seven *p'ien* and part of an eighth are spurious. Of the extant 152 *p'ien* in the *Nei ching*, 111 are completely or almost completely reproduced (not necessarily verbatim) in the incomplete *T'ai su*, 23 are reproduced in part, and only 28 have no counterpart. Conversely, every surviving *p'ien* in *T'ai su* has a counterpart in *Su wen* or *Ling shu* or both.

Scholars who have studied most deeply the textual history of the *Nei ching* accept — with reservations — Huang-fu Mi's equation of the *Huang ti nei ching* listed in *Han shu* 30, p. 1776, with the *Su wen* and *Chen ching* available to him (Okanishi 1958, 1–48, 1974, 1–11, Ma Chi-hsing 1990, pp. 70–85). Huang-fu Mi complains that the books were no longer intact, and parts were disordered. By *c.* 503, when Ch'üan Yüan-ch'i annotated the *Su wen*, *chüan* no. 7 had been lost, so his version, entitled *Huang ti su wen*, contains only 8 *chüan* and 68 *p'ien*. It is recorded in the bibliographical treatises of the Sui through Sung histories, but did not survive into the Yüan period.

Wang Ping's commentary accompanies a considerably re-arranged text in 24 *chüan*. He admits that he has added and excised text as his judgment dictated, and supplemented the incomplete Ch'üan version from other sources. His additions were originally inscribed in red, but this feature was not reproduced in any known printed edition. The choice by a government committee of the Wang text and commentary for further editing, printing, and official promulgation in 1026/1027 and 1067 ensured its survival and, no doubt, was responsible for the extinction of the Ch'üan version (for a *p'ien*-by-*p'ien* comparison of the two see Okanishi 1958, pp. 11–14, or Ma 1990, pp. 71–74). It is also pertinent that the T'ang medical examinations prior to 760 did not include any part of the *Nei ching*, and in 760 required study only of *Su wen*, perhaps an early version of that submitted by Wang Ping to the throne in 762. This situation may be compared to that in Korea from 692 on, when *Su wen* and *Chen ching* were required, and that in Japan in 757, when *T'ai su* was included in the curriculum (Miyashita 1963; Kosoto *et al.* 1981:VIII, 344–345).

There has been no major new edition of the *Su wen* since 1067. There is a great need for one that systematically compares quotations in early sources and parallels in *T'ai su* and *Ling shu* with the Wang text.

The career of the text now called *Huang ti nei ching ling shu* or simply *Ling shu ching* is more obscure between the Han and the Sung periods. In *Chia i ching* the quotations labelled *Huang ti* consistently correspond to the present *Ling shu* (and to parallels in *T'ai su*). *Sui shu* 34, p. 1040, lists a *Huang ti chen ching* in 9 *chüan*, adding in a note that the Liang imperial library included a *Huang ti chen chiu ching* 黃帝鍼灸經 in 12 *chüan*. The former title in 10 *chüan*, and the latter in 12, appear in *Chiu T'ang shu* 47, pp. 2046, 2047 and *Hsin T'ang shu* 59, p. 1565, along with several vaguely similar titles which have led Okanishi to suspect that many diverse versions were circulating in the Sui and T'ang (1974, p. 9).

Wang Ping's preface to *Su wen* uses 'Ling shu' for the second of the two texts that make up the *Nei ching*. In his commentary, he sometimes refers to this title and sometimes to either 'Chen ching' or 'Ching' (e.g., cf. quotations of the same passage in *chüan* 6, *p'ien* 20, p. 118, col. 9 and *chüan* 17, *p'ien* 62, p. 306, col. 12). Assertions that *Ling shu* possessed a preface by Yang Shang-shan (*Yü hai* 玉海 63, 9b–10a) or that the book was fabricated by Wang Ping (*Tao ku t'ang wen chi* 道古堂文集, 26, 6a–6b) have not been backed by plausible evidence, and are generally disregarded. But Wang's *Su wen* commentary copiously quotes from a version of the *Ling shu*, and he is the first to call it that.

Early in the eleventh century the Koryō government began importing Chinese medical books, a *Huang ti chen ching* among them (Jeon 1974, pp. 259–60). But neither *Chen ching* nor *Ling shu* were included alongside the *Su wen* in the great series of pre-Sung medical classics collated and printed under imperial Chinese auspices in 1026–1069, although the editors of the 1067 *Su Wen* were ordered to include *Ling shu* as well as *T'ai su* (see *Su Wei-kung wen chi* 蘇魏公文集, 65, 995 and the Sung editors' preface to *Chia i ching*). The editors of the 1067 *Su wen* note that 'since the *Ling shu* is no longer complete, we can no longer be sure' whether Wang always uses 'Ling shu' to refer to the Needling Canon. *Chen ching* was requested from Korea in 1091 and delivered in 1093 (*Yü hai* 63, 23b; Sohn 1959). The book was promulgated with no change of title, but there is no evidence that it was printed until 1155, when Shih Sung 史崧, 'regretting that *Ling shu* has long been out of circulation,' submitted to the government a 24-*chüan* edition he had prepared by comparing a copy 'preserved in his family' with parallel passages in other works. His preface stresses similarities, particularly to *Nan ching* and *Chia i ching*. His use of the title *Ling shu*, following Wang Ping, was followed in later editions, all evidently based on his recension. *Sung shih* 207, p. 5303, records both *Chen ching* and *Ling shu* in 9-*chüan* versions; possibly these are variant titles for the version recovered from Korea.

Because, so far as we know, *Ling shu* was not revised by either Wang Ping or the Editorial Bureau for Medical Books of the Northern Sung, its content remained close to its pre-T'ang state. One sign that it was less extensively edited than either of the other *Nei ching* books is that it retains a larger number of obvious copyist's errors. No commentary imposed a consistent interpretation upon the text as Wang's did for *Su wen*. That does not imply that *Ling shu* is closer to the Han *Nei ching* than is *T'ai su*. On the contrary, in language and in use of abstract concepts *Ling shu* does not differ greatly from *Su wen*. Maruyama Masao 丸山昌朗 (1965) has argued, after comparing twelve analogous *p'ien* in *Su wen* and *Ling shu*, that the latter is more mature and its use of Yin-Yang and Five Phases more consistent.

6. Traditional commentaries, evaluations

The earliest extant commentary on *Su wen*, that of Wang Ping, was officially adopted from the T'ang onwards for medical instruction. That gave it such authority that the text has rarely been read without it. It both explains and interprets. Although Wang devoted much effort to textual matters, he was prodigal in improving the text, to the point that 'when monarch and minister, engaged in questioning, violate good form, I have given thought to the relations between superior and inferior and made additions that illuminate their intentions' (Preface). Lin I 林億 and his co-workers in the Editorial Bureau for Medical Books, being more scrupulous, recorded textual differences as they resolved them. The state in which they left the text was still far from satisfactory. As Jen Ying-ch'iu 任應秋 has observed, 'it is regrettable that few among the *Nei ching*'s commentators have been good critical philologists.' He lists ten that he approves, but none published textual emendations on more than a small part of *Su wen* or *Ling shu*. Jen also evaluates a dozen commentaries (1984, pp. 354–61); Fu Ching-hua 傅景華 and Fu Ching-ch'un 傅景春 describe and assess thirty-nine, mostly Ming and Ch'ing (1985, pp. 30–61). These are noteworthy:

(a) Ma Shih 馬蒔, *Huang ti nei ching ling shu chu cheng fa wei* 黃帝內經靈樞注證發微 and *Huang ti nei ching su wen chu cheng fa wei* (1586?), in 9 *chüan* each, are often unreliable. The former is the oldest extant commentary on *Ling shu*, and, because Ma was expert in acupuncture, is considered superior to the latter.

(b) Wu K'un 吳崑, *Nei ching su wen Wu chu* 內經素問吳注 (1594), is exceptionally clear in its explanations, and grounded in deep experience of practice.

(c) Chang Chieh-pin 張介賓, *Lei ching* 類經 (1624), re-arranges *Su wen* and *Ling shu* in a judicious topical order, and incorporates what is in many respects the best-informed and most useful commentary on both. Chang was one of the leading physicians of his time, and a prolific author.

(d) Yao Shao-yü 姚紹虞, *Su wen ching chu chieh chieh* 素問經注節解 (1667), is an interesting example of Ch'ing philology both for its critical approach to previous annotators and its attempt to restore the text by rearranging it and excising redundant and corrupt portions. Yao compiled a similar work on *Ling shu* that did not survive.

(e) Chang Chih-ts'ung 張志聰, *Huang ti nei ching su wen chi chu* 黃帝內經素問集注, (1670) and *Huang ti nei ching ling shu chi chu* (1672), are called 'collected annotations' because Chang and his disciples worked together on them. These books often take up thorny problems ignored by their predecessors.

(f) Kao Shih-shih 高世栻, *Su wen chih chieh* 素問直解 (1695), is valued primarily as a clear, understandable digest of earlier annotations, including those of his teacher Chang Chih-ts'ung. Kao annotates the two 'lost sections' as well as the received text (see 7b below).

(g) Tamba no Motoyasu 丹波元簡, *Somon shiki* 素問識 (1806) and *Reisu shiki* 靈樞識 (by 1808), provide an excellent choice of Chinese and Japanese commentaries with the compiler's judicious assessments. They are widely used in China as well as Japan.

(h) Ch'eng Shih-te 程士德 *et al.*, *Su wen chu shih hui ts'ui* 素問注釋匯粹 (1982), is the best of many modern compendia of annotations to *Su wen*. Like most, it is printed in simplified characters. It provides not only explanations but a short comment on each section.

Yang Shang-shan's commentary on *T'ai su* remains unique. Hsiao Yen-p'ing 蕭廷平 (1924) supplemented it with notes comparing the text available in China with parallel passages in other books. They are reprinted in the 1965 Peking editions (see *Huang ti nei ching t'ai su*, under 10 (a) below).

7. Editions

There is only one recension of *T'ai su*. The only usable edition is the detailed photographic reproduction in *Tōyō igaku zempon sōsho* 東洋醫學全本叢書 (Kosoto 1981). All of the Chinese printed editions are based on imperfect copies of the Ninnaji MS. They omit many portions that are readable in the 1981 edition.

Since from the Southern Sung *Su wen* and *Ling shu* have been the foundation of medical education, hundreds of editions and commentaries survive (Chung kuo Chung i yen chiu yüan 中國中醫研究院 1991: items 1–213 are an incomplete listing). The most important editions that followed Wang Ping's annotated *Su wen* (672) and Shih Sung's *Ling shu* (1155) are:

(a) The critical editions of *Su wen* prepared in the palace by the Bureau for Critical Editions of Medical Books in 1027, 1035, and 1067. The first and third were printed, but only the latter, entitled *Ch'ung kuang pu chu Huang ti nei ching su wen* 重廣補注黃帝內經素問, in 12 *chüan*, survived to become the basis for extant later editions.

(b) The Ku lin shu t'ang 古林書堂 *Hsin k'an pu chu shih wen Huang ti nei ching su wen* 新刊補注釋文黃帝內經素問 of 1339 and *Ling shu ching* of 1339–1340, is the oldest extant combined edition. It reprints the last item and the Shih Sung *Ling shu*, its 24 *chüan* being rearranged into 12. Appended are *Su wen i p'ien* 素問遺篇 in 1 *chüan* and *Su wen ju shih yün ch'i lun ao* 素問入式運氣論奧 (1099) in 3 *chüan*.

(c) Two versions in the *Cheng t'ung tao tsang* 正統道藏: (i) *Huang ti nei ching su wen pu chu shih wen* 黃帝內經素問補註釋文 in 50 *chüan* (Schipper no. 1018, vols. 649–660) is an arbitrary redivision of the 1067 edition. (ii) *Huang ti su wen ling shu chi chu* 黃帝素問靈樞集註 in 23 *chüan* (no. 1020, vols. 661–663), despite the title, is merely the unannotated Shih Sung text of *Ling shu* with altered *chüan* divisions.

(d) A 1474 reprint of (b) by the Fukien medical publisher Hsiung Chün 熊均, better known as Hsiung Tsung-li 熊宗立. He added his *Su wen yün ch'i t'u k'uo ting chü li ch'eng* 素問運氣圖括定局立成 (1465), 1 *chüan*.

(e) The mid-sixteenth-century Chao fu 趙府 edition, prepared under the patronage of King K'ang 康王. Its *Huang ti su wen* was based on (b), and its *Huang ti ling shu ching* on the 12-*chüan* T'ien Ching 田經 edition, putatively Sung but recently shown to have been printed in the early Chia ching era (1522/1566; Mao Ch'un-hsiang 1962, p. 104).

(f) An anonymous Ming reprint of the 24-*chüan Su wen* alone, probably from a 1228/1233 version of the 1067 edition. The 1550 edition of Ku Ts'ung-te 顧從德, based on it but reproducing the title of the 1067 edition, became the basis of all later 24-*chüan* editions. The *Ssu pu ts'ung k'an* edition is based on this version, with *Ling shu* from (e). The *Ssu pu pei yao* reproduces an 1876 recension of this version, with *Ling shu* from (h).

(g) The Chou Yüeh 周曰 edition of 1584, with *Su wen* based on (f) and a *Ling shu* in 24 *chüan* greatly inferior to other Ming recensions (see the tabular comparison in Okanishi 1974, p. 66).

(h) The Wu Mien-hsüeh 吳勉學 edition entitled *Huang ti su wen ling shu ho chi* 黃帝素問靈樞合集, included in Wang K'en-t'ang's 王肯堂 (1549–1613) influential *I t'ung cheng mo ch'üan shu* 醫統正脈全書 of 1601, but not in the spurious 1923 'reprint.'

(i) The most widely used edition, a critical text which collates (f), (h), and one other version, is the punctuated and typeset *Huang ti nei ching su wen: fu Ling shu ching* 黃帝內經素問。附靈樞經 (Shanghai: Shang wu, 1955, with numerous reprints in China and Taiwan). The same text without Wang Ping's annotation is the basis of Jen Ying-ch'iu's index (1986), which makes reference by section numbers possible.

In summary, although the formidable resources of Ch'ing critical philology were applied with good effect in commentaries on *Su wen* and *Ling shu*, these made no important contribution to the state of the text. For comprehensive discussions of editions see Okanishi 1958, pp. 19–32, 38–44, and 1974, pp. 40–46, 57–66.

8. Translations

No published translation of any substantial part of *Huang ti nei ching* meets current standards for the establishment of a critical text, philological accuracy, and a faithful depiction of concepts. The special difficulties that face translators of medical classics are discussed by scholars of greatly varying linguistic competence, none magisterial, in Unschuld (ed.) 1988. The translations of seven individual chapters by Claude Larre, S.J., and Elisabeth Rochat de la Vallée are superior to other European translations in point of the third criterion. They are not philological in approach, and do not consult parallels in *T'ai su* and other texts. Highly interpretive, they are meant primarily for acupuncturists and other practitioners. They provide not only literal translations but excerpts from the Wang and occasionally other commentaries, expanded paraphrases, and explanations of underlying ideas.

The several complete translations into Japanese and Chinese have little value for textual, historical, or philosophical research. All are designed for medical practitioners whose understanding of classical medicine has been greatly influenced by Western bio-medical thought. They tend to scant the exact meaning of Chinese technical terms which do not have bio-medical counterparts, or which in modern medicine have very different meanings. For instance, *hsüeh* 血 in *Huang ti nei ching* sometimes refers to blood as seen issuing from the human body, but more usually to the yin aspect of vital *ch'i* (Sivin 1988, pp. 51–52).

Modern Chinese translations equate the term with *hsüeh yeh* 血液, the
bio-medical term for blood. They translate the old terminology for the
emotions into modern psychological terms, and ignore mentions of
divinities, possession and other forms of 'superstition.' Two of the best
examples of this genre are by Kuo Ai-ch'un 郭靄春 (1981, 1982). Both
include indifferent texts in simplified characters, variorum notes that
draw on diverse texts, and explanatory notes. Kuo is more systematic
than other recent translators in his coverage of variations. Okuri Eiichi
小栗英一 and Yabuuchi Kiyoshi 藪內清 have translated about a third
of the *Su wen* for a general Japanese readership (1975).

9.   Research aids

Many of the available reference works are meant for medical practitioners, and are of little or no use to scholars of the humanities. The index of
technical terms in Kitasato Kenkyūjo 1979 cites one or more occurrences
of each term in *Su wen* more or less at random, and that of Ku Chih-
shan 顧植山 1988 is based on widely available but mostly unsatisfactory
editions of four Han classics. A significant exception, Jen Ying-ch'iu
1986, includes not only all phrases in *Su wen* and *Ling shu* but their technical terminology. Its numbering of sections and subsections provides a
standard for concise citation.

Of the many introductory studies of the *Nei ching*, Jen Ying-ch'iu and
Liu Ch'ang-lin 劉長林 1982 and Jen 1984 are least superficial. Fu Wei-
k'ang 傅維康 and Wu Hung-chou 吳鴻洲 1988 combines background
essays and annotated excerpts with vernacular translations.

Recent attempts to apply new perspectives to studies of the Inner
Canon are gathered in Wang Ch'i 王琦 (1985). Chao Hung-chün 趙洪
鈞 has made a noteworthy first attempt to reconstruct the cultural and
intellectual background of the *Nei ching* (1985). A splendid set of reference tools appears in Kosoto 1981, vol. VIII. They include finding lists for
parallel passages in the various *Huang ti nei ching* texts and other early
medical books, as well as indexes of persons, books, and acupuncture
loci cited. Among Japanese authors, Fujiki Toshirō (1976, 1979) has written two straightforward introductory books. The essays of Maruyama
Masao (1977) are consistently original and percipient. For bibliographic
reference the works of Okanishi (1958, 1974) remain unparalleled.

New publications on the *Nei ching* are surveyed and abstracted annu-
ally in the yearbook *Chung i nien chien* 中醫年鑒, compiled by the
Shanghai College of Chinese Medicine. For a detailed conspectus of recent reference works for the history of Chinese medicine see Sivin 1989.

10. References

(a) *Primary sources*

Chia i ching 甲乙經. See *Huang ti chia i ching*.

Huang ti chen chiu chia i ching 黃帝鍼灸甲乙經. See *Huang ti chia i ching*.

Huang ti chia i ching 黃帝甲乙經, by Huang-fu Mi 皇甫謐 completed 256/282, 10 *chüan*. In *I t'ung cheng mo ch'üan shu* 醫統正脈全書 under the common later title *Huang ti chen chiu chia i ching*. 'Chia i,' or 'A–B,' refers to the use of the ten Celestial Stems to designate chapters in an early version.

Huang ti nei ching ling shu chi chu 黃帝內經靈樞集注, by Chang Chih-ts'ung 張志聰, 1670, 9 *chüan*. Shanghai: Shang hai k'o hsüeh chi shu, 1957.

Huang ti nei ching ling shu chu cheng fa wei 黃帝內經靈樞注證發微, by Ma Shih 馬蒔, 1580, 9 *chüan*, *I pu ch'üan shu* 醫部全書. Pan-ch'iao, Taiwan: Yee Wen, 1977.

Huang ti nei ching su wen chi chu 黃帝內經素問集注, by Chang Chih-ts'ung, 1672, 9 *chüan*. Shanghai: Shang hai wei sheng, 1959.

Huang ti nei ching su wen chu cheng fa wei, 1586, by Ma Shih, 9 *chüan*; in *I pu ch'üan shu*.

Huang ti nei ching t'ai su 黃帝內經太素, by Yang Shang-shan 楊上善, 666/683, 30 *chüan*. Text in Kosoto 1981, vols. I–III. For the variorum notes taken from comparison with many early texts by Hsiao Yen-p'ing 蕭延平 in 1924, see the Peking, Jen min wei sheng 1965 ed., the text of which is not only incomplete but not edited according to normal practice.

Huang ti pa shih i nan ching 黃帝八十一難經, anonymous, probably second century A.D., 81 *p'ien*. In *Nan ching pen i* 難經本義 of 1361, Taipei: Hsüan feng, 1976. Usually referred to as *Nan ching*.

Ku chin i t'ung 古今醫統. By Hsü Ch'un-fu 徐春甫, 1556, 100 *chüan*. Taipei, Hsin Wen feng 新文豐 reprint of Ming Ko Sung-li 葛宋禮 ed. A topical anthology.

Lei ching 類經. By Chang Chieh-pin 張介賓, 1624, 32 *chüan*, 4 *chüan* of supplementary essays, 11 *chüan* of diagrams. In *Ssu k'u ch'üan shu chen pen* (fifth series).

Mo ching 脈經. Wang Shu-ho 王叔和, c. A.D. 280, 10 *chüan*; in *I t'ung cheng mo ch'üan shu*.

Nan ching 難經. See *Huang ti pa shih i nan ching*.

Nan ching ching shih 難經經釋. By Hsü Ta-ch'un 徐大椿 1727, 2 *chüan*. In *Hsü Ling-t'ai i shu ch'üan chi* 徐靈胎醫書全集, vol. 1. Reprint, 4 vols. Taipei: Ch'eng wen, 1972.

Nei ching su wen Wu chu 內經素問吳注, by Wu K'un 吳崑, 1594, 24 *chüan*. Critical text based on 1609 and other eds. Chi-nan: Shan tung k'o hsüeh chi shu, 1984.

Reisu shiki 靈樞識, by Tamba no Motoyasu 丹波元簡, by 1808, 6 *chüan*. Peking: Jen min wei sheng, 1984.

Somon shiki 素問識, by Tamba no Motoyasu, 1806, 8 *chüan*. Peking: Jen min wei sheng, 1959.

Su Wei-kung wen chi 蘇魏公文集, by Su Sung 蘇頌, compiled 1139, 72 *chüan*. 2 vols. Peking: Chung hua, 1988.

Su wen chih chieh 素問直解. By Kao Shih-shih 高世栻, 1695, 9 *chüan*. Critical text based on 1695 and 1887 eds. under title *Huang ti su wen chih chieh*; Peking: K'o hsüeh chi shu wen hsien, 1980.

Su wen ching chu chieh chieh 素問經注節解, by Yao Shao-yü 姚紹虞, 1667, 9 *chüan*. Peking: Jen min wei sheng, 1963.

Su wen chu shih hui ts'ui 素問注釋匯粹, by Ch'eng Shih-te 程士德 *et al.* 2 vols. Peking: Jen min wei sheng, 1982. Modern ed. with 'lost sections' and explanation of phase energetics in appendices.

Tao ku t'ang wen chi 道古堂文集. By Hang Shih-chün 杭世駿, printed 1776, 48 *chüan*, in Sao yeh shan fang 掃葉山房 lithograph ed. of *Tao ku t'ang ch'üan chi* 道古堂全集.

Tsu pi shih i mo chiu ching 足臂十一脈灸經. Anonymous MS, before 168 B.C.; in Ma-wang-tui 1985; text, 1–4, transcription, 1–6.

Yin yang shih i mo chiu ching 陰陽十一脈灸經. Anonymous, before 168 B.C.; two MSS, in Ma-wang-tui 1985; text, 5–10, 43–45, transcription, 7–13, 87–91.

Yü hai 玉海. Wang Ying-lin 王應麟, before 1296, 240 *chüan*. Taipei: Ta hua, 1977 reprint of 1352 edition.

(b) *Secondary sources*

Akahori, Akira 赤堀昭, 1978. 'Shin shutsudo shiryō ni yoru Chūgoku iyaku koten no minaoshi 新出土資料による中國醫藥古典の見直し'. *Kampō no rinsō* 25, 11–12:1–16.

Akahori, Akira, 1979a. 'On'yō jūichi myaku kyūkyō to Somon — Somon no seiritsu ni tsuite no ikkōsatsu 陰陽十一脈灸經と素問 —— 素問の成立についての一考察'. *Nihon ishigaku zasshi* 25, 3:277–290.

Akahori, Akira, 1979b. 'Kleiner beitrag. Medical Manuscripts Found in Han Tomb No. 3 at Ma wang tui'. *Sudhoffs Archiv* 63:297–301.

Akahori, Akira, 1981. 'On'yō jūichi myaku kyūkyō no kenkyū 陰陽十一脈灸經の研究'. *Tōhō gakuhō* (Kyoto) 53:299–339.

Chao Hung-chün 趙洪鈞, 1985. *Nei ching shih tai* 內經時代. Shih-chia-chuang: Ho-pei Chung i hsüeh yüan. Tentative edition.

Chiu, Martha Li, 1986. Mind, Body, and Illness in a Chinese Medical Tradition. Ph.D. dissertation, History and East Asian Languages, Harvard University.

Chung kuo Chung i yen chiu yüan 中國中醫研究院, 1991. *Ch'üan kuo Chung i t'u shu lien ho mu lu* 全國中醫圖書聯合目錄. Peking: Chung i ku chi. Enumerates every known edition of over 12,000 titles in 113 Chinese libraries with the most extensive medical holdings. Stroke order and Pinyin indexes of titles and authors.

Fan Hsing-chun 范行準, 1951. 'Wu yun liu ch'i shuo ti lai yüan 五運六氣說的來源, *Chung hua i shih tsa chih* 中華醫史雜誌', 3.1:3–15.

Fu Ching-hua 傅景華 and Fu Ching-ch'un 傅景春, 1985. 'Nei ching hsü lu 內經敘錄', in Wang Ch'i 1985, pp. 16–81.

Fu Wei-k'ang 傅維康 and Wu Hung-chou 吳洪洲, 1988. *Huang ti nei ching tao tu* 黃帝內經導讀. Cheng-tu: Pa Shu.

Fujiki Toshirō 藤木俊郎, 1976. *Somon igaku no sekai—kodai Chūgoku igaku no tenkai* 素問醫學の世界──古代中國醫學の展開. Tokyo: Sekibundo.

Fujiki Toshirō, 1979. *Shinkyū igaku genryū kō. Somon igaku no sekai* 鍼灸醫學源流考。素問醫學の世界II. Tokyo: Sekibundo.

Graham, A. C. 1986. *Yin-Yang and the Nature of Correlative Thinking*. Occasional Paper and Monograph Series, vol. 6. Singapore: Institute of East Asian Philosophies.

Jen Ying-ch'iu 任應秋, 1984. 'Nei ching shih chiang 內經十講'. In *Jen Ying-ch'iu lun i chi* 任應秋論醫集, 335–87. Peking: Jen min wei sheng. Essays on medical practice, doctrine, and history. This tractate was published for internal circulation in 1978, and reprinted without its useful appendixes in Jen and Liu 1982.

Jen Ying-ch'iu, editor, 1986, *Huang ti nei ching chang chü so yin* 黃帝內經章句索引. Peking: Jen min wei sheng.

Jen Ying-ch'iu and Liu Ch'ang-lin 劉長林, 1982. *Nei ching yen chiu lun ts'ung* 內經研究論叢. Wu-chang: Hu pei jen min. Medical and historical studies.

Jeon, Sang-woon, 1974. *Science and Technology in Korea. Traditional Instruments and Techniques* (The MIT East Asian Science Series, vol. 4). Cambridge, Mass.: MIT Press.

Keegan, David, 1988. *Huang-ti nei-ching*. The Structure of the Compilation, the Significance of the Structure. Ph.D. dissertation, History, University of California, Berkeley.

Kitasato Kenkyūjo fuzoku Tōyō igaku sōgō kenkyūjo rinsō koten kenkyūhan 北里研究所附屬東洋醫學總合研究所臨床古典研究班, editors, 1979. *Somon rinsō sakuin shū* 素問臨床索引集. Tokyo: Kokusho.

Kosoto Hiroshi 小曾戶洋 editor-in-chief, 1981. *Tōyō igaku zempon sōsho* 東洋醫學善本叢書. 8 vols. Osaka: Tōyō igaku kenkyūkai.

Ku Chih-shan 顧植山, 1988. *Chung i ching tien so yin* 中醫經典索引. Hofei: An-hui k'o hsüeh chi shu.

Kuo Ai-ch'un 郭靄春, 1981. *Huang ti nei ching su wen chiao chu yü i* 黃帝內經素問校注語譯. Tientsin: T'ien-chin k'o hsüeh chi shu. Simplified characters.

Kuo Ai-ch'un, 1982. *Ling shu ching chiao shih* 靈樞經校釋. Peking: Jen min wei sheng. Simplified characters.

Larre, Claude, translator, 1987. *La voie du ciel. Huangdi, l'Empereur Jaune, disait . . . La médecine chinoise traditionnelle.* Paris: Desclée de Brouwer. A series of meditations on classical doctrine, with special attention to Ch. 1–2 of the *Inner Canon of the Yellow Lord*.

Larre, Claude, and Elisabeth Rochat de la Vallée, translators, 1983. 'Plein ciel. Les authentiqués de haute antiquité. Texte, présentation, traduction et commentaire du («Su Wen»), chap. I'. *Méridiens*, 61–62: 13–67. Translation of *p'ien* 1.

Larre, Claude, and Elisabeth Rochat de la Vallée, translators, 1983–1986. 'Vif. Texte, présentation, traduction et commentaire du "Su Wen", chap. III'. *Méridiens*, 1983, 69–70:39–90; 1985, 71–72:15–71; 1986, 73–74: 13–78.

Larre, Claude, and Elisabeth Rochat de la Vallée, translators, 1984. 'Assaisonner les esprits. Texte, présentation, traduction et commentaire du Su Wen, chap. II. Part 2'. *Méridiens*, 67–68:13–54.

Larre, Claude, and Elisabeth Rochat de la Vallée, translators, 1985. *Par cinq. Discours méthodique sur les phénomènes et comment ils repondent au yin/yang. Texte, présentation. traduction et commentaire du Suwen chapitre 5.* Paris: Institut Ricci.

Larre, Claude, and Elisabeth Rochat de la Vallée, translators, 1986–1987. 'Fil. Texte, présentation, traduction et commentaire du "Suwen", chap. VIII'. *Méridiens*, 1986, 75–76:13–44; 1987, 77:13–44.

Larre, Claude, and Elisabeth Rochat de la Vallee, translators, 1988–1989. 'Cascade. Texte, présentation, traduction et commentaire du Lingshu, chap. 8'. *Méridiens*, 1988, 81:25–44; 83:13–43; 1989, 85:17–41; 87:17–37.

Lu Gwei-Djen and Joseph Needham, 1966/1970. Medicine and Chinese Culture. In Needham, *Clerks and Craftsmen in China and the West*, pp. 263–293. Cambridge: Cambridge University Press.

Lu Gwei-Djen and Joseph Needham, 1980. *Celestial Lancets. A History and Rationale of Acupuncture and Moxa.* Cambridge: Cambridge University Press.

Lung Po-chien 龍伯堅, 1957. 'Huang ti nei ching ti chu tso shih tai 黃帝內經的著作時代'. *Chung hua i shih tsa chih* 2:106–113.

Ma Chi-hsing 馬繼興 and Li Hsüeh-ch'in 李學勤, 1975. 'Wo kuo hsien i fa hsien ti tsui ku i fang — po shu "Wu shih erh ping fang" 我國現已發現的最古醫方——帛書《五十二病方》. *Wen wu* 1975.9, 49–60. The authors use the *noms de plume* Chung I-yen 鍾益研 and Ling Hsiang 凌襄.

Ma Chi-hsing 馬繼興, 1990. *Chung i wen hsien hsüeh* 中醫文獻學. Shanghai: Shang hai k'o hsüeh. No index.

Ma-wang-tui Han mu po shu cheng li hsiao tsu 馬王堆漢墓帛書整理小組, 1985. *Ma-wang-tui Han mu po shu.* Vol. IV. [Medical MSS]. Peking: Wen wu.

Mao Ch'un-hsiang 毛春翔, 1962. *Ku shu pan pen ch'ang t'an* 古書版本常談. Peking: Chung hua.

Maruyama Masao 丸山昌朗, 1965. 'Reisu no seiritsu ni tsuite 靈樞の成立に就て'. *Nihon tōyō igaku kaishi* 日本東洋醫學會誌 15.3:83–88. Reprinted in 1977:262–75.

Maruyama Masao, 1977. *Shinkyū igaku to koten no kenkyū. Maruyama Masao tōyō igaku ronshū* 鍼灸醫學と古典の研究.丸山昌郎東洋醫學論集. Osaka: Sogensha. 2d ed., 1979.

Miyashita Saburō 宮下三郎, 1963. Zui-Tō jidai no iryō 隋唐時代の醫療. In *Chūgoku chūsei kagaku gijutsu shi no kenkyū* 中國中世科學技術史の研究. Tokyo: Kadokawa.

Okanishi Tameto 岡西爲人, 1958. *Sung i ch'ien i chi k'ao* 宋以前醫籍考. Peking: Jen min wei sheng. A pastiche of carefully selected information in Chinese. Originally published in part, 4 vols., Feng-t'ien: Man chou i k'o ta hsüeh, 1936–1944.

Okanishi Tameto, 1974. *Chūgoku isho honzō kō* 中國醫書本草考. Osaka: Minami Osaka.

Okuri Eiichi 小栗英一 and Yabuuchi Kiyoshi 藪內清, translators, 1975. *Kōtei naikyō somon* 黃帝內經素問. In *Chūgoku no kagaku* 中國の科學, ed. Yabuuchi. Tokyo: Chūō kōronsha.

Porkert, Manfred, 1974, *The Theoretical Foundations of Chinese medicine: Systems of correspondence.* Cambridge: MIT Press.

Rochat de la Vallée, Elisabeth, translator. n.d. *Toux, Texte, présentation, traduction et commentaire du Suwen, chapitre 38 (Kelun) et autres textes se rapportant au sujet.* Paris: Institut Ricci.

Sakurai Kensuke 櫻井謙介, 1985. 'Shin shutsudo iyaku kankei bunbu-tsu ni tsuite' 新出土醫藥關係文物について. In Yamada ed. 1985, II, 347–368.

Shang hai Chung i hsüeh yüan 上海中醫學院, 1984– . *Chung i nien chien* 中醫年鑒. Peking: Jen min wei sheng. Annual.

Sivin, N., 1988. *Traditional Medicine in Contemporary China* (Science, Medicine and Technology in East Asia, vol. 2). Ann Arbor: Center for Chinese Studies, University of Michigan.

Sivin, N., 1989. 'A cornucopia of Reference Works for the History of Chinese Medicine.' *Chinese Science*, 9:29–52.

Sivin, N., Forthcoming. On the Dates of Yang Shang-shan and the *Huang ti nei ching t'ai su*. In *Chinese Science*.

Sohn, Pow-key, 1959. 'Early Korean Printing.' *Journal of the American Oriental Society* 79.2:99–103.

Soothill, William Edward, 1951. *The Hall of Light, A Study of Early Chinese Kingship* (Missionary Research Series, vol. 18). London: Lutterworth.

Sun Man-chih 孫曼之, 1988. 'Huang ti nei ching ch'eng shu nien tai' 黃帝內經成書年代. *Chung hua i shih tsa chih* 18.1:54–55.

Unschuld, Paul U., editor, 1988. *Approaches to Traditional Chinese Medical Literature. Proceedings of an International Symposium on Translation Methodologies and Terminologies*. Boston: Kluwer. Essays from a 1986 conference.

Wang Ch'i 王琦, editor, 1985. *Huang ti nei ching chuan t'i yen chiu* 黃帝內經專題研究. Chi-nan: Shan-tung k'o hsüeh chi shu. Twenty essays on thought and context, mostly by Wang and collaborators.

Wang Yü-ch'uan 王玉川, 1988. 'Wu tsang p'ei wu hsing, wu wei chi ch'i t'a' 五臟配五行, 五味及其他. *Pei-ching Chung i hsüeh yüan hsüeh pao*, 1:7–12.

Wei Yao-hsi 委堯西, 1983. 'Ling shu ch'eng shu shih tai' 靈樞成書時代. *Chung hua i shih tsa chih* 13.2:88–92. Novel arguments, several specious.

Wu K'ao-p'an 吳考槃, 1983. 'Huang ti nei ching Su wen Ling shu k'ao' 黃帝內經素問靈樞考. *Chung hua i shih tsa chih* 13.2:85–87. Argues against identifying the extant *Su wen* and *ling shu* with original *Nei ching*.

Yamada Keiji 山田慶兒, 1979a. 'Kōtei naikyō no seiritsu' 黃帝內經の成立. *Shisō* 662:94–108.

Yamada Keiji, 1979b. 'The Formation of the *Huang-ti nei-ching*'. *Acta Asiatica* 36, 67–89. Translation of 1979a.

Yamada Keiji, 1980. 'Kyukū hachifū setsu to Shōshiha no tachiba' 九宮八風說と少師派の立場. *Tōhō gakuhō* (Kyoto) 52:199–242.

Yamada Keiji, editor, 1985. *Shin hakken Chūgoku kagakushi shiryō no kenkyū* 新發現中國科學史資料の研究. 2 vols. I. Annotated translations. II. Essays. Kyoto: Jimbun kagaku kenkyūjo.

Yang Shou-ching 楊守敬, 1901. *Jih pen fang shu chih* 日本訪書志. Reprint in *Shu mu ts'ung pien* 書目叢編, vol. 17.

Yao Ch'un-fa 姚純發, 1982. 'Ma-wang-tui po shu Tsu pi shih i mo chiu ching ch'u t'an' 馬王堆帛書足臂十一脈灸經初探. *Chung hua i shih tsa chih* 12.3:171–174.

— Nathan Sivin

I ching 易經 (*Chou I* 周易)

1. The place of the work in the Chinese tradition and its strata

It is almost inevitable that students of Chinese culture encounter this text, which is perhaps the single most important work in China's long intellectual history. Traditionally regarded as the inspired product of the 'Four sages', i.e. Fu Hsi 伏羲, King Wen 文王, Chou kung and Confucius, this enigmatic text was used in its earliest form as a manual of divination. Since at least the Han dynasty, when it was given first place among China's classics, the work has become the foundation on which innumerable commentators have erected moralistic, metaphysical, apocalyptic and soteriological constructs. While these philosophical exegeses are not without value or interest, for those who are concerned with early, i.e. pre-imperial, China they may often tend to obscure the meaning of the work in its original context.

Even in the pre-Han period the original divination text had already undergone a long process of interpretation and re-interpretation, resulting in the incorporation of a group of commentaries, the so called 'Ten Wings' (*shih i* 十翼), into what was to become one of the classical texts. By virtue of their canonical status, these commentaries, which reflect the world view of the late Warring States or Han periods, ensured that thereafter even the original stratum of the text would be interpreted according to moralistic concerns. Considerations of the context of the work that have been forthcoming in China during the past fifty years have demonstrated the anachronistic nature of this interpretation and have begun to suggest what the original meaning of the hexagram and line statements (to be explained below) must have been. For this reason, care is necessary in speaking of the *Book of Changes* as a single text. It is perhaps convenient to use the title *Chou i* to refer to the original parts (i.e. the hexagram and line statements), with special reference to the original context in which they were composed; and to use the title *I ching* as referring to the complete canonical text (i.e., inclusive of the 'Ten Wings'), with the entire text being understood as one of the Classics. This convention will be followed hereafter.

2. Content of the *Chou i*: the hexagram and line statements

The *Chou i* is organized around 64 permutations of six broken or solid lines (e.g. ䷀, ䷁) usually referred to as hexagrams, which have been regarded traditionally as resulting from combining two of eight basic trigrams (☰, ☷, ☳, ☵, ☶, ☲, ☴, ☱). However, recent research on *pa kua* 八卦 numerical symbols that have been found primarily on Western Chou bronzes but also on a few late Shang oracle bones suggests perhaps that the tradition of a development from a symbol of three lines to one of six lines lacks historical basis. These numerical symbols, which long antedate the earliest attested appearance of the solid and broken lined trigrams and hexagrams, regularly appear in sets of six; and those sets of three that do appear invariably date later than the sets of six. (See Chang Cheng-lang 張政烺, 'Shih shih Chou ch'u ch'ing t'ung ch'i ming wen chung ti I kua' 試釋周初青銅器銘文中的易卦, *KKHP* 1980:4, 403–15; translated in *EC* VI (1980–81), 80–96; and Chang Ya-ch'u 張亞初 and Liu Yü 劉雨 'Ts'ung Shang Chou pa kua shu tzu fu hao t'an shih fa ti chi ko wen ti' 從商周八卦數字符號談筮法的幾個問題, *KK* 1981:2, 155–63 and 154; translated in *EC* VII (1981–82), 46–54).

Each of these 64 hexagrams is given a name, usually derived from the most prominent image of the text which follows and which is found just after the the hexagram itself, and at the head of the 'hexagram statement' (*kua tz'u* 卦辭). This statement is normatively composed of certain formulaic divination determinations, of which the best known are the four characters *yuan heng li chen* 元亨利貞. During the Spring and Autumn and Warring States periods these terms were interpreted in a moralistic sense, as the 'four virtues' of 'sublimity', 'penetration', 'benefit' and 'steadfastness' (see *Tso chuan*, Duke Hsiang 9th year; Legge, *The Chinese Classics*, vol. V, p. 440), but modern critics have demonstrated that such an interpretation is anachronistic. Although no consensus has been attained regarding these terms, comparison of two translations ('primary receipt: beneficial to divine'; and 'perform the great sacrifice: a beneficial divination') at least illustrates agreement that the terminology is explicitly related to the practice of divination (see Edward L. Shaughnessy, 'The composition of the *Zhouyi*'; PhD. dissertation, Stanford University, 1983, 124–33 ; and Kao Heng 高亨, *Chou i ta chuan chin chu* 周易大傳今注; Chi-nan: Ch'i Lu shu she, 1973, p. 53). The usage of *chen* 貞 in particular, which is defined in the *Shuo wen chieh tzu* as *pu wen* 卜問 'to enquire by crack making' and which regularly appears in Shang oracle bone inscriptions as a general term for divination, suggests that this term is related to such practices.

Following the hexagram statement there come six 'line statements' (*yao tz'u* 爻辭), each of which is introduced by a systematic two word tag designating the position of the line and its nature. Thus, *ch'u* 初 represents the bottom line; *shang* 上 the top; and the characters *erh* 二, *san* 三, *ssu* 四 and *wu* 五 the respective intervening lines; *chiu* 九 represents a solid line and *liu* 六 a broken line. These systematic identifications presumably appeared only in the third century B.C. While they are found in the manuscript version of the text from Ma-wang-tui 馬王堆 (168 B.C.; for this item see below), they do not occur in citations of the text included in such early to mid-Warring States works as the *Tso chuan* and the *Kuo yü*. In such passages, reference to a line is made by relating the original hexagram to the hexagram that would be created if the line in question were to change from solid to broken or *vice versa*; e.g., '*Ch'ien*' *chih* '*Kou*' 乾之姤 refers to the bottom line (i.e. *ch'u chiu* 初九) of the hexagram *Ch'ien* 乾☰, which, if changed from a solid to a broken line, would create *Kou* 姤☴.

The line statement itself is composed of an 'image' (e.g., the 'submerged dragon' of the bottom line of *Ch'ien*) and one or more of several types of mantic terms (e.g., *chi* 吉 'auspicious'; *hsiung* 凶 'inauspicious'; *wu chiu* 无咎 'no harm'; *hui wang* 悔亡 'trouble gone'; *li yung pin yü wang* 利用賓于王' beneficial herewith to have audience with the king'). Usually the line statements cohere around a single theme and often they are differentiated in a natural progression (for the best examples, see hexagrams nos. 31 *Hsien* 咸 and 52 *Ken* 艮).

The images of the line statements have been subject to the same type of re-interpretation as that seen in the hexagram statements. If one example may be cited, the various 'dragon' (*lung* 龍) images of *Ch'ien* are interpreted in the 'Ten Wings' as allusions to the moral nature or proper conduct of a 'gentleman'; recent scholaship, on the other hand, has convincingly associated this 'dragon' with the 'Green dragon' (*ts'ang lung* 蒼龍), a constellation of the eastern quadrant of the Chinese firmament, thus giving it a concrete rather than an abstract referent. In general it can be said that while moralistic implications are not necessarily absent in the *Chou i*, no coherent or developed philosophy is presented in the text.

Finally it should be noted that the sequence of the text is based on paired hexagram units, one hexagram following another either on the basis of inversion (e.g., *Chun* 屯☵ is followed by *Meng* 蒙☶); or, when such an inversion would produce an identical hexagram, by a change in nature of all six lines (e.g., *Ch'ien* 乾☰ is followed by *K'un* 坤☷). While the texts of these individual 'hexagram pairs' are often related (e.g., *Sun*

損䷨ and *I* 益䷩ hexagrams 41 and 42; or *Chi chi* 既濟䷾ and *Wei chi* 未濟䷿ nos. 63 and 64), no organisation of the text is discernible beyond these basic units.

The existence of these 'hexagram pairs' takes on great significance in a consideration of the sequence of units in the text, and in this respect the manuscript copy from Ma-wang-tui, which is the earliest known version, differs radically from that of the received versions. The ordering of the manuscript version is according to strictly mechanical combinations of the eight trigrams, arranged in two groups, each member of one group combining in turn with each of those of the second group.

3. Date and authenticity of the *Chou i*

The first significant achievement of modern criticism directed to the *Chou i* was the demonstration that the text could not have been composed by King Wen or Chou kung. Nevertheless, early critics accepted an attribution to early Western Chou as the probable date of the text's creation. Subsequent studies have suggested that it did not attain its final form until late in Western Chou, perhaps in the latter part of the 9th century B.C. The most persuasive points of this argument are linguistic, as seen in comparisons, first of the poetic usage of parts of the text with passages in the *Ya* 雅 sections of the *Shih ching*; and, second, of formulaic phrases with those found in Western Chou bronze inscriptions. There has been little or no attempt to link the composition of the text with a specific author, but it is generally assumed that the *Chou i* represents the accumulated experiences of divination of Western Chou court scribes (*shih* 史).

No one who is familiar with the text would argue that it has survived from this period in absolutely pristine form, if indeed there ever were an absolutely pristine form; and yet the quotations of the hexagram and line statements that are found in the *Tso chuan* and *Kuo yü*, and attributed there to the 7th century B.C., substantially accord with the received text. Known textual transmission from the Han dynasty to the present also suggests that there is no reason to suspect the authenticity of most of the text.

4. Content of the *I ching*

The *I ching* includes seven distinct commentaries in addition to the hexagram picture, the hexagram name, the hexagram statement and the line statements, as described above. Three of these seven ((a),(b) and (d) below) are regularly divided into two portions (*shang* 上 and *hsia* 下),

thus rounding the number of commentarial portions to ten, and giving rise to the term 'Ten Wings'. The seven commentaries are as follows:

(a) *T'uan* 彖; explanations of the hexagram statements, usually combining elements of paronomastic lexicology, trigram symbolism and 'line position' (*yao wei* 爻位) theory.

(b) *Hsiang* 象; which are distinguished as 'Greater' (*ta* 大) and 'Lesser' (*hsiao* 小); of these the Greater *hsiang* are explanations of the hexagram statement and the Lesser *hsiang* correspond to each of the six line statements. The Greater *hsiang* are virtually always comprised of an explanation of the trigram symbolism, followed by a moralistic maxim that is related to the hexagram text. The Lesser *hsiang* take 'line position' and 'line virtue' (*yao te* 爻德) as primary heuristic devices.

(c) *Wen yen* 文言; complete and multi-faceted commentaries for the first two hexagrams *Ch'ien* and *K'un*.

(d) *Hsi tz'u* 繫辭; often referred to as the 'Great Treatise' (*Ta chuan* 大傳); a synthetic explanation of the text, its composition, function and meaning. The significance of this commentary reached its highest point in the metaphysical thought of the Sung Neo-Confucians.

(e) *Shuo kua* 說卦; in two parts; of these the first is a philosophical account of the creation of the hexagrams; the second lists attributes (e.g., type of personality, animal, bodily element, social status) for the eight trigrams. In the text found at Ma-wang-tui, the first of these parts is found embedded within the *Hsi tz'u* commentary with which it is indeed similar in format.

(f) *Hsü kua* 序卦; a moralistic attempt to explain the order in which the hexagrams are found.

(g) *Tsa kua* 雜卦; random one word or one phrase characterizations of each half of the 32 hexagram pairs.

There have been two traditions regarding the distribution of these commentaries within the text. Most editions place the glosses of the *T'uan*, *Hsiang* and *Wen yen* commentaries immediately after the hexagram or line statement to which they correspond, with the other four commentaries appended at the end of the text. A separate textual organization, wherein the three line commentaries are separated from the line texts and placed together at the end of the basic text, was suggested by the Sung classical scholars Lü Tsu-ch'ien 呂祖謙 (1137–1181) and Chu Hsi 朱熹 (1130–1200). Evidence from both the Han stone classics versions (A.D. 175) of the *I ching* and the Ma-wang-tui manuscript (168 B.C.) suggests that this latter organisation was indeed the original format of the *I ching*, with the more usual interspersing of commentary deriving from the textual tradition of Fei Chih 費直 (*c.* 50 B.C.–A.D. 10) and Cheng Hsüan 鄭玄 (127–200).

5. Date and authenticity of the *I ching*

As evidence that the canonical *I ching* commentaries derived from the sages, most traditional classical scholars have pointed to the following comment of Ssu-ma Ch'ien 司馬遷 (?145–?86 B.C.) *Shih chi* 47, p. 1937):

> Late in life, Confucius enjoyed the *I*, putting in order the *T'uan, Hsi* [*tz'u*]*, Hsiang, Shuo kua* and *Wen yen*, thrice wearing out the leather binders in reading the *I*.

However, beginning with Ou-yang Hsiu 歐陽修 (1007–1072), these commentaries have often been regarded with suspicion. Ou-yang Hsiu's own argument about the authenticity of the Confucian authorship can be summarized in three points: (a) the inclusion of divergent, at times contradictory, statements demonstrates that the commentaries are not from one hand; (b) that the glosses are frequently mundane, and sometimes nonsensical, suggests that they could not have come from the hand of the great sage; and (c) the occurrence of the expression *tzu yüeh* 子曰 proves that the texts come from the hands of later disciples.

A millennium later, scholars of the *Ku shih pien* 古史辨 movement of the 1920's and 1930's attempted to prove that not only was Ou-yang Hsiu correct in his rejection of the Confucian authorship, but that moreover virtually all of the texts were products of the Han dynasty. With the recent discovery of the Han Ma-wang-tui manuscript version of the text (168 B.C.) complete with the *Hsi tz'u*, it now appears that these modern scholars were rather over zealous in their suspicions of the past. Still, there can be no question that the commentaries were not produced by Confucius. Although each one remains to be dated independently, in general it would seem that they attained their present form in the mid-third to the early second century B.C., with the probable exception of the *Hsü kua* which would seem to date from the Later Han period.

6. Textual history

The process whereby the text was transmitted suggests some of the reasons for the divergent uses to which it was put, first in its original form for purposes of divination, and later as a classical fount of wisdom. Presumably the text of the *Chou i* was created by the scribes of the Western Chou court; but there is at least some suggestion in the *Tso chuan* (Duke

Chao, year 2; Legge, *The Chinese Classics*, vol. 5, p. 583) that the circulation of the text was still relatively circumscribed up to the middle of the
sixth century B.C. Thereafter, if the evidence of the *Tso chuan* can be
considered to be historically reliable, that century marked a widening
usage of the *Chou i*, both as a manual of divination that was open to
others as well as the nobility, and as a wisdom text that was susceptible
of rhetorical quotation. It is also to this time that the first moralistic re-
interpretations of the text date, as in the use of the 'four virtues' to
explain the phrase *yüan heng li chen* 元亨利貞.

That this period also coincides with the lifetime of Confucius may or
may not be fortuitous. Traditionally, Confucius was considered to be
the transmitter and editor of the basic text and the author of the 'Ten
Wings'. It has already been shown that this last association is due to
later hagiographical tradition, but there is some evidence in the *Analects*
(XIII, 22; see Legge, *The Chinese Classics*, vol. 1, p. 272) to suggest that
Confucius both knew the text and subscribed to the moralistic re-
interpretation of his own time. Regardless of Confucius' personal involvement in the transmission of the text, members of his school are
said to have been directly concerned.

Chapter 88 ('Ju lin chuan' 儒林傳) of the *Han shu* (88, p. 3597) traces
the transmission of the text from Confucius' first generation disciple
Shang Chü 商瞿 (b. 523 B.C.) through five generations to T'ien Ho 田何
(*c.* 202–143 B.C.), at the beginning of the Han dynasty. Having survived
the burning of the books in Ch'in by virtue of its functional nature as a
manual for divination, the text was passed from T'ien Ho to four disciples, the most important in the chain of transmission being Ting K'uan
丁寬 (*c.* 180–140 B.C.). Ting's text was in turn passed to T'ien Wang-sun
田王孫 (*c.* 140–90 B.C.), and thence to Shih Ch'ou 施讎, Meng Hsi 孟喜
and Liang-ch'iu Ho 梁丘賀 (all *c.* 90–40 B.C.). The texts of these three
scholars, all members of the Imperial Academy, were then accepted as
orthodox; one further recension, that of Ching Fang 京房 the younger
(77–37 B.C.), who was a second generation disciple of Meng Hsi, was
also subsequently accepted as being orthodox.

By the end of the later Han dynasty these traditions had apparently
lost currency. The textual traditions of Shih Ch'ou and Liang-ch'iu Ho
died out in the third century, and while the Meng and Ching texts were
still extant as late as the Sui dynasty, they appear to have had little or no
influence. Meanwhile a separate tradition, characterized as *ku wen* 古文
and deriving from one Fei Chih 費直 (*c.* 50 B.C.–A.D. 10) appeared towards the end of the Former Han period. Though receiving no official
recognition, this tradition gained in ascendancy during the two centu-

ries of Later Han through such notable adherents as Ma Jung 馬融 (79–166), Cheng Hsüan 鄭玄 (127–200), Hsün Shuang 荀爽 (128–190) and Lu Chi 陸績 (188–219). This was in turn the textual tradition used by Wang Pi 王弼 (226–249), author of the earliest commentary that still survives in its entirety. By the time of K'ung Ying-ta 孔穎達 (574–648), Wang Pi's commentary and text were recognised as orthodox, and from that time on virtually all of the hundreds of commentaries and studies still extant are based on Wang Pi's text.

Several archaeological discoveries of the present century have revived interest in these earlier textual traditions. Two segments of an early T'ang manuscript of Wang Pi's commentary were found at Tun-huang (see Lo Chen-yü 羅振玉 (1866–1940), *Tun-huang ku hsieh pen Chou i Wang chu* 敦煌古寫本周易王注; and Wang Chung-min 王重民, *Tun-huang pen Chou i Wang chu chiao chi* 敦煌本周易王注校記; both in *I ching chi ch'eng*, as cited under 12 (d) below, vol. 167). Shortly afterwards there followed the publication of rubbings of pieces of the Han stone classics, inscribed between A.D. 175 and 183. To date some 20 percent of this text, which has been identified as that of the Liang ch'iu school, has been recovered, and facsimiles and transcriptions have been published in Ma Heng 馬亨 (1881–1955) *Han shih ching chi ts'un* 漢石經集存 (Peking: K'o hsüeh, 1957); for the most complete discussion of these fragments see Ch'ü Wan-li 屈萬里 (1907–79), *Han shih ching Chou i ts'an tzu chi cheng* 漢石經周易殘字集證 (Nan-kang: Academia Sinica, 1961).

Undoubtedly the most important discovery was made in 1973, when a complete manuscript copy of the text, written on silk and dating from *c.* 168 B.C., was discovered in tomb no. 3 Ma-wang-tui (for photographs, see *WW* 1974.7, Plate I and *WW* 1984.3, Plates I, II; for a transcription, see *WW* 1984.3, 1–8). Finally, a second manuscript which is closely contemporary with the text from Ma-wang-tui was found at Fu-yang 阜陽 (An-hui) in 1977; this was written on some 300 wooden or bamboo strips (see *WW* 1983.2, p. 22).

7. Critical recensions

Since the canonical status enjoyed by the text from the Han dynasty onwards has served to ensure its faithful transmission; and since the text of Wang Pi is the basis of all extant editions, there are relatively few problems of recension involved in reading the *I ching*. Nevertheless three critical recensions should be mentioned as being the most complete; the *I ching i wen shih* 易經異文釋 of Li Fu-sun 李富孫 (1764–1843); the *Chou i chiao k'an chi* 周易校勘記) of Juan Yüan 阮元 (1764–1849); and the

Chou i i wen k'ao 周易異文考 of Hsü Ch'in-t'ing 徐芹庭 (Taipei: Wu-chou, 1975). At present, Hsü's study is the most rewarding, based as it is on both Ch'ing scholarship and also on such recently discovered sources as the Han stone classics and the manuscript from Tun-huang; but even this study requires revision in light of the later finds.

8. Principal commentaries

Fragments of more than a score of Han commentaries can be culled from three T'ang sources: the *Chou i cheng i* 周易正義 of K'ung Ying-ta; the *Chou i chi chieh* 周易集解 of Li Ting-tso 李鼎祚 (8th century); and the *Ching tien shih wen* 經典釋文 of Lu Te-ming 陸德明 (556–627). Selections of a number of these have been compiled by Ch'ing scholars such as Ma Kuo-han 馬國翰 (1794–1857).

For the pre-Sung period, certainly the most important and influential commentary is the *Chou i chu* 周易注 of Wang Pi, completed by Han K'ang-po 韓康伯 (d. *c.* 385). Perhaps more than any other treatment in the history of the text, Wang's systematic explanation made the *I ching* the cornerstone of Chinese philosophy. His explanation was elaborated during the Sung period, when the commentaries of Ch'eng I 程頤 (1033–1107), *Chou i Ch'eng shih chuan* 周易程氏傳, and Chu Hsi 朱熹, *Chou i pen i* 周易本義, stand out among many excellent works. But just as Wang Pi's interpretation represented a reaction against the orthodoxy of the Han scholars, so too did the new Sung orthodoxy precipitate a reform movement; in this case this was an attempt to return to the original meaning of the text.

One of the first notable proponents of this movement was the Ming scholar Lai Chih-te 來知德 (1525–1604), whose work was entitled *Chou i Lai chu t'u chieh* 周易來註圖解. Subsequently, the movement came to full flower during the Ch'ing period, with such works as the *I yin* 易音 of Ku Yen-wu 顧炎武 (1612–81), the *Chou I shu* 周易述 of Hui Tung 惠棟 (1697–1758), and the *I chang chü* 易章句 of Chiao Hsün 焦循 (1763–1820). Another work of the Ch'ing period that is worthy of mention is the *Chou i che chung* 周易折中 of Li Kuang-ti 李光地 (1642–1718). Prepared as a result of an imperial decree in 1715, this item acquired significance in Western studies of the *I ching* as the text used by both James Legge and Richard Wilhelm in their translations. Of the hundreds of commentaries written in recent years, the *Chou i ku ching chin chu* 周易古經今注 of Kao Heng 高亨, one of the field's pre-eminent context critics, has almost certainly been the most influential in scholarly circles; for details, see under 12 (a) below.

9. Recent editions

The foregoing list of commentaries should be considered only as a beginning to the vast wealth of Chinese secondary literature on the I ching. Virtually every notable thinker in China's intellectual history, and many who are not so notable, have had occasion to discuss the text. Fortunately, modern scholars have made some attempt to gather together the richest contributions to this wealth. By far the most valuable of these efforts is the Wu ch'iu pei chai I ching chi ch'eng 無求備齋易經集成 compiled by Yen Ling-feng 嚴靈峯 (Taipei: Ch'eng-wen, 1975). This 195 volume collection consists primarily of photographic reproductions of the oldest extant editions; it contains 362 works by 319 different scholars from the Han to the Republican period. The works are arranged chronologically according to the following categories: commentaries, comprehensive discussions, occasional notes, questions and answers, phonologies, diagramatic discourses, general examples, divination texts, apocrypha, textual recensions, commentarial redactions and miscellaneous works. While it would be possible to fault the I ching chi ch'eng for certain omissions (particularly in respect of recent works from Taiwan), it does conveniently assemble nearly all of the most important traditional Chinese studies of the I ching, and provides at least some introduction to all of its principal exegetical traditions.

10. Translations

The first complete published rendering of the I ching into a Western language was the Latin translation of the Jesuit priest Jean-Baptiste Regis (1663–1738), which was published in two volumes in 1834 and 1839. But the text will be encountered by most English speaking students in one of two translations: (a) that of Legge, Sacred Books of the East, vol. 16; reissued on numerous occasions; and (b) that of Richard Wilhelm (The I Ching or Book of Changes; translated by Cary F. Baynes; 2 vols., Bollingen Series 19, New York, 1950). Wilhelm's translation is certainly the more readable of the two, and while it cannot be used for any historical study of the text, it has the virtue of faithfully presenting the text as it was understood by traditional Chinese Confucian scholars towards the end of the Ch'ing dynasty. Some care is necessary in distinguishing between the different parts of the Chou i, the 'Ten Wings' and Wilhelm's own comments.

An exhaustive list of the many translations that have been published in recent years may be found in Hellmut Wilhelm, 'The Book of Changes in the Western Tradition' (Parerga 2, 1975).

11. Japanese editions

A. *Kambun taikei;* no.16, 1913, edited by Hoshino Tsune and Itō Tōgai (Nagatane).

B. *Kanseki kokujikai zensho;* nos. 3, 4, 1910, edited by Mase Chūshū and Matsui Rashū.

D. *Kokuyaku kambun taisei;* no. 2, 1922, edited by Uno Tetsuto.

E. *Kambun sōsho,* 1927, edited by Tsukamoto Tetsuzō and Hayashi Taisuke.

F. *Keisho taikō;* no. 8, 1939 (*Hsi tz'u chuan* only).

H. *Shinshaku kambun taikei;* nos. 23, 24, 63 edited by Imai Usaburō.

J. *Chūgoku no shisō;* no. 7, 1965, edited by Maruyama Matsuyuki.

K. *Chūgoku koten bungaku taikei;* no. 1, 1972, edited by Akatsuka Kiyoshi.

L. *Chūgoku koten shinsho,* 1974, edited by Akatsuka Kiyoshi.

M. *Shintei Chūgoku koten sen;* no.1, edited by Honda Wataru.

12. Recent studies and research aids

(a) Any listing of recent historical studies of the *I ching* necessarily begins with the third volume of the *Ku shih pien,* edited by Ku Chieh-kang 顧頡剛 (1893–1980) published in 1931. Containing studies by Ku Chieh-kang, Ch'ien Mu 錢穆, Hu Shih 胡適 (1891–1962), Li Ching-ch'ih 李鏡池, Yü Yung-liang 余永梁 and others, this volume established criticism of the work in its context as the most important branch of modern studies of the *I ching.* Mention of the most recent of the numerous works of that type that have appeared in the intervening fifty years would include:

   (i) Kao Heng, *Chou i ta chuan chin chu* 周易大傳今注; Chi-nan: Ch'i Lu, 1979; this is a revised version of the author's *Chou i ku chin chu* (1947), expanded to include discussion of the 'Ten Wings'.

   (ii) Li Ching-ch'ih, *Chou i t'an yüan* 周易探源 (Peking: Chung hua, 1978); a collection of Li's seminal essays on *I ching* context criticism.

   (iii) Chang Li-wen 張立文, *Chou i ssu hsiang yen chiu* 周易思想研究; Hu-pei: Hu-pei jen min, 1980, with historical studies of both the *Chou i* and *I ching.*

   (iv) Kao Huai-min 高懷民, *Liang Han i hsüeh shih* 兩漢易學史 Tai-pei: *Chung kuo hsüeh shu chu tso chiang chu wei yüan hui ts'ung shu,* 54, 1970; the first, and still the most important, study of *I ching* scholarship during the Han period.

(b) Noteworthy studies in Western languages include:

(i) Waley, Arthur, 'The Book of Changes'; *BMFEA* 5 (1933), 121–42.

(ii) Wilhelm, Hellmut, *Change: Eight Lectures on the I ching*; translated by Cary F. Baynes; London: Routledge and Kegan Paul, 1961.

(iii) Wilhelm, Hellmut, *Heaven, Earth and Man in the Book of Changes*; Seattle and London: University of Washington Press, 1977.

(iv) Shchutskii, Iulian K., *Researches on the I Ching*, translated by William L. MacDonald, Tsuyoshi Hasegawa and Hellmut Wilhelm; London and Henley: Routledge and Kegan Paul, 1980.

(v) Schmitt, Gerhard, *Sprüche der Wandlungen auf ihrem geistesgeschichtlichen Hintergrund*; Berlin: Deutsche Akademie der Wissenschaften zu Berlin, Institut für Orientforschung, Nr 76, 1970.

(vi) Ch'en Ch'i-yün, 'A Confucian Magnate's Idea of Political Violence: Hsün Shuang's (A.D. 128–190) Interpretation of the *Book of Changes*'; *TP* 54 (1968), 73–115.

(vii) Peterson, Willard J., 'Making Connections: "Commentary on the Attached Verbalizations" of the *Book of Changes*'; *HJAS* 42:1 (June 1982), 67–116.

(c) A number of doctoral (PhD) dissertations regarding the early history of the text have been written in recent years:

(i) Swanson, Gerald W., 'The Great Treatise: Commentatory Tradition to the Book of Changes'; University of Washington, 1974.

(ii) Shaughnessy, Edward L., 'The Composition of the *Zhouyi*'; Stanford University, 1983.

(iii) Kunst, Richard A., 'The Original *Yijing*: a Text, Phonetic Transcription, Translation, and Indexes, with Sample Glosses'; University of California, Berkeley, 1985.

(iv) Goodman, Howard L., 'Exegetes and Exegeses of the *Book of Changes* in the Third Century A.D.: Historical and Scholastic Contexts for Wang Pi'; Princeton University, 1985.

(v) Fendos, Paul George Jr., 'Fei Chih's Place in the Development of *I-ching* Studies'; University of Wisconsin, 1988.

(d) The most valuable research aids are:

(i) *A Concordance to Yi Ching*: Harvard-Yenching Index no. 10; first edition Peiping: 1935; reprinted Taipei: Ch'eng wen, 1966.

(ii) *I hsüeh lun ts'ung* 易學論叢; Taipei, 1971; this volume includes the most complete bibliographical studies of the text.

(iii) Yen Ling-feng, ed., *I ching chi ch'eng* 易經集成; Taipei: Ch'eng-wen, 1975; volume 1 includes the table of contents for the set of 195 volumes, brief biographical notes on the authors and bibliographical information on the editions selected.

(iv) Wilhelm, Hellmut, 'The Book of Changes in the Western Tradition'; see under (10) above; a selective bibliography of Western translations and studies of the *I ching*.

13.   Indexes

(a) See under (12) (d) above.

(b) *A Concordance to the Zhou yi* 周易逐字索引, ed. D.C. Lau and Chen Fong Ching; *ICS* series, Hong Kong: Commercial Press, forthcoming 1994.

— Edward L. Shaughnessy

I Chou shu 逸周書 (*Chou shu*)

1. Title of the work

The text is commonly named by three different titles, *I Chou shu*, *Chi chung Chou shu* 汲冢周書 and simply *Chou shu*. The term *I* 逸, as in the first of these three, derives from the tradition that the text is a compendium of passages that were not included by Confucius among the one hundred chapters of the *Book of Documents*. *Chi chung* derives from a second tradition, according to which the text had been among the writings on bamboo strips that were unearthed *c*. 280 from the tomb of King Hsiang 襄 of Wei 魏 (reigned 318–296 B.C.), in Chi hsien 汲縣, Ho-nan. Since both of these traditions can be shown to be without foundation, and since the earliest citations of the text uniformly refer to it as *Chou shu*, there is now a general scholarly consensus that the title of the text should in fact read simply as *Chou shu*.

2. Content of the work

The text originally consisted of seventy separate *p'ien* together with a preface modelled on the pseudo K'ung An-kuo 孔安國 'Preface to the Documents' (*Shu hsü* 書序). Fifty-nine of those *p'ien* are still extant, and in each one the title ends with the term *chieh* 解. Although there is no discernible organisation of the text, in which there is a considerable number of *lacunae*, it has been demonstrated that 32 of these *p'ien* are remarkably consistent in both language and thought, and should be regarded as the basic core of the text. These 32 are named as follows (with *chieh* following in each case):

1	*Tu hsün* 度訓	12	*Ch'eng tien* 程典
2	*Ming hsün* 命訓	21	*Feng pao* 豐保
3	*Ch'ang hsün* 常訓	22	*Ta k'ai* 大開
4	*Wen cho* 文酌	23	*Hsiao k'ai* 小開
6	*Wu ch'eng* 武稱	24	*Wen ching* 文儆
7	*Yün wen* 允文	25	*Wen chuan* 文傳
8	*Ta wu* 大武	26	*Jou wu* 柔武
9	*Ta ming wu* 大明武	27	*Ta k'ai wu* 大開武
10	*Hsiao ming* 小明	28	*Hsiao k'ai wu* 小開武

29	*Pao tien* 寶典	37	*Ta k'uang* 大匡
30	*Feng mou* 酆謀	38	*Wen cheng* 文政
31	*Wu ching* 寤儆	45	*Wu ching* 武儆
32	*Wu hsün* 武訓	46	*Wu ch'üan* 五權
33	*Wu mu* 武穆	47	*Ch'eng k'ai* 成開
34	*Ho wu* 和寤	50	*Ta chieh* 大戒
35	*Wu wu* 武寤	57	*Pen tien* 本典

These 32 *p'ien* consist predominantly of treatises on government and military affairs. The other 27 extant *p'ien* are heterogeneous texts, some of which relate, or purport to relate, to historical events of the Western Chou period; some enunciate Confucian or military thought of the War- ring States period; there are 'stars and seasons' texts; and some texts also appear in other repositories such as the *Li chi* and the *Ta Tai li chi*.

3.   Date of composition

The date of the *Chou shu*'s composition is a somewhat complicated topic, as it would seem that the text actually underwent two processes of redaction. The first of these was the composition, probably by a single hand, in the late 4th or early 3rd century B.C. of the 32 'core' *p'ien*. Not only do these *p'ien* display linguistic and intellectual features that are characteristic of this period; but the extant *Chou shu* is also quoted in texts such as the *Tso chuan*, *Han fei tzu*, *Lü shih ch'un ch'iu* and *Chan kuo ts'e*. Two important considerations are that all the passages that are thus quoted derive from the 'core' *p'ien*, and that at least the last three works uniformly attribute the passages to a *Chou shu*. This demonstrates both that the texts were already in existence by the third century B.C., and also that they had already been collected into an integral unit.

This first composition could not have resulted in the received text of 70 *p'ien*; while among the heterogeneous chapters there are examples of texts that are earlier than those of the core, there are also several *p'ien* which can be dated no earlier than Former Han. Thus, the redaction of the text as we have it today could have taken place no earlier than the middle part of the Former Han period. The supposition that the author of the text's preface was also responsible for the text's final redaction also supports this conclusion. Since the preface is clearly modelled on the pseudo K'ung An-kuo 'Preface to the Documents', which gained cir- culation only late in the second century B.C.; and since Liu Hsiang 劉向 (79–8 B.C.) took note of it, it is reasonable to suppose that both the preface and the final redaction must have been completed in the first half of the first century B.C. However, owing to the extremely heteroge- neous nature of the text, the date of its final redaction is often of little consequence to scholars working with individual chapters. Aside from the 32 'core' *p'ien*, each unit of text must be examined independently and dated according to its internal evidence.

4. Textual history

In its section that starts with the *Shang shu*, the *Han shu* (30, p. 1705) includes an entry for the *Chou shu* in 71 *p'ien*. The note attached to the entry amplifies this as *Chou shih chi* 周史記; and Yen Shih-ku's 顏師古 (581–645) comment cites Liu Hsiang's description of the work, as follows; 'The solemn statements and orders of the Chou period; they are in fact the residue of the hundred *p'ien* discussed by K'ung tzu'. The *Sui shu* (33, p. 959) lists a *Chou shu* in 10 *chüan*, with a note describing the text as deriving from Chi chung (i.e. the tomb of the Wei king, as noted above); the *Chiu T'ang shu* (46, p. 1995) lists a *Chou shu* in 8 *chüan*, under *tsa shih* 雜史, with a note describing this text as annotated by K'ung Ch'ao 孔晁 (mid. 3rd century); Fujiwara Sukeyo enters a copy in 8 *chüan* from the Chi tomb. These entries are followed by those of the *Hsin T'ang shu*, under *tsa shih*, which are for (a) a *Chi chung Chou shu*, in 10 *chüan*; and (b) a *Chou shu* in 8 *chüan*, annotated by K'ung Ch'ao (see *Hsin T'ang shu* 58, p. 1463). Finally, from the lists of the *Sung shih* onwards, there is only the single entry for the *Chi chung Chou shu* in 10 *chüan* (see *Sung shih* 202, p. 5042, under the category for *Shu ching*).

In addition to these bibliographic entries, comments by two early T'ang scholars shed light on the textual history of the *Chou shu*. In his comment to the entry in the *Han shu*, Yen Shih-ku noted that in his time only 45 of the original 71 *p'ien* were still extant; at about the same time Liu Chih-chi 劉知幾 (661–721) explicitly mentioned in his *Shih t'ung* 史通 that all 71 chapters were still extant (*Shih t'ung t'ung shih* 史通通釋, SPPY ed., 1.2a). Combined with the contradictory listings of the bibliographies, especially in the *Hsin T'ang shu*, these statements demonstrate that two separate texts must have existed until the T'ang period, one being in 8 *chüan* and associated with K'ung Ch'ao, and one, in 10 *chüan*, thought to have come from Chi chung. It would seem that the assimilation of the two editions must have taken place during the Northern Sung period; and from citations in the Sung encyclopaedias it can be surmised that the loss of the eleven units now missing must have occurred before the middle of the Southern Sung period.

The tradition linking the text to the tomb of King Hsiang of Wei (see *Chin shu* 3, p. 70 and 51, p. 1432) has been notably persistent since the early part of the T'ang period, but there are several reasons to suspect its historicity. First, the text is quoted by name in Han sources such as the

Shih chi, Shuo wen and Cheng Hsüan's commentaries to the three compendia on *li* 禮. This demonstrates that the text was known well after the interment of King Hsiang in 296 B.C. Of greater importance, there are *p'ien* such as *Chih fang* 職方 and *Shih hsün* 時訓, which were indubitably composed after the unification of Ch'in; i.e. well after the closure of King Hsiang's tomb. It is also doubtful whether K'ung Ch'ao, author of the earliest extant commentary on the text and the apparent source of one textual tradition, could have consulted the bamboo or wooden documents which made their appearance *c.* A.D. 280. While there is no source to give the dates of K'ung Ch'ao's birth or death, he was a contemporary of Wang Su 王肅, who died in 256, and the last date for which there is any mention of K'ung Ch'ao is found in an imperial invitation of 266 (*Chin shu* 47, p. 1320). In addition to this chronological difficulty, there is no mention of K'ung Ch'ao's name among the detailed list of scholars said to have worked on deciphering the bamboo strips.

These considerations suggest that the extant *Chou shu* could not have been among the texts buried with King Hsiang. But they do not preclude the possibility of another *Chou shu* having been buried in the tomb. Included in the contemporary inventories of the 75 *p'ien* discovered at Chi chung were 19 *p'ien* described as 'miscellaneous texts' (*tsa shu* 雜書), and further specified by the following passage (*Chin shu* 51, p. 1342): 周食田法周書論楚事周穆王美人盛姬死事. Clearly, *Chou shih t'ien fa* and *Chou Mu wang mei jen sheng chi ssu shih* are independent titles. Furthermore, in a separate contemporary account of the find, there is mention of a *Lun Ch'u shih* 論楚事. For this reason, it would seem that the *Chou shu* here mentioned is indeed a separate title; but that is not to say that it is necessarily the *Chou shu* in 71 *p'ien* with which we are concerned. It is probable that this *Chou shu* is to be identified with a text elsewhere quoted as *Ku wen Chou shu* 古文周書, containing primarily narratives about King Mu of Western Chou.

5. Principal commentators and studies

The earliest commentator to the text was K'ung Ch'ao, whose explanations of 42 *p'ien* are still extant. K'ung Ch'ao's remarks are often frustratingly oblique, but they remain an important aid in reading the text. Other commentaries which are important for general use derive from Ch'ing scholarship.

The edition of Lu Wen-ch'ao 盧文弨 (1717–1796) is still the best recension, based as it is on eight Yüan and Ming editions, and twelve earlier Ch'ing commentaries. First printed in the *Pao ching t'ang ts'ung shu*, and reproduced in the *Ts'ung shu chi ch'eng*, this version was used in the *Ssu pu pei yao* series. The *Ssu pu ts'ung k'an* reproduces a print of the text by Chang Po 章檗, with K'ung Ch'ao's notes (preface dated 1543); Ch'en Feng-heng's 陳逢衡 (1778–1855) *I Chou shu pu chu* 逸周書補注 is often more helpful for its glosses. The *I Chou shu kuan chien* 逸周書管箋 of Ting Tsung-lo 丁宗洛 (preface 1825) provides a complete commentary, and also valuable synthetic studies of the text which include tables of variant readings, chronology and proper names. The *I Chou shu fen pien chü shih* 逸周書分編句釋 of T'ang Ta-p'ei 唐大沛 (preface 1836; reproduced Taipei: Tai wan hsüeh sheng, 1969) is important as the first attempt to re-organize the traditional order of the text. T'ang divided the 59 extant *p'ien* into three collections (*pien* 編) each one of which was further sub-divided into philosophical, narrative, governmental and military texts. Finally, mention must be made of the *Chou shu chi hsün chiao shih* 周書集訓校釋 of Chu Yu-tseng 朱右曾 (preface 1846), which is considered to be the best available commentary to the entire text.

Owing to the heterogeneous nature of the *Chou shu*, recent scholarship has often been devoted to studies of isolated *p'ien*. The more important contributions include:

(a) Liu Shih-p'ei 劉師培 (1884–1919), '"Wang hui" p'ien pu shih' 王會篇補釋; *Kuo ts'ui hsüeh pao* 3.9, 12 (1907).

(b) Hsiao Ming-lai 蕭鳴籟, 'Tu *Chou shu* "Yin chu chieh"' 讀周書殷祝解; *Hsüeh wen* 1.2 (1931), 42–44.

(c) Ku Chieh-kang 顧頡剛 (1893–1980), 'Tu *Chou shu* "Kuan chih" p'ien' 讀周書官職篇; *Yü kung* 7. 6–7 (1937), 327–32.

(d) Ku Chieh-kang, '*I Chou shu* "Shih fu" p'ien chiao chu hsieh ting yü p'ing lun' 逸周書世俘篇校注寫定與評論; *Wen shih* 2 (1963), 1–42.

(e) Huang P'ei-jung 黃沛榮, *Chou shu 'Chou yüeh' p'ien chu ch'eng ti shih tai chi yu kuan san cheng wen t'i ti yen chiu* 周書周月篇著成的時代及有關三正問題的研究; Taipei: Taiwan University, 1972.

(f) Finally, although there has been a marked lack of work which treats the text synthetically, fortunately the one study that is available is excellent; the present writer wishes to acknowledge that the foregoing description is based substantially on this study: Huang P'ei-jung, '*Chou shu* yen chiu 周書研究'; dissertation for the degree of Ph.D, presented to Taiwan University (1976).

6. Index

A Concordance to the Yizhoushu 逸周書逐字索引, ed. D.C. Lau and Chen Fong Ching; *ICS* series, Hong Kong: Commercial Press 1992.

— Edward L. Shaughnessy

I li 儀禮

1. Name of the text

The classic now known as the *I li* did not come to bear that name until well after the end of the Han dynasty. During the Han period it was known variously as:

(a) *Shih li* 士禮. This name is given to the *chin wen* text, of 17 *p'ien*, mentioned in *Han shu* 30, p. 1710, and stated to have originated in its known, transmitted form with a person named Kao T'ang-sheng 高堂生 of Lu 魯 (see also *Han shu* 88, p. 3614).

(b) *Ch'ü li* 曲禮. In his *San li chu* 三禮注 Cheng Hsüan 鄭玄 (127–200) referred to a text under this name.

(c) *Li ku ching* 禮古經. *Han shu* 30, p. 1709, lists the *ku wen* text of the *I li*, in 56 *chüan*, under this name. It is said to have been found in the wall of a house, allegedly that of Confucius, when this was being demolished in the Former Han period.

(d) *Li (ching)* 禮(經). When Han texts refer simply to the *Li*, or to the *Li ching*, they mean the *I li*, as opposed to the *Chou li* or the later *Li chi*. Even the name *Li chi* 禮記 in Han texts refers to the *Li ching*, i.e., the *I li*, together with the incorporated *chi* 'records'; the term does not refer to what is known today as the *Li chi*.

(e) *I li*. The term *I li* was first used in reference to this text in the *Lun heng* 12 (36, 'Hsieh tuan 謝短'), p. 563 (Huang Hui ed.). Between the end of the Han and the Sui periods, this became the standard name for the text, as may be seen in *Hou Han shu* 35, p. 1212 (biography of Cheng Hsüan) and in *Sui shu* 32, p. 919, which both use the term as the standard name for the text with its associated commentaries.

2. Content and structure

Of the various names by which the text was known during the Han dynasty that of *Shih li* most accurately represents the content of the work. The text consists largely, though not exclusively, of detailed and specific descriptions of the ritual ceremonies of a *shih* 士, i.e. a low level member of the aristocracy. There are no accounts concerned with imperial or

234

court ritual or ceremony except for those that deal with the court visit and audience of a *kung* 公. The ceremonies and formalities described are otherwise those pertinent to the state officers from the *shih* level up to the *kung*.

The seventeen *p'ien* that comprise the transmitted text of the *I li* are given here in the order in which they occur, and with the names that they carry, in the standard, received text. As will be seen below, differences in the names and the sequences of these seventeen *p'ien* rather than the actual content are the main distinguishing features of the various Han versions of the text.

1. *Shih kuan li* 士冠禮: capping rites for [the son of] a common officer.
2. *Shih hun li* 士昏禮: nuptial rites for a common officer.
3. *Shih hsiang chien li* 士相見禮: rites attendant on the meeting of common officers with each other.
4. *Hsiang yin chiu li* 鄉飲酒禮: rites of the district symposium.
5. *Hsiang she li* 鄉射禮: rites of the district archery meet.
6. *Yen li* 燕禮: banquet rites (at state, not imperial, level).
7. *Ta she* 大射: the great archery meet (state level).
8. *Pin li* 聘禮: rites of courtesy calls [state to state].
9. *Kung shih tai fu li* 公食大夫禮: rites of the *kung* feasting a great officer.
10. *Chin li* 覲禮: rites of the [imperial] audience. This is the only *p'ien* of the *I li* that deals with ceremonies or rites that specifically involve the emperor and the royal court.
11. *Sang fu* 喪服: mourning attire. This *p'ien* describes those customs governing mourning attire for all levels of the aristocracy, irrespective of rank. Details that apply to only one particular level or another, usually becoming increasingly elaborate the higher the rank, are not included. Of the seventeen *I li* sections only this one has been extracted and treated as a separate text, both in having a wealth of commentaries written expressly for it alone, and in having an early transmission of its own, independent of the *I li* as a whole. This independent status is nowhere more apparent than in the *Sui shu* (32, p. 919) which lists a total of four entries for the *I li* itself but no fewer than forty-five separate titles for the *Sang fu* text.
12. *Shih sang li* 士喪禮: mourning rites for the common officer.
13. *Chi hsi* 既夕: [mourning procedures of] the evening preceding burial. This *p'ien*, without the title *Chi hsi*, appears in Liu Hsiang's 劉向 (79–8 B.C.) *Pieh lu* 別錄 version (see below) as the second part of the preceding section.

14. *Shih yü li* 士虞禮: post-burial rites for a common officer.

15. *T'e hsing kuei shih li* 特牲饋食禮: rites of the single victim food offering. A single victim is specified because at the level of a *shih* one was permitted to sacrifice only to a father and grandfather (i.e. two generations), and only with the offering of a pig, the most common of the sacrificial animals.

16. *Shao lao kuei shih li* 少牢饋食禮: rites of the secondary pen victim food offering. These are the rites for the great officers (*tai fu* 大夫 and *ch'ing* 卿) who were entitled and expected to sacrifice to the 'Great Ancestor' (i.e., the primary ancestor who represents all generations prior to the immediately preceding two, as well as the father and grandfather's generations). He was to use both pigs and sheep in his sacrificial offerings, the two together being known as the 'lesser' or 'secondary' pen victims, as opposed to the 'great' pen victims (*t'ai lao* 太牢), which included an ox.

17. *Yu ssu ch'e* 有司徹 'The servant clearing the way': this title derives from the first three words of the text and it is not particularly revealing of the contents of the *p'ien*. The text is concerned with the ceremonies of courtesy shown to the individual who has served as the impersonator of the deceased in the funeral rites just concluded. This *p'ien* is in effect a description of the last stage of the complex of funeral ceremonies and rites that are the subject of *p'ien* nos. 11 to 17. In Liu Hsiang's *Pieh lu* version this *p'ien* bears no separate title, being designated as the *hsia* 下 section of the preceding *p'ien* 'Shao lao'.

In addition to the basic descriptive part of the text, most *p'ien* also contain portions called *chi* 記 'records' or 'notes'. Moreover, no. 11 (*Sang fu*) contains numerous passages designated as *chuan* 傳 'transmitted comments' that are integrated within it. While it has been speculated that these *chi* and *chuan* parts are later additions to the basic text of the *I li*, there is no conclusive evidence to support such a conjecture. *Sang fu*, with its *chuan*, is a special case, being the only *p'ien* with such passages, and because its text has been treated independently, apart from the rest of the *I li* proper.

It has been suggested that perhaps Cheng Hsüan was responsible for the *chuan*. Two of the three manuscript copies of the *Sang fu* text dating from the end of Former Han and found at Wu-wei 武威 include *chuan* passages; one does not. This suggests that the *chuan* may be formed of later additions to the text; but it also proves that such additions could not have been the work of Cheng Hsüan.

3.   Origin and authenticity

As with the *Chou li*, there is a tradition, now generally recognised as untenable, that the *I li* dates from the time when Chou kung 周公 assumed the regency, and that it was he who was responsible for the compilation of the text. This tradition is recounted in the preface of Chia Kung-yen 賈公彥 (*fl.* 650) to his *I li shu* 儀禮疏 and in that of K'ung Ying-ta 孔穎達 (574–648) to the *Li chi cheng i* 禮記正義. It seems to be based on a statement in the *Li chi* ('Ming t'ang wei 明堂位'; *Shih san ching chu shu* 31, 4b), where Chou kung is credited with having 'made the Li "ceremonies" and created the Yüeh "Music"' *chih li tso yüeh* 制禮作樂. If the expression *chih li* is taken to refer to the *li* texts (i.e., *I li* and *Chou li*), the passage would appear to be the textual basis for the claim for his authorship, and it would imply that *tso yüeh* refers to his compilation of the now lost 'Classic of Music'. There is no real reason to assume that the terms *li* and *yüeh* refer to texts.

While several different passages in both the *Shih chi* and the *Han shu* make it clear that the text which we know as *I li* was known to have existed prior to the burning of books by Ch'in, no details of its pre-Han provenance are ascertainable. The most explicit passage regarding the appearance of the *I li* in the Han period is found in *Shih chi* 121 ('Ju lin chuan'), p. 3126 'Of the many scholars who discoursed on the Li, Kao T'ang-sheng of Lu was the most authoritative'. The *Shih chi* observes that in their transmission from the time of Confucius, the Li texts had become incomplete; with the book-burning of Ch'in the texts became even more defective, scattered and destroyed, so that by Han there was only the *Shih li* that was extant, and Kao T'ang-sheng was the one who was most able to discourse on it.

As mentioned above, *Shih li* is one of the names of the *chin wen* version of the text, in 17 *p'ien*. As the name suggests, it is basically a description of those ceremonies of the *shih* level, i.e. the lowest level of the aristocracy. The *Shih chi's* 'Ju lin' chapter implies that there were once, at the time of Confucius according to tradition, more *li* texts, later lost. We might presume that these lost *li* texts would have been the *p'ien* dealing with the ceremonies and rites pertaining to other ranks and levels of the aristocracy, comparable with those for the *shih* now extant in the *Shih li*. However this may be, it seems reasonable to accept as likely the supposition that the extant *I li* is in origin a part of a larger corpus of similar ceremonial and ritual texts dating from pre-Han times, perhaps as early as the time of Confucius; that much of this was lost by Han; and that some may have come to be preserved in the text known today as the *Li chi*.

4.   The *I li* in Former Han

According to *Sui shu* 32, p. 925, at the beginning of the Han period both a *chin wen* and a *ku wen* version of the *I li* existed. The earliest and most specific account of the appearance of the *ku wen* version comes in a letter of Liu Hsin 劉歆 (46 B.C.–A.D. 23; see *Han shu* 36, p. 1969). This is to the effect that, at the time when Confucius' house was being demolished, 39 *p'ien* of 'lost' (*i* 逸) *li* texts were found in the wall. We know from *Han shu* 30, p. 1709 that the *ku wen* version had a total of 56 *p'ien*, so it is usually assumed that it must also have included seventeen sections, matching the 17 *p'ien* of the *chin wen* version of Kao T'ang-sheng. Those, together with the 39 'lost' *p'ien* referred to in Liu Hsin's letter would make a total of 56. According to *Sui shu* 32, p. 925, the *ku wen* text was acquired by Ho-chien Hsien wang 河間獻王 (reigned 155–129 B.C.), who in turn presented it to the Han Imperial Library.

Both *Han shu* 30, p. 1710 and *Sui shu* 32, p. 925 state that the *chin wen* version of the *I li* was transmsitted from Kao T'ang-sheng to Hou Ts'ang 后倉 or 蒼 (*fl.* 70 B.C.), who, for his part, had three followers in the study of the *Li*, i.e., Tai Te 戴德 (known as Ta 大 Tai), Tai Sheng 戴聖 (known as Hsiao 小 Tai) and Ch'ing P'u 慶普; each one of these developed his own recension of the *Li* text, and each was established as an official scholar for that work. There thus came to be three recensions or versions of the *chin wen* text of the *I li* in Former Han. This statement is further elaborated in *Han shu* 88, p. 3615. *Hou Han shu* 79A, p. 2545 does not include Ch'ing P'u among the *chin wen* scholars of the *Li* in Former Han; there is thus some doubt as to the certainty of the third *I li* position that is supposed to have been established at the Han court.

From Cheng Hsüan's record of the contents of the *I li* as included in his *San li mu lu* 三禮目錄, and preserved in Chia Kung-yen's *shu* to the *I li*, we know that the differences between the two Tai versions of the text were largely in the precise names of the *p'ien* and their sequence within the work. We can presume that the version of Ch'ing P'u was likewise distinct in these respects, although Cheng Hsüan does not mention this recension. He does mention a third version said to have been that of Liu Hsiang, as included in his *Pieh lu*, and different in these same respects from both of the Tai versions. Liu Hsiang was not an advocate of *ku wen* texts, unlike his son Liu Hsin; and in fact the clear-cut opposition in doctrinal terms would be somewhat anachronistic if applied to him; for he still had easy access to the texts collected in the imperial library, and would thus have known of the *ku wen* version of the *I li* that had been deposited there by Ho-chien Hsien wang. It is possible, then, that the version of the text registered in his *Pieh lu* is that of those 17 *p'ien* of the *ku wen* text that find their counterparts in the *chin wen* version.

The following table gives the order of the *p'ien* according to the three versions we know from Former Han. As has been noted, the order of the Ch'ing P'u version is not known:

	Ta Tai	Hsiao Tai	Liu Hsiang
1.	士冠	士冠	士冠
2.	昏禮	昏禮	士婚
3.	相見	相見	士相見
4.	士喪	鄉飲	鄉飲酒
5.	既夕	鄉射	鄉射
6.	士虞	燕禮	燕禮
7.	特牲	大射	大射
8.	少牢	士虞	聘禮
9.	有司	喪服	公食大夫
10.	鄉飲酒	特牲	覲禮
11.	鄉射	少牢	喪服
12.	燕禮	有司徹	士喪
13.	大射	喪	士喪(下)
14.	聘禮	既夕	士虞
15.	公食	聘禮	特牲饋食
16.	覲禮	公食	少牢饋食
17.	喪服	覲禮	少牢(下)

The fact that Liu Hsiang has *Shih sang, hsia* in place of *Chi hsi*, and *Shao lao, hsia* in place of *Yu ssu ch'e*, combined with the fact that the content of *Chi hsi* and *Yu ssu ch'e* are very much of a kind respectively with that of *Shih sang* and *Shao lao*, suggests the possibility that these were in origin not different *p'ien*, but each pair was a single *p'ien*, and that the original version of the *I li*, therefore, would have had only 15 sections, at least in names, if not also in number of *p'ien*.

5. Commentaries and editions

The two principal commentaries to the *I li* are the *chu* by Cheng Hsüan and the *shu* by Chia Kung-yen. The latter is probably derived from, and in part at least based on, the earlier works of Huang Ch'ing 黃慶 (*fl.* 479–501) and Li Meng-hsi 李孟悊 (*fl.* 589–617); see *Chih chai shu lu chieh t'i* 2, 20a. Cheng Hsüan elected to use the order in Liu Hsiang's *Pieh lu* as the basis for his recension and commentary. He also collected the *chin wen* text with the matching 17 *p'ien* of the *ku wen* text, which had not, as far as is known, passed through the hands of any editors, but which was still extant in his time. He chose freely from either the *chin wen* or the *ku wen* versions where they differed, according to his best judgment; and he carefully specified the alternative in his notes. Thus the *I li* of Cheng Hsüan is truly a critical recension, reflecting both the *chin wen* and the *ku wen* versions as Cheng Hsüan saw fit. This is the text that constitutes the basis for all later studies and editions.

Unlike the *Chou li* there is no record that the *I li* was annotated or edited in the Han period other than by Cheng Hsüan, save for a commentary by Ma Jung 馬融 (79–166), now lost, to the separately transmitted *Sang fu*. Wang Su 王肅 (195–256) compiled two texts dealing with the *I li*, namely *San Li chieh* 三禮解 and *I li sang fu chuan* 儀禮喪服傳. Both were critical of Cheng Hsüan's editing and annotation, reflecting Wang Su's disenchantment in general with Cheng Hsüan's work on pre-Han texts. In the course of his criticism of Cheng Hsüan's work on the *I li*, Wang Su made the *chin wen* and *ku wen* versions even more inextricably intertwined than they had been in Cheng Hsüan's own work, so that from the third century the status of the *I li* as a pristine *chin wen* text was irrevocably lost.

Wang Su's scholarship on the *I li* predominated during the Western Chin period. During the Nan pei ch'ao period Cheng Hsüan became more respected in the north, while both he and Wang Su vied as equals in the south. When, in the T'ang period, Chia Kung-yen took Cheng Hsüan's *I li chu* as the basis for his *shu*, the latter's critical recension of the text became the basis for all subsequent scholarship.

Like the *Chou li*, in the K'ai ch'eng period (836–40) the text of the *I li* was carved in stone as one of the classical texts, now on display in Hsian. Again, like the *Chou li*, the *I li* was first printed from wood blocks as ordered in 932 and completed in 953. This text is now known as the *Wu tai chien pen I li* 五代監本儀禮. Like the *Chou li*, the *I li* was adopted within the classical canon by the time that printing was evolved, and its early printing history is generally that of the *Chou li*. Chia Kung-yen's *shu* for both works was collated and edited by imperial decree between 996 and 1001, when imperial orders were given for block printing in Lin-an 臨安. When the two were printed, they appeared as texts that were separated from the classics themselves.

The printing history of the *I li* differs from that of the *Chou li* in that there was no *Ch'a yen ssu* 茶鹽司 edition, nor a derivative 'ten column edition' *Shih hang pen* 十行本. In general fewer editions and printings were made of the *I li* than the *Chou li*; the *I li* is usually regarded as a more difficult text to read, with a higher degree of textual inaccuracy than the *Chou li*.

A new edition of Cheng Hsüan's *I li chu* was prepared in 1172. Chang Ch'un 張淳 (late 12th century) participated in the textual collation for the project, and as a result of his researches he compiled his own *I li shih wu* 儀禮識誤, cataloguing the errors that he had found. For further details, see Etienne Balazs and Yves Hervouet, *A Sung Bibliography (Bibliographie des Sung)*, (Hong Kong: The Chinese University Press, 1978), p. 31; also pp. 27–37 for other Sung studies of the *I li*.

Of early Ch'ing scholarship on the *I li*, Chang Erh-ch'i's 張爾岐 (1612–78) *I li Cheng chu chü tu* 儀禮鄭注句讀 is the most important. It was first printed in 1743 and is incorporated in Juan Yüan's 阮元 (1764–1849) *I li chu shu fu chiao k'an chi* 儀禮注疏附校勘記. Notable items among later Ch'ing studies include the *Li ching shih li* 禮經釋例 of Ling T'ing-k'an 凌廷堪 (1757–1809) and the *I li cheng i* 儀禮正義 by Hu Pei-hui 胡培翬 (1782–1849).

As with other classical texts, the single most important work of late Ch'ing textual scholarship is that of Juan Yüan, as cited immediately above. According to the preface of this work, the best printed edition of the *I li* from the Sung period is the so-called *Yen chou* 嚴州 edition of the second half of the twelfth century, re-cut and reprinted with a few corrections in the period 1532–1567, and known as the *Hsü* 徐 edition. Juan Yüan also used the *Yung huai t'ang* 永懷堂 edition (Ming), which he identifies with that of Li Yüan-yang 李元陽 (*fl.* 1550), both being known as the *Chiu hang pen* 九行本 and as the *Min* 閩 edition. The *Yung huai t'ang* edition is the basis for the *Ssu pu pei yao* print, and the *Hsü* edition is that adopted for the *Ssu pu ts'ung k'an* series.

6.   Extant stone fragments and manuscripts

Seventy-nine fragments of the *I li* survive from the stone classics of A.D. 175. Most of these bear a few characters each, with a few extending to 40 or 50; but owing to the physical nature of the pieces, there are no continuous and uninterrupted passages of that length. One fragment includes the title of one of the *p'ien* as *Hsiang yin chiu*, with its number as 10 鄉飲酒第十. It is thus evident that the text on which the inscription was based was probably that of the Ta Tai recension, as that is the only one where that *p'ien* comes as number 10; elsewhere it is number 4.

Of much greater importance is the cache of wooden and bamboo strips comprising more than seven full *p'ien*, in three separate manuscripts, found at Wu-wei 武威 (Kansu province) in 1959. These were discovered in the tomb of an unidentified official who had apparently been posted to Ku-ts'ang 姑臧, and it has been suggested, on the basis of some of the fragments found in the tomb, that he may have been the *li yüan* 禮掾, or chief instructor in *li*, of the area. Other evidence shows that the tomb must post-date Wang Mang's period. The editors of these strips conclude that the manuscripts of the *I li* represent a version of the text which was current at the end of Former Han; the three different manuscripts have been named as *chia* 甲, *i* 乙 and *ping* 丙 (for references, see *Wu-wei Han chien*, under (7) below).

(a) The *chia* manuscript consists of seven *p'ien* on wide wooden strips, written in large characters. Each *p'ien* carries a title and a number, showing that the order differs from those of the three versions listed above, and indicating that a fourth version was current at the end of Former Han. The seven *p'ien* are as follows:

> 3 *Shih hsiang chien chih li* 士相見之禮 / 第三
> 8 *Fu chuan* 服傳 / 第八
> 10 *T'e hsing* 特牲 / 第十
> 11 *Shao lao* 少牢 / 第十一
> 12 *Yu ssu* 有司 / 第十二
> 13 *Yen li* 燕禮 / 第十三
> 14 *T'ai she* 泰射 / 第十三 [i.e., 四]

Except for *Yen li*, the title is on the reverse side of the first strip and the number on that of the second; for *Yen li* both title and number are on the reverse side of the first strip. The editors speculate that this manuscript represents the Ch'ing P'u version of the *chin wen* tradition.

(b) The *i* manuscript carries the *Fu chuan p'ien* written in small characters on 37 narrow wooden strips.

(c) The *ping* manuscript carries the *Sang fu p'ien* written in large characters on 34 bamboo strips.

That part of the work named *Sang fu* in the received text and in the *ping* manuscript is identical with the text that is named *Fu chuan* in the *chia* and *i* manuscripts. There are other minor differences in the names of the various *p'ien*, but none for which the equivalents are not easily recognizable.

7. Translations, studies and reference works

(a) Translations

> (i) de Harlez, Charles Joseph, *Cérémonial de la Chine antique avec extraits des meilleurs commentaires*; Paris: Jean Maisonneuve, Éditeur, 1890.
> (ii) Couvreur, Séraphin, *Cérémonial*; Hsien hsien: Imprimerie de la Mission Catholique, 1916; 2nd ed. 1928; reprinted Paris: Cathasia, 1951.

(iii) Steele, John, *The I li, or Book of Etiquette and Ceremonial*; London: Probsthain and Co., 1917, 2 vols.

(b) Studies

(i) Hung Yeh 洪業 (William Hung), *I li yin te hsü* 儀禮引得序 (preface to the item under 8. below), 1932.

(ii) Hung Yeh, *Li chi yin te hsü* 禮記引得序; preface to the *Li chi yin te* (Harvard-Yenching Institute Sinological Index Series No. 27). Sub-titled *Liang Han li hsüeh yüan liu k'ao* 兩漢禮學源流考, this appeared originally in *Shih hsüeh nien pao* 史學年報 3:3 (1936, 1–31). Though a preface to the index to the *Li chi*, this essay discusses the question of the *I li*'s text in Han times in considerable detail.

(Both of these items are reprinted in *Hung Yeh lun hsüeh chi* 洪業論學集, Peking: Chung hua, 1981, pp. 41–50 and 197–220).

(iii) *Wu-wei Han chien* 武威漢簡, edited by Kan-su sheng po wu kuan 甘肅省博物館 and Chung kuo k'o hsüeh yüan k'ao ku yen chiu suo 中國科學院考古研究所; Peking: Wen wu, 1965.

(iv) Matsu'ura Yoshisaburō 松浦嘉三郎, *Girai no seiritsu ni tsuite* 儀禮の成立につ就て; *Shinagaku* 5:4 (1929), pp. 77–101.

(v) Kawahara Jūichi 川原壽市, *Girai shakukō* 儀禮釋攷; Kyoto: Hōyū-shoten, 1973; 15 vols.

8. Indexes

(a) *I li yin te* 儀禮引得; Harvard-Yenching Institute Sinological Index Series no. 6; Peking, 1932; reprinted Taipei: Ch'eng wen, 1966.

(b) *A Concordance to the Yili* 儀禮逐字索引, ed. D.C. Lau and Chen Fong Ching; *ICS* series, Hong Kong: Commercial Press, forthcoming 1994.

— William G. Boltz

Kuan tzu 管子

1. Contents and arrangement

The *Kuan tzu*, which bears the name of Kuan Chung 管仲 (d. 645 B.C.), a famous minister of Duke Huan 桓公 of Ch'i 齊, is one of the largest of China's early politico-philosophical texts, exceeding 135,000 characters in length. The table of contents lists 24 *chüan* containing the titles of 86 *p'ien*, of which ten are now missing (nos. 21, 25, 34, 60–63, 70, 82, and 86). Of the remaining 76 chapters nos. 6 and 9 are identical except for a different arrangement of their subsections; no. 50 is identical with a passage on the Feng 封 and Shan 禪 sacrifices in *Shih chi*, 28; no. 20, which concerns the careers of Duke Huan and Kuan Chung, is very similar in language and content to *chüan* 6, 'Ch'i yü' 齊語, of the *Kuo yü*; and nos. 63–67 consist of explanations (*chieh* 解) of other chapters located elsewhere in the text. In addition to being grouped in 24 *chüan*, the various chapters have also been arranged under eight named sections. The reason for this is not at all clear, but it may have something to do with the source from which particular chapters were taken to form the present *Kuan tzu*.

Put together in its present form by Liu Hsiang 劉向 (79–8 B.C.) in about 26 B.C., the present text contains a wide mixture of material written by a number of unnamed writers over a long period of time. Some chapters may date from as early as the fifth century B.C., while others clearly belong to the early Han period, perhaps as late as the middle of the first century B.C. Most of the chapters deal primarily with government and the art of rulership, and many of these are usually described as presenting a Legalist point of view. However, while law and the impartial implementation of a system of rewards and punishments is the primary concern of a number of these chapters, in general, their tone is less strident than that presented in the classic Legalist work attributed to Shang Yang 商鞅 (385–338 B.C.), the *Shang chün shu*. In general considerable importance is attached to traditional Confucian virtues and a number of chapters present a blending of Legalist, Confucian, and Taoist doctrines that is now frequently referred to as Huang-Lao 黃老 thought. As is appropriate to a work with its title, a number of these political chapters are devoted to stories about Kuan Chung and how he was able to make Duke Huan lord protector to the king of Chou.

The *Kuan tzu* is also noted for its wealth of material concerning early Chinese economic thought, especially its concept of *ch'ing chung* 輕重 'light and heavy', which, in its advocacy of using money to control the supply of grain and other commodities, may constitute the world's earliest statement of quantitative theories of money. Chapter 35 also presents a highly unusual, by Chinese standards, theory advocating extravagance in spending as a way to promote a state's economic development and well-being.

In addition to these politico-economic materials, the *Kuan tzu* also contains a particularly rich store of materials dealing with military theory, Taoist quietism, Yin-Yang and Five Phases thought, and early folk belief. Of special interest also are chapters such as no. 58, which is perhaps the world's earliest attempt at a systematic study of soils and plant ecology, no. 57, one of the earliest discussions in Chinese literature of irrigation and flood control, and no. 59, a very revealing discussion of the duties of the student and traditional Chinese education.

2. Earliest references to the *Kuan tzu*

In what appears to be the earliest reference to the work (*Han fei tzu* 19, 'Wu tu' 五蠹, Ch'en Ch'i-yu ed. p. 1066), it is stated that '[Every] household has those who preserve the laws of Shang [Yang] and Kuan [Chung]', but it is by no means certain that this passage alludes specifically to actual written records. The *Hsin shu* of Chia I 賈誼 (201–169 B.C.) quotes passages that are to be found in the extant *Kuan tzu*, identifying them with the words *Kuan tzu yüeh* 管子曰 (*Hsin shu* 4.9a and 6.8b).

The first clear and specific reference to the 'writings' of Kuan Tzu (*Kuan tzu shu* 管子書) occurs in the *Huai nan tzu* (21.9a, Liu Wen-tien ed.), but it is Ssu-ma Ch'ien 司馬遷 (?145–?86 B.C.) who provides the first available information about the actual contents of a collection of such writings as it existed before the first century B.C. (*Shih chi* 62, p. 2136). He names several *p'ien* of the *Kuan tzu*, including two (nos. 1 and 2) which can be identified as being part of the extant text; he adds that the writings of Kuan Chung were readily available in his time. Thus we know that by the second century B.C. there existed the beginnings of a collection of works attributed to Kuan Chung.

The diverse contents of the *Kuan tzu* created a problem of classification for early Chinese cataloguers. In *Han shu* 30, p. 1729, it is listed under *tao chia* works with 86 *p'ien*, in *Sui shu* (34 p. 1003) it appears under *fa chia* with 19 *chüan*, and in subsequent Chinese lists it is classified in that way. In Fujiwara Sukeyo's list it appears with 20 *chüan*, again under *fa chia*.

3. Liu Hsiang's editorial work

In a preface which is printed in most current editions of the *Kuan tzu*, Liu Hsiang tells how he set about collecting and editing the received text. He writes:

> The books of *Kuan tzu* which Your Servant has collated consisted of 389 bundles (*p'ien*) in the palace, twenty seven bundles belonging to the Imperial Counsellor Second Class, Pu Kuei 卜圭, forty-one bundles belonging to Your Servant Fu Ts'an 富參, eleven bundles belonging to the Colonel of the Bowmen Guards Li 立 and ninety-six bundles in the office of the Grand Astrologer, making a total of 564 bundles of books inside and outside the palace. In collating them, he has eliminated 484 duplicate bundles and made 86 bundles the standard text. This he has written on bamboo strips to form a basis for exact copies.

In this connection it may be noted that fragments of bamboo strips found at Yin-ch'üeh shan 銀雀山, Lin-i 臨沂 (Shantung) carry text which can be identified as deriving from a *p'ien* entitled *Wang ping* 王兵 and which is closely related to various passages in the *Kuan tzu* (*p'ien* nos. 6, 8, 27 and 28). Altogether this text would cover 23 complete strips. A transcription is given in *Wen wu* 1976.12, 36–43, with corresponding passages from the *Kuan tzu* printed alongside; for photographs of the strips, see *Wen wu* 1976.12 Plate 4; also *Wen wu* 1974.2 Plate 3, nos. 27, 28.

For further information concerning Liu Hsiang's editing of the *Kuan tzu* and its transmission to modern times, see P. van der Loon, 'On the transmission of *Kuan tzu*' (*TP* XLI:4–5, 1952, 357–93), from which the foregoing translation is adapted; W. Allyn Rickett, *Kuan-tzu, a Repository of Early Chinese Thought* (Hong Kong: Hong Kong University Press, 1965), pp. 13–31; and Rickett, *Guanzi: Political, Economic, and Philosophical Essays from Early China; A Study and Translation*; 2 vols.; Vol. I Princeton: Princeton University Press, 1985; Vol. II, forthcoming 1994.

4. Origins of the *Kuan tzu*

At least as early as the third century A.D. Chinese scholars recognized that Liu Hsiang's *Kuan tzu* contains a great many historical and ideological references to periods later than the 7th century B.C., that it is written in a literary style which did not appear before the fifth century B.C., and therefore could not have been written by Kuan Chung, at least not in its entirety. It has also long been recognized that it could not be the work of any single individual or single time because of its heterogeneous content, including conflicting statements in different parts of the work, and its varied style of writing.

In spite of these considerations many Chinese writers have persisted in maintaining that the received version of the *Kuan tzu* was indeed the work of Kuan Chung or his immediate followers: see, e.g., Lou Liang-lo 婁良樂, *Kuan tzu p'ing i* 管子評議, privately printed in Taiwan *c.* 1972. Other scholars have maintained that while the work is the product of later writers most of it represents the thought of Kuan Chung; see, e.g., Kung-chuan Hsiao, *A History of Chinese Political Thought*, vol. 1, translated by F.W. Mote, Princeton: Princeton University Press, 1979, pp. 320–2; and Yü Tun-k'ang 余敦康, *Lun Kuan Chung hsüeh p'ai* 論管仲學派 in *Chung kuo che hsüeh*, second collection (Peking: San lien shu tien, 1980), pp. 39–67 (translated in *Chinese Studies in Philosophy*, Winter 1982–83, 3–60). An intense debate on this subject has also been carried on in the quarterly *Kuan tzu hsüeh k'an* 管子學刊, published in Tzu-po 淄博 (Shantung) beginning in 1987.

Given the diverse nature of the *Kuan tzu*, it is necessary to deal with questions of dating and authorship for each chapter individually. So far, only Lo Ken-tse 羅根澤 in his *Kuan tzu t'an yüan* 管子探源 (Chung hua, 1931) has attempted to do this for the entire text. Although Lo's assessments concerning individual chapters may be questioned, most scholars today accept his basic conclusion that none of the *Kuan tzu* chapters predates the Warring States period, and that most of them come from the end of that period or the time of the Han dynasty, i.e. from the fourth to the first centuries B.C. Since Lo's work, a number of scholars have tried to date individual chapters with varying degrees of success (see the introductory comment to the various chapters in Rickett, 1985 and 1994.)

During the Warring States period, it seems that Kuan Chung had become the hero of a body of romance literature (see chapters nos. 18, 20) as well as the spokesman for various political and philosophical points of view. Kuan Chung's name appears in some 27 of the extant 76 chapters of the book and these twenty-seven are clearly of mixed origins. Most of them consist of dialogues seen as taking place between Kuan Chung and Duke Huan in which Kuan Chung enlightened his prince on matters of statecraft and political economy.

The primary source of the various political and philosophical writings in the *Kuan tzu* seems to have been scholars attached to the Chi hsia 稷

下 Academy, which flourished at Lin tzu 臨淄, the Ch'i capital at the time of king Hsüan 宜王 (reigned 319–301 B.C.). During the three quarters of a century that the Academy was in operation hundreds of scholars from all over China are said to have visited there, including Mencius, Hsün Tzu, Tsou Yen 鄒衍, Sung Hsing 宋銒, T'ien P'ien 田駢, Chieh Yü 接輿, Huan Yüan 環淵, P'eng Meng 彭蒙, Yin Wen 尹文 and probably Chuang Tzu as well as Shen Tao 慎到, representing a wide diversity of intellectual, social, political, and literary inclinations and predispositions. Most of the many works produced by these Chi hsia scholars were lost during the Ch'in and early years of the Han period, but according to a widely accepted theory, some of them came to be associated with parts of the *Kuan tzu* historical romance literature about 250 B.C., to form what Gustav Haloun has called the proto-Kuan tzu (see Haloun, 'Legalist Fragments: Part 1: Kuan-tsi 55 and related texts', *Asia Major*, NS 2, Pt 1, April 1951, 96). This 'proto-*Kuan tzu*' seems to have served as a core around which various other texts were later added to form the work known to Han Fei, Chia I and Ssu-ma Ch'ien and the basis of the collection edited by Liu Hsiang.

The process of adding to the collection may have continued right up to Liu Hsiang's time. The explanatory chapters (63–67) and most of the so-called *Ch'ing chung* chapters (68–86) are clearly of late origin, the latter dating no earlier than the middle of the second century B.C. It is also highly likely that several *p'ien* of the *Kuan tzu* are the product of writers from the state of Ch'u 楚 and had entered the Han imperial library through the collection of Liu An 劉安, king of Huai-nan, after his death in 122 B.C. Scholars at the court of Liu An are known to have had a special interest in the early culture of the Ch'u region, and given the fact that Kuan Chung was a native of Ying-shang 潁上, an area belonging to Ch'u, the *Kuan tzu* would have been a likely text to attract their attention. Furthermore, the *Huai nan tzu* and other texts associated with Ch'u, such as the *Wen tzu* 文子, contain a number of passages parallel to the *Kuan tzu* and share similarities in rhyme usage (see Rickett, forthcoming 1994).

In addition, a connection may be discerned between the *Kuan tzu* as received and the four texts prefixed to the *Lao tzu* (Manuscript B from Ma-wang-tui). Several chapters of the *Kuan tzu* (nos. 13, 36, 38, 49, 52) employ a similar rhyme scheme to that of those four texts and would appear to have been written by persons who, at least originally, came from the same region, i.e. the old land of Ch'u. Moreover some ten chapters of the *Kuan tzu* (nos. 8, 12, 15, 17, 36, 37, 38, 42, 49, 55) contain passages that are either identical with or similar to passages in these texts, thus indicating an affinity that is too close to be a matter of chance (see T'ang Lan 唐蘭: 'Ma-wang-tui ch'u t'u Lao tzu i pen chüan ch'ien ku i shu ti yen chiu' 馬王堆出土老子乙本卷前古逸書的研究, *K'ao-ku hsüeh-pao* 1975.1, 7–38; and Lung Hui 龍晦: 'Ma-wang-tui ch'u t'u Lao tzu i pen ch'ien ku i shu t'an yüan' 馬王堆出土老子乙本前古逸書探原, *K'ao-ku hsüeh-pao* 1975.2, 23–32.

5. Editions

The somewhat complex history of various editions of the *Kuan tzu* from the time of Liu Hsiang until recently is covered in detail in van der Loon, 'On the transmission of *Kuan tzu*' (*TP* 41, pp. 357–393). See also Kuo Mo-jo 郭沫若 and Hsü Wei-yü 許維遹, *Kuan tzu chi chiao* 管子集校 (Peking: K'o hsüeh, 1956), Rickett 1965 and 1985. The two most important editions that are readily available are (a) a Sung or Yüan reprint, containing a preface by Yang Ch'en 楊忱 (*c.* 1224) and a colophon by Chang Nieh 張嶸, and reproduced in the *Ssu pu ts'ung k'an* series; and (b) a Ming edition, by Chao Yung-hsien 趙用賢, reprinted in the *Ssu pu pei yao*, *Wan yu wen k'u* and *Kuo hsüeh chi pen ts'ung shu* series.

6. Commentaries and studies

The standard commentary printed in most editions is attributed to Fang Hsüan-ling 房玄齡 (578–648), but this was in all probability written by Yin Chih-chang 尹知章, who died in 718. This commentary should be used with some caution, since Yin was inclined to ignore obvious mistakes in transcription and to force a reading of the text no matter how inappropriate. Following Yin, a number of scholars have commented on the *Kuan tzu*, especially since the end of the Ming period. For many years the major collected commentary was that of Tai Wang 戴望, (1783–1863) *Kuan tzu chiao cheng* 管子校正 of 1873. This work, reprinted in many editions that include the *Kuo hsüeh chi pen ts'ung shu*, has now been superseded by the monumental two-volume *Kuan tzu chi chiao* 管子集校 of Kuo Mo-jo and Hsü Wei-yü. In addition, there are two important commentaries by Ma Fei-pai 馬非百, *Kuan tzu ch'ing chung p'ien hsin ch'üan* 管子輕重篇新詮 (Peking: Chung hua, 1979), and his posthumously published *Kuan tzu Nei yeh p'ien chi chu* 管子內業篇集注 (*Kuan tzu hsüeh k'an*, 1990, 1, 2, and 3). For detailed notes on these and other commentaries, see van der Loon (*op. cit.*) and Rickett, 1985 and forthcoming 1994. There have also been two excellent commentaries by Japanese scholars: (a) Igai Hikohiro 豬飼彥博 (1761–1845) and (b) Yasui Sokken 安井息軒 (Mamoru 衡; 1799–1876). The latter's *Kanshi sanko* 管子纂詁 is perhaps the most useful running commentary on the complete text yet available, and has served as the basis for most Japanese editions of the *Kuan tzu* (see below).

For an older study of the content of the *Kuan tzu*, see Liang Ch'i-ch'ao 梁啓超 (1873–1929), *Chung kuo liu ta cheng chih chia* 中國六大政治家, (Shanghai: Kuang chih 1911), section 1. More recent studies are to be found in the *Kuan tzu hsüeh k'an* (see especially bibliographies of Chinese, Japanese, and Western works in the first three issues of 1988) and two collections of conference papers published by the editors of this journal, *Kuan tzu yen chiu* 管子研究 (1987) and *Kuan tzu yü Ch'i wen hua* 管子與齊文化 (1990). See also two recent studies of economic thought in the *Kuan tzu*, both of which are entitled *Kuan tzu ching chi ssu hsiang yen chiu* 管子經濟思想研究, by Wu Pao-san 巫寶三 (Peking: Chung kuo she hui k'o hsüeh, 1989), and Chao Shou-cheng 趙守正 (Shanghai: Ku chi, 1989).

7. Translations

The first attempt to translate the *Kuan tzu* into a western language appears to be that of M.C. de Harlez, in French (*Journal Asiatique*, Series IX: vol. vii, 1896, 26–99). Unfortunately de Harlez found himself totally defeated by the difficulty of the text and his work is of little value. Thereafter, translations of brief passages began to appear in various western works on Chinese philosophy, but it was not until the 1930s that any substantial translation was made; e.g., see Gustav Haloun, 'Das Ti-tsï-tsï Fragmente II' in *Asia Major* 9 (1933), 467–502; and 'Legalist Fragments: Part I Kuan-tsï and Related texts', in *Asia Major* NS II (April 1951), 85–120. Haloun apparently collaborated with Joseph Needham in other translations which were never published but are mentioned in Needham, *Science and Civilisation in China*, (Cambridge: Cambridge University Press, 1956), vol. II, p. 630. For chapter no. 39, see Needham, *op. cit.* vol. II, pp. 42–5, and for chapter no. 54, see Burton Watson *Early Chinese Literature* (New York and London: Columbia University Press, 1962), pp. 181–83. In 1954 Lewis Maverick, in conjunction with two Chinese graduate students T'an Po-fu and Wen Kung-wen, published a translation of some thirty chapters dealing with political and economic theory, entitled *Economic Dialogues in Ancient China: Selections from the Kuan-tzu* (Carbondale, Illinois, 1954). Although this work is often more of a paraphrase than an actual translation it is very useful for understanding early Chinese economic theory. There is also a partial translation of many of the chapters that are covered by Maverick into Russian, by Viktor M. Shteyn, under the title *Guan-tze: Issledovanie i perevod* (Moscow: Izdatelstvo Vostochnoi Literaturi, 1959). Rickett's *Kuan-tzu: a repository of early Chinese thought* has been superseded by his two-volume *Guanzi*, the second volume of which is due for publication in 1994.

In 1989 Chao Shou-cheng published (Peking: Ching chi hsüeh yüan) his excellent two-volume annotated translation into modern Chinese, *Kuan tzu t'ung chieh* 管子通解. This work thus supersedes his earlier two-volume partial translation, *Kuan tzu chu i* 管子注譯 (Nan-ning: Kuang hsi jen min, 1982 and 1987). There are two other partial translations into modern Chinese: (a) *Kuan tzu ching chi p'ien wen chu i* 管子經濟篇文注譯 (Kiangsi jen min, 1980) by the Chung kuo jen min ta hsüeh, Kuan tzu ssu hsiang yen chiu tsu 中國人民大學管子思想研究組; and (b) Wu Pao-san, *Chung kuo ching chi ssu hsiang shih tzu liao hsüan chi, hsien Ch'in pu fen* 中國經濟思想史資料選集先秦部分 (Chung kuo she hui k'o hsüeh, 1989), vol. I, pp. 98–259.

8. Japanese editions

A. *Kambun taikei*; no. 21, 1916. edited by Koyanagi Shikita and Yasui Sokken.

B. *Kanseki kokujikai zensho*; nos. 18, 19, 1911, edited by Kikuchi Sankurō (Bankō).

D. *Kokuyaku kambun taisei*; no. 19, 1924, edited by Kimida Rentarō.

E. *Kambun sōsho*, 1928.

F. *Keisho taiko*; nos. 22, 23.

H. *Shinshaku kambun taikei*; nos. 42, 43, 52, edited by Endō Tetsuo.

J. *Chūgoku no shisō*; 1965, edited by Matsumoto Kazuo.

L. *Chūgoku koten shinsho*, 1970, edited by Kakimura Takashi.

9. Indexes

(a) Wallace Johnson, *Kuan tzu yin te* 管子引得 *A concordance to the Kuan-tzu*; Taipei: Chinese Materials and Research Aids Center, 1970. The references are to the *K'uo hsüeh chi pen ts'ung shu* print of Chao Yung-hsien's edition.

(b) *A Concordance to the Guanzi* 管子逐字索引, ed. D.C. Lau and Chen Fong Ching; *ICS* series, Hong Kong: Commercial Press, forthcoming 1996.

         — W. Allyn Rickett

Kung-sun Lung tzu 公孫龍子

1. Content

The *Kung-sun Lung tzu* is the only extant book ascribed to one of the sophists. Its supposed author is Kung-sun Lung, who was a client of Chao Sheng 趙勝, Lord of P'ing-yüan 平原 (died 251 B.C.). The first *p'ien* 'Chi fu 跡府' ('Storehouse of traces') consists of three extracts from no longer existing sources, concerning the life of Kung-sun Lung, i.e.:

(a) A sketch of Kung-sun Lung's teaching, including a summary of his argument that a white horse is not a horse. A shorter version of the passage appears in the *T'ai-p'ing yü-lan* (*SPTK* 464.5a), where it is attributed to the *Hsin lun* 新論 of Huan T'an 桓譚 (*c.* 43 B.C.–A.D. 28).

(b) The story of a controversy between Kung-sun Lung and K'ung Ch'uan 孔穿, a descendant of Confucius. The anecdote about the king of Ch'u's 楚 bow quoted by Kung-sun Lung appears also in *Shuo yüan* 24.4a (*SPTK*).

(c) A second version of the same story. The opening sentences addressed to Kung-sun Lung by K'ung Ch'uan are quoted in the commentary of the *Wen hsüan* (*SPTK* 39.7b) as from the *Hsin hsü* 新序 of Liu Hsiang 劉向 (79–8 B.C.), in which it is no longer to be found. In this version Kung-sun Lung quotes an anecdote about Yin Wen 尹文 (4th, 3rd century B.C.), found also in *Lü shih ch'un ch'iu* 16, 19b–20b (*SPTK* ed.).

A conflation of (a) and (b), including a refutation of the 'White Horse' argument by K'ung Ch'uan, which is missing in the *Kung-sun Lung tzu*, appears in the *K'ung ts'ung tzu* 孔叢子 (*SPTK* ed. 1.72a–76a).

The remaining five *p'ien* are essays on problems of dialectics:

> No. 2: *Pai ma lun* 白馬論; 'Essay on the white horse'.
> No. 3: *Chih wu lun* 指物論; 'Essay on pointings and things'.
> No. 4: *T'ung pien lun* 通變論; 'Essay on understanding changes'.
> No. 5: *Chien pai lun* 堅白論; 'Essay on the hard and the white'.
> No. 6: *Ming shih lun* 名實論; 'Essay on names and objects'.

252

2. History of the text

The bibliographical list in the *Han shu* (30, p. 1736) enters a *Kung-sun Lung tzu* in 14 *p'ien*, under *ming chia* 名家. An item under this title is missing in the bibliography of the *Sui shu*, which however includes a *Shou pai lun* 守白論 in one *chüan*, under *Tao chia* 道家 (*Sui shu* 34, p. 1002). A work with this title is ascribed to Kung-sun Lung by Ch'eng Hsüan-ying 成玄英 (*fl.* 630–60) in *Nan hua chen ching chu shu* 南華眞經 注疏 (*Tao tsang* 35.46b), and said there to be still current. The opening sentences of the extant book do in fact describe Kung-sun Lung as writing essays on *shou pai* 'clinging to the white'; the phrase is probably a corruption of the term *chien pai* 堅白 'hard and white', as in the *Hsin lun* parallel.

The item *Kung-sun Lung tzu* is entered in *Chiu T'ang shu* (47, p. 2031) and *Hsin T'ang shu* (59, p. 1532), under *ming chia*, as consisting of 3 *chüan*, without annotation. The *Chiu T'ang shu* also includes two entries for the work in 1 *chüan*, with annotation by Chia Ta-yin 賈大隱 (*fl.* 676) and Ch'en Ssu-ku 陳嗣古 respectively. These are also mentioned in the *T'ung chih* 通志, but by the time of the *Ssu k'u* editors they had disappeared. In the anonymous *Ni Kung sun Lung tzu lun* 擬公孫龍子論 (*Wen yüan ying hua* 758) the author states that in 672 he saw a *Kung-sun Lung tzu* in 1 *chüan*, consisting of 6 *p'ien*; he alludes to the titles of all the six that are in the extant text. The work does not feature in Fujiwara Sukeyo's list.

All references from the T'ang period onwards are to the 6 *p'ien* grouped as either 1 or 3 *chüan*. The earliest surviving printed edition, that of 1445 in the *Tao tsang*, has the work in 3 *chüan*, with an anonymous commentary but no preface. The text on which the *Ssu k'u ch'üan shu* editors reported was in a single *chüan*, with a preface ascribed to Hsieh Chiang 謝絳 (Hsi-shen 希深; 995–1039), who is also credited with the commentary. This version is reproduced from the *Shou shan ko ts'ung shu* (ed. Ch'ien Hsi-tso 錢熙祚 1801–44) in the *Ssu pu pei yao* series. Ch'ien had taken it from the *Mo hai chin hu* of Chang Hai-p'eng 張海鵬 (1755–1816); it is also available in the *Tzu hui*, dated at 1577. The ascription of the commentary to the author of the preface is certainly mistaken. It observes the T'ang taboos; it is echoed, together with the text, in Yang Liang's 楊倞 commentary to *Hsün tzu* 1.21b (*SPTK* ed.; preface dated 819); and its recurrent references to *shou pai* suggest that the book still carried the title *Shou pai lun*. Presumably this is one of the two old commentaries noted in the T'ang bibliographies. For a proposal to divide it between the two T'ang commentators, see Kandel, as cited under (5) below, p. 290.

There is evidence of serious textual dislocation in *p'ien* no. 2 and perhaps elsewhere. A re-arrangement of the text of that *p'ien* is proposed in A.C. Graham, 'Two dialogues in the *Kung-sun Lung tzu*, "White horse" and "Left and Right"' (*Asia Major*, New Series, 11:2 (1965), 128–52); for a re-arrangement of all five *p'ien*, see Amano Shizuo's edition, as cited under (6) below.

3. Authenticity

In his *Ku chin wei shu k'ao* 古今偽書考 , Yao Chi-heng 姚際恆 (b. 1647) suspected the *Kung-sun Lung tzu* to be a forgery, on the grounds of its absence from the Sui bibliography. The identification of the work with the *Shou pai lun* of that bibliography has removed this objection, and modern Chinese and Japanese scholars are content to accept the extant six *p'ien* as the remains of the item that was named *Kung-sun Lung tzu*, with 14 *p'ien*, in the *Han shu*. The issue was re-opened in A.C. Graham, 'The composition of the Gongsuen Long Tzyy' (*Asia Major*, New Series, 5:2 (1957), 147–83), which called attention to marked differences between *p'ien* nos. 2 and 3 (*Pai ma lun* and *Chih wu lun*) and the remaining *p'ien*.

(a) *P'ien* nos. 2 and 3 are purely dialectical, without moral or political interest; *p'ien* nos. 4–6 make no comparable effort to organise arguments in logically impeccable form, and each one ends up by making a moral or political point.

(b) The difference in the thought is reflected in the style. *P'ien* nos. 2 and 3 are written in long sentences with complex and firm syntax; *p'ien* nos. 4–6 are written in short clauses which tend to run in parallels, almost as rigid as those of the parallel prose of the Six Dynasties. The difference shows also in the details of vocabulary and grammatical usage.

(c) *P'ien* nos. 2 and 3 resemble in thought and style the dialectical writing of the Mohist Canons, but without direct parallels. But *p'ien* nos. 4, 5 and 6 are full of such parallels, some being grossly misunderstood and even linked together nonsensically.

(d) There is firm evidence of the existence of *p'ien* no. 2 (*Pai ma lun*) back to the time of Huan T'an; but commentators to the *Chuang tzu*, *Huai nan tzu* and *Shih chi*, in explaining references to 'the hard and the white', show their ignorance of the essay of that name, right up to the fifth century A.D.

The preface of Lu Sheng 魯勝 (*fl.* 291) to his lost edition of the Mohist Canons, which is preserved in his biography (*Chin shu* 94, pp. 2433–34) states explicitly that all writings of the sophists had disappeared, except for materials in miscellaneous collections which he had assembled in 'two *p'ien* on forms and names 刑名二篇'. It is therefore concluded that the *Kung-sun Lung tzu* was forged between A.D 300 and 600, but that it preserves at least two genuine essays of the pre-Han sophists (*Pai ma* and *Chih wu*), possibly with the 'Left and Right' dialogue at the beginning of *p'ien* no. 4, as well as the three extracts from lost sources on Kung-sun Lung's life and thought that are put together now in *p'ien* no. 1. This argument has not, however, attracted the attention of Chinese and Japanese scholars, who continue to take the integrity of the book for granted. In the west, J.E. Kandel, while accepting the argument that *p'ien* nos. 4–6 were written after A.D. 300, holds that they preserve authentic thought of the pre-Han sophists (see Kandel, as cited below, p. 205).

Materials for the history of the book and the life of Kung-sun lung are conveniently assembled in Hu Tao-ching 胡道靜, *Kung-sun Lung tzu k'ao* 公孫龍子考 (Shanghai: Shang wu, 1934). A revised version of 'The composition of the *Gongsuen Long tzyy*', and translations and annotations of the essays and dialogue identified as genuine, appeared in A.C. Graham, *Studies in Chinese philosophy and philosophical literature* (Institute of East Asian Philosophies, National University of Singapore, 1986; reprinted New York: State University of New York Press, 1990, pp. 125–215).

4. Modern editions (including versions in modern Chinese)

(a) Wang Kuan 王琯, *Kung-sun Lung tzu hsüan chieh* 公孫龍子懸解; original edition Peiping; Chung hua, 1927; facsimile by Taipei: Chung hua, 1971.

(b) Chin Shou-shen 金受申, *Kung-sun Lung tzu shih* 公孫龍子釋; Shanghai: Shang wu, 1930.

(c) Ch'en Chu 陳柱, *Kung-sun Lung tzu chi chieh* 公孫龍子集解; Shanghai: Shang wu, 1937.

(d) T'an Chieh-fu 譚戒甫, *Kung-sun Lung tzu hsing ming fa wei* 公孫龍子刑名發微; Peking: K'o hsüeh, 1957.

(e) Wang Ch'i-hsiang 王啓湘, *Kung-sun Lung tzu chiao ch'üan* 公孫龍子校詮; Taipei: 1958.

(f) Wang Tien-chi 汪奠基, *Chung kuo lo chi ssu hsiang shih liao fen hsi* 中國邏輯思想史料分析; Peking: Chung hua, 1961; vol. 1, pp. 196–253.

(g) Hsü Fu-kuan 徐復觀, *Kung-sun Lung tzu chiang shu* 公孫龍子講疏; Taichung: Ssu li Tung hai ta hsüeh, 1966.

(h) Ho Ch'i-min 何啓民, *Kung-sun Lung yü Kung-sun Lung tzu* 公孫龍與 公孫龍子; Taipei: Chung kuo hsüeh shu chu tso chiang chu wei yüan hui, 1967.

(i) Ch'en Kuei-miao 陳癸淼, *Kung-sun Lung tzu shu shih* 公孫龍子疏釋; Taipei: Lan t'ai, 1970.

(j) P'ang P'u 龐朴, *Kung-sun Lung tzu i chu* 公孫龍子譯注; Shanghai; Jen min, 1974.

(k) P'ang P'u, *Kung-sun Lung tzu yen chiu* 公 孫 龍 子 研 究; Peking: Chung hua, 1979.

(l) Ch'ü Chih-ch'ing 屈志清, *Kung-sun Lung tzu hsin chu* 公孫龍子新 注; Hupei: Jen min, 1981.

(m)Luan Hsing 欒星, *Kung-sun Lung tzu ch'ang chien* 公孫龍子長箋; Honan: Chung chou, 1982.

(n) Hsiao Teng-fu 蕭登福, *Kung-sun Lung tzu yü ming chia* 公孫龍子與 名家; Taipei: Wen chin, 1984.

(o) Yang Chün-kuang 楊俊光, *Kung-sun Lung tzu li ts'e* 公孫龍子蠡測; Chinan: Ch'i Lu, 1986.

(Yü Yüeh's 俞樾 (1821-1907) annotation appears in the *Chu tzu p'ing i*).

5.   Translations

(a) Forke, A., 'The Chinese sophists'; *Journal of the China Branch of the Royal Asiatic Society* vol. XXXIV (1901–02), 1–100, Appendix 3.

(b) Perleberg, Max, *The works of Kung-sun Lung tzu*; Hong Kong: 1952.

(c) Mei, Y.P., 'The Kung-sun Lung-tzu'; *HJAS* 16 (1953), 404–37.

(d) Kou Pao-koh, Ignace, *Deux sophistes chinoises: Houei Che et K'ong-souen Long*; Paris: Presses Universitaires, 1953.

(e) Chan, Wing-tsit, *A source-book of Chinese philosophy*; Princeton: Princeton University Press, 1963 (for *p'ien* 2–6).

(f) Kandel, J.E., *Ein Beitrag zur Interpretationsgeschichte des abstrakten Denkens in China: Die Lehren des Kung-sun Lung und deren Aufname in der Tradition*; Höchberg, 1976; (see pp. 61–114 for *p'ien* nos. 2–6).

Translations of *p'ien* no. 3 differ radically according to different interpretations of its key concept of *chih* 指 'pointing', and of the structure of the argument. Specialised studies of this problem include; A.C. Graham, 'Kung-sun Lung's Essay on Meanings and Things', *Journal of Oriental Studies* 2:2 (1955), 282–301; Janusz Chmielewski, 'Notes on Early Chinese Logic', *Rocznic Orientalistyczny* 26–32 (especially 26:1 (1962) 7–22); Cheng Chung-ying and Richard H. Swain, 'Logic and Ontology in the Chih Wu Lun of Kung-sun Lung-tzu', *Philosophy East and West* 20:2 (1970),

137–54; and A.C. Graham, *Later Mohist logic, ethics and science*: Hong Kong, Chinese University Press, and London: School of Oriental and African studies, 1978, pp. 457–68.

6. Japanese editions

D. *Kokuyaku kambun taisei;* no. 18, 1924, edited by Koyanagi Shikita.
L. *Chūgoku koten shinsho*, 1967, edited by Amano Shizuo.

7. Index

A Concordance to the Yinwenzi, Kongcongzi, Gongsun Longzi and Dengxizi 尹文子, 公孫龍子, 鄧析子逐字索引, ed. D.C. Lau and Chen Fong Ching; *ICS* series, Hong Kong: Commercial Press, forthcoming 1995.

— A.C. Graham

K'ung tzu chia yü 孔子家語

1. Content

The *K'ung tzu chia yü* consists of two parts which should be sharply distinguished from each other, intermingled though they are throughout the work:

(a) A compilation made up from the principal pre-Han and early Han traditions about Confucius, as handed down by followers of his school with the purpose of providing a complement to the *Lun yü*. This aim is stated explicitly in the postface (see under (2) below). Two other early texts on Confucius were omitted from consideration in the *Chia yü*, probably because at the time of the latter's compilation they were already being transmitted independently. These are the *Tseng tzu wen* 曾子問 and the *K'ung tzu san ch'ao chi* 孔子三朝記, now seen respectively as *Li chi* 7 and *Ta Tai li chi* 67-70 and 74-76. The main character of the bulk of the text is that it is in the nature of a compilation.

(b) A number of passages, sentences and phrases were probably interpolated during the 3rd century A.D. These were probably added by Wang Su 王肅 (195-256), editor of the text as handed down, in order to furnish authoritative evidence for his arguments against the tenets of Cheng Hsüan 鄭玄 (127-200). This part, which is interspersed among the rest of the text, constitutes only a minor portion of the whole.

The *Chia yü* is thus basically a collection of ancient lore centering around the figure of Confucius, his teachings and his principles, and the events in his life. Much of the text shows the Confucianist stress on the ethical side of human conduct, often illustrating such points by means of parable or metaphor. The single subject which recurs most frequently is that of ritual or the rites, and their relation to social order and proper human behaviour.

For a short survey of the contents, see R.P. Kramers, *K'ung tzu chia yü, the School Sayings of Confucius* (Leiden: E.J. Brill, 1950), pp. 1-14. Since practically the entire text of the *Chia yü* consists of materials found also in other sources, parallel versions with a considerable number of other pre-Han and early Han texts have been preserved (see Kramers, *op. cit.*, pp. 170f., and Table of Parallels, pp. 361f.).

2. Date of composition and authenticity

In his preface to his annotated edition, Wang Su writes that he was engaged in controversy with the school of Cheng Hsüan over the interpretation of a number of ritual traditions. A descendant of Confucius and former pupil of Wang Su one day brought him a copy of the *Chia yü* that had been preserved in his family, and Wang Su was delighted to find that the text contained passages in support of his own views. A number of passages of the *Chia yü* occur in the fragmentary account of a public disputation between Wang Su and representatives of Cheng Hsüan's school, which is entitled *Sheng cheng lun* 聖證論.

If Wang Su's preface is to be believed, the *Chia yü* must have been compiled at an earlier date. The only evidence for the earlier existence of a work thus named is to be found in *Han shu* 30, p. 1716, which includes an entry for the *K'ung tzu chia yü* in 27 *chüan*, along with the *Lun yü* and associated works.

There is also a postface to the received text, which consists of three parts:

(a) An account is given of the nature and early history of the text, its faulty transmission and the intermixture of other texts. It is noted how it came into the hands of K'ung An-kuo 孔安國, Confucius' descendant in the 12th generation (d. *c.* 100 B.C.).

(b) There is a genealogy of the K'ung family down to K'ung An-kuo, followed by an account of the latter's unsuccessful attempts to secure official recognition for his old texts.

(c) Finally, a memorial is quoted by K'ung Yen 孔衍, grandson of K'ung An-kuo, protesting against the failure to accord due recognition to his grandfather's merits.

Since Yen Shih-ku 顏師古 (581–645) questioned whether the work that was available in his own time was identical with the item listed in the *Han shu* (*Han shu* 30, p. 1717), the claims of both the preface and the postface have been held in doubt by later scholars. The prevailing opinion is that, either Wang Su himself was responsible for the present compilation; or that, having obtained an earlier text, he then added his own interpolations in order to suit his arguments. If, as seems to be likely, the latter opinion is correct, the actual compilation of the *Chia yü* may date back to some time before the end of the Former Han dynasty, when it was recorded among the documents in the imperial library. It can also be accepted that Wang Su did obtain a copy of the work and proceeded with some heavy editing. The main reason why the compilation may be regarded as being older than Wang Su's time is the existence of numerous small textual differences with a number of parallel texts. This suggests that both versions go back independently to an older tradition. Those parts of the text that must have been subject to alteration by Wang Su are easily recognisable thanks to their composite nature.

Wang Hsien-ch'ien 王先謙 (1842–1918; see *Han shu pu chu* 30.20a) took the view that it cannot be held that the book was a creation of Wang Su. The reasons why the latter may have forged parts of the *Chia yü* may have been due to a reaction that was setting in against Han 'theology', as still represented in the school of Cheng Hsüan. In particular, there are indications of a more 'rational' attitude in interpreting Confucius as a human saint as against the more hagiographic views that were held of him in Han times.

3.   Textual history

Sui shu 32, p. 937 and Fujiwara Sukeyo's catalogue mention a *K'ung tzu chia yü* in 21 *chüan*, as against entries in *Chiu T'ang shu* 49 p. 1982, and *Hsin T'ang shu* 57, p. 1443 which record the work in 10 *chüan*. A fragment from Tun-huang reveals yet another division into *chüan*, but these differences are unimportant, since the older division into 44 *p'ien* is attested in the fragments. From the Sung bibliographies we may see the beginning of a demotion of the *Chia yü*, in so far as henceforth it was no longer listed in the canonical category of *Lun yü*, but as the first work in the division of 'Philosophers'. This demotion must have continued under the Yüan dynasty, for the reconstructed official Yüan catalogue mentions no more than a work which must obviously be a selection of parts of the *Chia yü*, in 3 *chüan*, along with a translation into Jurchen, also in 3 *chüan*. During the Ming dynasty, several scholars tried to reconstruct the complete text with varying degrees of success. One Ming reprint of a Sung version, edited by a certain Wu Shih-yung 吳時用 and reproduced in the *Ssu pu ts'ung k'an* series, lacks the final three paragraphs and the postface; it also contains a number of copyist's errors, especially in the second half of the text. The *Ssu pu pei yao* print was also based on this copy.

Towards the end of the Ming period, Mao Chin 毛晉 (1599–1659) prepared a complete edition of the *Chia yü* from two Sung prints which he had obtained at different times. This Mao edition has been reprinted several times, and its text is identical with that of a beautiful Sung edition of Liu Shih-heng 劉世珩 (1875–1926) in 1898. This latter edition was included in the *Yü hai t'ang ying Sung ts'ung shu*, and both it and the Mao edition are superior to the *Ssu pu ts'ung k'an*. The Mao text was recently included in volume 21 of the series *Chung kuo tzu hsüeh ming chu chi ch'eng* 中國子學名著集成 (Taipei: 1978–80), together with a beautifully illustrated set of selections from the text in 5 *chüan*, under the title *K'ung tzu chia yü chün* 孔子家語雋; this had been edited, with a commentary, by Chang Nai 張鼐 (*chin shih* 1604).

4. Studies and translations

Four full length critical studies deserve mention:

(a) An annotated edition by Ho Meng-ch'un 何孟春 (*chin shih* 1493) was first published in 1505; additional notes by Lu Wen-ch'ao 盧文弨 (1717–96) were appended in 1767; these are available in a reprint of 1873.

(b) Fan Chia-hsiang 范家相 (*chin shih* 1754), *Chia yü cheng wei* 家語證偽; re-edited text, with addition of parallel texts and Fan's own notes; published in various *ts'ung shu*, including *K'uai chi Hsü shih shu shih lou*.

(c) Sun Chih-tsu 孫志祖 (1737–1801), *Chia yü shu cheng* 家語疏證. Like Fan, Sun believed Wang Su to have been the compiler of the entire text. An edition of this work is to be found in the *Chiao ching shan fang ts'ung shu* (1904).

(d) Ch'en Shih-k'o 陳士珂 (*fl.* 1818), *K'ung tzu chia yü shu cheng* 孔子家語疏證; the author copied out the entire text with all known parallels alongside, enabling readers to judge for themselves whether the *Chia yü* was a complete forgery; he himself did not believe this. The work is included in the *Hu pei ts'ung shu* and *Ts'ung shu chi ch'eng* (punctuated).

Japanese contributions include:

(e) Nishijima Rankei 西島蘭溪 (1780–1835), *Kōshi kego kō* 孔子家語考, with additional notes.

(f) Hattori Unokichi's introduction to his *kambun* version discusses a number of the problems of the work (see under (5) below).

(g) Fujiwara Tadashi's 藤原正 introduction to his translation discusses similar problems (see under (5) below).

(h) Takeuchi Yoshio 武內義雄, 'Toku Kego zasshi 讀家語雜識' (see the collection of his essays entitled *Rōshi genshi* 老子原始 Tokyo: Kōbundō, 1926) pp. 302–15.

These later scholars believe that the main body of the text was compiled before Wang Su's time.

Western contributions include:

(i) Haloun, Gustav, 'Fragmente des Fu-tsï und des Tsin-tsï: Früh-Konfuzianische Fragmente I' (*Asia Major* 8, 1932, 437–509); in setting out to prove that a passage of the *Chia yü* was the source of its parallel text, the author looks at the problem of authenticity from a new angle.

(j) The introduction to R.P. Kramers (*op. cit.*) is still the most exhaustive treatment of the subject; translations are given for *p'ien* nos. 1–10. A review of this work by Wolfram Eberhard (*Oriens*, IV, 1951, 142–45) opens the way for further enquiries on the ramifications of forgeries and their motivation.

(k) Wilhelm, Richard, *Kung Futse, Schulgespräche (Gia yü)*; published posthumously by Helmut Wilhelm (Düsseldorf-Köln: Eugen Diederichs Verlag, 1961); the work includes a complete translation, apart from those passages whose parallels are well known and have been translated by Richard Wilhelm elsewhere.

5.   Japanese editions

A. *Kambun taikei;* no. 20, 1915, edited by Hattori Unokichi.

E. *Kambun sōsho,* 1927.

H. *Shinshaku kambun taikei;* no. 53, edited by Uno Seiichi (forthcoming).

L. *Chūgoku koten shinsho;* no. 27, 1971, edited by Kiyota Kiyoshi.
Fujiwara Tadashi, *Kōshi kego;* Tokyo: Iwanami bunko, 1933.

6.   Index

A Concordance to the Kongzi Jiayu 孔子家語逐字索引, ed. D.C. Lau and Chen Fong Ching; *ICS* series, Hong Kong: Commercial Press, 1992.

— R.P. Kramers

Kuo yü 國語

1.   Origin of the work and its relation to the *Tso chuan* 左傳

Verbatim accounts of the sayings of rulers and prominent persons, which were drawn up for the various states of the Spring and Autumn period and subsequently supplemented from other sources, were usually termed *Kuo yü*, i.e., dialogues or discourses of the state. Of such a type and origin is the extant work of that name, whose contents show that it should be regarded as a compilation of several authors rather than the creation of a single one. Possibly it was Tso Ch'iu-ming 左丘明 (5th century B.C.), as mentioned in *Shih chi* 130, p. 3300, who put this work together and should therefore be regarded as the editor rather than the author. Ssu-ma Ch'ien 司馬遷 (?145–?86 B.C.) writes that the work was completed after Tso Ch'iu-ming had lost his sight, but it is nonetheless feasible that it was composed from memory. Identification of the actual author of any one of the existing sections of the *Kuo yü* is hardly possible. According to the account of the *Shih chi*, when he was about 20 years old, Tso Ch'iu-ming met an elderly Confucius, and he complied the *Kuo yü* when he was about 70; if this was so, the work could not have come into being before *c.* 425 B.C.

For the question of Tso Ch'iu-ming's authorship of the *Tso chuan*, see under the entry for *Ch'un ch'iu, Kung yang, Ku liang,* and *Tso chuan*. The theory that as the contents of the *Kuo yü* and the *Tso chuan* are in many cases very similar, the latter was extracted from the former has now been generally refuted. Some scholars take the view that the two documents derived from one and the same hand, but this cannot be possible, if it is allowed that the received version of the *Kuo yü* originated from several authors rather than from a single one. While it might appear that it would have been possible for Tso Ch'iu-ming to have written the one work and edited the other, the grammatical differences in the language of the two texts, as observed by Karlgren ('On the Authenticity and Nature of the *Tso chuan*'; Göteborg Högskolas Arsskrift XXXII:3, 1926) bring this suggestion into question. For the question of the relationship of the two texts, see Chang I-jen 張以仁, 'Lun Kuo yü yü Tso chuan ti kuan hsi' 論國語與左傳的關係, (*BIHP* 33, 1962, 233–86).

2. Contents and date of compilation

The 21 *chüan* of the *Kuo yü* include eight sections for the states of Chou
周, Lu 魯, Ch'i 齊, Chin 晉, Cheng 鄭, Ch'u 楚, Wu 吳 and Yüeh 越;
the section for Chin, with 9 *chüan*, is the longest; the sections for Ch'i,
Cheng and Lu, each with one *chüan*, are the shortest. There are altogether 240 separate items in the record.

The principal aim of the work is to record discourses, which are
linked with certain events; but records of events as such are of a supplementary nature. For each state the material is arranged chronologically,
e.g., that for Chou starts with the time of Mu wang 穆王 (956–918 B.C.)
and extends to the time of Ching wang 敬王 (reigned 519–476 B.C.).
Each item that is recorded is independent and complete in itself, without
being linked to other items. The choice of material and its layout do not
always follow the same form. The section for Ch'i is concerned exclusively with Kuan Chung 管仲 and the assistance that he rendered to
Huan kung to enable him to become an overlord, while the section for
Cheng deals entirely with the discourses of Shih Po 史伯. The records
of the sections for Wu and Yüeh centre completely around the struggle
of the two states for supremacy. Even where the overall pattern seems
to be generally uniform, there are some noticeable differences. Thus, all
the records in the 90 or so items for Chou, Lu and Ch'u seem to be
accounts of direct discourse. In the long section for Chin, discourse and
historical event are interspersed one with another. For Ch'i and Cheng,
discourse predominates; in the sections for Wu and Yüeh records of discourse and historical events are mixed together.

In a long study, which accompanies a similar investigation of the
Ch'un ch'iu and the *Tso chuan* (*Ku shih yen chiu* 古史研究; Shanghai:
Hsin yüeh shu tien, 1928), Wei Chü-hsien 衛聚賢 (1898–) considered
the problems of date, place of origin, identity of author and authenticity. He concludes that authorship can be distinguished as follows:
(see *Wei shu t'ung k'ao*, p. 628f.):

(a) The *Chou yü* and *Ch'u yü*: dated in 431 B.C.
(b) The *Ch'i yü* and *Wu yü*: between 431 and 384 B.C.
(c) The *Lu yü* and *Chin yü*: between 384 and 336 B.C.
(d) The *Yüeh yü* (*shang* 上): after 384 B.C.
(e) The *Cheng yü*: after 314 B.C.
(f) The *Yüeh yü* (*hsia* 下): after 314 B.C.

He also concludes that the detailed records of the affairs of Wu and
Yüeh, together with other indications, suggest that the book was a product of Ch'u.

3. Traditional evaluation

While the scope of the *Kuo yü* overlaps to a considerable extent with that of the *Ch'un ch'iu* and the *Tso chuan*, the emphasis that is placed on particular speeches or events and their treatment varies between the works. Traditionally, Chinese scholars have regarded the *Tso chuan* as a formal, and the *Kuo yü* as an informal, commentary on the *Ch'un ch'iu*, as is borne out by the description of the *Kuo yü* as *wai chuan* 外傳. This term appears in the earliest surviving notice on the work, by Wei Chao 韋昭 (d. 273), and it is retained in the titles of a number of items in the traditional catalogues from the *Sui shu* onwards (i.e., it is entered as *Ch'un chiu wai chuan kuo yü* 春秋外傳國語). The work was never accorded the same degree of respect as that shown toward the *Tso chuan*.

Wei Chao wrote that the work, which extended over the period from Mu wang of Chou to the execution of Chih Po 知伯, was concerned with the rise and fall of the various states, together with the memorable speeches of the day, the incidence of universal cycles and the relationship between the appointed seasons of Heaven and the affairs of mankind. He continued that the value of the book lies in the way in which it 'plumbs the depths of fortune and misfortune, brings to the fore the abstruse and the subtle and displays examples of good and bad.' At a later stage, Liu Tsung-yüan 柳宗元 (773–819) criticised the *Kuo yü* in a precisely contrary way as being a work which is devoid of moral principle; see his essay 'Fei Kuo yü' 非國語, in *Liu Ho-tung chi* 柳河東集 (SPPY ed.), ch. 44, 45; and *Liu Tsung-yüan chi* (Peking: Chung hua, 1979, pp. 1265–1297 and 1299–1328) for preface and critique of a total of 67 passages. Liu Tsung-yüan was apparently answered by Yeh Chen 葉真, whose 'Shih Kuo-yü' 是國語 is entered in *Sung shih* 202, p. 5058, with 7 *chüan*.

4. Early notices and commentators.

In all the early bibliographical lists, the *Kuo yü* is placed within the category of *Ch'un ch'iu*. In the *Han shu* (30, p. 1714), where it is said to have consisted of 21 *p'ien*, there is a further entry of *Hsin Kuo yü* 新國語 in 54 *p'ien*, with the somewhat enigmatic note: *Liu Hsiang fen Kuo yü* 劉向分國語.

Entries in the *Sui shu* (32, p. 932), *Chiu T'ang shu* (46, p. 1979) and *Hsin T'ang shu* (57, pp. 1437, 1440) usually describe the work as *Ch'un ch'iu wai chuan kuo yü*. Both of the T'ang histories include an item of 20 *chüan*, whose compilation is specifically ascribed to Tso Ch'iu-ming. An item with a length of 21 or 22 *chüan* carried the *Chang chü* 章句 of Wang Su

王肅 (195–256), which appears as a separate item of one *chüan* in the *Sui shu*. Other items refer to the comments of Chia K'uei 賈逵 (30–101), Yü Fan 虞翻 (164–233), Wei Chao 韋昭 (d. 273), K'ung Ch'ao 孔晁 (3rd century) and T'ang Ku 唐固 (d. 225). The single entry in Fujiwara Sukeyo's catalogue is for an item in 21 *chüan*, compiled by Wei Chao.

Of these commentaries, only that of Wei Chao survives, including as it does some of the important points made by some of the other early writers. The fragments of their remarks and of those of Cheng Chung 鄭衆 (d. A.D. 83), earliest of all commentators, are assembled in the *Yü han shan fang chi i shu* and in the *Han hsüeh t'ang ts'ung shu*.

5.   Principal editions

(a) *Kuo yü ting pen* 國語定本, with explanations (*chieh* 解) by Wei Chao and notes by Sung Hsiang 宋庠 (style Kung hsü 公序; 996–1066) on phonology; Osaka: Nakao Shinsuke 中尾新助; for Sung Hsiang's supplementary notes, see *Hu-pei hsien sheng i shu*.

(b) The *Ssu pu ts'ung k'an* series includes a facsimile of Yeh Te-hui's 葉德輝 (1864–1927) copy of a Ming print of 1522–67; this is known as the Kung hsü 公序 or the Chin li 金李 edition.

(c) *Kuo yü fu cha chi* 國語附札記, the appended notes of Huang P'ei-lieh 黃丕烈 (1763–1825) being in either 1 or 3 *chüan*; based on a copy known as *T'ien shen Ming tao* 天聖明道 of 1800, and available in the *Shih li chü Huang shih ts'ung shu* (1800); reproduced, e.g., by Hu-pei ch'ung wen shu chü and used as the basis for the *Ssu pu pei yao* print.

(d) *Kuo yü Wei chieh pu cheng* 國語韋解補正, edited by Chu Yüan-shan 朱元善; Shanghai: Shang wu, 1909.

(e) *Kuo yü cheng i* 國語正義, by Tung Tseng-ling 董曾齡; published by K'uai chi Chang shih shih hsün t'ang 會稽章氏式訓堂, 1880.

(Items (a) to (e) above all consist of 21 *chüan*.)

6.   Later commentaries

(a) Hung Liang-chi 洪亮吉 (1746–1809), *Kuo yü Wei Chao chu shu* 國語韋昭注疏.

(b) Wang Yin-chih 王引之 (1766–1834), *Kuo yü shu wen* 國語述聞.

(c) Wang Yüan-sun 汪遠孫 (1794–1836), *Kuo yü chiao chu pen san chung* 國語校注本三種 (1826), which included (i) *Kuo yü san chün chu chi ts'un* 國語三君注輯存 (4 *chüan*); (ii) *Kuo yü fa cheng* 國語發正 (21 *chüan*; also included in *Huang Ch'ing ching chieh hsü pien*); (iii) *Kuo yü Ming tao pen k'ao i* 國語明道本攷異 (4 *chüan*). A further work, *Kuo yü k'ao i* 國語攷異 is appended to the *Ch'ung wen shu chü* edition of the text.

(d) Yü Yüeh 俞樾 (1821–1906), *Kuo yü p'ing i* 國語平議.

(e) Ch'en Chuan 陳瑑 (Ch'ing period), *Kuo yü i chieh* 國語翼解, 6 *chüan*; in *Kuang ya shu chü ts'ung shu*.

(f) Shen Jung 沈鎔 and Wang Mou 王懋, *Kuo yü hsiang chu* 國語詳註 1916.

(g) Chin Ch'i-yüan 金其源, *Kuo yü kuan chien* 國語管見.

(h) Yang Shu-ta 楊樹達, *Tu Kuo yü hsiao shih* 讀國語小識.

(i) Chang I-jen 張以仁, *Kuo yü chiao cheng* 國語斠證; Taipei: Shang wu, 1969.

7. Translations

(a) *Guo yu: Propos sur les Principautés I: Zhouyu*; traduction d'André d'Hormon, complements par Rémi Mathieu; Paris: Collège de France, Institut des Hautes Études Chinoises, 1985.

(b) *Go Iui (Rechi tsarstv)*; translation and introduction and commentary by V.S. Taskin; Moscow, Nauka, 1987.

8. Japanese editions

B. *Kanseki kokujikai zensho* nos. 41, 42, 1917; edited by Katsura Koson.

D. *Kokuyaku kambun taisei*; no. 17, 1923, edited by Hayashi Taisuke.

E. *Kambun sōsho*, 1927, edited by Tsukamoto Tetsuzō and Nakamura Kyūshirō.

H. *Shinshaku kambun taikei*; nos. 66, 67, 1975, 1978, edited by Ōno Takashi.

K. *Chūgoku koten bungaku taikei* no. 7, 1972, edited by Tsuneishi Shigeru.

L. *Chūgoku koten shinsho*, 1969, edited by Ōno Takashi.

9. Indexes

(a) Suzuki Ryūichi 鈴木隆一, *Kokugo sakuin* 國語索引, Tokyo: Daian, 1943, reprinted 1967; based on the Ming tao edition, as reproduced in the Shih li chü print.

(b) Bauer, Wolfgang, *Kuo yü yin te*, 2 vols., Taipei: China Materials and Research Center, 1973; the index, which is based on the numbers of the characters in Morohashi *Dai Kanwa jiten*, follows the *Ts'ung shu chi ch'eng* edition (reproduced in vol. 2) of Huang P'ei-lieh's text of 1800. Volume 2 includes a frequency count of the characters which discriminates between (i) appearances in narrative, direct speech or quotations within direct speech and (ii) appearances within the eight groups of chapters for the various states.

(c) Chang I-jen, *Kuo yü yin te* 國語引得; Taipei: Institute of History and Philology, 1976; based on the photoprint (Taipei: Shih chieh), of the 1800 recut of the *T'ien sheng ming tao* edition by *Tu wei chien shu chai* 讀未見書齋.

(d) *A Concordance to the Guoyu* 國語逐字索引, ed. D.C. Lau and Chen Fong Ching; *ICS* series, Hong Kong: Commercial Press, forthcoming 1996.

— Chang I-jen, William G. Boltz and Michael Loewe

Lao tzu Tao te ching 老子道德經

This text may be called either the *Lao tzu*, on analogy with the *Chuang tzu*, the *Lieh tzu*, the *Mo tzu*, etc., or the *Tao te ching*. Here we shall normally refer to it as the *Lao tzu*. No difference in the text is attached to the choice of name.*

1. Structure of the text

The *Lao tzu* is a comparatively short work, sometimes called the *Wu ch'ien wen* 五千文 'The Five thousand character [classic]', and is in fact of about that length. It consists of eighty-one sections (*chang* 章), and is divided into two parts of roughly equal length, known as the *Tao ching* 道經 (nos. 1–37) and the *Te ching* 德經 (nos. 38–81), hence the alternative name *Tao te ching* for the work as a whole. All of the sections are short; none more than two printed pages, and most less than one. Some are rhymed. The division between the *Tao ching* and the *Te ching* parts does not vary from edition to edition, though the Han silk manuscript versions from Ma-wang-tui (see 4 (b) below) reverse their order, and vary the sequence of a few of the individual sections.

Because all of the sections are short, sometimes rhymed, and are sparing in their use of grammatical particles, especially in the transmitted versions, the work as a whole is sometimes referred to as poetry, though in the Chinese literary tradition it has never been formally classed as a type of poetry. Traditionally the *Lao tzu* is found in the *tzu* 子 category of the *ssu pu* 四部 classification scheme.

2. Authorship and date of composition

The *Lao tzu* is conventionally said to be the work of a person named Lao tzu, an apparent sobriquet meaning simply 'The Old Fellow', who was ostensibly an older contemporary of Confucius. Ssu-ma Ch'ien 司馬遷 (?145–?90 B.C.) gives what purports to be a biography of Lao tzu in *Shih*

---

* For the secondary works and their characters that are cited in this entry, see under (9) below.

chi 63, identifying him as an archivist serving the Chou court, a native of Ch'u, surnamed Li 李, with the given name of either Tan 聃 or Erh 耳. None of this can be historically documented, and indeed Ssu-ma Ch'ien's biography of Lao tzu contains virtually nothing that is demonstrably factual; we are left no choice but to acknowledge the likely fictional nature of the traditional Lao tzu figure.

According to widespread and enduring legend, seen already in the early portion of his *Shih chi* biography, Lao tzu is said to have been approached by Confucius, the latter seeking instruction on various points of 'ceremony' (*li* 禮). It has thus automatically been inferred that both Lao tzu the person and *Lao tzu* the text pre-date Confucius and the *Analects*. Stories following this model, of Confucius inquiring of Lao tzu about *li*, are found in, e.g., the *Li chi* ('Tseng tzu wen' 曾子問), elsewhere in the *Shih chi* (ch. 47, the 'K'ung tzu shih chia' 孔子世家), and in the *K'ung tzu chia yü*, all respectably ancient and venerable texts, but none significantly pre-Han in composition or provenance.

Slightly at variance with the theme of asking instruction in ceremony is the substance of an indirect encounter between Confucius and Lao tzu preserved in the *Chuang tzu* ('Te ch'ung fu' 德充符), where Lao tzu counsels a way of life that Confucius is portrayed as being too dim-witted to fathom. (See J. Boltz 1987a under (9) below, for a discussion of this aspect of Lao tzu lore.)

To assign authorship of the *Tao te ching* to Lao tzu is to say no more than that some respectable soul compiled, if not singly composed, the text. It says nothing about who that figure may have actually been, or when the compilation was achieved.

Ku Chieh-kang (1932) and D. C. Lau (1963/1982: Appendix I; see under 7(d) below) have both concluded on the basis of language, style, content, and the nature of apparent *Lao tzu* citations in other texts, that there is every reason to date the compilation of the work in its final form to the late third century B.C. Ku Chieh-kang shows in considerable detail the extent to which the *Lao tzu* text conforms to the language, terminology, and spirit of the *Lü shih ch'un ch'iu* and of the *Hsün tzu*, the compilation of both of which can be dated with confidence to the middle of the third century B.C. Ku proposes that the similarities between the *Lao tzu* and these two texts, rather than being due to borrowing in one direction or the other, are the result of the fact that all three texts arose and took shape at the same time, being products of the same intellectual milieu, breathing the same philosophical air, so to speak, and thus suffused with the same social and political concerns. He concludes that the *Lao tzu* is a *mixtum compositum* that reflects 300 or more years and many schools of intellectual and speculative thought, and that it was compiled in its final form in the period between the late third and early second centuries B.C. He arrives at this dating by noticing that, while the *Lü shih ch'un ch'iu* contains many passages similar to or identical with passages in the *Lao tzu*, it never cites the *Lao tzu* by name, whereas it regularly cites other texts by name when it quotes them. He takes this as an indication that while the textual substance of what was to be the *Lao tzu's* content was already well formed, the text called the *Lao tzu*, and attributed to a certain Lao Tan, was not yet established at the time of the compilation of the *Lü shih ch'un ch'iu*, which we know to have been *c.* 239 B.C.

The *Huai nan tzu*, in contrast to the *Lü shih ch'un ch'iu*, cites the *Lao tzu* text by name at least a dozen times, in passages nearly identical with the received text. This, Ku says, shows that by the time of the compilation of the *Huai nan tzu* in the second century B.C. the *Lao tzu* must have become an established text. Ku's conclusion is that the text of the *Lao tzu* was compiled in its final form in the second half of the third century B.C., and became widely circulated and well known in the second century B.C.

D.C. Lau for his part identifies the *Lao tzu* as a work that was compiled in a fixed form and associated with the person of Lao tzu only in the last quarter of the third century B.C., and is in origin no more than a 'collection of passages with only a common tendency in thought,' reflecting a genre of aphoristic and cryptic sayings of the preceding century or more, associated with legendary 'wise old man' figures, known sometimes as 'Lao Lai tzu' 老來子, 'Lao Ch'eng tzu' 老成子, or 'Cheng Chang che' 鄭長者 in addition to the sobriquet 'Lao tzu' (Lau 1963, pp. 133–134).

3. Principal transmitted versions and commentaries

(a) The Yen Tsun 嚴遵 version

The Yen Tsun version of the *Lao tzu* text originally accompanied the commentarial essay by Yen Tsun called [*Tao te*] *Chih kuei lun* 道德指歸論, and is now extant only for the *Te ching* part of the text. When we speak of the 'Yen Tsun version' or the 'Yen Tsun *Lao tzu*' we mean only that this is the text of the *Lao tzu* that has been transmitted together with the Yen Tsun essay *Tao te chih kuei lun*. We do not mean to imply, much less to claim, that Yen Tsun himself had any hand in editing the *Lao tzu* text, or in establishing the version that accompanies his *Chih kuei lun*.

Yen Tsun (*c.* 80 B.C.–*c.* A.D. 10), also known as Yen Chün-p'ing 嚴君平, was actually surnamed Chuang 莊, but Pan Ku 班固 (32–92) altered this to the synonymous Yen out of deference to Ming ti, whose given name (*ming* 名) was Chuang (*Han shu* 72, pp. 3056–3057). Thus, when the *Chih kuei lun* text says *Chuang tzu yüeh* 莊子曰 it is to be understood as Yen Tsun referring to himself, not as a reference to the well-known pre-Han text or (legendary) person of Chuang tzu.

Yen Tsun was a contemporary of Liu Hsiang 劉向 (79–8 B.C.), and probably used, Shima Kunio suspects (1973, p. 8), Liu's version of the *Lao tzu* text. Apart from short citations of the *Lao tzu* in other Former Han works, that of Yen Tsun can claim to be the earliest transmitted version of the *Tao te ching*.

There are now two different redactions of the *Chih kuei lun* extant: (i) the *Tao tsang* redaction (*HY** 693) which carries a commentary by a certain Ku Shen-tzu 谷神子, and (ii) one derived from Hu Chen-heng's 胡震亨 *Mi ts'e hui han* 秘冊彙函 redaction of the late Ming. Of the two, only the *Tao tsang* redaction includes the actual *Lao tzu* text; the Hu redaction, now found in the *Chin hsüeh t'ao yüan* 津學討原 collection of Chang Hai-p'eng 張海鵬 (1755–1815), lacks it. In addition to these two the *I lan t'ang ts'ung shu* 怡蘭堂叢書 (1922) includes a version copied by T'ang Hung-hsüeh 唐鴻學 (b. 1876) from a manuscript copy. Chu Ch'ien-chih 朱謙之 (1975, p. 1) suggests that this was the Ming manuscript of Yao Shun-tzu 姚舜咨. It is not clear how this version is related to the two redactions already mentioned, but Chu considers it superior to both of them, although he does not give any basis for this judgment.

Exactly when the *Tao ching* portion of Yen Tsun's work was lost is not known. Ch'ao Kung-wu's 晁公武 (d. 1171) notes in the *Ch'ün chai tu shu chih* (late twelfth century) suggest that the copy he saw in thirteen *chüan*, with the Ku Shen-tzu commentary, was complete. But the preface that Hu Chen-heng gives as that of Ku Shen-tzu says that the *Tao ching* part of the work was lost between the Ch'en and the Sui periods. This claim is suspect not only because Ch'ao Kung-wu makes no mention of the work being defective, but also because the relevant lines of the Ku Shen-tzu preface as given by Hu Chen-heng do not appear in the *Tao tsang* version of the same preface. It seems likely that the Yen Tsun version of the *Lao tzu* was wholly extant up to the end of the twelfth century, and that the *Tao ching* portion was lost sometime between 1200 and when the *Tao tsang* version was cut in 1445.

Ch'ao Kung-wu suspects that Ku Shen-tzu is in fact the person called Feng K'uo 馮廓, named in *Chiu T'ang shu* 47 (p. 2027) as the compiler (*chuan* 撰) of a *Tao te chih kuei lun* in thirteen *chüan*, the same number as

---

in the Ku Shen-tzu version. Modern scholarship has taken him to be Cheng Huan-ku 鄭還古 (*fl.* 827), the compiler of the *Po i chih* 博異志 and the *Tu tzu ch'un chuan* 杜子春傳, who gave himself the sobriquet (*hao* 號) 'Ku Shen-tzu'.

What we now have of the Yen Tsun *Lao tzu* varies significantly in a few places from the standard, received text, i.e., the Ho-shang Kung version (see (b) below), sometimes in ways matching extant Tun-huang manuscripts, other times matching the Ma-wang-tui silk manuscripts. There are a number of places where the section divisions of the Yen Tsun version vary from the standard, though the overall order of the text is the same. Ch'ao Kung-wu said that the *chang chü* (章句) varied noticeably from other versions, and gave as an example the fact that what are in most versions the final seventeen characters of ch. 22 are in the Yen Tsun version the opening passage of ch. 23. This is clearly a difference of section division rather than of wording, and it is not known if Ch'ao also had variation in wordings in mind when he said that the *chang chü* are often not the same as other versions. It does show, in relation to the date when the *Tao ching* part of the Yen Tsun text was lost, that that part must still have been extant *c.* 1200 since Ch'ao could cite ch. 22 and 23 from it. Robinet (1977, pp. 11–23) gives a thorough introduction to the content of the Yen Tsun commentary and its place in both Han and *Lao tzu* thought.

(b) The Ho-shang Kung 河上公 version

The Ho-shang Kung *Lao tzu* is the version that has been transmitted accompanying the Ho-shang Kung commentary. As with the Yen Tsun version, there is no suggestion that anyone named Ho-shang Kung had anything to do with the actual editing of the *Lao tzu* text. In fact the name Ho-shang Kung is, like the name Lao tzu, clearly fictional, and nothing is known about the real person responsible for the Ho-shang Kung commentary.

The transmitted Ho-shang Kung *Lao tzu* carries a preface attributed to Ko Hsüan 葛玄 (164–244), the substance of which is also found in the *Shen hsien chuan* 神仙傳 (attributed to Ko Hung 葛洪 (283–343), grand nephew of Ko Hsüan), which is the source for the well known legend surrounding the figure of Ho-shang Kung. He is said to have been a contemporary of Han Wen ti (r. 180–157 B.C.), and to have built a reed hut on the bank of a river (or the Yellow River) where he lived as a recluse, studying the *Tao te ching*. Officials from the court of Wen ti approached Ho-shang Kung with an invitation from the Emperor to come to court as an authority on the meaning of the *Lao tzu* text. Ho-shang Kung declined the invitation with a certain uncamouflaged aloofness, and is said to have been subsequently visited by Wen ti himself, who pressed the point with a combination of offers of wealth and status and hints that he who resists the wishes of his sovereign does so at his own peril. Ho-shang Kung is reputed then to have leapt into the air, faced Wen ti from a position suspended magically between heaven and earth, and asked rhetorically what use he could possibly have for the material trappings of wealth and position, so much a part of the confused mortal realm. Wen ti realized at once Ho-shang Kung's divine nature and humbled himself before him. As a result Ho-shang Kung is said to have prepared this commentary expressly for the Emperor.

Apart from this apocryphal account, there is no evidence for the existence of such a person, or of the commentary, at the time of Wen ti, or for that matter at any time before the fifth century A.D. If the Ko Hsüan preface and the *Shen hsien chuan* passage are genuine, it would mean that the commentary existed in the third century A.D. This would be consistent with the view suggested by Takeuchi Yoshio 武內義雄 (cited by Cheng Ch'eng-hai 1971, preface) to the effect that the Ho-shang Kung commentary, because of the nature of its content, finds its ideological origin in the 'metaphysical milieu' of Ko Hsüan and Ko Hung. Even if the Ko Hsüan preface and the *Shen hsien chuan* text are later compilations, spuriously attributed retroactively to Ko Hsüan and Ko Hung respectively, as is generally conceded, Takeuchi's opinion would still be a reasonable supposition. In surveying the same data, Pelliot concludes that the Ho-shang Kung commentary must be dated sometime between the third century A.D. and the early Sui (1912, p. 368).

The Ko Hsüan preface that regularly accompanies the Ho-shang Kung *Lao tzu* is a part of, but not the entirety of, the text known from later sources as the *Lao tzu tao te ching hsü chüeh* 老子道德經序訣 (*HY* 395). The portion of this latter work that attempts to establish a line of transmission of the *Lao tzu* associated with the Ling pao 靈寶 legacy, from Ko Hsüan through his disciple Cheng Ssu-yüan 鄭思遠 (Cheng Yin 鄭隱) to Ko Hung, is not included in the Ho-shang Kung preface. The *Lao tzu tao te ching hsü chüeh* is also attributed to Ko Hsüan, but clearly is not genuinely by him; see Ōfuchi 1978, pp. 246–250.

E. Erkes (1950) claims that the Ho-shang Kung commentary must have been known to Kao Yu 高誘 (*c.* 168–212) because of similarities with parts of the latter's commentary to the *Huai nan tzu*. While this is theoretically possible, the similarities are more curious than definitive, and may arise from the fact that both commentaries reflect the same 'metaphysical milieu' referred to above, that characterized these centuries. (See Hung 1957, fn. 76.)

The commentary is directly attested in the extant written record first in the note in *Sui shu* 34, p. 1000, which enters two relevant items: (i) a *Ho-shang Kung chu Lao tzu* 河上公注老子 said to be from the time of Han Wen ti, clearly a reflection of the account involving Wen ti in Ko Hsüan's preface, and (ii) a *Ho-shang Chang-jen chu Lao tzu* 河上丈人注老子 of the Warring States period, in 2 *chüan*. This second item is said to be from one of the now lost bibliographical records of the Liang (early sixth century), on which the *Sui shu* 'Ching chi chih' drew. The designation Ho-shang Chang-jen 'the senior person of the riverside' is usually taken as an alternative reference to Ho-shang Kung. The same sobriquet occurs in Ssu-ma Ch'ien's personal note to *Shih chi* 80, p. 2436, where he traces the lineage of teachers of Yüeh Ch'en-kung 樂臣公, an individual said to have been well versed in the teachings of Huang ti and Lao tzu, to a Ho-shang Chang-jen, about whose origins Ssu-ma Ch'ien then says he knows nothing (*pu chih ch'i so ch'u* 不知其所出; *Shih chi* 80, p. 2436.) The likeliest explanation for these facts seems to be that there was a Han-time tradition of a reclusive figure, here named Ho-shang Chang-jen, who was well versed in Huang-Lao teachings, and that, when the Ho-shang Kung commentary was compiled in the period between the end of the Han and the reunification of the Sui, that tradition and that figure, under the slightly altered name of Ho-shang Kung, came to be associated with this commentary.

Shima Kunio (1973, pp. 25–26, summarized in Herforth 1989 [1980]) argues that the Ho-shang Kung commentary can be no earlier than the late fifth century because it refers to other *Lao tzu* commentaries, including the work of Ku Huan 顧歡 (390–453). By the same token, Huang K'an 皇侃 (488–545) cites the Ho-shang Kung commentary in his *Lun yü i shu* 論語義疏, so the text must have existed by that time. Shima concludes that the Ho-shang Kung commentary must have been compiled sometime between the end of the fifth and the early part of the sixth centuries. He considers the Ko Hsüan account, in both of its versions, as a later, fictional, creation, not really by either Ko Hsüan or Ko Hung. William Hung takes the same sceptical position in regard to the composition of the Ko Hsüan preface (1957, fn. 76).

Whether the Ho-shang Kung commentary dates from as early as A.D. 300 or as late as A.D. 500, it was by A.D. 700 very much the predominant commentary to the *Lao tzu* text. The outcome of what William Hung has called the 'bibliographic controversy' at the T'ang court shows clearly that the Ho-shang Kung *Lao tzu* enjoyed a favoured status in comparison with the Wang Pi 王弼 version (see below).

The most important consequence of this predominance is that the text of the *Lao tzu* proper that was transmitted with the Ho-shang Kung commentary had a considerable influence on the *Lao tzu* text that accompanied the Wang Pi commentary as well, to the point where one can say that the *textus receptus* of the·Wang Pi *Lao tzu* is in fact a version of the Ho-shang Kung line of transmission, and could not have been the version that Wang Pi had to hand and commented upon. This has been shown in Shima 1973, W. Boltz 1985, and most fully in Wagner 1989. Even though the Wang Pi and Ho-shang Kung commentaries are very different from each other, the *Lao tzu* texts accompanying them are very similar, and can both be considered exemplars of the Ho-shang Kung *Lao tzu*. The import of this is that the current received text of the *Lao tzu* is, irrespective of whether we are referring to a Ho-shang Kung version or to a Wang Pi version, essentially the Ho-shang Kung *Lao tzu*.

The Ho-shang Kung commentary typically approaches the *Lao tzu* text as a kind of manual of conduct, both personal and political, the goal of which is, in part at least, the good order and longevity of the person and the state alike. It gives to each chapter of the *Lao tzu* a title that suggests the particular practice with which the chapter is ostensibly concerned; e.g., ch. 1 is called 'T'i tao' 體道 'Embodying the Tao'; ch. 2 is called 'Yang shen' 養身 'Nurturing the self'. The commentary then proceeds to interpret the text of each chapter in a way consistent with the title given it, and with the practice in question. At the same time the commentary suggests *inter alia* that these practices have the capacity to bring stability and longevity to the state, when adopted by the ruler, just as to the individual. (See Robinet 1977, pp. 30–31.)

Cheng Ch'eng-hai (1971), who has made a very thorough text critical study of the Ho-shang Kung *Lao tzu* text and commentary, collating all available versions of the text, including the several Stein and Pelliot manuscripts from Tun-huang, says that in his opinion the Sung Chien-an Yü shih chia shu 宋建安虞氏家塾 edition is, of all transmitted versions, the least beset with corruptions and errors. Wang Chung-min 王重民 expresses the same judgment (1979 [1958], p. 233). This edition is reproduced in facsimile in the *Ssu pu ts'ung k'an*, and in Yen Ling-feng's 嚴靈峯 *Wu ch'iu pei chai Lao tzu chi ch'eng* 無求備齋老子集成. Cheng lists altogether 33 versions of the text that he has consulted.

No critical edition of the Ho-shang Kung *Lao tzu* has yet been established, so it is impossible to single out any one version as the 'best' in any meaningful sense. Shima Kunio and Cheng Ch'eng-hai in the studies referred to above both discuss the various extant versions. For descriptive and collation notes on the various Tun-huang manuscripts of the Ho-shang Kung *Lao tzu* see the Cheng and Wang works just mentioned. For a review, and additional notes, of Cheng's study of the Ho-shang Kung text, see Kusuyama 1972.

(c) The Wang Pi 王弼 version

Unlike the circumstances of the Ho-shang Kung commentary, there is no doubt that the Wang Pi commentary is the work of the famous and precocious third century scholar Wang Pi (226–249), best known perhaps for his commentary to the *I ching*, and one of the most important figures of the post-Han intellectual milieu. Where the Ho-shang Kung commentary was written in a simple and straightforward everyday language and was concerned with physical techniques and practices designed to explain the *Lao tzu* as a guide to the good order and longevity of the self and the state alike, the Wang Pi commentary is altogether intellectual, interpretive, and scholarly, having been written in a sophisticated and learned style from the perspective of a distinct Juist orthodoxy.

The current received version of the Wang Pi *Lao tzu* is traceable no earlier than to its *Tao tsang* version (1445, *HY* 690). As noted above, the most important feature to recognize about this text is that it is in all likelihood not the text that originally accompanied the Wang Pi commentary, or the one that Wang Pi had before him.

There seems to have been a kind of competition between the Wang Pi and the Ho-shang Kung commentaries not just at the court of T'ang Hsüan tsung, but in general ever since the latter first appeared. The Ho-shang Kung commentary seems always to have been predominant in that competition overall, probably because of its simple language on the one hand and its overtly religious character on the other. The Wang Pi commentary seems to have had a somewhat less popular appeal thanks to the refinement and literary elegance of its language and to the abstruse and intellectual nature of its content. Even so, the Wang Pi commentary has always had a following of highly regarded partisans and defenders, from Lu Te-ming 陸德明 (556–627) to Liu Chih-chi 劉知幾 (661–721) (see Hung 1957), to Yao Nai 姚鼐 (1732–1815) and Ma Hsü-lun 馬敘倫 (1884–1970) (see Ma 1924).

The most important modern studies of Wang Pi and of the Wang Pi *Lao tzu* are those by Rudolf Wagner (1986 and 1989) and Hatano Tarō 波多野太郎 (1953–54) and (1959). In the first of his two articles Wagner shows that the anonymously transmitted *Lao tzu wei chih li lüeh* 老子微指例略 (*Tao tsang, HY* 1245) is the work of Wang Pi, and he gives a full translation of that text. In the latter article he demonstrates, as we have mentioned, that the *Lao tzu* text transmitted along with the Wang Pi commentary is not Wang Pi's original *Lao tzu* text, but is instead a version of the *Lao tzu* very closely allied with the Ho-shang Kung version. Wagner also shows that, of all extant versions of the *Lao tzu*, the text most likely to represent the one on which Wang Pi based his commentary, and that we could therefore call the original Wang Pi text, is the version that has since the Sung dynasty been known as the *Ku pen Lao tzu* 古本老子 (on which see immediately below). Hatano 1953–54 is essentially a *variorum* study of the Wang Pi *Lao tzu*; the 1959 article is a supplement to that study.

For a discussion of Wang Pi's own intellectual and philosophical inclinations, and of the related third century school of *hsüan hsüeh* 玄學, see Robinet 1977, pp. 56–76. For a translation of the received Wang Pi *Lao tzu* and Wang Pi's commentary see Lin 1977 (see under 7(f) below; this item is not a textually critical or rigorous study or translation.)

(d) The *Ku pen* 古本 version

There are two distinct, but closely related, redactions of the so-called *Ku pen* 'old text' *Lao tzu*, (i) one as edited and established by Fu I 傅奕 (*c.* 558–*c.* 639) of the T'ang, and (ii) the other as edited and established by Fan Ying-yüan 范應元 (Sung period).

(i) The Fu I *Ku pen* redaction

Fu I served as *T'ai shih ling* 太史令 'Grand Astrologer' in the early T'ang court. He had a reputation for being avidly interested in the *Lao tzu* text, and is reported to have gathered as many different versions of the text as he could. Hsieh Shou-hao 謝守灝 (1134–1212) registered in his *Hun yüan sheng chi* 混元聖紀 (*Tao tsang*, HY 769, on which see J. Boltz 1987b, pp. 133–134) that among the versions of the *Lao tzu* text to which Fu I had access there was one which was reputed to have come from the tomb of Hsiang Yü's 項羽 consort, which had been opened in 574. Hsiang Yü died in 202 b.c., and it is likely that his consort died before him, otherwise she would probably not have had a tomb of any note. Thus, if we can trust Hsieh Shou-hao's report, Fu I would have had access to a manuscript copy of the *Lao tzu* likely dating from slightly before 200 b.c., and clearly a version of inestimable value in establishing a critical edition.

The Fu I text is preserved in the *Tao tsang* as HY 665, and is reproduced in facsimile in Yen Ling-feng's *Wu ch'iu pei chai Lao tzu chi ch'eng*, first series, volume 17. Pi Yüan 畢沅 (1730–1797) relied on the Fu I text heavily in the course of preparing his *Tao te ching k'ao i* 道德經考異.

(ii) The Fan Ying-yüan *Ku pen* redaction

In the Sung dynasty Fu I's *Ku pen Lao tzu* was edited anew by Fan Ying-yüan, a person sometimes described as a 'Taoist master' (*tao shih* 道士), but otherwise an obscure figure about whom little is known. The opening page of Fan's redaction of the *Ku pen Lao tzu* identifies him as the 'former Instructor-in-charge at the Yü-lung Wan-shou temple' (前玉隆萬壽宮掌教), the 'Senior Lecturer of the Shou-ning Abbey at Nan yüeh (Heng shan)' (南岳壽寧觀長講). Fan provides his redaction with collation notes and exegetic comments in connection with the Yen Tsun, Wang Pi, Ho-shang Kung, and Fu I versions of the text, as well as notes reflecting other, later commentators, including Liang Chien-wen Ti 梁簡文帝 (503–551), Lu Te-ming, Ch'eng Hsüan-ying 成玄英 (*fl.* 630–660), and Su Ch'e 蘇轍 (1039–1112), and entitles it *Lao tzu tao te ching ku pen chi chu* 老子道德經古本集注.

Fan's redaction of the *Ku pen Lao tzu* differs from the Fu I *Ku pen* text in about one hundred places, according to Wagner's study (1989 p. 37). At least one of the reasons that Fan's version differs from Fu I's is that Fan uncritically adopted a number of Hsüan tsung's idiosyncratic emendations to the text. (See, e.g., Chu 1975, 1 for an example from ch. 20.) In spite of these differences between the two *Ku pen* versions, Wagner correctly observes that 'their common deviation against other extant texts is substantially higher [in number of variants, than between each other]'. These two exemplars, in other words, define a single line of transmission distinct from all others.

Fan's *Ku pen Lao tzu* was published by the Han fen lou 涵芬樓 library of rare books in volume 17 of the *Hsü ku i ts'ung shu*. This text was based on the Sung woodblock print that was in the Chiang-an Fu-shih Shuang chien lou 江安傅氏雙鑑樓 collection, i.e., the personal library of Fu Tseng-hsiang 傅增湘 (1872–1949), who is known to have provided a number of rare Sung and Yüan woodblock prints to the Han fen lou for facsimile reproduction in the early part of this century.

The text of Fan's *Ku pen Lao tzu* is not included in the *Tao tsang*. For a facsimile of the *Hsü ku i ts'ung shu* copy see *Wu ch'iu pei chai Lao tzu chi ch'eng*, vol. 59. Apart from Wagner's study discussed above, identifying the *Ku pen Lao tzu* with the original Wang Pi text, the fullest modern study of the *Ku pen* version is Lao Chien 1941.

(e) The T'ang *yü chu* 唐御注 'Imperial commentary' version

The so-called 'bibliographic controversy' at the court of T'ang Hsüan tsung (see Hung 1957) involved, among other classics, a competition between the Wang Pi *Lao tzu* and the Ho-shang Kung *Lao tzu* commentaries. Because there was no clear-cut basis established at the termination of the debate for choosing between these two, Hsüan tsung opted to produce his own commentary and sub-commentary (*shu* 疏). These were published in 735. At the same time he established an 'edited' version of the *Lao tzu* text, based largely on his personal choice of readings from either the Ho-shang Kung version or the *Hsiang erh* 想爾 version (on which see below). Because his text was not critically established in any scholarly way, and combines readings capriciously from other versions, it has no independent value for the establishment of a critical edition (Shima 1973, summarized in Herforth 1989 [1980], p. 19). Still, because of the nature and stature of the source of the Imperial commentary, Hsüan tsung's *Lao tzu* supplanted both the Wang Pi and Ho-shang Kung versions for T'ang civil service examination purposes, and to a considerable general extent as well (Hung 1957, n. 146).

To enforce his order that the *yü chu Lao tzu* should be the version of choice Hsüan tsung had both text and commentary inscribed on an eight-sided stone *ch'uang* 幢 in 738, erected in front of the Lung hsing kuan 龍興觀 of I chou 易州 (not to be confused with the *pei* 碑 of 708 found at the same site which carried only the *Lao tzu* text proper, nor with the *ch'uang* carrying both the *Lao tzu* text and the Imperial commentary, erected in 739 at the Lung hsing kuan of Hsing chou 邢州). Good quality photographs of the texts of these stone inscriptions can be found in Ho 1936. (See 5, nos. 2 and 3 below.)

Both Hsüan tsung's *Lao tzu yü chu* and his *shu* 'sub-commentary' are found in the *Tao tsang*, HY 677 and 678/679, respectively.

These are the five principal transmitted textual versions of the *Lao tzu* proper; innumerable notes, commentaries, and interpretive textual studies of all kinds have accrued to the text from as early as the Han dynasty. Most important of these early works are the two sections of the *Han fei tzu* known as 'Chieh Lao' 解老 and 'Yü Lao' 喻老 (sections 20 and 21, in chapters 6 and 7 respectively) that give exegetic notes to numerous lines from the *Lao tzu*. As early as the Later Han the *Lao tzu* seems to have become a fundamental part of the sacred canon of Taoism, a status it continues to enjoy today. During the reigns of T'ang Hsüan tsung and Sung Hui tsung the *Lao tzu* was, with Taoism in general, especially predominant. Those two periods produced many important works that bear on the *Lao tzu*, but they are generally more pertinent to the social, literary, political, and religious environment out of which they arose than they are to the *Lao tzu* text itself. For a survey of these materials from the Sung on, see J. Boltz 1987b, pp. 214–228.

4. Manuscript versions

Extant *Lao tzu* manuscripts fall into two categories: (a) Tun-huang manuscripts, and (b) the early Han silk manuscripts, commonly known as
the Ma-wang-tui manuscripts.

(a) Tun-huang manuscripts

There are at least fifty-three identified Tun-huang manuscripts of the
Lao tzu, in varying degrees of completeness. Twenty-five of them are
'Pelliot' manuscripts (abbreviated P.), now in the Bibliothèque Natio-
nale. These are:

> P.2255, P.2329, P.2347, P.2350, P.2370, P.2375, P.2417, P.2420, P.2421,
> P.2435, P.2517, P.2577, P.2584, P.2594, P.2599, P.2639, P.2735, P.2823,
> P.2864, P.3235, P.3237, P.3277, P.3592, P.3725, and P.3864.

Descriptions of individual manuscripts are given in the *Catalogue des
manuscrits chinois de Touen-houang* (Fonds Pelliot chinois), vol. 1: nos.
2001–2500 (1970); vol. 3: nos. 3001–3500 (1983); and vol. 4: nos. 3501–4000
(1991). (Vol. 2: nos. 2501–3000 has not yet [early 1992] appeared.)

Fifteen of the fifty-three are 'Stein' manuscripts (abbreviated S.), now
in the Oriental and India Office Collections division of the British Library. Publication of high quality photographic reproductions is being
undertaken jointly by the British Library and the Ssu-ch'uan jen min
ch'u pan she. *Lao tzu* Stein manuscripts are:

> S.189, S.477, S.602, S.783, S.792, S.798, S.2060, S.2267, S.3926, S.4365,
> S.4430, S.4681, S.5920, S.6453, and S.6825.

Descriptions of these Stein manuscripts are found in Giles 1957.

The remaining known *Lao tzu* Tun-huang manuscripts are found in
various private and public libraries and collections, mainly in China,
Hong Kong, Japan, and Russia.

The Tun-huang *Lao tzu* manuscripts are sometimes treated as a group,
as if they collectively represent a single textual line of transmission.
They are actually no more than several centuries worth of accumulated
copies, of disparate origin and purpose, that happened to be coffered in
the Tun-huang grottos. Still, because many of them date from before the
time of Hsüan tsung, they often represent a stage of the transmission of
the text that was free of post-T'ang emendations and corruptions. Thus,
they show occasional curious, but as a group fortuitous, matches with
one or another of the less common versions of the *Lao tzu*; e.g., the *Ku
pen* text or the Ma-wang-tui manuscripts.

Cheng Liang-shu 鄭良樹 (1987) concludes that the Tun-huang *Lao tzu* manuscripts as a whole do not follow any consistent textual pattern, but in small sub-groups they often show an affinity with one or another of the identifiable versions. A much earlier, but still important, textual study of pre-T'ang and T'ang *Lao tzu* manuscripts from Tun-huang is T'ang Wen-po 唐文播 (1944), which examines twelve of the Pelliot *Lao tzu* manuscripts, and tries to establish their relation to known transmitted versions. The best work on *Lao tzu* manuscripts from Tun-huang that are not included in either the Stein or Pelliot collections is Lo Chen-yü's 羅振玉 two-part study of 1921, *Tao te ching k'ao i* 道德經考異 and *Lao tzu k'ao i pu i* 老子考異補遺, in which he identifies and discusses variant readings in ten pre-T'ang and T'ang manuscripts and in four T'ang stone inscription versions (Lo 1921). Ōfuchi Ninji 大淵忍爾 has published detailed textual notes, including collation notes, and photographic reproductions, for nearly all of the Tun-huang 'Taoist' texts, including the *Lao tzu* manuscripts (Ōfuchi 1978). In this work he treats all of the Stein and most of the Pelliot manuscripts listed above, as well as numerous Tun-huang *Lao tzu* manuscript fragments from other collections.

Two Tun-huang manuscripts of the *Lao tzu* call for special comment:

(i) The So Tan 索紞 *Lao tzu* (sometimes read Su Tan)
    This manuscript has a colophon in the hand of the original scribe, a certain So Tan, who was a member of a well-known clan of scholars in the Tun-huang area in the third century (biography in *Chin shu* 95). The colophon is dated *Chien heng erh nien keng yen wu yüeh wu jih* 建衡二年庚寅五月五日 corresponding to 10 June A.D. 270, and says that this copy was made by So Tan at Tun-huang. This makes the So Tan *Lao tzu* the oldest of all of the Tun-huang manuscripts of any kind, as far as is known. The text of the manuscript is incomplete, beginning in the middle of ch. 51 and extending to the end of the work; thus comprising about three-fourths of the *Te ching* section, and including none of the *Tao ching*.

    The manuscript was recovered from Tun-huang by an official of the Ch'ing Ministry of Education sometime after Stein and Pelliot had already removed their materials out of China. It was taken to Peking where it passed from private owner to private owner. It was for a time in the Yurin-kan 有鄰館 collection of the Fujii Saisei 藤井齋成會 Association in Kyoto, and later came into the possession of Chang Ku-ch'u 張谷雛 who made it available to Jao Tsung-i 饒宗頤 for a complete study (Jao 1955). Sometime prior to April, 1986, it was turned over to the custody of Princeton University, and placed on long-term loan in the University Art Museum there (Mote 1986).

    Jao's 1955 study includes a good quality photographic reproduction of the whole manuscript. He concludes that the work is in the 'Ho-shang Kung tradition', based on the manuscript's agreement with five of eight citations of the Ho-shang Kung text given in Lu Te-ming's *Ching tien shih wen*.

(ii) The Hsiang erh chu 想爾注 *Lao tzu*

The Hsiang erh chu *Lao tzu* (S.6825) consists of all of the *Tao ching* portion of the work, save for the first two and a half *chang* (章) which are missing through damage at the beginning of the document. It ends with ch. 37, i.e., the end of the *Tao ching*. It does not include any of the *Te ching*.

The Hsiang erh chu *Lao tzu* is well-known and widely studied not primarily because of its *Lao tzu* text proper, though that also has its interesting points, but because of its lengthy commentary, which is directly associated with Chang Tao-ling 張道陵, Chang Lu 張魯, and the founding of the Way of the Celestial Masters (*t'ien shih tao* 天師道) in the second century A.D. It is at the same time, and for related reasons, closely allied with those versions of the *Lao tzu* text said to total exactly 5000 characters. (Transmitted versions of the *Lao tzu* typically exceed this figure by about 10%.)

As with the So Tan *Lao tzu*, the fullest textual study of the Hsiang erh chu *Lao tzu* is by Jao Tsung-i (Jao 1956, with a subsequent study in 1969). It has also been the subject of major studies by Ch'en Shih-hsiang (1957) and Fukui Kōjun (1967). (See also Boltz 1982, which writes 相爾 erroneously for 想爾 throughout.) A very useful concordance of the Hsiang erh chu *Lao tzu* text and commentary together has been prepared by Mugitani Kunio (1985; see under 6(a) below). For a full discussion of the text, including other Tun-huang manuscripts of the *Lao tzu* that seem to fall into the Hsiang erh textual tradition, and an explanation of the name 'Hsiang erh' see Shima 1973: 11–24.

(b) The Ma-wang-tui 馬王堆 manuscripts

Two virtually complete manuscript copies of the *Lao tzu*, written on pieces of silk that also contain other so-called 'Taoist', or 'Huang-Lao' texts, were among the 1973 finds from Ma-wang-tui (Hu-nan province). They both suffer from damage to the fabric in numerous places, but are still remarkable textual finds of inestimable value for the study of the *Lao tzu*. These manuscripts have come to be known collectively as the Ma-wang-tui manuscripts, and as the *chia* 甲, or 'A', and *i* 乙, or 'B' manuscripts individually.

On the basis primarily of the use or avoidance of certain characters appearing in the names of the first few Former Han emperors, the A and B manuscripts can be dated to about the first and third decades of the second century B.C., respectively. Both must ante-date 168 B.C., since that is the year when the tomb in which they were found is known to have been closed. The calligraphic style of each manuscript is consistent with these dates; the A manuscript is written in a style of script that seems to be transitional between the earlier *hsiao chuan* 'small seal' script and later *li shu* 'clerical script', while the B manuscript is written in a typical *li shu* form.

The texts of the two Ma-wang-tui *Lao tzu* manuscripts both put the *Te ching* section first and the *Tao ching* section second, the reverse of the order in all other known versions, transmitted and manuscript alike. In other respects the texts of the two manuscripts are not identical with each other, but are closer to each other than either one is to any other textual lineage or tradition. This would suggest that they represent a genuine textual lineage, rather than being just an isolated textual anomaly. In any case, the richness of the data that they provide calls for a thorough and rigorous text critical study, a task still (early 1992) awaiting attention.

The original announcement of the Ma-wang-tui manuscript finds, together with preliminary discussions and transcriptions, can be found in Hu-nan sheng po-wu-kuan 1974, Hsiao Han 1974, T'ang Lan 1974, and Kao Heng and Ch'ih Hsi-chao 1974. Complete photographic facsimile reproductions, revised transcriptions, and textual notes, are found in Kuo-chia wen-wu chü, Ku wen-hsien yen-chiu shih 1980. Major western studies and translations (marked 'tr.') include Henricks 1980, 1989 (tr.), Lau 1982 (tr.; see Under 7(c) and (d) below), and Boltz 1984.

5. Stone inscriptions

There are eleven important completely or partially extant stone inscription texts of the *Lao tzu*, dating from the early T'ang to the Yüan. The single fullest and most detailed modern study of these is the work published in 1936 by the K'ao ku tsu of the Shih hsüeh yen chiu hui (Kuo li Pei-p'ing yen chiu yüan). While no author is identified as such in this work, the preface is signed by Ho Shih-chi 何士驥, and the work is entered in (9) below under this name. This work is in three volumes, the third consisting of good quality photographic reproductions of all eleven texts. In addition to introductory facts about each inscription, the first two volumes give complete collations of the texts of each one, taking the Wang Pi *Lao tzu* as the standard against which variation is noted. The data given in the summaries below are based on this work, supplemented occasionally by the notes in Chiang 1937 and Chu 1975.

The eleven inscription texts of the *Lao tzu*, in chronological order, are as follows:

1. The I lung 易龍 stele, dated Ching lung 2 (708), located at the Lung hsing 龍興 abbey of I hsien 易縣 (Ho-pei). Complete; also known as the Ching lung 景龍 stele, and the Lung hsing kuan 龍興觀 stele. This last name is not recommended because of the potential for confusion with the next two. Shima Kunio (1973, *passim*) considers this to belong to the Hsiang erh textual tradition; included in Lo 1921.

2. The I hsüan 易玄 eight-sided stele, dated K'ai yüan 26 (738), located at the same Lung hsing abbey as the preceding; complete. This inscription reflects the T'ang Hsüan tsung, i.e., the Imperial, version of the text. It is also known as the Imperial text stele, and as the K'ai yüan stele. These alternative names could also apply to the next item, but in practice they do not; included in Lo 1921.

3. The Hsing hsüan 邢玄 eight-sided stele, dated K'ai yüan 27 (739), located at the Lung hsing abbey in Hsing t'ai 邢台 (Ho-pei); not complete. The text of this inscription is, like the preceding item, that of T'ang Hsüan tsung.

4. The Chiao shan 焦山 eight-sided stele, dated Kuang ming 1 (880), located at Chiao shan 焦山, Chen-chiang 鎮江 (Chiang-su); very defective. Also known as the Kuang ming stele; included in Lo 1921.

5. The I fu 易福 stele, dated Ching fu 2 (893), located at the Lung hsing abbey in I hsien (Ho-pei); defective. Also known as the Ching fu 景福 stele. Shima (1973, passim) classes this as a text in the Ho-shang Kung tradition; included in Lo 1921.

6. The Ch'ing yang 慶陽 eight-sided stele, dated Ching yu 4 (1037), located at the T'ien chen 天眞 abbey in Ch'ing yang 慶陽 (Kan-su); quite defective.

7. The Hang chou 杭州 eight-sided stele, date obliterated, but known to be a Sung inscription, carrying the version of the *Lao tzu* established by Sung Kao tsung. Located in Hang-chou (Che-chiang) at the Wu shan ch'ung i tz'u 吳山崇義祠; very incomplete, preserving little more than 100 characters.

8. The Lou ku 樓古 stele, dated Chih yüan 27 (1290), located at the Lou kuan t'ai 樓觀臺 (the Shuo ching t'ai 說經臺), in Chou-chih 盩厔 (Shen-si); complete. Calligraphy by Kao Tao 高翿, therefore also known as the Kao Tao stele, or just the Kao stele.

9. The Pan-hsi 蟠溪 eight-sided stele, dated Ta te 3 (1299), located at the Pan-hsi temple in Pao chi 寶雞 (Shen-si); complete.

10. The Chao Meng-fu 趙孟頫 incised stones, dated Yen yu 3 (1316); a set of ten stones said to have been set up at the Pai yün kuan 白雲觀 Taoist abbey in Peking. Complete; carved in the calligraphic style of Chao Meng-fu (1254–1322).

11. The Lou cheng 樓正 stele, undated, said by Wang Yen 王言 in his *Chin shih ts'ui pien pu lüeh* 金石萃編補略 (1882, see Chu 1975:1) to be a T'ang inscription, but dated to the Yüan in Ho 1936; located at the Lou kuan t'ai 樓觀臺 in Chou chih hsien (Shen-si); complete.

The locations given above for the various stelae are the original sites, but they may not match present locations. Apart from these eleven items, Lu Kung 路工 (1981) reports the discovery in 1962 of a rubbing from a stone inscription of the *Lao tzu* text edited by Yü Shih-nan 虞世南 (558–638) on instructions from T'ang T'ai tsung (r. 627–649). This text thus ante-dates the earliest of the extant stone inscription texts by almost a century. Yü's own preface to the text states that he based his edition on the Wang Pi version, taking into account variants in the Ho-shang Kung version and in the 'Chieh *Lao*' and 'Yü *Lao*' sections of the *Han fei tzu*.

6. Reference works

(a) Mugitani Kunio 麥谷邦夫. 1985. *Rōshi Sōjichū sakuin* 老子想爾注索引. Kyoto: Hōyū shoten.

(b) Müller, C.C., and R.G. Wagner, editors. 1968. *Konkordanz zum Lao-tzu*. Publikationen der Fachschaft Sinologie München No. 19. Munich: Fachschaft des Seminars für Ostasiatische Sprache- und Kulturwissenschaft der Universität München.

(c) *Rōshi sakuin* 老子索引. Kyōtō Daigaku Jimbun kagaku kenkyūjo 京都大學人文科學研究所, Koten no kōchū to sakuin hensan-ban 古典の校注と索引編纂班, preface dated 25 October 1950; a concordance in the fashion of the Harvard-Yenching Institute concordance series, with indexes arranged according to pronunciation (separately by Wade-Giles and *chu yin fu-hao*), and by total stroke count.

(d) Ts'ai T'ing-kan 蔡廷幹. 1922. *Lao tzu, Tao te ching* 老子道德經. N.p. Running title: *Lao chieh Lao* 老解老; a concordance to the *Lao tzu* text.

(e) Wang Chung-min 王重民. 1927. *Lao tzu k'ao* 老子考, 2 volumes. Peking: Chung hua t'u shu kuan hsieh hui 中華圖書館協會; the most replete catalogue of works on the *Lao tzu* yet; modelled on Chu I-tsun's 朱彝尊 (1629–1709) *Ching i k'ao* 經義考. Volume 1 covers the period from the earliest notices of the text through the Sung, volume 2 from the Yüan through the twentieth century.

(f) Yamamuro Saburō 山室三良 and Hikita Keiyu 疋田啓佑. *Rōshi mokuroku* 老子目錄. Kyūshu Daigaku bungaku-bu, Chūgoku tetsu-gaku kenkyū shitsu-nai: Chūgoku no shisō to bunka no kai 九州大學文學部中國哲學研究室內中國の思想と文化の會, no. 2. n.d.

(g) Yen Ling-feng 嚴靈峯. 1957. *Chung wai Lao tzu chu shu mu lu* 中外老子著述目錄. Taipei: Chung-hua ts'ung shu 中華叢書; this is a very useful bibliography, arranged in three parts: (i) textual notes and exegeses, (ii) essays and studies, and (iii) studies by foreign scholars.

(h) Yen Ling-feng. 1965a. *Lao, Lieh, Chuang san tzu chih chien shu mu* 老列莊三子知見書目, 3 volumes. Taipei: Chung-hua ts'ung shu. Volume 1 contains the bibliographic material for the *Lao tzu*; it largely supersedes the previous item.

(i) Yen Ling-feng. 1965b. *Wu ch'iu pei chai Lao tzu chi ch'eng ch'u pien* 無求備齋老子集成初編. Pan-ch'iao (Taiwan): I-wen; this collection, in 160 volumes (*ts'e* 冊), includes both essays on various aspects of the *Lao tzu* text, usually on specific versions of the text, by Yen Ling-feng, and reproductions of numerous copies of the *Lao tzu*, representing all of the transmitted versions.

(j) Yen Ling-feng. 1965c. *Wu ch'iu pei chai Lao tzu chi ch'eng hsü pien* 無求備齋老子集成續編. Pan-ch'iao (Taiwan): I-wen; in 280 volumes; supplements the preceding, and collects together Ch'ing, Republic, and Japanese works on the *Lao tzu*.

7. Translations

The *Lao tzu*, as is widely known, has been translated into Western languages innumerable times. It is neither feasible nor necessary to try to give anything approaching a comprehensive list of translations here. New translations, often recreational rather than scholarly, issue regularly from both the commercial and academic publishing houses of the day. For some sense of the varieties of recent translations available, and how they might be viewed, the reader is referred to the review article by Stephen Durrant, 'Packaging the *Tao*', *Rocky Mountain Review of Language and Literature* 45.1–2 (1991), pp. 75–84. The few items listed here are either well-known classics, useful recent translations, or works that are under reference above.

(a) Chan, Wing-tsit. 1963. *The Way of Lao tzu*. Indianapolis & N.Y.: Bobbs-Merrill Co., Inc.; well annotated.

(b) Chen, Ellen M. 1989. *The Tao Te Ching, A New Translation with Commentary*. N.Y.: Paragon House; annotated, with interpretive essays on various aspects of the work.

(c) Henricks, Robert G. 1989 *Lao-tzu, Te-tao ching*. N.Y.: Ballantine Books; well annotated; based on the Ma-wang-tui manuscripts, which reverse the traditional *Tao ching—Te ching* order, hence the title. This and the D.C. Lau translation (item (d) immediately below) are the only two serious attempts yet (early 1992) to translate the text in the light of these early Han manuscripts.

(d) Lau, D.C. 1963/1982 *Chinese Classics, Tao Te Ching*. Hong Kong: The Chinese University Press. Part I of this is a very slightly revised reprinting of the author's 1963 translation of the transmitted text; part II is his translation of a conflated version of the two Ma-wang-tui manuscripts. See the comment under (c) above.

(e) Legge, James. 1891 *The Texts of Taoism, the Tao Te ching*. Oxford: Oxford University Press. Reprints: N.Y.: The Julian Press, 1959, and in the series *The Sacred Books of the East*, Delhi: Motilal Banarsidass, 1966.

(f) Lin, Paul J. 1977 *A Translation of Lao tzu's* Tao Te Ching *and Wang Pi's Commentary*. Michigan Papers in Chinese Studies, no. 30. Ann Arbor: The University of Michigan Center for Chinese Studies; to be used with caution.

(g) Waley, Arthur. 1934 *The Way and Its Power*. London: George Allen & Unwin; reprint: N.Y.: Grove Press (Evergreen Book), 1958.

8. Japanese editions

A. *Kambun taikei*; no. 9, 1911, edited by Hattori Unokichi.
B. *Kanseki kokujikai zensho*; no. 9, 1910, edited by Yamamoto Tōun.
D. *Kokuyaku kambun taisei*; no. 7, 1920, edited by Kimida Rentarō.
E. *Kambun sōsho*, 1928.
F. *Keisho taikō*; no. 9, 1938.
H. *Shinshaku kambun taikei*; no. 7, 1966, edited by Abe Yoshio, Yamamoto Toshio, Ichikawa Yasuji, and Endō Tetsuo.
J. *Chūgoku no shisō*; no. 6, 1964, edited by Okudaira Takashi and Ōmura Masuo.
K. *Chūgoku koten bungaku taikei*; no. 4, 1973, edited by Kanaya Osamu.
L. *Chūgoku koten shinsho*, 1967, edited by Yamamuro Saburō.
M. *Shintei Chūgoku koten sen*; no. 6, 1968, edited by Fukunaga Mitsuji.

9. List of works cited, and additional important studies

Boltz, Judith M. 1987a. Lao-tzu. *The Encyclopedia of Religion*. Vol. 8, pp. 454–459. Edited by Mircea Eliade *et al*. N.Y.: Macmillan.
Boltz, Judith M. 1987b. *A Survey of Taoist Literature, Tenth to Seventeenth*

Centuries. China research monograph 32. Berkeley: University of California, Institute of East Asian Studies.

Boltz, William G. 1982. 'The religious and philosophical significance of the 'Hsiang erh' *Lao tzu* in the light of the Ma-wang-tui silk manuscripts', *BSOAS* XLV.1, pp. 95–117.

Boltz, William G. 1984. 'Textual criticism and the Ma wang tui *Lao tzu*', *HJAS* 44.1, pp. 185–224.

Boltz, William G. 1985. 'The *Lao tzu* text that Wang Pi and Ho-shang Kung never saw', *BSOAS* XLVIII.3, pp. 493–501.

Catalogue des manuscrits chinois de Touen-houang (Fonds Pelliot chinois). Vol. 1: nos. 2001–2500. 1970. Comp. J. Gernet and Wu Ch'i-yü on the basis of notes by P. Pelliot and Wang Chung-min; ed. by Marie-Rose Seguy and Helene Vetch under the direction of Marie-Roberte Guignard. Paris: Bibliothèque Nationale.

Catalogue des manuscrits chinois de Touen-houang (Fonds Pelliot chinois de la Bibliothèque Nationale). 1983. Vol. 3: nos. 3001–3500. Ed. Michel Soymié. Paris: Fondation Singer-Polignac.

Catalogue des manuscrits chinois de Touen-houang (Fonds Pelliot chinois de la Bibliotheque Nationale). 1991. Vol. 4: nos. 3501–4000. Ed. Michel Soymié. Paris: Fondation Singer-Polignac.

Chan, Alan K.L. 1991. *Two Visions of the Way, A Study of the Wang Pi and the Ho-shang Kung Commentaries on the* Lao tzu. Albany (N.Y.): State University of New York Press.

Ch'en Shih-hsiang 陳世驤. 1957. '"Hsiang erh" Lao-tzu Tao ching Tun-huang ts'an chüan lun cheng 想爾老子道經燉煌殘卷論證', *Ch'ing hua hsüeh pao* 清華學報, n.s., 1.2, pp. 41–62.

Cheng Ch'eng-hai 鄭成海. 1971. *Lao tzu Ho-shang Kung chu chiao li* 老子河上公注斠理. Taipei: Chung-hua.

Cheng Liang-shu 鄭良樹. 1987. *Tun-huang Lao-tzu hsieh chüan t'an wei* 敦煌老子寫卷探微. *Wang Li hsien-sheng chi nien lun wen chi* 王力先生紀念論文集, *Chung wen fen ts'e* 中文分冊. Pp. 281–293. Hong Kong: San lien.

Chiang Hsi-ch'ang 蔣錫昌. 1937. *Lao tzu chiao ku* 老子校詁. Shanghai: Shang wu.

Chu Ch'ien-chih 朱謙之. 1975. *Lao tzu chiao shih* 老子校釋. Tai-nan (Taiwan): P'ing p'ing.

Erkes, Eduard. 1950. *Ho-shang-kung's Commentary on Lao-tse*. Ascona (Switzerland): Artibus Asiae.

Fukui Kōjun 福井康順. 1967. *Rōshi Sōjichū kō* 老子想爾注考. *Waseda daigaku daigakuin bungaku kenkyūka kiyō* 早稻田大學大學院文學研究科紀要, pp. 1–20.

Giles, Lionel. 1957. *Descriptive Catalogue of the Chinese Manuscripts from Tunhuang in the British Museum*. London: British Museum.

Grill, Julius. 1911. 'Zur mandschurischen Übersetzung des *Tao-te-king*'; *ZDMG* 65, pp. 759–770.

Hatano Tarō 波多野太郎. 1953/54. *Rōshi Ōchū kōsei* 老子王注校正. *Yokohama shiritsu daigaku kiyō* 横濱市立大學紀要 A-2, A-3, A-8, nos. 15 and 27.

Hatano Tarō. 1959. 'Rōshi Ōchū kōsei ho-i 老子王注校正補遺', *Shinagaku kenkyū* 支那學研究 24/25, pp. 13–25.

Hatano Tarō. 1976. 'Ma-ō-tai shutsudo Rōshi kō' 馬王堆出土老子考, *Tōhō shūkyō* 東方宗教 47, pp. 1–11.

Henricks, Robert G. 1980. 'Examining the Ma-wang-tui silk texts of the *Lao tzu*', *TP* LXV, 4–5, pp. 166–199.

Henricks, Robert G. 1982. 'On the chapter divisions in the *Lao tzu*', *BSOAS* XLV.3, pp. 501–524.

Herforth, Derek D. 1989 [1980]. 'Two Philological Studies on the Ma-wangdui Lao Tzu Manuscripts'. Unpublished M.A. thesis, University of British Columbia, 1980; revised 1989.

Ho Shih-chi 何士驥. 1936. *Ku pen Tao-te-ching chiao k'an* 古本道德經校刊. Kuo li Pei-p'ing yen chiu yüan, shih hsüeh yen chiu hui 國立北平研究院史學研究會. *K'ao ku chuan pao ti i chüan, ti erh hao* 考古專報第一卷第二號.

Hsiao Han 曉菡. 1974. 'Ch'ang-sha Ma-wang-tui Han mu po shu kai shu' 長沙馬王堆漢墓帛書概述, *Wen wu* 文物 1974.9, pp. 40–44.

Hu-nan sheng po wu kuan 湖南省博物館. 1974. 'Ch'ang-sha Ma-wang-tui erh san hao Han mu fa chüeh chien pao' 長沙馬王堆二三號漢墓發掘簡報, *Wen wu* 文物 1974.7, pp. 39–48, 63.

Hung, William. 1957. 'A bibliographical controversy at the T'ang court A.D. 719', *HJAS* 20.1–2, pp. 74–134.

Imaeda Jirō 今支二郎. 1975. 'Ma-ō-tai shutsudo "Rōshi" koshabon ni tsuite' 馬王堆出土老子古寫本について. *Taishō daigaku kenkyū kiyō* 大正大學研究紀要 61, pp. 249–262.

Jao Tsung-i 饒宗頤. 1955. 'Wu Chien-heng erh nien So Tan hsieh pen Tao-te-ching ts'an chüan k'ao cheng' 吳建衡二年索紞寫本道德經殘卷考證. *Tung fang wen hua* 東方文化 2, pp. 1–71.

Jao Tsung-i. 1956. *A Study on Chang Tao-ling's Hsiang-er Commentary of Tao Te Ching*. Hong Kong: Tong Nam.

Jao Tsung-i. 1969. 'Lao tzu Hsiang erh chu hsü lun' 老子想爾注續論. *Tōyō bunka ronshū: Fukui Hakase shōju kinen* 東洋文化論集福井博士頌壽紀念; pp. 1155–1171. Tokyo: Waseda University Press.

Kao Heng 高亨 and Ch'ih Hsi-chao 池曦朝. 1974. 'Shih t'an Ma-wang-tui Han mu chung ti po shu Lao tzu' 試談馬王堆漢墓中的帛書老子, *Wen wu* 文物 1974.11, pp. 1–7.

Kao Ming 高明. 1978. 'Po shu "Lao tzu" chia i pen yü chin pen "Lao tzu" k'an chiao cha chi' 帛書老子甲乙本與今本老子勘校札記. *Wen wu tzu liao ts'ung k'an* 文物資料叢刊 no. 2, pp. 209–221.

Karlgren, Bernhard. 1975. 'Notes on Lao-tse', *BMFEA* 47, pp. 1–18.

Ku Chieh-kang 顧頡剛. 1932. 'Ts'ung Lü shih ch'un ch'iu t'ui ts'e Lao tzu chih ch'eng shu nien tai' 從呂氏春秋推測老子之成書年代. *Shih hsüeh nien pao* 史學年報 1.4, pp. 13–46.

Kuo-chia wen-wu chü, ku wen hsien yen chiu shih 國家文物局古文獻研究室. 1980. *Ma-wang-tui Han mu po shu* 馬王堆漢墓帛書 vol. 1. Peking: Wen wu.

Kusuyama Haruki 楠山春樹. 1972. 'Tei Sei-kai cho "Rōshi Kashōkō chū kōri"' 鄭成海著老子河上公注斟理, *Tōhō shūkyō* 東方宗教 40, pp. 47–51.

Lao Chien 勞健. 1941. *Lao tzu ku pen k'ao* 老子古本考. N.p.

Lo Chen-yü 羅振玉. 1921. *Tao te ching k'ao i* 道德經考異; and *Lao tzu k'ao i pu i* 老子考異補遺. *Yung-feng hsiang jen tsa chu hsü pien* 永豐鄉人雜著續編, reprinted in *Lo Hsüeh-t'ang hsien sheng ch'üan chi ch'u pien* 羅雪堂先生全集初編, vol. 3, pp. 1025–1075. Taipei: Wen hua, 1968.

Lu Kung 路工. 1981. 'Yü Shih-nan chiao hsieh pen "Lao tzu" chi ch'i shih k'o t'o pen' 虞世南校寫本老子及其石刻拓本, *Shih chieh tsung chiao yen chiu* 世界宗教研究 1981.4. pp. 45–53.

Ma Hsü-lun 馬敘倫. 1924. *Lao tzu chiao ku* 老子校詁. Reprinted: Hong Kong: T'ai p'ing, 1965, 1973.

Mote, Frederick. 1986. 'The Oldest book at Princeton', *Gest Library Journal* 1.1, pp. 34–44.

Ōfuchi Ninji 大淵忍爾. 1978. *Tonkō Dōkyō* 敦煌道經, 2 volumes. Tokyo: Fukutake shoten 福武書店.

Pelliot, Paul. 1912. 'Autour d'une traduction sanscrite du Tao tö king', *TP* 13 (1912), pp. 351–430.

Robinet, Isabelle. 1977. *Les Commentaires de Tao tö king jusqu'au VIIe siècle*. Mémoirs de l'Institut des Hautes Études chinoises V. Paris: Collège de France.

Shima Kunio 島邦男. 1973. *Rōshi kōsei* 老子校正. Tokyo: Kyūko shoin 汲古書院.

Shima Kunio. 1976. 'Ma-ō-tai Rōshi kara mita Kashōkō hon' 馬王堆老子からみた河上公本. *Shūkan Tōyōgaku* 集刊東洋學 36, pp. 1–26.

T'ang Lan 唐蘭 *et al.* 1974. 'Tso t'an Ch'ang-sha Ma-wang-tui Han mu po shu' 座談長沙馬王堆漢墓帛書, *Wen wu* 文物 1974.9, pp. 45–57.

T'ang Wen-po 唐文播. 1944. 'Pa-li so ts'ang Tun-huang Lao-tzu hsieh pen tsung k'ao' 巴黎所藏敦煌老子寫本綜考, *Chung-kuo wen hua yen chiu hui k'an* 中國文化研究彙刊, no. 4, pp. 95–124.

Wagner, Rudolf G. 1986. 'Wang Bi: "The structure of the Laozi's pointers"', *TP* 72, pp. 92–129.

Wagner, Rudolf G. 1989. 'The Wang Bi recension of the *Lao tzu*', *EC* 14, pp. 27–54.

Wang Chung-min 王重民. 1958. *Tun-huang ku chi hsü lu* 敦煌古籍敘錄. Reprinted: Peking: Chung hua, 1979.

Wulff, K. 1942. *Acht Kapitel des Tao-te-king.* Edited by Victor Dantzer. Copenhagen: Eijnar Munksgaard. Det Kgl. Danske Videnskabernes Selskab. Historisk-filologiske Meddelelser. XXVII, 4.

10.   Indexes

(a) See under 6 (a), (b), (c) and (d) above.

(b) *A Concordance to the Daozang Wang Bi ben Laozi and Heshang Gong ben Laozi ji Heshang Gong zhu* 道藏王弼本老子, 河上公本老子及河上公注逐字索引, ed. D.C. Lau and Chen Fong Ching; *ICS* series, Hong Kong: Commercial Press, forthcoming 1995.

— William G. Boltz

Li chi 禮記

The *Li chi* is a ritualist's anthology of ancient usages, prescriptions, definitions and anecdotes. Unlike the other two ritual titles of the canon, the *Chou li* and the *I li*, there is no apparent overall structure to the work. Nor does it seem that its forty-nine sections originated at the same time or in the same scholastic context. The date of each section and its provenance are subjects of considerable dispute, just as the date and origin of the *Li chi* as a whole have proved to be controversial throughout Chinese intellectual history.

1. Date of compilation

The first attempt to sort out the facts of the text's compilation was that of Ch'en Shao 陳邵 (late 3rd century). A consensus, which was based in part on Ch'en's account and reached by about the sixth century, is seen in numerous works of the mediaeval period and may be represented by the authoritative judgements of the compilers of *Sui shu* 32 (see p. 925):

> At the start of the Han, king Hsien of Ho-chien 河間獻王 obtained 131 [sic] *p'ien* of *chi* 記 recorded by the disciples of Confucius and their later students. He submitted them to the imperial throne.... When Liu Hsiang 劉向 [79–8 B.C.] studied and edited the canons and records, he discovered the 130 *p'ien* which he then set in order and epitomized; he also obtained the *Ming t'ang yin yang chi* 明堂陰陽記, in 33 *p'ien*; the *K'ung tzu san ch'ao chi* 孔子三朝記, in 7 *p'ien*; the *Wang shih shih chi* 王史氏記, in 21 *p'ien*; and the *Yüeh chi* 樂記 in 23 *p'ien*; in all five works, totalling 214 *p'ien*. Tai Te 戴德 excised those parts that were duplicated, and combined and recorded the rest, making 85 *p'ien*, which were entitled *Ta Tai chi* 大戴記; and Tai Sheng 戴聖 eliminated more text from the documents of *Ta Tai*, making 46 *p'ien* which were entitled *Hsiao Tai chi* 小戴記. At the close of the Han period, Ma Jung 馬融 [79–166] subsequently transmitted the studies of Tai the Lesser. [Ma] Jung further affixed the *Yüeh ling* 月令 in 1 *p'ien*, the *Ming t'ang wei* 明堂位 in 1 *p'ien* and the *Yüeh chi* 樂記 in 1 *p'ien*, bringing the total to 49 *p'ien*. Cheng

Hsüan 鄭玄 inherited the work from [Ma] Jung and made a commentary for it.

Thus goes the traditional litany on the text. It is for the most part a fabulation constructed to reconcile various works mentioned in the section on *li* in *Han shu* 30, pp. 1709–10, with the text in 49 *p'ien*, which is not listed there, and to show how these works preceded and led in rational fashion to the contemporary redaction. There is little in the account that is reliable; some of it is to be rejected outright.

While we may assume that the extant *Li chi* is perhaps to be connected with the various texts listed in *Han shu* 30, there is no reason to identify the 131 *p'ien* of the *Sui shu*'s account with the corpus of of *ku wen* texts obtained, in some accounts, by king Hsien of Ho-chien, who died in 129 B.C. It is true that Tai Te and his nephew Tai Sheng, together with Wen Jen T'ung Han 聞人通漢 and Ch'ing P'u 慶普 were disciples of the famous Han ritual master Hou Ts'ang 后倉 (*fl.* 70 B.C.) and were thus primarily responsible for the transmission and interpretation of the *I li*; we know that Tai Sheng and Wen Jen T'ung Han, at least, were familiar with material now found in the *Li chi*, since they quote some of it in the *Shih ch'ü ko* 石渠閣 debates of 51 B.C.; and there is good reason to assume that the schools associated with their names in Later Han continued to preserve and utilize this same textual material in the various debates on the canon of that period. But there is nothing in *Han shu* ch. 88 ('Ju lin chuan' 儒林傳) to suggest that they played a role in editing the *Ta Tai li chi* and the *Li chi*. Neither their names nor the redactions of 85 and 46 *p'ien* that are associated with them in the *Sui shu* are mentioned in connection with the ritual *chi* in *Han shu* 30. Contrary to the *Sui shu*'s reconstruction of events, the period of their activity preceded the bibliographic work of Liu Hsiang (79–8 B.C.).

The earliest evidence that we have that Tai Te and Tai Sheng were instrumental in the editing of the *Ta Tai li chi* and the *Li chi* is found in the *Liu i lun* 六藝論 of Cheng Hsüan 鄭玄 (127–200), now lost except for fragments. According to parts that are quoted in K'ung Ying-ta's 孔穎達 (574–648) preface to the *Li chi*, 'Tai Te transmitted *Chi* in 85 *p'ien*; Tai Sheng transmitted *Li* in 49 *p'ien*'. Since this fact is not mentioned in *Han shu* ch. 30 or elsewhere in Former Han sources, there is no evidence to support the great commentator's statement. It appears, in fact, that as late as the White Tiger Hall debates of 79 the critical editing which separated out the 49 *p'ien* of the present *Li chi* had not yet taken place, since sections from that text, from the *Ta tai li chi* and others not occurring now in either of these, are simply quoted by the title of their *p'ien* and are not identified as coming from one or the other collection. According to *Hou Han shu* 35A, p. 1205, Ts'ao Pao 曹褒 (d. 102), who was a member of the Ch'ing P'u school, transmitted a *Li chi* of 49 *p'ien*. It is perhaps to him, his era and his school that we are to trace the present compilation.

2. Content

The 49 *p'ien* of the text are extremely diverse and miscellaneous in their style and contents as well as in the origins of the materials of which they are constituted. According to quotations in Cheng Hsüan's *San li mu lu* 三禮目錄, Liu Hsiang divided the sections of an earlier recension into eleven categories, mostly according to their subject. Of these the largest single group is that of the 'Comprehensive discourses' ('T'ung lun' 通論), comprising sixteen *p'ien*. The name of the category suggests that its various parts are edited records of Han scholastic court debates; and that they are thus comparable with the records of the *Shih ch'ü ko* debates, of which only a few fragments survive, and the expurgated account of the *Pai hu t'ung* debates. Other large categories are those of 'Weights and measures', 'Mourning vestments', 'Sacrifices' and 'Auspicious activities'.

Many of the sections of the *Li chi*, especially those labelled 'Comprehensive discourses' by Liu Hsiang, are in the form of lists of definitions of ritual terms. It seems likely that their composition, or their preservation in the *Li chi*, was partly due to their inclusion of proper glosses on the old religious vocabulary. Several of the *Li chi* logomachies are devoted to explaining the terms and usages set forth in the *I li*. Another feature which many such passages have in common is their connection with Confucius. Most contain at least one mention of the sage. Others purport to transmit his teachings, or to reveal rather secret aspects of his life and career, and little known facts about his family. These references assume that Confucius enjoyed high status and seem to be a reflection of the systematic process of elevating the standing of his teachings during Former Han. Much of this material subsequently found its way into the *K'ung ts'ung tzu* 孔叢子 and the *K'ung tzu chia yü*.

Comparison with other texts makes it possible to suggest the diverse origins of some of the *p'ien* of the *Li chi*. For example, parts of the 'San nien wen' 三年問 and of the *Yüeh chi* 樂記 appear to have originated in the *Hsün tzu*. The 'Yüeh ling' 樂令 is an altered version of the 'Annals of the monthly observances' which are seen in the *Lü shih ch'un ch'iu* and in the *Huai nan tzu*. On the other hand we cannot be too hasty in assuming that parts of the *Li chi* originated in pre-Han texts. Contrary to the often stated conjecture, the 'Chung yung' 中庸 was not incorporated in the *Li chi* as a loan from the *Tzu ssu tzu* 子思子, a text that is associated with Confucius' grandson and is now lost. Although it may have been composed as part of an effort to explain the teachings of the latter person, we should perhaps identify it with the 'Chung yung shuo' 中庸說, which is listed in the ritual section of *Han shu* 30 (p. 1709). Similarly the 'Ch'ü li' 曲禮 is perhaps to be associated with the *Ch'ü t'ai chi* 曲臺記 attributed to Hou Ts'ang (*Han shu* 30, p. 1709; 88, p. 3615).

3. Editions

The standard edition of the text is that of Juan Yüan's 阮元 (1764–1849) *Shih san ching chu shu* 十三經注疏. This contains the glosses of Cheng Hsüan, notes on textual variants and pronunciation incorporated from the *Ching tien shih wen* 經典釋文 of Lu Te-ming 陸德明 (556–627), and the supplementary commentary of K'ung Ying-ta, which contains essential references to authorities on the text of the Six Dynasties period. The *Li chi chi shuo* 禮記集說 (preface 1322), edited with additional commentary by Ch'en Hao 陳澔 (1261–1341) contains the reading notes of a number of Sung scholars.

4. Recent studies and research aids

(a) *Li chi yin te*; Harvard-Yenching Index No. 27 (Peking, 1937; reprinted Taipei, 1966).
(b) Tsuda Sōkichi 津田左右吉, 'Raiki oyobi Tai Tai Raiki no hensan jidai ni tsuite' 禮記及び大戴禮記の編纂時代について; *Shigaku zasshi* 42 (1931), 131–70.
(c) Hung Yeh 洪業 (William Hung); preface to (a).
(d) Kimura Eiichi 木村英一, 'Zen Kan ni okeru raigaku no denju ni tsuite' 前漢に於ける禮學の傳授について; *Ritsumeikan bungaku* (1960), 610–27.
(e) Fujikawa Masakazu 藤川正數, *Kan dai ni okeru raigaku no kenkyū* 漢代における禮學の研究; Tokyo: Kazama shobō, 1968.

5. Translations

(a) Legge, *Sacred Books of the East*, vols. xxvii–viii; reprinted 1926 and 1967 (New York, with introductory material by Ch'u Chai and Winberg Chai).

(b) Couvreur, Séraphin, *Li Ki ou Mémoires sur les bienséances; texte Chinois avec une double traduction en Francais et en Latin;* 2 vols. ; 2nd ed., Ho Kien Fou: Mission catholique, 1913, reprinted 1928.

For the *Ta hsüeh* and *Chung yung,* see Legge, *The Chinese Classics,* vol. I.

6. Japanese editions

A. *Kambun taikei;* no. 17, 1913, edited by Hattori Unokichi.
B. *Kanseki kokujikai zensho;* nos. 26, 27, 1914, edited by Katsura Koson (Isoo).
D. *Kokuyaku kambun taisei;* no. 4, 1921, edited by Yasui Kotarō.
E. *Kambun sōsho;* 1927, edited by Tsukamoto Tetsuzō and Hayashi Taisuke.
F. *Keisho taikō;* no. 25, 1940.
H. *Shinshaku kambun taikei;* nos. 27–29, 1971–79, edited by Takeuchi Teruo.
L. *Chūgoku koten shinsho,* 1973, edited by Shimomi Takao.

In addition, the *Ta hsüeh* and *Chung yung* are included as follows:

A. *Kambun taikei;* no. 1, 1909, edited by Hattori Unokichi and Yasui Sokken.
B. *Kanseki kokujikai zensho;* no. 1, 1909, edited by Nakamura Tekisai.
C. *Kōchū kambun sōsho;* no. 3, 1913, edited by Mōri Teisai and Kubo Tenzui.
D. *Kokuyaku kambun taisei;* no. 1, 1922, edited by Hattori Unokichi and Komaki Masanari.
E. *Kambun sōsho,* 1927.
F. *Keisho taikō;* no. 18, 1939.
H. *Shinshaku kambun taikei;* no. 2, 1967, edited by Akatsuka Kiyoshi.
L. *Chūgoku koten shinsho;* 1968, edited by Matano Tarō.

7. Indexes

(a) See under 4 (a) above.
(b) *A Concordance to the Liji* 禮記逐字索引, ed. D.C. Lau and Chen Fong Ching; *ICS* series, Hong Kong: Commercial Press, 1992.

— Jeffrey K. Riegel

Lieh tzu 列子

1. Content and traditional evaluation

The *Lieh tzu* is a work in eight *p'ien*, corresponding to the eight *chüan* in which it has been transmitted up to the present. The content throughout is Taoist in its inspiration with the exception of the seventh section, which, under the name of the philosopher Yang Chu 楊朱, expounds a type of hedonism. As in the *Chuang tzu*, philosophical exposition is combined with a large number of parables and dialogues. Unifying themes may be detected within a single section (especially the sixth, *li ming* 力命, which is devoted to fatalism), but the connexions between the many anecdotes are not made explicit. The book takes its name from the sage Lieh Yü-k'ou 列禦寇, a figure mentioned in the *Chuang tzu* and also in many of the dialogues of the *Lieh tzu* itself, whose thought the Taoist sections of the work supposedly reflect.

The *Lieh tzu* first attracted commentary towards the end of the fourth century and was designated a Taoist classic together with the *Lao tzu* and *Chuang tzu* in the mid-eighth century. At this time it was given the honorific title *Ch'ung hsü chen ching* 沖虛眞經; in 1007 this was further expanded to *Ch'ung hsü chih te chen ching* 沖虛至德眞經. But within a half-century or so from the date of its elevation to the status of a Taoist classic doubts began to be expressed as to its textual integrity and eventually as to its authenticity as a whole. It has long been recognized that it shares material with the *Chuang tzu* and other early works, and also that it contains material suggesting a date even later than the Han dynasty, but Chinese scholarship of the Ch'ing dynasty and the present century has been divided as to whether it is an ancient work with later interpolations or a forgery confected from ancient sources.

As a result considerable secondary literature on the *Lieh tzu* has been produced. Yen Ling-feng 嚴靈峯 (b. 1904), *Chou Ch'in Han Wei chu tzu chih chien shu mu* 周秦漢魏諸子知見書目, vol. 2 (hereafter Yen, 1975), devotes sixty pages of bibliography to this. Yen has also reprinted a substantial number of editions of the *Lieh tzu* and secondary studies in his *Wu ch'iu pei chai Lieh tzu chi ch'eng* 無求備齋列子集成 (Taipei: I wen, 1970; hereafter *LTCC*). The most comprehensive listing and comparison

298

of editions of the *Lieh tzu* may be found on pp. 661–779 of a Japanese monograph by Kobayashi Katsundo 小林勝人, *Resshi no kenkyū* 列子の 研究 (Tokyo: Meiji, 1981; hereafter Kobayashi, 1981). Most important secondary writings on the *Lieh tzu* are also included in Yang Po-chün 楊 伯峻, *Lieh tzu chi shih* 列子集釋 (originally published 1958; references here are to Peking: Chung hua, 1979; hereafter Yang, 1979).

2. Authenticity and date of composition

To judge from the *Lieh tzu*, the *Chuang tzu* and other texts that mention his name, Lieh Yü-kou was believed to have lived around 400 B.C. Arguments as to whether portions of the text may be attributed to the date of the supposed author have mainly revolved around the passages shared between the *Lieh tzu* and other texts of undeniably early date, as well as the linguistic usage of the *Lieh tzu* itself. The only study to exploit both these approaches fully is A. C. Graham, 'The Date and Composition of *Liehtzyy*', *Asia Major*, n.s. 8 (1960–61), 139–198; hereafter Graham, *Liehtzyy*.

The earliest evidence we possess of a book named '*Lieh tzu*' is the report of Liu Hsiang 劉向 (79–8 B.C.) dated 14 B.C. which once formed part of his *Pieh lu* 別錄 (see Yang, 1979, pp. 277–278.) This mentions his collation of the text in eight *p'ien* based upon five shorter texts and gives the names of four *p'ien* exactly as in the present work; it also describes the work as rare. Though some have doubted the authenticity of this document Graham ('*Liehtzyy*', pp. 147–8) accepts it as genuine. *Han shu* 30, p. 1730, known to be based on Liu's work, also mentions the *Lieh tzu* in eight *p'ien*. Thereafter there is no trace of it until the fourth century when Chang Chan 張湛 produced the commentary to the present version of the *Lieh tzu*, with the single apparent exception of a reference to it in the *Po wu chih* 博物志 of Chang Hua 張華 (232–300). (See Kobayashi, 1981, pp. 178–9.) Graham does not mention this specific reference, but shows that the *Po wu chih*, which is far from being in its original state, absorbed portions of the *Lieh tzu* in the course of its transmission ('*Liehtzyy*', p. 145, n. 33.)

The only account of the history of the *Lieh tzu* text after Liu Hsiang and prior to Chang Chan is to be found in the latter's preface to his own commentary (see Yang, 1979, pp. 275–80). Chang claims that the text had been transmitted in his family since the time of his grandfather at the start of the fourth century. Graham shows that this ostensible text history is designed to provide a plausible explanation of its transmission prior to its promotion by Chang, but actually it leaves much room for doubt ('*Liehtzyy*'; pp. 145–6). It is noteworthy that the present *Lieh tzu* contains a story very similar to one in a Buddhist sutra translated in 285 and shows parallels as well to the *Mu T'ien tzu chuan*, discovered in *c.* 281 ('*Liehtzyy*', p. 142).

All parallels from early texts are listed by Graham and the main correspondences are investigated to determine which text is primary in each case. No cases where the *Lieh tzu* is clearly primary can be found; in many it is unambiguously secondary. At n. 60 Graham mentions two studies which attempt to prove the contrary, but adds that he disagrees with the criteria that they use. More recent studies of the same kind have been produced by Yamaguchi Yoshio 山口義男, *Resshi kenkyū* 列子研究 (Tokyo: Kazama, 1976), and Kobayashi Katsundo, in Kobayashi, 1981, pp. 65–133.

Graham next investigates the remaining three quarters of the text for linguistic evidence of late date, taking ten commonly used words and constructions. He shows the material examined to be in the main both homogeneous and late. In a more recent study, Yü Jo-chao 余若昭 independently lists eleven examples of late types of usage; see the preface to his grammatical description in *Lieh tzu yü fa t'an chiu* 列子語法探究 (Taipei: Wen shih che, 1973.) Both Graham and Yü refer back to the earlier findings by Yang Po-chün.

Graham then turns to the problem of unidentified early materials in the *Lieh tzu*, armed with the knowledge that whoever was responsible for incorporating the known early materials in his text did not adapt them to his own linguistic usage. Chang Chan indicates that he was aware of parallels in the *Lieh tzu* to several works now lost, and hence not readily identifiable. Graham identifies several passages in the Yang Chu section in particular as deriving from early material. They are dealt with separately by him in 'The dialogue between Yang Ju and Chyntzyy' (*BSOAS* 22.2 (1959), 291–9.) He argues that apart from this early material and other passages with parallels in surviving early works, the Yang Chu section and the preceding fatalist section are both the responsibility of the same hand that produced the rest of the work, and are designed to conform with the brief references to them in Liu Hsiang's report. He suggests finally that though Chang Chan shows a suspicious familiarity in his commentary with the presence of early material in the work, his knowledge in this respect is not entirely perfect and he occasionally misunderstands the text. The guiding hand responsible for putting the *Lieh tzu* together cannot have been Chang Chan himself but may well have been his grandfather or father.

It follows that the *Lieh tzu* cannot be used as a source for pre-Ch'in

Chinese thought without proof that the specific passage involved was incorporated into it from an earlier work of that period. It may be used as evidence for the form in which such early material was known in the fourth century A.D., and is thus of some importance for textual studies. Graham's work on the dating of the *Lieh tzu* is either unknown, or at least not utilized by Chinese and Japanese scholars, whose opinions are still divided as to the authenticity and authorship of the work.

3. Commentaries and textual history

(a) Chang Chan 張湛

The preceding discussion suggests that the text of the *Lieh tzu* has only been known as transmitted with the commentary of Chang Chan, though under the Ming editions were produced without it. Chang's commentary is of a philosophical type, and is comparable to those of Kuo Hsiang 郭象 (d. 312) and Hsiang Hsiu 向秀 (?221–?300) on the *Chuang tzu*, the latter commentary known largely through its quotation by Chang. The presence of notes on parallel texts and their commentaries and of some phonological information also makes Chang's work in some ways of greater value than the *Chuang tzu* commentaries, despite its later date.

Two fragmentary manuscripts of the *Lieh tzu* with Chang's commentary were found at Tun-huang. One, S.0777, probably of pre-T'ang date, is of a portion of the Yang Chu section, and restores a *lacuna* occurring in all printed editions. This restoration is incorporated in Yang, 1979. The other, S.6134 and P.2495, is of little value for collation purposes, since here the *Lieh tzu* is combined with the *Chuang tzu* in a summarized version, with much of the main text reproduced in double columns as though it were commentary, with little regard for textual accuracy. The date of this manuscript would appear to be late seventh century.

(b) Lu Ch'ung-hsüan 盧重玄

The commentary of Lu Ch'ung-hsüan was originally entitled *Lieh tzu* (or *Ch'ung hsü chen ching chu* 沖虛眞經注), as was that of Chang Chan, but it is sometimes termed the *Lieh tzu chieh* 列子解, since it has been transmitted only through a compilation of four commentaries in the Taoist canon (*Tao tsang*) bearing the title *Ch'ung hsü chih te chen ching ssu chieh* 沖虛至德眞經四解 (*HY** 732). It was recovered thence by Ch'in

---

* *HY*: Harvard-Yenching Institute Sinological Index Series No. 25 *Tao Tsang tzu mu yin te* 道藏子目引得; Peking: 1935; rpt. Taipei: 1966.

En-fu 秦思復 (1760–1843) and published separately in 1803. Ch'in's preface, readily available in the *LTCC* reproduction of his edition, notes that one source records that the office designation preceding Lu's name in the commentary was held by him in 735. This cannot be taken as an exact indication of the date of the work, which must have been written in 739–42, to judge by the honorific title peculiar to that period under which the emperor is mentioned in Lu's own preface. The commentary contains a greater proportion of philosophical interpretation than that of Chang and is correspondingly less useful in uncovering the original intention of the text.

(c) Yin Ching-shun 殷敬順

The *Lieh tzu shih wen* 列子釋文 of Yin Ching-shun is a philological commentary comparable to the *Ching tien shih wen* of Lu Te-ming 陸德明 (556–627). A decaying T'ang manuscript of it was discovered by Ch'en Ching-yüan 陳景元, a Taoist priest and scholar known for his work on the *Chuang tzu*, in the T'ien-t'ai 天臺 mountains in 1069. Ch'en copied this out and added supplementary notes of his own. This revised version, together with his preface, which gives an account of his work, may still be found in the *Tao tsang* (*HY* 738). From the Southern Sung onwards a substantial part of Yin's work was incorporated into editions of the *Lieh tzu* with Chang Chan's commentary, but Yin's notes were not distinguished from those of Chang. In 1787 Jen Ta-ch'un 任大椿 (1738–1787) reprinted the *Tao tsang* edition together with supplementary philological observations of his own, the *Lieh tzu shih wen k'ao i* 列子釋文考異.

In a postface written in 1796 on the earliest surviving (Northern Sung) printed copy of the *Lieh tzu*, Huang P'ei-lieh 黃丕烈 (1763–1825) asserted that the *Lieh tzu shih wen*, rather than deriving from a T'ang manuscript as Ch'en Ching-yüan would have us believe, must have been composed under the Sung after this printing since the readings of this Northern Sung copy correspond to variants noted in Yin's work. But a mid-ninth century quotation from Yin's commentary shows this to be false, although there are some internal indications confirming that Ch'en did in fact supplement the work to a certain extent. The original date of composition is unclear, but Yin must have been writing later than 819, since as Jen Ta-ch'un observes he quotes Yang Liang's 楊倞 commentary on *Hsün tzu*, which had been completed in that year.

Yin's commentary is extremely valuable for its textual notes and for its philological observations, which include quotations from several lost works and extend to remarks on Chang Chan's commentary. But Jen's edition (now in *LTCC*) does not correct some obvious errors in the *Tao tsang* text, whilst a quotation of Yin by Ch'u Po-hsiu 褚伯秀 (*c.* 1230–after 1287) on p. 4a of his preface to the *Nan hua chen ching i hai tsuan wei* 南華眞經義海纂微 in the *Tao tsang* (*HY* 734) contains two characters missing in the present text, suggesting that even after its rediscovery by Ch'en Ching-yüan this commentary suffered somewhat in the course of its transmission.

(d) Sung and Ming commentaries

The *Tao tsang* contains four Sung commentaries on the *Lieh tzu*, including one by Hui-tsung 徽宗 (reigned 1101–27) dated 1118 (*HY* 731). Full details may be found in Yen, 1975. All these commentaries approach the text as a religious classic, but the *Ch'ung hsü chih te chen ching k'ou i* 沖虛至德眞經口義 of Lin Hsi-i 林希逸 (*c.* 1200–*c.* 1273), dated 1261, at least provides a paraphrase of the text in simple language. This gave it unusual popularity, as is made clear by the large number of reprintings in China and Japan discussed in Kobayashi, 1981, pp. 703–730. Kobayashi's discussion neglects a possible Korean background to the seventeenth century Japanese reprints suggested by the presence of a Korean edition in movable type among the books once owned by Tokugawa Ieyasu 德川家康 (1543–1616). See Sugiura Toyoji 杉浦豐治, *Hōsa Bunko tenseki sōroku* 蓬左文庫典籍叢錄 (Nagoya: Kinjo Gakuin Daigaku Jimbun Kagaku Kenkyūkai, 1975), p. 213. Lin's work further formed the basis of a version with added remarks by Liu Ch'en-weng 劉辰翁 (1231–1294). Ming commentaries on the *Lieh tzu*, to judge from those included in *LTCC*, are also marked by clarity of exposition, but the modern student will find them to be of little value in comparison with the work of Ch'ing philologists incorporated in recent editions.

4. Important editions

(a) The Northern Sung edition

This is the edition upon the sole surviving copy of which Huang P'ei-lieh wrote the postface mentioned above. It eventually became part of the *T'ieh ch'in t'ung chien lou* collection, and since its first facsimile reprinting in the *T'ieh hua kuan ts'ung shu* in 1883, it has been reproduced in the *SPTK, LTCC* and elsewhere. It contains the commentary of Chang Chan, but lacks his preface and Liu Hsiang's report at the head of the edition. Where these are found in reproductions they are taken from a Ming edition.

Ch'en Ching-yüan in his preface to Yin Ching-shun's commentary mentions a printing of the *Lieh tzu* in the period 1004–07, and Yen (1975),

p. 6, notes a reference in the *Yü hai* of Wang Ying-lin 王應麟 (1223–96) to a 'new printing' in 1012, but not enough information exists to link the present copy to either of these. Huang does, however, remark on its superiority to a manuscript facsimile of a Sung copy already in his possession. The Northern Sung edition is both the earliest extant edition of the *Lieh tzu* and also one of the most readily available, and so remains the main edition for reference among most scholars.

(b) The Southern Sung edition

This edition is known from a copy in the Sonkeikaku 尊經閣 formerly in the Kanazawa bunko 金澤文庫. This does not include Liu Hsiang's report, but has Chang Chan's preface and commentary, together with Yin Ching-shun's notes. Though made available in reproduction in Japan in 1949 and most recently in the *LTCC*, it has been used for collation purposes by Japanese scholars only.

(c) The Shih te t'ang 世德堂 edition

This edition was produced in 1530 by the publishing house from which it takes its name as part of a reprinting of six pre-Ch'in philosophers. It contains Chang Chan's and Yin Ching-shun's comments as in the Southern Sung edition, together with Liu Hsiang's report; a reproduction is included in the *LTCC*. The Shih te t'ang edition was widely known to Ch'ing scholars and to scholars of Tokugawa and Meiji Japan, where it was reprinted three times, in 1747, 1791, and 1883. These reprintings are listed by Kobayashi, 1981, pp. 745–6, who notes that the first reprinting is also available in a recent photolithographic reproduction. All are identical with their 1530 original except for a preface and two dozen textual notes by Hattori Nankaku 服部南郭 (1683–1759) of little intrinsic value. Hattori's remarks in his preface and in the notes show that he was already exercised by the unsatisfactory condition of the Ming text, but he did not have the editions available to remedy the situation. Despite its shortcomings the Shih-te t'ang edition has been used as the basis of the *SPPY* and *CTCC* editions.

(d) The *Hu hai lou ts'ung shu* 湖海樓叢書 edition

This edition was produced in 1813 by Wang Chi-p'ei 汪繼培 (b. 1775), and represented the first attempt to improve upon the preceding edition by using a facsimile copy of a Sung edition and the *Tao tsang* text of Yin Ching-shun to separate Chang Chan's commentary from later work. Reference was also made to a further Ming edition and to the textual notes of Lu Wen-ch'ao 盧文弨 (1717–1796) on the *Tao tsang* editions.

Though now available once more in *LTCC* subsequent scholarship has improved upon it considerably through collation with quotations of the *Lieh tzu* in encyclopaedias and other texts, so that it is now of less importance than previously.

(e) The *Kambun taikei* edition

This edition, which was published in 1912, was prepared by Hattori Unokichi. Apparently unaware of Wang Chi-p'ei's work (see preceding item), Hattori also referred to the Northern Sung edition to separate Chang Chan's commentary from the portions of Yin Ching-shun's work mixed into the Shih te t'ang edition. The result in this case is simply the Shih te t'ang text (typeset, punctuated and provided with *kaeriten*) with its two layers of commentary distinguished; no collation with the Northern Sung edition is provided. Hattori does incorporate into the commentary the *Resshi kō* 列子考 of Morokuzu Kishun 諸葛歸春 (1783–1847), which provides some cross-references to the work of Lin Hsi-i as well as Morokuzu's own observations, but this work (as Hattori recognized) had also been improved upon by subsequent scholarship even at the time of printing. Hattori's additional observations fail to make the edition much more comprehensive.

(f) Yang Po-chün 楊伯峻, *Lieh tzu chi shih* 列子集釋

The Chung hua edition (Peking, 1979) is by far the most comprehensive and convenient produced to date. Yang's work was first published by Lung men lien ho Press in Shanghai in 1958 and was reprinted by the T'ai ping Book Company in Hong Kong in 1965, and twice more in Taiwan. (See Yen, 1975, p. 38). The 1979 Chung hua edition incorporates additional material both in the textual notes and in the three addenda, which consist of a collection of sources on Chang Chan, a collection of the main prefaces connected with the *Lieh tzu*, and a collection of the main writings on its authenticity.

In the body of the work the main text of the *Lieh tzu* is based on that established by Wang Chi-p'ei, followed by the commentaries of Chang Chan and Lu Ch'ung-hsüan, the latter indicated by the character *chieh* 解. Textual notes from various Ch'ing and twentieth century critics are put in third place, followed by Yin Ching-shun's *Shih wen* and Jen Ta-ch'un's additional comments. Yang intersperses his own textual and other observations on all these as appropriate.

Yang has incorporated the criticism of a large number of scholars, including such excellent work as the *Lieh tzu pu cheng* 列子補正 of Wang Shu-min 王叔岷, first published by the Shang wu Press in Shanghai in

1947; but he has not been able to make use of some recent publications from Taiwan, such as T'ao Kuang's 陶光 *Lieh tzu chiao shih* 列子校釋, first published, probably privately, in Taipei in 1953. This last, together with one or two other works overlooked by Yang, is available in the *LTCC*. In general Yang's edition is remarkably complete. The main disadvantage to the user is the difficulty of distinguishing the various types of annotation on the page; Yang's indications are occasionally misleading in this respect.

(g) *Resshi soshō* 列子疏證

This critical edition of the *Lieh tzu* by Kakimura Shigematsu 柿村重松, published by the Meiki kaikan in Tokyo in 1926, is highly praised by Japanese scholars but would seem to be unavailable in libraries in Great Britain and North America.

5.   Reference works and translations

One substantial index to the *Lieh tzu* has been produced: Yamaguchi Yoshio 山口義男, *Resshi sakuin* 列子索引 (Nishinomiya: Mukogawa Joshi Daigaku Chūgoku Bungaku Kenkyū shitsu 武庫川女子大學中國文學研究室, 1960). It is based on the *CTCC* text, and notes variants between this and the *SPTK* text. The text precedes the index, and characters are listed by stroke order. Although not a full concordance, it is nevertheless extremely valuable.

The *Chou Ch'in Han Wei chu tzu chih chien shu mu* of Yen Lin-feng probably constitutes the single most valuable reference work for the study of the *Lieh tzu*, superseding earlier bibliographies by the same author, though a complete listing of editions has been deferred until the appearance of the sixth volume of the work. Some misprints occur. The dates given for Lu Ch'ung-hsüan and Yin Ching-shun are based on incorrect inferences, and it is now necessary to consult also Yen's supplement to his own work, 'Wu ch'iu pei chai hsin shou Lao Lieh Chuang san tzu shu mu' 無求備齋新收老列莊三子書目, *Shu mu chi k'an* 18.3 (December, 1984), pp. A3–A21. Yen's reluctance to include publications in periodicals may be remedied, in the case of the Chinese mainland materials, by consulting the listing given in *Chung kuo che hsüeh* 11 (January, 1984), pp. 522–3. The coverage, especially of Chinese works, is otherwise generally good, and even the listing of printed Tokugawa commentaries and modern Japanese translations is almost complete.

One Japanese version overlooked by Yen is the *Kambun* transcription by Hattori Unokichi in the *Kambun sōsho*, but this is by no means im-

portant. Far superior to other translations in the thoroughness of its annotations and its careful discussion of the problem of authenticity is that
by Fukunaga Mitsuji 福永光司 in volume four of *Chūgoku koten bungaku
taikei*. Secondary studies in Japanese periodicals are totally ignored by
Yen's bibliography and are often hard to locate, though the monographs
of Yamaguchi and Kobayashi mentioned above do refer to some earlier
Japanese scholarship.

Kobayashi would be useful not only for his listing of editions but also
for his statistical comparisons of textual variations between them, were
it not that he takes a late Ch'ing printing of the Shih te t'ang edition as
his standard. Nevertheless his own textual notes, in Classical Chinese,
on pp. 783–877, should not be overlooked. Nor should the best modern
Chinese translation of the *Lieh tzu*, Chuang Wan-shou's 莊萬壽 *Lieh tzu
tu pen* 列子讀本 (Taipei: San min, 1979), be ignored either. Despite the
implication of the title, this represents a substantial and conscientious
piece of work. It includes besides the translation a thoroughly annotated version of the text, preceded by a forty-seven page introduction,
all based on a wide reading of earlier scholarship.

Yen's bibliography also attempts to list studies and translations in
Western languages, but it is far from complete and is poorly printed. A
much more thorough bibliography by M. Soymié and F. Litsch may be
found in *Dōkyō kenkyū* 3 (1968), pp. (47–49). It would appear from this
that a translation into Russian included in L. Pozdneeva, *Ateisty, materia-
listy i dialektiki drevnego Kitaya* (Moscow: Nauka, 1967) is the most recent
version of the *Lieh tzu* in a Western language, but this does not seem to
be available in British libraries. Next most recent in date is B. Grynpas,
Lie tseu, Le vrai classique du vide parfait (Paris: Gallimard, 1961), who
adopts an impossibly conservative attitude to the date of the *Lieh tzu*
and translates from an unidentified reprint of the Shih te t'ang edition.
Worse still, it has been accused of arbitrary rearrangement of the text,
and K. M. Schipper has shown in *TP* 51.2–3 (1964), pp. 293–4, that it
relies to an unacceptable extent on the outdated French translation of
L. Wieger.

Undoubtedly the best translation into a Western language to date is
A.C. Graham, *The Book of Lieh-tzu* (London: John Murray, 1960). Although criticized in some quarters for underestimating the religious element in the *Lieh tzu* it has been generally very well received. Based on
the 1958 edition of Yang's *Lieh tzu chi shih*, it appends a page of concise
textual notes. The translation itself contains very few explanatory notes,
but each section is preceded by a brief summary of the main ideas,
whilst a general survey of the work and its background is provided in a

thirteen page introduction. Several partial translations into Western languages have been made. A recent example is a translation into Polish of the Yang Chu section: T. Zbikowski, 'Jang Czu', *Przeglad Orientalistycy* 1976.4, 441–456.

6. Japanese editions

A. *Kambun taikei;* no. 13, 1912, edited by Hattori Unokichi (see under 4 above).
B. *Kanseki kokujikai zensho;* no. 9, 1910, edited by Ōta Genkyū.
D. *Kokuyaku kambun taisei;* no. 7, 1920, edited by Kimida Rentarō.
E. *Kambun sōsho;* 1928, edited by Hattori Unokichi.
F. *Keisho taikō;* nos. 9, 10, 1938.
H. *Shinshaku kambun taikei;* no. 22, 1967, edited by Kobayashi Nobuaki.
J. *Chūgoku no shisō;* no. 6, 1964, edited by Okudaira Takashi and Ōmura Masuo.
K. *Chūgoku koten bungaku taikei;* no. 4, 1973, edited by Fukunaga Mitsuji.
L. *Chūgoku koten shinsho;* 1969, edited by Anazawa Tatsuo.

7. Indexes

(a) See under (5) above.
(b) *A Concordance to the Liezi* 列子逐字索引, ed. D.C. Lau and Chen Fong Ching; *ICS* series, Hong Kong: Commercial Press, forthcoming 1995.

— T. H. Barrett

Lun heng 論衡

1. Content

The *Lun heng* of Wang Ch'ung 王充 (A.D. 27–*c*. 100) is concerned with a variety of questions raised in philosophy, history, literature and natural science. In discussing natural phenomena and their implications or causes, matters of popular belief and misconception and political issues, the book is often written in polemical form. A controversial statement is made, to be followed by the author's critical rebuttal, which is often supported by quotations from earlier writings. In many ways the *Lun heng* may be regarded as an encyclopaedic collection of the claims and beliefs of Chinese religion, thought and folklore. The title of the work is variously rendered, e.g., as 'Disquisitions' or 'Discourses weighed in the balance'.

2. Date of composition and authenticity

The *Lun heng* may possibly have been completed between 70 and 80, on the basis of earlier writings or collections of essays that were each concerned with a particular problem. The authenticity of the work has not been brought into question.

Although there is an internal reference to the 100 or more *p'ien* of which the book consisted, there survive no more than 84, arranged in 30 *chüan*; the title of one further *p'ien* (no. 44: 'Chao chih' 招致) survives without the text. Possibly the text of the remaining 15 of the supposed number of 100 has been incorporated into some of the other *p'ien*, which now form parts of the received text. *P'ien* no. 85, which consists of biographical information about Wang Ch'ung, may well have been compiled by another hand at a later date. The terms *Chüeh ning* 覺佞, *Neng sheng* 能聖, *Shih sheng* 實聖 and *Sheng pao* 盛褒 which are quoted in *p'ien* nos. 33, 60 and 84 may be titles of *p'ien* that have now been lost.

The *Lun heng* mentions other writings by Wang Ch'ung which may have been incorporated, in part, in the present book. Thus, works entitled 'Chi su' 譏俗 and 'Chieh i' 節義 may now be represented in *p'ien* such as 'Pu shih' 卜筮 (no. 71) or 'Chieh ch'u' 解除 (no. 75); *p'ien* nos. 42

and 52, 'Ch'ien kao' 譴告 and 'Shih ying' 是應, may have derived from a separate text entitled 'Cheng wu' 政務. The nine *p'ien* (nos. 16–24) whose titles include the term *hsü* 虛 (false), the three (nos. 25–27) whose titles include the term *tseng* 增 (exaggerated), and three (nos. 28–30) which set out to criticise K'ung Tzu 孔子, Han Fei 韓非 and Meng Tzu 孟子 probably derived from a set of specifically philosophical writings, i.e. *Lun heng*, which has given its name to the present collection of 84 *p'ien*. *P'ien* nos. 78 and 79, 'Shih chih' 實知 and 'Chih shih' 知實, belong to a work or collection known as 'Shih lun' 實論. From these considerations it seems likely that the *Lun heng* as received represents an anthology of Wang Ch'ung's writings which were composed at different times and subsequently put together as one book; see Timoteus Pokora, 'The works of Wang Ch'ung,' *Archiv orientální* 36 (1968), 122–34.

3. Textual history

The *Pao p'u tzu* 抱朴子 (*p'ien* no. 43, opening statement) refers to the *Lun heng* of 'some 80 *p'ien*'; *Sui shu* 34, p. 1006 lists the work, with 29 *chüan*, among miscellaneous writers; the figure of 30 *chüan* is given in Fujiwara Sukeyo's catalogue and in both of the T'ang histories (*Chiu T'ang shu* 47, p. 2033; *Hsin T'ang shu* 59, p. 1534).

In the first known printed edition a certain Yang Wen-ch'ang 楊文昌, whose preface is dated in 1045, called on seven partial and two complete copies, mostly in poor condition. He states that he corrected the readings of 11,259 characters, i.e. some five percent of the whole; he does not indicate the changes that he introduced. While Yang's version has served as the basis for all succeeding editions, it has itself long been lost.

A copy of a good edition, dated between 1190 and 1194, in which *chüan* nos. 8–10 are missing, is available in the Imperial Library, Tokyo; for 18 editions that are subsequent to that of Yang, see Pelliot's review of Forke's translation (see under 6 below), in *Journal Asiatique* Series X, vol. xx (1912), 156–71, and Huang Hui's edition (1969 print; see under 4 below), pp. 1317–43. In addition, the re-organisation of the Ch'ing archives in 1929 revealed a printed text of *chüan* nos. 14–17, from an edition that probably predated 1068.

The most commonly quoted early editions today are those in (i) Ch'eng Jung's 程榮 (1447–1520) *Han Wei ts'ung shu* (1592); and (ii) the T'ung chin ts'ao t'ang 通津草堂, 1522–66, reproduced in the *Ssu pu ts'ung k'an* series. The *Ssu pu pei yao* text was based on a Ming edition and included prefaces by Shen Yün-chi 沈雲揖 (1588) and Yü Ch'un-hsi 虞淳熙 (*cs* 1853).

4. Annotated editions

No commentaries to the *Lun heng* appear to have been written before the nineteenth century, when notes were compiled by Yü Yüeh 俞樾 (1821–1907), Sun I-jang 孫詒讓 (1848–1908) and Yang Shou-ching 楊守敬 (1835–1915). Subsequent editions, with notes accompanying the text, include:

(a) Huang Hui 黃暉 (b. 1930), *Lun heng chiao shih* 論衡校釋, preface dated 1935; first edition, Ch'ang sha: Shang wu, 1938; reproduced text from a copy marked by Hu Shih's 胡適 (1891–1962) manuscript annotation, Taipei: Taiwan Shang wu, 1964, reprinted 1969. Huang Hui's notes systematically quote citations of the *Lun heng* which appear in pre-Sung sources, thus throwing light on the textual changes introduced by Yang Wen-ch'ang. The appendix includes citations of lost fragments of text; the principal dates of Wang Ch'ung's life and career; comments to and evaluation of the *Lun heng* from the *Pao p'u tzu* 抱朴子 onwards; Hu Shih's essay on the *Lun heng* (first published in *Hsien tai hsüeh sheng* 現代學生 (Shanghai) 1.6, 8, 9 (1930–31); bibliographical notes; and prefaces, beginning with that of Yang Wen-ch'ang.

(b) Liu P'an-sui 劉盼遂 (b. 1899), *Lun heng chi chieh* 論衡集解; preface dated 1932; Peking: Ku chi, 1957; reprinted Taipei, 1964. Liu P'an-sui's extensive notes are included with the text. The appendix covers much the same ground as does that of (a).

For the foregoing two works, see Timoteus Pokora, 'Two recently commented editions of the Lun-heng,' *Archiv orientální* 34 (1966), 593–601.

(c) Pei ching ta hsüeh li shih hsi 'Lun heng' chu shih hsiao tsu, *Lun heng chu shih* 論衡注釋, 4 vols.; Peking: Chung hua, 1979. The text, in simplified characters, is preceded by summaries of the argument for each *p'ien*, and followed by notes, which frequently include a version of the text in modern Chinese. The appendix includes the biography of Wang Ch'ung from *Hou Han shu* 49, pp. 1629–30; citations of lost text; bibliographical information, including prefaces and postfaces; a select list of Chinese and Japanese secondary studies; and an index of proper names of persons mentioned in the text.

5. Secondary studies

(a) T'ien Ch'ang-wu 田昌五, *Wang Ch'ung—ku tai ti chan tou wei wu lun che* 王充——古代的戰鬥唯物論者; [Peking]: Jen min, 1958; second edition Shanghai: Jen min, 1973. Select portions of this booklet have been translated by Elma E. Kopetsky, in *Chinese Studies in Philosophy* VII.1-2 (Fall-Winter 1975-76), 1-197.

(b) Ch'en Kung 陳拱, *Wang Ch'ung ssu hsiang p'ing lun* 王充思想評論; T'ai chung: Ssu li tung hai ta hsüeh, 1968.

(c) Karlgren, Bernhard, 'Excursions in Chinese grammar,' *BMFEA* 23 (1952), 107f.; pp. 114f. refer to features of linguistic usage in the *Lun heng*.

(d) Leslie, Donald, 'Contribution to a new translation of the *Lun heng*,' *TP* 44 (1956), 100-49.

6. Translation

The only complete translation into English is that of Alfred Forke, *Lun-heng: Part I Philosophical essays of Wang Ch'ung; Part II Miscellaneous essays of Wang Ch'ung*, 2 vols.; Shanghai: Kelly and Walsh; London: Luzac; Leipzig: Harrassowitz, 1907 and 1911; reprinted, New York: Paragon Book Gallery, 1962. The order of the *p'ien* has been rearranged so as to fit categories of subject matter, e.g., metaphysical, physical or ethical. This translation appeared previously in *MSOS* IX (1906), 181-400; X (1907), 1-172; and XI (1908), 1-188.

7. Japanese editions

H. *Shinshaku kambun taikei*, nos. 68, 69 and 94, edited by Yamada Katsumi.
I.   *Tōyō bunko*, no. 46, edited by Otaki Kazuo.
K. *Chūgoku koten bungaku taikei*, no. 7, 1972, edited by Otaki Kazuo.
L. *Chūgoku koten shinsho*, 1983, edited by Wakamoto Makoto.

8. Indexes

(a) *Lun heng t'ung chien (Index du Louen Heng)*; Centre franco-chinois d'études sinologiques no. 1, Peking, 1943; reprinted Taipei; Ch'eng wen, 1968.

(b) *Ronkō jirui sakuin* 論衡事類索引, edited by Yamada Katsumi 山田勝美 and others; Tokyo: Taitō bunka kenkyūjo, 1960.

(c) *Ronkō koyūmeishi sakuin fu Kunaichō shoryōbu zō Sōbun kōkanki* 論衡固有名詞索引附宮內廳書陵部藏宋本校勘記, edited by Yamada Katsumi and others; Tokyo: Daitō bunka kenkyūjo, 1961.

(d) *A Concordance to the Lunheng* 論衡逐字索引, ed. D.C. Lau and Chen Fong Ching; *ICS* series, Hong Kong: Commercial Press, forthcoming 1995.

— Timoteus Pokora
— Michael Loewe

Lun yü 論語

1. Content

The *Lun yü* is probably the best known of the Confucian Classics and can be said to be an essential part of every person's culture in China, even today. In *Han shu* 30, p. 1717, Pan Ku 班固 (32–92) writes:

> The *Lun yü* contains the replies made by Master K'ung to his disciples and contemporaries, and the discussions between the disciples or the words that they heard from the Master. At that time each disciple held his own record, so that when the Master died, his followers put their notes together to make a compilation, thus called the *Lun yü*.

For the meaning of the two terms *lun* and *yü*, see Huang K'an 黃侃 as cited in 7 (a) below.

The *Lun yü* would thus appear to be a 'compilation of the words' of Confucius (traditional dates 551–479 B.C.). The work is in fact mainly composed of rather short pieces of dialogue, most frequently conducted by the Master and his disciples; these endow the work with a uniquely vivid and colourful character, quite at variance with that of other classical works. The chief value of the *Lun yü* is probably that of providing an insight into the behaviour and daily life of Confucius and his disciples. Through these dialogues, we also get a general idea of his personality and teaching, which is concerned essentially with problems of individual and social ethics, whose two levels are in constant interaction. Thus the utmost ideal of 'humanity' (*jen* 仁) that should be embodied by the 'man of good' (*chün tzu* 君子) finds its expression on the political plane in the humane government of the enlightened ruler. The ideal of *jen* defines a type of Confucian humanism that places great faith in, first, man's capacity for self-improvement; and, secondly, in the wisdom of ancient sages and the cultural tradition; these lead respectively to the fundamental role of education, and the frequent references to Yao, Shun or the early mythical rulers of China. Such themes receive comparatively short treatment in the *Lun yü*, as compared with the longer references in the classical texts.

The received text comprises twenty *p'ien*, each being traditionally split into two halves, and each being divided into sections (*chang* 章). The order of the *p'ien*, and of the sections within the *p'ien*, is most often purely haphazard. Some sentences are duplicated in different parts of the work; some ideas recur frequently. The titles of the *p'ien* do not indicate dominant themes; they merely consist of the first characters that occur at the beginning of each *p'ien*. The overall impression is that of an absence of a definite plan or organised scheme on the part of the compilers.

2. Authorship and date of composition

The heterogeneous nature of the *Lun yü* as received precludes the hypothesis that there was a single author. The idea that seems to have predominated under the Han is that the *Lun yü* was compiled after notes had been made by the direct disciples of Confucius. This is asserted by Liu Hsiang 劉向 (79-8 B.C.), as cited by Ho Yen 何晏 (190-249) in his *Lun yü chi chieh hsü* 論語集解序, and taken over by Pan Ku in his *I wen chih*. In a lost *hsü* 序 reproduced by Liu Pao-nan 劉寶楠 (1791-1855), Cheng Hsüan 鄭玄 (127-200) even specifies that the work was actually compiled by Chung Kung 仲弓, Tzu Hsia 子夏, Tzu Yu 子游 and others. In the T'ang dynasty, Liu Tsung-yüan 柳宗元 (773-819; see *Liu Ho-tung chi* 柳河東集; Shanghai: Jen min, 1974, pp. 68-9) affirmed the idea that the compilation had been due to second generation disciples, in particular Tseng tzu 曾子 and Yu tzu 有子, to whom the text of the *Lun yü* refers as 'Master'. This opinion was repeated by Chu Hsi 朱熹 (1130-1200), who quotes Ch'eng I 程頤 (1033-1107), in his *Lun yü hsü shuo* 論語序說.

Modern scholarship tends to conceive of less well defined or even anonymous authorship; the *Lun yü* is regarded as a composite work of various layers contributed by different hands, and being compiled at a more recent date (see Waley, *Analects of Confucius*, pp. 21f.). Ch'ien Mu 錢穆 (b. 1895) places the date of composition between the end of the Chou and the start of Ch'in, owing to traces of interpolations of the Warring States period. In a recent article Chu Wei-cheng 朱維錚 even goes as far as to suppose that the *Lun yü* could have been written down in Former Han, between 157 and 87 B.C., just as the *Kung yang chuan* had been compiled at that time in order to respond to the new degree of praise accorded to Confucianism (see Chu Wei-cheng, as cited in 7 (a) below). Most scholars agree that the title of the work was probably coined at the beginning of the Han period, thus confirming Wang

Ch'ung's 王充 (*c.* 27–100) testimony to that effect (see Chao Chi-pin, as cited in 7 (a) below). Originally the work had been referred to as the *K'ung tzu* 孔子, in the same way as writings of other masters of the Warring States period.

3. Textual history

As a text the *Lun yü* can be said to have passed through three main stages of elaboration; first in the Han and Six Dynasties period; secondly from the Sung to the Ming periods; and thirdly by way of scholastic scrutiny and textual criticism during the Ch'ing dynasty.

The process whereby the text was elaborated during the Han and Six Dynasties was somewhat involved. In the Former Han, there were three versions of the work. Quoting Liu Hsiang, Ho Yen distinguishes between a *Lu lun* 魯論 and a *Ch'i lun* 齊論 resulting from two different lines of transmission, and both in *chin wen* 今文. The two versions differed in the first place according to the number of chapters; the former version amounted to 20 *p'ien*, the latter to 22, with the two extra chapters being entitled *Wen wang* 問王 and *Chih tao* 知道. Ho Yen goes on to remark that, for the 20 *p'ien* which were common to both versions, the exegesis (*chang chü* 章句) was somewhat more abundant for the *Ch'i lun* than for the *Lu lun*.

Ho Yen mentions a third version, the *Ku wen Lun yü* 古文論語, i.e. the *Lun yü* in ancient script, that was supposedly re-discovered during the reign of Ching ti 景帝 (r. 157–141 B.C.) in the wall of Confucius' former house at Lu 魯. The text had been accompanied by copies of the *Shang shu* 尚書, *Li chi* 禮記 and *Hsiao ching* 孝經, all in ancient script, and the discovery followed the demolition of the house by Lu Kung wang 魯恭王 (r. 153–128 B.C.) in order to build his own palace (*Han shu* 30, p. 1706). The *Ku lun* is said to have consisted of 21 *p'ien*, the extra chapter resulting from the division of the last one into two. The main difference between the *Ku lun* and the other two, *chin wen*, versions lay not so much in the number of chapters as in the considerable textual variations, which, according to Huan T'an's 桓譚 (*c.* 43 B.C.–A.D. 28) statement may have affected over 400 words, and the organisation of the chapters (see Huang K'an). Ho Yen observes that the academician K'ung An-kuo 孔安國 (d. *c.* 100 B.C.) was the only one to make glosses on the text, but these were not handed down.

Doubts have been raised regarding the authenticity of these glosses, as in Ch'en Chan 陳鱣 (1753–1817), *Lun yü ku hsün* 論語古訓 of 1796. According to Shen T'ao 沈濤 (*fl.* 1820), *Lun yü K'ung chu pien wei* 論語孔

注辨僞, the glosses were by Ho Yen himself. Ting Yen 丁晏 (1794–1875), in his *Lun yü K'ung chu cheng wei* 論語孔注證僞, attributes them to Wang Su 王肅 (195–256); the latter is also accused of having forged the *Ku wen shang shu* 古文尙書, supposedly edited by K'ung An-kuo. Fragments of the *Ku lun* and the *Ch'i lun* are collected in the *Yü han shan fang chi i shu*. Wang Mo's 王謨 (*cs* 1778) *Han Wei i shu ch'ao* 漢魏遺書鈔 includes fragments of a lost *Lun yü*, i.e., quotations in the *Shuo wen chieh tzu* 說文解字 that are not present in the received text.

The basis of the modern version of the *Lun yü* seems in fact to be the result of a rather fortuitous attempt at syncretism made by Chang Yü 張禹 (d. 5 B.C.) (see *Han shu* 81, p. 3347f.). In about 48 B.C. he was acting as teacher of the *Lun yü* to the heir apparent. After the latter's accession as Ch'eng ti 成帝 (r. 33–7 B.C.), Chang Yü was ennobled as Marquis of An-ch'ang 安昌 (25 B.C.), and for this reason he is sometimes designated as Marquis Chang (Chang hou). He seems to have compiled his own commentary (*chang chü* 章句) by taking the Lu version as the basic text, making references to the Ch'i version whenever he deemed them to be necessary. This work was intended to serve as a handbook for the heir apparent. Known as the *Chang hou lun*, the book eventually took precedence over other commentaries; it enjoyed such prestige among the Han literati that it was this version of the *Lun yü* which was selected for engraving on stone, along with the other classical texts of the *chin wen* tradition in A.D. 175. The quality of this text was strongly questioned by Ch'ing scholars such as Ts'ui Shu 崔述 (1740–1816), but it represents a major landmark in that it was the first attempt to edit the *Lun yü* in a unified version.

According to Ho Yen, this text formed the basis for other commentaries, by Pao Hsien 包咸 (*fl.* A.D. 10; see *Hou Han shu* 79B, p. 2570) and a certain Chou shih 周氏 about whom nothing is known. Lu Te-ming 陸德明 (556–627) states that these two exegetical works were studied as official commentaries at the Imperial academy and 'that Cheng [Hsüan] collated the Chang, Pao and Chou glosses on the Lu version, comparing this with the Ch'i and the Ku versions, and that he added his own commentary'. The Chou glosses or commentaries, otherwise unknown, could have been a transition between the *Chang hou lun* and Cheng Hsüan versions.

The *Sui shu* (32, pp. 935–36) and *Chiu T'ang shu* (46, p. 1981) include respectively three and two entries for the *Lun yü* with Cheng Hsüan's commentary. Fragments of this work were collected by Ch'ing scholars such as Sung Hsiang-feng 宋翔鳳 (1776–1860) and Yüan Chün 袁鈞 (*fl.* 1796–1820), but the full text has long since been lost. Parts of a manuscript copy which is dated to the T'ang period and which was discovered recently at Tun-huang testify to the fact that Cheng Hsüan's commentary refers to the *Lu lun* as established by Chang Yü, and perhaps Chou shih, with corrections based on the Ch'i and Ku versions. This manuscript has been studied by Ishizuka Harumichi 石塚晴通 and Wang Su 王素.

It now appears that the received text of the *Lun yü* is the result of a gradual process of several centuries. The three versions of the early Han period have been compared by some specialists with the triple version of some chapters of the *Mo tzu*, probably representing three different transmissions. When, in the reign of Wu ti 武帝 (141-87), Confucianism came to the fore, the study of the *Lun yü* together with the *Hsiao ching* seems to have been regarded as a form of preparation for the study of the Five Classics.

Cheng Hsüan's synthesis was consolidated in the *Lun yü chi chieh* 論語集解, of 10 *chüan*, which was compiled by Ho Yen and three other scholars, with a preface dated in 242. This work is based on Cheng Hsüan's version, while taking into account the best of the commentaries of the Han and the Wei periods. The influence of the *hsüan hsüeh* 玄學 school of thought, of which Ho Yen was an eminent representative, can also be felt. Thereafter the Cheng and the Ho versions were studied concurrently until the T'ang period, when the Ho tradition eclipsed that of Cheng. Huang K'an's 黃侃 (488-545) *Lun yü i shu* 論語義疏, written in 10 *chüan* during the Liang 梁 period and based on Ho's commentary, doubtless contributed greatly to the success of that version on the eve of the Sui and T'ang dynasties. The work lists thirteen commentators of the Chin period, of whom Huang K'an had taken account in his own commentary, and it is through the work of Ho and Huang that it is possible to trace the textual and exegetical traditions of the *Lun yü* during the Han period and the Six Dynasties.

Except for Lu Te-ming's phonological commentary (*yin i* 音義), there were no exegetical departures in the T'ang period. According to the *Ssu k'u ch'üan shu tsung mu t'i yao*, in 999 orders were given to Hsing Ping 邢昺 (931-1010) to make a new edition, based on the work of Huang K'an, that would serve as a handbook for official examinations; this took the form of a sub-commentary to Huang's work.

Chu Hsi's interpretation, in his *Ssu shu chi chu* 四書集注 is of far greater importance. As the name of this work indicates, it collects preceding commentaries, by the brothers Ch'eng I 程頤 (1033-1107) and Ch'eng Hao 程顥 (1032-1085), Chang Tsai 張載 (1020-1077) and other major Sung thinkers, but it is not always possible to identify the source of an opinion. While Chu Hsi in no sense ignores questions of exegesis, his interpretations tend to be framed so as to accord with his philosophical views. Chao Shun-sun's 趙順孫 (1215-1276) *Ssu shu tsuan shu* 四書纂疏 may be used as a sub-commentary to Chu Hsi's *chi chu*, but it is thanks to the latter work that the *Lun yü* gained its place and title among the classics, and that Chu Hsi's version was to remain the current edition from the Sung to the Ch'ing periods. By the Yüan dynasty, it had become a basic requirement for the imperial examinations, completely eclipsing the editions of Huang K'an and Hsing Ping. During the Ming period it was felt necessary to produce a second version of the *chi chu*, which would include Sung and Yüan commentaries; the resulting work, by Hu Kuang 胡廣 (1370-1418) and others, was entitled *Ssu shu chi chu ta ch'üan* 四書集注大全.

The Ch'ing reaction to the work of the Sung and Ming Neo-Confucian scholars began with books such as Wang Fu-chih's 王夫之 (1619-1692) *Tu Ssu shu ta ch'üan shuo* 讀四書大全說. There followed a decisive turn in the preoccupations of scholars, who were no longer interested in speculating on the philosophical implications of classical texts, but wished increasingly to return to the Han tradition (*Han hsüeh* 漢學), with particular reference to the philological aspects that had been inherited from Cheng Hsüan. It was within this perspective that fragments of Han and Six Dynasties works were re-assembled in large compilations such as the *Yü han shan fang chi i shu*, and Wang Mo's *Han Wei i shu ch'ao*.

Other large collections gathered extant exegetical works. Thus, Chu I-tsun's 朱彝尊 (1629-1709) *Ching i k'ao* 經義考 (1701) collects 463 works on the *Lun yü*, ranging from the Han to the early Ch'ing period. Ch'ing scholarship is fully represented in the *Huang Ch'ing ching chieh* 皇清經解 (1829) of Juan Yüan 阮元 (1764-1859), and in the supplement to that work (*hsü pien* 續編 1888) by Wang Hsien-ch'ien 王先謙 (1842-1918). Textual variants are considered in Ch'en Chan's 陳鱣 (1753-1817) *Lun yü ku hsün* 論語古訓, Feng Teng-fu's 馮登府 (1783-1841) *Lun yü i wen k'ao cheng* 論語異文考證 and Chai Hao's 翟灝 (*cs* 1754) *Ssu shu k'ao i* 四書考異.

The most valuable and authoritative attempt at reconsidering the text of the *Lun yü* as a whole remains the *Lun yü cheng i* 論語正義 of Liu Pao-nan, completed by his son Liu Kung-mien 劉恭冕 (1824-1883). The text and glosses basically follow Hsing Ping's edition, but textual variants from the Han and T'ang stone classics, the *i shu* by Huang K'an, and Lu Te-ming's *shih wen* have been included in the glosses. In his postface (1866), Liu Kung-mien states that the *cheng i* was composed after the pattern of Chiao Hsün's 焦循 (1763-1820) *Meng tzu cheng i* 孟子正

義, and that his father had not discriminated between the Han and the Sung traditions; all that could serve the cause of scholarship had been worth using and taking into account.

For collected studies of and notes on the *Lun yü*, reproduced in facsimile, see Yen Ling-feng 嚴靈峯, *Lun yü chi ch'eng* 論語集成 (*Wu ch'iu pei chai* 無求備齋 series; Taipei: I wen, 1966).

4. Manuscript copies

A cache of bamboo strips found at tomb no. 40, Ting hsien 定縣 Ho-pei, included parts of the text; see *Wen wu* 1981.8, 11–12; see p. 10 for identification of the site as the tomb of Liu Hsiu 劉修, king of Chung shan 中山 who died in 55 B.C. The paper roll found at Turfan, which measures 5.38 by 0.27 metres, was dated by the twelve year old boy who wrote it in 710; see *Wen wu* 1972.2, 13–15. For items from Tun-huang, see Ishizuka and Wang Su, as cited in (7) below. Shimada Kan 島田翰 (see (7) below) mentions two Japanese manuscripts, the one with the *chi chieh* of 1327, and the other with the *i shu*, of 1338–42.

5. Current editions

The *Ssu pu pei yao* print is based on a Ming edition by Chin P'an 金蟠 (17th century) and Ko Tzu 葛鼏 (*fl.* 1523), of 1639, and Ho Yen's *chi chieh*. It includes the *Ch'ung k'an Sung pen shih san ching chu shu fu chiao k'an chi* 重刊宋本十三經注疏附勘記 of Juan Yüan, who had provided a late Sung edition by Yüeh K'o 岳珂 (1183–1240) to remedy the pitiful state of the extant Ming editions. The *Lun yü* is given there with Ho Yen's *chi chieh* and Hsing Ping's *shu* 疏.

The *Ssu pu ts'ung k'an* reproduces a *Lun yü* in 10 *chüan*, with Ho Yen's *chi chieh* only, from the *Ku i ts'ung shu*; this is in fact a facsimile of an early Japanese print, of the Shōhei 正平 period (1346–69). According to Shimada Kan this was in turn based on a Northern Sung edition, which had originated from the stone classics of the T'ang period (836–41); see Yen K'o-chün 嚴可均 (1762–1843), *T'ang shih ching chiao wen* 唐石經校文. The Shōhei edition formed the basis for a number of subsequent Japanese versions.

The *Ts'ung shu chi ch'eng* reproduces the *Lun yü*, with the *chi chieh* and *i shu*, from the *Chih pu tsu chai ts'ung shu*, which was originally based on a Japanese edition of 1750 that had been kept in the Ashikaga 足利 school library. It is to this edition that the *Ssu k'u t'i yao* refers in connection with a *Lun yü chi chieh i shu* in 10 *chüan*: 'Ever since the Southern Sung, this work has been long lost. This copy was brought back from

Japan, and is probably an ancient document handed down from T'ang. The text of the classic and its commentaries differs greatly from that of the modern edition'.

6. Modern annotated editions

Attention is drawn to the following, out of a large number of modern editions:

(a) Ch'eng Shu-te 程樹德, *Lun yü chi shih* 論語集釋, 3 vols.; preface dated 1939; Peking: Kuo li Hua pei pien i kuan, 1943, reprinted Taipei, 1965. With quotations from some 480 works related to the *Lun yü* which are listed at the end, this edition probably includes the most exhaustive annotations to be found in a modern edition.

(b) Yang Shu-ta 楊樹達, *Lun yü shu cheng* 論語疏證; Peking: K'o hsüeh, 1955, re-issued Shanghai: 1986. This commentary throws light on the text with the help of a large amount of material dated before the Six Dynasties.

(c) Yang Po-chün 楊伯峻, *Lun yü i chu* 論語譯注; Peking: Ku chi, 1958, re-issued 1980.

(d) Ch'ien Mu 錢穆, *Lun yü hsin chieh* 論語新解; Hong Kong: Hsin ya, 1963.

(e) Wang Shu-lin 王書林, *Lun yü i chu chi i wen chiao k'an chi* 論語譯注及異文校勘記; 2 vols., Taipei: Shang wu, 1982.

7. Secondary studies

The very large extent of publications on this text precludes mention of more than a few select works and those to which reference has been made above.

(a) Chinese

    (1) Chai Hao 翟灝, *Ssu shu k'ao i* 四書攷異; preface 1769.

    (2) Chao Chi-pin 趙紀彬, 'Lun yü hsin lun tao yen' 論語新論導言; *Chung kuo che hsüeh* 10, 1983, 49–62.

    (3) Chao Shun-sun 趙順孫 (1215–76), *Ssu shu tsuan shu* 四書纂疏.

    (4) Ch'en Chan 陳鱣, *Lun yü ku hsün* 論語古訓, 1796.

    (5) Chiao Hsün 焦循 (1763–1826), *Meng tzu cheng i* 孟子正義.

    (6) Ch'ien Mu 錢穆, *Lun yü yao lüeh* 論語要略; Shanghai: Shang wu, 1930.

    (7) Chu Hsi 朱熹 (1130–1200) *Lun yü hsü shuo* 論語序說.

    (8) Chu Hsi, *Ssu shu chi chu* 四書集注, 1177.

(9) Chu I-tsun 朱彝尊, *Ching i k'ao* 經義考, completed 1701.

(10) Chu Wei-cheng 朱維靜, 'Lun yü chieh chi ts'uo shuo' 論語結集脞說; *K'ung tzu yen chiu* 1, 1986, 40–52.

(11) Feng Teng-fu 馮登府, *Lun yü i wen k'ao cheng* 論語異文考證, 1890.

(12) Ho Yen 何晏, *Lun yü chi chieh [hsü]* 論語集解[序], 242.

(13) Hsing Ping 邢昺, *Lun yü chu shu* 論語注疏, 999.

(14) Hu Kuang 胡廣, *Ssu shu chi chu ta ch'üan* 四書集注大全, 1415.

(15) Huang K'an 黃侃 (488–545), *Lun yü i shu* 論語義疏.

(16) Juan Yüan 阮元, *Huang Ch'ing ching chieh* 皇清經解, 1829.

(17) Juan Yüan, *Ch'ung k'an Sung pen shih san ching chu shu fu chiao k'an chi* 重刊宋本十三經注疏附校勘記, 1806.

(18) Liu Pao-nan 劉寶楠, *Lun yü cheng i* 論論正義, completed 1866.

(19) Liu Tsung-yüan 柳宗元 (773–819), *Liu Ho-tung chi* 柳河東集.

(20) Lu Te-ming 陸德明 (556–627), *Ching tien shih wen hsü lu* 經典釋文敘錄.

(21) Shen T'ao 沈濤, *Lun yü K'ung chu pien wei* 論語孔注辨偽, 1821.

(22) Sung Hsiang-feng 宋翔鳳 (1776–1860), *Lun yü Cheng shih chu* 論語鄭氏注.

(23) Ting Yen 丁晏, *Lun yü K'ung chu cheng wei* 論語孔注證偽, preface 1881.

(24) Ts'ui Shu 崔述, *Chu ssu k'ao hsin lu* 洙泗考信錄, 1810.

(25) Wang Fu-chih 王夫之 (1619–92), *Tu ssu shu ta ch'üan shuo* 讀四書大全說.

(26) Wang Hsien-ch'ien 王先謙, *Huang Ch'ing ching chieh hsü pien* 皇清經解續編, 1888.

(27) Wang Mo 王謨, *Han Wei i shu ch'ao* 漢魏遺書鈔, 1798.

(28) Wang Su 王素, 'Tun-huang wen shu chung ti ti ssu chien "Lun yü Cheng shih chu"' 敦煌文書中的第四件 "論語鄭氏注", *Wen wu* 1984.9, 62–64.

(29) Yen K'o-chün 嚴可均, *T'ang shih ching chiao wen* 唐石經校文, 1797.

(30) Yüan Chün 袁鈞, *Cheng shih i shu* 鄭氏佚書, 1888.

(b) Japanese

(1) Ishizuka Harumichi 石塚晴道, 'The texts of *Lun yü*, with commentaries by Cheng Hsüan, discovered in Tun-huang and Turfan'; *Journal Asiatique* 269 (1981), 101–08.

(2) Morohashi Tetsuji 諸橋轍次, *Rongo no kōgi* 論語の講義; Tokyo: 1939.

(3) Nagasawa Kikuya 長澤規矩也, *Ashikaga gakkō iseki toshokan*

kosho bunrui mokuroku 足利學校遺蹟圖書館古書分類目錄; Ashikaga shiyakusho, 1966; revised edition Tokyo, 1975.

(4) Shimada Kan 島田翰, *Kobun kyūsho kō* 古文舊書考; Tokyo: Minyūsha, 1905.

(5) Takeuchi Yoshio 武內義雄, *Rongo no kenkyū* 論語の研究; Tokyo: Iwanami, 1939.

8. Translations

(a) Legge, *The Chinese Classics*, vol. I; also available in *The Four Books*, printed and reprinted variously.

(b) Soothill, William, *The Analects of Confucius*; London: Oxford University Press, 1937 (first published Yokohama, 1910).

(c) Waley, Arthur, *The Analects of Confucius*, London: George Allen and Unwin Ltd., 1938.

(d) Lau, D.C., *Confucius The Analects (Lun yü)*; Harmondsworth: Penguin Books, 1979; reprinted, with Chinese text, Hong Kong: Chinese University Press, 1979.

(e) Couvreur, Séraphin, *Entretiens de Confucius*; in *Les Quatre Livres*; Chinese text, translation in Latin and French, third edition, Sien Hsien: Mission Catholique, 1930.

(f) Cheng, Anne, *Entretiens de Confucius*; Paris: Éditions du Seuil, 1981.

(g) Ryckmans, Pierre, *Les Entretiens de Confucius*; Paris: Gallimard, 1987.

9. Japanese editions

A. *Kambun taikei*; no. 1, 1909, edited by Hattori Unokichi and Yasui Sokken.

B. *Kanseki kokujikai zensho*; no. 1, 1909, edited by Nakamura Tekisai.

C. *Kōchū kambun sōsho*; no. 1, 1913, edited by Mōri Teisai and Kubo Tenzui.

D. *Kokuyaku kambun taisei*; no. 1, 1922, edited by Hattori Unokichi and Kimida Rentarō.

E. *Kambun sōsho*, 1927.

F. *Keisho taikō*, nos. 1, 2, 1938–39.

H. *Shinshaku kambun taikei*; no. 1, 1960, edited by Yoshida Kenkō.

J. *Chūgoku no shisō*; no. 9, 1970, edited by Kume Sakao.

K. *Chūgoku koten bungaku taikei*; no. 3, 1970, edited by Kimura Eiichi and Suzuki Kiichi.

L. *Chūgoku koten shinsho*; 2 vols., edited by Uno Tetsuo.

M. *Shintei Chūgoku koten sen*; nos. 2, 3, 1965–66, edited by Yoshikawa Kōjirō.

10. Indexes

(a) *Lun yü yin te* 論語引得 (A concordance to the Analects of Confucius); *Harvard-Yenching Institute Sinological Index Series*, supplement no. 16, Peking: 1940; chief editor William Hung.

(b) Morimoto Kakuzō 森本角藏, *Shisho sakuin* 四書索引; Tokyo: Meguro shoten, 1921.

(c) Yeh Shao-chün 葉紹鈞, *Shih san ching so yin* 十三經索引, Shanghai: K'ai-ming, 1934.

(d) Gotō Toshimizu 後藤俊瑞, *Shushi shisho shūchū sakuin* 朱子四書集註索引; Hiroshima: Hiroshima daigaku bungakubu Chūgoku tetsugaku kenkyūshitsu, 1954.

(e) *A Concordance to the Lunyu* 論語逐字索引, ed. D.C. Lau and Chen Fong Ching; *ICS* series, Hong Kong: Commercial Press, forthcoming 1994.

— Anne Cheng

Lü shih ch'un ch'iu 呂氏春秋

1. Compilation

The *Lü shih ch'un ch'iu*, of about 239 B.C., has been ascribed to Lü Pu-wei 呂不韋, a merchant from Han 韓 who finally became chancellor of Ch'in 秦, and committed suicide in 235 B.C. (*Shih chi* 85, pp. 2505f.). While his association with the work can hardly be brought into question, it is not known what part he took in its compilation, and it is probable that the scholars whom he directed wrote a great proportion of the work. Its authenticity as a pre-Ch'in text is generally accepted.

The *Lü shih ch'un ch'iu* is unique among early works in that it is well organised and comprehensive, containing extensive passages on such subjects as music and agriculture, which are unknown elsewhere. It is also one of the longest of the early texts, extending to something over 100,000 characters. To the usual description of its language as 'homogeneous' there must be added the qualifications that there is considerable borrowing from other texts with differing grammatical characteristics, and the fact that in different parts of the book there are different patterns of word usage. The purpose for which the *Lü shih ch'un ch'iu* was written is subject to question. In the traditional Chinese view, the book was regarded as a repository of thought and knowledge derived mainly from the *ju chia* 儒家, *mo chia* 墨家 and *tao chia* 道家.

2. Content and structure

The book is divided into three major parts, or sections, characterised as (a) *chi* 紀, (b) *lan* 覽, and (c) *lun* 論, each of which is sub-divided in various ways according to a definite system.

(a) The first of the three parts, *chi*, is divided into 12 *chüan*, each one of which contains 5 *p'ien*. Apparently this arrangement was intended to reach a total of 60, i.e., the number of terms in the sexagenary cycle. The 12 *chüan* correspond with the months of the year and set out the activities that correspond thereto appropriately. Although the names of the *p'ien* have been standardised since Pi Yüan's 畢沅 (1730–97)

edition of 1789, a few *p'ien* bear different titles in earlier editions. Within the '*chi*' part of the book, there are thus 3 *chüan* assigned to each of the four seasons, and each group of 3 is characterised by a general topic; i.e., that of life, for the spring; music and learning, for the summer; war and strategy, for the autumn; and death, for the winter. In the received text the *Hsü i* 序意, or postface, follows the *chi* section of the book and belongs thereto.

In each of the 12 *chüan* the initial *p'ien* states the actions and prescriptions that are, or ought to be, performed at the appropriate times of the year to ensure that the state runs smoothly; the four succeeding *p'ien* of each *chüan* include disquisitions on the appropriate concept for the season that is concerned. The twelve initial *p'ien* were borrowed from a chapter of the *I chou shu* that is now lost, but which is termed 'Yüeh ling' 月令 in that book's table of contents. The same text occurs in the *Li chi* (again as 'Yüeh ling') and in the *Huai nan tzu*, with some differences. Grammatically, these 'Yüeh ling' chapters are quite different from others in this major part of the *Lü shih ch'un ch'iu*.

(b) The second of the three major parts includes 8 *chüan*, with the term *lan* appearing in the title of each one. Each *chüan* includes 8 *p'ien* (except that one *p'ien* is missing in the first *chüan*), which thus reach a total of 64, and suggest the 8 trigrams and 64 hexagrams and their treatment in the *Chou i*. The 8 *lan* form the longest and most varied section of the whole work, living up to their name or description of 'panoramic surveys'.

(c) The third major part includes 6 *chüan*, whose titles incorporate the term *lun*. Each of the six includes 6 *p'ien*, but the numerological significance has not been explained. Aside from the last four *p'ien* of the sixth *lun*, the behaviour of good and worthy rulers forms the underlying theme. In the last 4 *p'ien*, on agriculture, the emphasis lies in evaluating good conditions for plants or soil, thus continuing the pattern of analogies between nature and society that occurs throughout the work.

The comprehensive nature of the material and its systematic presentation have led to the suggestion that the *Lü shih ch'un ch'iu* formed an encyclopaedia of knowledge for the time. While this idea serves as a description of the book, it carries no implication regarding the purpose for which it was written. It seems certain that the work was intended for those persons who were already in, or might come to be in, positions of authority.

3. Composition and sources of the work

It has been supposed that much of the *Lü shih ch'un ch'iu* is not original, being gathered from other sources that are sometimes no longer extant. Ssu-ma Ch'ien 司馬遷 (?145–?86 B.C.) wrote that Lü Pu-wei had the scholars whom he had assembled 'each write what he had heard' (*Shih chi* 85, p. 2510). Frequently passages of the *Lü shih ch'un ch'iu* appear in other texts, either of earlier or of later date, with little or no differences; e.g., passages seen in the *Tso chuan* or in the 'Yüeh ling'. Some passages such as those on music, whose grammatical usage suggests that they had been borrowed from elsewhere, cannot be found in other sources. Passages which are introduced with the formula 'Hou chi 后稷 says', or 'Huang ti 黃帝 says' are also probably borrowed.

In general the *chi* section seems to have been compiled by wholesale borrowing from other texts and by fitting passages together in a way that satisfied the compiler. Moreover in the three *chüan* from the autumn months the topics of discussion move from one *chüan* to the next without structural or logical break, as if the compiler had made divisions in a text that had originally formed a whole. Like a clever collage, the *chi*, though made up of many pieces, creates a unified effect. In spite of its many borrowings only two texts are cited explicitly: the *Shih ching* and the *Shang shu*.

In the *lan* section, on the other hand, many books are cited, and short quotation from, e.g., the *Ch'un ch'iu* (which is never mentioned by name) is regular. Of the many passages that have been copied from elsewhere, the longest to show a distinctive grammar is seen in the second half of the *p'ien* 'Pen wei' 本味 in *chüan* no. 14. Not only does the plan of the *lan* section seem to be less detailed than that of the *chi*; many more names and places are mentioned. Text is sometimes repeated from elsewhere in the *lan* or indeed from the *chi* section. In general the *lun* section resembles the *lan* section.

In spite of these differences, the consistency of certain patterns of expression and the persistence of various grammatical features in the whole work seem to confirm its basic unity. Wilhelm and Naitō have suggested that the *lan* and the *lun* sections might have been written slightly later than the *chi*, on whose general concepts they called.

Carson (Michael F. Carson, 'The language of the *Lü shih ch'un ch'iu*: some characteristic features of grammar and style in a third century B.C. text'; PhD. dissertation, University of Washington, 1980) provides a general discussion of the work, a textual history, a study of some characteristics of grammar and style and a chapter on loan words. On the basis of the investigations of grammar and style, it was found that certain passages of the book are set aside from the others (e.g., the initial *p'ien* in each of the first twelve *chüan*). The *chi* section as a whole was found to have certain features that, in turn, separate it from the *lan* and the *lun* sections. The patterns of the use and non-use of certain words in the three sections lends verisimilitude to one of Ssu-ma Ch'ien's statements about the multiple authorship of the work. Linguistic investigation supports the conclusions reached by Wilhelm and Naitō that are mentioned above.

4. Textual history

The earliest and most instructive references to the *Lü shih ch'un ch'iu* are to be found in the *Shih chi*. In one passage (*Shih chi* 85, p. 2510), Ssu-ma Ch'ien relates something of the book's authorship and composition; the use of the term *Lü lan* 呂覽 to refer to the book originates from *Shih chi* 130, p. 3300; and a further reference is seen in *Shih chi* 14, p. 510. A complete text history will be found in Carson, pp. 39–70.

The text seems to be relatively well preserved (see Carson, pp. 52–53; 68), with some *lacunae* and displaced passages that have been noted by various commentators. Part of one of the 161 *p'ien* (probably entitled 'Lien hsiao' 廉孝) has been lost. The remaining part of that *p'ien* was joined to the *hsü i* that follows the *chi* chapters, of which some portion has also probably been lost (see Hsü Wei-yü 許維遹, pp. 1216–17). The order of the three sections of the *Lü shih ch'un ch'iu* is given by Ssu-ma Ch'ien as *lan, lun* and *chi*; but in the preface to his annotated edition Kao Yu 高誘 (*c.* 168–212) corrected this to *chi, lan* and *lun*, as now seen in the received text and questioned only rarely. Both Li Shan's 李善 (d. 689) commentary to the *Wen hsüan* 文選, and the *T'ai p'ing yü lan* 太平御覽 quote frequently from the *Lü shih ch'un ch'iu* with only slight textual discrepancies.

The earliest and best known commentator to the work is Kao Yu. In *Han shu* 30, p. 1741, the book is listed under *tsa chia* 雜家 with 26 *p'ien* [sic]. In *Sui shu* 34, p. 1006 and *Hsin T'ang shu* 59, p. 1533 it is given in the same category, in 26 *chüan*, with Kao Yu's annotation; *Chiu T'ang shu* 47, p. 2032 enters the work, compiled by Lü Pu-wei, again in 26 *chüan*. Fujiwara Sukeyo's catalogue includes a copy in 26 divisions (neither *p'ien* nor *chüan* are specified) with Kao Yu's notes. An entry in the *Chung hsing kuan ko shu mu* (late 12th century) gives the number of *p'ien* as 160, as it is in the received text. The loss of one *p'ien*, in the first *lan*, must be presumed to have occurred much earlier.

5. Editions

Although there are reports of Sung editions, the earliest surviving
printed versions date from the Chih cheng 至正 period (1341–68).
Eleven different editions which were printed during the Ming period
are known by various titles which do not always incorporate the name
of the collator or editor; most of these are known to have been based on
Sung or Yüan editions. Descriptions may be found in *Shan pen shu shih
ts'ang shu chih*, vol. 7, ch. 18:15b–17b; and in *T'ien lu lin lang shu mu hou
pien*, vol. 9 16:6a–b. In his *Lü shih ch'un ch'iu chiao shih* (see below), Ch'en
Ch'i-yu lists the following editions:

(a) The Yüan print, of between 1341 and 1367; sometimes termed the
    'Yüan print in large characters'.
(b) A print copied from (a), dated 1498, by Li Han 李瀚 (1453–1533).
(c) Hsü Tsung-lu's 許宗魯 (1495–1569) print of 1528.
(d) Chang Teng-yün's 張登雲 (*cs* 1571) print of 1579.
(e) Chiang Pi's 姜璧 (*cs* 1571) print of 1579.
(f) The edition of Sung Pang-i 宋邦義 (Ming period) and others, which
    was used for the *Ssu pu ts'ung k'an* series. Pi Yüan (see below) refers
    to a print made by Sung Ch'i-ming 宋啓明 (Ming period) which
    was a copy of this edition.
(g) Liu Ju-ch'ung's 劉如寵 (*cs* 1580) print of 1596.
(h) Wang I-luan's 汪一鸞 print of 1605.
(i) Ling Chih-lung's 凌稚隆 print of 1620.
(j) A late Ming print by Chu Meng-lung 朱夢龍, judged inferior by Pi
    Yüan owing to its arbitrary inclusion of readings from other texts.
(k) A Ming print by Huang Chih-shen 黃之寀.
(l) A Japanese print which bears the title of Sung Pang-i's edition, but
    which is similar to Chu Meng-lung's print.

The most important edition after the Ming period is that of Pi Yüan
畢沅, and this is regarded as the most authoritative collation of the *Lü
shih ch'un ch'iu* that exists. It was based on eight earlier editions, one of
the Yüan and seven of the Ming period; Pi Yüan's preface is dated in
1789. This edition, which was taken as the basis for the *Ssu pu pei yao*
print, also provides the basis for the now standard edition of Hsü Wei-
yü 許維遹 (1905–51). Pi Yüan and his co-editors are usually careful to
explain how they have decided on a particular reading and to cite
variants. A set of supplementary studies (*fu k'ao* 附攷) at the end of the
edition contains the prefaces of Kao Yu and pertinent remarks by Ssu-
ma Ch'ien, together with the collected notes and comments of other
editors, commentators and catalogues that were produced right up to Pi
Yüan's own time.

In his *Lü shih ch'un ch'iu chi shih* 呂氏春秋集釋 of 1935 (Peking: Kuo li Ch'ing hua ta hsüeh, 1935; reissued, Wen hsüeh ku chi k'an hang she, 1955), Hsü Wei-yü added to Pi Yüan's annotation notes that had been culled from a number of sources; not infrequently he lists several commentaries or notes and endorses one of them, giving his reasons for so doing. Some recourse is made to graphical analysis and archaic phonology. However, Hsü seems unwilling to make any changes to Pi's text, no matter how strong the evidence against it may be. The *fu k'ao* has been enlarged to include material that is dated after 1789 and entries from the later catalogues.

A punctuated edition by Ch'en Ch'i-yu 陳奇猷 is entitled *Lü shih ch'un ch'iu chiao shih* 呂氏春秋校釋, 2 volumes (Shanghai: Hsüeh lin, 1984). The text is based on Pi Yüan's edition. The notes of the earlier commentators are followed by Ch'en Ch'i-yu's own additional annotation, which takes account of earlier editions (including one Japanese reprint), inscriptions and archaeological finds. An appendix includes citations of the work that appear elsewhere but are no longer to be found in the received text; a list of twelve editions (see above); a list of works cited in the notes, amounting to 120 items; and a collection of references to the *Lü shih ch'un ch'iu* in the Standard Histories, traditional commentators and bibliographical lists and catalogues, ranging from the *Shih chi* to Ch'en Ch'i-yu's earlier publications.

6. Translation

The only complete translation is that of Richard Wilhelm, (*Frühling und Herbst des Lü Bu we; aus dem Chinesischen verdeutscht und erläutert*; Jena: Eugen Diederichs, 1928; reprinted, with a new preface by Hellmut Wilhelm, 1971), for which Pelliot's review (in *TP* 27, 1930, 68–91) should be consulted. The work contains valuable notes and explanations, together with an index of the names and places that occur in the text. In the new edition Wilhelm's introduction has been replaced by a preface by Wolfgang Bauer; otherwise the two editions are without change. Uchino and Nakamura's Japanese edition, which is principally concerned with the philosophical aspects of the *Lü shih ch'un ch'iu*, includes translations of twenty select chapters.

7. Modern Chinese versions

(a) Ho Ling-hsü 賀凌虛, *Lü shih ch'un ch'iu ti cheng chih li lun* 呂氏春秋的政治理論; Taipei: Shang wu, 1970.

(b) Hsia Wei-ying 夏緯瑛, *Lü shih ch'un ch'iu shang nung teng ssu p'ien chiao shih* 呂氏春秋上農等四篇校釋; Peking: Chung hua, 1956.

(c) Lin P'in-shih 林品石, *Lü shih ch'un ch'iu chin chu chin i* 呂氏春秋今
註今譯; Taipei: Shang wu, 1985.

8. Japanese editions

D. *Kokuyaku kambun taisei*, no. 20, 1924, edited by Fujita Toyohachi.
E. *Kambun sōsho*, 1928, edited by Okada Masayuki.
L. *Chūgoku koten shinsho*, 1976, edited by Uchino Kumaichirō and
Nakamura Shōhachi.

9. Research aids

(a) Carson, Michael F., 'The battle of words in ancient China'; *Asian
Culture Quarterly*, vol. XI, no. 2 (1983).
(b) Hsü Fu-kuan 徐復觀, 'Lü shih ch'un ch'iu chi ch'i tui Han tai hsüeh
shu yü cheng chih ti ying hsiang' 呂氏春秋及其對漢代學術與政
治的影響, *Hsin ya shu yüan hsüeh shu nien k'an* 新亞書院學術年刊
14 (1972), pp. 1–53.
(c) T'ien Feng-t'ai 田鳳台, 'Lü shih ch'un ch'iu shu mu lieh chü hsi
yao' 呂氏春秋書目列舉析要, *Shu mu chi k'an* 書目季刊 14.1 (June
1980), pp. 91–104.
(d) T'ien Feng-t'ai, *Lü shih ch'un ch'iu t'an wei* 呂氏春秋探微; Taipei:
Hsüeh sheng, 1986.

10. Indexes

(a) *Lü shih ch'un ch'iu t'ung chien* 呂氏春秋通檢 (*Index du Liu Che
Tch'ouen Ts'ieou*); Centre franco-chinois d'études sinologiques Index
no. 2; Peking, 1943; reprinted Taipei: Ch'eng wen, 1968).
(b) Carson, Michael F., *A concordance to Lü-shih ch'un-ch'iu*, vol. 1; Taipei:
Chinese materials Center, 1985.
(c) *A Concordance to the Lü shi chunqiu* 呂氏春秋逐字索引, ed. D.C. Lau
and Chen Fong Ching; *ICS* series, Hong Kong: Commercial Press,
forthcoming 1994.

— Michael Carson
— Michael Loewe

Meng tzu 孟子 (Mencius)

1. The date of Meng K'o

The *Meng tzu* is a collection of the sayings of Meng K'o 孟軻 (Mencius) and the conversations that he had with the leaders of the states, his other contemporaries and his disciples. Unmistakable evidence in *chüan* 1 shows that he must have travelled to the states of Liang 梁, Ch'i 齊 and Lu 魯 around 320 B.C. As king Hui 惠 of Liang addressed Meng K'o as '*sou* 叟' (literally 'old man'), he could not have been a young man at the time when he saw him; it is evident that in *chüan* 1 of the received collection, at least, we have the mature views of this philosopher.

In the earliest account of Meng K'o (*Shih chi* 74, pp. 2343f.) it is said that he received instruction from a follower of Tzu ssu 子思, a grandson of Confucius; from what we know of his teachings it is probably true that Meng K'o studied with someone in his school.

2. Authenticity and extent of the work

Two points may be noted regarding the entry for the *Meng tzu* in *Han shu* 30, p. 1725, which reads '*Meng tzu*; 11 *p'ien*', i.e. (a) no commentaries are mentioned; and (b) the work is described as consisting of 11 *p'ien*.

According to the preface (*T'i tz'u* 題辭) of Chao Ch'i 趙岐 (d. 201), the posts of academician (*po shih* 博士) were established in the time of Han Wen ti (reigned 180–157 B.C.) for the *Lun yü, Hsiao ching, Meng tzu* and *Erh ya* (for Chao Ch'i's statement, see p. 4 of the preface, in the *Kambun taikei* edition). It would thus seem to be unlikely that by the time when *Han shu* 30 was being compiled there was still no commentary to the *Meng tzu*. Although the *Sung shih* (205, p. 5172) includes an entry for *Ssu chu Meng tzu* 四註孟子 in 14 *chüan*, Chu I-tsun 朱彝尊 (1629–1709) considered this to be a later fabrication (see *Ching i k'ao* 經義考, *chüan* 232, 1a; *SPPY* ed.). Be this as it may, it may be noted that Yang Hsiung 揚雄 (53 B.C.–A.D. 18) figures among the four commentators in this work; there is some evidence in the *Fang yen* 方言 to show that Yang Hsiung was interested in glosses to the *Meng tzu*. In a chapter of the *Lun heng* entitled *Tz'u Meng* 刺孟, Wang Ch'ung 王充 (27–*c.* 100) raises objections to a number of passages in the *Meng tzu*.

The earliest extant commentary to the *Meng tzu* is that of Chao Ch'i, who was married to a niece of Ma Jung 馬融 (79–166) and was an older contemporary of Cheng Hsüan 鄭玄 (127–200). The text which he transmitted is noteworthy for two reasons. First, it stands out, among classical writings, for its soundness; and secondly, at the time of Chao Ch'i the *Meng tzu* consisted of 7 *p'ien* of 'inner' documents or books (*shu* 書), and 4 *p'ien* of 'outer' documents; together these make up the 11 *p'ien* as listed in *Han shu* 30, p. 1725. In his preface, Chao Ch'i states that he excised the outer books from the work, as 'these books, lacking in width and depth, bear no resemblance to the inner books and are likely to be the spurious work of a later age rather than the authentic work of Meng tzu.' The seven 'inner' books, perhaps because of their length, were each divided into two parts, thus together amounting to the 14 books listed as *chüan*, in the *Sung shih* 205, pp. 5171, 5173–5174; the arrangement into 14 *chüan* persists in most editions. The *Chiu T'ang shu* (47, p. 2024), *Hsin T'ang shu* (59, p. 1510) and Fujiwara Sukeyo's list include copies in either 14 or 7 *chüan*.

The question therefore arises of whether Chao Ch'i was justified in his excision of the 'outer' books, and in this connection it is only possible to conjecture. There are today two collections of sayings of Mencius which, while being quoted in various works, are not to be found in the received text; these are by Li T'iao-yüan 李調元 (1734–1803) and Ma Kuo-han 馬國翰 (1794–1857) respectively. For those works that preceded Chao Ch'i or were contemporary with him, there are no more than a dozen quotations; and what is of greater importance, none of these are significant in content. Of the 180 quotations from the *Meng tzu* in the *T'ai p'ing yü lan*, of 983, only 4 are not to be found in the received text. Even if these were all to have been derived from the 'outer' books, this would only show that there was little there that was worthy of quotation; if they had all come from the 'inner' books, this would suggest that the received text is basically sound.

3. Commentaries

The *Meng tzu* was not included in the canon of classical writings until the Sung period. It has however attracted a considerable body of writings, of which only a few can be mentioned here.

The various scholars who were in general contemporaries of Chao Ch'i and wrote commentaries on the *Meng tzu* included Cheng Hsüan,

Kao Yu 高誘 (*c.* 168–212) and Liu Hsi 劉熙 (*c.* 200); quotations from their writings are included in Ma Kuo-han's *Yü han shan fang chi i shu*. Lu Te-ming 陸德明 (556–627) did not include the *Meng tzu* among the books which he treated, and attempts to fill this gap by Chang I 張鎰 (d. 783) in his *Meng tzu yin i* 孟子音義 and Ting Kung-chu 丁公著 (759–822) in his *Meng tzu shou yin* 孟子手音 are no longer extant; a few citations from these works survive in the *Meng tzu yin i* of Sun Shih 孫奭 (962–1033). The extant standard sub-commentary (*shu* 疏) to Chao Ch'i's work is also said to have been written by Sun Shih, but according to Chu Hsi 朱熹 (1130–1200) this had been written by a person known to Ts'ai Yüan-ting 蔡元定 (1135–98); he criticised it on the grounds that it was not what was to be expected of a *shu*, being more concerned with Chao Ch'i's explanations than with the *Meng tzu*. The best known of the many commentaries by Neo-Confucian scholars is Chu Hsi's own *Meng tzu chi chu* 孟子集注, written in 1177; this remained the authoritative commentary on the *Meng tzu* until the revival of classical learning in the Ch'ing period.

As part of the attempt by the Ch'ing scholars to write new sub-commentaries that would replace those of the T'ang and Sung periods, Chiao Hsün 焦循 (1763–1820) spent his last three years writing the *Meng tzu cheng i* 孟子正義, but the transcription of the final draft of this work was not quite finished when he died. As a philologist, Chiao Hsün was bound to differ in his interpretation from that of Chao Ch'i; of some importance is the fact that as a philosopher he was greatly influenced by Tai Chen 戴震 (1724–77), whose re-interpretation of the thought of Mencius seems to be contrary to the spirit of Confucian philosophy.

There are variant readings for the *Meng tzu*, as there are for other works; for these, see (i) *Shichi kei Mōshi kōbun* 七經孟子考文 by Yamai Konron 山井崑崙 (Kanae 鼎; d. 1728), with a supplement by Ogyū Hokkei 荻生北溪 (Bukkan 物觀), published in 1731 (available in the *Ts'ung shu chi ch'eng* series); and (ii) Juan Yüan 阮元 (1764–1849) *Meng tzu chiao k'an chi* 孟子校勘記 (1806).

4. Translations

(a) Couvreur, Séraphin, *Oeuvres de Meng Tzeu*, in *Les Quatres Livres*; Ho Kien Fou, Mission catholique, 1895; second ed. 1910.

(b) Dobson, W.A.C.H., *Mencius, a New Translation Arranged and Annotated for the General Reader*; London: Oxford University Press, 1963.

(c) Giles, Lionel, *The Book of Mencius* (abridged); London: John Murray, 1942.

(d) Lau, D.C., *Mencius*; Harmondsworth: Penguin Books, 1970; bilingual revised edition, Chinese University of Hong Kong Press, 1984.
(e) Legge, *The Chinese Classics*, vol. II.
(f) Lyall, Leonard A., *Mencius*; London: Longmans, Green and Co., 1932.
(g) Ware, James R., *The Sayings of Mencius*; New York: Mentor Books, 1960.
(h) Wilhelm, Richard, *Mong Dsi* (Mong Ko); Jena: Eugen Diderichs, 1916.

5. Versions in modern Chinese

(a) Lan-chou ta hsüeh chung wen hsi 蘭州大學中文系 (ed.), *Meng tzu i chu* 孟子譯注; Peking: Chung hua, 1960.
(b) Hsieh Ping-ying 謝冰瑩 et al., *Meng tzu hsin i* 孟子新譯; in *Ssu shu hsin i* 四書新譯; Taipei: 1966.
(c) Shih Tz'u-yün 史次耘, *Meng tzu chin chu chin i* 孟子今注今譯; Taipei: Shang wu, 1973.

6. Japanese editions

A. *Kambun taikei*; no. 1, 1909, edited by Hattori Unokichi and Yasui Sokken.
B. *Kanseki kokujikai zensho*; no. 2, 1910, edited by Nakamura Tekisai.
C. *Kōchū kambun sōsho*; no. 2, 1913, edited by Mōri Teisai and Kubo Tenzui.
D. *Kokuyaku kambun taisei*; no. 1, 1922, edited by Hattori Unokichi and Kimida Rentarō.
E. *Kambun sōsho*, 1927.
F. *Keisho taikō*; nos. 3, 18, 1939.
H. *Shinshaku kambun taikei*; no. 4, 1962, edited by Uchino Kumaichirō.
J. *Chūgoku no shisō*; no. 3, 1964, edited by Imasato Tadashi.
K. *Chūgoku koten bungaku taikei*; no. 3, 1970, edited by Tōdō Akiyasu and Fukushima Chūzō.
L. *Chūgoku koten shinsho*; 1971, edited by Watanabe Takashi.
M. *Shintei Chūgoku koten sen*; no. 5, 1966, edited by Kanaya Osamu.

7. Indexes

(a) *Meng tzu yin te (A Concordance to Meng tzu)*; Harvard-Yenching Institute Sinological Index Series supplement no. 17; Peking, 1941; reprinted Taipei; Ch'eng-wen, 1966.

(b) Gotō Toshimizu 後藤俊瑞, *Shusi shisho shūchū sakuin* 朱子四書集註索引; Hiroshima: Hiroshima daigaku bungakubu Chūgoku tetsugaku kenkyūshitsu, 1954.

(c) Morimoto Kakuzō 森本角藏, *Shisho sakuin* 四書索引; Tokyo: Meguro shoten, 1921; 2nd ed., 1933; 3rd ed., 1937.

(d) *A Concordance to the Mengzi* 孟子逐字索引, ed. D.C. Lau and Chen Fong Ching; *ICS* series, Hong Kong: Commercial Press, forthcoming 1994.

— D.C. Lau

Mo tzu 墨子

1. Content

Mo tzu is the corpus of the Mohist school (*Mo chia* 墨家), the earliest rivals of the followers of Confucius, founded by Mo Ti 墨翟 in the late 5th century B.C. The school was a highly organized community of teachers, craftsmen and soldiers which survived until the late 3rd century, when according to *Han fei tzu* ch. 50 it had split into three sects. It distinguished itself by ten specific doctrines, which are listed in a discourse ascribed to Mo Ti in ch. 49, Sun 299/4–8. (References are to the edition of Sun I-Jang; see under (5) below). The seventy-one *p'ien* (eighteen of them lost) may be divided into six groups.

(a) 1–7, miscellaneous essays and dialogues.
(b) 8–37, the 'core chapters', ten triads of essays expounding the ten doctrines of the school, 'Elevating worth' (*Shang hsien* 尚賢), 'Conforming to superiors' (*Shang t'ung* 尚同), 'Universal love' (*Chien ai* 兼愛), 'Rejecting aggression' (*Fei kung* 非攻), 'Thrift in expenditure' (*Chieh yung* 節用), 'Thrift in funerals' (*Chieh tsang* 節葬), 'The will of Heaven' (*T'ien chih* 天志), 'Elucidating the spirits' (*Ming kuei* 明鬼), 'Rejecting music' (*Fei yüeh* 非樂), 'Rejecting destiny' (*Fei ming* 非命). The name of Mo Ti is frequently evoked, as though these are records of his teachings but not written by his hand. The essays in each triad run closely parallel but without continuing verbal identity. They are probably versions of a common oral tradition as written down in the three sects mentioned in *Han fei tzu*. Seven of the essays are missing. Of the rest, ch. 17 is a fragment of the missing conclusion of ch. 26, and ch. 14 and 20 are mere digests. There is linguistic as well as other evidence that these were added to make up for the loss of three essays, and that their intrusion has pushed the three series out of alignment. See A.C. Graham, *Divisions in early Mohism reflected in the core chapters of Mo-tzu*, Singapore: Institute of East Asian Studies, 1985.

    The dislocated last triad (ch. 35–37) shows further evidence of transpositions that have intermingled the three versions. In ch. 35, Sun 170/8 (from *kai* 蓋) –171/4 should probably be exchanged with Sun 175/2 (from *huo* 或) –10 (to *ming tsai* 命哉) in ch. 36, and Sun

Chapter Triads	Digests and Fragments	First Series	Second Series	Third Series
8–10		8	9	10
11–13		11	12	13
14–16	14	15	16	
17–19	17	18	19	
20–22	20	21	(22)	
23–25	(23)	(24)	25	
26–28		26	27	28
29–31	(29)	(30)	31	
32–34	?	?	32	?
35–37		35	36	37

171/5–173/2 (to *hui yeh* 毀休) belongs somewhere in ch. 37. The three series when re-aligned reveal clear doctrinal differences.

(c) Ch. 38, 39, 'Rejecting the *ju chia*' (*Fei ju* 非儒), a polemic against *ju chia* ideas.

(d) Ch. 40–45, the 'Dialectical Chapters', corrupt and difficult writings on the disciplines of logic, ethics, geometry, optics, and mechanics seldom discussed elsewhere in pre-Han literature. The heart of this section is the 'Mohist Canons', the *ching* 經 'Canons' and *ching shuo* 經說 'Explanations of the Canons' (ch. 40–43).

(e) Ch. 46–51, collections of dialogues between Mo Ti and others, and a single extended narrative (ch. 50), the story of Mo Ti using his skill as a military engineer to save the state of Sung from the rival engineer Kung-shu Pan 公輸盤.

(f) Ch. 52–71, the 'Military Chapters', as corrupt and difficult as (d); Mo Ti's instructions in the technique of defensive warfare addressed to his chief disciple Ch'in Ku-li 禽滑釐.

2. Date of composition and authenticity

No part of the book claims to be written by Mo Ti himself. Nevertheless, except in the Military Chapters, and possibly in ch. 1 and 2, it displays everywhere the distinctive thought of the Mohist school, which died out in the second century B.C. The Military Chapters were condemned as a Han forgery by Chu Hsi-tsu 朱希祖 (*Ku shih pien* v. 4, pp. 261–271), but have been generally accepted by more recent scholars such as Watanabe Takashi 渡邊卓 , *Bokka no heigikōsho ni tsuite* 墨家の兵技巧書について, *Tōkyō shinagaku hō* 3 (1957), 1–19. The only serious question is where to place the different parts of the corpus in the history of the Mohist school. The expositions of the ten Mohist doctrines in the Core

Chapters have a crudity of argument and style which suggests that they go back in substance to the beginnings of the school, although this has been questioned by Watanabe, who argues that these doctrines emerged at successive stages in the school's history down to the very latest period. (*Bokka no shūdan to sono shisō* 墨家の集團とその思想, *Shigaku zasshi* 70 (1961), 1198–1231, 1351–1385; *Bokushi shohen no chosaku nendai* 墨子諸篇の著作年代, *Tōyō gakuhō* 45.3 (1962), 1–38: 45.4 (1962), 20–38. The Dialectical Chapters represent a late and sophisticated stage in Mohist thought, and discuss issues raised towards the end of the fourth century B.C. by the Sophists and by Chuang Tzu.

3. Text history and editions

Almost all the major Chinese editions and studies of *Mo tzu* are assembled in Yen Ling-feng 嚴靈峯 (b. 1904), *Wu ch'iu pei chai Mo tzu chi ch'eng* 無求備齋墨子集成, 46 vol., I wen: Taipei, 1975. (Abbreviation: *MTCC*). The major Ming and early Ch'ing editions are collated in Wu Yü-chiang 吳毓江, *Mo tzu chiao chu* 墨子校注, Chungking: Tu-li, 1944 (*MTCC* v. 43, 44). They are described and to some extent affiliated in an appendix.

In all, *Mo tzu* is composed of seventy-one *p'ien* (of which eighteen are missing) grouped in fifteen *chüan*. The complete text was nearly unknown from the T'ang to the early Ming, having been driven out of circulation by a text of the first thirteen *p'ien* (in three *chüan*) with commentary by Yüeh T'ai 樂臺 (alternatively Yüeh I 樂壹; ?6th century A.D.). It survived in the Taoist Canon, from which it was returned to circulation during the Ming. The earliest complete editions are therefore late, and can be listed as follows:

(1) *Tao tsang* edition of 1445 (*MTCC* v. 1).

(2) T'ang Yao-ch'en 唐堯臣 edition of 1553 (*SPTK*; *MTCC* v. 2), with preface by Lu Wen 陸穩 and postface by T'ang Yao-ch'en. This derives directly from (1) and has no independent value.

(3) Mao K'un 茅坤 edition of 1581 (*MTCC* v. 3). A cognate edition edited by Lu Wen in 1552, long confused with the almost simultaneous edition of T'ang Yao-ch'en for which he wrote the preface, is reported and collated by Wu Yü-chiang. This Lu-Mao textual tradition is independent of the Ming Taoist Canon, but goes back to a common Sung exemplar. All three of the above-mentioned editions replace a taboo character in the name of the first Sung emperor by an identical note (ch. 49, Sun 296/–4).

(4) The Japanese Hōryaku 寶曆 edition of 1757, based on the Mao edi-

tion, but with both readings and quoted variants taken from manu-scripts preserved in Japan (*MTCC* v. 4).

The common Sung exemplar was presumably the Sung Taoist Canon version. For an independent tradition we have only the Yüeh T'ai text of ch. 1–13, preserved (but without his commentary) in the 'Yü 俞 manu-script' in the National Library of China, catalogued as *Mo tzu san chüan Ming ch'ao pen Huang P'ei-lieh pa* 墨子三卷明抄本黃丕烈跋. This is not included in *MTCC* but is collated by Wu Yü-chiang.

For a bibliography of *Mo tzu*, see Yen Ling-feng, *Mo tzu chih chien shu mu* 墨子之見書目, Taipei: Hsüeh sheng, 1969. This includes Japanese and Western items as well as Chinese.

4. Manuscript fragments

A tiny fragment of text identified as from ch. 70 (Sun 361/11, 12) was included among the large consignment of strips, mostly concerning military matters, that was found in tomb no. 1, Yin-ch'üeh-shan 銀雀山 Lin-i 臨沂 (Shantung), dated 140–118 B.C.; see *Wen wu* 1974.2, 18 and Plate 8 no. 80. For the relationship of other texts found at this site with parts of the *Mo tzu*, see *Wen wu* 1985.4, 27 and 28 (note 1); and Yin-ch'üeh-shan Han mu chu chien cheng li hsiao tsu 銀雀山漢墓竹簡整理小組 (ed.) *Yin-ch'üeh-shan Han mu chu chien* 銀雀山漢墓竹間, 1 (Peking: Wen wu, 1985), p. 129, note 1.

5. Textual studies

The text of *Mo tzu* is notoriously corrupt. The earliest corrected and an-notated version (1797) is that of Pi Yüan 畢沅 (1730–97), reprinted in the *Ssu pu pei yao* collection, (*MTCC* v. 7, 8). Pi Yüan's edition was super-seded in 1894 by the magnificent *Mo tzu chien ku* 墨子閒詁 of Sun I-jang 孫詒讓 (1848–1908), one of the greatest achievements of Ch'ing textual scholarship, reprinted in Peking in 1954 (*MTCC* v. 12–15). The Harvard-Yenching index to *Mo tzu* follows Sun's emended text; the apparent variants at the foot of the page are often the only readings attested in the Taoist Canon and other unemended editions. The danger of being deceived by the accumulating inheritance of misprints and conjectural emendations in later editions may be avoided by consulting the collation of the major Ming and early Ch'ing editions in Wu Yü-chiang. Variants from quotations and parallel passages are collected by Wang Shu-min 王叔岷, *Mo tzu chiao cheng* 墨子校證, *BIHP* 30.1 (1959), pp. 71–102.

Apart from Wu Yü-chiang, the only Chinese commentator on the whole book since Sun I-jang is Chang Ch'un-i 張純一, *Mo tzu chi chieh*

墨子集解, first edition 1931 (*MTCC* v. 23–26). Progress has come rather in specialized studies.

Of the more problematic parts of the book, the Military Chapters have been largely neglected, with the notable exception of Ts'en Chung-mien 岑仲勉, *Mo tzu ch'eng shou ko p'ien chien chu* 墨子城守各篇簡注, Peking: Ku chi, 1959 (*MTCC* v. 45). The Dialectical Chapters, little studied in the West until recently, have been treated in a long succession of works beginning with the *Mo tzu ching shuo chieh* 墨子經說解 (*MTCC* v. 9) of Chang Hui-yen 張惠言 (1761–1802). The following are especially important.

(1) Liang Ch'i-ch'ao 梁啓超 (1873–1929), *Mo ching chiao shih* 墨經校釋 Shanghai: Shang wu, 1922 (*MTCC* v. 19). Commentary on ch. 40–43. This makes the crucial point overlooked by Sun I-jang, that the start of every *shuo* 'Explanation' is marked by repeating the first character of the Canon in question.

(2) Luan T'iao-fu 欒調甫, *Mo tzu yen chiu lun wen chi* 墨子研究論文集, Peking: Jen min, 1957 (*MTCC* v. 33), essays valuable for taking an overall rather than the more usual piecemeal approach to the textual problems.

(3) T'an Chieh-fu 譚戒甫, *Mo pien fa wei* 墨辯發微, Peking: K'o hsüeh, 1958, revised in 1964 (*MTCC* v. 35), commentary on the whole of ch. 40–45.

(4) Kao Heng 高亨, *Mo ching chiao ch'üan* 墨經校詮, Peking: K'o hsüeh, 1950 (*MTCC* v. 41). Commentary on ch. 40–43, vitiated by a tendency to solve all problems by conjectural graphic emendation.

For a recent study of the 'core chapters', see Erik W. Maeder, 'Some observations on the composition of the "core chapters" of the *Mozi*'; *EC* 17 (1992), 27–82.

6. Research aids and translations

There is a complete German translation by Alfred Forke, *Me Ti des Sozialethikers und seiner Schüler philosophische Werke*, Berlin: Kommissionsverlag der Vereinigung wissenschafticher Verleger, 1922. For the Dialectical and Military Chapters, at least, this was premature. For a more recent translation into German of chapters 1–39 see Helwig Schmidt-Glintzer, *Mo ti: Solidarität und allgemeine Menschenliebe*, and *Mo ti: Gegen den Krieg* (Düsseldorf-Köln: Eugen Diederichs Verlag, 1975.) There are three selective translations in English:

(a) Mei, Y.P., *The ethical and political works of Motse*, London: A. Probsthain, 1929. (Ch. 1–39, 46–50 only).

(b) Watson, Burton, *Mo Tzu: basic writings*, New York: Columbia University Press, 1963 (one or more chapters in each of the triads in ch. 8–37, also ch. 39).
(c) Sjöholm, Gunnar, *Readings in Mo ti: chapters XXVI–XXVIII on the will of heaven*, Helsingborg: Plus ultra, 1982.)

Western scholars have only recently ventured into the more problematic parts of the Dialectical and Military Chapters. A.C. Graham, *Later Mohist logic, ethics and science*, Hong Kong and London: Chinese University Press, 1978, re-edits the Chinese text and translates in full *Mo tzu* ch. 40–45, after a detailed analysis of the textual and grammatical problem. The problems of the Military Chapters are investigated by Robin Yates, *Towards a reconstruction of the tactical chapters of Mo-tzu*, which includes a textual reconstruction of chapters 52–67 (MA thesis, University of California, Berkeley, 1975). The modern Chinese version of Li Yü-shu 李漁 叔, *Mo tzu chin chu chin yi* 墨子今註今譯, Taipei: Shang wu, 1974, covers only ch. 1–39 and 44–50.

7. Japanese editions

A. *Kambun taikei*; no. 14, 1913, edited by Koyanagi Shikita.
B. *Kanseki kokujikai zensho*; nos. 20, 21, 1911, edited by Makino Kenjirō (Sōshū).
D. *Kokuyaku kambun taisei*; no. 8, 1921, edited by Koyanagi Shikita.
E. *Kambun sōsho*; 1928, edited by Koyanagi Shikita.
F. *Keisho taikō*; nos. 16, 17, 1938–39.
H. *Shinshaku kambun taikei*; nos. 50, 51, 1975, 1987, edited by Yamada Taku.
J. *Chūgoku no shisō*; no. 5, 1964, edited by Wada Takeshi.
K. *Chūgoku koten bungaku taikei*; no. 5, 1968, edited by Yabuuchi Kiyoshi.
L. *Chūgoku koten shinsho*; 1967, edited by Takata Atsushi.

8. Indexes

(a) The major reference work is *Mo tzu yin te* 墨子引得 (*Concordance to Mo tzu*), Peking: Yenching University Press, 1948; Harvard-Yenching Institute Sinological Index Series, supplement no. 21.
(b) *A Concordance to the Mozi* 墨子逐字索引, ed. D.C. Lau and Chen Fong Ching; *ICS* series, Hong Kong: Commercial Press, forthcoming 1996.

— A.C. Graham

Mu t'ien tzu chuan 穆天子傳

1. Content

Claiming to be a biography of one of the kings of Chou, the *Mu t'ien tzu chuan* reports certain incidents that are supposed to have occurred during the life of King Mu (reigned 956–918 B.C.) as part of his private, political and diplomatic activities and his relations with women. The work is in fact in the nature of an historical romance, being the first of its sort in China. If historical facts are mentioned, they serve no more than as a pretext for presenting a romantic tale, which is marked by exaggeration, grandiloquence and sentiment. Possibly the work should be regarded as one of the few successful attempts to produce an epic in ancient Chinese literature (see F. Tökei, *Naissance de l'élégie chinoise*; Paris: Gallimard, 1967, p. 56).

While the value of the text *qua* literature is somewhat limited, its significance lies in the way that it reveals different aspects of the life of a sovereign of the Chou period. In addition the work includes considerable information about relations between the Chinese and other peoples, and between king and vassal. Finally, the value of the text lies in its inclusion of allusions to a mythology other than that of the supermen of the *Shang shu* or the *Tso chuan*. Thanks to its theme of a journey to the west, the book reflects a Chinese attempt to take possession of the whole earth, and raises the question of the control that a sovereign and his court may exercise over all people under the skies.

2. Date of composition and authenticity

This problem has been subject to considerable controversy. The text, which was found in *c.* 281 in the tomb of Hsiang 襄 (or Ai Hsiang 哀襄; for this name, see under *Chu shu chi nien*), king of Wei 魏 (reigned 318–296 B.C.), certainly dates from *c.* 350 B.C., but it is necessary to distinguish between its different parts. Both the *Sui shu* (ch. 33, p. 964) and Fujiwara Sukeyo's catalogue enter the book as the text found in the tomb, together with the later notes of Kuo P'u 郭璞 (276–324), in six *chüan*; the received version consists of six *chüan*. While the authenticity of the first

four *chüan* lies beyond doubt, it is very likely that *chüan* 5 was an interpolation added by the scholars of the Chin court, who were responsible
in *c.* 281 for re-establishing the order of the strips on which the text had
been written and for completing its defective parts. Both syntactical
analysis and the statement of the *Chin shu* (ch. 51, p. 1433) suggest that
chüan 6 was most probably compiled from elements of 19 other *chüan* of
text that were found in the tomb, such as the *Chou Mu wang mei jen
Sheng Chi ssu shih* 周穆王美人盛姬死事. Different themes thus obtrude
in different parts of the work. While a remarkable unity, i.e. the theme
of King Mu's journey to the west, links *ch.* 1–4 together, *ch.* 6 is not to be
placed within the same context, being concerned with the short story of
the king's love for Sheng Chi.

3.   Textual history

The early history of the text remains unknown, with no other versions
other than that of the Chin scholars being available in traditional
sources of literature or being found in recent archaeological excavation.
It may perhaps be surmised that during the Warring States period other
histories of King Mu may have existed, of which we now possess no
more than traces. It does appear that the version of the Chin dynasty
has been subject to considerable loss. Ch'ao Kung-wu 晁公武 (d. 1171;
Chün chai tu shu chih 9.1b) refers to its 8514 characters; the received version amounts to no more than 6641 characters.

4.   Editions

The following are the more important editions and prints; more complete lists are given in item (h) below (supplement, pp. 1f.) and Wei
T'ing-sheng's book (see under (6) below; vol. I, pp. 114f.)

(a) From the *T'ien i ko* 天一閣 collection; format 9 by 18, with inter-
    columnar notes by Kuo P'u; prefaces by Wang Chien 王漸 (Hsüan-
    han 玄翰) dated 1350, and Hsün Hsü 荀勗, who had been involved
    in the discovery of this and the other texts in *c.* 281; reproduced in
    the *Ssu pu ts'ung k'an* series.

(b) *Han Wei ts'ung shu* (ed. Ch'eng Jung, 1592); format 9 by 20, with Kuo
    P'u's notes, and prefaces as in (a). A copy of this print which was
    owned by Huang P'ei-lieh 黃丕烈 (1763–1825) and carries his manu-
    script annotation was reproduced by the Shantung Provincial
    Library in 1934.

(c) *Tseng ting Han Wei ts'ung shu* (ed. Wang Mo, 1791); format 9 by 20;

preface by Wang Chien (Hsüan-han); postface by Wang Mo (1788); Kuo P'u's notes.

(d) *Han Wei ts'ung shu ts'ai chen* 漢魏叢書採珍 (*Lung wei pi shu* 龍威秘書 series I, 1794); format 9 by 20, with Kuo P'u's notes and Wang Chien's preface; annotator Wang Ming-chi 汪明際.

(e) *Ku chin i shih*; format 10 by 20, with Kuo P'u's notes and Hsün Hsü's preface; editor Wu Kuan 吳琯 (*chin shih* 1571).

(f) Hung I-hsüan's 洪頤煊 (1765–1837) annotated edition of 1800, in the *P'ing chin kuan ts'ung shu*, including Hung's own notes, together with those of Kuo P'u, and Hsün Hsü's preface; format 11 by 20. Bibliographical notices, from the *Sui shu* to those of the *Ssu k'u* editors, are printed after the text. This edition was reprinted in the *Lung hsi ching she ts'ung shu*, in the *Ssu pu pei yao* series and, with punctuation, in the *Ts'ung shu chi ch'eng*.

(g) *Fu chiao Mu t'ien tzu chuan* 覆校穆天子傳, with notes by Chai Yün-sheng 翟云升, and Kuo P'u's notes included in part; in *Wu ching sui pien chai chiao shu san chung* 五經歲徧齋校書三種 (preface 1838).

(h) Ku Shih 顧實, *Mu t'ien tzu chuan hsi cheng chiang shu* 穆天子傳西征講疏; Shanghai: Shang wu, 1934; reprinted Taipei, 1976; punctuated text including earlier commentators' annotations and Ku Shih's own notes; seven maps.

Of the most easily available editions, that of the *Ssu pu pei yao* (reproduced in Mathieu's translation: see below) is the most easy to read, although the absence of markings alongside proper names may present a difficulty to those who are not experienced with this text. The characters of the *Ts'ung shu chi ch'eng* are less easy to read; there is little of special note in the *Ssu pu ts'ung k'an* and *Han Wei ts'ung shu* editions. For those embarking on a systematic study of the *Mu t'ien tzu chuan*, Ku Shih's edition is indispensable for *chüan* 1–4, being printed with highly legible characters and with punctuation that is almost free of error. The list of editions and secondary studies runs to 52 pages. The best traditional commentaries are those of Kuo P'u, which draws on glosses from the *Shan hai ching* and the *Erh ya*, and Hung I-hsüan, but these notes are not always sufficient to elucidate the two most important problems of the book, i.e. the identification of place-names and the interpretation of the myths to which reference is made.

5. Translations

As far as is known, no versions in modern Chinese or translations into Japanese have been published. The oldest translation into English is that of E. J. Eitel (*China Review* XVII, 1888, 223–40 and 247–58), but as is the case with a number of translations of the nineteenth century, the English version does not follow the original text too closely. This version is short of notes and some errors have been included. A second English translation, by Cheng Te-k'un, (*JNChBrAS* LXIV, 1934, 124–42 and LXV, 128–49) is of better quality, with, however, an even more brief annotation than that of Eitel. Part of the text was translated by Léopold de Saussure, as 'La Relation des voyages du roi Mou (au Xe siècle avant J-C.)' in *Journale asiatique*, second series XVII (1921) 247f.; this does little more than reproduce Eitel's work (see Paul Pelliot's review in *TP* 21, 1922, 98–102). For a fully annotated translation with introduction and a facsimile of the *Ssu pu pei yao* text, see Rémi Mathieu, *Le Mu Tianzi zhuan: traduction annotée: étude critique*; Paris: Collège de France, Institut des hautes études Chinoises, 1978. This volume includes a concordance based on the *Ssu pu pei yao* print.

6. Studies published without the text

(a) In European languages

> (i) Tökei, F., 'A propos du genre du Mou t'ien-tseu tchouan'; *Acta Orientalia* 9 (1958), 45–9.
>
> (ii) Hulsewé, A.F.P., 'Texts in tombs'; *Asiatische Studien* 18/19 (1965), 78–89; see especially pp. 86f.
>
> (iii) See also references by Chavannes, in *Mémoires Historiques* vol. II, pp. 6f. and vol V, pp. 480f.

(b) In Chinese

> (i) Chang Kung-liang 張公量 published a series of articles in *Yü kung* 1:5, 6f.; 2:5, 31f.; 2:6, 18f.; and 3:4, 31f. (1934–35).
>
> (ii) Wei Chü-hsien 衛聚賢, 'Mu t'ien tzu chuan ti yen chiu 穆天子傳的研究'; *Ku shih yen chiu* 1 (1931), 187–245.
>
> (iii) Ku Chieh-kang 顧頡剛, 'Mu t'ien tzu chuan chi ch'i chu tso shih tai 穆天子傳及其著作時代'; *Wen shih che* 1, (July 1951) 63–8.
>
> (iv) Wei T'ing-sheng 衛挺生 (b. 1890), *Mu t'ien tzu chuan chin k'ao* 穆天子傳今攷, 3 vols; Taipei: Chung hua hsüeh yüan, 1970. In this self styled 'modern scientific study of King Mu's travels', the author considers the chronology of King Mu, events of Chou history and geographical problems posed by the text; he concludes that the data prove the authenticity of the book. Volume 3 includes chronological tables and maps.

(v) Wang Fan-chih 王範之, 'Mu t'ien tzu chuan yü suo chi ku tai ti ming ho pu tsu 穆天子傳與所記古代地名和部族'; *Wen shih che* 6 (1963).

(vi) Ting Ch'ien 丁謙; see *Ti li tsa chih* 6 (1915) and 11 (1920).

(vii) Tu Erh-wei 杜而未, 'Mu t'ien tzu chuan yü Shan hai ching 穆天子傳與山海經'; in *Shan hai ching shen hua hsi t'ung* 山海經神話系統; Taipei: Hsüeh sheng, 1976, pp. 137–41.

(c) In Japanese

(i) Ogawa Takuji 小川琢治 'Shū Boku ō no sai sei 周穆王の西征'; in *Shina rekishi chiri kenkyū zokushū* 支那歷史地理研究續集; Tokyo: Kōbundō, 1929, pp. 165f.

(ii) Ogawa Takuji, 'Boku tenshi den kō 穆天子傳考'; in *Kano Kyō-ju kanreki kinen* 狩野教授還歷記念; Tokyo: Kōbundō, 1928.

(iii) Ogawa Takuji, 'Boku tenshi den no Saiōbo 穆天子傳の西王母'; in *Shina rekishi chiri kenkyū I*; Tokyo: Kōbundō, 1928–29, pp. 239f.

7. Index

A Concordance to the Yan danzi, Shanhaijing and Mu tianzi zhuan 燕丹子, 山海經, 穆天子傳逐字索引, ed. D.C. Lau and Chen Fong Ching; *ICS* series, Hong Kong: Commercial Press, forthcoming 1994.

— Rémi Mathieu

Pai hu t'ung 白虎通

1. Compilation

The compilation of the *Pai hu t'ung* is mentioned in three passages of the *Hou Han shu*, with somewhat different details. According to the longest passage (*HHS* 3, pp. 137f.), an imperial decree of A.D. 79 reviewed the steps that had been taken to promote official attention to the Five Classical Texts and took note of the differences in interpretation that had come into existence from the time of the establishment of the academicians (124 B.C.). The decree referred to the growth of various schools of study; the discussions that had taken place in 51 B.C. in the Pavilion of the Stone Canal (Shih ch'ü ko 石渠閣); the decree of A.D. 56 that expressed concern over the complexity of current interpretations; and the plea made for a re-examination of the principal issues, put forward in a memorial dated A.D. 58. The passage implies that the conference which was duly called for this purpose in 79 owed its origin to that plea. The conference was to be attended by counsellors of state and academicians, and other dignitaries and scholastics, who were to meet in the White Tiger Hall (Pai hu kuan 白虎觀) to discuss the differences in the Five Classics. Wei Ying 魏應 was ordered to assume responsibility for seeing that appropriate questions would be considered, and Shun-yü Kung 淳于恭 was to draw up the replies. The emperor himself (Chang ti 章帝) participated personally in the meetings to pronounce decisions, on the basis of the precedent set by Hsüan ti 宣帝 in 51 B.C. An account of the proceedings entitled *Pai hu i tsou* 白虎議奏 'Memorials on the White Tiger Discussions' was drawn up.

A second reference, which is considerably shorter (*HHS* 79A, p. 2546), adds that the discussions lasted for several months and that orders were given for the compilation of 'An account of its general significance' (*t'ung i* 通義). In the third passage, which occurs in the biography of Pan Ku 班固 (32–92; *Hou Han shu* 40B, p. 1373), it is stated that the emperor ordered an assembly of scholars to expound the Five Classics and to compose the *Pai hu t'ung te lun* 白虎通德論; and that orders were given to Pan Ku to compile an account of the affair from the collected material.

2.   Title and length

Different details are given for the title and length of the work. In *Sui shu* 32, p. 937, it is entered as *Pai hu t'ung* in 6 *chüan*. In Fujiwara Sukeyo's catalogue the book is entered likewise, but with 10 *chüan*, and authorship is ascribed to Pan Ku and others. A later hand inserted the character *wu* 五 in a crucial position in the text, but it is not clear whether this was intended to emend the entry to read 5 or 15 *chüan*. In the *Chiu T'ang shu* (46, p. 1982) the work is still entitled *Pai hu t'ung*; it is given as amounting to 6 *chüan*, and Chang ti is named as the compiler in the note. In the *Hsin T'ang shu* (57, p. 1445) there is an entry for *Pai hu t'ung i* 白虎通義 in 6 *chüan*, and it is here for the first time in a native Chinese list that authorship is ascribed to Pan Ku and others.

The *Ch'ung wen tsung mu* 崇文總目 lists an item as *Pai hu t'ung te lun* 白虎通德論 in 10 *chüan*, by Pan Ku, being in all 14 *p'ien*; possibly the figure 14 was due to a scribal error for 44. The *T'ung chih* 通志 enters *Pai hu t'ung* in 6 *chüan*, by Pan Ku and others; the *Chün chai tu shu chih* 郡齋讀書志 records the work as *Pai hu t'ung te lun*, in 10 *chüan*, by Pan Ku; and the *Chih chai shu lu chieh t'i* 直齋書錄題解 refers to the *Pai hu t'ung* in 10 *chüan*, amounting in all to 44 *men* 門. Most of the entries in these lists and catalogues appear in sections which concern the exegesis of the classical texts and the *Lun yü*.

In recent editions the book is divided into 2, 4 or 10 *chüan*. In each case the table of contents lists 44 titles of the separate *p'ien*, including two that are given respectively as *San kang* 三綱 and *Liu chi* 六紀. These entries are erroneous, *San kang liu chi* together forming the title of a single *p'ien* and being given as such in the main body of the text.

3.   Origin and authenticity of the work

The following summary of this subject may be supplemented by reference to the full study of Tjan Tjoe Som (1903–69), as cited under 6 (j) below.

The authenticity of the *Pai hu t'ung*, as received, has been brought into question for two reasons. First, a citation that is ascribed to it in the commentary to the *Hsün tzu* is not to be found in the received text; the *Ssu k'u* editors do not accept this as a significant indication of forgery. In the second and more demanding instance, the somewhat different accounts of the work's compilation and the use of different titles have raised doubts regarding the relationship of the received text to an original piece of writing of the first century. In this respect the *Ssu k'u* editors observe that the proper title of the book should be *Pai hu t'ung i*; they imply that use of the term *Pai hu t'ung te lun* is mistaken, and that it should be applied solely to notes of the discussions that were made prior to the compilation of an ordered, comparatively short account, by Pan Ku. This opinion is partly shared by Chou Kuang-yeh 周廣業 (1730–98), who believed that use of the term *Pai hu t'ung te lun* arose from an erroneous conflation of two works written by Pan Ku, i.e. *Pai hu t'ung* and *Kung te lun* 功德論; he prefers the title *Pai hu t'ung*.

Chuang Shu-tsu 莊述祖 (1751–1816) emphasised the distinction between an original set of notes on the proceedings, amounting, as he believed, to over 100 *chüan*, and the received text, whose chapters he believed to be a later forgery. Sun I-jang 孫詒讓 (1848–1908) agreed in discriminating between two sets of records; he suggested that a similar procedure took place in A.D. 79 to that which had followed the earlier discussions on the subject, in 51 B.C. On both occasions accounts of the questions raised and the answers that were reached were drawn up in respect of each one of the classical texts that was under review. Such records were extensive, running to about 100 *chüan*; they were written in the form of memorials to the throne, and they had been lost by the fourth century. A second record, of matters that were of general concern to a number of classical works, was compiled in a different form, being entitled *Pai hu t'ung i*. More recently, Liu Shih-p'ei 劉師培 (1884–1919) expressed his general agreement with Sun I-jang's views, with some modifications. He stressed that the *Pai hu t'ung i* consisted of a summary of the discussions, the decisions pronounced by the emperor and a personal contribution by Pan Ku.

As against these views which accept that the received text derived from Pan Ku's part in drawing up an account of the discussions of A.D. 79, William Hung 洪業 suggests that the work is a later compilation. Citing material of a comparable nature, including passages in Pan Ku's own *Han shu*, he concludes that the received text came from a later intellectual background, and relied on material (including apocryphal texts) of the latter part of the second, or the early part of the third century. He places its compilation between 213 and 245, the ascription to Pan Ku being accepted from the fourth or fifth centuries. The extant work reflects ideas that were current towards the end of the Han dynasty or slightly later, rather than those expressed during the discussions of 79.

William Hung's conclusions, however, are rejected by Tjan Tjoe Som as being invalid, on the grounds that his arguments apply only to parts of the book and do not impugn its general authenticity. Comparison with other texts does not suffice to prove that the received text is a forgery, although it is possible to identify some cases of interpolation of material dating from the second century or later. Citations in encyclopaedias and by early commentators lead to the conclusion that a more complete text than that available today may have existed up to 516. In a subsequent note (*HJAS* 20, 1957, 110–11, note 50) William Hung takes account of Tjan's views and re-affirms his own opinion that the *Pai hu t'ung* was compiled between 213 and 245.

4. Contents

The received text is described as being faulty, prone to the inclusion of incomplete quotations and by no means always clear. Much of the text takes the form of questions directed to the meaning or authority of a passage from the classical works, followed by an answer that is itself backed by a further citation. Usually the New Text versions are quoted.

A summary of the arguments of the book is set out in Tjan's work (see pp. 71–72), where there is also a detailed account of the subjects of the 43 *p'ien* (pp. 195–216). The text concerns human relationships (e.g., the correct use of ranks, names and titles; a king's treatment of his subjects; marriage); religious and philosophical topics (e.g., deities to be worshipped; divination; sacrifices; the Five Phases; the significance of calamities; the idea of destiny); features of the natural world (e.g., the four seasons; sun and moon; the relation of heaven to earth); matters of imperial or state ceremony (e.g., archery; ploughing; inspections; ritual presents; conduct of the rites and of music); and imperial government (e.g., the capital city; punishments; admonitions; education).

5. Editions

The following notes are in general limited to editions that have been available for inspection. A more complete list of editions will be found in the *Harvard-Yenching Index*, pp. xix–xx.

In the absence of further information, it has been assumed by a number of scholars that the extant prints of the work, whether entitled *Pai hu t'ung, Pai hu t'ung i* or *Pai hu t'ung te lun*, derived from a print of 1305, which carried prefaces by Yen Tu 嚴度 and Chang K'ai 張楷 that were dated in that year. According to Chang K'ai, that print was itself based on a rare copy of the work which was owned by Liu Shih-ch'ang 劉世常 (P'ing-fu 平父), and which is sometimes described as a Sung edition (e.g., in the editorial note to the *Ssu pu ts'ung k'an* print). Extant copies may be considered in three groups.

(a) In 10 *chüan*, with format of 9 x 17; available in:

   (i) The *Ssu pu ts'ung k'an* series.

   (ii) A manuscript copy held in the National Library, Peking.

   (iii) The *Sui an Hsü shih ts'ung shu hsü pien*. The regular format is occasionally subject to change (e.g., *chüan* 10.7 a,b carries columns of 18 or 19 characters).

Copy (ii), from which the *Ssu pu ts'ung k'an* was not taken, bears a note stating that it was made from the print of 1305 in reduced size, with a number of imperfections being rectified. It also states that the format of the 1305 edition was 8 x 17, and that a number of additions to the text, made during the Ming period, were relegated in this copy to a place below the columns of the text. This manuscript copy was made in 1841, along with a similar copy of the *Feng su t'ung i* 風俗通義. As far as it is possible to determine, the text of (ii) is identical with that of (i). The text of (iii) is not entirely identical with that of (i) and (ii), but it varies far less frequently from those two than it does, in common with (i) and (ii), from the text given in the *Liang ching i pien*, to be discussed immediately below. Copies (i), (ii) and (iii) all include the prefaces of Yen Tu and Chang K'ai.

(b) In 2 *chüan*. This text is included in the *Liang ching i pien* (1582) and is stated to have been edited by Yang Hu 楊祜. The format is 9 x 17; no prefaces are included. In seven sample *p'ien* that have been examined, the text does not vary from that of an edition held in the National Library Peking, which is described as a Ming reprint of the edition of 1305. This rare copy is in 10 x 16 format and includes the prefaces of Chang K'ai and Yen Tu, in that order.

A large number of variants may be observed between copies listed under (a) above, in 10 *chüan*, and these two copies in 2 *chüan*. Thus, in 45 cases noted in 7 *p'ien*, the *Ssu pu ts'ung k'an* and the two other associated copies are clearly in error as compared with the text of the *Liang ching i pien* and the 10 x 16 print, on at least 28 and possibly 33 occasions (e.g., *hsia* 下 and *Liu* 劉 appear in place of *yen* 言 and *chao* 剑 respectively). The *Liang ching i pien* and the 10 x 16 print are in obvious error as compared with the others on three occasions only (e.g., *t'ai tzu* 太子 in place of *t'ien tzu* 天子).

(c) Copies printed with a column length of 20 characters.

   (i) In the *Ku chin i shih* (1571–76), edited by Wu Kuan 吳琯 (*cs* 1571); in 2 *chüan*, of 10 x 20 format, with prefaces by Chang K'ai and Yen Tu. This text was reproduced, apparently without change, in the *Pi shu nien i chung* (1668), except that Wang Shih-han 汪士漢 is named as the editor and his preface is included.

(ii) In the *Han Wei ts'ung shu*, edited by Ch'eng Jung 程榮 (1592); in 2 *chüan* of 9 x 20 format, with prefaces by Chang K'ai, Yen Tu and Leng Tsung-yüan 冷宗元 (*fl.* 1520). Leng's preface refers to corrections made to the text by Fu Yüeh 傅鑰 (Hsi-chün 希準; attained *chin shih* degree 1506–21).

(iii) In the *Kuang Han Wei ts'ung shu*. According to an entry in the *Ts'ung shu shu mu hui pien* (p. 472), the *Pai hu t'ung* in 4 *chüan* was included in the *Han Wei ts'ung shu* of 76 *chung* 種. This is presumably a reference to the *Kuang Han Wei ts'ung shu* of Ho Yün-chung 何允中 (1628), and it is likely that this was the earliest edition to be printed in 4 *chüan*, forming the basic text that was available to Lu Wen-ch'ao 盧文弨 (1717–96) and Ugai Sekisai 鵜石參 (see below). The format of the *Pai hu t'ung te lun* in this collection is 9 x 20. On the first folio of the text Wang Tao-k'un 王道焜 is named as the editor; he is possibly to be identified with Wang Tao-k'un (Chao-p'ing 昭平) of the early sixteenth century. Chang K'ai's preface is included.

(iv) In the *Tseng ting Han Wei ts'ung shu*, edited by Wang Mo 王謨 (1791–92); in 4 *chüan*, of 9 x 20 format, and punctuated. The preface of Chang K'ai is included and there is an undated post-face by Wang Mo; Chao I-lun 趙宜崙 is named as the editor.

In general these editions carry the same text as that of the *Liang ching i pien*, being thus free of the errors which occur in the *Ssu pu ts'ung k'an* print. The *Ku chin i shih*, *Han Wei ts'ung shu*, *Kuang Han Wei ts'ung shu* and *Tseng ting Han Wei ts'ung shu* all carry unique individual variants or errors.

These three groups of prints observe the taboo on the character *heng* 恒 (personal name of Sung Chen tsung 宋真宗, reigned 998–1022); *huan* 桓 (personal name of Ch'in tsung 欽宗, reigned 1126–27) is sometimes given in full, sometimes in an abbreviated form. The *Han Wei ts'ung shu* retains *k'uang* 匡 (personal name of T'ai tsu 太祖, reigned 960–75) in its complete form; in the *Ssu pu ts'ung k'an* and the *Liang ching i pien* practice is varied.

From the foregoing considerations it may be concluded that the version of the 1305 print that is least subject to error is the one to be found in the *Liang ching i pien* and the Ming print of 10 x 16 format, a copy of which is held in Peking.

6. Annotations and commentaries

(a) Lu Wen-ch'ao's annotated edition was published in the *Pao ching t'ang ts'ung shu* and reproduced in facsimile in the *Ts'ung shu chi ch'eng* series (no. 238). In his preface (1784), Lu Wen-ch'ao acknowledges his debt to Chuang Shu-tsu who had started the work of correcting existing copies before 1777. He also refers to a copy of the work in 'small characters', which had been made available by Wu Ch'a-k'o 吳槎客 (18th century). In his supplementary notes to his edition, Lu Wen-ch'ao described this as having a format of 12 x 23 and expressed the view that it was dated before the Southern Sung period. It was possibly from this copy that at one point he inserted a column of 23 characters in the text (see *Ts'ung shu chi ch'eng* reprint p. 285; *SPTK* 10.8b; *Liang ching i pien* A.72a). Lu also mentions a further copy in small characters belonging to Chu Wen-yu 朱文游, and the edition of 1305. However, these last were not available to him when he was preparing his edition, and he was able to refer to them only in the supplementary notes that are printed after the text.

It is not possible to identify the edition in 'small characters' seen by Lu; it would seem that the 1305 edition which he eventually saw had greater affinity to the text printed in the *Liang ching i pien* than to that of the *Ssu pu ts'ung k'an*. In making the notes to his edition, Lu had been able to call on a number of Ming and Ch'ing prints which he lists. The works that were available to him included a contribution by Fu Yüeh of 1522 (see above, under *Han Wei ts'ung shu*), Ch'eng Jung's *Han Wei ts'ung shu*, Chou Kuang-yeh's supplementary notes and Ho Yün-chung's text in 4 *chüan*. He writes that he corrected a number of errors in that edition. His emendations to the text of the *Pai hu t'ung* are often based on citations that appear in encyclopaedias or on similar evidence.

Lu Wen-ch'ao's text is divided into 4 *chüan*, each one of which is split into two parts. He writes that the original division of the book in 6 *chüan* was extended into 10 *chüan* in the Sung edition, but that in the more usual prints the text had been set out in 4 *chüan*. Without access to earlier copies, he had chosen to retain the arrangement of 4 *chüan*. In the list of titles of the 43 *p'ien*, Lu Wen-ch'ao inserted an analytical summary of the contents or argument of each one.

In this edition the text of the *Pai hu t'ung* is set out with divisions between the separate sections of each *p'ien*; intercolumnar notes provide explanations to the text and reasons for the readings that have been adopted. Sometimes a radical emendation may be introduced (e.g., the title of the 26th *p'ien* is changed from Wen chih 文質 to Jui chih 瑞贄). Lu's edition includes the prefaces of Chang K'ai and Yen Tu, together with one of his own; there is also Chou Kuang-yeh's account of the book, and Lu Wen-ch'ao's own postface (undated) to the edition of 1305. Following the main text, there is a section of collected fragments, assembled by Chuang Shu-tsu and Lu himself; thereafter there are the supplementary notes, with information that became available only when Lu's main work had been completed.

(b) An edition with a new and extensive commentary by Ch'en Li 陳立 (1809–69) entitled *Pai hu t'ung shu cheng* 白虎通疏證 is available in several versions. An independent print, undated, carries a final note that it was annotated by Yang To 楊鐸; a different print, which is included as items 1265–76 in the *Huang Ch'ing ching chieh hsü pien* 皇清經解續篇 of Wang Hsien-ch'ien 王先謙 (1888) incorporates annotation at the end of each of the 12 *chüan* into which the book is divided. This is ascribed variously to Wu Ta-pin 吳大彬, Wang Chih-ch'ang 汪之昌, Ho Hsi-hua 何錫驊, Kuan Li-ch'ang 管禮昌 and Liu Yü-chia 劉毓家. Ch'en Li's preface is dated in 1832 [sic]. He divides each *p'ien* into sections, to which he appends by way of short description the notes that are given in Lu Wen-ch'ao's table of contents. Tjan Tjoe Som describes the edition as being highly valuable, supplying a large extent of commentary which, however, did not include the notes of Hung I-hsüan 洪頤煊 (1765–1837).

(c) Sun Hsing-hua's 孫星華 edition is divided into 4 *chüan*, followed by 4 *chüan* of critical notes (*Chiao k'an chi* 校勘記), which at times comment on Lu Wen-ch'ao's views; the final note by Sun Hsing-hua is dated at 1895. This edition was first published in the *Fu chou shu chü*'s 福州書局 reprint of the *Wu ying tien chü chen* 武英殿聚珍 collection; it was reproduced in the *Kuan chung ts'ung shu*, where there is a postface signed by Sung Lien-k'uei 宋聯奎, Wang Chien 王健 and Wu T'ing-hsi 吳廷錫, dated in 1934. The text does not follow exclusively that of any of the editions mentioned above.

(d) Hung I-hsüan's notes to a few problems sometimes include a refutation of Lu Wen-ch'ao's views; see *Tu shu ts'ung lu* 16.14a–18a (1821).

(e) Sun I-jang's notes were made on the basis of the 1305 edition, with attention to the views of Lu Wen-ch'ao and Ch'en Li; Sun sometimes rejects the readings that Lu Wen-ch'ao adopted. These notes appear in his *Cha i* 10.1a–6a, and in his collected works. In addition, Sun published his conclusions regarding the compilation of the work in the *Kuo ts'ui hsüeh pao* 55 (She shuo 社說) 1a–4a, under the title *Pai hu t'ung i k'ao* 白虎通義考 (1909).

(f) Tjan Tjoe Som refers (p. 4 note 16) to two works of Wang Jen-chün 王仁俊 (1866–1913) that have not been traced.

(g) Liu Shih-p'ei 劉師培 (1844–1919) added considerably to the work of earlier scholars by publishing textual notes, comments on the explanations given by Lu Wen-ch'ao, Hung I-hsüan, Ch'en Li and Sun I-jang and studies of defective or lost passages of the work. His writings are best available in *Liu Shen-shu hsien sheng i shu* 劉申叔先生遺書 33 and 34.

(h) Chin Te-chien 金德建 published two articles in *Ku chi ts'ung k'ao* 古籍叢考 (Shanghai: Chung hua, 1941): (i) 'Pai hu kuan yü i chu ju hsüeh p'ai k'ao' 白虎觀與議諸儒學派考; this lists 14 participants in the discussions with notes on their scholastic achievements; pp. 139–56; dated 1937; (ii) 'Pai hu t'ung i yü Wang Ch'ung Lun heng chih kuan hsi' 白虎通義與王充論衡之關係; this discusses the relationship between the *Pai hu t'ung* and the *Lun heng*; pp. 157–66.

(i) For other items that are not all generally or easily available, see *Shin Kan shisō kenkyū bunken mokuroku*, items 0904, 0906, 0909, 0923 and 0925.

(j) The most comprehensive study of the *Pai hu t'ung* in English is that of Tjan Tjoe Som (1903–69), entitled *Po hu t'ung, the Comprehensive Discussions in the White Tiger Hall* (2 vols.; Leiden: E.J. Brill, 1949, 1952). In a lengthy introduction, the author examines the bibliographical history of the work, its contents and its place within the context of classical studies during the Han period. In what is a monumental work, Tjan pays attention to critical assessments of the *Pai hu t'ung*'s authenticity; to the different interpretations of the Classical texts and to the controversies between the New Text and the Old Text Schools. The translation of the work takes note of the *Ssu pu ts'ung k'an* edition and the comments of Lu Wen-ch'ao and Ch'en Li. English translation of four *p'ien* is included in volume 1; that of the remainder, together with the fragments, is included in volume 2. Annotation is more extensive in volume 1 than in volume 2.

7. A *kambun* edition

It has been noted above that the work was included in Fujiwara Sukeyo's catalogue, and the title also appears in the lists of books imported into Nagasaki during the Edo period. In a *kambun* text, which was probably based on that of the *Kuang Han Wei ts'ung shu*, a colophon names Ugai Sekisai 鵜石參 (Nobuyuki 信之) and Iida Chūbei 飯田忠兵衞 as the editors, and dates the print at 1662. The text, in 4 *chüan* with 9 x

20 format, is furnished with *kunten* 訓點 and *kaeriten* 返り點, and carries the prefaces of Chang K'ai, Yen Tu and Leng Tsung-yüan, together with further notes by way of introduction by Wang Yen-chou 王弇州 (?17th century) and Chin Fu-fu 金府父 (?17th century).

8. Indexes

(a) *Pai hu t'ung yin te* 白虎通引得; Harvard-Yenching Institute Sinological Index Series No.2, 1931, based on the *Ssu pu ts'ung k'an* print.

(b) *Byakkotsū sakuin* 白虎通索引 (Fu hombun 附本文); no.3 in the series 'Source Materials for Chinese Philosophy', compiled by the Research Group for Chinese Philosophy, Hokkaidō; edited by Itō Tomoatsu 伊東倫厚, *et al.*; Tokyo: Tōfū shoten, 1979. The index is preceded by an introduction which discusses the history of the text and its editions. References are to the punctuated text that is included in the volume, being based on Lu Wen-ch'ao's edition.

(c) *A Concordance to the Baihu tong* 白虎通逐字索引, ed. D.C. Lau and Chen Fong Ching; *ICS* series, Hong Kong: Commercial Press, forthcoming 1995.

— Michael Loewe

Shan hai ching 山海經

1. Structure and contents

The *Shan hai ching* is a *descriptio mundi* with three main textual layers compiled and assembled by different authors over a period of some six to eight centuries.[*] The received text, of about 31,000 characters, is divided as follows:

(a) *(Wu tsang) shan ching* 五臧山經: *chüan* nos. 1–5, for south, west, north, east and centre.
(b) *Hai wai ching* 海外經: *chüan* nos. 6–9, for south, west, north and east.
(c) *Hai nei ching* 海內經: *chüan* nos. 10–13, for south, west, north and east.
(d) *Ta huang ching* 大荒經: *chüan* nos. 14–17, for east, south, west and north.
(e) *Hai nei ching* 海內經: *chüan* no. 18.

The compilers conceived the earth as being divided into three concentric rectangles (see Fracasso, 'Teratoscopy', as cited under (7) below), i.e. (i) a central territory, 28,000 *li* in length, 26,000 *li* in height; (ii) four seas, encompassing the central lands; and (iii) a 'great wilderness', stretching from the sea-shore to un undetermined limit.

Chüan nos. 1–5 are divided into 26 subsections and describe 447 mountains of the central lands. The description of each mountain consists, as a minimum, of its name, its distance from the preceding mountain and information about its flora, fauna and minerals. Some cases include remarks about the *numina* and miraculous beings that dwell on a mountain or group of mountains and certain mythological events. When a river is associated with a mountain, the text specifies its source and mouth, the direction in which it flows and the material or objects that may be found within it. At the end of 24 subsections the text supplies some prescriptions of ritual that concern the cult of the mountain spirits; such entries are of paramount importance for a study of early

---

[*] For a detailed bibliography of this work, see R. Fracasso, 'The Shanhaijing: a bibliography by subject'; *CINA* xxiii (1991), 81–104.

Chinese religion (see Itō, 'Yamagawa no kamigami', as cited under (7)
below). These *chüan* also contain valuable information on popular medicine and the practice of divination on the basis of portents. Many of the
geographical names that are mentioned (especially in *chüan* no. 5) may
be identified with comparative certainty; many others remain subject to
controversy.

The contents of *chüan* nos. 6 to 18 are somewhat different. Geographical names are hardly recognizable; botany and zoology give place to fictional ethnology; medical, mantic and ritual prescriptions are no longer
found, and mythological accounts become more numerous. Genealogies
form a distinctive feature of *chüan* nos. 14 to 18 (see Wu Han, as cited in
(7) below).

A considerable *lacuna* in *chüan* 13 has been filled (possibly by Kuo P'u
郭璞 276–324) with text from a *Shui ching* 水經 of Ch'in or Han date that
is unrelated to the rest of the book. Several passages of *chüan* 6–9 and
10–13 recur, in slightly different and expanded form, in *chüan* 14–17 and
18. This lends credibility to the hypothesis of Ku Chieh-kang 顧頡剛
(1893–1980) and Hou Jen-chih 侯仁之, that nos. 14–18 should be regarded as a parallel version of nos. 6–13, being appended to the *Shan hai
ching* at a later time.

2. Classification of the work

Owing to the miscellaneous nature of its contents, classification of the
Shan hai ching has been, and remains, a matter of controversy. According
to the preface of Liu Hsiu 劉秀 (i.e. Liu Hsin 歆), the *Shan hai ching* was
highly esteemed in Former Han as being a handbook on prodigies; in
Han shu 30, p. 1774, it is listed under *hsing fa* 形法, together with five lost
works on geomancy and assessment of physiognomy. In Later Han it
was evidently regarded as a reliable geographical text, being included
among the books given to Wang Ching 王景, when engaged in repair-
ing the dykes of the Yellow River (A.D. 69; see *Hou Han shu* 76, p. 2465).
In the bibliographical chapters of the *Sui shu*, *Chiu T'ang shu* and *Hsin
T'ang shu*, Fujiwara Sukeyo's list and works such as the *Chih chai shu lu
chieh t'i* the book is entered under geographical texts; in the *Sung shih* it
is listed under 'wu hsing 五行'. Hu Ying-lin 胡應麟 (1551–1602) described the *Shan hai ching* as the 'ancestor of old and new literary
oddities' (see *Ssu pu cheng o* 四部正訛, ed. Ku Chieh-kang, Peiping: Pei
ching shu chü, 1929, 3, p. 55); this judgment foreshadowed the inclusion
of the work among *hsiao shuo* 小說 in the *Ssu k'u* 四庫 project.

In recent times the work has been described variously as 'a traveller's
guide' (Schlegel, and Chiang Shao-yüan 江紹源, p. 41); a 'geographical

gazetteer' (Schiffeler); a 'record of exploration (Wei T'ing-sheng 衛挺生 b. 1890); a 'shamanic text' (Lu Hsün 魯迅 1881–1936; see *Chung kuo hsiao shuo shih lüeh* 中國小說史略, Peking: Pei hsin shu chü, 1925, p. 11); the 'secret records of Ch'in and Han *fang shih* 方士' (Kao Ch'ü-hsün 高去尋); or the 'forerunner of *chih kung t'u* 職貢圖' (Wang I-chung 王以中). There are elements of truth in all these descriptions, but not one of them is complete; they appear to reflect the interests and sensibility of each of the authors rather than give a correct idea of the whole work. The *Shan hai ching* cannot in fact be ascribed in its entirety to any single category of writing.

3. Authorship, date and place of composition.

Traditionally the *Shan hai ching* has been ascribed to Yü 禹 the Great and his assistant I 益, as may be seen in the *Lun heng* and *Wu Yüeh ch'un ch'iu* and in Liu Hsin's memorial on the book. This view was upheld by scholars such as Yang Shen 楊慎 (1488–1559) and Pi Yüan 畢沅 (1730–97). Others have expressed doubts, beginning with Yen Chih-t'ui 顏之推 (531–*c*. 591). Yen noticed the presence of Han geographical names in the text, and thought that they had been added after the destruction of literature under Ch'in or by Tung Cho 董卓 (assassinated 192). Other scholars who have attributed the work to the Ch'un ch'iu or Chan kuo periods have included Tu Yu 杜佑 (735–812), Chu Hsi 朱熹 (1130–1200), Yu Mao 尤袤 (1127–93), Ch'en Chen-sun 陳振孫 (*c*. 1190 to after 1249) and Hu Ying-lin. Yao Chi-heng 姚際恆 (b. 1647) placed the book in Ch'in or Han; Pi Yüan accepted an original composition by Yü and I, with alterations during the Chou and Ch'in periods; for these views, see *Wei shu t'ung k'ao*, pp. 688f.

Terrien de Lacouperie, who was the first scholar to discriminate between different strata of the work, dated the *chüan* of the *Wu tsang shan ching* to Shang, those of the *Hai wai ching* and *Hai nei ching* to Chou and those of the *Ta huang ching* and *Hai nei ching* to later periods, with Kuo P'u's interpolation in *chüan* 13. While no certain agreement has been reached, most scholars now regard the *Wu tsang shan ching* as being the oldest part of the work (Chan kuo), with Meng Wen-t'ung 蒙文通 and Yüan K'o 袁珂 taking this to be later than the *Ta huang ching* and the *Hai nei ching*. Karlgren (in *BMFEA* 18, 1946, 204–05) defined the *Shan hai ching* as a 'product of the Han era, in parts not even of the early Han'; Shih Ching-ch'eng 史景成 placed the composition of the work between 290 B.C. and the compilation of the *Lü shih ch'un ch'iu* (*c*. 240 B.C.). The place of composition is variously identified with the states of Ch'u, Ch'i, Shu or Pa, or with Lo-yang. Inconclusive evidence has been adduced to

The Main Theories Concerning the Date and Place of Composition for Sections of the *Shan hai ching*

| Sources | WTSC | Date of Composition | | THC/HN | Place of Composition |
		HWC	HNC		
Ogawa (1926)	Eastern Chou	Pre-Ch'in (?)	Late Chan-kuo	Pre-Ch'in (?)	–
Hsüan Chu (1928) Cheng Te-k'un (1932)	Eastern Chou	Ch'un-ch'iu / Chan-kuo		Pre-Ch'in	Lo-yang (WTSC)
Lu K'an-ju (1929) Hou Jen-chih (1937)	Chan-kuo		Western Han	Eastern Han/ Wei-Chin	Ch'u (WTSC)
Ho Kuan-chou (1930)	Chan-kuo		Ch'in / Han	Post-Han	Ch'i (WTSC)
Hsü Ping-ch'ang (1946)	Late Chan-kuo	Prior to Han Wu-ti (141) B.C.			–
Karlgren (1946)		Han	(partly late	Han)	–
Yüan K'o (1982)	Eastern Chou	Ch'un-ch'iu / Chan-kuo		Early Han	–
Meng Wen-t'ung (1962)	Ch'un-ch'iu / Chan-kuo		Western	Chou	Pa (THC/HN) Shu (HNC) Ch'u (WTSC/HNC)
Shih Ching-ch'eng (1974)		Between	290 and	240 B.C.	Ch'u
Yüan K'o (1982)	Late Chan-kuo		Early Han	Early Chan-kuo	Ch'u
Mathieu (1983)	Late Chan-kuo		Han	Han (with Chin interpolations)	–

Key: HN: *Hai nei ching* (*chüan* 18)   HWC: *Hai wai ching* (*chüan* 6–9)   WTSC: *Wu tsang shan ching* (*chüan* 1–5)
       HNC: *Hai nei ching* (*chüan* 10–13)   THC: *Ta huang ching* (*chüan* 14–17)

support these various theories, and many of the problems that are raised call for the help of archaeological research. A detailed analysis of current opinion is planned for publication in a forthcoming work.

4. Textual transmission

Before reaching its present form, the *Shan hai ching* suffered from interpolation and re-arrangement of the text. The title appears for the first time in *Shih chi* 123, p. 3179, but without specification of the structure or size of the book. Liu Hsin's statement that he produced a definitive text of 18 *p'ien* out of a total of 32 conflicts with the entry in *Han shu* 30, p. 1774, for 13 *p'ien*. After the Han period the book apparently fell into oblivion, and its partially disarranged text was reconstructed in various ways. Entries in the catalogues vary from those for 23 *chüan* (*Sui shu* 33, p. 982, and *Hsin T'ang shu* 58, p. 1504) to 21 (Fujiwara Sukeyo), or 18 (*Chiu T'ang shu*, 46, p. 2014; *Sung shih*, 206, p. 5257, *Chün chai tu shu hou chih* and *Chih chai shu lu chieh t'i*). Some Southern Sung editions are in 3 *chüan*. The extent to which these changes may have affected the contents of the work can only remain a matter of speculation. The division into 18 *chüan* has remained generally unaltered from the Yüan period until the present day.

The following entry, which is to be found in the *Chung hsing shu mu*, is of considerable interest: '*Shan hai ching* in 18 *chüan*, with commentary by Kuo P'u; altogether 23 *p'ien*'. Two versions of the work, one in 23 and one in 18 *chüan* are mentioned in the *T'ung chih*. The extent of the variations that have been due, both in the text itself and in Kuo P'u's commentary, to losses, interpolation and confusion of text and notes may be measured by comparing the figures given for the length of the work in different editions, such as 'Ch'ih yang chün chai', *Tao tsang*, *Ssu pu ts'ung k'an*, *Shan hai ching hsin chiao cheng* and *Ssu pu pei yao* (for details of these editions see under (6) below).

5. Illustrations

In view of its contents, the text of the *Shan hai ching* has always been closely associated with illustrations, and it is even possible that some illustrations, or maps, existed prior to the text and inspired its composition. In *Wen hsüan* 5.6b (*SPPY* ed.), Tso Ssu 左思 (third century) wrote that some of the beings described in the *Shan hai ching* had originally featured on the nine tripods cast by Yü the Great; Ou-yang Hsiu 歐陽修 (1007–72) and Yang Shen shared this view.

Some scholars have regarded the *Shan hai ching* as being a set of explanatory notes that accompanied maps (Pi Yüan) or tribute maps (Wang I-chung). Yüan K'o and others have believed that the text was partly derived from the pictures of supernatural beings used by shamans in Ch'u 楚. There is no certain evidence with which to support these hypotheses. The first possible allusion to illustrations is to be found in Liu Hsin's preface, where it is stated that the *Shan hai ching* could be 'used for enquiring into auspicious and portentous beings and for looking at the customs of far-away countries'; these two sentences seem to refer to the *chüan* of (a) *Wu tsang shan ching* and (b) *Hai wai ching* and *Hai nei ching* respectively.

Illustrations certainly existed by the third century. Besides mentioning them in his commentary, Kuo P'u wrote over 250 appraisals, known as *Shan hai ching t'u tsan* 山海經圖讚 (see 6 (a) below) , which are included in the *Tao tsang* and *Ssu pu pei yao* editions. Chang Chün 張駿 wrote a similar work, entitled *Shan hai ching t'u hua tsan* 山海經圖書讚, which is lost entirely, apart from one citation (*Ch'u hsüeh chi*, Peking; Chung hua, 1962, 29(4), p. 704). T'ao Ch'ien 陶潛 (365–427) speaks of himself as glancing over some of the illustrations (*t'u*) of the *Shan hai ching*. It cannot be known whether the illustrations seen or mentioned by these three scholars and poets existed in the Han period or were drawn subsequently.

The most famous set of illustrations, no longer extant, was that made by Chang Seng-yu 張僧繇 (sixth century), which included 247 pictures, arranged in 10 *chüan*. A damaged copy of Chang's work was discovered in the Imperial Library by Shu Ya 舒雅 (born before 940, died 1009), who made a second drawing from what was left; he produced a further *Shan hai ching t'u* in 10 *chüan*, but it is not known what became of that work. In his preface to *Shan hai ching kuang chu* 山海經廣注, Ch'ai Shao-ping 柴紹炳 (1667) claimed that the blockprints therein were based on Shu Ya's copies; this claim remains unsupported by evidence. The oldest sets of illustrations that are extant are of Ming and Ch'ing date; some of these were published together with the text in editions mentioned below. In addition, separate sets of illustrations with short captions were circulated independently in Ch'ing times (see Fracasso, 'Illustrations', as cited under (7) below).

6. Commentaries and principal editions

The only commentary to be compiled before the Ming period was that of Kuo P'u (early third century). Taken as the standard, this has been reprinted in almost every edition of the *Shan hai ching*. Its transmission has thus been closely related to that of the text itself, with which it has probably become confused on a number of occasions.

The oldest extant printed copy is the Southern Sung edition termed *Ch'ih yang chün chai* 池陽郡齋, and edited by Yu Mao 尤袤 (1127–93) in 1180. A rare copy of this print is preserved in Peking, and the work has been reprinted with a valuable preface by Wang Yü-liang 王玉良 (Peking: Chung hua, 1984). Other Sung editions that Yu Mao mentions (see his *Sui ch'u t'ang shu mu*), such as Mi ko 秘閣 and Ch'ih chou 池州, are now lost. A Yüan edition by T'ien Tzu-chih 田紫芝 exists in the form of a manuscript copy made by Wu K'uan 吳寬 in 1465.

A list of the principal Ming, Ch'ing and modern editions follows; for fuller details, see Ho Tz'u-chün and Ogawa, as listed under (7) below.

(a) *Tao tsang*, 18 *chüan*, published 1445, without *chüan* 14–15; each section of the text is followed by Kuo P'u's appraisals.

(b) *Ssu pu ts'ung k'an*, 18 *chüan*, first published by the Imperial Academy, 1468, and probably based on a Sung copy. The *Ssu pu ts'ung k'an* reprint includes the *chiao k'an chi* 校勘記 of Lin Chih-hsüan 林志烜 (preface 1929).

(c) *Shan hai ching shih i* 山海經釋義, 18 *chüan*, commentary by Wang Ch'ung-ch'ing 王崇慶; printed 1537, after 1538 and 1597. The third edition included a set of poor woodcuts. Wang's notes are in general negligible, but they include a few valuable suggestions.

(d) *Shan hai ching pu chu* 山海經補注, 1 *chüan*; a collection of 107 short glosses of mediocre value compiled by Yang Shen and edited by Chou Shih 周爽 in 1554.; included in several *ts'ung shu* such as *Han hai* and *Pai tzu ch'üan shu*.

(e) *Shan hai ching kuang chu* 山海經廣注, 18 *chüan*, commentary by Wu Jen-ch'en 吳任臣 (?1628–?1689); first published 1667 with 5 *chüan* of illustrations; reprinted on several occasions and included without illustrations in the *Ssu k'u ch'üan shu*. Wu's notes are a rich source of bibliographical information but they have been criticized for being inconclusive.

(f) *Shan hai ching ts'un* 山海經存, 9 *chüan* (18 *p'ien*), commentary by Wang Fu 汪紱 (1692–1759), printed posthumously 1895. The text is apparently based on a Sung original and is enriched by a generally reliable commentary and a set of 431 illustrations (420 drawn by Wang himself).

(g) *Shan hai ching hsin chiao cheng* 山海經新校正, 18 *chüan*, commentary by Pi Yüan; first printed 1781; reprinted in *Erh shih erh tzu* and elsewhere, and with 5 *chüan* of woodcuts (Taipei: Hsin hsing, 1962). Pi

Yüan paid particular attention to geographical names and proposed a number of reliable identifications, based both on literary evidence and his own personal inspection. For a translation of Pi Yüan's preface, his study on the textual history of the work and Sun Hsing-yen 孫星衍's (1753–1818) postface, see Eitel, as listed under (7) below.

(h) *Shan hai ching chien shu* 山海經箋疏, 18 *chüan*, commentary by Hao I-hsing 郝懿行 (1757–1825); available in the *Ssu pu pei yao* series. The first edition, known as *Lang huan hsien kuan* 琅嬛仙館 (Yang-chou: 1809; reprinted Taipei: Yeewen, 1974), included a preface by Juan Yüan 阮元 (1764–1849) and was published with 1 *chüan* of illustrations (not included in the *Ssu pu pei yao* reprint). The edition includes the main prefaces, Kuo P'u's *t'u tsan*, and a chapter of textual emendations (*Shan hai ching ting o* 山海經訂訛) compiled by Hao himself.

(i) *Tsu pen Shan hai ching t'u tsan* 足本山海經圖讚, ed. Chang Tsung-hsiang 張宗祥 (Shanghai: Ku tien, 1958); a typeset edition of the *Shan hai ching t'u tsan*, based on a manuscript in the Palace Museum, Taipei, without illustrations.

(j) *Shan hai ching chiao chu* 山河經校注, 18 *chüan*, commentary by Yüan K'o 袁珂: Shanghai: Ku chi, 1980; review by R. Mathieu in *Asiatische Studien*, XXXVII:1 (1983), 62–6. The work is in two parts: (one) *Hai ching hsin shih* 海經新釋 (pp. 181–475), with detailed commentary on *chüan* 6–18. This part was originally conceived as an independent work, with preface dated 1963; (two) *Shan ching chien shih* 山經柬釋 (pp. 1–180), with a succinct and often unsatisfactory commentary on *chüan* 1–5, preface dated 1978. The value of the two parts is thus somewhat different. The text is punctuated and there are some 150 illustrations, taken mostly from (e) above. The book includes a useful index, compiled by Chang Ming-hua 張明華.

Editions (h) and (j) are indispensable for the study of the *Shan hai ching*, and these may be fruitfully supplemented by (e) and (g) and Mathieu's translation (see under (8) below). For comment on the geographical problems, see the following works, where a number of identifications are not as certain as the writers supposed:

(k) Lü T'iao-yang 呂調陽, *Wu tsang shan ching chuan* 五臧山經傳 and *Hai nei ching fu chuan* 海內經附傳; in *Kuan hsiang lu ts'ung shu* 觀象廬叢書 (1888).

(l) Wu Ch'eng-chih 吳承志, *Shan hai ching ti li chin shih* 山海經地理今釋; in *Ch'iu shu chai ts'ung shu*.

(m) Wei T'ing-sheng 衛挺生 and Hsü Sheng-mo 徐聖謨, *Shan ching ti li t'u k'ao* 山經地理圖考 (Taipei: Hua kang, 1974).

7. Textual and secondary studies

(a) Chang Kung-liang 張公量, 'Mu chuan shan ching ho cheng 穆傳山經合證'; *Yü kung* 1:5 (1934), 126–35.

(b) Cheng Te-k'un 鄭德坤, '*Shan hai ching chi ch'i shen hua* 山海經及其神話'; *Shih hsüeh nien pao* 4 (1932), 127–51.

(c) Chiang Shao-yüan 江紹源, *Chung kuo ku tai lü hsing chih yen chiu* 中國古代旅行之研究; Taipei: Shang wu, 1966.

(d) Chung kuo Shan hai ching hsüeh shu t'ao lun hui pien chi 中國山海經學術討論會編輯, *Shan hai ching hsin t'an* 山海經新探; Ch'eng-tu: Ssu ch'uan Academy of Social Sciences, 1986.

(e) de Lacouperie, Terrien, *Western Origin of the Early Chinese Civilisation from 2300 BC to 200 AD*; London: Asher and Company, 1894.

(f) Eitel, E. Joseph, 'Prolegomena to the *Shan Hai King*'; *China Review* XVII (1888), 330–348.

(g) Fracasso, Riccardo 'Teratoscopy or Divination by Monsters, Being a Study on the *Wu-tsang Shan-ching*'; *Han hsüeh yen chiu* 1:2 (December 1983), 657–700.

(h) Fracasso, Riccardo 'The Illustrations of the *Shan hai jing* (1). From Yu's Tripods to Qing Blockprints'; *Cina* 21 (1988), 93–104.

(i) Ho Kuan-chou 何觀洲, 'Shan hai ching tsai k'o hsüeh shang chih p'i p'an chi ch'i tso che chih shih tai k'ao 山海經在科學上之批判及其作者之時代考'; *Yen ching hsüeh pao* 7 (1930), 1347–75.

(j) Ho Tz'u-chün 賀次君, 'Shan hai ching chih pan pen chi kuan yü Shan hai ching chih chu shu 山海經之版本及關於山海經之著書'; *Yü kung* 1:10 (1934), 9–20, 311–22.

(k) Hou Jen-chih 侯仁之, 'Hai wai ssu ching Hai nei ssu ching yü Ta huang ssu ching Hai nei ching pi chiao 海外四經海內四經與大荒四經海內經比較', *Yü kung* 7 (1937), 319–26.

(l) Hsü Ping-ch'ang 徐炳昶, *Chung kuo ku shih ti ch'uan shuo shih tai* 中國古史的傳說時代; Shanghai, 1946; reprinted Taipei:1978.

(m) Itō Seiji 伊藤清司, 'Yamagawa no kamigami – Sangai kyō no kenkyū 山川の神神 —— 山海經の研究'; *Shigaku* 41:1 (1969), 31–61; 42:2 (1969), 29–78; and 42:4 (1969), 73–106.

(n) Itō Seiji, 'Kodai Chūgoku no minkan iryō – Sangai kyō no kenkyū 古代中國の民間醫療 —— 山海經の研究'; *Shigaku* 42:4 (1969), 41–62; 43:3 (1970), 17–33; 43:4 (1971), 39–87.

(o) Kao Ch'ü-hsün 高去尋 (ed.), *Shan hai ching yen chiu lun wen chi* 山海經研究論文集; Hong Kong: Chung shan, 1974.

(p) Ku Chieh-kang, 'Wu tsang shan ching shih t'an 五臧山經試探'; *Shih hsüeh lun ts'ung* 1 (1934).

(q) Ling Chun-sheng 凌純聲, *Shan hai ching hsin lun* 山海經新論; Taipei: Orient Cultural Service, 1970.

(r) Mänchen-Helfen, O. 'The Later Books of the *Shan hai ching*'; *AM* 1 (1924), 550–586.

(s) Meng Wen-t'ung 蒙文通, 'Lüeh lun Shan hai ching ti hsieh tso chi ch'i ch'an sheng ti yü 略論山海經的寫作及其產生地域'; *Chung hua wen shih lun ts'ung* 1 (1962), 43–70.

(t) Ogawa Takuji 小川琢治, 'Sangai kyō kō 山海經考'; translation in Chiang Hsia-an 江俠菴, *Hsien Ch'in ching chi k'ao* 先秦經籍考, vol. 3; Shanghai: Shang wu, 1931; reprinted Taipei, 1970.

(u) Ou Hsieh-fang 歐纈芳, 'Shan hai ching chiao cheng 山海經校正'; *Wen shih che hsüeh pao* 11 (1962), 203–338.

(v) Schiffeler, John Wm., 'Chinese Folk Medicine: a study of the Shan-hai ching'; *Asian Folklore Studies* XXXIX:2, (1980) 41–83.

(w) Schlegel, Gustave, 'Problèmes Géographiques: les Peuples étrangers chez les historiens Chinois'; the first of this series of articles is in *TP* 3 (1892), 101f.

(x) Shen Yen-ping 沈雁冰 (Hsüan Chu 玄珠), *Chung kuo shen hua yen chiu ch'u t'an* 中國神話研究初探; Shanghai: 1928; reprinted Taipei: Oriental Culture, 1971 (see chapter 2).

(y) Shih Ching-ch'eng 史景成, 'Shan hai ching hsin cheng 山海經新證'; see Kao Ch'ü-hsün, above, pp. 1–77.

(z) Wang I-chung 王以中, 'Shan hai ching t'u yü chih kung t'u 山海經圖與職貢圖'; *Yü kung* 1:3 (1934), 5–10; reprinted Kao Ch'ü-hsün, 94–99.

(aa) Wu Han 吳晗, 'Shan hai ching chung ti ku tai ku shih chi ch'i hsi t'ung 山海經中的古代故事及其系統'; *Shih hsüeh nien pao* 1;3 (1931), 81–105.

(ab) Yüan K'o, *Chung kuo ku tai shen hua* 中國古代神話; Shanghai: 1960; reprinted Peking: Chung hua, 1981.

(ac) Yüan K'o, *Shen hua lun wen chi* 神話論文集; Shanghai: Ku chi, 1982, pp. 1–44.

8. Translations

(a) European languages:

(i) Finsterbusch, Käte, *Das Verhältnis de Schan Hai Djing zur bildenden Kunst*; index with translations of large parts of the work; Berlin: Sächs. Ak. der Wissenschaften zu Leipzig/Phil.-Hist. Kl., Band 46, heft 1, 1952.

(ii) Finsterbusch, Käte, '*Shan-hai ching*, Buch 13: Das Buch vom

osten innerhalb des Meeres'; translation of *chüan* 3, with two
maps; *Asiatica — Festschrift für F.Weller*; Leipzig, 1954.

(iii) Mathieu, Rémi, *Étude sur la mythologie et l'ethnologie de la Chine
ancienne*; vol. I *Traduction annotée*; vol. II Index; Paris; Collège
de France, 1983.

(iv) *Katalog Gor i Morei: Shan' hai tszin*; introduction, translation
and commentary by E.M. Ianshina; Moscow, Nauka, 1977.

(b) Versions in modern Chinese:

(i) Fu Hsi-jen 傅錫壬, *Pai hua Shan hai ching* 白話山海經; reprinted Taipei: Ho lo, 1980.

(ii) Li Feng-mou 李豐楙, *Shan hai ching: shen hua ti ku hsiang* 山海
經: 神話的故鄉; includes a version of *Wu tsang shan ching*;
Taipei: 1983.

(iii) Yüan K'o, *Shan hai ching chiao i* 山海經校譯; Shanghai: Ku chi,
1985.

9. Japanese editions

K. *Chūgoku koten bungaku taikei*; no. 8, 1969, edited by Kōma Miyoshi,
with illustrations.
Maeno Naoaki 前野直杉, *Sangai kyō*; Tokyo: Shūeisha, 1975.

10. Indexes

(a) *Shan hai ching t'ung chien (Index du Chan Hai King)*; Centre franco-
chinois d'études sinologiques no. 9, Peking, 1948; reprinted Taipei:
Ch'eng wen, 1968; edited Nieh Ch'ung-ch'i 聶崇岐 and Hung Yeh
洪業 (William Hung).

(b) Sugawa Terukazu 須川照一, Nakamura Takashi 中村喬 and
Tamada Tsuguo 玉田繼雄, *Sangai kyō sakuin* 索引; Kyoto: Rinsen
shoten, 1961.

(c) *A Concordance to the Yan danzi, Shanhaijing and Mu tianzi zhuan* 燕丹
子, 山海經, 穆天子傳逐字索引, ed. D.C. Lau and Chen Fong
Ching; *ICS* series, Hong Kong: Commercial Press, forthcoming 1994.

See also Finsterbush and Mathieu, under (8) above.

— Riccardo Fracasso

Shang chün shu 商君書

1. Contents and structure

The book is concerned with the development of legalist theory; order can be maintained in a state by means of a system of ruthless punishments, so as to keep the population on the right track; secondary activities, that are of low priority, are to be suppressed; agriculture is to be promoted; and the martial virtues are to be encouraged, for use in wars of conquest. Within this context a whole variety of social and economic problems are likely to arise.

The work is divided into five *chüan*, and the text is missing for two (nos. 16 and 21) of its twenty-six *p'ien*, each one of which bears its own title. Some of the *p'ien* (e.g., nos. 1 and 26) are in dialogue form; others take the form of addresses submitted to a king; yet others are in the form of essays. There is some duplication between different *p'ien*, and the work is marked by a lack of homogeneous treatment. There are some inconsistencies within a single *p'ien*.

2. Authorship

The title of the book bears the name of its reputed author, i.e. Shang Yang 商鞅 or Kung-sun Yang 公孫鞅, sometimes known as Wei Yang 衛鞅, who was a member of the royal house of Wei 衛 and served as minister to Duke Hsiao 孝 of Ch'in from 359 B.C. until his death in 338 B.C. Shang Yang was one of the boldest reformers of his age, and he may be described as the architect of Ch'in's economic and military supremacy. Biographical details may be found in *Shih chi* 68, pp. 2227–39, with further information on the man and his work in *Shih chi* 5, pp. 202f., *Chan kuo ts'e* ('Ch'in' 1 and 3; 'Ch'i' 4 and 5; 'Ch'u' 4 and 'Wei' 1) and other writings of the Ch'in and Han periods. For a recent study of Shang Yang's biography, see Léon Vandermeersch, *La Formation du Légisme* (Paris: École Francaise d'Extreme Orient, 1965), pp. 27–44.

3. Date of compilation and authenticity

Two entries are included in *Han shu* 30: (a) *Shang chün*, 29 *p'ien*, under *fa chia* 法家 (p. 1735); and (b) *Kung-sun Yang*, 27 *p'ien*, under *ping* 兵, *ch'üan mo* 權謀 (p. 1757). According to the *Pieh lu* of Liu Hsiang 劉向 (79–8 B.C.), as cited by Yen Shih-ku 顏師古 (581–645) (*Han shu* 30, p. 1743 note), a work entitled *Shen nung* 神農 probably included some of Shang Yang's theories. It cannot be known whether these entries refer to entirely different books, or whether there were some parts of Shang Yang's writings which were repeated from one collection to another. The two works which are entered in *Han shu* 30, however, both disappeared at an early stage. According to Duyvendak (*The Book of Lord Shang*; see under (9) below, p. 131), *p'ien* nos 10, 11 and 12 of the received text, which are concerned with warfare, may have been parts of the book which is entered among works on strategy.

The received text cannot derive in entirety from the hand of Shang Yang. It has been regarded as suspect since the Sung period (see *Chou shih she pi* 周氏涉筆, as cited in the *fu k'ao* 附攷 to Yen K'o-chün's 嚴可均 (1762–1843) edition, described under (6) below), and Maspero believed it to be a product of the Six Dynasties. *P'ien* nos. 1, 9, 15, 20 and 26, which allude to institutions, incidents or events that postdated Shang Yang's death cannot have been written entirely by him. However, even though they are of different authorship and period, the various parts of the work are all prior to the Han period.

Shang Yang's writings were widely distributed during the Warring States period, and the received text retains considerable fragments of that time. Some *p'ien* quite possibly derive from Shang Yang's own hand, i.e.:

(a) *Chin ling* 靳令 (no. 13); authenticity has been in doubt, owing to the presence of similar passages in the *Han fei tzu*. However, that work also includes a direct citation, attributed to Shang Yang, in *p'ien* no. 30 'Nei chu shuo 內諸說', *shang* 上 (Ch'en Ch'i-yu ed.,p. 543). It would be surprising if Han Fei were to quote himself when attributing his ideas to Shang Yang. In addition, in a passage which is concerned with Shang Yang's policies, the *Yen t'ieh lun* makes use of an expression which is close to one which is found in this *p'ien*.

(b) *Ching nei* 境內 (no. 19); there is a somewhat free citation, attributed to Shang Yang, in *Han fei tzu* 43 'Ting fa 定法' (Ch'en ed., p. 907).

(c) *Wai nei* 外內 (no. 22); the title is cited, in reverse order, in the *Han fei tzu*; however, the passage there is ambiguous, and can be interpreted in a different way. In *Yen t'ieh lun* 7 'Fei Yang 非鞅' (Wang Li-ch'i ed., p. 50) the terms *nei* and *wai* are used in a context that is analogous to that of *Wai nei*, as a means of defining Shang Yang's policies.

(d) *K'ai sai* 開塞 (no. 7); Ssu-ma Ch'ien 司馬遷 (?145–?86) wrote that he had read Shang Yang's *K'ai sai* (*Shih chi* 68, p. 2237.) There is a reference to Shang Yang's *Ch'i sai* 啓塞 in *Huai nan tzu* 20, 22b (Liu Wen-tien ed.), and there are allusions in *Yen t'ieh lun* (Wang Li-ch'i ed., p. 52) and possibly in *Han fei tzu* 13 'Ho shih 和氏' (Ch'en ed., pp. 238–39).

(e) *Nung chan* 農戰 (no. 3); Ssu-ma Ch'ien mentions a work known under the similar title of *keng chan* 耕戰 among Shang Yang's writings (*Shih chi* 68, p. 2237).

(f) *Li pen* 立本 (no. 11); critical remarks in *p'ien* no. 6 'Fei shih erh tzu 非十二子' of the *Hsün tzu*, although ascribed to two other legalists, are similar to those of the *Shang chün shu*; the opening phrase, which is designed to refute the views of Shen Tao and T'ien P'ien 田駢, can only be understood by reference to the theories expressed in *p'ien* no. 11 of the *Shang chün shu*.

During the third century, and in the Han period, new material that was related in some ways to the works and personality of Shang Yang was appended to his writings to form a book. Even though all the *p'ien* of the received text are not the work of the minister of Ch'in, they date from before the Han period, and cannot be said to be in conflict with the principles of the *Shang chün shu*.

4. History of the text

Shang Yang's writings were widely distributed during the Ch'in and Han periods and still enjoyed considerable popularity during the Three Kingdoms and Six Dynasties. In his will, Liu Pei 劉備 (161–223) enjoined his son to read this text, and a reference in the *Chin shu* (50, p. 1393) to Shang Yang's 'Six vermin' shows that it was known during the Chin period; there is also a reference in the *Wen hsin tiao lung* 文心雕龍.

At the beginning of the T'ang period the text was in a more complete state than it is today, but it was not available in entirety. The *Ch'ün shu chih yao* (ed. Wei Cheng 魏徵 631) cites part of a *p'ien* entitled *Liu fa* 六法, to be placed before *p'ien* no. 14 as now received; *Liu fa* is not known from other sources. Fujiwara Sukeyo's catalogue carries the simple entry, under *fa chia*, of '*Shang chün shu san* 商君書三, compiled by Wei Yang'. In *Chiu T'ang shu* 47, p. 2031, the item appears as '*Shang tzu wu chüan* 商子五卷, by Shang Yang'; in *Hsin T'ang shu* 59, p. 1531 it appears as '*Shang chün shu wu chüan*, also termed *Shang tzu*'. The substitution of the title *Shang tzu* in place of *Shang chün shu* at the close of the T'ang period remained usual practice until Yen K'o-chün's edition (see under (6) below).

Certain *p'ien* disappeared between the T'ang and the Sung periods,

Cheng Ch'iao 鄭樵 (1104–62), Ch'ao Kung-wu 晁公武 (d. 1171) and Wang Ying-lin 王應麟 (1223–96) noting with regret the loss of three. Ch'en Chen-sun 陳振孫 (*c.* 1190 to after 1249) wrote in the *Chih chai shu lu chieh t'i* of '28 *p'ien*, of which one has been lost', and it is therefore possible that two versions existed in the Sung period, being of 27 and 26 *p'ien* respectively. However, it is by no means impossible that the figure of 28 was a copyist's error for 26, and that Ch'en's reference was to a total of 26 *p'ien*, of which one had been lost, rather than to a text of 28 *p'ien*.

Whatever the facts may have been, the text was in a highly corrupt state from the beginning of the Sung period, being hardly comprehensible to some scholars (see *Chou shih she pi*, and Huang Chen 黃震 (1213–80) *Huang shih jih ch'ao* 黃氏日鈔). The situation deteriorated yet further during the Yüan period, with the disappearance of *p'ien* nos. 16 and 21; the title of the latter was missing in all editions except that of the *Mien miao ko* 緜眇閣. Of the original 29 *p'ien*, no more than 24 survived in the earliest printed edition to be mentioned, which dated from the Yüan period and was known only to Yen K'o-chün.

5. Early prints

The Yüan edition just mentioned is the earliest to survive before the Ming period. All editions consist of 26 *p'ien*, with the text of nos. 16 and 21 missing; the work is divided into five *chüan*, except in Chu Wei-jan's 朱蔚然 edition, which is of two *chüan*. There are no variants other than those of individual characters, and the filiation of the different editions is extremely difficult to determine; they may well all derive from a single manuscript version. A distinction may be drawn between (a) independent prints and (b) prints included in the major collections.

(a) Independent prints

(i) A copy which was included in the T'ien i ko 天一閣 library of Fan Ch'in 范欽 (1506–85) was widely known during the Ming period and in the time of Yen K'o-chün. It was apparently derived from the edition of the Yüan period and is reproduced in the *Su pu ts'ung k'an* series; format: 9 by 18.

(ii) Feng Chin's 馮覲 (*cs* 1544) edition, so named after his annotations; published in 1559.

(iii) Ch'in Ssu-lin's 秦四麟 edition, published between 1573 and 1620; singled out by Yen K'o-chün as the best edition that he was able to consult.

(iv) Cheng Ts'ai's 鄭寀 edition, unquestionably of the Ming period, and used by Yü Yüeh 俞樾 (1821–1907) and Sun Hsing-yen 孫星衍 (1753–1818) in their critical notes. Duyvendak's statement (seeunder (9) below, p. 135) that this was a Sung edition, printed between 1241 and 1253, rests on a confusion between two scholars of the same name.

(b) Editions included in collections

(i) Of Feng Meng-chen 馮夢楨 (1546–1605); in *Hsien Ch'in chu tzu ho pien* (Mien miao ko, 1573–1620).

(ii) Of Wu Mien-hsüeh 吳勉學; in *Erh shih tzu* 1573–1620.

(iii) Of Ch'eng Jung 程榮 (1447–1520); in *Han Wei ts'ung shu* 1573–1620.

(iv) Of Kuei Yu-kuang 歸有光 (1506–71); in *Chu tzu hui han* 1621–27; very much like the edition of Feng Chin.

(v) Of Ch'en Jen-hsi 陳仁錫 (c. 1580–c. 1635); in *Chu tzu ch'i shang* 諸子奇賞 1621–27.

(vi) Of Chu Wei-jan 朱蔚然; in *Ho chu ming chia p'i tien chu tzu ch'üan shu*; notes by Ku Ch'i-yüan 顧起元 (1565–1628), with text established by Chu Wei-jan and critical comments of Yang Shen 楊慎; printed between 1621 and 1627. As distinct from other editions, the text is divided into two *chüan* (no. 1 with *p'ien* nos. 1–14; no. 2 with nos. 15–26).

(vii) Of Ch'en Shen 陳深; in *Chu tzu p'in chieh* 諸子品節.

(viii) The *Ch'ung wen shu chü* edition, in *Chu tzu pai chia* 諸子百家; used by T'ao Hung-ch'ing 陶鴻慶 (1859–1918) in his critical notes.

6. Major critical editions of the Ch'ing period

(a) Yen K'o-chün, *Shang chün shu chiao* 商君書校. Yen K'o-chün was the first scholar to establish the text on the basis of philological study. He did so with the help of the Yüan edition, the copy held in the T'ien i ko library and the editions of Ch'in Ssu-lin and a certain Mr. Yeh 葉 (probably Ming; no details provided). Yen's edition was printed in 1793 with a preface and a table of contents, followed by a note of the editions consulted. Appendicial notes (*fu k'ao* 附攷) which follow the text include some of the references to Shang Yang and his writings that appear in early works and bibliographical lists. Yen's textual emendations are sometimes somewhat rash, with no note being given of the editions which had been used.

A manuscript copy of Yen's work was available to Sun I-jang 孫詒

讓 (1848–1908), being perhaps superior to a printed copy which was in circulation. The *Ssu pu pei yao* print is based on a re-issue of this edition by the *Che-chiang shu chü*, as is also the text that is included, with punctuation, in the *Chu tzu chi ch'eng* 諸子集成 (Shanghai: Shih chieh, 1935). These do not include Yen's list of the editions that were available to him.

(b) Sun Hsing-yen 孫星衍 (1753–1818), *Shang chün shu chiao* 商君書校; text established by Sun Hsing-yen and Sun P'ing-i 孫馮翼 (*fl.* 1800) on the basis of the Mien miao ko edition, *Erh shih tzu*, the *Han Wei ts'ung shu* and the editions of Chu Wei-jan and Cheng Ts'ai; published (1803) in the *Wen ching t'ang ts'ung shu*, with Sun Hsing-yen's postface which concerns the editions consulted.

(c) Ch'ien Hsi-tso 錢熙祚 (1801–44), *Shang chün shu chiao* 商君書校, included in the *Chih hai*, with a postface; mid nineteenth century.

7. Recent critical editions

(a) Wang Shih-jun 王時潤, *Shang chün shu chiao ch'üan* 商君書斠詮; published 1915 by the *Hung wen t'u shu she* in the *Wen chi hsien ts'ung shu*; notes include the work of late Ch'ing scholars, with some emendations. Duyvendak's translation was based on this edition.

(b) Yin T'ung-yang 尹桐陽, *Shang chün shu hsin shih* 商君書新釋; in the *Ch'i sheng chai ts'ung shu* of 1918, re-edited 1922; Duyvendak writes (p. 140) that 'little good can be said of this edition'.

(c) Chu Shih-ch'e 朱師轍, *Shang chün shu chieh ku* 商君書解詁; punctuated text, first published 1921 by *Kuang i shu chü*; improved edition, with a new *apparatus criticus*, under the title *Shang chün shu chieh ku ting pen* 商君書解詁定本 (Canton: Chung hua, 1948; reprinted Peking, Hong Kong 1956, 1974). The text is preceded by prefaces of the author (1916 and 1947), of Hu P'u-an 胡樸安 (Yün-yü 韞玉) and of Yin Yen-wu 尹炎武, and by explanatory notes to the edition. Appendixes include: (i) the prefaces and other material from the edition of Mien miao ko and of Yen K'o-chün, and postfaces by Sun Hsing-yen and Ch'ien Hsi-tso; and (ii) passages from other works which concern Shang Yang and his writings. These are followed by Sun I-jang's emended text of *p'ien* no. 19 (*ching nei* 境內), and a list of editions used by Chu Shih-ch'e himself. This is a valuable edition, despite some errors of interpretation and punctuation.

(d) Ch'en Ch'i-t'ien 陳啓天, *Shang chün shu chiao shih* 商君書校釋, in the *Hsüeh sheng kuo hsüeh ts'ung shu* (Shanghai: Shang wu, 1935); punctuated text, established in the light of earlier commentators' work. The notes are intended to assemble comments of a number of scholars published in various series and not easily available. The text of the *Liu fa* 六法, known only from the *Ch'ün shu chih yao*, is also included at the end of the book.

(e) Kao Heng 高亨 (b. 1900), *Shang chün shu chu i* 商君書注譯, Peking: Chung hua, 1974; text in simplified characters and punctuated, on the basis of earlier, and some more recent, editions. The title of each *p'ien* is followed by an explanation of its main ideas and a discussion of authenticity. The text is followed by annotation and a *pai hua* version. A long introduction on the subject of Shang Yang and his thought, as interpreted in accordance with contemporary ideology, is followed by a list of the editions consulted and a critical account of the book's authenticity. References to Shang Yang and his writings in Ch'in and Han sources are appended, together with Kao Heng's own critical notes (*Shang chün shu hsin chien* 商君書新箋), hitherto unpublished.

(f) Chang Shih-t'ung 章詩同, *Shang chün shu*; text in simplified characters and punctuated, for the use of peasants, workers and soldiers at the time of the *P'i Lin P'i K'ung* campaign; Shanghai: Jen min, 1974.

8. Annotations printed without text

(a) Yü Yüeh 俞樾 (1821–1907); in *Chu tzu p'ing i* 20 (first published 1870).

(b) Sun I-jang 孫詒讓 (1848–1908); in *Cha i* (1894).

(c) Yü Ch'ang 于鬯 (1894–1910), *Hsiang ts'ao hsü chiao shu* 香草續校書; punctuated edition by Chang Hua-min 張華民, Peking: Chung hua, 1963.

(d) T'ao Hung-ch'ing 陶鴻慶, 'Tu Shang chün shu cha chi 讀商君書札記'; in *Tu chu tzu cha chi* 讀諸子札記, Shanghai: Chung hua, 1959, pp. 406–20.

(e) Yang Shu-ta 楊樹達; *Chi wei chü tu shu chi* 積微居讀書記; Peking: Chung hua, 1962, pp. 188–90.

9. Translations

(a) Duyvendak, J.J.L., *The Book of Lord Shang*; London: Arthur Probsthain, 1928; reprinted Chicago: Chicago University Press, 1963, and London: Unesco's collection of representative works, Chinese series, 1963. There is a long introduction with a study of Shang Yang's thought and the authenticity of the work, and there is considerable annotation to the text. There are some errors of interpretation.

(b) Levi, Jean, *Le Livre du prince Shang*; Paris: Flammarion, 1981.

10. Japanese editions

D. *Kokuyaku kambun taisei;* no. 9, 1921, edited by Koyanagi Shikita.
L. *Chūgoku koten shinsho*, 1970, edited by Shimizu Kiyoshi.

11. Research aids and critical studies

Most of the recent studies are concerned more with Shang Yang's practical politics than with his writings, which are sometimes considered within the somewhat more general studies of legalism (e.g., see entries under *Han fei tzu*, (9) and (1) for works by Liang Ch'i-ch'ao 梁啓超 (1873-1929) and Vandermeersch). For Shang Yang's political theories, see Duyvendak and Levi, as cited above, and Yuan Shao-chi 袁紹基, 'Some Reflections on Shang Yang and his Political Philosophy', in *Chinese Culture* 9:3 (1968), 81-92; for critical editions and textual history, see, in addition to the works listed above, Ch'en Ch'i-t'ien, 'Fa chia shu yao 法家述要', in *BIHP* 40:2 (1969), 865-66.

   Shang Yang's political principles and contribution to Chinese statecraft have prompted comment by a number of writers, including Su Shih 蘇軾 (1036-1101) in 'Lun Shang Yang 論商鞅', and more recently by Yang K'uan 楊寬, in *Shang Yang pien fa* 商鞅變法 (Shanghai: Jen min, 1955, re-issued 1975, with changes to take account of the contemporary political situation in China).

   For bibliography, evaluation and translation of some recent contributions, see Li Yu-ning (ed.), *Shang Yang's Reforms and State Control in China*; White Plains, New York: M.E. Sharpe, Inc., 1977. See also Vitaly A. Rubin, *Individual and State in Ancient China: Essays on Four Chinese Philosophers*, translated by Steven I. Levine (New York: Columbia University Press, 1976), Chapter 3 'The Theory and Practice of a Totalitarian State; *Shang Yang and Legalism*'.

12. Index

A Concordance to the Shang jun shu 商君書逐字索引, ed. D.C. Lau and Chen Fong Ching; *ICS* series, Hong Kong: Commercial Press, 1992.

— Jean Levi

Shang shu 尚書 (Shu ching 書經)

The *Shang shu*, also commonly referred to as the *Shu ching* (whence the titles *Document Classic* or *Book of Documents* most commonly used in the West), was recognized during the Han dynasty as one of the 'Five Classics' and has served for more than two-thousand years as the foundation of Chinese political philosophy. The text contains the earliest writings in China's traditional literature, with some chapters dating nearly a thousand years before its recognition as a classic. But other chapters are much later; indeed, nearly half the text was systematically forged early in the fourth century A.D. Because of this heterogeneous nature, the *Shang shu* has long been the focus of China's most important philological debate and, perhaps more so than with any other early Chinese text, requires familiarity with the later scholarship for an accurate understanding of the text.

1. Content

The *Shang shu* is found in one of two formats, depending on the date of the edition and the editor's position in the debate on the text's authenticity. In the 'orthodox' organization, there is first a 'Greater Preface' (*Ta hsü* 大序, also commonly referred to as the 'K'ung Preface' (*K'ung hsü* 孔序), ostensibly written by K'ung An-kuo 孔安國 (d. *c.* 100 B.C.) in the second century B.C. This preface describes K'ung's discovery of the text of the *Shang shu*, written in an 'Old Text' (*ku wen* 古文) script, in the wall of Confucius' home. There then follow fifty separate documents in fifty-eight chapters (four chapters, the 'T'ai Chia' 大甲, 'P'an Keng' 盤庚, 'Yüeh ming' 說命 and 'T'ai shih' 泰誓, are each divided into three discrete sections, with each section counted as a separate chapter), each chapter preceded by a brief preface, referred to usually as the 'Preface to the Documents' (*Shu hsü* 書序), and traditionally supposed to have been composed by Confucius. According to the same tradition, Confucius had originally selected one hundred documents to be in the *Shang shu*; the chapters no longer extant are each represented, in their proper sequence, by that portion of the 'Preface to the Documents' describing their background. Also included in all 'orthodox' editions of the *Shang shu* is a commentary also ostensibly written by K'ung An-kuo and referred to as the 'K'ung Commentary' (*K'ung chuan* 孔傳).

The second usual arrangement of the work, first seen in the *Shang shu tsuan yen* 尙書纂言 of Wu Ch'eng 吳澄 (1247–1331), and best known in the West by the translation of Bernhard Karlgren, includes only the 28 (or sometimes 29) 'New Text' (*chin wen* 今文, for this term see below) chapters, that are now generally considered to be authentic. The arrangement differs also by collecting the 'Preface to the Documents' into a single integral chapter, which may be placed at either the beginning or end of the complete text, and by deleting both the 'K'ung Preface' and the 'K'ung Commentary'.

In both schemes of arrangement the text is set out in chronological sequence as follows, corresponding with the four earliest periods of Chinese history:

	'Old Text' editions	'New Text' editions
Yü shu 虞書	5 chapters	2 chapters
Hsia shu 夏書	4	2
Shang shu 商書	17	5
Chou shu 周書	32	19 or 20

Most of the chapters are in the form of addresses, either by kings or their ministers. These are conventionally divided by title into five types, i.e. (i) Consultations (*mo* 謨), which represent dialogues between the king and his ministers; (ii) Instructions (*hsün* 訓), ministers' advice for the king; (iii) Announcements (*kao* 誥), pronouncements by the king to the people at large; (iv) Declarations (*shih* 誓), battlefield speeches by kings; and (v) Commands (*ming* 命), entitlements of royal responsibilities and privileges conferred on a single individual.

2. Date and authenticity

The *Shang shu* is divided into 'Old Text' and 'New Text' chapters, and it is generally agreed that the 'Old Text' chapters were deliberately forged in the early fourth century A.D. Since demonstration of the spurious nature of these chapters requires a survey of the textual history of the *Shang shu*, a detailed discussion will be reserved until the following sections. Here it is necessary to discuss only the 28 or 29 'New Text' chapters. Although long protected from philological scrutiny by their 'New Text' pedigree, recent scholarship has shown that even many of these chapters were composed well after the events they purport to record.

There is now general agreement that the 'Yao tien' 堯典 and 'Kao Yao mo' 皋陶謨 chapters of the 'Yü shu' 虞書 and the 'Yü kung' 禹貢 and 'Kan shih' 甘誓 chapters of the 'Hsia shu' certainly do not date from the time of the semi-legendary emperors Yao 堯 and Yü 禹, but rather were composed in the last centuries of the Chou dynasty and, especially in the case of the 'Yü kung', perhaps as late as the Ch'in dynasty. Arguments for the date of the 'Yao tien' often hinge on astronomical information provided in that text, but unfortunately this is subject to various interpretations, which lead to a wide range in proposed dates of composition. On the basis of its language and thought, the text would appear to date no earlier than the late Spring and Autumn period.

There are five documents of the *Shang shu* 商書. Of these, the 'T'ang shih' 湯誓, which is ostensibly the earliest, is generally agreed to date to the Chou period. Although there is no consensus as to when, in that period, it was written, many scholars argue that, since the text justifies the Shang conquest of Hsia, it could have been created by the Chou founders to justify their own conquest of Shang. The next chapter, the 'P'an Keng', is a lengthy address exhorting the Shang people to follow their king P'an Keng in moving the capital to Yin 殷, present day An-yang 安陽. This chapter is considered by many scholars to be the earliest document in the text and, thus, the earliest document in Chinese history, pre-dating even the Shang oracle-bone inscriptions. Despite this, there are many indications, such as the use of 'Yin' to refer to the Shang capital and people and the expression of a developed concept of 'heaven' (*t'ien* 天), that this text was also written during the Chou dynasty, perhaps also to justify the Chou conquest and forced migration of the Shang people. The final three chapters, 'Kao tsung jung jih' 高宗肜日, 'Hsi po k'an Li' 西伯戡黎, and 'Wei tzu' 微子, all appear to be written by a single hand, probably late as the Warring States period, although they do seem to be based on records of actual events.

The next section, the 'Chou shu' 周書, which is not to be confused with the text of the same title, often referred to as the *I Chou shu* 逸周書, comprises the bulk of the *Shang shu*. The 19 or 20 of the 28 or 29 'New Text' documents that are in this section include the first chapters to be generally regarded as contemporary records of the events that are described. However, not all of the chapters of this section are regarded as being authentic. The first chapter, the 'T'ai shih', which is the only document to be found in radically different versions in the 'Old Text' and some 'New Text' editions of the *Shang shu*, has been reconstituted on the basis of quotations in early works. Despite being included among the 'New Text' chapters during the Han dynasty, the 'T'ai shih' does not share the same provenance as the other chapters and is generally regarded as a forgery of the Han period. The next three chapters, the 'Mu shih' 牧誓, 'Hung fan' 洪範, and 'Chin t'eng' 金縢, all attributed to the time of King Wu 武 (r. 1045–1043 B.C.), are also generally regarded as later creations, although they are certainly much earlier than the 'T'ai shih'.

It is with the 12 chapters generally attributed to the reign of King Ch'eng 成 (r. 1042/35–1006 B.C.), and especially the first seven years of that reign during which time the Duke of Chou acted as regent, that the heart of the authentic *Shang shu* is found. The titles of the these chapters are, in the order in which they appear: 'Ta kao' 大誥, 'K'ang kao' 康誥, 'Chiu kao' 酒誥, 'Tzu ts'ai' 梓材, 'Shao kao' 召誥, 'Luo kao' 洛誥, 'Tuo shih' 多士, 'Wu i' 無逸, 'Chün Shih' 君奭, 'Tuo fang' 多方, 'Li cheng' 立政 and 'Ku ming' 顧命. Although various scholars reject certain of these chapters (the 'Wu i' and 'Li cheng' are most often suspected of being later compositions), almost no scholar questions the authenticity of the five 'announcement' (*kao*) chapters, questionable as their date of composition may be. The 'K'ang kao' and 'Chiu kao' are both addresses made to Feng 封, the ninth of King Wen's 文 ten direct-line sons, upon the occasion of his appointment to govern the capital area of the former Shang dynasty. All early references to these texts clearly date them to the period of the Duke of Chou's regency, just after the suppression of the Wu Keng 武庚 rebellion. Because these two documents both purport to record the words of the king, being introduced with the formulaic phrase 'the king seemingly said' (*wang juo yüeh* 王若曰), and because in the 'K'ang kao' Feng is addressed as the speaker's younger brother (*chen ch'i ti* 朕其弟), beginning in the Sung dynasty scholars such as Su Shih 蘇軾 (1036–1101) and Chu Hsi 朱熹 (1130–1200) proposed that the documents should not be attributed to King Ch'eng, the nephew of Feng; they must rather date to the reign of King Wu, who was in fact Feng's elder brother. This argument is inconsistent with all of the reliable evidence regarding the establishment of the Chou dynasty. In addition its two primary points of evidence are equally satisfied by considering the Duke of Chou, also an elder brother of Feng, as speaking on behalf of the young King Ch'eng, which is implied by the formula 'the king seemingly said', and which was affirmed by Ssu-ma Ch'ien 司馬遷 (?145–?86 B.C.). Despite these two points, the argument has been accepted by many subsequent scholars. Not only has this led to confusions regarding the historical context of the texts themselves, it has also led to the curious, and equally indefensible, view of those who maintain the traditional date that, during the time he was regent, the Duke of Chou had usurped the title of 'king'.

The final four chapters of the 'New Text' *Shang shu*, the 'Lü hsing' 呂刑, 'Wen hou chih ming' 文侯之命, 'Fei shih' 費誓 and 'Ch'in shih' 秦誓, are a medley of texts from early in the Spring and Autumn period. Of these, only the 'Lü hsing', which purports to date to the reign of King Mu 穆 (r. 956–918 B.C.), pretends to be earlier and is still accepted as such by many scholars. The date of the 'Wen hou chih ming', which bears a remarkable resemblance to the text of standard late Western Chou investiture inscriptions, has also been the focus of some debate. Whereas the 'Preface to the Documents' and most early commentators state that the text is a command given by King P'ing 平 (r. 770–720 B.C.) to a Lord of Chin 晉, Ssu-ma Ch'ien attributed it instead to King Hsiang's 襄 (r. 651–619 B.C.) command to Ch'ung-erh 重耳, lord of Chin, following his victory at the battle of Ch'eng-p'u 城濮 in 632 B.C. Most scholars now accept the date given in the 'Preface to the Documents'.

3.   Textual history

The history of the *Shang shu*'s transmission from the Former Han until the early part of the T'ang dynasty is probably more complex than that of any other work in Chinese literature. And because of the great status accorded to the text, its transmission was often bitterly, and sometimes unscrupulously, contested. Indeed, in many ways the story of the *Shang shu*'s transmission reflects the broader developments in the intellectual world of that period. A study of the problem may be found in Paul Pelliot, *Mémoires concernant l'Asie Orientale*, vol. II, Paris, 1916; for an abbreviated account, see Bernhard Karlgren, *Philology and Ancient China*, Oslo: Aschehoug, 1926, pp. 95–101.

The *Shang shu* is frequently cited in pre-Ch'in texts and apparently already by the time of Confucius was regarded as a venerable guide to political philosophy. However, most of the citations in these early works do not accord with the present text of the *Shang shu*; in one survey, only 45 of 137 citations were found in the received text. Among pre-Ch'in texts that cite the *Shang shu*, only the *Hsün tzu* does not quote from any text other than those in the received text. Coupled with the probable Ch'in date for the latest chapters in the 'New Text' *Shang shu*, this suggests perhaps that a text roughly resembling the received text (of the 'New Text' chapters) was edited about the middle of the third century B.C.

Shortly thereafter, however, the First Ch'in Emperor's purge of literature and scholars nearly brought an end to the transmission of the *Shang shu*, some chapters of which had already been in existence for more than eight-hundred years. Fortunately, at least one scholar of the time, Fu Sheng 伏勝, more often referred to simply as Fu sheng 伏生, took the precaution of secreting the bamboo strips on which his copy of the text was written in a wall of his home, in the vicinity of present day Chi-nan 濟南. After the fall of the Ch'in dynasty, Fu excavated the bamboo strips, discovering that only 28 chapters of the original corpus were still legible. Undaunted, he made those texts the focus of his teaching. It was not until somewhat later, during the reign of Wen ti 文帝 (r. 179–157 B.C.), that the imperial court secured a copy of Fu's text, written in the *li shu* 隸書 script of the Ch'in dynasty. This is the basis for the 'New Text' version of the *Shang shu*. During the reign of Wu ti 武帝 (r. 141–87 B.C.), this text was recognized as a classic; a post of Academician (*po shih* 博士) was established with specific responsibility for interpreting and expounding it, under the tutelage of Ou-yang Kao 歐陽高. Eventually, academicians were appointed to represent the textual traditions of Hsia-hou Sheng 夏侯勝 (*fl.* 70 B.C.), usually called the Elder (Ta 大) Hsia-hou, and his son Hsia-hou Chien 夏侯建, usually called the Younger (Hsiao 小) Hsia-hou. Both of these were also based on the Fu Sheng text, and recognized as orthodox. See Tjan Tjoe Som, *Po hu t'ung i: the Comprehensive Discussions in the White Tiger Hall*, vol. I, Leiden: E.J. Brill, 1949, pp. 82 f.

At about the time that the Fu Sheng 'New Text' tradition was being recognized as orthodox, two other texts are said to have been discovered in the walls of houses. One of these discoveries, variously said to have been made during the reign of Wu ti or Hsüan ti 宣帝 (r. 74–49 B.C.), was a text of the 'T'ai shih' chapter. This was quickly incorporated into the various 'New Text' versions, making a total of 29 (or, according to a different way of counting allowing for the multiple enumeration of some chapters, 34) chapters.

Also during the reign of Wu ti, a renovation of the ancestral home of Confucius in present day Ch'ü-fu 曲阜 (Shantung) is said to have produced another complete text of the *Shang shu*, this one written in the 'tadpole script' (*k'o tou wen* 科斗文), that was current before the Ch'in script-reform. K'ung An-kuo 孔安國 (d. *c.* 100 B.C.), a direct descendant of Confucius, deciphered this text and discovered that it contained, in addition to the same 28 chapters originally present in Fu Sheng's text, a radically different version of the 'T'ai shih' and 16 other documents (in 24 chapters), giving a total of 45 documents in 58 chapters, the same number as in the present 'orthodox' text. According to the account provided in the *I jang T'ai ch'ang po shih shu* 移讓太常博士書 of Liu Hsin 劉歆 (46 B.C.–A.D. 23), when K'ung attempted to present his text to the court, the emperor's pre-occupation with an on-going witchcraft purge precluded official recognition, and the text was simply accepted into the imperial library. Liu Hsin's account of this presentation has provoked suspicions on several counts, the most important being that K'ung An-kuo is reported to have died no later than 100 B.C., well before the famous witchcraft purge of 91 B.C. to which it is assumed that Liu was referring. If this story is not completely apocryphal, it is possible that Liu Hsin was in fact referring to a separate witchcraft purge, which took place in 130 B.C.

Whatever the actual provenance of K'ung An-kuo's text, there would seem to be no question that when Liu Hsin and his father Liu Hsiang 劉 向 (79–8 B.C.) were given responsibility for producing an inventory of the imperial library, there was contained therein both a 'New Text' and an 'Old Text' version of the *Shang shu*. According to their collation, in addition to the 16 extra documents in the 'Old Text' version and the different texts of the 'T'ai shih', the 28 documents common to the two texts also differed in the following ways:

(a) Two bamboo strips were misplaced in the 'New Text' version.
(b) Three bamboo strips were missing from the 'New Text' version.
(c) Several tens of individual graphs were missing in the 'New Text' version.
(d) As many as 700 individual graphs differed.

In another inventory of the imperial library undertaken during the reign of Ming ti (r. 59–75), Chia K'uei 賈逵 (30–101) and Pan Ku 班固 (32–92), among others, confirmed that the 'New Text' versions of the *Shang shu* were exactly as Liu Hsin had reported, but that the 'Old Text' version now had only 57 chapters, the 'Wu ch'eng' 武成 chapter apparently having been lost during the reign of Kuang-wu ti 光武帝 (r. 25–57).

There is considerable evidence that the 'Old Text' *Shang shu* was gaining in popularity and circulation at about this time; aside from these librarian's notices, however, there is little evidence for the existence of its 15 or 16 extra documents. For instance, in his *Shuo wen chieh tzu* 說文解字, Hsü Shen 許慎 (c. 55–c. 149) quoted the 'Old Text' *Shang shu* 159 times, but not one of these quotations came from other than the 28 chapters that were common to both textual traditions. Indeed the only evidence of these chapters is found in the *Shang shu chu* 尙書注 commentary of Cheng Hsüan 鄭玄 (127–200). While this commentary, which now exists only in modern recensions, was also restricted only to the 28 chapters common to both versions, Cheng Hsüan occasionally cited passages from the other chapters, suggesting that they were in fact available in the imperial library. In any event, the recognition of the 'Old Text' tradition by a scholar as influential as Cheng Hsüan seems to have been sufficient to win it the status of orthodoxy. This can be seen by a comparison of the two great ventures in 'publishing' of this era.

In 175, Ling ti 靈帝 (r. 168–189) ordered the 'Classics' to be engraved in stone, the so-called 'Hsi-p'ing Stone Classics' (*Hsi p'ing shih ching* 熹 平石經). For the text of the *Shang shu*, the 'New Text' tradition was selected, the Ou-yang version apparently serving as the base text, with *variora* from the two Hsia-hou texts also noted. This engraving project was completed in 183, the full text of the *Shang shu* coming to 18,500 graphs, and the stones were erected in front of the lecture hall of the imperial academy at Lo-yang. Within ten years, however, when the disturbances that resulted in the downfall of the Han dynasty brought about the destruction of the capital, the 'Hsi p'ing Stone Classics' were also destroyed; pieces of stone bearing about 1,000 graphs from this engraving have now been recovered (see Ma Heng 馬衡, *Han shih ching chi ts'un* 漢石經集存; Peking: K'o hsüeh yüan, 1957).

Sixty years later, during the Cheng shih 正始 (240–249) era of the Wei 魏 dynasty, the classics were again carved in stone, in a project usually referred to as the 'Three Styles Stone Classics' (*san t'i shih ching* 三體石 經), and by that time the 'Old Text' tradition had become orthodox. Unfortunately again, in 311 the Chin court, inheritor of these engravings, was defeated and not only were the 'Three Styles Stone Classics' destroyed, with very little left to survive today, but the imperial library was also lost.

With the re-establishment of Chin rule in 317, a call was made for contributions to a new imperial library. One of those who responded to this call, Mei Tse 梅賾 (*fl.* 317–322), presented a text entitled the *K'ung An-kuo Shang shu* 孔安國尙書. Apparently this text was readily accepted as orthodox, and remained current thereafter, eventually being taken as the basis for the *Shang shu cheng i* 尙書正義, definitively published in 653 under the nominal editorship of K'ung Ying-ta 孔穎達 (574–648). The *Shang shu cheng i*, in turn, served as the basis for the 'K'ai-ch'eng Stone Classics' (*K'ai ch'eng shih ching* 開成石經), engraved by imperial decree in 837. This third engraving has not suffered the fate of the two preceding projects and for over a millennium has provided an unvarying text for the *Shang shu*.

4.   Critical recensions

Since the 'K'ai-ch'eng Stone Classics' text of the *Shang shu* has remained available as an unvarying source for all subsequent editions of the work, and since no complete text prior to the *Shang shu cheng i*, on which it was based, is extant, in some ways the need for a systematic critical recension of the *Shang shu* is less pronounced than for most texts. In other ways, however, the need has been very great indeed; a great number of Ch'ing dynasty scholars did much to fill this need, reconstructing in large measure the Han dynasty text of the *Shang shu*. Mention of just the more important of their works would have to include the following:

(a) Chiang Sheng 江聲 (1721–1799), *Shang shu chi chu yin shu* 尙書集注 音書
(b) Wang Ming-sheng 王鳴聲 (1722–1798), *Shang shu hou an* 尙書後案
(c) Tuan Yü-ts'ai 段玉裁 (1735–1815), *Ku wen Shang shu chuan i* 古文尙 書撰異
(d) Sun Hsing-yen 孫星衍 (1753–1818), *Shang shu chin ku wen chu shu* 尙 書今古文注疏

and especially:

(e) Ch'en Ch'iao-ts'ung 陳喬樅 (1809–1869), *Chin wen Shang shu i shuo k'ao* 今文尙書遺說考

Important though these efforts to reconstruct the Han dynasty text of the *Shang shu* have been, they appear as but a post-script to the most important issue regarding the recension of that text; i.e., the debate over the authenticity of the 16 (17 including the 'T'ai shih' chapter) 'Old Text' documents that appear only in the text Mei Tse produced in the early fourth century. The first scholar to recognize problems with these 'Old Text' chapters was Wu Yü 吳棫 (d. 1155). In a work entitled *Shu pi chuan* 書裨傳, he noted that whereas the 28 chapters that had originally been transmitted by Fu Sheng were difficult to read, the 17 chapters exclusive to the 'Old Text' tradition were quite easy to read. Although this text is no longer extant, Wu's views reached a wide audience through their acceptance by his younger contemporary Chu Hsi 朱熹 (1130–1200). In addition to agreeing that the 'Old Text' chapters were forged, Chu went further to cite text-historical reasons suggesting that both the purported K'ung An-kuo 'Preface' and 'Commentary' were also written not during the Han but during the Chin dynasty.

The great renown of Chu Hsi won a certain amount of recognition for this position during the following Yüan and Ming dynasties, as seen in Wu Ch'eng's 吳澄 (1247–1331) *Shang shu tsuan yen* 尙書纂言 and the *Shang shu p'u* 尙書譜 and *Shang shu k'ao i* 尙書考異 of Mei Chuo 梅鷟 (*fl.* 1513). But it was in the early stages of the Ch'ing dynasty that the 'Old Text' chapters were definitively shown to be forgeries. The most

influential work in this regard was the *Ku wen Shang shu shu cheng* 古文
尚書疏證 of Yen Jo-chü 閻若璩 (1636–1704). In this work Yen cited 128
specific instances demonstrating the spurious nature of the texts presented by Mei Tse. For instance, in the 'K'ung Commentary' the place
name 'Chin-ch'eng' 金城 is mentioned, but this city was not established
until the reign of Chao ti 昭帝 of Han (r. 87–74 B.C.), after the time when
K'ung An-kuo is reported to have died. Shortly after Yen's work was
published (posthumously, in 1745), Hui Tung 惠棟 (1697–1758) published a still more detailed study, the *Ku wen Shang shu k'ao* 古文尚書考,
following which it has been rare indeed for any serious scholar to
consider the 'Old Text' writings as authentic.

No consensus has yet been reached regarding the identity of the person who was responsible for this forgery. Many scholars (e.g., Mei Chuo
and Wang Ming-sheng) initially suspected Huang-fu Mi 皇甫謐 (215–
282), or Wang Su 王肅 (195–256), first accused by Ting Yen 丁晏 (1794–
1875) in his *Shang shu yü lun* 尚書餘論, but these figures have since
been shown never to have used these documents. More recently, Ch'en
Meng-chia 陳夢家 (1911–1966) argued that another K'ung An-kuo (d.
408) who lived during the Eastern Chin could have been the perpetra-
tor, but he subsequently rejected this suggestion in a posthumously
published article included in the second edition of his *Shang shu t'ung
lun* 尚書通論. Perhaps the most likely culprit remains Mei Tse himself, a
suggestion made already by Yen Jo-chü and Hui Tung.

5.   Commentaries and studies

As one might expect for a classic such as the *Shang shu*, numerous important commentaries have been produced during a period of over two
millennia. The first commentary likely to be encountered is that attributed to K'ung An-kuo and included in all 'orthodox' editions of the
Shang shu. As suggested already, this commentary was almost certainly
spuriously written in the fourth century A.D. and is of little scholarly
value. On the other hand, a sort of commentary entitled *Shang shu ta
chuan* 尚書大傳, attributed to the other figure central to the transmission of the *Shang shu*, Fu Sheng, is a text of considerable historical
importance in its own right.

Although the *Shang shu ta chuan* may have been written by his students rather than by Fu Sheng himself, it was certainly produced during
the second century B.C.; it is quoted in the *Ch'un ch'iu fan lu* and was
apparently consulted by Ssu-ma Ch'ien. *Han shu* 30, p. 1705 includes an
entry entitled 'chuan' in 41 *p'ien*, which is presumably to be identified

with this work. A century later, Cheng Hsüan wrote a commentary to this work itself, expanding the number of *p'ien* to 83. The *Shang shu ta chuan* continued to be listed in the bibliographic monographs of the *Sui shu* and two T'ang histories, but by the Sung dynasty it had apparently already been lost. In the case of this work too a great debt is owed to scholars of the Ch'ing dynasty who culled quotations from various early works to produce the recension that is now available. The best text is certainly the *Shang shu ta chuan chi chiao* 尙書大傳輯校 of Ch'en Shou-ch'i 陳壽祺 (1771–1834), which in turn was based on the work of Lu Wen-ch'ao 盧文弨 (1717–96) and other earlier scholars. The text is included in the *Huang Ch'ing ching chieh hsü pien* 皇清經解續編 (ch. 354–356) and also in the *Ssu pu ts'ung k'an*. Although in the fragmentary state in which it now exists the *Shang shu ta chuan* cannot be considered as a systematic commentary to the text of the *Shang shu*, it is still very important for the general background information it gives for individual chapters.

Other Han dynasty commentaries that have been reconstituted on the basis of quotations in early texts were written in the early second century A.D. by Ma Jung 馬融 (79–166) and his still more illustrious student Cheng Hsüan. In addition to the intrinsic interest of any work by these two great scholars, their commentaries on the *Shang shu* are particularly interesting for their synthesis of both 'New Text' and 'Old Text' traditions of interpretation. In addition, as noted above, Cheng Hsüan's *Shang shu chu* is also important as the only work to quote the 16 extra chapters of the authentic K'ung An-kuo text.

Other commentaries of this period and slightly later are extensively quoted in the *Shang shu cheng i*, nominally edited by K'ung Ying-ta but actually written by Wang Te-shao 王德韶 and Li Tzu-yun 李子雲 (both *fl.* 653). After this monumental 'orthodox' work of the early T'ang period, the next influential commentary was not to appear for more than 500 years when Ts'ai Chen 蔡沈 (1167–1230), a disciple of Chu Hsi, produced a work generally referred to simply as the *Ts'ai chuan* 蔡傳. The work is important for making explicit Chu Hsi's suspicions of the authenticity of the 'Old Text' chapters. As discussed above, studies of the *Shang shu*'s authenticity came to fruition during the Ch'ing dynasty. So too it was at that time that the best commentaries were produced. Four items are generally considered to stand out among a great number of works that exemplify the best exegetical scholarship; i.e.: Chiang Sheng, *Shang shu chi chu yin shu*, Wang Ming-sheng, *Shang shu hou an*, Sun Hsing-yen, *Shang shu chin ku wen chu shu* (which have been mentioned above with regard to their contributions to the critical recension of the text); P'i Hsi-jui 皮錫瑞 (1850–1908) *Chin wen Shang shu k'ao cheng* 今文尚書考證, which is especially important for the historical perspective it brings to the 'New Text' 'Old Text' controversy.

Since the definitive demonstration of the spurious nature of the 'Old Text' chapters during the Ch'ing dynasty, and with the increasing corpus of early epigraphic materials in the form of oracle-bone and bronze inscriptions, the focus of most recent *Shang shu* scholarship has been to determine the date and authenticity of the various 'New Text' chapters. A work that pioneered the historical and linguistic comparison of the *Shang shu* to oracle-bone and bronze inscriptions was the *Shang shu hsin cheng* 尚書新證 of Yü Hsing-wu 于省吾 (1897–1984). Two other scholars renowned primarily for their palaeographic research subsequently produced works that are now probably the most authoritative studies of all aspects of the *Shang shu*: Ch'en Meng-chia's *Shang shu t'ung lun* 尚書通論 (originally published in Shanghai: Shang wu, 1956; re-issued with important appendices Peking: Chung hua, 1985), and the *Shang shu shih i* 尚書釋義 and *Shang shu chin ku chin i* 尚書今詁今譯 of Ch'ü Wan-li 屈萬里 (1907–79). Finally, mention must be made of an incomplete study by Ku Chieh-kang 顧頡剛 (1893–1980), at least two chapters of which have now been published separately:

> '*Shang shu* "Ta kao" chin i (chai yao)' 尚書大誥今譯(摘要), *LSYC* 1962.4:26–51.

and

> '*Shang shu* "Hsi po k'an li" chiao shih i lun' 尚書西伯戡黎校釋譯論, *Chung kuo li shih wen hsien yen chiu chi k'an* 中國歷史文獻研究集刊 I (1980), 46–59.

Ku is also important for having edited a concordance to the *Shang shu* (see under (8) below). His major disciple Liu Ch'i-yü 劉起釪 has recently published an exhaustive history of scholarship on the *Shang shu*: *Shang shu hsüeh shih* 尚書學史 (Peking: Chung hua, 1989). For a recent study of the 'Hung fan', see Michael Nylan, *The Shifting Center: The Original "Great Plan" and Later Readings*; Institut Monumenta Serica, Sankt Augustin; Nettal: Steyler Verlag, 1992.

6. Translations

The *Shang shu* was first translated into a Western language by Father Antoine Gaubil, under the title *Shu ching* (Paris: 1770), and by Walter Henry Medhurst, as *Shu ching, Ancient China; the Shoo King, or the Histori-*

cal Classic; being the most ancient authentic record of the annals of the Chinese Empire, illustrated by later commentators: (Shanghai: 1846). The most commonly used translations are those of James Legge (1815–1897) and Bernhard Karlgren (1889–1978), the latter of which is supplemented by 'Glosses' published separately.

(a) Legge, *The Chinese Classics*, Vol. III, Parts I and II; *Sacred Books of the East*, Vol. III.
(b) Karlgren, Bernhard, 'The Book of Documents'; *BMFEA* 22 (1950), 1–81; re-issued as a separate volume under the same title Göteborg: Elanders, 1950.
(c) Karlgren, Bernhard, 'Glosses on the Book of Documents I', *BMFEA* 20 (1948), 39–315.
(d) Karlgren, Bernhard, 'Glosses on the Book of Documents, II', *BMFEA* 21 (1949), 63–206; re-issued as a single volume: *Glosses on the Book of Documents* (Göteborg: Elanders, 1970).

Legge's translation is a credible representation of the 'orthodox' interpretation of the complete text, inclusive of both 'New Text' and 'Old Text' chapters. Legge provides both a lengthy introduction and copious notes in which he demonstrates considerable awareness of the exegetical controversies surrounding the text. Although he is almost certainly mistaken in regarding the 'Old Text' chapters as authentic, the translation is generally reliable. Karlgren, on the other hand, has translated only the 28 chapters attributed to Fu Sheng. The translation is generally considered to represent more accurately the archaic language of these chapters and his 'Glosses' conveniently assemble and evaluate the best of the Ch'ing dynasty commentaries.

7. Japanese editions

A. *Kambun taikei*; no. 12, 1911, edited by Hattori Unokichi and Hoshino Tsune.
B. *Kanseki kokujikai zensho*; no. 6, 1910, edited by Ōta Kinjō.
D. *Kokuyaku kambun taisei*; no. 2, 1922, edited by Hattori Unokichi and Yamaguchi Satsujō.
E. *Kambun sōsho*; 1927, edited by Hayashi Taisuke.
F. *Keisho taikō*; nos. 4, 5, 1938–39.
H. *Shinshaku kambun taikei*; nos. 25, 26, 1983, 1985; no. 25 edited by Katō Jōken; no. 26 edited by Onozawa Seiichi.
K. *Chūgoku koten bungaku taikei*; no. 1, 1972, edited by Akatsuka Kiyoshi.
L. *Chūgoku koten shinsho*; 1974, edited by Nomura Shigeo.

Katō Jōken, *Shin kobun Shōsho shūshaku* 眞古文尙書集釋 (Tokyo: Meiji shoin, 1964) treats the 28 'New Text' chapters only.

8. Indexes

(a) *Shang shu t'ung chien* 尙書通檢, ed. Ku Chieh-kang; Peking: Harvard-Yenching Institute, 1936; re-issued Peking: Shu mu wen hsien ch'u pan she, 1982.

(b) *A Concordance to the Shang shu* 尙書逐字索引, ed. D.C. Lau and Chen Fong Ching; *ICS* series, Hong Kong: Commercial Press, forthcoming 1994.

(c) *A Concordance to the Shang shu da zhuan* 尙書大傳逐字索引, ed. D.C. Lau and Chen Fong Ching; *ICS* series, Hong Kong: Commercial Press, forthcoming 1994.

— Edward L. Shaughnessy

Shen chien 申鑒

1. Content

The received text of the *Shen chien* probably includes no more than parts, or even fragments, of the original work. We now possess a miscellany of long treatises, short essays, dialogues and short notes, bearing on moral, political, ritual, educational, financial and military matters, with some measure of historical, literary and religious criticism. The somewhat confused, inconsistent and ill-ordered way in which the book discusses philosophical questions and alludes to historical facts reflects the bewilderment of an author who was writing during the confused conditions of China in the period from 196–220.

2. Authorship

According to *Hou Han shu* 62, pp. 2049 and 2058f., Hsün Yüeh 荀悅 (148–209), style Chung Yü 仲豫, was a descendant in the twelfth generation of Hsün Ch'ing 荀卿 (*c.* 335–*c.* 238 B.C.); for this reason Hsün Yüeh himself and at times his work the *Shen chien* were sometimes termed the *Hsiao Hsün tzu* 小荀子. Hsün Yüeh's uncle, Hsün Shuang 爽 (128–90) was a scholar of classical learning, who was appointed to be *Ssu k'ung* 司空 (Minister of Works) in 189. During the *tang ku* 黨錮 persecutions (166–84), Hsün Shuang had lived in hiding; Hsün Yüeh had also lived in seclusion, being little known to his contemporaries, except for his cousin Hsün Yü 荀彧 (163–212) who held him in high esteem. When Hsün Yü became principal adviser to Ts'ao Ts'ao 曹操 (155–220) and acting head of the secretariat (*Shang shu ling* 尚書令), Hsün Yüeh was appointed to office, finally becoming Palace Attendant (*shih chung* 侍中). Together with Hsün Yü and the prominent scholar K'ung Jung 孔融 (153–208) he gave lectures and conducted discussions inside the palace. At that time the court was under the control of Ts'ao Ts'ao, and Hsien ti 獻帝 was powerless. Finding that his principles were not acceptable, Hsün Yüeh wrote the *Shen chien*, or 'Extended reflections', in five *p'ien*, 'presenting comprehenssive and penetrating discourses on the basic principles of government'. The work was valued by the emperor, who ordered Hsün Yüeh to write an abbreviated version of Pan Ku's 班固

(32–92) *Han shu;* the results of that order are discussed under the entry for *Han chi.*

3.　Date of composition and traditional assessments

The *Hou Han shu,* which does not specify when the *Shen chien* and the *Han chi* were compiled, may give the erroneous impression that Hsün Yüeh had completed the *Shen chien* before embarking on the *Han chi.* According to the preface of the *Han chi,* Hsün Yüeh was ordered to compile that work in 198, and he completed it in 200. According to the *Hou Han chi* 後漢記 of Yüan Hung 袁宏 (328–376; see *SPTK* ed. 29.14b), Hsün Yüeh completed the *Shen chien* and submitted it to the emperor in 205. For detailed studies of Hsün Yüeh and his works, see Chi-yun Chen, *Hsün Yüeh (A.D. 148–209): the life and reflections of an early medieval Confucian* (Cambridge: Cambridge University Press, 1975); and Ch'i-yün Ch'en, *Hsün Yüeh and the mind of late Han China; a translation of the Shenchien with introduction and annotations* (Princeton: Princeton University Press, 1980).

From the third to the eighth century, Hsün Yüeh and his works were highly praised, but from the eleventh century his reputation became somewhat eclipsed. Huang Chen 黃震 (1213–80) considered the *Shen chien* to be 'wordy, inconsequential, inconsistent and of a humiliatingly weak style'; and he questioned whether the text was the genuine work of Hsün Yüeh (see *Tz'u hsi Huang shih jih ch'ao fen lei* 慈溪黃氏日抄分類 57.6b–7a). In his preface (dated 1519) to the annotated edition of the *Shen chien* by Huang Hsing-tseng 黃省曾 (1490–1540), Wang Ao 王鏊 (1450–1524) cautioned the editor against further involvement with the work. Yang Ch'i-kuang 楊琪光 (Ch'ing period) criticized Hsün Yüeh as being disloyal to the Han dynasty (see *Pai tzu pien cheng* 百子辨正 1.23). While the bias of Sung opinion against Hsün Yüeh is obvious enough, the content of the received text of the *Shen chien* does not seem to warrant the excessive praise that it had received previously. This consideration raises the serious question of whether the received text is authentic or how far it varies from a version that had been available earlier.

Several passages of the *Shen chien* and the *Han chi* are included in the *Hou Han shu* which states (62, p. 2063) that Hsün Yüeh had also written a number of other works; these are now not traced.

4.　Textual history

Beginning with the *Sui shu* (34, p. 998, under *ju chia* 儒家), most bibliographical lists include entries for the *Shen chien,* but these do not appear

in the *Ch'ung wen ts'ung mu* 崇文總目, the *Chün chai tu shu chih* 郡齋讀
書志 or the bibliographical treatise of the *Sung shih* 宋史; nor is there an
entry in Fujiwara Sukeyo's catalogue. Despite Huang Chen's doubts, it
is nonetheless clear that the received text cannot be a forgery of the
Sung period or later and it is unlikely that it had been forged before
then.

There is evidence to show that all of Hsün Yüeh's works were subject
to tampering during the process of re-compiling or re-editing. Some
parts of the *Shen chien* may have become mixed with Hsün Yüeh's
essays in the *Han chi*; some of his other essays may have been included
in the *Shen chien*. In his supplement to the *Chün chai tu shu chih* (preface
dated 1250), Chao Hsi-pien 趙希弁 listed the work as a 'miscellany by
individual authors'; Yu Mao 尤袤 (1127–1193), in the earliest extant
postscript to the *Shen chien*, of 1182 (retained in the *Tzu hui* edition),
simply mentions the text as one of Hsün Yüeh's writings. These
remarks, together with the designation of the work as *Hsiao Hsün tzu*,
suggest that the work derived from Hsün Yüeh's hand; but it remains
uncertain how far the received text embodies the original book.

5. Editions

(a) A Sung edition, probably to be identified as including Yu Mao's
    postscript and as being essentially identical with the text that was
    criticized by Huang Chen, is reproduced in the *Tzu hui* (1576–77)
    under the title *Hsiao Hsün tzu*; it is reprinted in the recent *Han fen lou*
    涵芬樓 edition.
(b) Huang Hsing-tseng's annotated edition (preface 1519), allegedly
    made by collation of a text with an edition of an earlier date than (a),
    has been reproduced in the *Liang ching i pien*, the *Ssu pu ts'ung k'an*
    and various editions of the *Han Wei ts'ung shu*. Of these last, Wang
    Mo's 王謨 (*cs* 1778) print (1791) was used as the basis for the *Ssu pu
    pei yao* series. Prefaces by Wang Ao (1519) and Ho Yüan-fu 何元父,
    and a postface by Ch'iao Yü 喬宇 are also included. Huang Hsing-
    tseng's edition was used as the basis for the text in the *Lung hsi ching
    she ts'ung shu*, which appends Lu Wen-ch'ao's 盧文弨 (1717–1796)
    notes and citations from the *Shen chien* that appear in the *Ch'ün shu
    chih yao* 群書治要.
(c) The best of the collated editions is that of Ch'ien P'ei-ming 錢培名
    in the *Hsiao wan chüan lou ts'ung shu* (postface dated 1852); special
    attention is paid in the collation notes to the quotations in the *Ch'ün
    shu chih yao*.

6. Research aids and secondary studies.

Heinrich Busch, 'Hsün Yüeh, ein Denker am Hofe des letzen Han-Kaisers' (*Monumenta Serica* 10 (1945), 58–90) presents a comprehensive survey of Hsün Yüeh's life and thought. Other studies include Yoshinami Takashi 好並隆司, 'Jun Etsu no shakai haikei to sono seisaku ni tsuite' 荀悦の社會背景とその政策について (*Okayama shigaku* 岡山史學 2 (1956), 68–86); Hihara Toshikuni 日原利國, 'Jun Etsu no kihan ishiki ni tsuite' 荀悦の規範意識について (*Tōhōgaku* 東方學 18 (1959), 9–20); and Chang Mei-yü 張美煜, *Hsün Yüeh Shen chien ssu hsiang yen chiu* 荀悦申鑒思想研究 (Taiwan: Taiwan Normal University, 1962). Ch'en Ch'i-yün's two books, which include an English translation, are the most detailed studies that are available.

7. Indexes

(a) *Shen chien t'ung chien* 申鑒通檢 (*Index du Chen Kien*), Centre franco-chinois d'études sinologiques no. 8 (Peking: 1947), is based on the *Ssu pu pei yao* edition, and includes a summary of the contents of the work.

(b) *A Concordance to the Shen jian, Zhong lun and Xin yu* 申鑑, 中論, 新語 逐字索引, ed. D.C. Lau and Chen Fong Ching; *ICS* series, Hong Kong: Commercial Press, forthcoming 1995.

— Ch'i-yün Ch'en

Shen tzu 申子 (Shen Pu-hai 申不害)

1. Nature of the text

Since 1616 no complete copy of this work is known to have existed. All that we possess are fragments, that are quoted in various works and alleged to have once formed part of a text of this name. We do not know the order in which these fragments occurred in the text, if indeed they did so, nor the length or the number of the chapters of an original work. It is generally believed that it had consisted of six *p'ien*, of which three were named *Chün ch'en* 君臣, *Ta t'i* 大體 and *San fu* 三符 respectively.

If one may judge from the fragments, the *Shen tzu* probably did not consist of long essays, but was made up chiefly of relatively brief, and frequently cryptic, aphorisms.

2. Content

The book was supposedly a record of the sayings of Shen Pu-hai 申不害, who was born in Cheng 鄭 around 400 B.C. In 375 B.C. that state was conquered and annexed by Han 韓, where Shen was appointed chancellor, probably in 354. Shen re-organized the somewhat disordered government of Han so that it functioned well, and managed by skilful diplomacy to neutralize the powerful military threats from other states. He continued as chancellor for at least some fifteen years, until his death; this is usually dated in 337, but it may possibly have occurred as early as 340. Shen left Han in a strong state and it was able to survive until 230 B.C. when it was conquered by Ch'in.

Shen's success focussed attention on his ideas, especially those concerning administration, and we find clear evidence of their influence in various works of the Warring States Period. Even Hsün Ch'ing 荀卿 (*c.* 335–*c.* 238 B.C.) shows such influence, although he overtly denounced Shen and rejected some of his principles. Hsün Ch'ing must have resented the fact that his two most famous pupils, Han Fei 韓非 (280–*c.* 233 B.C.) and Li Ssu 李斯 (?280–208 B.C.), were not known as followers of Confucius but as advocates of the ideas of Shen Pu-hai and Shang Yang 商鞅 (*c.* 385–338 B.C.).

Although Han Fei spoke of a 'school' of Shen Pu-hai, there is little other evidence that such a school existed in the Warring States period. Li Ssu appears to have played the principal role in devising the governmental machinery of the Ch'in dynasty, which became the foundation for the imperial system; and he said that he had drawn upon two principal sources, Shang Yang for law and Shen Pu-hai for administrative technique. Although these two had been clearly distinguished in the early days, once they had been classified as *fa chia* the differences between their ideas became obscured. Han Fei explicitly criticized Shen Pu-hai for giving exclusive attention to administrative technique, and neglecting law. In the early years of Former Han, there was great concern with the machinery of government and much interest was shown in the philosophy of Shen Pu-hai. In 141 B.C. when adherents of certain philosophies were excluded from service in government, students of 'the words of Shen Pu-hai' were named first on the list. Thereafter, while Shen's doctrines continued to be studied by some scholars, high officials and even, occasionally, by an emperor, they seem never again to have received widespread attention.

Presumably the *Shen tzu* embodied the 'words of Shen Pu-hai'. We can deduce the general outline of his philosophy of administration from remarks that were made about it in various early works. Essentially, he believed that the ruler should delegate all conduct of government to officials chosen for their ability. While not himself engaging in any of the routine business of administration, he must maintain the most vigilant supervision over his subordinates, and be prepared to intervene decisively when necessary. Shen also devoted considerable attention to practical psychology. The biography and philosophy of Shen Pu-hai are discussed in Herrlee G. Creel, *Shen Pu-hai, A Chinese Political Philosopher of the Fourth Century B.C.* (Chicago and London: Chicago University Press, 1974).

3.   Date of composition, and authenticity

It is impossible to say when, or by whom, the *Shen tzu* was written. Although there was much talk of Shen's doctrines, there seems to be no mention of writings in connection with him until the *Huai nan tzu* (completed 139 B.C.). That work suggests, though it does not say clearly, that when he became chancellor Shen solved the administrative problems facing the state of Han by producing certain writings (*Huai nan tzu* 21.9b, Liu Wen-tien ed.). Elsewhere, when the same book (20.23a) speaks of the '*San fu* 三 符 of Shen tzu', this is thought to refer to one of the chapters of the *Shen tzu*. The book is not known by name until the *Shih chi*, which writes (63. p. 2146) 'Shen Pu-hai . . . wrote a book in two *p'ien* called *Shen tzu*'.

In 1951 Gustav Haloun briefly discussed the *Shen tzu* and announced his intention of publishing an edition of the fragments quoted by various works in a later article (see G. Haloun, 'Legalist Fragments, Part I: Kuan-tsï 55 and related texts'; *Asia Major*, New Series, II, 1951, 85–120), but unfortunately he did not live to do so. He had stated that the *Shen tzu* dated from '300 B.C. or after'; in his discussion of the origin of the text he leaves in doubt his opinion of the extent to which the *Shen tzu* actually derived from or was connected with Shen Pu-hai.

Since it appears that the *Shen tzu* was a short book, it is not impossible that even a busy administrator like Shen Pu-hai could have found time to write it. Alternatively, it may have consisted, like the Confucian *Analects*, of a collection of sayings made by or attributed to Shen that was compiled at some time after his death. Since Shen's philosophy appears to have differed sharply from that of his contemporaries, and most of the alleged quotations from the *Shen tzu* are in general agreement with descriptions of his philosophy in early works, it appears that the *Shen tzu* was at least based, in large part, on the ideas of Shen Pu-hai. It is normal for such works to come to incorporate some extraneous materials, and there is reason to believe that that may have occurred in the case in question.

4. Textual history

In a citation from the *Pieh lu* 別錄 that is given in the *Chi chieh* 集解 note to *Shih chi* 63, p. 2146, Liu Hsiang 劉向 (79–8 B.C.) observed 'the extant 2 *p'ien*, i.e. *shang* 上 and *hsia* 下, that are at present in general circulation and the 6 *p'ien* of the imperial library in each case fit in entirety [*ho* 合] to 2 *p'ien*'. *HS* 30, p. 1735, lists the *Shen tzu* with 6 *p'ien* under *fa chia*; and in the *Ch'i lu*, Juan Hsiao-hsü 阮孝緒 (479–536) lists it with 3 *chüan*. Thereafter it is regularly entered with 3 *chüan*.

The book does not appear in Fujiwara Sukeyo's catalogue. The note to the entry for the *Shang chün shu* in *Sui shu* 34, p. 1003 writes 'During the Liang dynasty [502–56] there existed the *Shen tzu* in three *chüan*, compiled by Shen Pu-hai, chancellor of Han, now lost'. Since there are many references to, and quotations from, the *Shen tzu* after that time, this entry raises the question of whether a forged *Shen tzu* had been substituted for a work that was actually lost.

There is another explanation. The bibliographical list of the *Sui shu* was compiled separately, and presented to the emperor 13 years after the death of Wei Cheng 魏徵 (d. 643), editor of that history. The compilers of the bibliographical list had apparently overlooked the fact that Wei Cheng himself, in compiling his *Ch'ün shu chih yao*, had quoted extensively from the *Shen tzu*. There is abundant evidence that the *Shen tzu* existed long after this pronouncement that it was lost; for details, see Creel, *op. cit.*, pp. 302–05.

Chiu T'ang shu 47, p. 2031 and *Hsin T'ang shu* 59, p. 1531 include the identical entry for '*Shen tzu*, 3 *chüan'*; thereafter the work is not listed in the official bibliographies, but it is still mentioned and quoted. The latest evidence that a copy still existed is probably the entry in Ch'en Ti's 陳第 (1541–1617) *Shih shan t'ang ts'ang shu mu lu*, of 1616.

5. Quotations from the *Shen tzu*

A number of works, beginning as early as the *Han fei tzu*, quote, or claim to quote, Shen Pu-hai and the *Shen tzu*, but it is sometimes impossible to distinguish quotations of the man from those of the book. These quotations are drawn chiefly from writings which take their place in books compiled at dates ranging from around 600 to 1400, and together they form a considerable body of material. If genuine, they would give us a substantial portion of the *Shen tzu*.

These quotations are not always in agreement, as the same passage occurs in two or sometimes three variant forms. Usually these differences are slight, but sometimes they alter the meaning significantly. Of greater importance, some of these quotations seem to have nothing to do with Shen Pu-hai or his philosophy, and the validity of the works in which they sometimes occur is variable.

For the most part, modern scholars have paid little attention to Shen Pu-hai, and the prevalent opinion seems to be that his *Shen tzu* is irretrievably lost. Definite reasons for rejecting the alleged quotations have been raised by Hu Shih 胡適 (1891–1962), in *Chung kuo che hsüeh shih ta kang* 中國哲學史大綱, vol. I (15th ed., Shanghai: Shang wu 1930), pp. 361–62, and Ch'en Ch'i-t'ien 陳啓天, in *Chung kuo fa chia kai lun* 中國法家概論 (Shanghai: Chung hua, 1936) pp. 237–38. These objections have been refuted in Creel, *Shen Pu-hai*, pp. 317–20, 356–57.

Several scholars have published compilations of alleged quotations from the *Shen tzu*. The first was by Yen K'o-chün 嚴可均 (1762–1843), in *Ch'üan shang ku san tai Ch'in Han san kuo liu ch'ao wen*. For a pioneering attempt this was a considerable achievement, although the work includes some errors and some liberties are taken with the text. The next attempt was made by Ma Kuo-han 馬國翰 (1794–1857), in *Yü han shan fang chi i shu*. This compilation omits some of the material included in Yen's corpus, which was indeed not published until after Ma's death; but it includes some additional passages. Ma's work improved on that of Yen in citing sources and in noting variant readings, but it also includes some errors. Huang I-chou 黃以周 (1828–99) made a compilation of alleged quotations of the *Shen tzu*, but it was apparently never published. We have no more than the preface (Huang I-chou, *Ching chi tsa chu* 儆季雜箸, 1873, *Tzu hsü* 子敘) in which he states that the compilation of Yen K'o-chün 'omitted a great deal', and that that of Ma Kuo-han fell short of complete excellence.

In Appendix C to his work, entitled 'The Shen Pu-hai fragments' (pp. 343–413), Creel attempted to include both every alleged direct quotation of Shen Pu-hai and every alleged quotation of the *Shen tzu*. Two or more forms of the same passage are collated so as to arrive at what the author believed, most probably, to have been the original passage. This material extends to 1346 characters, of which by far the greater part consists of alleged quotations from the *Shen tzu*. After subjecting all of this material to various tests, Creel expressed the opinion that 79 percent 'probably represents sayings of Shen Pu-hai in something close to the original form'. These fragments were published together with annotation and translation into English, with a concordance prepared by June Work.

6. Index

A Concordance to the Shenzi, Shenzi and Shizi 慎子, 申子, 尸子逐字索引, ed. D.C. Lau and Chen Fong Ching; *ICS* series, Hong Kong: Commercial Press, forthcoming 1996.

— Herrlee G. Creel

Shen tzu 慎子 (Shen Tao 慎到)

The *Shen tzu*, of which no more than fragments survive, is attributed to Shen Tao 慎到, one of the philosophers of the Chi hsia 稷下 group at the turn of the fourth and third centuries B.C. (?350–?275 B.C.). A reconstruction of the history of this work up to the time of its loss, the identification of fragments adequately attested in the indirect tradition, a critical presentation of the text of those fragments and a concordance of the edited text can be found in P.M. Thompson, *The Shen Tzu Fragments* (Oxford: Oxford University Press, 1979), to which readers are referred for fuller documentation of the account which follows.

1. Authenticity

Although there seem to be no reasons, bibliographical or textual, for doubting the authenticity of the *Shen tzu* from which the present fragments derive, there is serious cause for doubt concerning the claims of some of the alleged fragments. This has led historians of philosophy either to reject the modern collections of fragments out of hand (e.g., Henri Maspero, *China in Antiquity*, translated by Frank A. Kierman Jr; Folkestone: Wm Dawson and son, Ltd., 1978, p. 464, n. 19; see also Thompson, *op. cit.*, p. 7, n. 16) or to adopt an extremely cautious view (e.g., Hsiao Kung-chuan, *A History of Chinese Political Thought*; Princeton: Princeton University Press, 1979, p. 370).

The only alternative for most writers has been to rely exclusively on ancient testimony, which consists of (a) a small number of citations (in the *Lü shih ch'un ch'iu*, the *Han fei tzu*, the *Huai nan tzu* and the 'T'ien hsia' 天下 *p'ien* of the *Chuang tzu*) and (b) a few critical comments (in the *Hsün tzu*, the *Shih chi* and the 'T'ien hsia' *p'ien*).

Unfortunately, for many writers of whom Fung Yu-lan 馮友蘭 (1895–1990) is perhaps representative, this testimony appeared to be contradictory. The *Hsün tzu* and the *Han fei tzu* are concerned respectively with Shen Tao's concepts of *fa* 法 and *shih* 勢 and were felt to represent him as a 'Legalist', whereas the *Shih chi* (74, p. 2347) says that he studied the 'arts of Huang [ti] and Lao [tzu] and of the *tao* and the *te*'; and the 'T'ien hsia' *p'ien* describes him as one who rejects knowledge as being incompatible with the unity of the *tao*. Fung goes so far as to divide the already minimal early testimony into two parts and to treat Shen Tao as if he were entirely two different philosophers; see *A History of Chinese Philosophy* (London: George Allen and Unwin Ltd., 1952), vol. I, pp. 153–59, 318–19.

The identification of the genuine fragments of the *Shen tzu* makes it possible to reconcile this apparent contradiction and throws light on what was meant in the second century B.C. by 'Huang-Lao'.

2.　Transmission of the text

The Direct Tradition

Hsün Tzu's use of the expression Shen Mo 慎墨 (Shen Tzu and Mo Tzu) as a class term of opprobrium in his philosophical polemic suggests that Shen Tao's reputation was considerable in the generation after his death. That this reputation was sustained by a knowledge of his book is made likely by the early citations mentioned above, but it is not until the end of the second century B.C., in the *Shih chi*, that an explicit reference to the *Shen tzu* is to be found. In his account of the Chi hsia philosophers, Ssu-ma Ch'ien 司馬遷 (?145–?86 B.C.) says that 'Shen Tao wrote twelve discourses' (*lun* 論; *Shih chi* 74, p. 2347). Less than a hundred years later, the *Shen tzu* was amongst the books collated and re-copied by Liu Hsiang 劉向 (79–8 B.C.); the text in 42 *p'ien* is listed under *fa chia* 法家 (*Han shu* 30, p. 1735).

Possibly as early as Later Han, but certainly before the end of the fourth century, the text was supplied with a commentary by a certain T'eng Fu 滕輔. Parts of this commentary have survived in association with the fragments. Another commentary which has not survived is known to have been written in the South at the end of the fourth century by a scholar with the provocative name of Liu Huang-lao 劉黃老 (*Chin shu* 69, p. 1842). There is also testimony to the existence of the complete text of Liu Hsiang's redaction in 41 *p'ien*, probably in the form of a manuscript in the imperial library of Eastern Chin (see Hsü Kuang 徐廣 (352–425), as cited in P'ei Yin's 裴駰 note to *Shih chi* 74, p. 2347).

In the first half of the sixth century, the *Shen tzu*, accompanied by T'eng Fu's commentary, appears to have been held in the library of the Liang dynasty in the form of a manuscript on either silk or paper (see Thompson, *op. cit.*, pp. 54–5). This manuscript was in all probability the direct ancestor of the manuscripts known to have existed in the official collections of the Sui and T'ang courts (see *Sui shu* 34, p. 1003; *Chiu T'ang shu* 47, p. 2031; *Hsin T'ang shu* 59, p. 1531, where the work is listed under *fa chia*). In the case of the T'ang dynasty it is safe to assume, on general bibliographical grounds, that a number of copies were made and distributed among the various official libraries both in Ch'ang-an and Lo-yang; this guaranteed the survival of the text until at least the middle of the eighth century. When the Sung libraries were being established at the end of the tenth century no copy of the *Shen tzu* could be found.

Thompson has argued for the probability that the work was still available in public or private libraries until the fall of the T'ang dynasty, but reasoned objections to this argument have been raised by T.H. Barrett ('On the Transmission of the *Shen tzu* and of the Yang sheng Yao chi,' *Journal of the Royal Asiatic Society* 1980, 168–71). For the time being, therefore, the cautious dates that should be taken for the break in the direct tradition are 'after 755' and 'before 960'.

The Indirect Tradition

A definitive break in the direct tradition of the *Shen tzu* was obscured for some centuries by the re-appearance of a *Shen tzu* in one *chüan* in bibliographical sources from as early as the middle of the eleventh century. The history of this 'one *chüan*' *Shen tzu* is well documented and it can be identified with certainty with the *Shen tzu* in five *p'ien*, of which manuscripts and printed editions of Ming date survive. Thus, the manuscript held in the Central Library, Taipei (reproduced in Thompson, *op. cit.,* Plates VIII–XXVI) appears to be descended from a 12th or 13th century Ma sha 麻沙 print. It was however only in the early 19th century, after the recovery of Wei Cheng's 魏徵 (580–643) *Ch'ün shu chih yao* 群書治要, that it became clear that this text, in 1 *chüan*, was no more than a fragment of *chüan* 37 of the *Ch'ün shu chih yao*, in which extracts from seven *p'ien* of the *Shen tzu* had been preserved. These extracts make the *Ch'ün shu chih yao* the most important single source for the indirect tradition of the *Shen tzu*.

Fifteen further extracts from the *Shen tzu* are preserved in the *I lin* 意林 of Ma Tsung 馬總 (compiled before 787) and go back to the direct tradition probably by way of the *Tzu ch'ao* 子抄. The addition of these extracts to those of the *Ch'ün shu chih yao*, in the *Shen tzu* of one *chüan*, either in Ming times or earlier, represents the first attempt to compile a redaction of the fragments of the *Shen tzu*. This combination of fragments that derived from two sources occurs already in the manuscript that is held in Taipei (mentioned above), and in the redaction of the *Shen tzu* in the *Tzu hui* (1577), the *Nien erh tzu* (1875–77), the *Tzu shu pai chia* (1875) and the *Pai tzu ch'üan shu* (1919).

A much more ambitious collection of fragments appeared in the 16th

century, almost contemporaneously with the *Tzu hui* edition. This was
in a work entitled *Shen tzu nei wai p'ien* 慎子內外篇, which was first
published by Shen Mao-shang 慎懋賞 in 1579. The author, who
believed himself to be a descendant of Shen Tao, added to the 'five *p'ien*'
and the extracts of the *I lin* a number of genuine fragments, but in no
case did he identify his sources. With these he mixed a much greater
quantity of material that was not connected in any way with the *Shen
tzu*.

Before falling, as it almost instantly did, into the oblivion that it de-
served, this redaction supplied twenty items, including sixteen spurious
passages, to an anthology by Chiao Hung 焦竑 (1541–1620), called the
Chung yüan wen hsüan 中原文選, which does not seem to have survived.
Having acquired a temporary respectability by this transfer, these
passages were then copied, *en bloc*, in the early 17th century, into a redaction of the *Shen tzu* by a certain Fang I 方疑. This editor had drawn
on the *Tzu hui* for those parts which had derived from the *Ch'ün shu chih
yao* and the *I lin* (see the *Shih erh tzu*, as reproduced in Thompson, *op. cit.*,
Plates XLIV–LXII). In the 18th century a Ming print of this redaction of
Fang I was copied into the *Ssu k'u ch'üan shu*; in the early 19th century, it
was reprinted in the *Mo hai chin hu* of Chang Hai-p'eng 張海鵬 (1755–
1816; blocks cut in 1808).

Shortly afterwards Yen K'o-ch'ün 嚴可均 (1762–1843), who immediately grasped the significance of the complete text of the *Shen tzu*
extracts in the newly recovered *Ch'ün shu chih yao*, compiled a new
redaction consisting of the whole of the seven *p'ien* of that anthology
and forty-four passages which he had collected himself from other
sources of the indirect tradition. Blocks for an edition of this redaction
had been cut in 1815, but nothing is known of its publication and no
exemplar seems to have survived. It is almost certain, however, that Yen
K'o-chün's text was known to Ch'ien Hsi-tso 錢熙祚 (1801–1844), when
the latter was engaged on his revision of the *Mo hai chin hu*. The *Shen tzu*
in this revision (which was published in 1844 under the title *Shou shan
ko ts'ung shu*) included the additional material from the direct tradition
of the *Ch'ün shu chih yao* and the fragments newly discovered by Yen
K'o-chün. It also included the sixteen spurious passages which originated with Shen Mao-shang, and was therefore less satisfactory than
the redaction from which it had borrowed so much. Nevertheless it is
with the *Shou shan ko ts'ung shu* that the corpus of genuine fragments of
the *Shen tzu* is virtually complete.

The re-publication in this century of the long forgotten *Shen tzu nei
wai p'ien* of Shen Mao-shang raised the hopes of some that the direct

transmission of Shen Tao's work had been restored. This had been effected (i) in 1920, when the *Ssu pu ts'ung k'an* published a late 19th century manuscript; and (ii) in 1928, when Chung kuo hsüeh hui published an exemplar of the original edition. Most scholars who noticed the reappearance of this text were, however, sceptical. The issue was settled in the mid 1930s by the publication within a few months of each other of two new editions of Shen Mao-shang's *Shen tzu*. Of these, Wang Ssu-chün's 王斯睿 *Shen tzu chiao cheng* 申子校正 (Shanghai: Shang wu, 1935) ignored the superior edition of the *Chung kuo hsüeh hui* and presented the text as the authentic, directly transmitted work of Shen Tao; it attempted to account for obvious anachronisms as interpolations in the text received by Shen Mao-shang. Had Wang Ssu-chün seen the prefatory material in the original edition, which was not included in the *Ssu pu ts'ung k'an* reproduction, he would not thus have exceeded Shen Mao-shang's own claims for his book. The other edition (*Shen tzu shu cheng* 申子疏證, by Fang Kuo-yü 方國瑜; *Chin ling hsüeh pao* 金陵學報 4.2 (1934), 216–70) systematically identified the actual sources of most of the spurious material introduced by Shen Mao-shang. Fang Kuo-yü's study was conclusive; Shen Mao-shang has had no further partisans.

The only other modern edition of the *Shen tzu* fragments published in China is the *Shen tzu chi shuo* 申子集說 of Ts'ai Ju-k'un 蔡汝堃 (*Kuo hsüeh hsiao ts'ung shu*; Shanghai: Shang wu, 1940). While rejecting the *Shen tzu* of Shen Mao-shang, this edition also refuses to accept the testimony of the direct tradition of the *Ch'ün shu chih yao*; such a limitation greatly reduces its value.

3. Sources of the fragments

Thompson divides the fragments into 121 items attested in mediaeval sources and appends 5 items cited only in ancient sources. The independent mediaeval sources fall into three groups:

(a) Sources which are likely to be primary; i.e. whose relation to the direct tradition is immediate.

(b) Sources which, if not primary, are likely to be secondary; i.e. whose relation to the direct tradition is mediated by at least one other source.

(c) Sources which cannot be primary but are likely to be secondary.

The following table shows the sources in these groups and gives for each one the number of fragments for which it is the earliest complete source:

	Source	Date	Fragments
(a)	Commentary to *Lieh tzu*	late 4th century	1
	Ching tien shih wen	*c.* 625	1
	Pei t'ang shu ch'ao	early 7th century	1
	I wen lei chü	early 7th century	13
	Ch'ün shu chih yao	631	63
	Shang shu cheng i	early 7th century	2
	Commentary to *Hou Han shu*	late 7th century	1
	Commentary to *Wen hsüan*	late 7th century	10
	Ch'u hsüeh chi	726	1
(b)	*I lin*	late 8th century	10
	Commentary to *Hsün tzu*	early 9th century	4
	Pai shih liu t'ieh	early 9th century	1
(c)	*T'ai p'ing yü lan*	983	12
	Yün chi ch'i ch'ien	mid 11th century	1

By virtue of his argument (*op. cit.*) that the case for the survival of the *Shen tzu* into the ninth century is not proved, T.H. Barrett would by implication combine the latter two groups as secondary sources. In the same article he has made the useful contribution of identifying to a high degree of probability the primary source to which the *Yün chi ch'i ch'ien* 雲笈七籤 is ultimately indebted, namely the *Yang sheng yao chi* 養生要集, a 4th century work attributed to Chang Chan 張湛; this was the author of the earliest mediaeval primary source, the commentary to the *Lieh tzu*.

4. Index

A Concordance to the Shenzi, Shenzi and Shizi 慎子, 申子, 尸子逐字索引, ed: D.C. Lau and Chen Fong Ching; *ICS* series, Hong Kong: Commercial Press, forthcoming 1996.

— P.M. Thompson

Shih chi 史記

1. Contents

The *Shih chi*, known during the first centuries of its existence as *T'ai shih kung shu* 太史公書, is a history of China from the days of the mythical Yellow Emperor down to the author's own time, viz. the end of the second century B.C. It consists of 130 *chüan*. In contrast to the basically chronological arrangement of the early historical works like the *Ch'un ch'iu* and the *Chu shu chi nien*, the author of the *Shih chi* has divided his material into five groups: (a) 12 *chüan* of *pen chi* 本紀 or basic annals of the rulers of the successive dynasties; (b) 10 *piao* 表 or tables, mainly providing a chronological concordance of the rulers of the different pre-imperial states, as well as genealogies of the families that were ennobled during the first century of the Han period; (c) 8 *shu* 書, literally 'documents' but in fact treatises or historical surveys concerning subjects that were considered to be important for good government: e.g., ritual, music, the calendar and astronomy (or astrology), waterways, and agricultural economy (concentrating on taxation and coinage); (d) 30 chapters of *shih chia* 世家, hereditary families; in fact the histories of the major states of pre-Ch'in China, and the biographies of Confucius, as well as those of a few prominent figures in early Han; (e) 70 *chuan* 傳, literally 'traditions', but in fact biographies of prominent figures in all walks of life, including statesmen, military leaders, scholars and jesters. These chapters also include historical surveys of the foreign peoples with whom the Chinese had come into close contact during the early Han period; i.e., the Hsiung-nu, the peoples of the Western Regions, Korea, the South-East and the South-West. This division of historical materials has remained fundamentally normative for all succeeding dynastic histories.

2. Date of composition and authenticity

The *Shih chi* is traditionally accepted as having been initiated by the Grand Astrologer Ssu-ma T'an 司馬談 (died 110 B.C.) and continued and completed by his son and successor in office, Ssu-ma Ch'ien 司馬遷, *tzu* Tzu chang 子長 (?145–?86 B.C.). The latter is usually mentioned as the sole author. It is unknown when Ssu-ma Ch'ien completed his history, but it is known that during the century after his death (which date is likewise uncertain) several authors added to his work. Thus, passages in the present text that refer to events after c. 100 B.C. might be additions by later hands, and those that deal with the years after 90 B.C. certainly are. Only the passages added by Ch'u Shao-sun 褚少孫, who was active during the second half of the first century B.C. (?104–?30 B.C.), are clearly marked as such. Beyond this, already in the first century of our era it was noted that ten chapters were missing from the text. These gaps were filled later, see Yü Chia-hsi 余嘉錫 (1883–1955), *T'ai shih kung shu wang p'ien k'ao* 太史公書亡篇考 in *Yü Chia-hsi lun hsüeh tsa chu*, 余嘉錫 論學雜著 (Peking: Chung hua, 1963), pp. 1–108.

In modern times a further problem has arisen. This concerns the authenticity of the several dozen chapters of the *Shih chi* that deal with events and personalities of the first century of the Han dynasty, i.e. the 2nd century B.C. It has been suggested that, for unknown reasons, these chapters disappeared, to be reconstructed in the third or fourth century of our era from the related chapters in the *Han shu* with which they agree practically word for word; see Yves Hervouet, 'La valeur relative des textes du Che-ki et du Han-chou', in *Mélanges de sinologie offerts à Monsieur Paul Demiéville*, vol. 2 (Paris, 1974), pp. 55–76. So far, only a few chapters have been tested in this regard; see Hervouet, *op. cit.*; A.F.P. Hulsewé, 'The problem of the authenticity of *Shih chi* ch. 123, The Memoir on Ta Yüan', in *TP* 61 (1975), pp. 83–147; Ch'iu Ch'iung-sun 丘 瓊蓀, *Li tai yüeh chih lü chih chiao shih, ti i fen ts'e* 歷代樂志律志校釋, 第 一分冊 (Peking: Chung hua, 1964). For the contrary view see E.G. Pulleyblank, 'Chinese and Indo-Europeans', *JRAS* 1966, 9–39, and 'The Wu-sun and Sakas and the Yüeh-chih migration', *BSOAS* 33 (1979), 154–70. There are some indications that other chapters might also be suspected of being late reconstructions.

3. Sources

For the period preceding the Han, the *Shih chi* is based on works that the author considered to be of historical value, e.g. the *Shang shu*, the *Shih ching*, and, of course, the *Ch'un ch'iu*, with the *Tso (shih) chuan*, and texts resembling the present *Chan kuo ts'e*. It should be noted that this last-mentioned work was only compiled in its present form a century after the *Shih chi* had already been written. Of special importance is the use that Ssu-ma Ch'ien made of a history of the Ch'in state, now lost, and of a work, likewise lost, which described the wars out of which the Han dynasty arose, the *Ch'u Han ch'un ch'iu* 楚漢春秋.

For the Han period Ssu-ma Ch'ien was able to use official documents, because, as Grand Astrologer, he had access to the government archives. Thus he was able to draw on and even to quote imperial edicts and memorials addressed to the throne, as well as genealogies of royal and noble families and service records. He also collected local oral traditions during his extensive travels.

A survey of the works presumably consulted by Ssu-ma Ch'ien was published by Chin Te-chien in 1963 as cited under (8) c (ii) below.

4. Text history and early editions

In his extremely valuable, detailed study of the extant versions of the *Shih chi* (dated 1958), Ho Tz'u-chün 賀次君 (see (8) a (iii) below) discussed two pre-T'ang and nine T'ang manuscripts of isolated chapters, and complete editions of Sung, Yüan, Ming, and Ch'ing times, with references to modern reprints. It is to be noted that in the manuscripts and early prints the text of the *Shih chi* is accompanied either by the *chi chieh* 集解 of P'ei Yin 裴駰 (fifth century) alone, or by the *chi chieh* together with the *so yin* 索隱, by Ssu-ma Chen 司馬貞 (early eighth century). The earliest extant print to include the *cheng i* 正義 by Chang Shou-chieh 張守節 (preface dated 737) as well is that of 1196. P'ei Yin's *chi chieh* was also attached to a copy of the *Shih chi* in eighty *chüan* which is listed in Fujiwara Sukeyo's catalogue.

There do not seem to exist any clear-cut filiations that allow the division of the texts into distinct groups. The oldest nearly complete *Shih chi*, including the *chi chieh* commentary, is that of the Shao hsing period (1131–1162), which is a re-cut version of a Northern Sung edition. It was reproduced in Peking by the Wen hsüeh ku chi ch'u pan she in 1955 (see Ho Tz'u-chün, pp. 53–58, and P. van der Loon in *RBS* I (1955), p. 45, no. 73). Another, likewise incomplete, edition may be even older. It is included in the *Jen shou pen erh shih wu shih* 仁壽本二十五史 reproduced in Taipei in 1955–1956. This *Shih chi* with the *chi chieh* commentary may date essentially from the Ching yu period (1034–1038), but the printing blocks were repaired and partly replaced at the beginning of the Southern Sung (see the remarks by van der Loon in *RSB* III (1957), p. 37, no. 48). Ho Tz'u-chün mentions a Japanese *Jen shou* edition of the Twenty Five Histories, but only 41 *chüan* remain of the *Shih chi chi chieh* included there, although this is also attributed to the Ching yu period;

whereas the ancient part of the Taipei reprint consists of 115 *chüan* (see Ho Tzu-chün, 1958, pp. 29–32, and van der Loon, *op. cit.*).

The earliest edition that contains all three commentaries is that printed by Huang Shan-fu 黃善夫 (*ming* Tsung-jen, 宗仁) of Chien-an, during the Ch'ing yüan period (1195–1200), probably on the basis of a print made between 1111 and 1126, but otherwise unknown. This version is reproduced in the *Po na* edition of the Twenty Four Histories. An earlier re-edition of this version was made by Wang Yen-che 王延喆 in 1525. His text was cut anew in 1870 by the Ch'ung wen shu chü, and many mistakes in the 1525 edition were corrected (Ho Tz'u-chün, pp. 94 and 144).

In 1641 work was started on the *Shih chi* with the *chi chieh* commentary to be included in the Seventeen Histories of Mao Chin's 毛晉 (1599–1659) *Chi ku ko* 汲古閣. It was finished only in 1657. This edition is based on several Northern Sung prints (Ho, p. 191). Although not ideal, this version was one of the texts consulted by the editors of the Palace edition of 1739 (see below) and it formed the basis for the edition of the *Shih chi* and its three commentaries prepared by the Chin ling shu chü in 1870 (see below).

The *Shih chi* with its three commentaries in the so-called Palace edition, i.e. the Wu ying tien 武英殿 edition of 1739, is based on the Ming Kuo-tzu chien 國子監 edition of 1598, of Liu Ying-ch'iu 劉應秋 (*cs* 1538), a text with both mistakes and omissions (Ho, 1958, p. 173). This had been checked against three other editions: the Huang Shan-fu edition, the Wang Yen-che edition (for both see above), and the *Shih chi p'ing lin* 史記平林 by Ling Chih-lung 凌稚隆 of 1576. Ling Chih-lung had consulted Sung and Ming prints and presents a text which Ho Tz'u-chün considers to be rather good (p. 160 ff.) The editors of the Palace edition made many corrections, adding their text-critical remarks, *k'ao cheng* 考證, in an appendix to each chapter. According to Ho, the Palace edition is far better than the Ming prints, but it is still flawed (p. 207 ff.) It has been reprinted many times. During the Ch'ien lung period it was faithfully recut for the emperor's private collection, the *Ku hsiang chai ts'ung shu* 古香齋叢書.

The Palace edition was reproduced by the T'ung wen shu chü in 1884, the Wu-chou t'ung wen shu chü and the Shanghai Commercial Press. It was likewise reproduced by the T'u shu chi ch'eng shu chü in Shanghai in 1888. This is the edition used by Édouard Chavannes for his *Mémoires historiques* (see below). It was reprinted in moveable type by the Chung hua shu chü in the *Ssu pu pei yao*, and by the Kai ming shu tien in Shanghai in 1936.

In the opinion of Ho Tz'u-chün, the best of all Ming and Ch'ing editions is that of 1870, published by the Chin ling shu chü in Nanking, under the editorship of Chang Wen-hu 張文虎 (1808–1885) and T'ang Jen-shou 唐仁壽 (19th century). The basic text is a corrected Chi ku ko edition.

In 1934 Takigawa Kametarō 瀧川龜太郎 (b. 1865) published a punc-tuated edition of the *Shih chi* titled *Shiki kaichū kōshō* 史記會注考證 with his own commentary in Chinese. The text was initially based on Ling Chih-lung's *Shih chi p'ing lin* (see above), but later the Chin ling shu chü edition was adopted. Although extensive use was made of Chinese and Japanese scholarship, Ho Tz'u-chün reproaches the author for his fail-ure to consult some of the best authorities. He also notes that Takigawa's text of both the *Shih chi* and its commentaries is not free from mistakes (pp. 223 ff.)

A punctuated edition of the *Shih chi* without commentaries was pre-pared by Ku Chieh-kang 顧頡剛 (1893–1980) in collaboration with Hsü Chih-shan 徐之珊, and published as the *Shih chi, pai wen chih pu* 史記白文之部 in Peking in 1936 by the Kuo li Pei-p'ing yen chiu yüan, shih hsüeh yen chiu hui 國立北平研究院史學研究會. The text of this first edition was based on a new edition published in about 1870 by the Hu-pei shu chü of Wang Yen-che's recut print of the Huang Shan-fu ver-sion (see above). A revised version of Ku Chieh-kang's work, now based on the Chin ling shu chü edition was published in 1959 (Peking: Chung hua shu chü); further revised 1985.

5. Recent editions

The *Shih chi hsin chiao chu kao* 史記新校注稿, by Chang Sen-k'ai 張森楷 (1858–1928), reproducing the author's manuscript notes, was published in 1967 in Taipei by the Chung kuo hsüeh shu shih yen chiu hui 中國學術史研究會.

Annotations printed without the text include:

(a) Liang Yü-sheng 梁玉繩 (1745–1819), *Shih chi chih i* 史記志疑, chiefly a text-critical study, in 36 *chüan*; first published in 1787, and later re-printed in the *Kuang ya ts'ung shu*, and Peking: Chung hua, 1981 (*cf.* Ho Tz'u-chün), on the basis of the earliest, or one of the earliest editions.

(b) Mizusawa Toshitada 水澤利忠, *Shiki kaichū kōshō kōho* 史記會注考證校補, 9 vols.; (Tokyo: Shiki kaichū kōshō kōho kankō kai, 1957–1970). This work provides variant readings for the whole of the *Shih chi* and its three commentaries found in Chinese and Japanese manuscripts and printed editions.

(c) Ch'en Chih 陳直, *Shih chi hsin cheng* 史記新證, Tientsin: T'ien-chin Jen min, 1979; preface dated 1958, with a brief author's postscript of 1963.

(d) Wang Shu-min 王叔岷 (b. 1914), *Shih chi chiao cheng* 史記斠證, 10 vols. Taipei, Nankang: Academia Sinica, Institute of History and Philology; special publication no. 78, 1983. This is a text-critical study of the whole work, and recapitulates and supersedes the individual chapter studies that the author published between 1965 and 1982, mostly in the *Bulletin of the Institute of History and Philology*.

6. Translations

With few exceptions, all the chapters of the *Shih chi* have been translated. The most complete lists of such translations were published by Timoteus Pokora in *Oriens Extremus* 8 (1962), 159–73, and in volume VI of item (a) below, pp. 113–46. The following list refers only to translations that have appeared in book form.

Edition	*Chüan* nos.
(a) Chavannes, Édouard, *Les mémoires historiques de Se-ma Ts'ien*, in five volumes (Paris: Ernest Leroux, 1895–1905); an annotated translation; photographically reprinted, Paris: by Adrien Maisonneuve, 1969; with a sixth volume containing annotated translations of *Shih chi* 48–52.	1–47 48–52
(b) Watson, Burton, *Records of the Grand Historian of China* translated from the *Shih chi of Ssu-ma Ch'ien*, 2 vols. (New York and London: Columbia University Press, 1961. This is a highly readable translation with but a few explanatory notes, and no scholarly apparatus.	7–12, 16–20, 28–30, 48–59, 84, 89–104, 106–125, 127, 129.
(c) Watson, Burton, *Records of the Historian; the Shih Chi of Ssu-ma Ch'ien* (New York and London: Columbia University Press, 1969).	7, 8, 16, 29, 53– 55, 61, 66, 82, 85, 86, 92, 97, 99, 107, 109, 122, 123, 129

(d) Yang Hsien-i and Gladys Yang, *Selections from Records of the Historian* (Peking: Foreign Languages Press, 1979). This also appeared in 1974, published by the Commercial Press in Hong Kong. Both versions are called 'first edition', but they are in fact identical.   6, 7, 41, 47, 48, 55, 56, 65, 66, 68, 74–77, 79, 81, 82, 85, 86, 92, 100, 102, 106, 107, 109, 118, 120, 122, 124, 126, 129

(e) Viatkin, R.V. and V.S. Taskin, *Syma Cian, Istoričeskie zapiski — Siczi* (Moscow: Nauka, 1972–), 6 vols.   1–

(f) Dolby, William and John Scott, *Sima Qian, Warlords; translated with twelve stories from his Historical Records* (Edinburgh: Southside, 1974). Translations without annotation.   65, 75–78, 86, 126

(g) Haenisch, Erich, *Gestalten aus der Zeit der chinesischen Hegemoniekämpfe. Uebersetzungen aus Sze-ma Ts'ien's Historischen Denkwürdigkeiten.* Abhandlungen für die Kunde des Morgenlandes XXXIV, 2 (Wiesbaden: Franz Steiner, 1962).   75, 76, 77, 78

(h) Kierman, Frank Algerton Jr., *Ssu-ma Ch'ien's historiographical attitude as reflected in four late Warring States biographies* (Wiesbaden: Harrassowitz, 1962).   80, 81, 82, 83

(i) Taskin, V.S., *Materialy po istorii Syunnu (po kitaiskim istočnikam)* (Moscow: Nauka, 1968), vol. 1.   110, parts of 81, 93, 99, 109, 112

(j) Hervouet, Yves, *Le chapitre 117 du Che-ki; biographie de Sseu-ma Siang-jou* (Paris: Presses universitaires de France, 1972); translation accompanied by full scholarly apparatus and the Chinese text, with commentaries, reproduced from the Takigawa edition.   117

(k) de Groot, J.J.M., *Chinesische Urkunden zur Geschichte Asiens, zweiter Teil, Die Westlande Chinas in der vorchristlichen Zeit* (Berlin und Leipzig: Walter de Gruyter, 1926), pp. 9–45.   123

(l) Swann, Nancy Lee, *Food and Money in Ancient China* (Princeton, N.J.: Princeton University Press, 1950), pp. 419–464.   129

7. Japanese editions

A. *Kambun taikei*; nos. 6, 7, 1911, edited by Shigeno Yasutsugu (Chapters 61-130 only).

B. *Shiki kokujikai*; vols. 1-8, 1919-20. This is a special series whose arrangement of text and treatment is identical with that of the *Kanseki kokujikai* series; edited by Katsura Isoo (Koson), Kikuchi Sankurō (Bankō), Matsudaira Yasukuni and Makino Kenjirō (Sōshu).

C. *Kokuyaku kambun taisei*; nos. 13-16, 1922-23, edited by Kimida Rentarō and Yanai Watari.

E. *Kambun sōsho*; 1927, 6 vols., edited by Kuwabara Jitsuzō.

G. *Chūgoku koten bungaku zenshū*; nos. 4-5, 1958-59, edited by Noguchi Sadao.

H. *Shinshaku kambun taikei*; nos. 38-41 and 85-87, 1973-82, edited by Yoshida Kenkō; and nos. 88-92, edited by Mizusawa Toshitada (no. 88, 1992; nos. 89-91, forthcoming).

K. *Chūgoku koten bungaku taikei*; nos. 10-12, 1968-71, edited by Noguchi Sadao, Kondō Mitsuo, Rai Tsutomu and Yoshida Mitsukuni.

M. *Shintei Chūgoku koten sen*, nos, 10-12, 1966-67, edited by Tanaka Kenji and Ikkai Tomoyoshi (no. 10 includes text for Ch'un ch'iu, Chan kuo; no. 11 for Ch'u Han; no. 12 for Wu ti).

In addition to the volumes in the foregoing series, the *Shih chi* has been treated independently as follows:

(a) Kotake Fumio 小竹文夫 and Kotake Takeo 小竹武夫 Gendaigo-yaku Shiki 現代語譯史記, Tokyo: Kōbundō, 1956-1958.

(b) Kaizuka Shigeki 貝塚茂樹 and Kawakatsu Yoshio 川勝義雄 *Shiba Sen Shiki retsuden* 司馬遷史記列傳 in the series *Sekai no meicho* 世界の名著, Tokyo: Chūōkōron sha, 1968.

(c) Katō Shigeru 加藤繁, *Shiki Heijunsho, Kanjo Shokkashi yakuchū* 史記平準書, 漢書食貨志譯注, Tokyo: Iwanami shoten, 1942; nos. 3039-40 in the series Iwanami bunko.

8. Recent studies and research aids

The following items are selected from the large volume of material published on various aspects of *Shih chi* research.

(a) History of editions:

(i) Wang Chung-min 王重民, *Shih chi pan pen yü ts'an k'ao shu* 史記版本與參考書, in *T'u shu kuan hsüeh chi k'an* 1/4 (1926), pp. 555-577.

(ii) Chao Cheng 趙 證, *Shih chi pan pen k'ao* 史 記 版 本 考 in *Shih hsüeh nien pao* 1/3 (1931), pp. 107–146.

(iii) Ho Tz'u-chün 賀 次 君. *Shih chi shu lu* 史 記 書 錄 (Peking: Shang wu, 1958).

(b) Indexes to *Shih chi* studies:

(i) *Shih chi yen chiu ti tzu liao ho lun wen so yin* 史 記 研 究 的 資 料 和 論 文 索 引 (Peking: K'o hsüeh, 1957). This index contains titles of articles published up to 1937.

(ii) Sanae Yoshio 早 苗 良 雄, *Kandai kenkyū bunken mokuroku, hōbun hen* 漢 代 研 究 文 獻 目 錄, 邦 文 篇 (Kyoto: Hōyu shoten, 1979).

(c) Other studies:

(i) Cheng Ho-sheng 鄭 鶴 聲, *Shih Han yen chiu* 史 漢 研 究; Shanghai: Shang wu, 1930; discusses authorship and interpolations of the *Shih chi*, and compares the work with the *Han shu*.

(ii) Chin Te-chien 金 德 建, *Ssu-ma Ch'ien suo chien shu k'ao* 馬 司 遷 所 見 書 考 (Shanghai: Jen min ch'u pan she, 1963) discusses the ancient texts consulted by Ssu-ma Ch'ien.

(iii) *Ssu-ma Ch'ien yü Shih chi* 司 馬 遷 與 史 記, ed., Wen shih che tsa chih pien chi wei yüan hui 文 史 哲 雜 誌 編 輯 委 員 會 (Peking: Chung hua, 1957), contains some valuable articles, both on the author and on his work.

(iv) Watson, Burton, *Ssu-ma Ch'ien: Grand Historian of China* (New York and London: Columbia University Press, 1957).

(v) Kroll, Y.L., *Syma Cyan — istorik* (Moscow: Nauka, 1970).

(vi) Dzo Ching-chuan, *Sseu-ma Ts'ien et l'historiographie chinoise* (Paris: Presses universitaires de France, 1978).

(vii) Studies on particular *Shih chi* chapters assembled in *Erh shih wu shih pu pien*, vol. 1, pp. 1–134.

9. Indexes

(a) *Combined indices to Shih chi and the notes by P'ei Yin, Ssu-ma Cheng, Chang Shou-chieh and Takigawa Kametarō.* Harvard-Yenching Index no. 40 (1st ed. Peiping 1947; 2nd ed. Cambridge, Mass: Harvard University Press, 1955). This index is based on the T'ung wen edition.

(b) Wong Fook-luen 黃 福 鑾, *Shih chi so yin* 史 記 索 引 (Hongkong: The Chinese University of Hongkong, 1963). This is an index to both the *Ssu pu ts'ung k'an* and the *Ssu pu pei yao* edition of the *Shih chi*. The indexed items are divided into twenty-four groups (personal names,

geographical names, natural phenomena, wearing apparel, official
titles etc.), the items being arranged according to the number of
character strokes.
(c) Chung Hua 鍾華, ed., *Shih chi Jen ming so yin* 史記人名索引 (Peking:
Chung hua, 1977). Entries are arranged according to the four corner
system, and references are to the punctuated edition of the Chung
hua shu chü (Peking, 1959).
(d) *Shih chi so yin* 史記索引, edited by Li Hsiao-kuang 李曉光 and Li Po
李波; Peking, Chung hua kuang po tien shih, 1989. References in
this massive volume, printed in small type, are to the 1985 revised
print of the punctuated edition (Peking: Chung hua, 1959).
(e) Ts'ang Hsiu-liang 倉修良, *Shih chi tz'u tien* 史記辭典 (Shantung
Chiao-yü ch'u pan she, 1991). Set out in encyclopaedic form, this
work includes entries for proper names of persons and places, and
for technical terms that appear in the *Shih chi*, with short biographical, geographical or technical details, and dates for the individuals
listed. The entries themselves are given in unabbreviated characters;
references are to the pages of the *Chung hua shu chü* print.
(f) *Twenty-five Dynastic Histories Full Text Data Base* 廿五史全文資料庫;
Taipei: Institute of History and Philology, 1988.

— A.F.P. Hulsewé

Shih ching 詩經

1. The collection of the poems and the four schools

The *Shih ching*, or *Book of Songs*, includes 305 poems, which may be dated between *c.* 1000 and *c.* 600 B.C. Traditionally, these were said to have been collected by Confucius from a total of some three thousand items, some of which had originated in remote antiquity; according to another version, they had been collected by officials, commissioned to do so in order to discover the extent and depth of popular feeling. Arthur Waley observes (see under 7 (d) below, p. 18) that 'there is no reason to suppose that Confucius had a hand in forming the collection'. However, the inclusion of the work in the classical canon and its exploitation in imperial times as a vehicle for conveying Confucian teachings may well have served to perpetuate the tradition.

By the start of the Former Han period, the collection was known in the three officially recognised versions of Lu 魯, Ch'i 齊 and Han 韓, and in the private version of Mao Kung 毛公. Of these, the first three, later categorised as *chin wen* 今文 versions, were supported by the established posts of academicians who were responsible for their interpretation; the Mao school, later categorised as *ku wen* 古文, did not enjoy such backing, until it had been promoted in the time of P'ing ti (reigned 1 B.C. to A.D. 6). In the meantime, the school of Ch'i had come to include three sections, including those sponsored by Hou Ts'ang 后蒼 (*fl.* 70 B.C.) and a Mr. Sun 孫 (given name unrecorded); for the Han school there was both an inner and an outer tradition.

The *Han shu* (30, pp. 1707f.) includes entries for the texts of the four versions; it notes that the total for the six schools (i.e., the main four and the extra sections of the school of Ch'i) amounted to 416 *chüan*. The *Sui shu* (32, pp. 915f.) carries two entries for the school of Han and 35 for that of Mao, in addition to the supplementary text of the *Han shih wai chuan*; Fujiwara Sukeyo's catalogue includes the *Han shih wai chuan* and 14 items belonging to the school of Mao. There would thus be general verification for the statement of Lu Te-ming 陸德明 (556–627) that once the Mao version had been established and backed by Cheng Hsüan's 鄭

玄 (127–200) commentary (see below), the other three schools came to be abandoned, so that in his own time the Mao school was the sole survivor (*Ching tien shih wen* 經典釋文, *Ts'ung shu chi ch'eng* ed., 1, p. 32). The Ch'i version had probably been lost during the third century, with those of Han and Lu surviving respectively in the south and in the north for some time. A few fragments of the Lu version survive on the Stone Classics of 175, as may best be seen in Ma Heng 馬衡 (posthumous) *Han shih ching ts'un* 漢石經存 (Peking: K'o hsüeh, 1957). Other fragments of the other versions have been collected in Ma Kuo-han's 馬國翰 *Yü han shan fang chi i shu*, ch. 12, 13. For the history of these three versions or schools in Han times, see James R. Hightower, 'The *Han-shih wai-chuan* and the *san chia shih*', *HJAS* 11 (1948), 241–310.

The second of the entries for the Mao version in the *Han shu* reads *Mao shih ku hsün chuan san shih chüan* 毛詩故訓傳三十卷. In *Hou Han shu* 79B, p. 2569, and *Sui shu* 32, p. 916 Mao is identified as Mao Ch'ang 毛萇, of the Chan kuo state of Chao 趙; the statement in *Ssu k'u ch'üan shu tsung mu t'i yao* p. 293, under the entry for *Mao shih cheng i ssu shih chüan* 毛詩正義四十卷 that the *Hou Han shu* gives this as 長 is not borne out in the received editions of that text. Cheng Hsüan and Lu Chi 陸璣 (third century), however, ascribe the *hsün chuan* 訓傳 to Mao Heng 毛亨, of Lu, who duly transmitted it to Mao Ch'ang (see Lu Chi, *Mao shih ts'ao mu niao shou ch'ung yü shu* 毛詩草木鳥獸蟲魚疏 B, p. 70, in *Ts'ung shu chi ch'eng*'s facsimile of the text from the *Ku ching chieh hui han*). In subsequent texts the terms Greater and Lesser are applied somewhat differently to the two men. The editors of the *Ssu k'u* state clearly their view that the commentary was written by Mao Heng, regarding a compromise stance taken by Chu I-tsun 朱彝尊 (1629–1709) as being groundless.

2.   Form and contents

Each of the poems of the collection is usually known by its title, which is drawn from phrases that are usually found in its opening words. Each one is preceded by a short passage, known as its *hsü* 序, which explains or summarises its content or point. Exceptionally, for the first poem ('Kuan ch'ü' 關雎), this introductory passage is considerably longer, such that it is usually regarded as including two parts, (a) a short passage, comparable with those seen before the other poems; and (b) a much longer passage which is concerned with the aims and subjects of the songs in general. Distinctions have therefore been drawn between (a) the *Hsiao hsü* 小序, as seen for all the poems, including the first, and

(b) the *Ta hsü* 大序, as seen only for 'Kuan ch'ü.' Authorship of these passages, which are written in a completely different, and later, linguistic style from that of the poems themselves, has been variously ascribed to Confucius, his disciple Tzu Hsia 子夏 (Pu Shang 卜商), Mao Kung, Tzu Hsia in collaboration with Mao, Wei Hung 衛宏 (1st century), Mao's disciples, scribes of the various states or unnamed and unknown villagers (see the entry for *Shih hsü erh chüan* 詩序二卷 in *Ssu k'u ch'üan shu tsung mu t'i yao*, p. 291).

The collection of the 305 poems includes four parts:

(a) *Feng* 風, or *Kuo feng* 國風, or airs; 160 poems are concerned with 15 states of the north and may be described as lyrical expressions of emotion; they allude to the life-cycle of the common people, their festivals and daily lives. Two sections are entitled *Chou nan* 周南 and *Chao nan* 召南, the former being ascribed to an origin in Chou, the latter to the more distant areas of the South. The profuse reference to flora and fauna has prompted a considerable body of specialist study. Mao's comments impart a political interpretation to these folk songs.

(b) *Hsiao ya* 小雅, or odes, including 74 poems. The title of this section suggests a connection with the higher reaches of society and the content often concerns one of the courts of the land; some of the poems are interpreted as a series of complaints voiced against the authorities of the day.

(c) *Ta ya* 大雅, or odes, with 31 poems; many of these specifically concern the kingdom of Chou and the overthrow of Shang 商. There are some allusions to the mythology of an earlier period, e.g. that of Hou Chi 后稷; there is some criticism of contemporary times.

(d) *Sung* 頌, or hymns of praise, divided into sections for Chou, Lu, and Shang; 40 poems describe religious rites, feasts or musical performances, with an underlying message of the praise that is due to the house of Chou.

The *Ta hsü* introduces the term *liu i* 六義 as a means of classifying poems, under the categories of *feng, fu* 賦, *pi* 比, *hsing* 興, *ya* and *sung*, and sets out an explanation of the character and purpose of each type. The meaning of the term has been subject to a number of different interpretations. The terms *Pien feng* 變風 and *Pien ya*, i.e. the *feng* and *ya* that derive from change, also appear in the *Ta hsü*; they were applied by Cheng Hsüan to those poems of the Feng and Ya sections which concerned the times of the later kings of Chou and reflected the decadence of those reigns, as opposed to the *Cheng feng* 正風, which described the glories of Western Chou.

3.   Traditional commentaries and interpretations

In view of the voluminous extent of the scholarly attention paid to the *Shih ching*, it is possible to do no more than indicate the main trends of development.

(a) Cheng Hsüan contributed two types of study to the work, the *chien* 箋 or explanatory notes to the text, and the *p'u* 譜 or chronological record. He sought to relate the poems to the political circumstances of the states of the Chou and Ch'un ch'iu period, fastening on a few well-known heroes such as the first kings of Chou, and losing no opportunity to illustrate the faults of those kings who were notorious for their alleged depravities. His theme, of the emergence of the *pien feng* and *pien ya* as a measure of decline, is set out clearly in the preface to the *p'u*. In his explanation of the lines of the poems, Cheng Hsüan took the Mao version as his basic text, calling on the three other schools for purposes of elucidation.

In this work, Cheng Hsüan was formulating what was long to be the orthodox Confucian interpretation of the poems as direct allegories of political events, and warnings of activities that were questionable; it was long before a reaction set in against the violence that was being done thereby to the emotional and lyrical qualities of the songs.

(b) Wang Su 王肅 (195–256) found himself at variance with Cheng Hsüan, who, he thought, had misinterpreted some of Mao's interpretation. Controversies of this type continued during the San kuo and Nan pei ch'ao periods, resulting in a large number of written works which have nearly all disappeared. Lu Chi's study of the flora and fauna (as cited above) is an exception.

(c) In his *Ching tien shih wen* 經典釋文 Lu Te-ming 陸德明 (556–627) was concerned essentially with questions of scholarship rather than exegesis. His notes relate to problems of philology and phonetics, but not to the application of the poems to political or dynastic incidents.

(d) Following the plethora of interpretation that had appeared, the T'ang government took steps to establish a version and interpretation that was to be regarded as orthodox and approved. It was in response to a decree which called for the production of the necessary commentaries that K'ung Ying-ta 孔穎達 (574–648) compiled his *shu* 疏 or sub-commentary. In his preface he traces the emergence of the songs from the earliest times. He lists a number of scholars who had expressed views on the poems, and evaluates their interpretations, stating clearly that he is selecting those of Liu Cho 劉焯, 544–610, (*Mao shih i shu* 毛詩義疏) and Liu Hsüan 劉炫, d. 613, (*Mao shih shu i* 毛詩述義) as being those that were of outstanding value; the original works of those two scholars do not survive. His own contribution is essentially that of the orthodox point of view.

(e) Three types of comment took shape during the Sung period:

    (i) A school which was highly critical of the interpretations of Mao and Cheng Hsüan, and wished to abandon the shorter *hsü* that stood at the head of each poem as being unsuitable; these views were voiced by Ou-yang Hsiu 歐陽修 (1007–1072)Su Ch'e 蘇轍 (1039–1112), Cheng Ch'iao 鄭樵 (1104–1162) and others.

    (ii) A school which favoured retention of the *hsü* and the traditional exegesis; these views were expressed by Lü Tsu-ch'ien 呂祖謙 (1137–1181) and others.

    (iii) A school which may be termed that of *ming wu hsün ku* 名物訓詁, which focussed attention on the accuracy and precise meaning of some of the expressions of the text, thus acting as followers of Lu Chi and as precursors of the *k'ao cheng* 考證 school of the Ch'ing period. Scholars mentioned in this connection include Ts'ai Pien 蔡卞 (1058–1117) and Wang Ying-lin 王應麟 (1223–96).

In addition, Chu Hsi 朱熹 (1130–1200) saw the songs as a natural expression of emotion that cannot be voiced by other means, and stressed their value for educational purposes in so far as they placed a restraint on excessive displays of feeling. While wishing to see the *hsü* removed from the text, Chu Hsi retained some of the explanations of Mao and Cheng Hsüan.

(f) The principal name to bear in mind for the Ming period is that of Hu Kuang 胡廣 (1370–1418), who is said to have taken over the work of Liu Chin 劉瑾 (Yüan period). The period saw the eclectic adoption of the products of the Sung scholars, but few original contributions.

(g) The scholarly output of the Ch'ing period is seen first and foremost in the work of Ch'en Ch'i-yüan 陳啓源 (d. 1689), whose critical study reverted to that of the pre-T'ang scholars. The attention to Han learning and the development of *k'ao cheng* methods produced a wealth of critical notes on problems of phonetics and philology as well as exegesis, partly by way of reaction against the attitude of Chu Hsi and other Sung scholars. As part of the Han school of learning, Tai Chen 戴震 (1724–77) had adopted the interpretations of Mao and Cheng Hsüan, but some of the Ch'ing scholars were themselves critical of Cheng Hsüan. The culmination of Ch'ing scholarship is seen in the inclusion of Juan Yüan's 阮元 (1764–1849) *chiao*

k'an chi 校勘記 with the *Shih san ching chu shu* 十三經注疏 (1816).
Juan Yüan was anxious to eliminate those errors that had crept in as
a result of uncritical interpretations. The works of Ch'en Huan 陳奐
(1786–1863) and Yao Chi-heng 姚際恒 (b. 1647) are of particular
value (see under 6 below).

4. Manuscript copies

In addition to the surviving parts of the Han Stone Classics of 175 and
the T'ang Stone Classics of 837 (now on display in Hsi-an), discoveries
of engraved or manuscript copies of the text have been reported as
follows.

(a) Over 170 wooden strips or fragments from tomb no. 1 Fu-yang 阜陽
    (An-hui), dated 165 B.C.; the text varies from that of any of the four
    versions; see (i) *Wen wu* 1983.2, 21–22, and 1984.8, 1–12 and 13–21,
    and (ii) Hu P'ing-sheng 胡平生 and Han Tzu-ch'iang 韓自強, *Fu-
    yang Han chien Shih ching yen chiu* 阜陽漢簡詩經研究; Shanghai: Ku
    chi, 1988.
(b) Two further fragments of the Stone Classics of 175; see *Wen wu*
    1986.5, 1–6.
(c) For a mirror of *c.* A.D. 200 which is inscribed with a passage from the
    Lu version, see *Wen wu* 1980.6, 80 and *Chiang Han k'ao ku* 1985.4, 77.
(d) Paper fragments, of the T'ang period, found at Miran 米蘭 (Hsin-
    chiang); see *Hsin-chiang ch'u t'u wen wu* 新疆出土文物 (Peking:
    Wen wu, 1975), p. 69, no. 106.

5. The arrangement of the text and commentaries

As presented in the traditional editions, the text does not always separate the Greater from the Lesser *hsü*; nor is it always easy to draw a
distinction between the principal commentaries. This may be achieved
most clearly in the 1871 reprint of the Wu ying tien edition of the *Shih
san ching chu shu* of 1739, with the headings of *chuan* 傳, for Mao Heng's
explanations; *chien* 箋 for Cheng Hsüan's annotation; *yin i* 音義 for Lu
Te-ming's notes; and *shu* 疏 for K'ung Ying-ta's commentary. This latter
usually bears the introductory formula of *Cheng i yüeh* 正義曰; K'ung's
sub-commentary was written not only in respect of the text of the poems
themselves, but also for that of the earlier commentators mentioned.
The *k'ao cheng* of the Ch'ing scholars is appended in the 1871 print.

The *Ssu pu ts'ung k'an* copy, which is based on an unidentified Sung
print, and the *Ssu pu pei yao* include the *chuan*, *chien* and *yin i*, but the

distinctions are not recognised so easily. They do not include Cheng Hsüan's *p'u* or its preface, which is usually appended in other editions. The *p'u* itself appears in various forms of layout, having been subject to editing by Ou-yang Hsiu and Ting Yen 丁晏 (1794–1875). It is studied most easily in the *Han wei i shu ch'ao* or the *Shao wu Hsü shih ts'ung shu*. Juan Yüan's *Chiao k'an chi* is sometimes printed as a unit; sometimes it is separated and appears in different parts of the book. Chu Hsi's annotation, known either as *Shih ching chi chuan* 詩經集傳 or as *Shih ching chi chu* 詩經集註, is available with his own preface in a number of prints (e.g., see (8) below); such editions do not include the *hsü* to the poems in the main body of the text; sometimes these are appended in one of the margins.

6. Research aids

(a) For an introduction to the *Shih ching*, see (i) Burton Watson, *Early Chinese Literature* (New York and London: Columbia University Press, 1962), pp. 199–230, and P. Eugen Feifel, *Geschichte der Chinesischen Literatur* (i.e., a translation of Nagasawa Kikuya 長澤規矩也, *Shina Gakujutsu bungeishi* 支那學術文藝史; Tokyo: San shō, 1938); Darmstadt: Wissenschaftliche Buchgesellschaft, 1959, pp. 62–78. A summary of scholarly developments and a consideration of a number of problems will be found in Matsuzaki Tsuruo 松崎鶴雄, *Shikei kokufū hen kenkyū* 詩經國風篇研究 (Tokyo: Dai ichi, 1937).

(b) For philological problems, see Bernhard Karlgren, 'Glosses on the Book of Odes,' *BMFEA* 14 (1942), 16 (1944) and 18 (1946).

(c) For a modern annotated edition, see Ch'ü Wan-li 屈萬里 (1907–1979), *Shih ching shih i* 詩經釋義, 2 vols., Taipei: Chung hua wen hua, 1953.

(d) Yao Chi-heng 姚際恒, *Shih ching t'ung lun* 詩經通論 is a highly valuable critique, published first in 1837, and available in punctuated form (Peking: Chung hua, 1956).

(e) For the critical work of the school of Han learning, see Ch'en Huan 陳奐, *Shih Mao shih chuan shu* 詩毛氏傳疏, first printed c. 1850 (reprinted Taipei: 1968).

(f) For modern criticism, see (i) Wen I-to 聞一多 (1899–1946), *Ku tien hsin i* 古典新義 (Peking: Ku chi, 1956); (ii) Ch'en Shih-hsiang 陳世驤, 'The Shih ching: Its Generic Significance in Chinese Literary History and Poetics,' *BIHP* XXXIX.1 (1969), 371–413; and (iii) C.H. Wang, *The Bell and the Drum: Shih Ching as Formulaic Poetry in an Oral Tradition* (Berkeley: 1974).

7. Translations

(a) Legge, *The Chinese Classics*, Vol. IV, Parts I, II; *Sacred Books of the East*, Vol. III.

(b) Couvreur, S. S.J., *Cheu King. Texte chinois avec une double traduction, en francais et en latin*; Sien Hien: Mission Catholique, 1896; third ed., 1934.

(c) Granet, Marcel, *Fêtes et chansons anciennes de la Chine*; Paris: Biblothèque de l'école des hautes études, 1919, an interpretative study of the Songs from a literary and anthropological viewpoint, which includes translations from the *Kuo feng*; translated E.D. Edwards, as *Festivals and Songs of Ancient China* (London: Broadway Oriental Library, 1932).

(d) Waley, Arthur, *The Book of Songs; translated from the Chinese*; London: George Allen and Unwin Limited, 1937.

(e) Karlgren, Bernhard, *The Book of Odes: Chinese Text, Transcription and Translation*; Stockholm: Museum of Far Eastern Antiquities, 1950 (published originally in *BMFEA* 16 (1944) and 17 (1945)).

8. Japanese editions

A. *Kambun taikei*, no. 12, 1911, edited by Hattori Unokichi and Hoshino Tsune.

B. *Kanseki kokujikai zensho*, no. 5, 1909, edited by Nakamura Tekisai.

C. *Kōchū kambun sōsho*, no. 8, 1913, edited by Kubo Tenzui and Uno Tōzan.

D. *Kokuyaku kambun taisei*, no. 3, 1921, edited by Shaku Seitan.

E. *Kambun sōsho*, 1927.

F. *Keisho taikō*, nos. 6–8, 1938–39.

G. *Chūgoku koten bungaku zenshū*, no. 1, 1960, edited by Mekata Makoto.

H. *Shinshaku kambun taikei*, nos. 110–112 (forthcoming), edited by Ishikawa Tadahisa.

K. *Chūgoku koten bungaku taikei*, no. 15, 1969, edited by Mekata Makoto.

L. *Chūgoku koten shinsho*, 1984, edited by Ishikawa Tadahisa.

Of these editions, the *Kambun taikei* is perhaps the most valuable, including the *hsü*, Mao Heng's *chuan*, the *p'u* and *chien* of Cheng Hsüan and Lu Te-ming's *yin i* (headed by the formula *chi chuan* 集 傳). In general other *Kambun* versions exclude the *hsü*; Chu Hsi's preface is included in the *Kanseki kokujikai zensho*.

9. Indexes

(a) *Mao shih yin te* (*A Concordance to Shih Ching*); Harvard-Yenching Institute Sinological Index Series supplement no. 9; Peking, 1934; reprinted Tokyo: Tōyō Bunko, 1962 and San Francisco: Chinese Materials Center Inc., 1974.

(b) van der Loon, P., *Index to the Shih Ching; Register zum Shih Ching;* Leiden: E.J. Brill, 1943. The author describes this as 'an alphabetical index to all odes as they can be found in the translations of Legge, Couvreur, Granet and Waley'.

(c) *A Concordance to the Shijing* 詩經逐字索引, ed. D.C. Lau and Chen Fong Ching; *ICS* series, Hong Kong: Commercial Press, forthcoming 1994.

— Michael Loewe

Shih ming 釋名

1. Content and subject matter

The *Shih ming*, sometimes known as the *I ya* 逸雅, is an important lexicographical compilation attributed to Liu Hsi 劉熙 (style Ch'eng kuo 成國) and believed to date from *c.* 200. The text, in 8 *chüan*, consists of somewhat over 1500 individual lexical entries arranged under 27 major semantic categories (e.g., heaven, earth, body parts, kinship terms). For most of these entries the text supplies paronomastic (punning) glosses, which are generally followed in turn by short remarks that help to elucidate the point of the pun that is being posed in each gloss.

The importance of the *Shih ming* derives from the contemporary evidence that it preserves for theories of language of the Han period. Liu Hsi's preface categorically expounds the cardinal assumption that was at the centre of the Han view of language, and at the same time clearly localizes the content of the text within the confines of the traditional Chinese world view as it existed in the Han period. He does so in the following terms:

> In the correspondence of name with reality, there is in each instance that which is right and proper. The common people use names every day, but they do not know the reasons why names are what they are. Therefore I have chosen to record names for heaven and earth, *yin* and *yang*, the four seasons, states, cities, vehicles, clothing and mourning ceremonies, up to and including the vessels commonly used by the people, and have discussed these terms with a view to explaining their origin.

Each of the *Shih ming*'s paranomastic glosses attempts to illustrate this theory of language, and to implement its basic assumption, to the effect that 'in the correspondence of name with reality, there is in each instance that which is right and proper', on the two levels of phonology and semantics simultaneously. In order to do so, each one of Liu Hsi's punning glosses tries to capitalize on similarities in the pronunciation of two different words in order to illustrate the author's view of what constituted the 'right and proper' (*i lei* 義類) correspondence that words or names (*ming* 名) were supposed to have had in relation to reality (*shih* 實).

For the author of the *Shih ming*, as for all known Han scholars of language and linguistic theory, language was a sociological phenomenon of intrinsically profound ethical and moral significance. Words, i.e. names, were not simply arbitrary linguistic signs that had become attached to arbitrarily segmented parts of the real world through a gradually accumulating process of social convention. Rather, words were immutable cosmological entities, each one of which contained within itself a kernel of absolute moral and ethical principle; such principles in turn reflected much of what man was able to learn about the nature of the world and of the society in which he lived. It was the duty as well as the function of linguistic scholarship to discover and elucidate these principles; and it was this vital work of 'discovery and elucidation' to which the *shih* ('explanation') of the title of the work has immediate reference. The *Shih ming* was therefore a lexicographical compilation that aimed at the discovery and elucidation both of the reality and of the principles that the author believed to underlie all language. For Liu Hsi this was in turn co-extensive with his own version of Han period Chinese, i.e. the dialect of Ch'i 齊.

The paranomastic glosses of the *Shih ming* preserve important evidence for the pronunciation of the Chinese language during the first centuries of our era. Many of the punning associations between words can only be explained by the existence of initial consonant clusters in the language of the period. Such combinations of sounds were thereafter drastically simplified, with the result that soon after the compilation of this text the phonological basis behind many of the lexical equations that Liu Hsi proposed was obscured.

The same problems of methodology still attend the full exploitation of the *Shih ming* for the study of Chinese historical phonology. Such problems continue to complicate, when they do not actually stalemate, the utilization of similar evidence to be found in other Han lexicographical compilations, including the more extensive *Shuo wen chieh tzu* and the somewhat better-known, but still less adequately studied, *Fang yen* 方言. At best these texts present us with a large set of interlocking lexical equations, in which we are told that word x is somehow equivalent to word y in both sound and sense; but we are never given any unequivocal ground for determining just what the actual sound values were for either x or y, both of which terms necessarily remain phonologically indeterminate in each such equation, given the nature of the Chinese script.

In Liu Hsi's view of language, it is clear that the concept of historical etymology and the idea of linguistic relationships played no part. Such ideas were as unknown to him as they were to Han intellectual life in general and also to the later traditional Chinese world-view that grew out of it. Liu Hsi's paranomastic glosses do not pre-suppose the existence of earlier proto-forms connecting the x's and the y's of his equations, partly because he had no concept of such proto-forms, and partly because he would have had no way in which to recover them even if he had.

Nevertheless, and particularly when it is examined with proper respect for the intellectual basis and the linguistic concepts that underlie it, the *Shih ming* is able to provide us with important materials for the future study of the entire range of Han linguistic theory and speculation, and for investigating the seminal part that such theories played in early Chinese intellectual life, including their central role in the formulation of the later socio-political orthodoxy. Liu Hsi formulates his concept of the socio-linguistic role of his own native Ch'i dialect, as well as the roles of other apparently non-standard local varieties of language of the Han period, as compared with the dialect of officials of the central government that enjoyed prestige. Such a conceptualization is often an important factor not only for understanding the significance of individual entries in the *Shih ming* but also for interpreting their evidence correctly.

Thanks to Bodman's work (see under (4) below), almost all the information that may be extracted from the *Shih ming* relating to the probable pronunciation of initial consonant clusters during the Han period has been completely indexed, carefully weighed and meticulously studied. Furthermore, Bodman's monograph, limited though it is to the questions that concern the pronunciation of the initial consonant clusters in Liu Hsi's language, also provides the student of the *Shih ming* with important guidance to a wide variety of textual problems for future research in other linguistic aspects of the text. Bodman's work will also without question be of great value for furthering the more involved studies, still lying largely in the future, that eventually will attempt to relate the many other important facets of the *Shih ming* to an overall formulation of theories of language of the Han period.

2.   Authorship and extent of the book

In *Sui shu* 32, p. 937 and Fujiwara Sukeyo's catalogue, the *Shih ming* is entered as a work of 8 *chüan*, by Liu Hsi, in each case under *Lun yü*; in

Chiu T'ang shu 46, p. 1984, *Hsin T'ang shu* 57, p. 1447 and *Sung shih* 202, p. 5072 it is entered under *Hsiao hsüeh* 小學. The received text, of 8 *chüan*, includes 27 separate sections, each one being entitled for a particular topic. This arrangement was doubtless the significance of the note in the *Ch'ung wen tsung mu* that the work comprised a total of 27 items or categories (*mu* 目). The preface, which is written in Liu Hsi's name, refers to the 27 *p'ien* of the work; the *Chih chai shu lu chieh t'i* (*Ts'ung shu chi ch'eng* ed., p. 82, *s.v. Hsiao hsüeh*) refers to the book as being of 8 *chüan*, comprising 27 *p'ien*; the figure of 27 is repeated in a postface by Lü Nan 呂柟, which is dated 1524.

These references are to be distinguished from two statements: (i) that of *Hou Han shu* 80A, p. 2617, which refers to a *Shih ming* by Liu Chen 劉珍 (died shortly after 126), of 30 *p'ien*; and (ii) that of the *Ssu k'u ch'üan shu tsung mu t'i yao*, which specifies 20 *p'ien*. This latter notice avers that Liu Chen's book as mentioned in the *Hou Han shu* had long since been lost; it further suggests that the figure of 27 *p'ien* that was given by Cheng Ming-hsüan 鄭明選 (Wan li period) did not conform with the received version and that it had been changed thereto in error.

Ch'ien Ta-hsin 錢大昕 (1728–1804) was satisfied that Liu Hsi, who lived at the end of the Han period and fled for refuge to the south, had indeed been the author. Pi Yüan 畢沅 (1730–97) showed reason why it is unlikely that the received text can be dated as early as the time of Liu Chen. He also drew attention to a statement made by Wei Yao 韋曜, in a submission written from prison in 253, to the effect that he had seen Liu Hsi's book and found it wanting in some respects (*San kuo chih* 65, 'Wu', pp. 1462–63). Pi Yüan suggested the possibility that the the book had originated with Liu Chen; that it had been completed by Liu Hsi, either at the end of Han or during the San kuo period; and that it had been supplemented by Wei Yao.

The text is preceded by two prefaces, one attributed to Liu Hsi and one signed by Ch'u Liang-ts'ai 儲良材, which is dated in 1524.

3. Editions

By the time of the great T'ang and Sung encyclopaedias, the *Shih ming* text as we have it today was already well known, and parts of it were frequently cited *in extenso*. Apart from such early testimony, the tradition of the received text begins with a tracing of a Sung version, known today through a Ming copy that is reproduced in the *Ssu pu ts'ung k'an* series. Other editions are seen as follows:

(a) In the *Tseng ting Han Wei ts'ung shu*; unannotated.

(b) In the *Ku chin i shih,* edited by Wu Kuan 吳琯 (*chin shih* 1571).

(c) The *Lung hsi ching she ts'ung shu* includes the annotation of Wu Chih-chung 吳志忠, which was first published in 1829. It is also available in the *Hsiao hsüeh hui han* 小學彙函 and in the *Ts'ung shu chi ch'eng* series, with prefaces by Wang Yin-chih 王引之 (1766–1834) and Ku Kuang-ch'i 顧廣圻 (1776–1835).

(d) Annotation by Chou Li-ching 周履靖 (Ming period) is available in his *I men kuang tu* 夷門廣牘.

(e) Pi Yüan, *Shih ming shu cheng* 釋名疏證, in 8 *chüan,* preface dated 1789, is included in, e.g., the *Kuang ya shu chü ts'ung shu;* there is also a supplement and list of variant readings.

(f) For Sun I-jang's 孫詒讓 (1848–1908) notes, see his *Shih ming chiao* 釋名校 and his *Cha i* 札迻.

(g) Wang Hsien-ch'ien 王先謙 (1842–1918), *Shih ming shu cheng pu* 釋名疏證補, with supplement (1896), is available in *Ssu hsien shu chü k'an shu* 思賢書局刊書.

4. Recent studies

(a) Bodman, Nicholas Cleaveland, *A linguistic study of the* Shih ming, *Initials and consonant clusters;* in Harvard-Yenching Institute Studies XI; Cambridge, Mass.: Harvard University Press, 1954.

(b) Miller, Roy Andrew, review of (a), in *T'oung Pao* 44 (1956) 266–87.

(c) Miller, Roy Andrew, 'The Far East'; in Thomas E. Sebeok (ed.), *Current trends in linguistics,* vol. 13, *Historiography of Linguistics;* The Hague and Paris: Mouton, 1975, pp. 1213–64, esp. 1224–25.

5. Index

A Concordance to the Shi ming and Jijiu pian 釋名, 急就篇逐字索引, ed. D.C. Lau and Chen Fong Ching; *ICS* series, Hong Kong: Commercial Press, forthcoming 1996.

— Roy Andrew Miller (1980)

Shuo wen chieh tzu 說文解字

1. Authorship, date and circumstances of compilation

The *Shuo wen chieh tzu*, known usually as the *Shuo wen*, is the first comprehensive dictionary of Chinese characters that was ever compiled. Some of the earlier lexicographical works which are known to have existed are already mentioned in the *Postface* (*hsü* 敘) to the *Shuo wen* itself, but these are extant only through citations in later works and in fragments. In any case none of these was in any real sense comprehensive, even in its original full form, the *Erh ya* being more in the nature of a list of glosses; see Thern, under 7 (b) below, pp. 11f. The *Erh ya* is likely to be older than the *Shuo wen*, but it is much more a thesaurus than an analytic dictionary, and probably arose as an aggregate of scattered lexical glosses to the pre-Han Classics.

The *Shuo wen* was compiled by Hsü Shen 許慎 (*c.* 55 to *c.* 149; see *Hou Han shu* 79B, p. 2588 for a short biography, and Miller, 1953, p. 69). It was finished in 100, but was not presented to the throne until 121, when Hsü Ch'ung 許沖, the son of Hsü Shen, offered the work to An ti 安帝 accompanied by a suitable memorial. The reasons why the *Shuo wen* was held back for more than two decades after its completion are bound up with Hsü Shen's purpose in compiling the work and with the political and scholarly circumstances of the Han court during the last years of the first century and the early years of the second century A.D.

In A.D. 86 Chang ti 章帝, who had less than a decade previously sponsored the discussions in the White Tiger Hall, now showed a distinctly less accommodating attitude towards the world of letters. He dismissed the suggestion for further scholastic deliberations and codifications with the curt observation that scholars seem forever to debate, and never to conclude; and that if a 'single K'uei 夔 was enough for Yao 堯', why should he need a throng of tedious intellectuals and contending academics? (see *Hou Han shu* 35, p. 1203; Miller, 1953, p. 69). This disdainful attitude towards the learned bookmen of the day persisted unchanged for the next several decades through successive periods of rule by empresses and eunuchs (see Miller, 1953, pp. 7f).

On the recommendation of Ch'en Chung 陳忠 (*fl.* 120), An ti ordered the full re-instatement of scholars to the service of the court. With this restoration the long disfavour that the intellectuals had suffered came to an end, and academics recovered a respected status and received a genuine welcome by the government. The scene was now set for the first time since the *Shuo wen* had been completed for a favourable reception at court, and the work was thus presented to the throne on 19 September 121 (for full details of these circumstances and the reasons for the delay, see Miller, 1953, pp. 3–26).

In addition to the general disfavour with which scholars had been treated by the Han court up to 121, Hsü Shen was subject to a further disadvantage. He gave every appearance of being a partisan of the so-called Old Text School, and thereby of being in the popular ranks rather than in the officially sanctioned and administratively entrenched New Text camp.

The usual claim that Hsü Shen was an Old Text adherent stems most directly from his own statements in the *Postface* where he purports to follow the *ku wen* 古文 texts of, e.g., K'ung An-kuo's 孔安國 (d. *c.* 100 B.C.) *Shu ching*, and the *Tso chuan*. It is also apparent from the fact that the great majority of the citations from the classics within the *Shuo wen* are of *ku wen* versions (see Chou Tsu-mo, under 7 below, pp. 710–22, esp. 717). While Hsü was in fact an Old Text partisan, he was very idiosyncratic in his attitudes, 'holding remarkably independent views' within the Old Text School (see Miller, 1977–78, 1–21, esp. pp. 4, 20).

Hsü's compilation of the *Shuo wen* cannot be held to have arisen from a purely linguistic or lexicographical drive. He was motivated chiefly by his belief in the need to render the understanding of the ancient classics free of doubt, thereby putting the full force of their accumulated and sanctified wisdom at the service of the Han government in its very immediate objective of enforcing order in all areas of human activity through a dominant central authority (Miller, 1953, 27f.). It was lexicological and lexicographic studies that he saw as the means to this pragmatic end, and that culminated in the compilation of the *Shuo wen*.

Hsü Shen stresses in his *Postface* that the written language constitutes the foundation of all texts, classical and common alike, and that these are the starting point for proper government. It is, moreover, the vehicle whereby men of the present can know the truths of the past (Tuan Yü-ts'ai 段玉裁 (1735–1815) *Shuo wen chieh tzu chu* 說文解字注, *SPPY* ed. 15A, 14b). Recognising this, we can see that a proper understanding of the written language was for Hsü Shen a prerequisite for successful government, and for this reason, if for no other, codification and standardisation were necessary.

Beyond this simple, yet very central, concern was the added fact that as an Old Text adherent, and thus something of a rationalist, Hsü Shen seems to have been influenced by the same spirit of systematisation and standardisation that, starting in Ch'in, touched nearly every facet of Han society in some way (e.g., axle lengths, legal codes, weights and measures and script). Much of the later scientific systematisation of the middle Han years on the part of, e.g., *wu hsing* 五行 and *yin yang* 陰陽 theorists, can likewise be traced to the same prevailing spirit of unification of the time; Hsü Shen's *Shuo wen* is its major linguistic and lexicographical manifestation.

2. Organisation of the text

The *Shuo wen* is arranged according to 540 different graphic classifiers, called *pu shou* 部首, which correspond in function and structure to what are now commonly, but somewhat inaccurately, called 'radicals'. This is the first work ever to have classified Chinese characters by graphic structure, i.e., by identifying shared graphic components. Even if Hsü Shen had gone no further than this first step, it would have been, by virtue of the analytic presumptions on which it was based, a major conceptual innovation in the understanding of the Chinese writing system. He did, indeed, go further, categorizing and analyzing the characters according to six graphic structural types, the so-called *liu shu* 六書.

The basic analytical distinction drawn, as seen already in the title of the work, is between the *wen* 文 and the *tzu* 字. This bi-partite division is not directly correlated with either the overt organizational framework of the dictionary proper or with the *liu shu* that Hsü Shen identifies in his preface, and according to which he categorizes most of the individual entries in the body of the work. The *wen* are characters consisting of only a single graphic element, and they are thus not susceptible of analysis into constituent parts smaller than the graphs themselves. These are what Tuan Yü-ts'ai terms *tu t'i tzu* 獨體字 'single-bodied characters'. The *tzu* are characters that are made up of more than one identifiable graphic component, and are thus capable of analysis into those individual parts. They are the graphic derivatives, or 'progeny', so to speak, of the *wen*, termed by Tuan Yü-tsai *ho t'i tzu* 合體字 'joint-bodied characters'.

When Hsü Shen calls his work *Shuo wen chieh tzu*, he is reflecting this distinction; the intended meaning is 'commenting on the *wen*, analyzing the *tzu*'. The *wen*, because they are single-bodied, and not combinations of two or more graphic components, cannot be 'analyzed' (*chieh*); they can only be 'commented on' or 'explained' (*shuo*). The *tzu*, by contrast, are by definition precisely those characters that can be divided into constituent parts and are hence analyzable (see Boodberg, under 7 below, esp. p. 117).

In the actual entries in the *Shuo wen,* Hsü Shen does not expressly
label a character as a *wen* or a *tzu*; and although on the whole the *wen*
will themselves be classifiers, the converse is not true. Rather it is the *liu*
shu that form the basis for his scheme of classification. In his *Postface,*
Hsü Shen lists the *liu shu* in the following order:

(i) *Chih shih* 指事; graphs that suggest the meaning of the words for
which they stand through some kind of indicative graphic shape,
though not the concrete depiction of any thing.

(ii) *Hsiang hsing* 象形; 'pictographs', or better 'zodiographs'; graphs
which [in origin] were more or less realistic depictions of the
things corresponding to the words for which the graphs stand.

(iii) *Hsing sheng* 形聲, sometimes called *hsieh sheng* 諧聲, 'phonetic
compounds'; characters that include a graphic component that is
intended to suggest the pronunciation of the character in question, through a similarity to the pronunciation of that component
as it occurs in other characters.

(iv) *Hui i* 會意, 'etymonic compounds'; characters in which at least
one component serves to convey both phonetic and semantic information simultaneously.

(v) *Chuan chu* 轉注, 'graphically and etymonically related pairs of
characters'; i.e., a term suggesting words that are phonetically
similar, graphically related and for which the meaning of one is
somehow seen as an extended or derived sense of the other; see
Serruys, under 7 (b) below.

(vi) *Chia chieh* 假借, phonetic loan characters.

The first two of the *liu shu* categories are used to label individual
character entries in the *Shuo wen* explicitly. The formula for such an
entry generally is:

A B *yeh* . . . *chih shih (yeh)*   A B 也 . . . 指事 (也)
or A B *yeh* . . . *hsiang hsing (yeh)*   A B 也 . . . 象形 (也),

where A is the character being defined and classified, and B is the definition, which may be one or more characters in length. Both *chih shih*
and *hsiang hsing* characters tend to be *wen*, and are thus among those
merely commented on, but not analyzed in the dictionary.

The third category's name, *hsing sheng*, is never used as a label, but by
a large measure applies to the type of characters that is the most
numerous in the whole book. It is unambiguously identifiable from the
formulaic nature of the entry, where the pattern is:

A . . . *ts'ung* X, Y *sheng*   A . . . 從 X, Y 聲

meaning 'character A . . . is derived from component X, and component Y is the element which bears the sound' (i.e., conventionally termed 'phonetic'; hereunder termed 'phonophoric'). The crucial part of this formula is the word *sheng*, which indicates that Hsü Shen is claiming that the graphic element Y is serving to specify the pronunciation of character A. The pattern occasionally occurs with the variation:

A . . . *ts'ung* X, Y *sheng sheng*　　　A . . . 從 X, Y 省聲

where the phrase *sheng sheng* means 'abbreviated phonophoric'.

The fourth category, *hui i*, is only infrequently used as a label for a character; it is generally regarded as being implied by the formulaic analysis:

A . . . *ts'ung* X, *ts'ung* Y　　　A . . . 從 X 從 Y

'A is graphically derived from X and from Y', where neither X nor Y is explicitly invested with a phonetic role, but either, or sometimes both, may have one.

Neither the fifth nor the sixth categories, *chuan chu* and *chia chieh*, are used as labels, nor are they identifiable from the wording of the entry in the *Shuo wen*. They are included in the discussion of the *liu shu* in Hsü Shen's *Postface* because they are important principles of graphic derivation and usage, but structurally their analyses in the body of the dictionary may follow the same formulaic wording as that of the other categories. *Chuan chu* are by definition *tzu*, and therefore would be analyzed into constituent parts in the dictionary, whereas *chia chieh* can in principle be either *wen* or *tzu*, and are thus capable of description by any of the types of entry.

There are a few variations of the formulaic entries as outlined above. The most important is the pattern:

A . . . *ts'ung* X, Y　　　　A . . . 從 X, Y

It is often the case that this is a foreshortened variant of the *hsing sheng* formula *ts'ung* X, Y *sheng* , where the word *sheng* 聲 has been excised (in most cases probably by Hsü Hsüan 徐鉉 (916–91); see below). The likely reason for the deletion of this word is that, after more than eight centuries of phonetic change, the editors and scholars of the tenth century could not understand how a graph Y could be the phonophoric element in character A, despite the apparent statement of the *Shuo wen*. They therefore deleted the word *sheng*, regarding it as some kind of aberrant phonetic claim that, to their minds, was of untenable status and inexplicable origin.

A second variation that is not infrequently encountered is the pattern:

A . . . *ts'ung* X, *ts'ung* Y, Y *i sheng*　　　　A . . . 從 X 從 Y Y 亦聲

'A . . . is derived from X, and from Y, and Y is also the phonophoric'. Hsü Shen here seems to be attributing a dual role to Y in a way that he refrains from doing in the many cases of straight forward *hsing sheng* analysis, and for reasons that are not entirely clear.

Individual entries occasionally contain dialect information, citations from the pre-Han classics or other pre-Han texts, alternative graphic forms, and such additional phonetic information as, e.g., the specification *tu jo* 讀若 'read like'. In this last case the pronunciation of the character in question is indicated by saying that it is read like another character, presumably as a homonym. The best of a number of studies that concern the *tu jo* glosses is that of Coblin (see under 7 below), which includes a discussion and evaluation of some of the others.

Hsü Shen's lexicographical aims were twofold: the systematic analysis of the graphic structure of individual characters on the one hand, and the identification of alternative and equivalent graphic forms of the same word on the other. The work takes the *hsiao chuan* 小篆 'small seal' form of the Ch'in standardization as basic, and gives graphic alternatives in (a) the *chou wen* 籀文 script, a form traditionally said to be characteristic of Western Chou (also known as *ta chuan* 大篆 'large seal'); (b) *ku wen* 古文 forms; and (c) occasionally in other recognized variants, e.g., the so-called 'eccentric' forms that Hsü labels *ch'i tzu* 奇字, which seem to be considered a kind of off-shoot of the *ku wen* forms.

In his *Postface* Hsü Shen says that there is a total of 9353 characters defined and analyzed in his dictionary, with an additional 1163 alternative forms given (e.g., from *chou wen, ku wen*). Because of the vicissitudes of textual transmission over the centuries, the received text of the *Shuo wen* does not include exactly these numbers. In particular, in his recension of the work Hsü Hsüan (see under (4) below) added entries for characters that he found missing in the work as he knew it. His additional characters were appended at the end of the appropriate classifier section, being labelled as a category of *hsin fu tzu* 新附字. A total number is given at the end of each classifier section both for primary entries, called *wen* 'graphs', and for the graphic variants, called *ch'ung* 重 'duplicates' or 'doublets' for that section. In this context Hsü uses the term *wen* in respect of any character, and not in the specialised sense in which he uses it in the title of his work, as is discussed above. These totals are sometimes slightly inaccurate, suggesting the loss or accretion of a character or two in a given section, with an overall increase in the number of characters in current editions of the *Shuo wen* over the original figure of 9353 that is given by Hsü Shen in his *Postface*.

3. Textual history and principal recensions

Although the text of the *Shuo wen* was never irrevocably lost, there is no extant record of it for the period between the end of the Han and the political re-unification of the Sui and T'ang empires. The earliest known manuscript fragments are from the T'ang period, and they are slim indeed. There is a T'ang manuscript copy of about half of the *mu* 木 classifier section (*Shuo wen* classifier no. 206), containing 188 entries, and equal to about 2% of the entire text of the book. This fragment has been thoroughly studied by Mo Yu-chih 莫友芝 (1811–71) in his *T'ang hsieh pen Shuo wen chieh tzu mu pu chien i* 唐寫本說文解字木部箋異 (1863; included in *Hsü hsüeh ts'ung shu*, for which see under 7 (a) below). There are also extant two even more meagre samples of a part of the *k'ou* 口 classifier section (no. 22), one fragment with only twelve entries, the other with a mere four. For a study of the phonological implications of these fragments see Chou Tsu-mo, pp. 723–59.

The first post-Han scholar known to have studied and edited the *Shuo wen* is Li Yang-ping 李陽冰 (*fl.* 765–80) who is usually regarded as something of a *bête noire* of *Shuo wen* studies, owing to his idiosyncratic and somewhat capricious editing of the text. Li was by all accounts not well versed in the discipline of *hsiao hsüeh* 小學, i.e. language, text and script studies, which may be termed 'philology'. He nevertheless apparently felt himself qualified to undertake the wholesale revision of Hsü Shen's original text, introducing his own arbitrary and often baseless opinions, frequently in direct contradiction to Hsü's explanations and analyses. None of this would matter a great deal, except for the fact that no editions of the *Shuo wen* prior to Li's re-working of the text are extant. It is therefore felt that it was he who was responsible for the lack of a complete, authentic pre-T'ang version of the work (see Chou Tsu-mo, pp. 801–42).

4. Sung scholarship

After T'ang, *Shuo wen* scholarship can be divided into two parts, of the Sung and Ch'ing periods. The two most important Sung scholars were the brothers Hsü K'ai 徐鍇 (920–74; usually regarded as being of Southern T'ang rather than Sung)) and Hsü Hsüan 徐鉉 (916–91). Conventionally known as the 'younger' and the 'elder' Hsü, their most important contribution was the restoration and elucidation of the text that pre-dated Li Yang-ping. Through careful collation of all available versions, citations, fragments etc., they weeded out the excesses and ill-considered claims that had been the hallmark of the earlier Li Yang-ping edition. But they did not actually work as a team.

Hsü K'ai was intent on explaining the sense of Hsü Shen's original entries, and *chüan* 1 to 30 of his *Shuo wen hsi chuan* 說文繫傳 (in 40 *chüan*) are intended to do this. The remaining ten *chüan* deal with such analytical concerns as determining the rationale behind the order of the 540 classifiers, identifying apparent gaps, inconsistencies and discrepancies in the text. *Chüan* 36 specifically discredits the earlier mistaken claims of Li Yang-ping. In Chou Tsu-mo's view, the best edition of the *Shuo wen hsi chuan* is the woodblock print of Ch'i Chün-tsao 祁寯藻 (1793–1866; see Chou Tsu-mo, pp. 843–51, where Chün appears erroneously as Sui 雟).

Hsü Hsüan's textual work was the direct result of Sung T'ai tsung's commission of 986 to produce a corrected and authoritative edition of the book. Making no effort to duplicate his brother's investigation of the sense of the *Shuo wen*, he concentrated on a strictly text critical study. In the critical edition that he produced, entitled *Chiao ting Shuo wen chieh tzu* 校定說文解字, he divided each *chüan* into two parts (*shang* and *hsia*), added *fan ch'ieh* 反切 pronunciation formulas for each entry and, as already seen, appended to many of the sections a supplement giving characters that were not included in the original text as he knew it. For these additional characters he gave complete entries based exactly on the model of the *Shuo wen* itself; but he carefully distinguished these from the body of Hsü Shen's original text, by setting them in the clearly marked section of *hsin fu tzu* 新附字.

Hsü Hsüan is also held responsible for at least one inappropriate editorial change. This occurs in a number of cases where entries were originally of the form A . . . *ts'ung* X, Y *sheng* (the stock formula for *hsing sheng* characters). When it was not obvious to Hsü, in the light of the phonetic structure of his tenth century Chinese, that the graph Y could be phonophoric in A, he excised the character *sheng* 聲 from the entry, leaving the anomalous formula . . . *ts'ung* X Y.

Nevertheless it is to Hsü Hsüan in particular that we owe all subsequent editions of the *Shuo wen*, so that, as Miller has pointed out (1953, p. 166) Hsü Hsüan's edition is the closest thing that we possess to an *editio princeps*. It is from an undated copy of his *Chiao ting pen* (thought to be from the period 998–1022) that the late Ming edition of Mao Chin 毛晉 (1599–1659) and his son Mao I 毛扆 (1640 to after 1710) was made. And it is precisely with this edition in its turn that Tuan Yü-ts'ai worked. The best edition of Hsü Hsüan's *Chiao ting pen*, again according to Chou tsu-mo, is that of Sun Hsing-yen 孫星衍 (1753–1818) in the *P'ing chin kuan ts'ung shu*. The *Ssu pu ts'ung k'an* series contains a facsimile copy of a Sung woodblock edition of this recension.

5. Ch'ing scholarship

Shuo wen scholarship flourished in the Ch'ing period hand in hand with other textual studies, and the list of philologists who produced *Shuo wen* studies is long indeed. For a comprehensive and well organised survey of Ch'ing scholars, see Lin Ming-po 林明波, *Ch'ing tai Hsü hsüeh k'ao* 清代許學考 (Taipei: Chia hsin shui ni kung ssu, 1964). Four names stand out as pre-eminent: Tuan Yü-ts'ai 段玉裁 (1735–1815); Kuei Fu 桂馥 (1736–1805); Wang Yün 王筠 (1784–1834); and Chu Chün-sheng 朱駿聲 (1788–1858). Of these, Tuan Yü-ts'ai is the most important.

Hsü K'ai and Hsü Hsüan had set a rough kind of model for work on the *Shuo wen*. Hsü K'ai had been primarily concerned with the meaning of what he found in the text and with Hsü Shen's reasons for what he had written; such work may be termed an analytical, or exegetical study. By contrast Hsü Hsüan worked only to establish an authoritative critical edition, engaging himself thus in a straightforward text critical study. On the whole the Ch'ing scholars followed this distinction, only rarely encompassing both original textual criticism and exegesis in a single work. Tuan Yü-ts'ai is the outstanding exception to this pattern, and it is precisely for this reason, together with the depth and overall soundness of his scholarship, that he ranks as the greatest of the *Shuo wen* scholars (see Chou Tsu-mo, pp. 852–84).

Tuan Yü-ts'ai's *Shuo wen chieh tzu chu* 說文解字注 (originally called *Shuo wen chieh tzu tu* 說文解字讀) was begun in 1776 and was not finished until 1807. He did not automatically accept the prior authoritative edition of Hsü Hsüan, but rather insisted on checking questionable and doubtful passages against all the available evidence, i.e., in addition to that of other editions, citations in mediaeval texts such as the *Ching tien shih wen* of Lu Te-ming 陸德明 (556–627) of c. 625, the *I ch'ieh ching yin i*, of T'ang times, commentaries to the standard histories, the *Wen hsüan* and the classics, and such lexicographical works as the *Kuang yün* and the *Yü p'ien*. While still relying on Hsü Hsüan's basically sound text as a starting point, when necessary Tuan repeated much of the work of collating texts of the *Shuo wen* in order to establish his own authoritative edition.

At the same time his analytical and exegetic studies of the *Shuo wen* included an elucidation of some of the general organizational principles of the work, e.g., the order of the classifiers, the order of the characters within each classifier section, the structure of individual entries. He gave his opinions as general principles at appropriate places throughout his commentary to the entries. Thanks to his thorough familiarity with the traditions of lexical usage in the early classics, Tuan was also able to demonstrate the purport of Hsü Shen's definitions and to elaborate the meaning and usage of the words that were being defined.

Tuan Yü-ts'ai's endeavours were not limited to just these two matters of textual criticism and exegesis. His work went well beyond the scope of his predecessors, particularly in the realm of what may be termed 'semasiology'. Recognising the trilateral relation between graph, sound and meaning (*hsing* 形, *sheng* 聲, *i* 義) he was able to explain cases of semantic evolution or extension in ancient and mediaeval texts, where the meaning of a particular word diverged from Hsü Shen's glosses. Tuan's pioneering achievement was to take the related areas of semasiology, phonology and palaeography and make of them a single independent field of study where formerly each had been little more than an isolated adjunct to textual studies, especially to *ching hsüeh* 經學. Tuan Yü-ts'ai's *Shuo wen chieh tzu chu* has been reprinted many times and is widely available, often with a character index appended.

Kuei Fu's *Shuo wen chieh tzu i cheng* 說文解字義證 (50 *chüan*) codifies the author's efforts to trace the source of Hsü Shen's definitions. Thus the work falls into the analytical and exegetic category rather than into that of text criticism. Kuei worked on the *Shuo wen* at the same time as Tuan, but there is no evidence of collaboration between the two. Kuei's scope is considerably narrower than that of Tuan, and his aim is much more specific, viz., to show justification for every one of Hsü Shen's original statements about the meaning of the word in question. In this single-minded pursuit lie both his strongest and his weakest points. The strongest point, and the reason why Kuei's work stands out in importance, is the exceptionally comprehensive coverage of textual sources invoked to explain or justify a given definition. The weakest point is that Kuei never allows himself to question, much less to reject, anything that Hsü Shen had written. He believed every word of the original text as he perceived it to be, even in the face of clear evidence that Hsü Shen was, every now and again, wrong. He goes to extreme lengths to demonstrate textual support for what are patently incorrect glosses in the *Shuo wen*.

In his *Shuo wen chieh tzu chü tu* 說文解字句讀 (30 *chüan*, finished in 1850), Wang Yün integrated the work of Tuan Yü-ts'ai, Kuei Fu and Yen K'o-chün 嚴可均 (1762–1843), together with the results of his own studies, into a single comprehensive commentary. Wang's main effort in this work was to bring the results of these three scholars together into some kind of overall system and order through the judicious editing of each of their various notes; he hoped in this way to make *Shuo wen* scholarship more accessible to a wider community of learning than had been the case previously.

Wang Yün is also the author of the *Shuo wen shih li* 說文釋例 (20 *chüan*; 1865). This is a less comprehensive and more discursive work on graphic structure, and on the relation between graph, sound and meaning as he saw it, without reliance on or reference to classical texts for meanings and usages. The *Shih li* is organized as a collection of essays on various features of the *Shuo wen*, or of the graphic system that it represents, and does not follow the *Shuo wen*'s dictionary format. It was written before the *Shuo wen chü tu*, and it is generally regarded as the less significant of the two works, though this is not necessarily a fair judgement. In fact Wang's capacity for original observations and suggestions is perhaps more in evidence in the *Shih li* than in his later work. One of the important features of the *Shih li* is its recourse to bronze inscriptions in discussions on the relation between graph and sound.

Chu Chün-sheng's *Shuo wen t'ung hsün ting sheng* 說文通訓定聲 (1833) consists of eighteen sections. Each one is called a *pu* 部, and comprises a single one of the old Chinese rhyme groups; overall the eighteen sections match the eighteen *Shih ching* rhymes proposed by Tuan Yü-ts'ai, though with different names. Typically, but not always, an entry consists of four parts: (i) the definition and analysis of the *Shuo wen*, with Chu's own notes; (ii) a part that he labels *chuan chu* 轉注, by which term he seems to signify semantic specialisations and extensions in meaning; (iii) a part giving *chia chieh* 假借 usages in early texts; and (iv) a part listing rhyming contexts in pre-Han works. It is clear just from the arrangement of Chu's work that he had a very definite idea of the importance of pronunciation, and of the relation between graph and sound. He benefitted in particular from the conceptual work of Tuan Yü-ts'ai, but his treatment of the evidence is a step that is further developed and shows a keen recognition of the phonological versatility and complexity of the writing system, and in general reveals a very sophisticated understanding of the relation between writing and language. For his accomplishments in creative scholarly thinking Chu Chün-sheng ranks second only to Tuan Yü-ts'ai, and his *Shuo wen ting sheng* (as his work is often abbreviated) is as much a work of original scholarship as it is a commentary to the *Shuo wen*.

6. Twentieth century studies

Three important names should be added to those of Chou Tsu-mo, Miller and Serruys who are all mentioned above.

(a) Ting Fu-pao 丁福保 (1874–1952), whose monumental *Shuo wen chieh tzu ku lin* 說文解字詁林 was first published in 1932 (Shanghai: Shang wu; reproduced in 12 volumes, Taipei: Shang wu, 1959). Ting Fu-pao brought virtually all extant commentaries, exegeses and notes on the *Shuo wen* (a total of 182 works) together into a single encyclopaedic collection, so that under each entry the reader has at hand every pertinent known annotation or discussion. Moreover he added a section of *chia ku wen* 甲骨文 and *chin wen* 金文 forms of the graphs, as known until 1932, at the end of each entry. The *Ku lin* also reproduces all prefaces and *Postface*s to the various editions and studies that have been incorporated. A character index to the entries is arranged according to the conventional 214 classifiers. The sheer volume and comprehensive nature of this collection make it the single major work in *Shuo wen* studies of the twentieth century to date.

(b) In the 1950s Ma Tsung-huo 馬宗霍 (1898–) completed a set of four studies that cite passages from other pre-Han or Han texts and scholars:

    (i) *Shuo wen chieh tzu yin ching k'ao* 說文解字引經考; preface 1955; Peking: Ko hsüeh, n.d.; photo-reprint Taipei: Hsüeh sheng, 1971.

    (ii) *Shuo wen chieh tzu yin ch'ün shu k'ao* 說文解字引群書考; preface April 1956; Peking: K'o hsüeh, 1959; photo-reprint Taipei: Hsüeh sheng, 1973.

    (iii) *Shuo wen chieh tzu yin t'ung jen shuo k'ao* 說文解字引通人說考; preface June 1956; Peking: K'o-hsüeh, 1959; photo-reprint Taipei: Hsüeh sheng, 1973.

    (iv) *Shuo wen chieh tzu yin fang yen k'ao* 說文解字引方言考; preface 1957; Peking: K'o hsüeh, 1959.

In each of these works Ma Tsung-huo individually scrutinizes all entries in the *Shuo wen* that cite a line or phrase from the sources in question, collating the cited forms with the passages as they exist in the current, received versions, and discussing the differences and variations as they occur. After giving the comments and notes of earlier scholars on the citation at issue he concludes with his own suggestions and explanations or remarks.

(c) The third important Chinese *Shuo wen* scholar who deserves special mention is Ma Hsü-lun 馬敘倫 (1884–1970), with two major works.

    (i) *Shuo wen chieh tzu yen chiu fa* 說文解字研究法; Shanghai: Shang wu, 1929; reprinted Hong Kong: T'ai p'ing, 1970. This is a collection of essays on various aspects of *Shuo wen* studies, such as the history of the text, the different types of script preserved in the text, the classifiers, the correspondence between graph, sound and meaning, Han dialects, graphic structure and citations from other texts.

(ii) *Shuo wen chieh tzu liu shu shu cheng* 說文解字六書疏證; photocopy of the original manuscript, Peking: K'o hsüeh, 1957. This is a very large study of the *liu shu* 六書 analysis of the writing system as preserved in the *Shuo wen*, presented in an entry by entry examination of the whole of the text. In his preface, Ma Hsü-lun states that he began his work in 1911, and that by the time of his graduation in 1928 he did not consider the manuscript finished. In fact, even as it is now published a large part is simply a photo-copy of what is clearly a cursively written draft manuscript; the author makes it clear that he does not regard the work as definitive. It is, nevertheless, a voluminous and valuable work.

In 1939 a scholarly journal with the title *Shuo wen yüeh k'an* 說文月刊, founded, edited and personally financed by Wei Chü-hsien 衛聚賢, began publication in Shanghai. The journal moved to Chungking in the early 1940s, and seems to have ceased publication in 1945 after only five volumes had appeared. Contributors included such major scholars as Ting Fu-pao and Ma Hsü-lun. In spite of the implication of the title, the journal contains many articles that are not directly related to *Shuo wen* scholarship, but which deal with various topics that extend over the whole range of traditional Chinese textual, philological and linguistic research.

7. Research aids

(a) Other important research and reference materials include the following items.

(i) Chang Ping-hsiang 張炳翔, *Hsü hsüeh ts'ung shu* 許學叢書, 1887. This *ts'ung shu* contains fourteen titles of thirteen Ch'ing scholars, most of which are not found readily elsewhere; reprinted in Yen I-p'ing 嚴一萍 (ed.), *Pai pu ts'ung shu chi ch'eng* 百部叢書集成, Pan-ch'iao (Taiwan): I wen, 1965.

(ii) Shirakawa Shizuka 白川靜, Setsumon shingi 說文新義; Kyoto: Goten shoin, 1969; a voluminous, item by item study of every entry in the *Shuo wen*, by one of Japan's foremost scholars of Chinese language and texts.

(iii) Serruys, Paul L-M., 'On the system of the *pu shou* (部首) in the *Shuo wen chieh tzu*; *BIHP* 55 (1984), 651–754. This includes English translations for every one of the 540 *Shuo wen* classifiers, as well as meticulously detailed and thorough lexicographical notes for each item.

(b) Items under reference above.

(i) Boodberg, P.A., 'The Chinese script: an essay in nomenclature (the first hecaton)'; *BIHP* 29 (1957), 113–20.

(ii) Chou Tsu-mo 周祖謨, *Wen hsüeh chi* 問學集, 2 vols.; Peking: Chung hua, 1966: (a) *Hsü Shen chi ch'i Shuo wen chieh tzu* 許慎及其說文解字 (pp. 710–22); (b) *T'ang pen Shuo wen yü Shuo wen chiu yin* 唐本說文與說文舊音 (pp. 723–59); (c) *Li Yang-p'ing chuan shu k'ao* 李陽冰篆書考 (pp. 801–42); (d) *Hsü K'ai ti Shuo wen hsüeh* 徐鍇的說文學 (pp. 843–51); and (e) *Lun Tuan shih Shuo wen chieh tzu chu* 論段氏說文解字注 (pp. 852–84).

(iii) Coblin, W. South, 'The initials of Xu Shen's language as reflected in the *Shuowen duruo* glosses'; *Journal of Chinese Linguistics* 6 (1978), 27–75.

(iv) Miller, Roy Andrew, 'Problems in the Study of *Shuo wen chieh tzu*'; unpublished PhD dissertation, Columbia University, 1953.

(v) Miller, Roy Andrew, 'The Wu-ching i-i of Hsü Shen'; *MS* 33, 1977–78, 1–21.

(vi) Serruys, Paul L.M., 'A study of the chuan chu in Shuo wen'; *BIHP* 29 (1957), 131–95.

(vii) Thern, K.L., *Postface* of the *Shuo wen chieh tzu*; Madison, Wisconsin: University of Wisconsin, 1966.

A full bibliography of modern *Shuo wen* studies and scholarship can be found in sections 5.1.1.3 and 12.3.4 of Paul Fu-mien Yang, *Chinese Linguistics: a Selected and Annotated Bibliography*; Hong Kong: Chinese University of Hong Kong, 1974. This includes Chinese, Japanese and Western works up to the early 1970s.

8. Index

A Concordance to the Shouwen jiezi 說文解字逐字索引, ed. D.C. Lau and Chen Fong Ching; *ICS* series, Hong Kong: Commercial Press, forthcoming 1996.

— William G. Boltz

Shuo yüan 說苑

1. Content

The *Shuo yüan* is a collection of moral tales and political admonitions assembled by Liu Hsiang 劉向 (79–8 B.C.), with a received text that contains 639 items in 20 *chüan*. Like the *Hsin hsü*, the *Shuo yüan* mainly consists of material derived from earlier texts (see under *Hsin hsü*). Each of the 20 *chüan* is a chapter that pertains to a particular theme, and almost every *chüan* has a paragraph introducing the theme, followed by a series of illustrative stories. Many of the *chüan* centre round the idea that the ruler must employ talented and virtuous officials, and that he should not hesitate to accept their criticism and advice (nos. 12 and 7–9). No. 11 contains examples of model types of persuasion that illustrate the efficacy of heeding good advice; no. 16 is a collection of aphorisms that are mainly concerned with the proper conduct of rulers and officials. Other *chüan* discuss the necessity of caution and vigilance by individuals and the state (no. 10); tactics and schemes, which must be used only for the public good and not for self-interest (no. 13); the need for military preparedness in times of peace (no. 15); and the importance of proper ritual forms and music (no. 19), while maintaining simplicity and avoiding extravagance (no. 20).

2. Date of composition and authorship

In the entry for the *Shuo yüan* in the *Pieh lu* 別錄, Liu Hsiang states that he collated a group of texts called *Shuo yüan tsa shih* 說苑雜事, which were held in the imperial library, against texts in his own collection and those 'from the people'. He eliminated material that duplicated that which was found in the *Hsin hsü* and that which was 'superficial and not in accord with reason'; and he appended this to a collection of fanciful stories known as the *Pai chia* 百家; the remaining material he organised into a work that he named *Hsin yüan* 新苑.

Parts of Liu Hsiang's account present problems. It is not clear whether *Shuo yüan tsa shih* is the name of an actual book, or simply means 'congeries of persuasions and miscellaneus stories'. Furthermore, scholars

443

have noted that in spite of Liu Hsiang's claim to have removed material that duplicated the text of the *Hsin hsü*, the two works in fact do contain a number of almost identical entries. Finally, there is the variant title *Hsin yüan*. Hsü Fu-kuan 徐復觀 suggests that the original title was *Hsin yüan*, and that when Pan Ku 班固 (32–92) wrote Liu Hsiang's biography, he purposely or erroneously changed the title to *Shuo yüan*. However one understands the account in the *Pieh lu*, it is clear that, like the *Hsin hsü*, the *Shuo yüan* is basically a collection which was edited rather than composed by Liu Hsiang, who, as he states in the *Pieh lu*, selected 784 items (*chang* 章); organised them in 20 *p'ien*; gave titles to the chapters and presented the work to the throne in 17 B.C.

3. Textual history

According to the *Pieh lu*, the text consisted of 20 *p'ien*. The *Sui shu* (34, p. 997) and Fujiwara Sukeyo's catalogue list the work in 20 *chüan*; the *Chiu T'ang shu* (47, p. 2024) and the *Hsin T'ang shu* (59, p. 1510) record the *Shuo yüan* as a work of 30 *chüan*, but Lu Wen-ch'ao 盧文弨 (1717–1796) and others have suggested that the figure of 30 is a mistake for 20. In all these cases the work is entered under *ju chia* 儒家. By the Northern Sung period, a complete text no longer existed. The *Ch'ung wen tsung mu* notes that only a fragment of 5 *chüan* was preserved in the imperial library. In his preface, Tseng Kung 曾鞏 (1019–83) cites this as 5 *p'ien*; he states that he was able to obtain 15 *p'ien* from other scholars, and that he combined these with the original five *p'ien*, thereby restoring the work to 20 *p'ien*. However, the version that he established lacked no. 20 ('Fan chih' 反質); to create a text in 20 *p'ien*, Tseng Kung split no 19 ('Hsiu wen' 修文) into two parts. Later, no. 20 was supplied from a text obtained from Korea.

4. Editions

(a) The earliest known printed edition is a woodblock issued by Chen chiang fu hsüeh 鎮江府學 in 1265. Copies of this edition which had been 'repaired' during the Ming dynasty are held in the National Library of China and the Fu Ssu-nien Library in Taiwan; it is the basis for the text that is printed in the *Kuang Han Wei ts'ung shu*.

(b) The most important of the numerous Ming prints of the *Shuo yüan* include the *Liu shih erh shu* 劉氏二書, issued by Yang Mei-i 楊美益 in 1559, and a woodblock prepared by Wu Mien-hsüeh 吳勉學 during the period 1573–1620. A facsimile of a Ming manuscript of unknown provenance has been included in the *Ssu pu ts'ung k'an*; the *Ssu pu pei yao* is based on an unspecified Ming woodblock print.

(c) The work was included in the *Lung hsi ching she ts'ung shu*; the text of the *Han Wei ts'ung shu* was reprinted, with punctuation, in the *Ts'ung shu chi ch'eng* series.

(d) Liu Wen-tien 劉文典, *Shuo yüan chiao pu* 說苑斠補; Kunming: Yün-nan ta hsüeh, 1928.

(e) Tso Sung-ch'ao 左松超, *Shuo yüan chi ch'eng* 說苑集證; Taipei: Wen shih che, 1961.

5. Annotation without text

(a) Lu Wen-ch'ao 盧文弨 (1717–96), *Shuo yüan chiao cheng* 說苑校正; *Ch'ün shu shih pu* (*Pao ching t'ang ts'ung shu*).

(b) Sun I-jang 孫詒讓 (1848–1908), in *Cha i*.

(c) Chin Chia-hsi 金嘉錫, *Shuo yüan pu cheng* 說苑補正; Taipei: Taiwan Ta hsüeh, 1960.

6. Recent studies

See under *Hsin hsü* 7 (b), (e) (f) and (g), for works by Lo Ken-tse, Hsü Fu-kuan, Ikeda Shūzō and Yen Ling-feng.

7. Modern Chinese version

Lu Yüan-chün 盧元駿, *Shuo yüan chin chu chin i* 說苑今註今譯; Taipei: Shang wu, 1967.

8. Japanese editions

K. *Chūgoku koten bungaku taikei*, no. 6, 1974, edited by Iikura Shōhei.

L. *Chūgoku koten shinsho*, 1969, edited by Takagi Tomonosuke.

9. Indexes

(a) *Shuo yüan yin te* (*Index to Shuo Yüan*); Harvard-Yenching Index no. 1 (1st ed. Peiping, 1931; reprinted Taipei; Ch'eng wen, 1966).

(b) *A Concordance to the Shuoyuan* 說苑逐字索引, ed. D.C. Lau and Chen Fong Ching; *ICS* series, Hong Kong: Commercial Press, 1992.

— David R. Knechtges

Sun tzu ping fa 孫子兵法

1. Content and structure

The *Sun tzu ping fa*, also known as the *Sun tzu*, is the most important surviving treatise of the school of strategy (*ping chia* 兵家). The work describes various methods of warfare and conflict between states, including diplomacy, economic measures, and what we might call military intelligence. Being concerned with struggles between warring states, the book has long been regarded as a textbook on the achievement of supremacy over enemies or partners. Its theories were also applied to social relationships, political manoeuvres and the attainment of success in economic ventures, or even personal affairs and artistic creativity. As a theoretical basis for many techniques of fighting, the book is concerned with attaining mastery by any means, fair or foul. Its fundamental thesis is that war is based on deception, and it teaches the ways of manipulating adversaries or partners as a means of achieving superiority.

The work is set out in a strict logical manner such that successive paragraphs follow immediately from their predecessors. It is divided into thirteen *p'ien*, and many of its statements are preceded by the formula 'Sun tzu yüeh' 孫子曰 thus introducing Sun tzu's own teaching. *P'ien* no. 1, (*Shih*) *chi* (始) 計 stresses the need to evaluate the various factors that may lead to success or failure and to make due preparations; *p'ien* no. 2, *Tso chan* 作戰 analyses the economic aspect of war; no. 3, *Mou kung* 謀攻 recommends the avoidance of costly combat, if possible by political or diplomatic means. *P'ien* nos. 4, 5 and 6, (*Chün*) *hsing* (軍) 形, (*Ping*) *shih* (兵) 勢 and *Hsü shih* 虛實 concern methods of deceiving an enemy, manipulating human energy and the different uses of direct (*cheng* 正) and indirect (*ch'i* 奇) action; these themes are further discussed in *p'ien* nos. 7 and 8, *Chün cheng* 軍爭 and *Chiu pien* 九變. Nos. 9 to 13, *Hsing chün* 行軍, *Ti hsing* 地形, *Chiu ti* 九地, *Huo kung* 火攻 and *Yung chien* 用間 concern differences of terrain, exploitation of different types of situation and methods of discovering an enemy's intentions. Intelligence and sabotage, both military and political, are shown to be one of the decisive factors in waging war and achieving final success.

Analysis of the text shows that all of its parts can be dated to approximately the same period, but allowance must be made for editorial changes and some interpolation. There are some quotations from earlier military texts.

2. Origin and authenticity

According to an early tradition, mentioned in *Shih chi* 65, p. 2161, a text on military matters in 13 *p'ien* had been written before the imperial period by Sun Wu 孫武 of Ch'i 齊 and had been read by Ho Lu 闔廬 king of Wu 吳 (reigned 514–495 B.C.) There are also references in the *Han fei tzu* and the *Hsün tzu*. The authenticity of the received text has been sub]ect to controversy, at least since the time of Yeh Shih 葉適 (1150–1223), who cast doubt on the historical existence of Sun Wu, on the grounds that he is not mentioned in the *Tso chuan*. He further believed that the terms of the text applied more to the Warring States than to the Spring and Autumn period. His view that the work was written at the beginning of the Warring States period has been accepted by scholars of the Sung and Ch'ing periods and by modern Chinese, Japanese and western critics. In particular Liang Ch'i-ch'ao 梁啓超 (1873–1929) suggested that the work had been written by Sun Wu's descendant Sun Pin 孫臏 (?378–?301 B.C.). This view was supported by Ch'i Ssu-ho 齊思和 (b. 1907) whose comprehensive study of the authenticity of the work is listed under 5 (f) below. But as will be seen below, recently discovered evidence invalidates that conclusion.

Doubts regarding the work are also occasioned by the different records of its divisions and its size, as follows:

Shih chi 65, p. 2161	13 *p'ien*
Han shu 30, p. 1756	82 *p'ien* and 9 *chüan* of illustrations
Ch'i lu 七錄 (cited in *Sui shu* 34, p. 1012)	3 *chüan*, with notes by Ts'ao Ts'ao 曹操 (155–220).
	2 *chüan*, with notes by Meng Shih 孟氏.
	2 *chüan*, edited by Shen Yu 沈友.
	1 *chüan* of 'illustrations of Sun tzu's eight formations' *Sun tzu pa chen t'u* 孫子八陣圖.
Sui shu 34, p. 1012	2 *chüan*, with notes by Ts'ao Ts'ao.
	1 *chüan*, with notes by Ts'ao Ts'ao and Wang Ling 王凌.
	2 *chüan*, entitled *Sun wu ping ching* 孫武兵經 with notes by Chang Tzu-shang 張子尙.

Chang Shou-chieh 張守節 (note 2, *Shih chi* 65, p. 2162)	3 *chüan* as listed in the *Ch'i lu*; wherein 13 *p'ien* form the first *chüan*.
Fujiwara Sukeyo's list	2 *chüan*
Chiu T'ang shu 47, p. 2039	13 *chüan*, with Ts'ao Ts'ao's notes; this entry is evidently an error for 13 *p'ien*.
Hsin T'ang shu 47, p. 2039	3 *chüan*, with Ts'ao Ts'ao's notes.
Ch'ung wen tsung mu	1 *chüan*; separate copies with notes by Ts'ao Ts'ao, Hsiao Chi 蕭吉, Ch'en Hao 陳皞 and Chia Lin 賈林.
	2 *chüan*, with notes by Ho Yen-hsi 何延錫.
Chün chai tu shu chih 14, 7b	1 *chüan*, with Ts'ao Ts'ao's notes.
Wen hsien t'ung k'ao 221, p. 1788B	1 *chüan*, with Ts'ao Ts'ao's notes.

Two further considerations affect the question of authenticity.

(a) Ts'ao Ts'ao (155–220) is the earliest commentator to the book to be named, and his preface makes it clear that he edited the text, eliminating certain passages. The extent of his contribution and of the changes that he introduced thus remains subject to question.

(b) *Han shu* 30, pp. 1756–57 lists two items, viz. *Wu Sun tzu ping fa* 吳孫子兵法 and *Ch'i Sun tzu* 齊孫子, the latter being said to comprise 89 *p'ien*, with four *chüan* of illustrations. It must therefore be asked whether there were in fact two original and separate compilations, or two versions of the same text, and which version it was that survived for transmission.

Considerable light has been shed on these problems by the discovery in 1972 of several military documents on wooden strips in grave no. 1 of the Yin-ch'üeh-shan 銀雀山 site (Lin-i 臨沂, Shantung), which may be dated between 134 and 118 B.C. (see Michael Loewe, 'Manuscripts found recently in China: a preliminary survey'; *TP* 63:2–3 (1977), 131f.). These manuscripts included two texts which were entitled respectively (i) *Sun tzu ping fa* (sometimes called *Sun Wu ping fa* 孫武兵法) and (ii) *Sun Pin ping fa* 孫臏兵法. Of these the *Sun tzu ping fa* is earlier than the received version that had been edited by Ts'ao Ts'ao. The contents of the 13 *p'ien* of this newly found manuscript are matched very closely by those of the received version, and amount to about one-third of the latter. This also includes some text material that does not appear in the received version. To the extent that we can judge from this manuscript, it seems that Ts'ao Ts'ao did not introduce substantial changes. He may perhaps have been relying on a version different from that to which the received version should be traced, as his commentary suggests. There were also some apocryphal texts attributed to Sun tzu, as may be seen in a number of fragmentary strips found in Ch'ing-hai that carry passages from the text of the *Sun tzu* with some differences from the transmitted text; see *Wen wu* 1981.2, 21 and 25–26, and *TP* 72 (1986), 303–04.

Of greatest significance overall is the confirmation by the finds from Yin-ch'üeh-shan of the existence of the two separate texts, *Sun tzu ping fa* and *Sun Pin ping fa*. Sun Pin's work is unquestionably the later of the two, referring as it does to the *Sun tzu ping fa* whose ideas it explains and expands. It does not have any transmitted counterpart.

The finds fron Yin-ch'üeh-shan also confirm the existence of other writings on military subjects. It is possible that the copy of the *Sun tzu* which is listed in the *Han shu* with 82 *p'ien* may have included these other works; and that the copies that are noted in the later lists with 2 or 3 *chüan* may have included the 13 *p'ien* of the *Sun tzu* in the first *chüan*, with other writings being included in the second or third *chüan*. In the earliest printed edition now available the 13 *p'ien* are themselves set out in 3 *chüan*, and citations of the *Sun tzu* that appear in mediaeval books are derived exclusively from those 13 *p'ien*.

The newly excavated material supports the view that the 13 *p'ien* were compiled in their present form towards the end of the Spring and Autumn period. Cheng Liang-shu 鄭良樹 (b. 1940) dates authorship to between 496 and 453. Kuo Hua-jo 郭化若 concludes that the text had been shaped over a comparatively long period. These views are in general agreement with those expressed by Giles and Konrad.

3.   Early editions and versions

The choice of books for inclusion in the *Wu ching ch'i shu* 武經七書 was determined by Sung Shen-tsung 宋神宗 (reigned 1068–1085) in 1080. These were:

   (i) *Sun tzu ping fa;*
   (ii) *Wu tzu ping fa* 吳子兵法 (ascribed to Wu Ch'i 吳起 440–381);
   (iii) *Liu t'ao* 六韜 (probably Warring States period);
   (iv) *Ssu-ma fa* 司馬法 (ascribed to Ssu-ma Jang-chü 司馬穰苴 of the sixth century B.C., but in reality certainly much later, perhaps of the fourth century B.C.);
   (v) *San lüeh* 三略 (perhaps written in the fifth or sixth century A.D.);
   (vi) *Yü Liao tzu* 尉繚子 (ascribed to Yü Liao, *fl.* 335–319);
   (vii) *Li Wei Kung wen tui* 李衛公問對 (written in the T'ang period, as a dialogue between T'ang T'ai tsung 唐太宗 (reigned 627–49) and his general Li Ching 李靖 (571–649).

Of these the *Sun tzu ping fa* and the *Wu tzu ping fa* were always placed at the beginning of the collection, the former being accompanied by comments ascribed to Ts'ao Ts'ao.

(a) A Sung print of the *Wu ching ch'i shi* of 1080 included the *Sun tzu* in three *chüan* (13 *p'ien*) without annotation. This text is available in *Hsü ku i ts'ung shu*, 38, which reproduces an edition said to have been made by Ho Ch'ü-fei 何去非 (*c*. 1023–after 1095); this was made from a copy held in the Seikadō library. Reduced versions have been included in the *Sung Yüan Ming shan pen ts'ung shu shih chung* 宋元明善本叢書十種 (1935) and the *Chung kuo ping hsüeh ta hsi* 中國兵學大系 (preface 1957, edited by Li Yü-jih 李浴日). The *Sun tzu* was included (3 *chüan*) in the *Wu ching ch'i shu chih chieh* 武經七書直解 with annotation by Liu Yin 劉寅 1398. This edition with a preface by Li Min 李敏 of 1486 was reproduced in 1933 on the basis of a Japanese facsimile of 1864. More recently it has been reproduced in Taipei by the *Shih ti chiao yü ch'u pan she* (1972).

(b) *Wei Wu-ti chu Sun tzu san chüan* 魏武帝註孫子三卷; reproduction of a Sung print with Ts'ao Tsao's annotation, in *P'ing chin kuan ts'ung shu (chia)*, 1800. An edition of this text and notes, in two *chüan*, is included in some versions of the *Han Wei ts'ung shu* reprinted, with punctuation, in *Ts'ung shu chi ch'eng*.

(c) A text with annotations assembled from ten commentators beginning with Ts'ao Ts'ao and extending to scholars of the eleventh century was edited by Chi T'ien-pao 吉天保 (11th to 12th centuries), and has been published under various titles such as *Sun tzu shih chia chu shih san chüan* 孫子十家註十三卷. In addition to Ts'ao Ts'ao, Meng Shih, Ch'en Hao, Chia Lin and Ho Yen-hsi, as mentioned above, the ten included Li Ch'üan 李筌 (8th to 9th century), Tu Mu 杜牧 (803–52), Mei Yao-ch'en 梅堯臣 (1002–60), Wang Che (or Hsi) 王哲 (晳) and Chang Yü 張預. This edition has appeared in collections such as the *Tao tsang*, on the basis of which it was reprinted in the *Tai nan ko ts'ung shu*, with preface and annotation by Sun Hsing-yen 孫星衍 (1753–1818) and Wu Jen-chi 吳人驥 (*chin shih* 1766). Sun Hsing-yen made up deficiencies in the text with the help of citations found in the *T'ung tien* and the *T'ai p'ing yü lan*. Some of his notes were removed in the process of imperial censorship. The *Ssu pu pei yao* follows the text of the *Tai nan ko ts'ung shu*. The *Ssu pu ts'ung k'an* reproduces a copy that was printed in 1555, under the title *Sun tzu chi chu* 孫子集註.

A defective copy of this edition, entitled *Shih i chia chu Sun tzu* 十

一家註孫子, which is held in the Shanghai Library may be dated to the period 1195–1224. The figure of eleven commentators is given here owing to the inclusion of Tu Yu 杜佑 (735–812), who was not counted among the ten. Two other copies of this edition are held in the National Library, Peking. A complete text, assembled by collecting parts from all the copies, was published in facsimile by Kuo Hua-jo in 1961 (Shanghai: Chung hua; see under 4(f) below).

(d) *Sun tzu shu chiao chieh yin lei* 孫子書校解引類 compiled by Chao Pen-hsüeh 趙本學 (Ming period; commoner without official posting) and published by Liang Chien-meng 梁見孟 in the Wan-li 萬曆 (1573–1619) period with a preface signed by Kuo Li-hua 郭理化 dated 1615. A feature of this edition is the inclusion of specific historical examples to elucidate the text. It has been reproduced by Taipei: Chung hua, 1970.

4. Modern editions

(a) Ch'en Ch'i-t'ien 陳啓天, *Sun tzu ping fa chiao shih* 孫子兵法校釋; Shanghai: Chung hua, 1944.

(b) Yang Ping-an 楊炳安 *Sun tzu chi chiao* 孫子集校; Peking: Chung hua, 1959, with reprints in China and Hong Kong.

(c) Kuo Hua-jo 郭化若 *Chin i hsin pien Sun tzu ping fa* 今譯新編孫子兵法; Peking: Jen min, 1957; reprinted several times. A rather free version in modern Chinese accompanies the text (simplified characters).

(d) Kuo Hua-jo, *Sun tzu chin i* 孫子今譯; Shanghai: Ku chi, 1977; a modern version of the text precedes the text from Yin-ch'üeh-shan (annotated)

(e) Kuo Hua-jo, *Shih i chia chu Sun tzu fu chin i* 十一家注孫子附今譯; Shanghai: Chung hua, 1962; text with traditional commentators' notes and Kuo Hua-jo's modern version; republished 1978, in simplified characters, with the text from Yin-ch'üeh-shan (in an appendix).

(f) Kuo Hua-jo, *Sung pen shih i chia Sun tzu fu Sun tzu chin i* 宋本十一家孫子附孫子今譯; first edition Shanghai: Chung hua, 1961; second edition 1978, with modern version and text from Yin-ch'üeh-shan.

(g) Kuo Hua-jo, *Sun tzu i chu* 孫子譯注; Shanghai: Ku chi, 1984. Of all Kuo Hua-jo's works this is perhaps the most valuable. There is a revised description of the text with an account of authorship and its significance, a free modern translation, the original text with a literal modern Chinese translation, and detailed notes of all variants, including those of the copy from Yin-ch'üeh-shan.

(h) Wei Ju-lin 魏汝霖 *Sun tzu chin chu chin i* 孫子今註今譯; punctuated and annotated text is followed by a version in modern Chinese; Tai-pei: Shang wu, 1972.

(i) *Chung kuo ku tai ping fa* 中國古代兵法; Peking: Chün shih hsüeh yüan chün shih tzu liao shih 軍事學院軍事資料室, 1982.

(j) Wu Ju-sung 吳如嵩, *Sun tzu ping fa ch'ien shuo* 孫子兵法淺說; Shen-yang: Chieh fang chün, 1983.

(k) Yang Ping-an 楊炳安, *Sun tzu hui chien* 孫子會箋; [Sian]: Chung chou ku chi, 1986; this presents all existing versions of the text; the text excavated at Yin-ch'üeh-shan; so called 'lost texts' — quotations from *Sun tzu* preserved in various mediaeval sources; and an index of the characters with an explanation of their meanings and the phrases in which they appear.

(l) *Wu ching ch'i shu chu i* 武經七書注譯; Peking: Chieh fang chün, 1986; the work is included in this collection.

(m) Kao T'i-kan 高体乾 (ed.), *Chung kuo ping shu chi ch'eng* 中國兵書集成; Shen-yang: Chieh fang chün, vol. 1, 1987, vol. 12, 1990; various editions of the *Sun tzu* are included.

(n) Huang K'uei 黃葵, *Sun tzu tao tu* 孫子導讀; Cheng tu: Pa Shu, 1989; includes quotations from *Sun tzu* in various sources or from the texts ascribed to Sun Wu, and an index of characters and phrases in which they occur; excellent, despite some omissions.

(o) Wu Chiu-lung 吳九龍 (ed.), *Sun tzu chiao shih* 孫子校釋; Peking: Chün shih k'o hsüeh, 1990; refers to other versions of the text, ren-derings in modern Chinese and translations into English, Russian, Japanese and Italian.

(p) Hsü Pao-lin 許保林, *Chung kuo ping shu t'ung lan* 中國兵書通覽; Peking: Chieh fang chün, 1990. This work describes all traditional books on military affairs, including *Sun tzu* and its various editions.

(q) *Sun tzu hsin t'an: Chung wai hsüeh che lun Sun tzu* 孫子新探: 中外學者論孫子; Peking: Chieh fang chün, 1990. This includes the studies presented at the first International Symposium on Sun Tzu's *Art of War* (1989), with a highly useful bibliography of books and studies of between 1954 and 1988. Publication of the papers of the second symposium (1990) is planned.

5. Commentators and annotations

(a) Separate comments by Cheng Yu-hsien 鄭友賢 (Sung period) are appended to the *Tao tsang* and *Tai nan ko ts'ung shu* editions, and to some of the prints which include the notes of the ten or eleven scholars.

(b) The *Sun tzu* was included in the *Ch'i shu chiang i* 七書講義 of Shih Tzu-mei 施子美 (Chin 金 period). This work was lost in China and exists now principally in the form of a reprint made in Japan in 1863.

(c) Yü Yüeh 俞樾 (1821–1907); see *Chu tzu p'ing i*, ch. 3

(d) Sun I-jang 孫詒讓 (1848–1908), see *Cha i*, ch. 9

(e) Li Yü-jih 李浴日, *Sun tzu ping fa chih tsung ho yen chiu* 孫子兵法之綜合研究 Ch'ang-sha: Shang wu, 1938.

(f) Ch'i Ssu-ho 齊思和, 'Sun tzu chu tso shih tai k'ao' 孫子著作時代考; in *Yen ching hsüeh pao* 26 (1939) 175–90.

(g) Huang Chih-hsiang 黃志祥, 'Sun tzu (ping fa) shu mu chi lun wen p'ien mu' 孫子 (兵法) 書目及論文篇目; in *Shu mu chi k'an* 14:3 (1980), 78–87.

(h) Cheng Liang-shu 鄭良樹, 'Lun Sun tzu ti tso ch'eng shih tai' 論孫子的作成時代, in his *Chu chien po shu lun wen chi* 竹簡帛書論文集, Peking: Chung hua, 1982, pp. 47–86.

(i) Wang Hsien-ch'en 王顯臣 and Hsü Pao-lin 許保林, *Chung kuo ku tai ping shu tsa t'an* 中國古代兵書雜談, Peking: Chan shih, 1983.

6.   Studies of the Yin-ch'üeh-shan manuscript fragments

(a) Yin-ch'üeh-shan Han mu chu chien cheng li hsiao tsu 銀雀山漢墓竹簡整理小組 (ed.), *Yin-ch'üeh-shan Han mu chu chien Sun tzu ping fa* 銀雀山漢墓竹簡孫子兵法; Peking: Wen-wu, 1976.

(b) Yin-ch'üeh-shan Han mu chu chien cheng li hsiao tsu (ed.), *Yin-ch'üeh-shan Han mu chu chien*, vol. 1, Peking: Wen wu, 1985. This series will include plates, tracings and annotated transcriptions (using full-form characters) of the bamboo material found at Yin-ch'üeh-shan. Volume 1 includes *Sun tzu ping fa*, *Sun Pin ping fa*, *Yü Liao tzu*, *Yen tzu* 晏子, *Liu t'ao* and *Shou fa shou ling teng shih san pien* 守法守令等十三篇.

(c) Wu Chiu-lung 吳九龍, *Yin-ch'üeh-shan Han chien shih wen* 銀雀山漢簡釋文, Peking: Wen wu, 1985; transcriptions, in full characters, of all strips from tombs numbers 1 and 2 in serial order.

(d) Yin-ch'üeh-shan Han mu chu chien cheng li hsiao tsu (ed.), *Sun Pin ping fa*; Peking: Wen wu, 1975. This volume includes a transcription of the text in abbreviated characters together with some plates of the originals in reduced format. There follow reprints of the archaeological report on the site (for original, see *Wen wu* 1974.2, 15); of Wei Chin 衛今, 'Ts'ung Yin-ch'üeh-shan chu chien k'an Ch'in shih huang fen shu' 從銀雀山竹簡看秦始皇焚書 (for original, see *Hung ch'i* 1974, no. 7); and of the text of Sun Wu's biography in *Shih chi* 65.

A Japanese version of this book, *Son Hin heihō*, with transcription
(full characters) printed alongside tracings of the strips, followed by
punctuated and annotated text, was published by Kanaya Osamu
金谷治, Tokyo: Tōhō shoten, 1976. See also 7 (e) below.

7.   Translations

(a) Giles, Lionel, *Sun Tzu on the Art of War*; London: Luzac and com-
     pany, 1910.
(b) Griffith, Samuel B., *Sun Tzu the Art of War*; Oxford: Clarendon Press,
     1963, reprinted 1971.
(c) Konrad, N.I., *Sun Wu, Traktat o voennom iskusstve*; Moscow: Izdatel-
     stvo Akademii Nauk 1950; reprinted in the author's collected works
     Izbrannye trudy, Sinologija, Moscow: 1978.
(d) Cleary, Thomas, *Sun Tzu, The Art of War*; Boston-Shaftsbury: Sham-
     bala, 1988.
(e) Ames, Roger T., *Sun-tzu: the Art of Warfare: a New Translation Incor-
     porating the Recently Discovered Yin-ch'üeh-shan Texts*; New York:
     Ballantine Books, 1993. This includes a translation of (i) the received
     text, with due account of the manuscript from Yin-ch'üeh-shan; (ii)
     the additional texts of that find; and (iii) citations of other passages,
     in works such as the *T'ung tien* 通典. An introduction discusses the
     history, context, and philosophical concepts behind the work; an
     appendix concerns the excavations at Yin-ch'üeh-shan and their
     results.

8.   Japanese editions

A.   *Kambun taikei*; no. 13, 1912, edited by Hattori Unokichi
B.   *Kanseki kokujikai zensho*: no. 10, 1910 edited by Ogyū Sorai
C.   *Kōchū kambun sōsho*; no. 5, 1913, edited by Kubo Tenzui and Kanda
      Katsuhisa
D.   *Kokuyaku kambun taisei*; no. 7, 1921, edited by Kojima Kenkichirō
E.   *Kambun sōsho*; 1928, edited by Tsukamoto Tetsuzō and Koyanagi
      Shikita
F.   *Keisho taikō*; no. 24, 1938
H.   *Shinshaku kambun taikei*; no. 36, 1972, edited by Amano Shizuo
J.   *Chūgoku no shisō*; no. 10, 1965. edited by Murayama Makoto
K.   *Chūgoku koten bungaku taikei*: no. 4, 1973, edited by Murayama
      Yoshihiro
L.   *Chūgoku koten shinsho*: 1967, edited by Tadokoro Gikō (Yoshiyuki)

In addition to the volumes in the foregoing series, the text has been treated independently as follows:

1. Kimida Rentarō 公田連太郎 and Ōba Yahei 大場彌平, *Sonshi no heihō* 孫子の兵法 in *Heihō zenshu* 兵法全集 vol. 1; Tokyo: Chūō kōronsha, 1935; transcription in *kambun*, followed by Japanese version and annotation. The Chinese text is not included.
2. Andō Akira 安藤亮, *Sonshi no heihō* 孫子の兵法, Tokyo: Nihon bungeisha, 1969; transcription in *kambun* with explanatory notes, and Chinese text with *kambun* notation.

9. Indexes

(a) See under 4 (k) and (n) above.
(b) *A Concordance to the militarists (Sunzi, Yuliaozi, Wuzi, Simafa* 兵書四種 (孫子, 尉繚子, 吳子, 司馬法) 逐字索引, ed. D.C. Lau and Chen Fong Ching; *ICS* series, Hong Kong: Commercial Press, 1992.

— Krzysztof Gawlikowski
— Michael Loewe

Ta Tai Li chi 大戴禮記

1. Date of composition and authenticity

The *Ta Tai Li chi* is named after Tai Te 戴德 (1st century B.C.), one of the four disciples of Hou Ts'ang 後倉 (*fl.* 70 B.C.) who established officially recognised schools for the preservation and transmission of the *I li* in the first century B.C. (see *s.v. Li chi*). It appears, however, that the occurrence of Tai Te's name indicates no more than an attempt to give the text a respectable provenance. Contrary to some traditional accounts, there is no contemporary evidence to show that the Former Han ritualist had anything to do with the compilation of the text or that the *Ta Tai Li chi* is an earlier recension of the *Li chi*. Moreover, the *Ta Tai Li chi* is not listed as such in *Han shu* ch. 30, and it is doubtful whether it existed as an independent collection much before the beginning of the second century A.D.

2. Content and sources

It may be that the *Ta Tai Li chi* is derived to some extent from an earlier collection of *chi* in 131 *p'ien* that is listed in *Han shu* 30, p. 1709. Nevertheless, some parts of the *Ta Tai li chi* seem to have been written after the compilation of the essays of the *Li chi*; e.g., *Ta Tai Li chi*, *p'ien* no. 46 begins with a summary of the contents of *Li chi* 30; *p'ien* 41 is copied from *Li chi* 27; *p'ien* 52 contains part of *Li chi* 24. Most of the *p'ien* of the *Ta Tai Li chi* are pastiches of passages taken from a variety of pre-Han and Former Han sources. For example, *p'ien* 71 (*Kao chih* 誥志) is a version of material otherwise found in the almost eponymous *p'ien* 58 of the *I Chou shu*; the *Hsün tzu* contributed material to *Ta Tai Li chi*, *p'ien* nos. 42 and 64–6, which also include miscellaneous passages from the *Huai nan tzu*; *Ta Tai Li chi p'ien* nos. 46 and 48 depended largely on the writings of Chia I 賈誼 (201–169 B.C.); parts of *Huai nan tzu* 3 and 4 were borrowed for *Ta Tai Li chi* 58 and 81. Finally, it is important to note that *Ta Tai Li chi* 77, and to a lesser extent 63, rely on the *Chou li*. Since the *Li chi* consistently favours the *I li* over the *Chou li* on points where one contradicts the other, we may strongly question whether these *p'ien* could have derived from the same source which yielded the *Li chi*.

P'ien nos. 49–58 either bear the name of Confucius' disciple Tseng Tzu 曾子 in their titles or they record his teachings and conversations. It has been argued that these writings were taken from the now lost *Tseng tzu*, listed under *Ju chia* in *Han shu* 30 p. 1724 with 18 *p'ien*. When fragments of the *Tseng tzu* were assembled during the Ch'ing period, these *p'ien* were included. It is, however, unlikely that these materials were in fact borrowed from the book before it was lost. Many of the *p'ien* associated with Tseng Tzu in the *Ta Tai Li chi* can be shown to have been adopted from other sources. The remainder are probably fabrications of the Han dynasty which use Tseng Tzu's name for the prestige and orthodoxy that it might lend to the teachings which they espouse.

3. Textual history

The *Ta Tai Li chi* is listed in *Sui shu* 32, p. 921, as consisting of 13 *chüan*. This entry is repeated in the T'ang catalogues and official Sung bibliographies (*Chiu T'ang Shu* 46, p. 1973; *Hsin T'ang Shu* 57, p. 1430; *Sung Shih* 202, p. 5048) and it is consistent with the division of the extant editions. The text of ten *chüan* that the *Ch'ung wen tsung mu* mentions must have suffered loss owing to the existence of *lacunae*, but the extant editions shed no light on this anomaly.

A commentary to the *Ta Tai Li chi* was written by Liu Hsi 劉熙, *c.* 200, but according to the note in *Sui shu* 32, p. 921, it was lost. A surviving commentary is attributed to Lu Pien 盧辯 (*fl.* 519–57), who served under the Wei and Northern Chou dynasties. As this commentary is not mentioned in the Sui and T'ang bibliographies, it may be inferred that it did not merit establishment on an orthodox basis until Sung times.

The most severe damage to the text is traditionally assumed to have taken place sometime between the end of the Han and the Sui periods. According to a statement in the *Liu i lun* 六藝論 of Cheng Hsüan 鄭玄 (127–200), the *Ta Tai Li chi* consisted originally of 85 *p'ien*. Extant editions have no more than 39 *p'ien*, and it is assumed that this was also the case for the text which is listed in the *Sui shu*. The first *p'ien* in *chüan* no. 1 of the received text is identified as no. 39; the second *chüan* begins with no. 46, rather than 43; the seventh *chüan* begins with no. 62 and not 61, and the collection ends with *p'ien* no. 81. It would appear that altogether 46 *p'ien* of some earlier redaction were lost.

While it is quite possible that some parts of the text were lost before the compilation of the catalogue that is in the *Sui shu*, it is doubtful whether the *Ta Tai Li chi* was bereft of as many as 46 *p'ien*, as the present numbering would indicate. By Sui times it was believed that the *Ta Tai Li chi* was an earlier redaction, in 85 *p'ien*, of a *Li chi* in 46 *p'ien*; it was further assumed that the 46 *p'ien* common to the two collections had dropped out of the *Ta Tai Li chi* (see the passage from the *Sui shu* which is translated in the entry, above, for the *Li chi*). But there is nothing in Han dynasty bibliographical records to corroborate such a relationship between the two texts. Furthermore, several *p'ien* now in the *Ta Tai Li chi* repeat some of the contents of the *Li chi* and were not excised. It may be that the numbering of the *p'ien* of the *Ta Tai Li chi* was influenced by this unfounded version of the relationship between the *Ta Tai Li chi* and the *Li chi*, and further intended to confirm that the *Ta Tai Li chi* may be identified with the 85 *p'ien* of *chi* 記 said by Cheng Hsüan to have been transmitted by Tai Te.

4. Editions

The *Ssu pu ts'ung k'an* reproduces a Ming print with Lu Pien's commentary, and a preface of Han Yüan-chi 韓元吉 (b. 1118), dated 1175. The *Han Wei ts'ung shu* and the *Ya Yü t'ang ts'ung shu* also include editions of the text. All three are inferior to the *Wu ying tien* 武英殿 edition in movable type (1774–77), which served as the main source for the collated edition printed in the *Ts'ung shu chi ch'eng*.

In his annotated edition entitled *Ta Tai Li chi pu chu* 大戴禮記補注, K'ung Kuang-sen 孔廣森 (1752–86) includes an analytical table of contents which usefully summarises the textual parallels and sources for each *p'ien* of the *Ta Tai Li chi*. The edition is included in the *Chi fu ts'ung shu* and *Ts'ung shu chi ch'eng*. Another version of K'ung's work, with additional collation notes by Wang Shu-nan 王樹枏 (1857–1937), was published under the title *Chiao cheng K'ung shih Ta Tai Li chi pu chu* 校正 孔氏大戴禮記補注; this is also included in the *Ts'ung shu chi ch'eng*.

Sun I-jang 孫詒讓 (1848–1908) compiled a set of collation notes for selected lines of the text entitled *Ta Tai Li chi chiao pu* 大戴禮記斠補, which was published posthumously in 1914.

5. Recent studies and translations

(a) For the date of the *Ta Tai Li chi* and the critical question of its relationship to the *Li chi*, see Tsuda Sōkichi 津田左右吉, 'Raiki oyobi Tai Tai Raiki no hensan jidai ni tsuite 禮記及大戴禮記の編 纂時代について'; *Shigaku zasshi* 42 (1931), 131–70.

(b) A minimally annotated translation, which does not include *p'ien* nos. 77–79, may be found in Benedykt Grynpas, *Les écrits de Tai l'Ancien et le petit calendrier des Hia* (Paris, 1972). The contents of each part are summarized in an otherwise brief introduction; an appendix is concerned with *p'ien* no. 47 *Hsia Hsiao cheng* 夏小正, a ritual calendar which may be profitably compared with the *Yüeh ling* 月令 of the *Li chi* and with related almanacs.

(c) For a rendering in modern Chinese, see Kao Ming 高明, *Ta Tai Li chi chin chu chin i* 大戴禮記今註今譯; Taipei: Taiwan Shang wu, 1975.

6.   Japanese editions

H. *Shinshaku kambun taikei*; no. 113, edited by Kurihara Keisuke.

L. *Chūgoku koten shinsho*, 1972, edited by Nitta Daisaku.

7.   Indexes

(a) Suzuki Ryūichi 鈴木隆一, *Tai Tai rai sakuin* 大戴禮索引 (Tokyo: Dai-an, 1945; reprinted 1967); based on the edition of K'ung Kuang-sen.

(b) *A Concordance to the Dadai Liji* 大戴禮記逐字索引, ed. D.C. Lau and Chen Fong Ching; *ICS* series, Hong Kong: Commercial Press, 1992.

— Jeffrey K. Riegel

T'ai hsüan ching 太玄經

1. Content

Of the two prose works by Yang Hsiung 揚雄 (53 B.C.–A.D. 18), the *T'ai hsüan*, also known as the *T'ai hsüan ching* 太玄經 owing to the appendage of the last character by its admirers, is a far more difficult text than the *Fa yen*. Intending, on the model of the *I ching*, to set out a series of symbolical patterns covering all cosmic situations, the *T'ai hsüan* provides expository text to accompany 81 tetragrams, i.e., graphic patterns made by combinations of four lines of three types, unbroken, bisected or trisected. Yang Hsiung also composed his own commentaries to the text in eleven sections, which serve as counterparts to the 'Ten Wings' of the *I ching*. In its title, each tetragram alludes to a single aspect and stage of the evolving cosmic *Tao*. To the title is appended a poetic description of the effect of *yin* or *yang* energy upon the myriad things during one precise phase in the annual cycle. The nine Appraisals (*tsan* 贊) which follow direct the reader's attention to the interplay of eternal cosmic patterns and the changing circumstances that prompted divination. According to two sources, to complete this literary collection Yang Hsiung also wrote a series of chapter and verse (*chang chü* 章句) commentaries, but these have now been lost. A table of correspondences between extant parts of the *T'ai hsüan* and its protoype may be drawn up as follows:

T'ai hsüan ching	*I ching*
Chia 家	Kua 卦
Shou 首	T'uan 彖
Tsan 贊	Yao 爻
Ts'e 測	Hsiang 象
Wen 文	Wen yen 文言
Li 攡, Ying 瑩, I 掜, T'u 圖	Hsi tz'u 繫辭
Kao 告, Shu 數	Shuo kua 說卦
Ch'ung 衝	Hsü kua 序卦
Ts'o 錯	Tsa kua 雜卦

The *T'ai hsüan* provided inspiration and vocabulary for *Hsüan hsüeh*

玄學 Movement as this developed after the Han period and continued
to influence Chinese thought thereafter. However, certain prominent
Sung thinkers, including Su Hsün 蘇洵 (1009–60) and Chu Hsi 朱熹
(1130–1200), raised objections to Yang Hsiung on the grounds of his
service at the court of Wang Mang 王莽, his rejection of the Mencian
theory of human nature and his presumption in composing neo-classical
writings in imitation of Confucius. As a result, in the *Ssu k'u* catalogue
the *T'ai hsüan* was demoted from the category of *ju chia* and placed in
that of *shu shu* 數術, notwithstanding the respect that other famous
writers such as Ssu-ma Kuang 司馬光 (1019–86) had accorded to the
work.

2.　Early references and authenticity

The *Han shu* (30, p. 1727) records a total of 38 *p'ien* under Yang Hsiung's
name in the category of *ju chia*; a note appended to the entry states that
19 *p'ien* belong to the *T'ai hsüan*. A contemporary reference, in one of the
fragments of the *Hsin lun*, writes of a *T'ai hsüan*, with main text in 3 *p'ien*
and 12 *p'ien* of auto-commentaries. Entries in the later bibliographical
lists vary from 6 to 14 *chüan*, the difference depending on the commentaries accompanying the main text. One such entry, for 13 *chüan*, occurs
in Fujiwara Sukeyo's list, also under *ju chia*. The contents of the received
text of *T'ai hsüan* corresponds with the detailed description that is given
in Pan Ku's 班固 (32–92) biography of Yang Hsiung (*Han shu* 87A, B; see
especially pp. 3565, 3575). According to Pan Ku the work was completed
during the reign of Ai Ti 哀帝 (reigned 7–1 B.C.) The authenticity of the
received text has not been brought into question. Its formal nature, its
rhymed passages and its numerical layout preclude the possibility of
blatant interpolation or omission. For a consideration of the original
length of the *T'ai hsüan*, see under 3 (o) below.

3.　Commentaries and editions

(a) Yao Chen-tsung's 姚振宗 (1842–1906) reconstructed catalogue of the
palace library of Later Han lists a commentary to the *T'ai hsüan* by
Hou Pa 侯芭, who was one of Yang Hsiung's pupils, but this work
does not appear in the extant catalogues of the Standard Histories.
Only selected passages of commentaries by Sung Chung 宋衷 (2nd–
3rd century), Yü Fan 虞翻 (164–233) and Lu Chi 陸績 (188–219) survive, as cited in later annotations. There are a few fragments of an
imitation of Yang Hsiung's work by Yang Ch'üan 楊泉 of the Chin
晉 period.

(b) The commentary by Fan Wang 范望, of the Chin 晉 dynasty, which
draws on earlier commentaries, survives in its entirety. Fan Wang is
also credited with a re-arrangement of the text, whereby the sections
known as *shou* 首 (head texts), *tsan* 贊 (appraisals) and *ts'e* 測 (fa-
thomings), which had originally existed as separate sections, were
integrated as appropriate under the 81 tetragrams. This arrangement
has been followed by all subsequent editors. The *SPTK* reproduces
the earliest extant edition of this commentary, which was published
by the Wan yü t'ang 萬玉堂 in 1524; in its turn it had copied a Sung
edition, printed by Chang Shih 張寔. There is one report of a further
Ming print (dated to the period 1621–43), which was allegedly closer
to the original Sung edition. Extant editions which are based on the
commentary of Fan Wang include Lu Chi's 'Shuo hsüan' 述玄 and
Fan's own 'Chieh tsan' 解贊 before the main text. A diagram of uncertain authorship, Wang Ya's 王涯 'Shuo hsüan' 說玄 (of ?809) and
an anonymous 'Shih wen' 釋文 follow Yang's auto-commentaries.

(c) The second major commentary, which is by Ssu-ma Kuang, is accompanied by three introductory pieces, i.e., a preface, dated 1082,
and two essays entitled 'Shuo hsüan' 說玄 and 'Tu hsüan' 讀玄. In
his interpretation of the first six *chüan* of the text (the *shou*, *tsan* and
ts'e attached to the 81 tetragrams), Ssu-ma Kuang sporadically cites
from thirteen commentators; these include Sung Chung 宋衷 (whom
he terms Sung Tzu 宋子), Lu Chi, Fan Wang and Wang Ya. Later
editions interpolate remarks by Sung Wei-kan 宋惟幹 (Sung period;
termed Hsiao Sung 小宋), Ch'en Chien 陳漸 and Wu Mi 吳祕 (*cs*
1034). Whereas Fan Wang was mainly concerned with explaining
the cosmic interplay of the *wu hsing*, Ssu-ma Kuang believed that the
major focus of the *T'ai hsüan* lay in the five constant virtues that are
espoused in the earliest Confucian texts. To supplement the commentary of Ssu-ma Kuang, which covers only the first six *chüan*, the
annotations of Hsü Han 許翰 (d. 1133) on the final four *chüan* of the
auto-commentaries have been included in some editions; this arrangement dates from the early part of the 13th century. Most
editions also append the *T'ai hsüan li* 太玄曆, by way of explaining
Yang's dependence on the T'ai-ch'u 太初 calendar of Former Han,
and a chart showing the correlations between the tetragrams of the
T'ai hsüan and the hexagrams of the *I ching*.

  This text is reprinted in the *SPPY* series, on the basis of a copy of
the work which was made by Mr. T'ao 陶 in 1798; this was a Ming
tracing of a Sung print, that had once been in the possession of T'ang
Yin 唐寅 (1470–1524). Sun Chu's 孫澍 corrections to some 250 copy-

ists' errors that he found in the text are listed in his *Tseng pu T'ai hsüan chi chu* 增補太玄集注, now in the Taiwan National Palace Museum. Ssu-ma Kuang's commentary is also reprinted in the *Tao tsang*, and, along with punctuation and notes regarding variant readings, in Wu Ju-lun's 吳汝綸 (1840–1903) *Chu tzu chi p'ing* 諸子集評 (1886).

(d) Chang Hsing-ch'eng's 張行成 *I hsüan* 翼玄 of 1173 is included in the *Han hai* 函海 and reprinted in the *Ts'ung shu chi ch'eng* series. This commentary claims to follow the lead of Ssu-ma Kuang, Shao Yung 邵雍 (1011–77), and Ch'ao Yüeh-chih 晁說之 (1059–1129) in exploring the numerological and calendrical aspects of the *Tai hsüan ching*, with repeated reference to the treatises of the *Han shu*. In general, Chang attempts to demonstrate the inferiority of the *T'ai hsüan* when compared with the *I ching*.

(e) Yeh Tzu-ch'i's 葉子奇 *T'ai hsüan pen chih* 太玄本旨 of 1386 is available in the *Ssu k'u ch'üan shu chen pen*, series 3 (vol. 194). The work has been criticised in the *Ssu k'u ch'üan shu chien ming mu lu* for ignoring astro-calendrical explanations and the evidence of *Han shu* 87; nevertheless, the same book rightly credits it with valuable expositions of certain difficult passages.

(f) Chiao Yüan-hsi 焦袁熹 (1660–1735) *T'ai hsüan chieh* 太玄解 (original title *T'ai yüan chieh* 太元解) of c. 1700 is reprinted in the *Ts'ung shu chi ch'eng* series; clear and concise explanations of 36 difficult passages are given.

(g) Lu Wen-ch'ao's 盧文弨 (1717–96) *Yang Hsiung T'ai hsüan ching chiao cheng* 揚雄太玄經校證 took Fan Wang's commentary to Yang's work as a basis, adding a number of glosses drawn from the notes of earlier scholars, including Ch'en Jen-hsi 陳仁錫 (c. 1580–c. 1635) and Ho Ch'o 何焯 (1661–1722).

(h) Ch'en Pen-li's 陳本禮 (1739–1818) *T'ai hsüan ch'an mi* 太玄闡祕 is probably the most methodological exposition of the view that the *Tai hsüan ching* should be seen as a political satire aimed at Wang Mang and other prominent public figures in the last decades of Former Han. He reviews Yang Hsiung's biography in the *Han shu* in order to demonstrate the errors of all those who see in the *Mystery* no more than an imitation of the *I ching*. The work is valuable for its inclusion of supplementary materials, though its elucidations of difficult phrases are often farfetched.

(i) Yü Yüeh's 俞樾 (1821–1907) short notes in *Chu tzu p'ing i* 諸子平議 include emendations based on the requirements of parallel prose or internal rhyme, or as seen in citations of the early commentators; he has ascertained the sources of several obscure allusions.

(j) Sun I-jang 孫詒讓 (1848–1908) in *Cha i* provides glosses for no more than eleven passages, including three that are discussed by Yü Yüeh.

(k) Hsia Ching-kuan 夏敬觀, 'Tai hsüan ching k'ao' 太玄經考, in *I wen tsa chih* 1:2 (1936), 1–4, discusses the relation of the *T'ai hsüan* to the schools of interpretation of the *Changes* from the Han to the Sung.

(l) See *Chung kuo che hsüeh shih tzu liao hsüan chi* 中國哲學史資料選輯, (Peking: Chung hua, 1960), *Liang Han chih pu* 兩漢之部, A, pp. 179–89, for renderings in modern Chinese of three of Yang Hsiung's own commentaries to his text; and *Chung kuo che hsüeh shih chiao hsüeh tzu liao hui pien* 中國哲學史教學資料彙編, (Peking: Chung hua, 1964), *Liang Han pu fen* 兩漢部份, B, pp. 301–21 for annotations to four commentaries.

(m) Hsü Fu-kuan 徐復觀, 'Yang Hsiung lun chiu' 揚雄論究, in *Ta lu tsa chih* 50:3 (1975), 1–43. This article discusses a number of questions concerning Yang Hsiung's life and his biography in the *Han shu*. In pp. 13–22, which concern the *T'ai hsüan*, the author contrasts the motives behind its composition and that of the *Chieh nan fu* 解難賦 and the *Fa yen*. Hsü describes the structure of the *T'ai hsüan* and its relation to the calendar then in use; he discounts Fung Yu-lan's suggestion that Han numerology was borrowed from the Pythagoreans (see Fung Yu-lan, *A History of Chinese Philosophy*, vol. II, Princeton: Princeton University Press, 1953, pp. 93–96, 101–102).

(n) Cheng Wen 鄭文, 'T'ai hsüan hsüeh shuo ch'u t'an' 太玄學說初探; *Kan-su shih ta hsüeh pao* 1979:4, 59–70. In hoping to stimulate further study of Yang Hsiung's works and in seeking to explain his motives, the author provides clues to the traditional controversies surrounding the *T'ai hsüan*.

(o) Shu Ching-nan 束景南, 'T'ai hsüan ch'uang tso tai k'ao' 太玄創作代考; *Li shih yen chiu* 1981:5, 142–47. The author adduces arguments to reject the view that the work was a satirical attack on Wang Mang and discusses the problem of its original length.

(p) Han Ching 韓敬, 'Lun "T'ai hsüan" ti che hsüeh t'i hsi' 論太玄的哲學體系; *Chung kuo che hsüeh shih yen chiu* 6 (January, 1982), 49–59. Hampered as it is by a preoccupation with the use of Marxist terminology, this essay refutes Fung Yu-lan's equation of the key term *hsüan* with *ch'i* 氣.

(q) Cheng Wan-keng 鄭萬耕, 'T'ai hsüan yü tzu jan k'o hsüeh' 太玄與自然科學; *Chung kuo che hsüeh* 12 (April, 1984), 76–84. This article shows that the astronomical foundation of the *T'ai hsüan* rested on Hun-t'ien 渾天 theory and the San t'ung 三統 and T'ai ch'u 太初 calendars; it also shows the resemblance between the cosmogony of the *T'ai hsüan* and that found in contemporary apocryphal writings.

(r) Chang Tai-nien 張 岱 年, 'Yang Hsiung p'ing chuan' 揚 雄 評 傳 *Chung kuo che hsüeh shih yen chiu* 16 (July, 1984), 6–22. Drawing equally on the *Fa yen* and the *T'ai hsüan*, the author describes Yang's ideas of human nature, the Mandate of Heaven and the sequence of phenomenal change; Yang's philosophical antecedents and his debt to Hsün Tzu are discussed briefly.

(s) Cheng Wan-keng, 'Yang Hsiung wu shen lun ssu hsiang ti chi ko fan ch'ou' 揚雄無神論思想的幾個範疇, *Chung kuo che hsüeh shih yen chiu* 17 (October, 1984), 44–47. This essay analyses the various meanings attached to the terms *t'ien* 天 and *shen* 神 in Yang's work.

(t) Cheng Wan-keng, *T'ai hsüan chiao shih* 太玄校釋; Peking: Teacher's Normal University Publishing House, 1989. This annotated edition intends to be the definitive treatment of the work in modern Chinese. In many ways it succeeds. Preliminary essays and several appendices supplement Cheng's analysis of all 81 tetragram texts plus Yang's own commentaries. Unfortunately, the great achievements of the book are marred by a few failings. In the case of variant characters and interpretations, Cheng often fails to give reasons for his choice. Unusual characters are sometimes, but not always, provided with *Pinyin* readings. Particularly difficult lines tend to be ignored, or glossed over with vague remarks intended to convey the 'general idea' of the passage.

4. Studies by western scholars

(a) Forke, Alfred, 'The Philosopher Yang Hsiung'; *Journal of the North China Branch of the Royal Asiatic Society* 66 (1930), 108–110; and 'Chinesischer Bildersaal: der Philosoph Yang Hiung', in *Sinica* 7 (1932), 169–78; see also his *Geschichte der mittelalterlichen chinesischen Philosophie* (Hamburg: Friederischen, de Gruyter and Co., 1934). pp. 74–99.

(b) Knechtges, David R., *The Han Rhapsody* (Cambridge: Cambridge University Press, 1976); see pp. 7f. for the structure of the *T'ai hsüan* and pp. 90 f. for a translation of tetragram no. 47.

(c) Nylan, Michael and Nathan Sivin, 'The First Neo-Confucianism: an Introduction to Yang Hsiung's 'Canon of Supreme Mystery' (*T'ai hsüan ching, c.* 4 B.C.)'; in Charles Le Blanc and Susan Blader (eds.), *Chinese Ideas About Nature and Society: Studies in Honour of Derk Bodde* (Hong Kong: Hong Kong University Press, 1987), pp. 41–99. This article discusses the philosophical background to the *Canon*, its arrangement, problems of interpretation and its mathematical basis; it also includes sample translations of Head and Appraisal texts.

5. Translation

Nylan, Michael, *The Canon of Surpreme Mystery by Yang Hsiung*; Albany: State University of New York Press, 1993.

6. Japanese studies and editions

(a) Mitarai Masaru 御手洗勝, 'Yō Yū to Taigen' 揚雄と太玄; *Shinagaku kenkyū* 18 (1957), 22–32; Mitarai attempts to refute Hou Wai-lu's 侯外盧 opinion that the *T'ai hsüan* shows no originality of thought. Mitarai argues that the *T'ai hsüan* is, in fact, an improvement over the *I ching*, as it makes possible a more perfect correlation of graphic symbols with current *wu hsing* calendrical theory. The creativity of the text is also contrasted with the hackneyed scholastic treatises of the time.

(b) Suzuki Yoshijirō 鈴木由次郎; there are two works: (i) *Taigen no kenkyū* 太玄の研究 (Tokyo: Meitokusha, 1964) and (ii) a *kambun* version in the series *Chūgoku koten shinsho*, 1972. The long introduction in (i) reviews *I ching* theory of the Han period, where this is relevant; the structure of the *T'ai hsüan*; procedures for oracular consultation; and some of the possible implications of Yang Hsiung's work. In (i), notes follow the major divisions of the text. They are more conveniently placed, immediately after the Japanese version, in (ii), which does not handle the *ts'e* or the final nine of Yang Hsiung's own commentaries.

(c) Machida Saburō 町田三郎, 'Taigenkyō ni tsuite' 太玄經に就て; *Kyūshū daigaku tetsugaku kenkyūkai nempō* 37 (1978), 103–31. This article provides general background information by a scholar who had previously worked on the *Fa yen*. It reviews factionalism at the court at the close of Former Han, major philosophical influences on Yang Hsiung's thought, and the basic structure of the *T'ai hsüan* somewhat more concisely than is done in Suzuki's works.

7. Index

A Concordance to the Fayan and Taixuanjing 法言, 太玄經逐字索引, ed. D.C. Lau and Chen Fong Ching; *ICS* series, Hong Kong: Commercial Press, forthcoming 1995.

— Michael Nylan

Tu tuan 獨斷

1. The author and his writings

Ts'ai Yung 蔡邕 (133–92; style Po-chieh 伯喈; for biography, see *Hou Han shu* 60B, pp. 1979–2008) is best known for his proposals (170–71) for engraving the approved texts of the classical texts on stone tablets. In the course of his career he submitted a number of memorials criticising institutional practice and the conduct of public life, or giving his views on certain inauspicious events which had alarmed the court. At one time he was involved in activities which could be interpreted as being treasonable, but secured a pardon. Later he served as an adviser to Tung Cho 董卓 and died in prison after the latter's defeat (192). At the time a plea had been made to save him from punishment, in view of his familiarity with imperial institutions and the belief that he should be saved from the death penalty in order that he could perpetuate his knowledge in writing. According to his biography (p. 2007), Ts'ai Yung compiled Annals of Ling ti 靈帝 (reigned 168–89) and 42 *p'ien* of supplementary biographies, the greater part of which did not survive. Apart from this, altogether 104 *p'ien* of poems, epitaphs essays and other writings, including the *Tu tuan*, were transmitted to posterity. Some of these may be seen in the extant *Ts'ai Chung-lang chi* 蔡中郎集. One source (*Shang yu lu* 尚友錄 18) draws a distinction between two men named Ts'ai Yung, both with the style of Po-chieh 伯喈, who were contemporaries; the second one, known for his filial piety, lived as a recluse.

2. Contents of the work

The *Tu tuan* is usually divided into two parts or *chüan*. The first part sets out the different terms used in dynastic, imperial and official institutions and explains their distinctions, which very often reflect hierarchical practice. An introductory statement concerns the terms used to denote the emperor himself and his various actions or activities; the following 28 passages, usually preceded by a caption, or heading of the form . . . *chih pieh ming* 之別名, treat terms used in ritual or court practice and intended to convey or imply distinctions of rank. They mention details

467

both of Han imperial times and of the traditional usage ascribed to the monarchs of mythology.

The second part is not divided into captioned passages; and whereas the first part is concerned with distinguishing the use of correct terms, the second one includes descriptions of imperial practices and procedures, such as those held at the imperial shrines. The text refers to both Former and Later Han usage.

3.   Date of composition

The list of Han emperors that is included in the text (*Han Wei ts'ung shu* 漢魏叢書 ed. B, 1a–3a) ends with Ling ti; a note, which was apparently part of the original text, refers to events of the 22nd (according to *SPTK* text 20th) year of his reign, i.e., 189 (or 187). However, if credence is given to the suggestion of Lu Wen-ch'ao 盧文弨 (1717–96) that this entry was an interpolation, this list would end at 167. This view is partly supported by a passage (B, 6a) which concerns the imperial shrines, and again closes with with Huan ti 桓帝. However, a year specified as Yung-an 永安 7 is mentioned on B, 11b, but the first occasion when the regnal title of Yung-an was introduced was in 258 (for the kingdom of Wu 吳). This passage must presumably be regarded as either a corruption or an interpolation. It may perhaps be assumed that the original parts of the text were completed before the death of Ling ti in 189, and that references to his posthumous title or events of his reign and later are to be found only in insertions that were made by another hand subsequently; alternatively it may be suggested that Ts'ai Yung himself included the references to Ling ti between 189 and his own death in 192.

4.   Condition of the text

It is thus apparent that the state of the text may be in question, and the *Ssu k'u* 四庫 editors were quick to point out the existence of a number of textual errors, as already stated in the *Yu hai* 玉海 (51, 23a, in the Che chiang shu chü print, 1883) and the discrepancies that are to be seen in the counts of the years of Han emperors' reigns. They add that the inclusion of the term Hsien ti 獻帝, i.e. the posthumous title of the last emperor (abdicated 220) shows that the received text is not entirely the work of Ts'ai Yung, and has been subject to interpolation. The note also points out that the contents of the work places considerable reliance on the *Li chi* 禮記 but does not follow the *Chou kuan* 周官; and the correspondence of certain passages with the notes of Cheng Hsüan 鄭玄 (127–200) suggest that both works derived from the same source. There are also a number of differences between the received text and citations to be found, e.g. in commentaries to the *Hou Han shu* 後漢書 (*chih* 志) or the *Ch'u hsüeh chi* 初學記 of Hsü Chien 徐堅 (657–729), which may be explained either as incorrect citation or as errors in the received text. The existence of such errors had been noticed by scholars from at least 1180.

5.　Textual transmission and editions

In the preface to his annotated edition, which is dated in 1790, Lu Wen-ch'ao 盧文弨 observed that copies of the book were rare. He cited the *Ch'ung wen tsung mu* 崇文總目 (completed 1041; see under *I chu lei* 儀注類) as entering the work in 2 *chüan*, and stated that the book had been put in order by Yü Tse-chung 余擇中 in the period 1056–63, and given the title of *Hsin ting Tu tuan* 新定獨斷. The *Ssu k'u* editors, who had also noted this, added that this text had not been transmitted. Lu Wen-ch'ao added that the version in the *Han Wei ts'ung shu* 漢魏叢書, the only one which was available, was full of errors and was not necessarily that of Yü Tse-chung. However a friend had fortunately presented him with a Sung print, i.e. the text included in the *Pai ch'uan hsüeh hai* 百川學海 collection of 1273 by Tso Kuei 左圭. The *Tu tuan* is in fact the earliest text to be included in that work, and the print had derived from an edition of Lü Tsung-meng 呂宗孟, whose colophon, which is dated in 1180, referred to the many errors which he had corrected. In fact, Lu Wen-ch'ao added, there were only slight differences in the text. He expressed his thanks to his friends Tsang Yung 臧庸 (1767–1811) and Ku Ming 顧明 for their unstinted help in editing the text. The editions that are available today may be divided into two groups, i.e. (a) consisting of 2 *chüan* and (b) consisting of 1 *chüan*. The figure of 2 *chüan* is given not only in the *Ch'ung wen tsung mu* 崇文總目 of 1041, but also in the *Wen hsien t'ung k'ao* 文獻通考 (completed *c.* 1308; see ch. 1187, Shang wu yin shu kuan reprint, 1936; p. 1596A) and the *Yü hai* 玉海 of 1343–51 (*loc. cit.*)

Group (a) is represented in the two versions in the *Pai ch'uan hsüeh hai* 百川學海, (of 1265–74 and 1488–1505); the *Han Wei ts'ung shu* (of 1592); and, with some variations, in the print of 1503 that is reproduced in the *Ssu pu ts'ung k'an* 四部叢刊 series. This text was also adopted by Lu Wen-ch'ao. Group (b) is seen in the *Ku chin i shih* 古今逸史 of *c.* 1580; the *Shuo fu* 說郛; and the *Tseng ting Han Wei ts'ung shu* 增訂漢魏叢書 (1791), edited by Yen Ping-heng 嚴秉衡. The prints of group (a) carry the colophon of Lü Tsung-meng; those of group (b) do not. Other differences are as follows:

(A) In group (a) the captions are usually separated from the passages which they head, and which thus start in the next column; in group (b) there is no such separation.

(B) Textual differences may be noted consistently, e.g.:
  (i) In the section that is headed *T'ien tzu ming ling chih pieh ming*
      天子命令之別名, *Ku chin i shih* 6a, *Shuo fu* 11, and *Tseng ting
      Han wei ts'ung shu* read 一曰命二曰令三曰政; *Han Wei ts'ung
      shu* A, 6b, and other texts of group (a) omit 一曰, 二曰, 三曰;
  (ii) *Ku chin i shih* 3a reads: 無復言之者; *Han Wei ts'ung shu* A, 3a
      omits 復; other copies are consistent with this difference.
(C) In at least one instance the short annotation is placed differently; see
    Han Wei ts'ung shu A, 17a, where a note follows 五等爵之別名; in
    Ku chin i shih 15a this note, less one character, is placed at the close
    of the passage after 五十里.

Apart from the print of 1503, in the *Ssu pu ts'ung k'an*, all prints are
with a column length of 20; in the *Ku chin i shih* the half folios carry 10
columns; in the prints of group (a) the number of columns is either 9
(*Han Wei ts'ung shu*) or 12 (*Pai ch'uan hsüeh hai*). It seems likely that the
texts of both groups derived from the same source, into which a short
annotation had already been introduced; and there is no apparent reason to suggest why this cannot be traced to the 1180 print of Lü Tsung-
meng.

The 1503 print, which has a format of 10 by 21, includes a preface of
that date by Liu Hsün 劉遜 (presumably to be identified as the scholar
of that name who achieved his *chin shih* 進士 degree in 1478, rather than
the one who did so in 1427). The *Ssu pu ts'ung k'an* appends an undated
postface by Chang Yüan-chi 張元濟 (b. 1868) which refers to the prints
of the *Pai ch'uan hsüeh hai* and the *Ku chin i shih*. This is followed by a
table of variant readings, as between these copies, the *Han Wei ts'ung
shu* and Lu Wen-ch'ao's edition, which is available in the *Pao ching t'ang
ts'ung shu*, the *Lung hsi ching she ts'ung shu* and, reprinted with punctuation, in the *Ts'ung shu chi ch'eng*.

6.   Annotation

See Sun I-jang 孫詒讓 (1848–1908), *Cha i* 10.

7.   A *kambun* edition

The text of the *Han Wei ts'ung shu* was reproduced by Saitō Sanzaemon
齋藤三左衛門, with *kambun* notation, in 1669; this is now available in
Nagasawa Kikuya 長澤規矩也 (1902–80), *Wa koku bon Kanseki zuihitsu
shu* 和刻本漢籍隨筆集 vol. 10 (Tokyo: Koten kenkyūkai, 1974).

                                                    — Michael Loewe

Tung kuan Han chi 東觀漢記

In A.D. 72 Emperor Ming of the Later Han dynasty ordered a history of the reign of his late father, Kuang-wu (r. 25–57), to be compiled. The work was entrusted to Pan Ku 班固 (32–92), Ch'en Tsung 陳宗, Yin Min 尹敏 (*fl.* 30–60), Meng Chi 孟冀 (*fl.* 44), Ma Yen 馬嚴 (d. 98), and Tu Fu 杜撫. It was carried out on the Orchid Terrace, *Lan t'ai* 蘭臺, one of the libraries and archives in the Southern Palace compound of Lo-yang. The finished compilation in 28 *p'ien* was called the *Chien wu chu chi* 建武注記 and consisted of an Annal (*ti chi* 帝紀) for emperor Kuang-wu, Biographies (*lieh chuan* 列傳) for meritorious subjects, and Records (*tsai chi* 載記) for Kung-sun Shu 公孫述 (d. 36) and the troops from P'ing lin 平林 and Hsin shih 新市.

In A.D. 120, the Empress Dowager Teng 鄧 (81–121) instructed Liu Chen 劉珍 (d. after 126), Liu T'ao-t'u 劉騊騄 (*fl.* 110), Liu I 劉毅 (c. 58–125) and Li Yu 李尤 (d. after 135) to expand the *Chien wu chu chi*. They wrote Annals, Tables (*nien piao* 年表) and Biographies in the Eastern Lodge, *Tung kuan* 東觀, another library and archive of the Southern Palace. The history was thereafter known as the *Han chi* 漢記.

The second continuation was ordered by Emperor Huan in A.D. 151 or 152. Fu Wu-chi 伏無忌 (*fl.* 130–50), Huang Ching 黃景 (*fl.* 130–50), Pien Shao 邊韶 (*fl.* 155), Ts'ui Shih 崔寔 (c. 110–170), Chu Mu 朱穆 (100–163), Ts'ao Shou 曹壽, and Yen Tu 延篤 (d. 167) compiled in the Eastern Lodge further Annals, Tables, and Biographies, which expanded the *Han chi* to 114 *p'ien*.

The third continuation was ordered by Emperor Ling between A.D. 172 and 177. Ma Mi-ti 馬日磾 (d. 194), Han Yüeh 韓說 (*fl.* 180), Ts'ai Yung 蔡邕 (133–92), Lu Chih 盧植 (d. 192), and Yang Piao 楊彪 (142–225) improved or updated, again in the Eastern Lodge, the earlier sections of the work, wrote additional Annals and Biographies, and added a number of Treatises (*chih* 志). Henceforth, the history was called the *Tung kuan Han chi*.

The fourth and last continuation was privately compiled by Yang Piao after the fall of the Later Han in A.D. 220. He died in A.D. 225. The entire history consisted then of 143 *chüan*.

471

The *Tung kuan Han chi* was consequently written in five instalments, covering the periods from 22 to 57, 58 to 106, 107 to 146, 147 to 167, and 168 to 220. With the exception of the last instalment, it was the government-sponsored dynastic history of the Later Han. When Fan Yeh 范曄 (398–446) compiled his *Hou Han shu* 後漢書, he used the *Tung kuan Han chi* as his chief source. For the relationship of these two works to other historical accounts that were written for the Later Han dynasty, see Hans Bielenstein, *The Restoration of the Han Dynasty with Prolegomena on the historiography of the Hou Han shu* (Stockholm: Museum of Far Eastern Antiquities, 1954), pp. 9f.

After the *Tung kuan Han chi* had been superseded by the *Hou Han shu* as the standard dynastic history, large parts of it were lost. By Sui times, the original 143 *chüan* were still extant (*Sui shu* 33, p. 954), and such a copy had reached Japan by the ninth century. Elsewhere the book had been reduced to 127 or 126 *chüan* by T'ang times (*Chiu T'ang shu* 46, p. 1988; *Hsin T'ang shu* 58, p. 1454), and by Sung it included no more than 8 *chüan* (*Sung shih* 203, p. 5094). Later, surviving passages were reassembled from the early encyclopaedias and the *Yung lo ta tien* and printed together in the *Wu ying tien chü chen pan* 武英殿聚珍版 series, with prefaces dated in 1774 and 1777. The latter was signed by Lu Hsi-hsiung 陸錫熊 (1734–92), Chi Yün 紀昀 (1724–1805) and Yang Ch'ang-lin 楊昌霖 (*fl.* 1775). The text is arranged under the headings of Annals, Tables, Treatises, Biographies and Records, in 24 *chüan*; the final *chüan* includes notes of variants as between the *Tung kuan Han chi* and other works, mainly that of Fan Yeh. In addition, the text has been included in the *Ssu k'u ch'üan shu chen pen* (*pieh chi*) (nos. 106–07).

The *Wu ying tien* print was reproduced in the *Hu-pei hsien cheng i shu* 湖北先正遺書 and was used as a basis for the text printed in the *Ssu pu pei yao*, which is the best modern edition. A punctuated text was included in the *Ts'ung shu chi ch'eng*.

Index

A Concordance to the Dong kuan Han ji 東觀漢記逐字索引, ed. D.C. Lau and Chen Fong Ching; *ICS* series, Hong Kong: Commercial Press, forthcoming 1994.

— Hans Bielenstein
— Michael Loewe

Wu Yüeh ch'un ch'iu 吳越春秋

1. Content

The *Wu Yüeh ch'un ch'iu* is a romantic version, in chronicle form, of the conflict that took place between the states of Wu and Yüeh during the early part of the fifth century B.C. In its present form the text is divided into two equal halves, the first being devoted to Wu and the second to Yüeh. Each half of the book includes one *chüan* which relates to the legend of the states' ancestors (no. 1 for T'ai po 泰伯, of Wu, and no. 6 for Yü 禹 of Yüeh), followed by four *chüan* of annals. *Chüan* nos. 2–5 contain entries for the years 585–473 B.C., and these are based largely on the *Tso chuan* and the *Shih chi; chüan* nos. 7–10 cover the years 492–470 B.C., and rely more on the *Kuo yü* and the *Yüeh chüeh shu*. The first half, like its sources, is orientated more towards events; the second half is composed primarily of rhetorical exercises. Both parts contain what is patently fictional material, and there is not a single historical detail which cannot be traced to more reliable sources. The interest of the work is therefore thematic and literary but not historical.

Briefly stated, the work belongs to the category of texts such as the *Mu t'ien tzu chuan* or the *Lü shih ch'un ch'iu* which explore the nature of political legitimacy in more or less explicitly fictional manner. In so far as it is composed of historical and semi-historical anecdotes, the work resembles the *Lü shih ch'un ch'iu*; in so far as it attempts to string these anecdotes together to form a coherent story, it resembles the *Mu t'ien tzu chuan*. Thematically the *Wu Yüeh ch'un ch'iu* contrasts markedly with both of those books, for it treats the nature of power in an exceedingly negative manner.

The action takes place on the south-eastern fringes of classical China, in territories that were virtually 'barbarian', and in the decadent context of the hegemonic period. The general decline is further underscored by the contrast between the latter-day rulers of these fringe states and their virtuous ancestors. The very choice of venue was dictated by a pessimistic cosmological consideration; for the south-east is, in the words of the *Wu yüeh ch'un ch'iu*, the *ti hu* 地戶, the Door of the Earth, i.e. the cosmic drain. In this context of utter decadence, both temporal and spatial,

473

only the chief ministers retain a certain degree of virtue and intelligence. But their intelligence is employed for personal rather than for public ends. The one, Wu Tzu-hsü 伍子胥, is put to death unjustly as the result of the intrigues of a conspiring colleague; Fan Li 范蠡 the other, who is his counterpart in Yüeh, survives only because he has the intelligence to leave Yüeh before the king whom he has served murders him too. In sum, there is in these latter days no legitimate depository for political power, and the best that the individual can hope for is to serve the limited interests of a temporary hegemon, and then to move elsewhere.

2.   Date of composition and authenticity

The first record of copies of the *Wu Yüeh ch'un ch'iu*, in *Sui shu* 33, p. 960, lists three entries:

(a) *Wu Yüeh ch'un ch'iu*; 12 *chüan*, by Chao Yeh 趙曄 (date unspecified; for biography, see *Hou Han shu* 79B, p. 2575).
(b) *Wu Yüeh ch'un ch'iu hsiao fan* 吳越春秋削繁; 5 *chüan*, by Yang Fang 楊方 (early fourth century; for biography see *Chin shu* 68, pp. 1831f.).
(c) *Wu Yüeh ch'un ch'iu*; 10 *chüan*, by Huang-fu Tsun 皇甫遵 (seventh century).

This entry is repeated in the list of the *Chiu T'ang shu* 46, p. 1993; in Fujiwara Sukeyo's catalogue, the work appears under miscellaneous histories in 7 *chüan* (with some supplementary items), without specifying the author. In the *Hsin T'ang shu* 58, p. 1466, the work ascribed to Huang-fu Tsun is entitled *Wu Yüeh ch'un ch'iu chuan* 吳越春秋傳. The *Sung shih* (203, p. 5094) lists Chao Yeh's *Wu Yüeh ch'un ch'iu* with 10 *chüan*; it omits mention of Yang Fang's book and names Huang-fu Tsun's work as *Wu Yüeh ch'un ch'iu chu* 吳越春秋注. The *Liao shih* simply lists a *Wu Yüeh ch'un ch'iu yin chu* 吳越春秋音註 in 10 *chüan* by Hsü T'ien-hu 徐天祜 (*chin shih* degree in 1262). The only edition that is extant today is a *Wu Yüeh ch'un ch'iu* in 10 *chüan* attributed to Chao Yeh with commentary by Hsü T'ien-hu.

Wang Yao-ch'en 王堯臣 (1001–1056) was the first scholar to state explicitly the relationship between the three entries of the *Sui shu* and other works (see *Ch'ung wen tsung mu*):

> *Wu Yüeh ch'un ch'iu*, 10 *chüan*, annotated by Huang-fu Tsun of the T'ang period. Originally Chao Yeh wrote the *Wu Yüeh ch'un ch'iu* in 12 *chüan*. Thereafter Yang Fang, finding [Chao] Yeh's work too lengthy, abridged it and cut it down to 5 *chüan*. [Huang-fu] Tsun

then put the two authors' versions together, correcting and anno-
tating the whole.

It is thus very difficult to state how much of the received *Wu Yüeh
ch'un ch'iu* goes back directly to Chao Yeh, and it is open to question
how far Yang Fang altered the style of the work, or re-arranged the episodes. Nor do we know whether, in making what we can only suppose
is the text that we now possess, Huang-fu Tsun referred to the texts of
both Yang Fang and Chao Yeh. All these questions are further complicated by the fact that a good half of the *Wu Yüeh ch'un ch'iu* as received
seems to derive from the *Shih chi, Tso chuan, Kuo yü* and *Yüeh chüeh shu;*
there may well have been other sources, now lost or undetected, that
might have accounted for much of the remainder. It remains open to
question how much of the received text derived from such sources, and
neither from Chao Yeh's original work nor from Yang Fang's abridge-
ment.

In view of the citation of passages in various encyclopaedias and
commentaries, it can only be concluded that the *Wu Yüeh ch'un ch'iu*, as
now received, is at the very least an abridged version of Chao Yeh's
original work. The *T'ai p'ing yü lan*, in particular, contains a number of
passages that are ascribed to a *Wu Yüeh ch'un ch'iu* but which are not to
be found in the received text. If it is assumed that the *T'ai p'ing yü lan*
was citing from a version in 12 *chüan*, the fact that that work was compiled in 983 suggests that the *Hsin T'ang shu* (of 1060) was accurate in
recording a *Wu Yüeh ch'un ch'iu* by Chao Yeh in 12 *chüan*, which was undoubtedly still extant as such in early Sung times. In this connection it is
worthy of note that the *Wu chün chih* 吳郡志, of Fan Ch'eng-ta 范成大
(1126–93) seems to follow the same text as that used by Hsü T'ien-hu. In
defence of the antiquity of the received text it may be observed that by
far the greater proportion of the passages cited from the *Wu Yüeh ch'un
ch'iu* in the *T'ai p'ing yü lan* are still to be found there.

3. Editions

Of the many editions of the work, about half are in 10 and half are in 6
chüan. It might at first be supposed that the text in 6 *chüan* is the original
12 *chüan* version of Chao Yeh; but the 6 *chüan* version retains the
division into 10 parts, as does the 10 *chüan* version. This consideration
makes it more likely that some enteprising editor wished his readers to
believe that he was offering them the original text; and this impression
is supported by the fact that the 6 *chüan* edition first appears in the *Ku
chin i shih;* this dates from 1571–76, considerably later than the oldest

extant version in 10 *chüan*. In addition, the editions in 6 *chüan* all include Hsü T'ien-hu's notes, but without attributing them to him; such an editorial policy is in itself suspect. Finally, the text of the 6 *chüan* is identical to that of the 10 *chüan*, except for an increase in the number of textual errors.

Of the editions in 10 *chüan*, the earliest that is available is usually that of the *Ssu pu ts'ung k'an*, second series. This is a photolithographic copy of the edition cut by K'uang Fan 鄺璠 (1458–1521) in the Hung chih period (1488–1505), and it is to be distinguished from a different, and later, text that was used in the *Ssu pu ts'ung k'an* first series. Ch'ien Fu's 錢福 (1461–1504) preface, entitled 'Preface to a recutting of the Wu Yüeh ch'un ch'iu' provides the precise date, which corresponds with 17 May 1501.

Various bibliographers claim to have held or seen editions earlier than that of 1501. Thus, Chang Chin-wu 張金吾 (1787–1829) lists a *Wu Yüeh ch'un ch'iu* which, he records, was a 'traced copy of an edition cut in the Sung period'. According to Chang, the postface to that edition, which was written by Wang Kang 王綱 (13th century), dates to 1224 (see *Ai jih ching lu ts'ang shu chih* 14.10a). Yeh Te-hui 葉德輝 (1864–1927), however, doubts the existence of any editions prior to 1307 (see *Hsi yüan tu shu chih* 18a–20b). If an edition of 1224 such as that mentioned by Chang Chin-wu does still exist, it is in any case, according to Wang Kang's postface as cited by Chang, the version in 10 *chüan*.

4. Translations

(a) Eichhorn, Werner, *Heldensagen aus dem unteren Yangtze-Tal*; Wiesbaden: Franz Steiner, 1969; a relatively imprecise translation with little annotation.

(b) Lagerwey, John, *The Annals of Wu and Yüeh, Part I* (Ph.D. thesis, Harvard University); includes a complete study of the relationship of the *Wu Yüeh ch'un ch'iu* to its sources and a fully annotated translation of *chüan* nos. 1–5.

5. Index

A Concordance to the Wu Yue chunqiu 吳越春秋逐字索引, ed. D.C. Lau and Chen Fong Ching; *ICS* series, Hong Kong: Commercial Press, forthcoming 1993.

— John Lagerwey

Yen t'ieh lun 鹽鐵論

1. Content

The text, in dialogue form, is an expanded account of the court debate ordered by imperial edict in 81 B.C. While the discussion was ostensibly concerned with the merits of the government's monopolies of the salt and iron industries, the record of the debate ranges over a variety of controversial issues. The parties to the debate included spokesmen for the government, such as the *ta fu* 大夫, sometimes identified with Sang Hung-yang 桑弘羊, who held the post of *Yü shih ta fu* 御史大夫 from 87 to 80 B.C., and critics who are described as the *wen hsüeh* 文學 or by other titles. Some of the participants are mentioned by name in the final *p'ien* of the book, authorship of which is ascribed to Huan K'uan 桓寬, during the reign of Hsüan ti 宣帝 (74–49 B.C.). For a summary of the arguments that are presented, and which may well represent an idealised rather than a strictly factual account of the debate, see Michael Loewe, *Crisis and Conflict in Han China* (London: George Allen and Unwin Limited, 1974), chapter 3. Y.L. Kroll pays particular attention to the economic issues in 'Toward a study of the economic views of Sang Hung-yang' (*Early China*, 4 (1978–79) 11–18). See also Wu Hui 吳慧, *Sang Hung-yang yen chiu* (Chi-nan: Chi Lu shu she, 1981), especially chapter 6.

2. Date of composition, and authenticity

The entry for the book in *Han shu* 30.1727 lists it under *ju chia*, as a work of 60 *p'ien*. The received text is divided in this way, with each *p'ien* bearing its own title, and the book falling into three parts: (i) *p'ien* nos. 1–41, the formal debate; (ii) *p'ien* nos. 42–59, the subsequent discussions; and (iii) *p'ien* no. 60, Huan K'uan's postface. A reference in the *Lun heng* (*SPTK* ed. 29.5a) cites the book as an example of a work which presents opposing sides of an argument, compiled by Huan K'uan. There is no immediate reason to believe that parts of the text were interpolated after the original compilation during the reign of Hsüan ti; but it is possible that *p'ien* no. 29, which is not in dialogue form, may be citing from what was originally an independent piece of writing. Quotations from the book in commentaries, anthologies or encyclopaedias from the fifth to

477

the tenth centuries are essentially identical with the received text and corroborate the order of the *p'ien* that is known to-day.

3. Text history

Extant editions fall into two groups: (a) in 10 *chüan* and (b) in 12 *chüan*.

(a) The *Sui shu* 34, p. 997 lists the book in 10 *chüan*. This figure is also given in Fujiwara Sukeyo's list and in the *Yü hai*, which also lists the titles of the 60 *p'ien*. A print of 1501, with prefaces by T'u Chen 涂禎 and Tu Mu 都穆 (1458–1525), claimed to be based on an edition of 1202, which had become very rare by that time. T'u Chen's own edition had become scarce by 1807, when a copy was re-engraved and published by Chang Tun-jen 張敦江 (1754–1834), in 10 *chüan*. This edition was later incorporated in a number of *Ts'ung shu* (e.g., *Tai nan ko ts'ung shu* and *Ku shu ts'ung k'an*), usually with the addition of *k'ao cheng* notes by Ku Kuang-ch'i 顧廣圻 (1776–1835). The text was used as the basis for Wang Hsien-ch'ien's 王先謙 (1842–1918) edition of 1891, which was reprinted in the *Ssu pu pei yao* series, with Wang's own notes but without the *k'ao cheng*.

   A somewhat poor Ming print in 10 *chüan*, reproduced in the *Ssu pu ts'ung k'an* series, was erroneously regarded by some bibliographers of the 19th century as T'u Chen's print; its provenance has not been traced, but it is tentatively dated between 1506 and 1566. An edition in movable type, probably from the Hua 華 printing house, was almost certainly based on the print of 1202 or one of its immediate derivatives; this copy had been made carelessly with some omissions.

(b) An annotated edition in 12 *chüan* was published in 1554 by Chang Chih-hsiang 張之象 (1507–1587) with his own preface. This text probably derived from a print in 12 *chüan* of 1174, which was recognised to be very rare in the 19th century. Chang Chih-hsiang's edition does not include the prefaces of T'u Chen or Tu Mu. It was taken as a basis for the *Kuang Han Wei ts'ung shu*, the *Tseng ting Han Wei ts'ung shu* and the *Tzu shu pai chia*, and for the first copies to be made in Japan. These latter were published in the first instance under the auspices of Itō Tōgai 伊藤東涯 in 1708. Subsequent Japanese recuts of Chang Chih-hsiang's print have been made with the addition of *kambun* diacritical marks.

   Chang Chih-hsiang's text differs from those of group (a) as follows:

   (i) In group (a) the text of each *p'ien* is printed without divisions between the speeches of the different spokesmen. In Chang

Chih-hsiang's edition, a new column is started at the beginning of each speech; the speeches of the 'Confucian' critics of
the government are accorded special honour, by being ex-
truded to a higher level of print on the page. This edition
therefore requires greater space; it is understandable that it
would be more easily accommodated in 12 than in 10 *chüan*.

(ii) There are certain regular differences in the text; e.g., Chang
Chih-hsiang reads 坊, 澹, 冊 and 伯; the other editions read
防, 瞻, 策 and 霸.

(iii) There is one textual difference which may affect conclusions
regarding the date of the compilation of the *Yen t'ieh lun*. In
p'ien no. 29, Chang Chih-hsiang reads *Pi hsia* 陛下, whereas
the texts of group (a) read Hsüan ti 宣帝. Acceptance of the
latter reading as authentic would imply that compilation was
not complete until after the death of that emperor, in 49 B.C.

(iv) Quite apart from textual variants, the following points possibly suggest that Chang Chih-hsiang's version is more reliable
than that of other editions:

(A) In Chang Chih-hsiang's text, the title of *p'ien* no. 58 is given
correctly both *in situ* and in the table of contents; in other
editions there is an error in the table of contents, which
also appears in the *Yü hai*. (In all the basic prints the title of
p'ien no. 28 appears in two forms: as *kuo chi* 國疾 in the table
of contents; as *kuo ping* 國病 at the head of the *p'ien* itself).

(B) The points at which *p'ien* nos. 24, 27 and 29 close, and at
which nos. 25, 28 and 30 begin, are different. The arrangement is perhaps more logical and consistent in Chang
Chih-hsiang's edition.

(C) The attribution of the speeches is in one instance more likely to be correct in Chang Chih-hsiang's edition; i.e., in *p'ien*
no. 29, attribution to the assistant of the Chancellor *ch'eng
hsiang shih* 丞相史 is inherently more probable than to the
Chancellor *ch'eng hsiang*, as given in the texts of group (a).

4. Recent editions

(a) Within a series

The *Yen t'ieh lun* has been included in the *Han Wei ts'ung shu*, *Ssu pu
ts'ung k'an* and *Ssu pu pei yao* as described above. The *Ts'ung shu chi
ch'eng* reproduces Chang Tun-jen's text directly from the *Tai nan ko
ts'ung shu*. The same version has been reprinted, with added punctu-

ation and the *k'ao cheng*, in the series *Chu tzu chi ch'eng* (first published 1935; re-issued by Chung hua shu chü Peking, 1954). The *Chu
tzu chi ch'eng* print, followed by Yang Shu-ta's 楊樹達 notes (see
under (c) below) was reproduced in the series *Shih chieh wen k'u*
(Taipei: Shih chieh shu chü, 1958).

(b) Editions with new annotation or other features

(i) Lin Chen-han 林振翰, *Yen t'ieh lun*; in the Basic Sinological
Series, Shanghai: Shang wu, 1934. The text is based on that of
Wang Hsien-ch'ien's edition, being divided into separate paragraphs for each speech, and punctuated. The principal notes
include comments by a number of Ch'ing scholars; a separate
series of notes indicates differences with the text of Chang
Chih-hsiang.

(ii) Hsü Te-p'ei 徐德培, *Yen t'ieh lun chi shih* 鹽鐵論集釋, with
preface by Hsia Sun-t'ung 夏孫桐, dated 1939. The text is
based on that of Wang Hsien-ch'ien's edition, being printed
continuously. Intercolumnar notes include comments of
Ch'ing scholars collected from a number of sources, together
with Hsü Te-p'ei's own contribution. There are some printing
errors in the text.

(iii) Kuo Mo-jo 郭沫若 (1892–1978), *Yen t'ieh lun tu pen* 鹽鐵論讀
本, Peking: K'o hsüeh, 1957. The text, which is divided as in (i)
above, is punctuated and annotated. It incorporates a number
of textual variants not seen elsewhere, which are sometimes
introduced without remark or warning; reprinted, together
with annotations by Wang P'ei-cheng 王佩諍 and Yang Shu-
ta, Kyoto: Hōyū shoten, 1975.

(iv) Wang Li-ch'i 王利器, *Yen t'ieh lun chiao chu* 鹽鐵論校注,
Shanghai: Ku tien, 1958. The text is based on Chang Tun-jen's
version, punctuated and divided as in (i) above. This is probably the most valuable of the modern editions, as the annotation does full justice to variant readings, as collated from other
editions. The text is followed by the prefaces of all editions under consideration; reprinted Taipei: Shih chieh, 1979, together
with item (c) (i) below (Wang P'ei-cheng's annotation); revised
and enlarged edition, 2 vols., published T'ien-chin: Ku chi ch'u
pan she, 1983.

(v) *Yen t'ieh lun*; punctuated text in abbreviated characters, by an
unnamed editor, in 60 *p'ien*; Shanghai: Jen min, 1974. The text
is preceded by a reprint of an article 'Tu Yen t'ieh lun' 讀鹽鐵

論, by Liang Hsiao 梁效 (i.e., Peking and Ch'ing hua universities), first published in *Jen min jih pao* (18 May 1974) and *Hung ch'i* (1974 no. 5, 12–19).

(vi) Ma Fei-pai 馬非百, *Yen t'ieh lun chien chu* 鹽鐵論簡注, Peking: Chung hua, 1984. The text is printed in abbreviated characters; each *p'ien* is preceded by a short summary; extensive annotation is included after each speech.

(c) Annotations printed without the text

(i) Wang P'ei-cheng 王佩諍, *Yen t'ieh lun cha chi* 鹽鐵論札記, Peking: Shang wu, 1958; reprinted Taipei: Shih chieh, 1979.

(ii) Yang Shu-ta, *Yen t'ieh lun yao shih* 鹽鐵論要釋, Peking: K'o hsüeh, 1957; reprinted, with preceding text, Taipei: Shih chieh, 1958, and, enlarged, in *Yang shu-ta wen chi chih shih i* 楊樹達文集之十一, Shanghai: Ku chi, 1985.

For a reprint of the foregoing two items, see under (b) (iii) above.

(iii) Lin P'ing-ho 林平和, *Yen t'ieh lun hsi lun yü chiao pu* 鹽鐵論析論與校補; Taipei: Wen shih che, 1984. Essays on the background of the debate, the editions of the text and its commentaries precede the annotation, which is principally a list of variant readings; an analysis of the argument follows.

5. Translations

(a) Gale, Esson M., *Discourses on Salt and Iron*; published in the series *Sinica Leidensia*, vol. II (Leyden: E.J. Brill, 1931). An English translation of *p'ien* nos. 1–19 is accompanied by an index and glossary.

(b) Gale, Esson M., with Peter A. Boodberg and T. C. Lin, 'Discourses on Salt and Iron (Yen T'ieh Lun: Chaps: XX–XXVIII)', in the *Journal of the North China Branch of the Royal Asiatic Society*, vol. LXV (1934), 73–110.

Items (a) and (b) were re-issued in one volume as *Discourses on Salt and Iron*, by Ch'eng wen (Taipei), 1967.

(c) Walter, Georges, *Chine, An -81 Dispute sur le Sel et le Fer Yantie lun*; présentation par Georges Walter, traduit du Chinois par Delphine Baudry-Weulersse, Jean Levi, Pierre Baudry; collaboration de Georges Walter; Paris: Lanzmann & Seghers, 1978. A somewhat free translation in elegant style, which is addressed to the general reader rather than intended as a scholarly exercise. Regrettably some inaccuracies and loose renderings intrude. The book is divided into 42 chapters, which do not correspond with the textual divisions of the original, and there is no indication where translations of the different *p'ien* may be located. While it is stated that the translation is not of the complete text, no indication is given to show a reader where omissions occur.

6.   Japanese editions

I.   *Tōyō bunko*; 1970, edited by Satō Taketoshi.
L.   *Chūgoku koten shinsho*; 1967, edited by Yamada Katsumi; selections of the text only are included.

The work is also included in the Iwanami Bunko series (nos. 965–967), edited by Sogabe Shizuo 曾我部靜雄.

7.   Recent studies

(a) Lao Kan 勞幹, 'Yen t'ieh lun chiao chi' 鹽鐵論校記, in *BIHP* 5.1 (1935), 13–52; this article concerns the history of the editions and draws attention to a number of variant readings.
(b) Hsü Fu-kuan 徐復觀, 'Yen t'ieh lun chung ti cheng chih she hui wen hua wen t'i' 鹽鐵論中的政治社會文化問題; *Hsin ya hsüeh pao* 11 (September 1975) 337–418.
(c) Hsü Han-ch'ang 徐漢昌, *Yen t'ieh lun yen chiu* 鹽鐵論研究; Taipei: Wen shih che, 1983; essays on the composition of the text, the personalities of the debate, editions of the text and the background of the Former Han internal and external policies.

8.   Indexes

(a) Yamada Katsumi, *Entetsu ron sakuin*; Tokyo: Tōyō Daigaku Chūtetsubun kenkyūshitsu, 1970; this index is based on the *Ssu pu ts'ung k'an* text.
(b) *Entetsu ron sakuin* 鹽鐵論索引; no. 6 in the series 'Source materials for Chinese philosophy', compiled by the Research group for Chinese philosophy, Hokkaidō; edited by Itō Tomoatsu 伊東倫厚, *et al.*; Tokyo: Tōfū shoten, 1988. References are to the print in the *CTCC* series.
(c) *A Concordance to the Yantie lun* 鹽鐵論逐字索引, ed. D.C. Lau and Chen Fong Ching; *ICS* series, Hong Kong: Commercial Press, forthcoming 1994.

— Michael Loewe

Yen tzu ch'un ch'iu 晏子春秋

1. Content

The *Yen tzu ch'un ch'iu* is a collection of remonstrances delivered by Yen Ying 晏嬰 primarily to Duke Ching 景 of Ch'i 齊 (held the title 547–489 B.C.) and other miscellaneous anecdotes depicting Yen Ying's pious behaviour.* The text contains 215 short items (*chang* 章) which are distributed among 8 *p'ien*. The first six *p'ien* are entitled 'Inner', and the last two 'Outer' *p'ien*. The 'Outer' *p'ien* contain variants of items found in the 'Inner' *p'ien* along with other items that are of a strong anti-Confucian tone. Although the last two *p'ien* are termed simply 'Outer', the six 'Inner' *p'ien* carry further designations, i.e. *chien* 諫 1 and 2; *wen* 問 1 and 2; and *tsa* 雜 1 and 2. The arrangement of the content of each of the 'Inner' *p'ien* appears to be arbitrary, but within the book as a whole chapters tend to be arranged according to general topic; i.e., remonstrances aimed at the same type of indiscretion on the part of the Duke are placed together.

Yen Ying, known posthumously as P'ing chung 平仲, is an historical figure attested in works such as the *Lun yü*, *Mo tzu* and especially the *Tso chuan*. According to the *Shih chi* (32, p. 1505), Yen Ying died in 500 B.C.; he is first mentioned in connection with the death of his father in 556 B.C. Wang Keng-sheng 王更生 (pp. 20–21) has suggested that his life stretched for a full 90 years from 589 to 500 B.C.

2. Textual history and authenticity

In *Shih chi* 62, p. 2136 Ssu-ma Ch'ien 司馬遷 (?145–?86 B.C.) refers to the *Yen tzu ch'un ch'iu* by name and claims that many in his generation possessed copies of the text. In Liu Hsiang's 劉向 (79–8 B.C.) preface to the work and in the entry in *Han shu* 30, p. 1724, it is termed *Yen tzu*, with the title *Yen tzu ch'un ch'iu* re-appearing in Six Dynasties' sources such

---

* References to secondary works that are cited will be found under (5) and (6) below; see also Wu Tse-yü's edition of the work (5 (e) below), pp. 599f., 625f. for the text of many of the bibliographical notices and comments that are quoted.

as the *K'ung ts'ung tzu* 孔叢子 (*SPPY* ed., 5.8a; Wu Tse-yü, pp. 49–50). In his preface, Liu Hsiang wrote as follows:

> The imperial text of the *Yen tzu* which I collated had 11 *p'ien*. What I, Hsiang, carefully collated with [Fu] Ts'an [富] 參, Commandant of Ch'ang she 長社, were the Director of Astrology's text in 5 *p'ien*, my own text in 1 *p'ien* and Ts'an's text in 13 *p'ien*. Altogether the imperial and private texts amounted to 30 *p'ien*, forming 838 *chang*. I removed duplicates numbering 22 *p'ien* and 638 *chang*, establishing a text of 8 *p'ien* and 215 *chang*. . . .
>
> 6 *p'ien* of this book are all loyal remonstrations against a ruler; the composition is worthy of respect, the principles worthy of emulation. In all cases these agree with the doctrine of the Six Classics. In addition, there are repetitions with rather different phraseology which I dared not overlook and which have been further arranged in 1 *p'ien*. There are also those parts which disagree somewhat with the learning of the Classics, as if they were not the words of Yen Tzu. I suspect that they were produced by sophists of a later age, but again I did not dare to abandon them and have arranged them in 1 *p'ien*.

This preface informs us of several different collections of Yen Tzu lore, often with the same episodes being duplicated in each, which circulated during the Former Han period. 112 strips and fragments of one such collection that were discovered at Lin-i 臨沂 (see *Wen wu* 1974.2, 32–4) date from the early years of the Han dynasty and contain episodes which closely match passages from 7 of the 8 *p'ien* of the received text; *p'ien* no. 4 is not represented. Furthermore Liu Hsiang's description of his edition corresponds with the structure of the text as it appears today. Not only are the numbers of the items and the *p'ien* the same; the seventh *p'ien* of the modern editions indeed includes numerous duplicates of episodes recorded elsewhere in the text, and *p'ien* no. 8 has several items whose anti-Confucian content might well have offended Liu Hsiang and led to his characterization of this *p'ien* as 'disagreeing with the learning of the Classics'.

The transmission of the text is nonetheless not without problems. The *Sui shu* (34, p. 997), *Chiu T'ang shu* (47, p. 2023), *Hsin T'ang shu* (59, p. 1509) and Fujiwara Sukeyo's catalogue list the work with 7 *chüan*; the same figure is cited for the received text by Ssu-ma Chen 司馬貞 (early 8th century; see *Shih chi* 62, p. 2036 note); in the *Ch'ung wen tsung mu* and *Yü hai* it is noted as a work of 12 *chüan*. Liu Shih-p'ei 劉師培 (1884–1919) has explained these discrepancies by suggesting that the Sui and

T'ang editions may have combined the two *p'ien* termed *tsa* 雜 into a single *chüan*. He further suggests that the Sung editions split five of the 7 *chüan* into 2 each, leaving the two 'Outer' *p'ien* untouched, and thereby producing the edition in 12 *chüan*. While this suggestion is a matter of conjecture, Liu Shih-p'ei goes on to argue, more plausibly, that the Yüan editions in 8 *p'ien* might have been made by re-arrangement from the Sung editions, so as to reflect Liu Hsiang's description (Wu Tse-yü, pp. 635-36).

Several Chinese scholars have argued that the received versions of the *Yen tzu ch'un ch'iu* do not derive from the text that was edited by Liu Hsiang. For example, Wu Te-hsüan 吳德旋 (1767-1840) believed that the present text is a forgery of the Six Dynasties period; Kuan T'ung 管同 (1780-1831) assigned it to an even later time (see Wu Tse-yü, pp. 630-31). Many of the doubts concerning the work are either highly subjective, such as Kuan T'ung's attack on the literary style; or they arise from disaffection with the philosophical bias of the text, particularly the inclusion of several episodes in *p'ien* no. 8 which attack Confucius and duplicate sections of the notorious 'Anti-Confucian' chapter of the *Mo tzu*.

More serious questions of authenticity have been summarized by Wang Keng-sheng (pp. 41-72). (a) The text contains numerous anachronisms. (b) Many passages of the received text appear almost word for word in other sources and could easily have been assembled from such works. In this respect, Wang counts 23 *chang* which are paralleled in the *Tso chuan*, 1 in the *Li chi*, 1 in the *Meng tzu* and as many as 78 in late Chou, Ch'in and Han philosophical works, including 40 in the *Shuo yüan* and 8 in the *Han shih wai chuan*. (c) There are two chapters in the received text which were not in the copy seen by Ssu-ma Ch'ien. The latter states specifically (*Shih chi* 62, p. 2136) that his biography of Yen Ying includes only episodes not found in the *Yen tzu ch'un ch'iu*, but both of the anecdotes which he narrates form part of the received text. Wang thus concludes that the original text of Liu Hsiang may have been lost and reassembled much later from a number of different sources.

Other considerations, however, support the contention that the *Yen tzu ch'un ch'iu* does descend directly from Liu Hsiang's work, and that he, in turn, collected his text from authentic documents of the Chou period. The strips mentioned earlier provide conclusive proof that Yen Tzu lore had been assembled into collections at least by the early part of the Han period and that such collections resembled the received text. Moreover, preliminary grammatical studies by Richard Walker indicate that the *Yen tzu ch'un ch'iu* has a uniformity of grammar that would not be expected in a text gathered in the Six Dynasties from a multiplicity of

Chou and Han sources. The authenticity of the work is also supported by the very fact that many textual problems and questionable readings have been preserved as they stand. As Wang Nien-sun 王念孫 (1744–1832) has argued, this is precisely what to expect from a very ancient work which has not passed through the critical hands of commentators and editors (Wu Tse-yü, pp. 643–44).

From the time of Liu Hsiang until the philologists of the 18th century, there is no notice of commentaries or critical editions of the work. In this respect the textual history somewhat resembles that of the *Mo tzu* which, like the *Yen tzu ch'un ch'iu*, contains numerous problematical readings. Still another argument in favour of authenticity has been presented by Walker. The political milieu of the *Yen tzu ch'un ch'iu* is precisely what would be expected of a text deriving from Ch'i during the Spring and Autumn period. Such a verisimilitude of both geographical and political setting would not easily be reconstructed by a late forger.

3.   Date of composition

Although the greater weight of evidence indicates that the *Yen tzu ch'un ch'iu* is an authentic Chou text, there is considerable disagreement on the subject of dating. No one seriously contends that any portion of the text was written by Yen Ying himself. Sun Hsing-yen 孫星衍 (1753–1818) attributed the work to disciples of Yen Ying who collected the stories and words of their master from official state annals preserved in Ch'i and mentioned in *Mo tzu* 31 (Wu Tse-yü, pp. 639f.). That the *Yen tzu ch'un ch'iu* derives from such a source is unlikely, for it differs stylistically from state annals of the Chou period which have been preserved elsewhere. However, Sun's assertion that the text was produced by disciples of Yen Ying accords with the conclusions of major scholars such as Forke, Maspero (p. 359) and Walker, who states specifically that the text took form sometime before 400 B.C. All three of these scholars base their conclusions on a belief that the *Yen tzu ch'un ch'iu* versions predate and are the source for the parallels in the *Tso chuan*. Walker correctly notes that the wording of the *Yen tzu ch'un ch'iu* is consistently fuller than that of the *Tso chuan*, but Karlgren (pp. 171–76) has shown that this is by no means conclusive evidence of earlier authorship. Clearly a careful study of all passages of the *Yen tzu ch'un ch'iu* with their parallels elsewhere would go far towards establishing a probable date of authorship.

By contrast with such views, Liang Ch'i-ch'ao 梁啓超 (1873–1929; see Wu Tse-yü, p. 632) ascribed the *Yen tzu ch'un ch'iu* to the late Warring

States period. Although he gives little justification for such a date, the text does possess both style and content which fit the literary environment of the late Warring States, when historical romance and stories of clever political persuaders were much in vogue (see Maspero, pp. 357–65). Koga Dōan 古賀侗庵 (1788–1847) has cited a number of items of the *Yen tzu ch'un ch'iu* where the arguments are remarkably similar to some found in the *Chan kuo ts'e* (Wu Tse-yü, pp. 633–35).

4.　Classification and evaluation

Much of the work on the *Yen tzu ch'un ch'iu* has focused on its appropriate classification within the scheme of traditional Chinese bibliography. In the *Han shu, Sui shu, Chiu T'ang shu, Hsin T'ang shu* and Fujiwara Sukeyo's catalogue it is listed under *ju chia* 儒家. Liu Tsung-yüan 柳宗元 (773–819) objected to this classification and argued that the work is in fact Mohist, on the grounds that it emphasized principles such as 'Universal love', 'Opposition to music' and 'Frugality' (*Liu Ho-tung chi* 柳河東集, 4 ('I pien' 議辯; *BSS* ed., pp. 56–7). Liu Tsung-yüan was not suggesting that Yen Ying himself was a Mohist, which would be anachronistic, but rather that the text was written by a follower of Mo Tzu from the state of Ch'i who was familiar with Ch'i's traditions. Wang Ying-lin 王應麟 (1223–1296), Chiao Hung 焦竑 (1541–1620) and Chang Hsüeh-ch'eng 章學誠 (1738–1801) followed Liu Tsung-yüan's view (Wu Tse-yü, pp. 604–05). More recently Chang Ch'un-i 張純一 (preface to his edition; see 5 (d) below) has attempted a compromise, declaring the work to be 60 to 70% Mohist and 30 to 40% Confucian. Such debates assume a rigid classification of Chinese thought which cannot be justified.

　　The authors of the *Ssu k'u ch'üan shu tsung mu* avoid the problem by placing the *Yen tzu ch'un ch'iu* under history. They create a new problem by classifying the text in the sub-category of 'biography' (*chuan chi* 傳記) and claiming that it is the source of the Chinese genre of biography. In the strict sense of the term, however, the *Yen tzu ch'un ch'iu* should not be regarded as biography; the anecdotes and remonstrances are not even arranged chronologically. Maspero's description of the work (p. 360) as historical romance is apt, and his judgment concerning its literary merit holds: 'The author knows how to make his characters come alive, how to give them appropriate bearing and ways of speaking'.

5.　Editions and annotations

A number of editions should be consulted for a study of the book. For a complete list, see Wu Tse-Yü, pp. 43–8.

(a) A late Ming movable type edition, which is based upon a Yüan exemplar is reproduced in the *Ssu pu ts'ung k'an* series.

(b) An edition of 1602 by Feng Meng-chen 馮夢禎 (1546–1605), which is available in the *Hsien Ch'in chu tzu ho pien*, was supposedly based on woodblocks of the Sung period. When this is compared with (a), each is shown to possess both strengths and weaknesses (see Wu Tse-yü p. 43).

(c) Sun Hsing-yen was one of the most important of a host of Ch'ing scholars to turn their attention to the *Yen tzu ch'un ch'iu*. He prepared a new text based on two Ming editions (i) by Shen Ch'i-nan 沈啓南 in 1585; and (ii) by Wu Huai-pao 吳懷保, a late Ming text purportedly deriving from the same exemplar as (a); this was first published in 1788. Of greater importance, Sun prepared a series of notes entitled *yin i* 音意, which contain information on variant readings, problematical characters and phonological features such as rhymes. This text, together with Sun's addendum and a further series of notes on collation by Huang I-chou 黃一周 (1828–99) is available in the *Ssu pu pei yao* series. Lu Wen-ch'ao 盧文弨 (1717–1796), Wang Nien-sun 王念孫 (1744–1832) and Yü Yüeh 俞樾 (1821–1907) also wrote comments on the text.

For such comments and abundant notes on textual variants, see the following editions:

(d) Chang Ch'un-i, *Yen tzu ch'un ch'iu chiao chu* 晏子春秋校注; preface 1930; first published Shanghai: Shih chieh, 1936; reprinted in *Chu tzu chi ch'eng* series.

(e) Wu Tse-yü 吳則虞, *Yen tzu ch'un ch'iu chi shih* 晏子春秋集釋; 2 vols., Peking: Chung hua, 1962.

These two editions sometimes cite different sources and should be used in tandem; owing to its arrangement (e) is easier to use, and the author's judgments are usually more useful than those in (d).

(f) Wang Shu-min 王叔岷, 'Yen tzu ch'un ch'iu chiao cheng' 晏子春秋 斠證; *BIHP* XXVIII (1956), 55–105.

6. Secondary writings cited above

For citations from the following scholars, see Wu Tse-yü: Chang Hsüeh-ch'eng (p. 605); Chiao Hung (p. 604); Koga Dōan (p. 635); Kuan T'ung (pp. 630–31); Liang Ch'i-ch'ao (p. 632); Liu Shih-p'ei (pp. 635f. and 647f.); Wang Nien-sun (pp. 643–44); Wu Te-hsüan (p. 630); and Wang Ying-lin (p. 604). To these may be added:

(a) Forke, Alfred, 'Yen Ying, Staatsman und Philosoph, und das Yen-tse Tch'un-tsch'iu'; *AM*, Hirth Anniversary Volume (1923), 101–44.
(b) Karlgren, Bernhard, 'On the Authenticity of Ancient Chinese Texts'; *BMFEA* I (1929), 165–83.
(c) Maspero, Henri, *China in Antiquity*; translated by Frank A. Kierman Jr.; Folkestone: Wm Dawson, 1978.
(d) Walker, Richard, 'Some notes on the Yen tzu ch'un ch'iu'; *JAOS* 73 (1953), 156–63.
(e) Wang Keng-sheng, *Yen tzu ch'un ch'iu yen chiu* 晏子春秋研究; Taipei: Wen shih che, 1976.

7. Translations

No complete translation into a western language has yet appeared; translations of select parts may be found as follows:

(a) Kao, George, *Chinese wit and humor*; first published 1946; reprinted New York: Sterling Publishing Company, 1974; for the twelve episodes chosen from the *Yen tzu ch'un ch'iu*, see pp. 37–46.
(b) Lippe, Aschwin, 'Drei Geschichten aus dem "Frühling und Herbst des Yen Ying"'; *Studia Sino-Altaica; Festschrift für Erich Haenisch* (1961).
(c) Watson, Burton, *Early Chinese Literature*; New York: Columbia University Press, 1962; see p. 186.
(d) See also Forke, as cited under (6) above.

A manuscript translation into Manchu is held in the National Library of China, Peking.

8. Japanese editions

A. *Kambun taikei*; no. 21, 1916, edited by Koyanagi Shikita.
D. *Kokuyaku kambun taisei*; no. 18, 1924, edited by Fujita Toyohachi (Kempō).
E. *Kambun sōsho*, 1928.
L. *Chūgoku koten shinsho*, 1969, edited by Yamada Taku.

9. Index

A Concordance to the Yanzi Chunqiu 晏子春秋逐字索引, ed. D.C. Lau and Chen Fong Ching; *ICS* series, Hong Kong: Commercial Press, forthcoming 1993.

— Stephen W. Durrant

Yüeh chüeh shu 越絕書

1. Content

Along with the *Wu Yüeh ch'un ch'iu*, the *Yüeh chüeh shu* is usually included in the bibliographical lists under *tsa shih* 雜史. Both works take as their theme the lack of royal virtues in the pre-imperial states of Wu and Yüeh; both texts were apparently written during the Later Han period. Unlike the *Wu Yüeh ch'un ch'iu*, the *Yüeh chüeh shu* is a collection of individual essays on a variety of subjects; it has sometimes been described, and may even be regarded as, the earliest example of a local gazeteer.

The received text comprises 19 sections, whose titles may include the term *chuan* 傳 or *ching* 經, and which are distributed in 15 *chüan*. Some of the text bears a considerable affinity to that of other works, e.g., with the *Wu Yüeh ch'un ch'iu* to varying degrees in *chüan* no. 1 ('Ching P'ing wang' 荆平王), no. 2 ('Wu ti' 吳地), no. 3 ('Wu' 吳), no. 5 ('Ch'ing ti' 請糴), no. 8 ('Chi ti' 記地), no. 9 ('Chi ni' 計倪), no. 10 ('Chi Wu wang chan meng' 記吳王占夢), no. 11 ('Pao chien' 寶劍) and no. 12 ('Chiu shu' 九術); and with the *Kung yang chuan* in *chüan* no. 3 ('Wu'). 'Ch'en Ch'eng heng' 陳成恒, in *chüan* no. 7, is identical, almost verbatim, with text that appears in *Shih chi* 67.

Historical figures such as Wu Tzu-hsü 伍子胥, Fan Li 范蠡, and Kou Ch'ien 句踐, king of Yüeh, feature in much of the text, whose distinctive characteristics lie in its topographies; in its preservation of particular versions of the Wu Tzu-hsü legends and similar literary matter (see David Johnson, 'Epic and history in early China; the matter of Wu Tzu-hsü'; *JAS* 40, 1981, 255–71); in its treatment of philosophical concepts such as *wu hsing* 五行; in its philosophy of history (see Gustav Haloun, 'Die Rekonstruktion der chinesischen Urgeschichte durch die Chinesen'; *Japanisch-deutsche Zeitschrift für Wissenschaft und Technik* 3:7, 1925, 243–70); and in its preservation of certain words of an old language of Yüeh (for examples, see 3.27b and 8.75a, *SPTK* ed.).

2. Authenticity, authorship and title

It is likely that, as compared with an original version, the received text has both suffered loss and been subject to interpolation. The *Ch'i lu* 七

錄 and the bibliographical lists of the *Sui shu* (33, pp. 960, 962), *Chiu T'ang shu* (46, p. 1993) and *Hsin T'ang shu* (58, p. 1463) enter the work with 16 *chüan*; subsequent catalogues give the figure of 15, 14 or 10. *Chüan* no. 15 and 'Wai chuan pen shih' 外傳本事 in *chüan* no. 1 are clearly post Han additions. In view of its identity with text in the *Shih chi*, it is likely that 'Ch'en Ch'eng heng' did not derive from an original *Yüeh chüeh shu*. In addition, 'Hsü wai chuan chi' 敘外傳記 in *chüan* no. 15 appears to be misplaced. Something less than 15 of the sections are likely to have derived from an original Han work.

Ch'ien P'ei-ming 錢培名 (19th century) and Yü Yüeh 俞樾 (1821–1907) have collected citations ascribed to lost parts of the work, and Li Shan 李善 (d. 689) mentions a part that is entitled 'Wu Tzu-hsü shui chan ping fa nei ching' 伍子胥水戰兵法內經 (commentary to *Wen hsüan* 22.23a, *SPTK* ed.). In addition, the *Ku wei shu* 古微書 includes a text which supposedly originated from the *Yüeh chüeh shu* (see Max Kaltenmark, 'Ling-pao, note sur un terme du taoïsme religieux'; *Mélanges publiés par l'Institut des hautes études chinoises* II, 1960, 559–88). Finally, the *Ssu k'u* editors list the sections of two lost *chüan*, most of which are suspected of not being genuine.

The content and heterogeneous nature of the text refute the traditional ascription of the work to Confucius' disciple Tzu Kung 子貢 or to Wu Tzu-hsü. Attribution of authorship to a certain Yüan K'ang 袁康 (Later Han) or to Chao Yeh 趙曄 (Later Han; traditional author of the *Wu Yüeh ch'un ch'iu*) is little more than speculative. Recently scholars have tended to agree that the contents, ideas and style of the work do not conflict with the date of A.D. 52, the last year to be specified in *chüan* no. 2.21a. It may be supposed that the *Yüeh chüeh shu* was originally the work of one or more unknown writers or compilers of the Later Han period.

The meaning of the title *Yüeh chüeh shu* has been almost as elusive as the question of the book's authorship. One problem concerns the inclusion of Yüeh but absence of Wu in the title; secondly, the purpose of the term *chüeh* is somewhat puzzling. The title is often interpreted as meaning 'The account of Yüeh's bringing to an end [of Wu]'.

3. Textual history and editions

The earliest mention of the *Yüeh chüeh shu* is to be found in the form of a citation in the *chi chieh* 集解 commentary of P'ei Yin 裴駰 (5th century) to *Shih chi* 65, p. 2162. The comment of the *Cheng i* 正義 by Chang Shou-chieh 張守節 (*fl.* 737) to the same passage cites the *Ch'i lu*'s entry for the work.

The first printed edition evidently appeared in Shu 蜀 in 1220, with a subsequent reprint in K'uai-chi 會稽. Hsü Ting-fu 徐丁黼 (13th century), the editor, had collated three manuscript copies, but he suspected that the result of his efforts still differed from the original text.

In their recent editions, as described below, Chang Tsung-hsiang 張宗祥 and Yüeh Tsu-mou 樂祖謀 mention the print of 1220, that of 1212 by Wang Kang 汪綱 and one of 1306; none of these survive. There are records of two prints of the Ming period: (i) of 1509, with format of 8 x 16, of which a copy is held in the University Library, Hang-chou; and (ii) of 1545 by K'ung T'ien-yün 孔天允, of which a copy is held in the University Library, Peking. These are said to have followed Sung prints. An edition by Chang Chia-yin 張家胤 (?1527–88) followed the Yüan print, with format of 8 x 17, and this is reproduced in the *Ssu pu ts'ung k'an* series from the Shuang po t'ang 雙柏堂 print. It includes Chang's preface, dated 1554; an unsigned note on the nature of the work that appears in various other editions either as a preface or as a postface; and Hsü Ting-fu's postface of 1220. Another print of Chang's edition, which is punctuated, is included in the *Tseng ting Han Wei ts'ung shu*; this dates Chang's preface at 1552.

A copy of a different edition, by Ch'en K'ai 陳塏 (1502–88) of 1547 is held in the National library, Peking. A print which was reproduced in the *Ku chin i shih*, without preface or postface, was edited by Wu Kuan 吳琯 in the Wan li period. In the *Lung hsi ching she ts'ung shu* (1917) and the *Hsiao wan chüan lou ts'ung shu* (1854; text reprinted, with punctuation, in the *Ts'ung shu chi ch'eng*) Ch'ien P'ei-ming's 錢培名 *cha chi* 札記 follows the text. The *Ssu pu pei yao* follows an unidentified Ming print.

4.   Recent editions

(a) By Chang Tsung-hsiang (Shanghai: Shang wu, 1956), with an introduction which concerns the textual history and the contents of the book. An interlinear commentary to the punctuated text draws attention to variant readings and cites other early texts by way of explaining difficulties of interpretation. The appendix includes prefaces or postfaces by Hsü Ting-fu, Wang Kang, Tu Mu 都穆 (1458–1525), Yang Shen 楊慎 (1488–1509), Ch'en K'ai, Chang Chia-yin and Wang Mo 王謨 (*cs* 1788). This is followed by two sets of *cha chi*, by Ch'ien P'ei-ming and Yü Yüeh.

(b) By Yüeh Tsu-mou (Shanghai: Ku chi, 1985); punctuated text, in unabbreviated characters, based on the *Ssu pu ts'ung k'an*. A lengthy preface by Ch'en Ch'iao-i 陳橋驛 (dated 1982) considers authorship, the title and its meaning, the size and arrangement of the work, its value as historical source material and as a reflection of conditions of life in south China, and the retention of personal place names and a few words of the local language.

For a collection of all extant bibliographical and related information, see Hsü I-fan 徐益藩, 'Yüeh chüeh k'ao' 越絕考, in *Wen lan hsüeh pao* 文瀾學報 6 (1937): 1–36.

5. Index

A Concordance to the Yuejue shu 越絕書逐字索引, ed. D.C. Lau and Chen Fong Ching; *ICS* series, Hong Kong: Commercial Press, forthcoming 1993.

— Axel Schuessler
— Michael Loewe

Appendix I: Bibliographical Sources

Abbreviations

The following abbreviations are used in the text and indexes:

AM	*Asia Major*
BIHP	*Bulletin of the Institute of History and Philology*
BMFEA	*Bulletin of the Museum of Far Eastern Antiquities*
BSOAS	*Bulletin of the School of Oriental and African Studies*
BSS	*Basic Sinological Series (Kuo hsüeh chi pen ts'ung shu* 國學基本叢書)
CTCC	*Chu tzu chi ch'eng* 諸子集成
CYYY	*Chung yang yen chiu yüan li shih yü yen yen chiu so chi k'an* 中央研究院歷史語言研究所集刊
EC	*Early China*
HJAS	*Harvard Journal of Asiatic Studies*
HY	*Harvard Yenching Institute*
ICS	*The ICS Ancient Chinese Text Concordance Series: Hsien Ch'in liang Han ku chi chu tzu so yin ts'ung k'an* 先秦兩漢古籍逐字索引叢刊, ed. D.C. Lau 劉殿爵 and Chen Fong Ching 陳方正; The Chinese University of Hong Kong Institute of Chinese Studies; Hong Kong: the Commercial Press, 1992– ; responsibility for textual notes with D.C. Lau, as editor.
JAOS	*Journal of the American Oriental Society*
JAS	*Journal of Asian Studies*
JNChBrAS	*Journal of the North China Branch of the Royal Asiatic Society*
JRAS	*Journal of the Royal Asiatic Society*
KK	*Kaogu* 考古
KKHP	*K'ao ku hsüeh pao* 考古學報
Legge	(A) Annotated texts and translations: James Legge, *The Chinese Classics*; vols. I–III Hong Kong: at the author's, and London: Trübner and Co., 1861–65; vols. IV–V Hong Kong: Lane Crawford, and London:

Trübner and Co., 1871–72; 2nd edition, revised, Oxford: Clarendon Press, 1893–94; reprinted variously. (B) Translations without Chinese text: in F. Max Müller (ed.), *Sacred Books of the East*; Oxford: Clarendon Press, 1879–91, under the sub-title '*Sacred Books of China*' (a): *The texts of Confucianism*; (b) *The texts of Taoism*; rpt. Delhi: Varanasi, and Patna: Motilal Banarsidas, 1966.

LSYC	*Li shih yen chiu* 歷史研究
MS	*Monumenta Serica*
MSOS	*Mitteilungen des Seminar für orientalische sprachen*
RBS	*Revue bibliographique de sinologie*
SPPY	*Ssu pu pei yao* 四部備要
SPTK	*Ssu pu ts'ung k'an* 四部叢刊
THG	*Tōhō gakuhō* 東洋學報
TP	*T'oung Pao*
TPYL	*T'ai p'ing yü lan* 太平御覽
TSCC	*Ts'ung shu chi ch'eng* 叢書集成
TSK	*Tōyōshi kenkyū* 東洋史研究
WW	*Wen wu* 文物
ZDMG	*Zeitschrift der Deutschen Morgenländischen Gesellschaft*

Index of *Ts'ung shu* 叢書 and Other Major Studies

In the following list the title of a work is followed by the author, compiler or editor, where known, and the original date of compilation or publication; where the latter cannot be known for certain, dates of the author or editor are added in parenthesis.

Ai jih ching lu ts'ang shu chih 愛日精廬藏書志
    Chang Chin-wu 張金吾 1827
An-hui ts'ung shu 安徽叢書 1932–36
Cha i 札迻
    Sun I-jang 孫詒讓 1894
Cheng t'ung tao tsang 正統道藏 1445
Chi fu ts'ung shu 畿輔叢書
    Wang Hao 王灝 1879; rpt., Taipei 1966
Ch'i lu 七錄
    Juan Hsiao-hsü 阮孝緒 (479–536)
Ch'i sheng chai ts'ung shu 起聖齋叢書 1918

Ch'i shu chiang i 七書講義
    Shih Tzu-mei 施子美 (12–13th century); rpt. 1863
Chiao ching shan fang ts'ung shu 校經山房叢書
    Chu Chi-jung 朱記榮 1904
Chih chai shu lu chieh t'i 直齋書錄解題
    Ch'en Chen-sun 陳振孫 (*c.* 1190–after 1249)
Chih chin chai ts'ung shu 屍進齋叢書
    Yao Chin-yüan 姚覲元 1883
Chih hai 指海
    Ch'ien Hsi-tso 錢熙祚 1839–46
Chih pu tsu chai ts'ung shu 知不足齋叢書
    Pao T'ing-po 鮑廷博 1776–1823
Chin tai pi shu 津逮祕書
    Mao Chin 毛晉 1630-42; facsimile, Taipei 1966
Ching i k'ao 經義考
    Chu I-tsun 朱彝尊 1755
Ching tien shih wen 經典釋文
    Lu Te-ming 陸德明 *c.* 625
Ch'iu shu chai ts'ung shu 求恕齋叢書
    Liu Ch'eng-kan 劉承幹 1922
Chou Ch'in chu tzu chiao chu shih chung 周秦諸子斠注十種
    Ch'en Nai-ch'ien 陳乃乾
Chu tzu chi ch'eng 諸子集成 [*CTCC*]
    1935; rpt. 1958
Chu tzu hui han 諸子彙函
    Kuei Yu-kuang 歸有光 1626
Chu tzu pai chia 諸子百家 Ch'ing period
Chu tzu p'ing i 諸子平議
    Yü Yüeh 俞樾 1870
Ch'u hsüeh chi 初學記
    Hsü Chien 徐堅 726
Ch'un tsai t'ang ch'üan shu 春在堂全書
    Yü Yüeh 俞樾 1899
Ch'üan shang ku san tai Ch'in Han san kuo liu ch'ao wen 全上古三代秦漢
    三國六朝文
    Yen K'o-chun 嚴可均 1887–93
Chün chai tu shu chih 郡齋讀書志
    Ch'ao Kung-wu 晁公武 1151; supplement 1249
Ch'ün shu chih yao 群書治要
    Wei Cheng 魏徵 631
Ch'ün shu shih pu 群書拾補

Lu Wen-ch'ao 盧文弨 1787

Chung hsing (kuan ko) shu mu 中興 (館閣) 書目 late 12th century

Chung kuo hsüeh shu chu tso chiang chu wei yüan hui ts'ung shu 中國學術
著作獎助委員會叢書

Ch'ung wen shu chü hui k'o shu 崇文書局彙刻書
see *San shih san chung ts'ung shu* 三十三種叢書

Ch'ung wen tsung mu 崇文總目
Wang Yao-ch'en 王堯臣 1041

Erh shih tzu 二十子
Wu Mien-hsüeh 吳勉學 (*fl.* 1600)

Fujiwara Sukeyo 藤原佐世
see *Nihon koku genzai sho mokuroku* 日本國現在書目錄

Han hai 函海
Li T'iao-yüan 李調元 1778–84

Han hsüeh t'ang ts'ung shu 漢學堂叢書
Huang Shih 黃奭 1893

Han shu 'I wen chih' 漢書藝文志
Pan Ku 班固 (32–92) *et al.*

Han Wei i shu ch'ao 漢魏遺書鈔
Wang Mo 王謨 1798

Han Wei ts'ung shu 漢魏叢書
Ch'eng Jung 程榮 1592

Ho chu ming chia p'i tien chu tzu ch'üan shu 合諸名家批點諸子全書
early 17th century

Ho chung t'u shu kuan ts'ung shu 合衆圖書館叢書 1940–48

Hsi yin hsüan ts'ung shu 惜陰軒叢書
Li Hsi-ling 李錫齡 1846–58; facsimile Taipei,1967

Hsi yüan tu shu chih 郋園讀書志
Yeh Te-hui 葉德輝 1928

Hsiao wan chüan lou ts'ung shu 小萬卷樓叢書
Ch'ien P'ei-ming 錢培名 1854; facsimile Taipei,1968

Hsien Ch'in chu tzu ho pien 先秦諸子合編
Feng Meng-chen 馮夢禎 1602

Hsü hsiu ssu k'u ch'üan shu t'i yao 續修四庫全書提要 1971–72

Hsü ku i ts'ung shu 續古逸叢書
Chang Yüan-chi 張元濟 1922

Hsüeh chin t'ao yüan 學津討原
Chang Hai-p'eng 張海鵬 1805; rpt. 1922

Hsüeh sheng kuo hsüeh ts'ung shu 學生國學叢書

Hu hai lou ts'ung shu 湖海樓叢書
Ch'en Ch'un 陳春 1809–19; facsimile Taipei,1966

Hu-pei hsien sheng i shu 湖北先生遺書
    Lu Ching 盧靖 1923
Hu-pei ts'ung shu 湖北叢書
    Chao Shang-fu 趙尚輔 1891
Huang Ch'ing ching chieh 皇清經解
    Juan Yüan 阮元 1825–29
Huang Ch'ing ching chieh hsü pien 皇清經解續編
    Wang Hsien-ch'ien 王先謙 1888
I chia t'ang ts'ung shu 宜稼堂叢書
    Yu 郁 family (Shanghai) 1840–42
I ch'ieh ching yin i 一切經音義
    (a) Hsüan Ying 玄應 (627–49)
    (b) [P'ei] Hui-lin [裴] 慧琳 810
I lin 意林
    Ma Tsung 馬總 (8th century)
I wen lei chü 藝文類聚
    Ou-yang Hsün 歐陽詢 (557–641)
Jao p'u ts'ang shu t'i chih 蕘圃藏書題識
    Huang P'ei-lieh 黃丕烈 1919
Ku chin i shih 古今逸史
    Wu Kuan 吳琯 1571–76
Ku ching chieh hui han 古經解彙函
    Ch'en Li 陳澧 1872–74
Ku i ts'ung shu 古逸叢書
    Li Shu-ch'ang 黎庶昌 1882–84; facsimile, Taipei, 1965
Ku shu ts'ung k'an 古書叢刊
    Ch'en Yen 陳琰 1922
K'uai chi Hsü shih shu shih lou ts'ung shu 會稽徐氏述史樓叢書
    Hsü Wei-tse 徐維則 1875–1908
Kuan chung ts'ung shu 關中叢書
    Sung Lien-k'uei 宋聯奎 1934–36
Kuan ko shu mu 館閣書目
    see *Chung hsing (kuan ko) shu mu* 中興 (館閣) 書目
Kuang Han Wei ts'ung shu 廣漢魏叢書
    Ho Yün-chung 何允中 1628
Kuang ya shu chü ts'ung shu 廣雅書局叢書
    Hsü Shao-ch'i 徐紹棨 1875–1908
Kuang yün 廣韻
    Ch'en P'eng-nien 陳彭年 and others 1011
Kuo hsüeh chi pen ts'ung shu 國學基本叢書 1929–41
Kuo hsüeh hsiao ts'ung shu 國學小叢書 1940

Liang ching i pien 兩京遺編
    Hu Wei-hsin 胡維新 1573–1619
Liu Shen-shu hsien sheng i shu 劉申叔先生遺書
    Liu Shih-p'ei 劉師培 1936
Liu tzu ch'üan shu 六子全書
    Ku Ch'un 顧春 1573
Lü t'ing chih chien chuan pen shu mu 邵亭知見傳本書目
    Mo Yu-chih 莫友芝 1909
Lung hsi ching she ts'ung shu 龍谿精舍叢書
    Cheng Kuo-hsün 鄭國勳 1917
Mo hai chin hu 墨海金壺
    Chang Hai-p'eng 張海鵬 1817
    see *Shou shan ko ts'ung shu* 守山閣叢書
Nan Sung kuan ko shu mu 南宋館閣書目
    see *Chung hsing (kuan ko) shu mu* 中興 (館閣) 書目
Nien erh tzu ch'uan shu 廿二子全書 1833
    Wang Jang-t'ang 王纕堂
Nihon koku genzai sho mokuroku 日本國見在書目錄
    Fujiwara Sukeyo 藤原佐世 889–98 (reproduced from a copy in the
    imperial collection, postface by Yamada Yoshio 山田孝雄, 1925)
Pai pu ts'ung shu 百部叢書
Pai shih liu t'ieh shih lei chi 白氏六帖事類集
    Pai Chü-i 白居易 (772–846)
Pai tzu ch'üan shu 百子全書 1919
Pao ching t'ang ts'ung shu 抱經堂叢書
    Lu Wen-ch'ao 盧文弨 1782–97; rpt. 1923
Pei t'ang shu ch'ao 北堂書鈔
    Yü Shih-nan 虞世南 (558–638)
Pi shu nien i chung 祕書廿一種
    Wang Shih-han 汪士漢 1668
Pi sung lou ts'ang shu chih 皕宋樓藏書志
    Lu Hsin-yüan 陸心源 1882
Pi ts'e hui han 祕冊彙函
    Shen Shih-lung 沈士龍 and Hu Chen-heng 胡震亨 Wan-li period;
    facsimile, Taipei, 1966
P'ing chin kuan ts'ung shu 平津館叢書
    Sun Hsing-yen 孫星衍 (1753–1818)
San shih san chung ts'ung shu 三十三種叢書 also known as *Ch'ung wen*
    shu chü hui k'o shu 崇文書局彙刻書 1875
Shan pen shu shih tsang shu chih 善本書室藏書志
    Ting Ping 丁丙 1901

Shao wu Hsü shih ts'ung shu 邵武徐氏叢書
  Hsü Kan 徐幹 late nineteenth century
Shih erh tzu 十二子
  Fang I 方疑 c. 1625
Shih li chü Huang shih ts'ung shu 士禮居黃氏叢書
  Huang P'ei-lieh 黃丕烈 posthumous publication; items dated
  1800–23; facsimile rpt. 1887, 1922
Shih liu tzu 十六子
  Fang I 方疑 c. 1625
Shih shan t'ang ts'ang shu mu lu 世善堂藏書目錄
  Ch'en Ti 陳弟 1616
Shih t'ung 史通
  Liu Chih-chi 劉知幾 710
Shin Kan shisō kenkyū bunken mokuroku 秦漢思想研究文獻目錄
  Sakade Yoshinobu 坂出祥伸 1978
Shou shan ko ts'ung shu 守山閣叢書
  Ch'ien Hsi-tso 錢錫祚 1844 (revision of *Mo hai chin hu*) 墨海金壺
Shuo fu 說郛
  T'ao Tsung-i 陶宗儀 (b. 1316); supplement by T'ao T'ing 陶珽 (*cs*
  1610); rpt. Shanghai: Shang wu, 1927
Ssu hsien shu chü k'an shu 思賢書局刊書
  late nineteenth century
Ssu k'u ch'üan shu chen pen 四庫全書珍本
  eighteenth century
Ssu k'u ch'üan shu chien ming mu lu 四庫全書簡明目錄 1782
Ssu k'u ch'üan shu tsung mu t'i yao 四庫全書總目提要
  1782; supplement by Juan Yüan 阮元; rpt. Shanghai: Shang wu 1933
Ssu k'u t'i yao pien cheng 四庫提要辨證
  Yü Chia-hsi 余嘉錫 1958
Ssu pu pei yao 四部備要 [*SPPY*]
  Chung hua shu chu 中華書局 1936
Ssu pu ts'ung k'an 四部叢刊 [*SPTK*]
  Chang Yüan-chi 張元濟 1919; supplements 1934–36
Sui an Hsü shih ts'ung shu hsü pien 隨盦徐氏叢書續編
  Hsü Nai-ch'ang 徐乃昌 1916
Sui shu 'Ching chi chih' 隋書經籍志
  Wei Cheng 魏徵 (580–643)
Sung Yüan Ming shan pen ts'ung shu shih chung 宋元明善本叢書十種
  1935
Tai nan ko ts'ung shu 岱南閣叢書
  Sun Hsing-yen 孫星衍 (1753–1818) rpt. 1924

T'ai p'ing yu lan 太平御覽
　　Li Fang 李昉 983
T'ang Sung ts'ung shu 唐宋叢書
　　Chung Jen-chieh 鍾人傑 (Ming period) and Chang Sui-ch'en 張遂辰
　　(Ming period); facsimile Taipei, 1965
Tao tsang 道藏 1436–49; 1573–1619; and 1923–26
Tao tsang chi yao 道藏輯要 1906
T'ieh ch'in t'ung chien lou ts'ang shu mu lu 鐵琴銅劍樓藏書目錄
　　Ch'ü Yung 瞿鏞 1898
T'ieh hua kuan ts'ung shu 鐵華館叢書
　　Chiang Feng-tsao 蔣鳳藻 late nineteenth century
T'ien lu lin lang shu mu 天祿琳琅書目
　　1775; supplement 1797; printed 1884
T'ien lu lin lang shu mu hou pien 天祿琳琅書目後編
　　P'eng Yüan-jui 彭元瑞 1798
T'ien lu lin lang ts'ung shu ti i chi 天祿琳琅叢書第一集 1932
Tseng ting Han Wei ts'ung shu 增訂漢魏叢書
　　Wang Mo 王謨 1791
Ts'ung shu chi ch'eng 叢書集成 [TSCC]
　　Shang wu press 1935–37
Tu chu tzu cha chi 讀諸子扎記
　　T'ao Hung-ch'ing 陶鴻慶 1959
Tu shu tsa chih 讀書雜志
　　Wang Nien-sun 王念孫 1812–31
Tu shu ts'ung lu 讀書叢錄
　　Hung I-hsüan 洪頤煊 (1765–1837)
T'ung chih 通志
　　Cheng Ch'iao 鄭樵 (1104–62)
T'ung chih t'ang ching chieh 通志堂經解
　　Hsü Ch'ien-hsüeh 徐乾學, Na-lan Ch'eng-te 納蘭成德 (Singde) 1677
T'ung tien 通典
　　Tu Yu 杜佑 (735–812)
Tzu ch'ao 子鈔
　　Yü Chung-jung 庾仲容 (476–549)
Tzu hui 子彙
　　Chou Tzu-i 周子義 and others 1576–77
Tzu lüeh 子略
　　Kao Ssu-sun 高似孫 (c. 1160–c. 1230)
Tzu shu erh shih erh chung 子書二十二種
　　Che-chiang shu chü 1897
Tzu shu pai chia 子書百家

Ch'ung wen shu chü 1875

Wei shu t'ung k'ao 偽書通考
Chang Hsin-ch'eng 張心澂 1939; rev. ed. Shanghai; Shang wu 1957

Wen chi hsien ts'ung shu 聞雞軒叢書 1915

Wen ching t'ang ts'ung shu 問經堂叢書
Sun P'ing-i 孫馮翼 1797–1802

Wen hsien t'ung k'ao 文獻通考
Ma Tuan-lin 馬端臨 *c.* 1308

Wen yüan lou ts'ung shu 文淵樓叢書
Sung Hsing-wu 宋星五 and Chou Ai-ju 周藹如 1928

Wen yüan ying hua 文苑英華
Li Fang 李昉 987

Wu ying tien chü chen pan ts'ung shu 武英殿聚珍版叢書 1794

Ya yü t'ang ts'ung shu 雅雨堂叢書
Lu Chien-tseng 盧見曾 1756; facsimile Taipei, 1966

Yü hai 玉海
Wang Ying-lin 王應麟 (1223–96); published 1343–51

Yü hai t'ang ying Sung ts'ung shu 玉海堂景宋叢書

Yü han shan fang chi i shu 玉函山房輯佚書
Ma Kuo-han 馬國翰 1853

Yü p'ien 玉篇
Ku Yeh-wang 顧野王 543

Yüeh ya t'ang ts'ung shu 粵雅堂叢書
Wu Ch'ung-yüeh 伍崇曜 (mid 19th century; supplement 1875)

Yung lo ta tien 永樂大典 1403–07

Principal Periodicals Quoted

[Abbreviations that are used here are given in square brackets]

Acta Orientalia, Budapest: 1950–
Archiv Orientální, Prague: 1929–
Asia Major [*AM*], Leipzig: 1924–35; New Series, London: 1949–75; Third Series, Princeton: 1988–
Asiatische Studien, Bern: 1947–
Bibliography Quarterly see *Shu mu chi kan*
Bulletin of the Institute of History and Philology [*BIHP*], Peiping, Shanghai: 1928; Taipei: 1950–
Bulletin of the Museum of Far Eastern Antiquities [*BMFEA*], Stockholm: 1929–

Bulletin of the School of Oriental and African Studies [*BSOAS*], London:
  1917–
Chih yen yüeh k'an 制言月刊, Su-chou, Shanghai: 1935–40
China Review, Hong Kong: 1872–1901; London: 1931–38
Chin ling hsüeh pao 金陵學報, Nanking: 1931–45
Chinese Studies in Philosophy, White Plains: 1969–
Chūgoku kankei ronsetsu shiryō 中國關係論說資料, Tokyo: 1964–
Chung kuo che hsüeh 中國哲學, Peking: 1979–
Chung kuo che hsüeh shih yen chiu 中國哲學史研究, Tientsin: 1980
Chung kuo wen hsüeh chi kan 中國文學季刊, Shanghai: 1929–30
Chung shan ta hsüeh hsüeh pao 中山大學學報, Kuang-chou
Chung yang yen chiu yüan li shih yü yen yen chiu so chi k'an 中央研究院歷
  史語言研究所集刊 [*BIHP*], Peiping, Shanghai: 1928; Taipei: 1950–
Ch'ung hua 重華: 1931
Early China [*EC*], Berkeley: 1975–
Han hsüeh yen chiu 漢學研究: 1983–
Harvard Journal of Asiatic Studies [*HJAS*], Cambridge, Massachusetts:
  1936–
Hsin ya shu yüan hsüeh shu nien k'an 新亞書院學術年刊, Hong Kong:
  1956–
Hsüeh wen 學文, Peiping: 1930–32
I wen tsa chih 藝文雜志, Peiping: 1943–
Jen wen tsa chih 人文雜志, Hsi-an: 1957–
Jiang Han kaogu 江漢考古, Hupei: 1981–
Journal of the American Oriental Society, New York: 1843–
Journal of Asian Studies (formerly *Far Eastern Quarterly*), New York, 1941–
Journal Asiatique, Paris: 1822–
Journal of the China Branch of the Royal Asiatic Society, 1858–1905
Journal of Chinese Religions (formerly *Bulletin of the Society for the Study of
  Chinese Religions*), 1981–
Journal of the North China Branch of the Royal Asiatic Society [*JNChBrAS*],
  Shanghai, 1858–1948
Journal of Oriental Studies, Hong Kong: 1954–
Journal of the Royal Asiatic Society [*JRAS*], London: 1834–
Kambun gakkai kaihō 漢文學會會報, Tokyo: 1933–
Kaogu 考古 (formerly *K'ao ku t'ung hsün* 考古通訊) [*KK*], Peking: 1955–
Kao-hsiung shih fan hsüeh yüan hsüeh pao 高雄師範學院學報
K'ao ku hsüeh pao 考古學報 [*KKHP*], Peiping, Peking: 1936–
Ku shih pien 古史辨, Shanghai: 1926–41
Ku shih yen chiu 古史研究: 1931–
K'ung tzu yen chiu 孔子研究

Kuo ts'ui hsüeh pao 國粹學報, Shanghai: 1905–11

Kyōto daigaku bungakubu kenkyū kiyō 京都大學文學部研究紀要, Kyoto: 1952–63

Kyūshu daigaku tetsugaku kenkyūkai nenpō 九州大學哲學研究會年報

Mitteilungen des Seminars für Orientalistische Sprachen [MSOS], Berlin: 1898–1935

Monumenta Serica [MS], Peiping; Tokyo; Los Angeles, 1935–

Nan yang ta hsüeh hsüeh pao 南洋大學學報, Singapore: 1967–

Nihon joshi daigaku kiyō 日本女子大學紀要, Tokyo: 1951–

Okayama shigaku 岡山史學, Okayama:1955–

Oriens, Leiden 1948–

Pei p'ing t'u shu kuan yüeh k'an 北平圖書館月刊, Peiping: 1928–37

Revue bibliographique de sinologie [RBS], Paris: 1955–

Ritsumeikan bungaku 立命館文學, Kyoto 1947–

Shigaku 史學, Tokyo 1921–

Shigaku zasshi 史學雜志, Tokyo: 1889–

Shih hsüeh lun ts'ung 史學論叢, Peiping 1934–35

Shih hsüeh nien pao 史學年報, Peiping 1929–40

Shinagaku 支那學, Kyoto: 1920–42

Shinagaku kenkyū 支那學研究, Tokyo: 1929–45; Hiroshima 1950–65

Shina rekishi chiri kenkyū (zokushū) 支那歷史地理研究 (續集)

Shu mu chi k'an 書目季刊 (*Bibliography Quarterly*), Taipei: 1966–72

Sinica, Frankfurt a.M.: 1927–42

Sinica-Sonderausgabe

Ssu yü yen 思與言, Taipei: 1963–

Ta lu tsa chih 大陸雜誌, Taipei: 1950–

T'ai wan shih ta chiao yü yen chiu so chi k'an 臺灣師大教育研究所季刊

Ti li tsa chih 地理雜誌, Nanking: 1928–

Tōhō gaku 東方學, Tokyo: 1951–

Tōhō gakuhō 東方學報 [THG], (a) Kyoto: 1931– ; (b) Tokyo: 1931–44

Tōhō shūkyō 東方宗敎, Tokyo: 1951–

Tōkyō shinagaku hō 東京支那學報, Tokyo: 1955–

T'oung Pao [TP], Leiden and Paris: 1890–

Tōyō gakuhō 東洋學報, Tokyo: 1911–

Tōyōshi kenkyū 東洋史研究 [TSK], Kyoto: 1935–

T'u shu kuan hsüeh chi k'an 圖書館學季刊, Peiping:1926–37

T'u shu kuan hsüeh pao 圖書館學報, Taichung: 1959–71

Wen hsüeh i ch'an 文學遺產

Wen lan hsüeh pao 文瀾學報, Hangchow: 1935–

Wen shih 文史, Peking: 1962–

Wen shih che 文史哲, Shan-tung, 1951–66

Wen shih che hsüeh pao 文史哲學報, Taipei: 1950–

Wen wu 文物 (formerly *Wen wu ts'an k'ao tzu liao* 文物參考資料) [WW], Peking: 1950–

Yen ching hsüeh pao 燕京學報, Peiping: 1927–51

Yü kung 禹貢, Peiping: 1934–37

Zeitschrift der Deutschen Mörgenlandischen Gesellschaft [ZDMG], Leipzig, 1847–

Note on the *Kambun* 漢文 Editions

The following are the principal series to which references are made in the entries for the items that are treated here. As will be seen, the different series may include text with *Kambun* notation, with *Kambun* transcription or with translations of the text into free Japanese. The selection and extent of the *kaeriten* and *furigana* that are included in the *Kambun* notation may vary considerably. Varying styles of Japanese are used by the different editors, writing as they have been over the span of nearly a century. In general references are not included to the *Kambun* editions of early scholars such as Ogyū Sorai 荻生徂徠. Much of their pioneering work was in fact taken over by the editors of the series that are mentioned below and which are readily available, whereas the original prints of Japanese scholars of the seventeenth and eighteenth centuries are to be found only with difficulty. In a few cases, where a valuable Japanese edition has been published as a separate item, either prior to these series or independently, details are included in the appropriate entries. Of the thirteen series that are considered below, (A) is of greatest help for traditional Chinese scholarship; (H) is in many ways the easiest to use; (E) is the least informative.

A. *Kambun taikei* 漢文大系; Tokyo: Fuzambō, 1909–16; 22 volumes; Chinese text with intercolumnar notes of the traditional Chinese commentators, all marked with *Kambun* notation. Separate explanatory notes in Japanese are printed at the head of each page. Prefaces of the traditional Chinese editors are also included, with *Kambun* notation. Many of the volumes bear the name of Hattori Unokichi 服部宇之吉 as editor (reprinted, Fuzambō, 1972 and Taipei: Hsin wen feng, 1974).

B. *Kanseki kokujikai zensho* 漢籍國字解全書; Tokyo: Waseda University, 1909–17; 45 volumes; also *Shiki kokujikai* 史記國字解, 1919–20; 8 volumes; Chinese text with *Kambun* notation, followed by Japanese annotation and a Japanese version. The notes of traditional Chinese commentators, with *Kambun* notation, are included in some of the volumes of the series.

C. *Kōchū kambun sōsho* 校註漢文叢書; Tokyo: Hakubunkan, 1913-18; 12 volumes. This series was published under the general supervision of Kubo Tenzui 久保天隨, with due acknowledgement to the work of Nakamura Fusetsu 中村不折. The Chinese text, with *Kambun* notation and *kambun* transcription, is followed by Chinese and Japanese notes, the former with *Kambun* notation.

D. *Kokuyaku kambun taisei* 國譯漢文大成; Tokyo: Kokumin bunko; (a) 20 volumes (classics, philosophers and histories) 1920-24; (b) 20 volumes (literature) 1922-25. All items that are mentioned here are from (a), except for the *Ch'u tz'u*. There is a *Kambun* transcription of the text, with *furigana*, and explanatory notes in Japanese. Chinese text, with *Kambun* notation, is printed separately at the end of each volume.

E. *Kambun sōsho* 漢文叢書; Tokyo: Yūhōdō, 1927-29; 41 volumes. Tsukamoto Tetsuzō 塚本哲三 is regularly specified as the editor of the series, and his name has not been repeated in the entries of this book. Introductions are signed by other scholars, whose work is also seen in some of the other series. Chinese text, with somewhat slender *Kambun* notation, is printed at the head of the page; *Kambun* transcription, with *furigana*, is given below, with explanatory notes in Japanese. The volumes in this series do not bear serial numbers.

F. *Keisho taikō* 經書大講; Tokyo: Heibonsha, 1938-40; 25 volumes. Kobayashi Ichirō 小林一郎 is regularly specified as the editor, and his name has not been repeated in the entries of this book. Introductory remarks to the individual volumes are not signed. The Chinese text, with *Kambun* notation, is followed by *Kambun* transcription with *furigana*. The text is divided into short passages, which are followed by an expanded Japanese version.

G. *Chūgoku koten bungaku zenshū* 中國古典文學全集; Tokyo: Heibonsha, 1958-61; 33 volumes, in which only a few pre-Han and Han texts are included. In some of the volumes (e.g. no.1, which includes the *Shih ching* and the *Ch'u tz'u*) the Chinese text is printed without *Kambun* notation, followed by a Japanese version and Japanese annotation. In other volumes (e.g., nos 4 and 5, which include most chapters of the *Shih chi*) a Japanese version is printed without the Chinese text but with illustrations and maps.

H. *Shinshaku kambun taikei* 新譯漢文大系; Tokyo: Meiji shoin, 1960- ; 104 volumes projected, of which all but a few have been published;

Chinese text with *Kambun* notation, followed by *Kambun* transcription with *furigana*. An extended Japanese version is followed by explanatory notes in Japanese.

I. *Tōyō bunko* 東洋文庫; Tokyo: Heibonsha, 1963– . This large series, which extends to at least 456 volumes, includes Japanese versions of literary works of a number of cultures and languages. Not all the volumes include the complete text of the work that is handled, and Chinese text is not included. The Japanese versions may be accompanied by notes, illustrations or an index of proper names.

J. *Chūgoku no shisō* 中國の思想; Tokyo: Keiei shichō kenkyūkai, 1964–66; 13 volumes. Japanese versions of select chapters or passages are followed by Chinese text (without *Kambun* notation) and *Kambun* transcription; under the general supervision of Matsueda Shigeo 松枝茂夫 and Takeuchi Yoshimi 竹內好.

K. *Chūgoku koten bungaku taikei* 中國古典文學大系; Tokyo: Heibonsha, 1967-75; 60 volumes; Japanese version printed without Chinese text.

L. *Chūgoku koten shinsho* 中國古典新書; Tokyo: Meitoku shuppansha, 1967– ; 100 volumes; Chinese text with *Kambun* notation, *Kambun* transcription with *furigana*, and explanatory notes. The complete text of a work is not always included.

M. *Shintei Chūgoku koten sen* 新訂中國古典選; Tokyo: Asahi Shimbunsha, 1965-69; 20 volumes (original series in 12 volumes); Chinese text with *kaeriten* (not in all volumes), *Kambun* transcription and Japanese annotation; under the general supervision of Yoshikawa Kōjirō 吉川幸次郎.

Appendix II: Chronological Tables

Western Chou Kings*

King Wen 文王	r. 1099/1056–1050 B.C.
King Wu 武王	r. 1049/45–1043 B.C.
Duke of Chou 周公	1042–1036 B.C.
King Ch'eng 成王	r. 1042/35–1006 B.C.
King K'ang 康王	r. 1005/03–978 B.C.
King Chao 昭王	r. 977/75–957 B.C.
King Mu 穆王	r. 956–918 B.C.
King Kung 共王	r. 917/15–900 B.C.
King I 懿王	r. 899/97–873 B.C.
King Hsiao 孝王	r. ?872–866 B.C.
King I 夷王	r. 865–858 B.C.
King Li 厲王	r. 857/53–842/28 B.C.
(*Kung ho*) 共和	841–828 B.C.
King Hsüan 宣王	r. 827/25–782 B.C.
King Yu 幽王	r. 781–771 B.C.

*The editor is grateful to Professor Shaughnessy for providing these dates.

Eastern Chou Kings

King P'ing 平王	r. 770–720 B.C.
King Huan 桓王	r. 719–697 B.C.
King Chuang 莊王	r. 696–682 B.C.
King Li 釐王	r. 681–677 B.C.
King Hui 惠王	r. 676–652 B.C.
King Hsiang 襄王	r. 651–619 B.C.
King Ch'ing 頃王	r. 618–613 B.C.
King K'uang 匡王	r. 612–607 B.C.
King Ting 定王	r. 606–586 B.C.
KingChien 簡王	r. 585–572 B.C.
King Ling 靈王	r. 571–545 B.C.
King Ching 景王	r. 544–520 B.C.
King Ching 敬王	r. 519–476 B.C.
King Yüan 元王	r. 475–469 B.C.
King Chen-ting 貞定	r. 468–441 B.C.
King K'ao 考王	r. 440–426 B.C.
King Wei-lieh 威烈	r. 425–402 B.C.
King An 安王	r. 401–376 B.C.
King Lieh 烈王	r. 375–369 B.C.
King Hsien 顯王	r. 368–321 B.C.
King Shen-ching 慎靚	r. 320–315 B.C.
King Nan 赦王	r. 314–256 B.C.
(Tung Chou chün 東周君 770–720 B.C.)	

Former Han Emperors

Personal name	Dynastic title	Reigned
Liu Pang 劉邦	Kao-ti 高帝	202 B.C.* to 195 B.C.
Liu Ying 劉盈	Hui-ti 惠帝	195 to 188 B.C.
[Domination by Empress Lü 呂后:		188 to 180] B.C.
Liu Heng 劉恒	Wen-ti 文帝	180 to 157 B.C.
Liu Ch'i 劉啓	Ching-ti 景帝	157 to 141 B.C.
Liu Ch'e 劉徹	Wu-ti 武帝	141 to 87 B.C.
Liu Fu-ling 劉弗陵	Chao-ti 昭帝	87 to 74 B.C.
Liu Ho 劉賀	——	74 to 74 B.C. (deposed)
Liu Ping-i 劉病已	Hsüan-ti 宣帝	74 to 49 B.C. (also named Hsün 詢)
Liu Shih 劉奭	Yüan-ti 元帝	49 to 33 B.C.
Liu Ao 劉驁	Ch'eng-ti 成帝	33 to 7 B.C.
Liu Hsin 劉欣	Ai-ti 哀帝	7 to 1 B.C.
Liu Chi-tzu 劉箕子	P'ing-ti 平帝	1 B.C. to A.D. 6

*King of Han from 206 B.C.; assumed title Huang ti 皇帝 202

Hsin Dynasty

Wang Mang 王莽	9 to 23

Later Han Emperors

Personal name	Dynastic title	Reigned
Liu Hsiu 劉秀	Kuang-wu-ti 光武帝	25 to 57
Liu Yang 劉陽	Ming-ti 明帝	57 to 75 (also named Chuang 莊)
Liu Ta 劉炟	Chang-ti 章帝	75 to 88
Liu Chao 劉肇	Ho-ti 和帝	88 to 106
Liu Lung 劉隆	Shang-ti 殤帝	106 to 106
Liu Yu 劉祜	An-ti 安帝	106 to 125 (also named Hu 祜)
Liu I 劉懿	Shao-ti 少帝	125 to 125
Liu Pao 劉保	Shun-ti 順帝	125 to 144
Liu Ping 劉炳	Ch'ung-ti 沖帝	144 to 145
Liu Tsuan 劉纘	Chih-ti 質帝	145 to 146
Liu Chih 劉志	Huan-ti 桓帝	146 to 168
Liu Hung 劉宏	Ling-ti 靈帝	168 to 189
Liu Pien 劉辯	Shao-ti 少帝	189 to 189
Liu Hsieh 劉協	Hsien-ti 獻帝	189 to 220

Index of Chinese, Japanese and Western Scholars

(Characters are not included for Chinese authors whose names appear in romanized forms only.)

386, 415–22, 457, 468

Cheng Huan-ku 鄭還古 (*fl.* 827), 273

Cheng Kuo-hsün 鄭國勳 (20th cen.), 91–92, 500

Cheng Liang-shu 鄭良樹 (b. 1940), 10, 281, 289, 449, 453

Cheng Ming-hsüan 鄭明選 (15–16th cen.), 427

Cheng Ssu-yüan 鄭思遠 (Cheng Yin 鄭隱) (3rd cen.), 274

Cheng Te-k'un 鄭德坤 (d. 1992), 345, 360, 365

Cheng Ts'ai 鄭采 (Ming period), 372, 373

Cheng Wan-keng 鄭萬耕 (20th cen.), 464, 465

Cheng Wen 鄭文 (20th cen.), 464

Cheng Yin 鄭隱 *see* Cheng Ssu-yüan

Cheng Yu-hsien 鄭友賢 (Sung period), 452

Ch'eng Fa-jen 程發軔 (20th cen.), 46

Ch'eng Hao 程顥 (1032–85), 317

Ch'eng Hsüan-ying 成玄英 (*fl.* 630–60), 60–62, 253, 279

Ch'eng I 程頤 (1033–1107), 224, 314, 317

Ch'eng Jung 程榮 (1447–1520), 84, 164, 310, 352, 353, 498

Ch'eng Shih-te 程士德 (20th cen.), 205, 210

Ch'eng Shu-te 程樹德 (20th cen.), 320

Ch'eng Ta-ch'ang 程大昌 (1123–95), 81–82, 86

Ch'eng Yüan-min 程元敏 (20th cen.), xiii

Chi T'ien-pao 吉天保 (11–12th cen.), 450

Chi Yün 紀昀 (1724–1805), 472

Ch'i 齊: Ching kung 景公 (547–489 B.C.), 483; Hsüan wang 宣公 (319–301 B.C.), 56, 248; Huan kung 桓公 (685–643 B.C.), 244f.

Ch'i Chün-tsao 祁寯藻 (1793–1866), 436

Ch'i Po 岐伯 (discussant with Huang ti), 198

Ch'i Ssu-ho 齊思和 (b. 1907), 10, 66, 188, 447, 453

Ch'i Yü-chang 祁玉章 (20th cen.), 169

Chia I 賈誼 (201–169 B.C.), 49, 82, 137–38, 161f., 245, 248, 456

Chia K'uei 賈逵 (30–101), 27, 266, 382

Chia Kung-yen 賈公彥 (*fl.* 650), 26f., 237f.

Chia Lin 賈林, 448, 450

Chia Ta-yin 賈大隱 (*fl.* 676), 253

Chiang Chi 蔣驥 (early 18th cen.), 52

Chiang Feng-tsao 蔣鳳藻 (19th cen.), 156, 502

Chiang Hsi-ch'ang 蔣錫昌 (20th cen.), 289

Chiang Jun-hsün 江潤勳 (20th cen.), 168–69

Chiang Kuo-hsiang 蔣國祥 (*c.* 1696), 114

Chiang Liang-fu 姜亮夫 (b. 1901), 52–53

Chiang Pi 姜璧 (*cs* 1571), 328

Chiang Sheng 江聲 (1721–99), 384, 386

Chiang Shao-yüan 江紹源 (20th cen.), 358, 365

Chiang Weng 江翁 (1st cen. B.C.), 144

Chiang Yüan-t'ing 蔣元廷 (1755–1819), 192

Chiang Yung 江永 (1681–1762), 25, 29

Chiao Hsün 焦循 (1763–1820), 224, 318, 320, 333

Chiao Hung 焦竑 (1541–1620), 60, 402, 487

Chiao Yüan-hsi 焦袁熹 (1660–1735), 463

Ch'iao Yü 喬宇 (*fl.* 1521), 392

Kimida Rentarō 公田連太郎 (d. 1963), 65, 251, 288, 308, 322, 334, 412, 455

Kimura Ei'ichi 木村英一 (b. 1906), 296, 322

Kishi Yōko 岸陽子 (b. 1934), 66

Kiyama Hideo 木山英雄 (b. 1934), 194

Kiyota Kiyoshi 清田清 (b. 1900), 262

Knechtges, David R., 465

Knoblock, John, 187

Ko Hsüan 葛玄 (3rd cen.), 273f.

Ko Hung 葛洪 (c. 283–343), 273f.

Ko Sung-li 葛宋禮 (Ming period), 209

Ko Tzu 葛鼐 (c. 1523), 7, 73, 97

Kobayashi Ichirō 小林一郎, 507

Kobayashi Katsundo 小林勝人, 299f.

Kobayashi Nobuaki 小林信明, 308

Koga Dōan 古賀侗庵 (1788–1847), 487

Kohn, Livia, 58, 64

Kojima Kenkichirō 兒島獻吉郎 (b. 1931), 75, 177, 454

Kōma Miyoshi 高馬三良 (b. 1911), 367

Komaki Masanari 小牧昌業 (1843–1922), 297

Kondō Mitsuo 近藤光男 (b. 1921), 412

Konrad, N.I., 449, 454

Kopetsky Elma E., 312

Kornicki, P., xii

Kosoto Hiroshi 小曾戶洋 (b. 1950), 202, 211

Köster, Hermann, 187

Kotake Fumio 小竹文夫, 412

Kotake Takeo 小竹武夫, 412

Kou Ch'ien 句踐 (king of Yüeh), 490

Kou, Ignace Pao-koh, 256

Kow Mei-kao see Ku Mei-kao

Koyanagi Shikita 小柳司氣太 (1870–1940), 123, 251, 257, 341, 454, 489

Kraft, Eva, 193

Kramers, R.P., 258

Kroll, Y.L., 413, 477

Ku Ch'i-yüan 顧起元 (1565–1628), 372

Ku Chieh-kang 顧頡剛 (1893–1980), 28, 29, 31, 98, 226, 233, 290–91, 345, 358, 365, 376, 381, 385

Ku Ch'ien-li 顧千里 see Ku Kuang-ch'i 顧廣圻

Ku Chih-shan 顧植山 (20th cen.), 208, 212

Ku Ch'un 顧春 (fl. 1530), 102, 181, 183, 500

Ku Huai-san 顧櫰三 (19th cen.), 109–10

Ku Huan 顧歡 (390–453), 275

Ku Kuang-ch'i 顧廣圻 (Ch'ien-li 顧千里, 1776–1835), 5, 118–19, 122, 181, 183, 186, 191, 428, 478

Ku Mei-kao 辜美高 (Kow Mei-kao) (20th cen.), 177

Ku Ming 顧明 (18–19th cen.), 469

Ku Shen-tzu 谷神子, 272

Ku Shih 顧實 (b. 1876), 344

Ku Ts'ung-te 顧從德 (c. 1550), 206

Ku Yeh-wang 顧野王 (519–81), 503

Ku Yen-wu 顧炎武 (1612–81), 224

K'uai T'ung 蒯通 (c. 236–196 B.C.), 5

Kuan Chung 管仲 (d. 645 B.C.), 244f., 264

Kuan Feng 關鋒 (20th cen.), 56, 64

Kuan Li-ch'ang 管禮昌 (?19th cen.), 354

Kuan T'ung 管同 (1780–1831), 485

K'uang Fan 鄺璠 (1458–1521), 476

Kubo[ta] Chikusui 久保 [田] 築水 (Ai 愛, 1759–1832), 184, 188

Kubo Tenzui 久保天隨 (b. 1875), 297, 322, 334, 422, 454, 507

Kudō Moto'o 工藤元男 (b. 1950), 9

www.ingramcontent.com/pod-product-compliance
Lightning Source LLC
Chambersburg PA
CBHW020651270326
41928CB00005B/73